the Unofficial Guide® to

New York City

4th Edition

the Unofficial
Guide® to
New York City

4th Edition

Eve Zibart
Bob Sehlinger
with Rachel F. Freeman
and Lea Lane

WILEY

Please note that prices fluctuate in the course of time, and travel information changes under the impact of many factors that influence the travel industry. We therefore suggest that you write or call ahead for confirmation when making your travel plans. Every effort has been made to ensure the accuracy of information throughout this book, and the contents of this publication are believed correct at the time of printing. Nevertheless, the publishers cannot accept responsibility for errors or omissions or for changes in details given in this guide or for the consequences of any reliance on the information provided by the same. Assessments of attractions and so forth are based upon the author's own experience, and therefore, descriptions given in this guide necessarily contain an element of subjective opinion, which may not reflect the publisher's opinion or dictate a reader's own experience on another occasion. Readers are invited to write the publisher with ideas, comments, and suggestions for future editions.

Published by:

John Wiley & Sons, Inc.

111 River Street

Hoboken, NJ 07030

Produced by Menasha Ridge Press
Cover design by Michael J. Freeland
Interior design by Michele Laseau

For information on our other products and services or to obtain technical support please contact our Customer Care Department within the U.S. at (800) 762-2974, outside the U.S. at (317) 572-3993 or fax (317) 572-4002.

John Wiley & Sons, Inc. also publishes its books in a variety of electronic formats. Some content that appears in print may not be available in electronic formats.

ISBN 0-7645-4191-9

Manufactured in the United States of America

5 4 3 2 1

Contents

List of Maps

Acknowledgments

Many thanks to Lea Lane, Jim Leff, and Wonki Kim for their time, taste, and sometimes tableside companionship.

As always, thanks to the folks at Menasha Ridge, particularly Georgia, Molly, Clay, Holly, and Grace. Special thanks to Chris Mohney for his patience and painstaking transcription.

Many thanks to Laura Poole and Clay White, the people who read about our vacations but never have the chance to take one.

Special thanks to Ruben and a tip of the hat to Johnny, who made the Oak Bar my favorite Manhattan sanctuary.

Finally, this book is for my brother Michael, the best companion.

—*Eve Zibart*

About the Authors and Contributors

Eve Zibart has written more about dining and entertainment than most people experience in a lifetime. In her early years as the pop music and culture reporter for, first, the *Nashville Tennessean* and then for the *Washington Post,* Eve quickly exhibited a flair for scene and sensory detail coupled with an aptitude for grammar and an extensive vocabulary. She rapidly moved through the ranks of the *Post* as a Style feature writer, a Maryland columnist, the TV editor, and a Weekend assistant editor. Long known to friends and fans as "Dr. Nightlife," Eve has enough experience and knowledge to advise the Joint Chiefs of Staff on national trends. Currently, Eve is the restaurant critic for the *Washington Post's* Weekend section.

In addition to her responsibilities at the *Post,* Eve is a columnist for *Book Page* and has been a regular contributor to *USAir inflight, New England Financial Journal, Impress,* and *Four Seasons* magazines. She has also written for *Cosmopolitan, Town and Country,* and *Playboy.* Given an amazing ability to turn 24 hours into 30, Eve has found time to author several books, including *The Ethnic Food Lover's Companion; The Eclectic Gourmet Guide to Washington, D.C.; The Unofficial Guide to New Orleans; The Unofficial Guide to Walt Disney World for Grown-Ups;* and *Inside Disney: The Incredible Story of Walt Disney World and the Man Behind the Mouse.*

Bob Sehlinger is the creator and executive publisher of the *Unofficial Guide* series. He has authored over 20 books on travel and outdoor recreation.

Native New Yorker **Rachel F. Freeman** (Dining and Nightlife contributor) believes it is her duty to act as both foodie and nightowl. Having lived abroad for 11 years, she returned to New York with a renewed hunger for what the city has to offer, resisting the temptation to join the ranks of the jaded. She has written for guidebooks in Warsaw, Poland and has a passion for Edinburgh and the Highlands and Islands of Scotland. She has written for *Poland Business Guide, Wider Insider, Warsaw Insider,* and *Voyage* magazine.

Lea Lane is a hotel maven, visiting and researching perhaps 1,000 rooms around the world—including in The Big Apple—for many guidebooks and trade publications, such as *Birnbaum's United States, Zagat's Hotel and Resort Survey,* and *Star Service,* the premiere travel agent reference. In addition, Lea has been a columnist for Gannett Suburban newspapers, a TV travel and lifestyle reporter, managing editor of the newsletter *Travel Smart,* and co-author of a book on cruises. She is a major contributor to guidebooks about Geece, Naples, and the Amalfi Coast, and is the author of *The Unofficial Guide to Bed & Breakfasts and Country Inns in New England.*

Introduction

"New York, New York, It's a Helluva Town . . ."

If you're ever a passenger in a taxicab in New York, look at the city map affixed to the back of the driver's seat. Chances are, it will show only the tourist territories, cutting Manhattan off partway up Central Park, only hinting at Brooklyn, and likely dispensing with the Bronx, Long Island, and Staten Island altogether. So do most guidebooks about New York. They get you from the Staten Island Ferry (the departure point, at least) on the Battery to the Metropolitan Museum of Art at 82nd Street. Some less hidebound books mention Harlem and a few riverside attractions. But for the most part, it's "East Side, West Side" rather than "all around the town."

Worse, tour guides rarely draw connections, convey waves of progress, or point up ironies of development. In a city literally embraced by the spirits of multiculturalism—with the Statue of Liberty, that monumental icon of hope for immigrants, at one end, and the shrine of Mother Cabrini, their patron saint, at the other—most visitors peer through the most homogeneous of filters, the endless barrage of Big Apple boosterism and crime or inflation news trotted out every day. Watch enough TV and you'd think the whole city was painted with red ink, white ticker tape, and blue uniforms.

What a waste. New York City is one of the most original, elaborate, eccentric, and irresistible creatures—it clearly has a life of its own—you will ever encounter. And we want you to encounter it all, in not just three but four: underground, above the cloud line, and most definitely at street level, as well as seeing its past, present, and future. And for that, we need your cooperation. We need you to be open to the city's charm. And we need you to turn off that damn television.

We often speak of visiting a new place as "seeing" it. "See Rock City," read those famous barns. "Join the Navy and see the world." But the strange thing about sight-seeing is that people get too absorbed in the "sights" and forget about the "seeing." It may sound odd for an author to say, but having your nose buried in a book, even this book, is not the way to travel. And it certainly isn't the way to go looking for exactly that intersection or department store or luxury hotel you always see in the cop shows.

To experience New York fully, you need to give it the full attention of your eyes and your heart. This city is a romance, a record of both the finest moments and the darkest hours of our history. You need to respond to it, not just react to it. Start with our book, but don't stick to it. Admire the Empire State Building, but don't spend your whole day there. Join the crowds on the street, grab a coffee, see a show. Otherwise, you might just as well have stayed home.

Many guidebooks will tell you that New York is not for the faint-hearted; we would say that it is not for the unimaginative. Part of its fascination is its complexity: all the accents, the rhythms, the smells. For so famous a melting pot, New York has yet to produce a truly creole society; minorities here are not so much assimilated as incorporated. That means food, gifts, clothes, and "roots" of a hundred cultures. It's a permanent World's Fair, free for the strolling. Diversity isn't just a souvenir of Ellis Island or dim sum in Chinatown; it's daily life, the greatest attraction of them all.

New York is also the great silent witness to American culture. There is not a single block in the city, whether residential, renovated, commercial, or even crumbling, that does not speak of its restless and often reckless history: expansionist, extravagant, fickle, fashionable. All you have to do is look. Broadway or off-Broadway, here all the world truly is a stage.

And a stage set: If there had not been such a thing as a skyline, New York would have had to invent it. As it is, New York reconceived the horizon beyond the dreams of even the greatest medieval builders. Skyscrapers are the true cathedrals of Manhattan's private religion—not that there aren't exquisite churches and temples galore. You can almost relive the evolution of the city by glancing around at the architecture, from the 18th-century purity of St. Paul's Chapel to the 19th-century neoclassicism of Federal Hall, the French Renaissance of the Jewish Museum, and the Gothic Revival of St. Patrick's; from the Beaux Arts Grand Central Terminal (with staircases copied from the Paris Opéra) and the Art Deco Chrysler Building to the Wright-stuff Guggenheim and the Bauhaus Seagram Building.

Even "ordinary" office buildings have extraordinary features: friezes, carvings, gilding, capitals, cornice pieces, decorative sills—all the showy elements of European palaces, only bigger and brasher and designed to make aristocrats out of merchants. For these are the great palaces of trade, tributes to the variety and vitality of American industry. New York was one of the first cities to abandon class distinction, at least as far as the purveyors were concerned, between the carriage trade and the merchant class, between the custom-tailored and the store-fitted. It was the natural preserve of the department store, with its abundance of luxuries (which gradually became, by long acquaintance and by the nature of human ambition, necessities), and it fostered the democratization of service.

Here the great merchant princes—the Rockefellers, Guggenheims, Fricks, and Morgans—amassed great art collections and libraries that became public treasures. Today's corporate equivalents often act the patron role, too: There are Lichtenstein and Thomas Hart Benton murals in the lobby of the Equitable Center (Seventh at 51st); a mini-museum in the PaineWebber Building (Sixth and 52nd); an Alexander Calder sculpture outside IBM (Madison and West 57th); and a branch of the Whitney Museum of Modern Art in the Philip Morris Building (on Park Avenue, just across from the 42nd Street entrance to Grand Central).

On the other hand, there is far more "outdoors" to New York than you may have realized. Every borough has a large public park—and no, Central Park is not the largest—and four have botanical gardens. There are five zoos and an aquarium, a wildlife refuge, and beaches and marinas.

So this book is about seeing New York. Not just Midtown Manhattan, but the whole city. It's about shopping and art-gazing and theatergoing, of course, but mostly it's about looking past the sales pitches to the piers, beyond the boutiques to the brownstones, outside Times Square to Washington Square. It's about relaxing in the green spaces as well as the grand hotels, about going off-Broadway as far as Brooklyn and seeing as far back as its founding. If you want a top ten list of tourist attractions, you can find them on any corner and any souvenir stand; but it you want to know ten lovely things to do for yourself, ten splendors to share with your children, or ten places where beauty really is truth, read on.

About This Guide

How Come "Unofficial"?

Most guides to New York tout the well-known sights, promote the local restaurants and hotels indiscriminately, and leave out a lot of good stuff. This one is different.

Instead of pandering to the tourist industry, we'll tell you if the food is bad at a well-known restaurant, we'll complain loudly about high prices, and we'll guide you away from the crowds and traffic for a break now and then.

Visiting New York requires wily strategies not unlike those used in the sacking of Troy. We've sent in a team of evaluators who toured each site, ate in the city's best restaurants, performed critical evaluations of its hotels, and visited New York's wide variety of nightclubs. If a museum is boring, or standing in line for two hours to view a famous attraction is a waste of time, we say so—and, in the process, hopefully we will make your visit more fun, efficient, and economical.

Creating a Guidebook

We got into the guidebook business because we were unhappy with the way travel guides make the reader work to get any usable information. Wouldn't it be nice, we thought, if we were to make guides that are easy to use?

Most guidebooks are compilations of lists. This is true regardless of whether the information is presented in list form or artfully distributed through pages of prose. There is insufficient detail in a list, and prose can present tedious helpings of nonessential or marginally useful information. Not enough wheat, so to speak, for nourishment in one instance, and too much chaff in the other. Either way, these types of guides provide little more than departure points from which readers initiate their own quests.

Many guides are readable and well researched, but they tend to be difficult to use. To select a hotel, for example, a reader must study several pages of descriptions with only the boldface hotel names breaking up large blocks of text. Because each description essentially deals with the same variables, it is difficult to recall what was said concerning a particular hotel. Readers generally must work through all the write-ups before beginning to narrow their choices. The presentation of restaurants, nightclubs, and attractions is similar except that even more reading is usually required. To use such a guide is to undertake an exhaustive research process that requires examining nearly as many options and possibilities as starting from scratch. Recommendations, if any, lack depth and conviction. These guides compound rather than solve problems by failing to narrow travelers' choices down to a thoughtfully considered, well-distilled, and manageable few.

How Unofficial Guides Are Different

Readers care about the authors' opinions. The authors, after all, are supposed to know what they are talking about. This, coupled with the fact that the traveler wants quick answers (as opposed to endless alternatives), dictates that authors should be explicit, prescriptive, and above all, direct. The authors of the *Unofficial Guide* try to do just that. They spell out alternatives and recommend specific courses of action. They simplify complicated destinations and attractions and allow the traveler to feel in control in the most unfamiliar environments. The objective of the *Unofficial Guide* authors is not to give the most information or all of the information but to offer the most accessible, useful information.

An *Unofficial Guide* is a critical reference work; it focuses on a travel destination that appears to be especially complex. Our authors and research team are completely independent from the attractions, restaurants, and hotels we describe. *The Unofficial Guide to New York* is designed for individuals and families traveling for the fun of it, as well as for business travelers and conventioneers, especially those visiting the Big Apple for the first time. The guide is directed at value-conscious, consumer-oriented adults who seek a cost-effective, though not spartan, travel style.

SPECIAL FEATURES

The *Unofficial Guide* offers the following special features:

- Friendly introductions to New York's most fascinating neighborhoods.
- "Best of" listings giving our well-qualified opinions on things ranging from raw oysters to blackened snapper and 5-star hotels to 12-story views.
- Listings that are keyed to your interests, so you can pick and choose.
- Advice to sight-seers on how to avoid the worst of the crowds; advice to business travelers on how to avoid traffic and excessive costs.
- Recommendations for lesser-known sights that are away from Times Square but are no less worthwhile.
- A zone system and maps to make it easy to find places you want to go to and avoid places you don't.
- Expert advice on avoiding New York's notorious street crime.
- A hotel chart that helps you narrow down your choices fast, according to your needs.
- Shorter listings that include only those restaurants, clubs, and hotels we think are worth considering.
- A table of contents and detailed index to help you find things fast.
- Insider advice on best times of day (or night) to go places.

WHAT YOU WON'T GET

- Long, useless lists where everything looks the same.
- Information that gets you to your destination at the worst possible time.
- Information without advice on how to use it.

How This Guide Was Researched and Written

Although many guidebooks have been written about New York, very few have been evaluative. Some guides come close to regurgitating the hotels' and tourist offices' own promotional material. In preparing this work, we took nothing for granted. Each hotel, restaurant, shop, and attraction was visited by a team of trained observers who conducted detailed evaluations and rated each according to formal criteria. Team members conducted interviews with tourists of all ages to determine what they enjoyed most and least during their New York visit.

While our observers are independent and impartial, they did not claim to have special expertise. Like you, they visited New York as tourists or business travelers, noting their satisfaction or dissatisfaction.

The primary difference between the average tourist and the trained evaluator is the evaluator's skills in organization, preparation, and observation. The trained evaluator is responsible for much more than simply observing and cataloging. Observer teams use detailed checklists to analyze hotel rooms, restaurants, nightclubs, and attractions. Finally, evaluator ratings and observations are integrated with tourist reactions and the opinions of patrons for a comprehensive quality profile of each feature and service.

In compiling this guide, we recognize that a tourist's age, background, and interests will strongly influence his or her taste in New York's wide array of attractions and will account for a preference for one sight or museum over another. Our sole objective is to provide the reader with sufficient description, critical evaluation, and pertinent data to make knowledgeable decisions according to individual tastes.

Letters, Comments, and Questions from Readers

We expect to learn from our mistakes, as well as from the input of our readers, and to improve with each new book and edition. Many of those who use the *Unofficial Guides* write to us asking questions, making comments, or sharing their own discoveries or lessons learned in New York. We appreciate all such input, both positive and critical, and encourage our readers to continue writing. Readers' comments and observations will be frequently incorporated in revised editions of the *Unofficial Guide* and will contribute immeasurably to its improvement.

How to Write the Authors:

Eve and Bob
The Unofficial Guide to New York City
P.O. Box 43673
Birmingham, AL 35243
unofficialguides@menasharidge.com

When you write, be sure to put your return address on your letter as well as on the envelope—sometimes envelopes and letters get separated. And remember, our work takes us out of the office for long periods of time, so forgive us if our response is delayed.

Reader Survey

At the back of the guide you will find a short questionnaire that you can use to express opinions about your New York visit. Clip the questionnaire out along the dotted line and mail it to this address.

"Inside" New York for Outsiders

It's a funny thing about New York travel guides: Most of them tell you too much, and a few tell you too little. It's because it's such a complex city, so ornate and enveloping and layered with history and happenstance that it's hard to stop acquiring good stories and passing them on. And it's an endless voyage: The more time you spend there, the more you realize you don't know.

But the fact is, statistics show that the majority of visitors to New York stay only three or four days—and even that average span frequently includes time spent in business meetings or conventions. How much can you squeeze into a long weekend? How much do you want to see? This city's attractions are among the most frequently photographed in the world, yet packaged tours often haul you about the city as relentlessly as if you didn't already know what the Statue of Liberty or the horse-drawn carriages of Central Park looked like. Some tour books either skimp on shopping or endorse every dealer in town; some overlook any collection smaller than five stories tall. Some short-change any fine arts or theater productions outside Lincoln Center or Broadway, as if Midtown were the whole of Manhattan and restaurants were the sole form of nightlife. Some are too uncritical, some too "insider." Some have all the right stuff, but are poorly organized; some are easy to read, but oversimplified and boring.

Not only that, but most guidebook writers seem so attached to the modern stereotype of the city—the New York of loudmouthed cabbies, TV cop shows, the "if I can make it there" rat race, and Wall Street shark pool—that they don't express the great romance of this rich, inimitable, and electrifying metropolis. It's an asphalt wonder, sure, but there are cobblestones still to be seen; a world-famous skyline, yes, but an architectural creation, not just a higher-rent district. It's a magnet for immigration, but that also means it's a tapestry of ethnic revival. And in an era when the Statue of Liberty is animated for a deodorant commercial, it's too easy to forget what an icon it really is and has been to millions of Americans and would-be Americans. Okay, call us sentimentalists, but it's true: We do love New York, just not the one the hype artists are selling.

So as hard and heartbreaking as it is to limit a book like this, we have done so, by doubling up whenever possible. The neighborhood profiles in Part One, Understanding the City, are partly geographical descriptions and partly historical romances: They're designed to help you get your bearings, but they include enough sights and stories to give you the community's true flavor. In Part Seven, Sight-seeing, Tours, and Attractions, we've listed some attractions by type—family style, theatrical, genealogical, and so on—to help you customize your visit. Particular museums and entertainments in each zone are explored in more detail and rated for interest by age group. We've also listed some personal favorites that may not get as much publicity but that we think are first-rate. In Part Nine, Shopping in New York, we've combined best bets with do-it-yourself walking tours so you can see the sights and fill out your wish list at the same time. The zone maps are designed to help you with the logistics of arranging accommodations, dining, and sightseeing.

As for the hundreds of tourist attractions, well, we've tried to sort them into first-rate, special interest, and hype jobs, and we spend space on only the best. The truth is, even if you visit New York a dozen times, you won't be able to see even as much as we've described for you, and by then you'll have discovered your own favorite side to the city. But certainly we don't want you to waste any of that time, either. We take things easy, the way we think you will want to; but we don't forgive exploitation or boost unworthy distractions. If it isn't fun, if it isn't informative, if it isn't accurate, we don't want you to go. If there's a better alternative, we want you to know. We hope to keep the quality of your visit high and the irritation quotient low. And if we'd known that would turn into a poem, we'd have let you know.

We've covered these attractions in these various ways, often overlapping, because we want to make sure you can pick out the ones you'd most enjoy. And for those who don't wish to do it yourself at all, we have listed a number of commercial and customized tours that you can take tailored to almost any interest, also in Part Seven.

On the other hand, even granting that your time will be tight, we have included a list of opportunities for exercise or play. That's partly because we at the *Unofficial Guides* try to keep up with our workouts when we're on the road; and also because you may be visiting old friends, old teammates, and tennis players. Beyond that, although you may not think you'll want to make time for a run or ride, experience has taught us that sightseeing and shopping can be exhausting, make you stiff, make you long for a little outdoors—or at least a little calorie countering.

Please do remember that prices and hours change constantly; we have listed the most up-to-date information we can get, but it never hurts to double-check times in particular (if prices of attractions change, it is generally not by much). And remember, this is one of the busiest tourist towns in the world, drawing more than 30 million visitors a year, so make your reservations early and reconfirm at least once.

How Information Is Organized:
By Subject and by Geographic Zone

In order to give you fast access to information about the best of New York, we've organized material in several formats.

Hotels　Since most people visiting New York stay in one hotel for the duration of their trip, we have summarized our coverage of hotels in charts, maps, ratings, and rankings that allow you to quickly focus your decision-making process. We do not go on, page after page, describing lobbies and rooms that, in the final analysis, sound much the same. Instead, we concentrate on the specific variables that differentiate one hotel from another: location, size, room quality, services, amenities, and cost.

Restaurants We provide plenty of detail when it comes to restaurants. Since you will probably eat a dozen or more restaurant meals during your stay, and since not even you can predict what you might be in the mood for on Saturday night, we provide detailed profiles of the best restaurants in and around New York.

Entertainment and Nightlife Visitors frequently try several different clubs or nightspots during their stay. Since clubs and nightspots, like restaurants, are usually selected spontaneously after arriving in New York, we believe detailed descriptions are warranted. The best nightspots and lounges in New York are profiled by category in Part Eleven, "Entertainment and Nightlife."

Geographic Zones Once you've decided where you're going, getting there becomes the issue. To help you do that, we have divided the city into geographic zones:

Zone 1	Lower Manhattan, Wall Street, and the Battery	Zone 10	West Side
		Zone 11	East Side
Zone 2	Soho and Tribeca	Zone 12	Upper West Side
Zone 3	Chinatown, Little Italy, and the Lower East Side	Zone 13	Upper East Side
		Zone 14	Columbia University and Harlem
Zone 4	Greenwich Village		
Zone 5	The East Village	Zone 15	The Heights
Zone 6	Chelsea	Zone 16	Brooklyn
Zone 7	Gramercy Park and Madison Square	Zone 17	Queens
		Zone 18	The Bronx
Zone 8	Midtown West and the Theater District	Zone 19	Staten Island
Zone 9	Midtown East		

All profiles of hotels, restaurants, and nightspots include zone numbers. If you are staying in Lower Manhattan, for example, and are interested in restaurants within walking distance, scanning the restaurant profiles for restaurants in Zone 1 will provide you with the best choices.

Zones 1–13:
Manhattan
(See map on p. 12)

NE

10

New York Touring Zones

N

Zone 15

Zone 18

87

Bronx River Pkwy.

Boston Rd.

George
Washington
Bridge

95

Bronx

95

Long Island Sound

Henry Hudson Pkwy.

87

Zone 14

East River

295

LaGuardia
Airport

278

Whitestone Expwy.

Clearview Expwy.

25A

Northern Blvd.

Flushing Meadows
Corona Park

Kissena
Park

Cunningham
Park

Long Island Expwy.

295

Cross State Pkwy.

Grand Central Pkwy.

278

Forest
Hills

Interborough Pkwy.

Forest
Park

Merrick Blvd.

Zone 16

Atlantic Ave.

Rockaway Blvd.

678

Zone 17
Queens

Southern Pkwy.

Nassau Expwy.

Prospect
Park

Kings Hwy.

JFK
International
Airport

Flatbush Ave.

Shore Pkwy.

Jamaica Bay
Wildlife Refuge

878

Atlantic
Beach

27

Jamaica
Bay

Rockaway Inlet

ATLANTIC OCEAN

Zones 1–13:
Manhattan

Zones 1–5:
Lower
Manhattan

NE

13

Zones 6–9: Midtown Manhattan

NE

ZONE 8

Midtown West

W. 42nd St.

Port Authority Bus Terminal

Time Square

Madison Square Garden

Central Park S.

W. 57th St.

W. 53rd St.

W. 50th St.

W. 45th St.

W. 34th St.

Museum of Modern Art

Rockefeller Center

New York Public Library

E. 59th St.

E. 50th St.

Midtown East

E. 45th St.

United Nations

E. 42nd St.

ZONE 9

Bryant Park

Empire State Bldg.

Madison Ave.

Murray Hill

E. 34th St.

11th Ave.

10th Ave.

9th Ave.

8th Ave.

7th Ave.

Broadway

Avenue of the Americas

5th Ave.

Park Ave.

Lexington Ave.

3rd Ave.

2nd Ave.

1st Ave.

East River

W. 23rd St.

E. 23rd St.

ZONE 6

Gramercy Park

ZONE 7

Chelsea

W. 14th St.

Union Square

E. 14th St.

8 | 9

6 | 7

ZONE 4

W. 12th St.

ZONE 5

0   0.5 Mile

14

Zone 14

Cathedral Pkwy.

Henry Hudson Pkwy.

Riverside Dr.

West End Dr.

Columbus Ave.

Broadway

W. 96th St.

Upper
West Side

W. 86th St.

Riverside
Park

American Museum
of Natural History

W. 79th St.

Zone 12

W. 72nd St.

Zone 10

Freedom St.

Lincoln
Center

59th St.

57th St.

Fordham
University

W. 53rd St.

W. 50th St.

Zone 8

Lexington Ave.

3rd Ave.

E. 110th St.

Museo Del
Barrio

E. 106th St.

Museum of the City
of New York

Park Ave.

Madison Ave.

5th Ave.

East River

FDR Drive

E. 96th St.

International Center
of Photography

Cooper Hewitt
Museum

E. 91st St.

Guggenheim
Museum

Carl Schurz
Park

Metropolitan
Museum of Art

E. 84th St.

Upper
East Side

Yorkville

E. 79th St.

Zone 13

John Jay
Park

E. 72nd St.

E. 67th St.

E. 65th St.

Zone 11

E. 62nd St.

Central Park S.

E. 59th St.

Zone 9

12   13
10   11

0   0.5 Mile

**Zones 10–13:
East and West
Side Manhattan**

NE

15

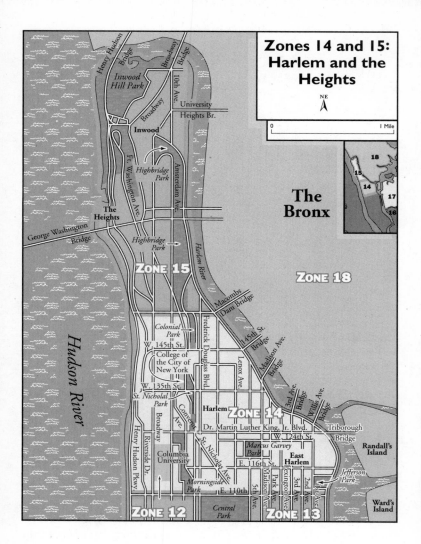

Part One

Understanding the City

Boroughs, Neighborhoods, and "Districts"

"New York, New York, it's a helluva town / The Bronx is up and the Battery's down / And the people ride in a hole in the ground." It's true, it's easy to remember . . . and you can dance to it. But it's only a little bit of the story.

When we say "New York," most of the time we really mean the island of **Manhattan,** and so does almost everybody else. Even those who live in other areas talk about going into "the city" when they mean going to Manhattan. In fact, however, Manhattan is just one of New York's five "boroughs," which are the equivalent of counties. The others are the **Bronx** to the north across the Harlem River, **Brooklyn** and **Queens** to the east on Long Island across the East River, and **Staten Island** to the south of the harbor. (Manhattanites, incidentally, refer to the other four jurisdictions as "the outer boroughs.")

Within all five boroughs are areas that have nicknames or historic designations, such as Prospect Park, the Theater District, and Union Square. And with the usual shifts of time and trend, some neighborhoods have merged with others, or upscaled, or run down, and so forth. For the purposes of this book, and to help focus your touring, we have combined some of these older neighborhoods in our zone system. For example, the Lower East Side, Zone 3, incorporates Little Italy and Chinatown; Midtown West, Zone 8, includes the Theater District and what is often called the Garment District.

We recommend that you also read, or at least skim, Part Six, New York's Neighborhoods, once before your visit; these profiles will not only help you frame your itinerary but also will give you a sense of the historical evolution of New York—how succeeding generations of immigrants, merchants, and millionaires gradually spread up from the southern tip of the island to the top of Central Park, each generation pushing the last before it, moving the less fortunate or simply less picturesque elements up and out away from the prow of prosperity; and how in the early 21st century, the process is repeating itself, so that areas once abandoned in the wake of this northward expansion are once again gathering strength and vitality.

Take the A Train . . . Carefully

Most of Manhattan is laid out on a grid, which is easy to master, but there are some irregular rules to remember. Occasionally streets change names as well, at least on the maps and signs. Sixth Avenue is officially dubbed "Avenue of the Americas," but you never hear anybody call it that except perhaps a city promoter. Where 59th Street runs along the south border of Central Park, it is called, not surprisingly, Central Park South; and when Eighth Avenue passes 59th/Central Park South on its way north along the western edge of the park, it becomes Central Park West. (Above that, in the Heights, it's officially named Frederick Douglass Boulevard, but it's more often still called Eighth Avenue.) East 110th Street, which runs along the top of Central Park on the Upper East Side, is called Central Park North along the park itself and Cathedral Parkway on the Upper West Side.

However—and these are the ones that can be more confusing—Fifth Avenue, which is the eastern border of Central Park, does not change its name; and Park Avenue, which a visitor might assume was a form of "Central Park East," is two blocks east of that. Columbus Avenue, which one might assume originated in Columbus Circle, is actually an avenue away; it is the extension of Ninth Avenue, whereas Columbus Circle is on Eighth. And West Street, which is over by the Hudson River in Lower Manhattan, Greenwich Village, and Chelsea, eventually runs over into Twelfth Avenue and becomes the West Side Expressway; don't confuse that with West End Avenue, which is the extension of Eleventh Avenue on the Upper West Side.

There is a Broad Street not far from Broadway in the Financial District, but it's less than half a mile long and a couple of blocks east of the real thing. On the other hand, there is a West Broadway that runs parallel to the "big" Broadway from Washington Square Park south to Battery Park, so Soho and Tribeca addresses can be tricky. In the East Village, it is possible to find yourself at such confusing intersections as 2nd and Second, meaning East 2nd Street and Second Avenue, but such addresses are fortunately rare.

Most of the avenues with "names"—Park, Lexington, and Madison—are on the East Side between Third and Fifth Avenues (Park was once Fourth). However, there are some places on the island that are farther east than First Avenue, namely York on the Upper East Side and Avenues A, B, C, and D—in order as they go toward the East River—in the East Village. Tenth Avenue becomes Amsterdam Avenue above West 72nd Street.

Finally, be careful about subway names as well: The Sixth Avenue subway does generally go below Sixth Avenue, but the famous A Train is on the West Side, a world (almost literally) away from Avenue A on the Lower East Side.

As for specific addresses, there are various ornate and unmemorizable mathematical equations for pinpointing the nearest cross street, but even these aren't always exactly the same. We suggest you either pick up one of the various pocket maps that have this formula, or just call ahead and ask; most businesses automatically supply the "between such and such" information.

For more tips see, Part Four, Arriving and Getting Oriented.

"And the Battery's Down"

We have divided Manhattan into 15 zones so that you can more easily pinpoint attractions, restaurants, and accommodations. (Each of the other four boroughs is a zone in itself.) Although they sound complicated, they block off into fairly obvious pieces; see the street borders in "How Information Is Organized" in the Introduction if you'd like to mark off a map.

However, it helps to have some general notion of up and down— meaning uptown and downtown, not that hole in the ground. If you think of the island of Manhattan as running north-south, which it very nearly does, you can fix it in your head as a sort of skinny, slightly bottom-heavy watch, a Salvador Dalí affair with an oversized stem, a squiggly right edge, and Central Park more or less at the center of the dial.

The northernmost part of Manhattan, which sticks up like the extra-long clock stem, is called the **Heights,** shorthand for the series of areas called Morningside Heights, Hamilton Heights, and Washington Heights. These are divided from New Jersey on the west by the Hudson River and across the top and east by the Spuyten-Duyvil Creek. The lower eastern bulge of this area, from about 12 to 1, is **Harlem.**

On either side of Central Park and matching it top and bottom are, logically, the **Upper East Side** and **East Side,** a long two o'clock hour, and the **Upper West Side** and **West Side** at ten. (Remember, the clock face is stretched out a little, so it's longer at the bottom.)

From the southern edge of Central Park (59th Street) it gets a little trickier, but if you imagine a line running down the middle of the rest of Manhattan—generally along Sixth Avenue and Broadway—then you can place **Midtown** at three o'clock, **Gramercy Park/Madison Square** at four, with the **East Village** and then the combined **Chinatown/Little Italy/Lower East Side** filling up from around 4:30 almost to 6, where **Lower Manhattan** and the **Battery** hang at the very tip.

Swinging back around from the bottom from about 6:30 toward 8 are **Soho/Tribeca** and **Greenwich Village,** then **Chelsea** at 8, **Midtown West/ the Theater District** at 9, and back to the West Side.

The **Bronx** is indeed "up"—it curves alongside the Heights above Harlem. In fact, if Manhattan were a pocket watch, the Bronx would be the fob it hung from. **Queens** is opposite the East and Upper East Side, **Brooklyn** a little southeast (4 to 5:30-ish), and **Staten Island** drops off almost directly below Manhattan, as if the tip of Lower Manhattan had let go a teardrop. Having these vague compass points in mind is especially helpful when you are trying to figure out which subway platform you want to be standing on, as most signs include "uptown," "downtown" or a borough name as a general direction. Of the five boroughs, only the Bronx is attached to the continental United States; and though most of the island's waterside culture has been almost obscured by modern development, it was integral to many areas of New York—and it also means that boats, and occasionally intrepid swimmers, can actually circumnavigate Manhattan.

A Very Short History
of an Extremely Complex City

New York is one of the oldest cities in the United States, the nation's first capital and still one of the financial and cultural capitals of the world, and as such it has all the ingredients of a rousing history: founding fathers, first brokers, big money, political corruption, cultural diversity, ethnic riots, artistic enterprise, struggling immigrants. It was the site of many of the legendary "firsts" of America: Robert Fulton's first steamboat was launched on the Hudson River in 1807; Samuel Morse sent the first telegraph message from New York in 1837; the first organized baseball team, the New York Knickerbockers, was organized in 1845; and the first World's Fair was held in Manhattan in 1853. The first real battles of the American Revolution were fought there. Even the first antitax uprising took place in Manhattan, led by merchant Jacob Leisler more than 300 years ago.

New York has always welcomed the iconoclast: It was not the first city to have a fine church built with the donations of a retired pirate (in this case, William Kidd, who contributed much toward the construction of Trinity Church), but colonial governor Lord Cornbury, who was appointed just after the turn of the 18th century, was surely the first public official in America to appear in drag.

New York is still the great melting pot; it only covers 300 square miles—Manhattan a mere 22—but it has a population of about 9 million, speaking between 90 and 100 languages. Sixty percent of city residents place their city of origin outside the United States. Add the parts of Connecticut, New Jersey, Pennsylvania, Long Island, and the upstate region considered the greater metropolitan area, and New York becomes a nation of more than 20 million speaking some 160 languages.

Colonialism and Capitalism

If it weren't for a determined jag of geography (or, rather, political arm-twisting), New York City might not even connect with the rest of the state. It's like the little tail on a stylized comma, or the pointed throat of some vulturous bird cutting down the Hudson River toward the Atlantic.

Before the arrival of the Europeans, the region was inhabited by two groups of related native tribes: the Algonquians (which included the Canarsie, who lent their name to a section of eastern Brooklyn, and the Delaware as well as the "Mohegans" or "Mahicans," immortalized by James Fenimore Cooper) along the Hudson and on Long Island; and the Iroquois Confederacy, among them the Mohawks and Seneca, who roamed to the west and upstate. Some historians theorize that the colony reportedly established in the year 1010 by Greenlander Thorfinn Karls-fensi was in fact on the island of Manhattan, but if so, the three years of his village's existence left no trace.

As was common in the 16th and 17th centuries, the explorers who sailed for one European empire were often citizens of another, so fascinated by the prospect of travel that they accepted commissions from rival powers. So John Cabot of Genoa became a citizen of Venice, then moved to Bristol and sailed for England; he landed in Newfoundland in 1497 and returned to the region in 1498. His son Sebastian, who may have reached the Hudson Bay a decade later, sailed for the Spanish. Venetian Giovanni da Verrazano, who sailed into New York Bay in 1524, was in the pay of the French. Esteban Gomez, who sighted Manhattan a year later, was a Portuguese Moor flying the Spanish flag. Henry Hudson, who was English, was working for the Dutch. At least Samuel de Champlain, who was also carrying the French flag when he mapped eastern Canada, was working in his own language.

With its fine natural port, access to Canada via the Hudson River, and the agricultural wealth of the surrounding territory—not to mention European dreams of a vast paradise of gold in the land beyond and a marine shortcut to the Asian trade—New York was destined to be the target of political and colonial struggles. Champlain and Hudson worked their way into almost the same area at the same time, in 1609, and left their names behind as a handy reminder: The Frenchman sailed south from Canada along what is now known as Lake Champlain to its tip, while the Englishman sailed north along the route, ever after called the Hudson River, nearly as far as modern Albany.

The French, who had earlier allied themselves with the Huron in Canada, immediately became embroiled in trade and territorial struggles with the tribes of the Iroquois, a strategy that would haunt them for more than a century. The Dutch, on the other hand, went right for the open water: In 1624, representatives of the newly created Dutch West Indies

Company famously acquired the land at the south end of the island of Manhattan from the easy-going Manates tribe for trinkets worth roughly $25, naming the settlement New Amsterdam. They were sometimes referred to as the Manhattan Indians, as they called the area Man-a-hatt-ta. However, that may have been a bad omen: One other possible interpretation of the word derives from "island of drunkenness," because Hudson's landing apparently turned into quite a party. Under a series of practical-minded Dutch administrators, the port prospered and expanded, and they almost certainly got their money's worth in the next 40 years. Workers, whether voluntary or involuntary, were highly desirable: the first African slaves were imported in 1625, and the first Jewish settlers arrived in 1664.

But during the Second Dutch War, England redeclared its right to the region, basing its claim on the voyages of John Cabot; in 1664, when the English fleet sailed into New York Harbor, then-governor Peter Stuyvesant struck his colors and quietly surrendered. (Actually, his constituents surrendered for him; a puritanical tyrant with a wooden leg, Stuyvesant ordered every tavern in the city to close by 9 p.m., which clearly proves he was in the wrong place.) He left behind the names of Wall Street (so called because a protective wall was raised there); Broadway (originally Breede Wegh), a cobbled route that ran the entire length of the island; the Bowery (from his own country home or "bouwerie") in the farmland a mile north and east of the city; Harlem; and of course, Stuyvesant Square. With one very brief resurgence of the Dutch, New York—now renamed in honor of King Charles's brother, the Duke of York (later James II)—was firmly in the hands of the British.

Back in Europe, the imperial and often internecine struggles between Britain and France only intermittently gave way to peace. So the colonial governor, Thomas Donegan, increasingly wary of French expansionism from the Canadian border, assiduously cultivated friendly relationships with the Iroquois. It was a good strategy, and the tribes were an invaluable ally during the decades of the French and Indian Wars that stretched from the late 17th century into the mid-18th. The Battery got its name early in those wars, when nearly a hundred cannon were lined up along the waterfront to prevent an attack on the harbor. The Treaty of Paris in 1763 confirmed the British domination of the North American territories, and the long and bitter campaigns gave way to a burst of settlement and expansion.

There was a brief period of self-satisfied prosperity. The area was covered in wheat fields and farms, like the one in the Bronx on which the Van Courtland House, now a museum, was built in 1748. King's College (now Columbia) was founded in 1754; St. Paul's Chapel was dedicated in 1766.

But then, in one of those ironies history is made of, the British crown tried to pay off its war debts by levying huge taxes on the very American colonies it had fought so hard to retain. With the passage of the Stamp Act in 1765, the resentment of many formerly loyal colonists reached a crisis. Shippers and "bolters" (millers) turned to smuggling and tariff-dodging. Fledgling Sons of Liberty took on the British authorities in the "Battle of Golden Hill" as early as 1770, and in 1774 they threw a "tea party" of their own in New York Harbor. Tensions increased to the point that many older landowners returned to England. William Tryon, the popular colonial governor of North Carolina, was transferred to New York in an attempt to contain the troubles, but he was forced out in 1775. Rebellion-minded New Yorkers—notably including English-born but radical-hearted Thomas Paine and 19-year-old Alexander Hamilton, whose eloquence would later be turned to persuading the colonies to ratify the Constitution—published scathing denunciations of the Crown's policies toward the colonies. With the capture of Fort Ticonderoga later that year, war was all but declared.

This was the crucial region of the American Revolution. Fully a third of all battles were fought in the state, including the tide-turning Battle of Saratoga. New York produced both America's first martyr, Nathan Hale, who was hanged in the city, and its most infamous traitor, Benedict Arnold.

But for all its cathartic rhetoric, New York City's active role in the Revolution was very short and not too sweet. General Washington suffered a series of defeats in the fall of 1776, including the battles of Long Island, Harlem Heights, and White Plains, and though the Americans held onto most of the upper and western part of the state, they eventually had to abandon the city to the British forces, who sailed into the harbor in a fleet of 500 ships and occupied it for the full seven years until the end of the war.

During the British occupation, unfortunately, the city was swept by two massive and somewhat suspicious fires, one right after the occupation that destroyed a thousand homes and Trinity Church, and the second in 1778. Consequently, there are few buildings from the colonial period visible outside Historic Richmondtown and the Alice Austen House, both on Staten Island; even the Fraunces Tavern, site of Washington's famous farewell to the troops in 1783, is a partial re-creation of the original.

The Empire State

Almost from the moment peace was pronounced, New York boomed—and bickered. From 1785 until 1790, New York served as the nation's capital; it was here that Washington was sworn in as the first president; and it was from here that Hamilton, John Jay, and Virginian James Madison published the so-called Federalist Papers, which eventually persuaded the states to ratify the Constitution. Hamilton, who had married the governor's daughter, served as Washington's secretary of the treasury and founded both the Bank of New York and the *New York Post*. But he and John Adams opposed the French Revolution, which widened the gap between the Federalists and the Jeffersonians, among whom were Hamilton's former collaborator Madison and the brilliant young senator Aaron Burr, strongman of the Tammany Society. (For an explanation of the Tammany Society, see the section on Zone 10 in Part Six, New York's Neighborhoods.) Burr succeeded in becoming Jefferson's vice president, but Hamilton's jealous maneuvering prevented Burr's becoming president instead; and when Hamilton later blocked Burr's election as governor, Burr challenged him to a duel. The 1804 shootout left both Hamilton and Burr's political career fatally wounded.

About the time that political power shifted, first to Philadelphia and then to the new capital at Washington, the New York Stock Exchange opened, and New York's indefinite term as a financial capital began. The agricultural order gradually began to yield to an industrial and shipping society. Staten Island ferry boy Cornelius Vanderbilt gradually bought up the local freight lines and built his shipping force into an empire, becoming a millionaire while still in his teens. German-born John Jacob Astor, whose China trading, land sales, and fur trade companies enjoyed comfortable monopolies in the nation, was the first in New York's long line of millionaire tycoons (and first to establish the city's philanthropic tradition by leaving money for what became the New York Public Library). Confident of its own importance as early as 1804, the city established the New-York Historical Society collection.

Already it was the largest city in the country, with more than 33,000 residents; ten years later the population had nearly doubled. In 1811, city planners tried to impose some order on the labyrinth of haphazard roads by laying out the famous Manhattan "grid" above 14th Street. A series of virulent epidemics—yellow fever, cholera, typhoid, smallpox—gradually drove residents from the old downtown area into what is now Greenwich Village; and another huge fire in 1835, which once again destroyed most of lower Manhattan, cleared the way for ever more ambitious construction. They also inspired the creation of Croton Reservoir in 1842, in the heart of Midtown where the New York Public Library is now; this project marked the beginning of fresh public water and a citywide sewer system.

The Erie Canal was completed in 1825, drawing even more trade, and immigrants as well, through its already booming port. The great potato famine forced a huge influx of Irish immigrants—at least 200,000—in the 1840s and 1850s. A wave of German immigrants followed in the 1860s; the Chinese began arriving in the 1870s; and in the 1880s, an estimated 1.5 million Eastern European Jews flooded the Lower East Side. They were accompanied by thousands of Italians, Irish, and displaced Southern blacks, and by 1900 the city held an astonishing 3.4 million people. That would double again, to 7 million, in just 30 years. And those were just the ones who settled down; an estimated 17 million more transient immigrants passed through the city between 1880 and 1910.

The widespread poverty and incredibly unsanitary living conditions of the underclass produced not only disease, but rampant and almost institutional crime—that is, street gangs at one level, and political machines at the other. The Five Points neighborhood, re-created by Martin Scorcese in his 2002 epic *Gangs of New York,* was only blocks from Cherry Street, where William "Boss" Tweed held court. Tweed and his Tammany Hall organization looted the city of more than $160 million over the years, though they did do the immigrants the favor of registering them as Democrats by way of maintaining control.

New York took on the role of intellectual capital as well. The rest of the state might be known to have a sort of wild and bucolic beauty, thanks to the efforts of such writers as Washington Irving, James Fenimore Cooper, and William Cullen Bryant, and the Hudson River School artists, including Thomas Cole and Frederick Church; but New York City was determined that everything be modern and smart.

Horace Greeley's *New York Tribune,* the most influential newspaper before and during the Civil War, was founded in 1841; the *New York Times* followed in 1851. The University of the City of New York was chartered in 1831; the Philharmonic Society of New York gave its first concert in 1842. The Crystal Palace, modeled on the pavilion erected for London's Great Exposition of 1851, hosted the first World's Fair in 1853 (and later burned to the ground, just as the London palace had). Numerous progressive and reformist movements made New York their headquarters, including the suffragettes (the first women's rights convention was held in Seneca Falls in 1848); Greeley's *Tribune* editorialized in favor of organized labor, profit sharing (both of which he instituted at his paper), abolition, and women's suffrage. The California gold rush electrified Wall Street in 1849; a scheme by Jay Gould to corner the gold market 20 years later would nearly bankrupt it.

And in 1858, one of New York's most beloved landmarks, Central Park, opened its gates, ensuring that even the poorest sweatshop employee in the city would always have a place to walk like a prince.

Civil War and the "Second Empire"

New York was no stranger to slavery. The first slaves had been imported by the Dutch in 1625, and in fact it was slave labor that built the original fortress, including the "wall" that was Wall Street. With painful irony, Wall Street also featured the first slave market, a mercenary operation that predated the Stock Exchange by nearly a century. But New York was also in the vanguard of the abolitionist movement, outlawing slavery in the city as early as 1799 (phasing it out over 30 years) and increasingly agitating for nationwide abolition. Frederick Douglass's influential *North Star* newspaper was headquartered in Rochester; Greeley's *Tribune* was the country's most vociferous antislavery mainstream paper (though originally a passivist one). It was the growing split between the outspoken antislavery and laissez-faire elements within the long-dominant Democratic Party that helped swing New York to the Republicans and Abraham Lincoln in 1860.

Nevertheless, while the progressive intellectual element in New York favored abolition, not even all of them—and even fewer members of the laboring class and immigrant communities, who could not hope to raise the $300 "replacement fee" that was the rich man's alternative to active service—supported a war to free the Southern slaves. With the passage of the Conscription Act, draft riots broke out all over the country; those in New York City, which lasted four days in July 1863 and resulted in the death or displacement of close to a thousand blacks, were the most serious. It required the mobilization of the police, navy forces, militia, and even West Point cadets, along with the troops already in the field, to restore order.

In general, however, New York vigorously supported the war effort, especially as the need for continual military supplies and transportation fueled the city's industries: battleships (including the ironclad *Monitor*) and freighters, textiles for uniforms and supplies, provisions, and, most important, the railroads that carried them. And for all the occasional Wall Street panics, the momentum never really slackened: the end of the war was for New York the beginning of what Mark Twain christened the "Gilded Age."

Luxury hotels such as the (original) Waldorf-Astoria and the Plaza opened their doors; so did the Metropolitan Museum of Art and the Metropolitan Opera House on Broadway. Fifth Avenue became known as "Mansion Row." Henry Villard, publisher of the *New York Evening Post* and founder of the Northern Pacific Railroad, began his gilded palace (now the New York Palace) at 50th Street in 1881; W. K. Vanderbilt built an Italianate mansion at 51st and Fifth, just one of a long line—or avenue—of Vanderbilt family extravagances leading up to his cousin Cornelius II's fantastic French Renaissance chateau at the foot of Central Park (the house seen in the painting in the Plaza Hotel's Oak Bar).

Elevated railroads, or "Els," running above Second, Third, Sixth, and Ninth Avenues suddenly made it easier to get uptown, and newly electrified streetlights made it safer. Telephone and telegraph wires crisscrossed the city, at least until the blizzard of 1888 ripped them down and launched the city on a buried-cable program. The first great luxury apartment building, the Dakota, designed by the architect of the Plaza, staked out a new frontier on Central Park West at 72nd Street. Henry Frick constructed his mansion on the east side of the park at 70th, within easy reach of the new Metropolitan Museum of Art. The Statue of Liberty, St. Patrick's Cathedral, the Brooklyn Bridge, Carnegie Hall—all these monuments to the New York spirit were in place within a quarter century of war's end.

And the city was stretching in other directions, too, especially to the southeast. The Brooklyn Academy of Music had been founded in 1858; Brooklyn's Prospect Park, designed by Central Park architects Frederick Olmsted and Calvert Vaux (and considered by many to be superior to the Manhattan park), was finished in 1867; the Brooklyn Museum of Art opened in 1897. In fact, Brooklyn was the third largest city in the country on its own—it would still be the fourth largest today—but in 1898, the modern city of New York, the combined five boroughs, was officially consolidated.

No economy—and no underground economy—benefited more than New York's during the postwar period. Shipping, trade, industry, government contracts, and, inevitably, corruption in the awarding of them, made millionaires out of manufacturers, mob bosses, political influence-peddlers, and sweatshop operators alike. Samuel Tilden became an early example of New York's periodic hero, the crusading reformer, when he prosecuted Boss Tweed of the Tammany Hall ring, but he made little real dent in the power of Tammany itself. (A few years later, city police commissioner Theodore Roosevelt would build a more successful political career on his reformist reputation.) The Republicans were not much cleaner, and the semi-underground power struggle led to a more overt political distance between the city's Democrats and the Republicans upstate.

The hundreds of thousands of immigrants who arrived near the end of the 19th century were herded into warehouses, mills, and industrial sweatshops, while labor leaders fought to establish minimal hour and wage (and age) standards. The tenement, the flophouse, the drug den, and the gang took up permanent positions in the city structure. Despite periodic catastrophes—most famously the Triangle Shirtwaist Factory fire of 1911, which killed 140—and the increase of institutionalized poverty, most New Yorkers were intoxicated by the flow of commercial goods and boastfully smug about the prosperity of the city.

To a great extent, both this vast prosperity and the narrowness of its beneficiaries is exemplified by the spread of the railroads and the great fortunes their owners made from them. And one way or another, most of the rail barons had New York connections. The gold rush of 1849 may have lured Collis Huntington from Oneonta, New York, to California; but he quickly realized that the real money was to be made in railroads stretching to the West Coast. The fortunes of Andrew Carnegie and his partner-turned-rival Henry Frick were forged in steel and railroading. "Commodore" Cornelius Vanderbilt expanded into railroads as well and became lord of the New York–Chicago routes. Jay Gould was forced out of the Erie Railroad and other state rails, but he merely headed west and wound up with four more.

New York stockbroker E. H. Harriman took over the Union Pacific, Southern Pacific, and Central Pacific. J. Pierpont Morgan, already extremely wealthy thanks to his financier father, J. S. Morgan, took a lesson from all of these preceding examples, wresting away control of Gould's eastern railway holdings, founding U.S. Steel with Frick, and lending gold to the federal government at usurious rates during the Panic of 1895. These families, along with the Astors and Villards and their financial rivals, built lavish mansions on the East Side, establishing Midtown and Central Park as the social center of Manhattan and defining what came to be known as the "Four Hundred," the city's social elite. (It may be worth remembering that the life of luxury need not be a safe one, however: John Jacob Astor went down on the *Titanic,* and a Vanderbilt died on the *Lusitania.*)

Of course, there was nonsteel money. John D. Rockefeller's fortune, grounded in the oil-refining business, was almost incalculable, well into the hundreds of millions by the turn of the century. And he was not alone. By 1900, 70% of the nation's corporations were headquartered in Manhattan, and 65% of all import trade passed through the harbor.

The Early 20th Century

In characteristic fashion, New York was too impatient to wait for the calendar to announce a new era. The age of American imperialism, such as it was, was hastened by New York newspaper tycoons William Randolph Hearst and Joseph Pulitzer, whose respective (if not entirely respectable) dailies the *Journal* and *World* so twisted coverage of Cuban-Spanish tensions that the United States was eventually lured into the Spanish-American War, from which it gained the Philippines, Guam, and Puerto Rico, not to mention the toothy New York–born hero Teddy Roosevelt.

Even so, 1900 was a landmark year. Ground for the first subway was broken in 1900; when it was completed, it was suddenly possible to cross the nine miles from City Hall to 145th Street in a little over 20 minutes. (A steam-driven version, a single car that rocketed about 300 feet along Broadway between Warren and Murray Streets and then was sucked backward, was constructed in 1870, but it made little impression.)

The city of the future had already been forged from the five boroughs in 1898. New Yorkers were so confident of their home's position as First City that the Vanderbilts launched a railroad line that ran back and forth between Manhattan and Chicago, the "Second City"; it was described as the overland version of a luxury liner, and it was grandly titled *The Twentieth Century.* The "new" Grand Central Station, the Beaux Arts beauty now restored to its original glory, was begun in 1903; Pennsylvania Station (the original, not the existing building) would follow only a few years later. The Staten Island Ferry made its first crossing in 1905; the first metered taxi challenged the old omnibus system in 1907.

The scramble for the skyline began with the construction of the 300-foot Flatiron Building at Broadway, Fifth, and 23rd Street in 1902; skeptics confidently predicted its collapse, though it stands proudly today as the symbol of its own "district." At 30 stories, the 1913 Gothic Woolworth Building at Broadway and Park reigned for 17 years, until the construction of the 77-story Chrysler Building in 1930, and that topped the city for only a few months, until the 102-story Empire State Building opened in 1931. It was getting so dark above that the city finally passed an ordinance restricting the height and size of buildings in 1913. (The limits were rescinded in 1961, hence the MetLife building that hovers over Grand Central Terminal.)

The Apollo Theater in Harlem opened in 1913. Blacks and Hispanics settled on the West Side, in an area of the 60s then called San Juan Hill (possibly in reference to Roosevelt's great victory in Cuba), and on the north side of Manhattan in Harlem. That had been a prosperous Jewish neighborhood, but it gradually became a center for black art, literature, and music during a period called the Harlem Renaissance. In the 1920s alone, Harlem's population increased from 83,000 to more than 200,000.

World War I only boosted the city's economy, which went into overdrive to supply the troops; stocks continued to rise throughout the 1920s, which roared in New York as nowhere else. Prohibition became the law in 1920, but just as war boosted profits, so did the relatively genteel, or at least socially tolerated, crime of bootlegging. Smart, brittle, and literary characters went hand in hand with Follies. American women were not only emancipated, in the phrase of the time, but were also finally enfranchised. (Women got the vote; movies found a voice.) The *New Yorker* debuted in 1925, with its quintessential Gilded Age fop of a symbol, Eustace Tilley, on the cover. Lindbergh crossed over the Atlantic in the *Spirit of St. Louis* while New Yorkers drove under the Hudson River through the brand-new Holland Tunnel. Big bands and Broadway filled the airways; so did Babe Ruth, who in 1927 hit 60 home runs for the Yankees. The Museum of Modern Art was founded in 1929, and the Guggenheim a year later.

Everything glittered until 1929, when New York once again led the nation, this time into disaster. The crash of the stock market on October 29 turned Central Park into a shantytown and the city's greatest artists into federal employees, thanks to the Works Progress Administration (WPA). At the same time, growing political tensions in Europe, particularly in Germany, inspired a whole new generation of writers and artists to emigrate to America. During the slow reconstruction of the 1930s,

Mayor Fiorella La Guardia, the "Little Flower," was able to institute a series of municipal reforms so that the poorer classes could also share in the recovery. He also persuaded President (and former New York governor) Franklin Roosevelt to provide New Deal funds to build the Triborough and Hudson bridges, the Battery Park tunnel, and dozens of other public projects. In 1939, multimillionaire philanthropist John D. Rockefeller, Jr. personally drove the final rivet into the beautiful Art Deco complex at Rockefeller Plaza, and a few months later, flush with visions of a bright new future, the New York World's Fair of 1939–1940 drew a staggering 45 million visitors to Queens.

The Modern Era

Once again, war fueled the economy. The outbreak of World War II kicked the stock market back into high gear, and it was not to slow for nearly 30 years. With the ending of the war, America the melting pot took its place at the head of international power as well; the United Nations headquarters were established in New York in 1946. Large numbers of Puerto Ricans and other Hispanic immigrants arrived, and many of them moved to the Upper East Side, to what became known as El Barrio or Spanish Harlem; the Chinese arrived in even greater numbers throughout the 1940s and 1950s. Builder and powerbroker Robert Moses remade the face of the West Side, culturally and physically, by sweeping away the crumbling buildings in the San Juan district and designing a huge arts complex, now Lincoln Center for the Performing Arts, in its place.

The 1960s were famously feverish in New York, in the arts world and in politics. The Beatles set foot on American soil for the first time at Kennedy Airport, and they played their first U.S. concert at Shea Stadium. Queens's Flushing Meadow hosted another World's Fair, and its symbolic Unisphere still holds up its one-world promise. Columbia University students staged famous sit-ins. *Hair* opened on Broadway, and Mikhail Baryshnikov and Rudolf Nureyev led the list of Russian dancers and artists who fled to the United States. New York's black intelligentsia, from Langston Hughes and Zora Neale Hurston to James Baldwin, Richard Wright, and Ralph Ellison, had been exposing racism in scathing essays, novels, and plays throughout the 1950s; now their writings and *The Autobiography of Malcolm X* became required reading. The flamboyant lifestyle of Harlem congressman Adam Clayton Powell and the charges of corruption and political favoritism that surrounded him were reminiscent of the Prohibition-era reign of Mayor Jimmy Walker. Militant civil rights groups, antigovernment radical political parties, anti-Vietnam demonstrators, and women's groups seemed to have transformed New York society top to bottom.

And perhaps it did—but in New York, money always seems to have more pull than politics. By the early 1970s, Nixon was beginning to withdraw the troops from Southeast Asia, the hippies were on the way out, and the yuppies had arrived. A burst of luxury hotel and apartment building and huge, showy corporate structures jacked the skyline ever higher (and led, though too late for Stanford White's Penn Station, to a greater appreciation of historic restoration and preservation).

Moreover, the expansion of New York, specifically the exodus of Manhattanites into the suburbs, began to drain the city of vital income. And as the upper middle class moved out, the city became a playground for the super-rich and a prison for the poor.

The pride of the 1970s nearly led to a great fall. Just as the World Trade Center was completed in 1973, the city began to spiral toward bankruptcy, a fate just barely averted with the fraternal assistance of Wall Street. The Great White Way and the entire rest of the city went dark in the Blackout of 1977. Stocks ballooned again, only to crash again. This time even Donald Trump, symbol of conspicuous consumption, had to resort to humble refinancing. But markets never stay slow in a city that never sleeps; and downtown construction, repair, and improvement of mass transit and the restaurant and entertainment industry are stronger than ever.

Heading into the millennium, and having celebrated its own official first century as a unified city, New York seemed to be turning over its own chronometers, spiritual and literal. That great symbol Ellis Island, which reopened as the Immigration Museum in 1990, is already one of the most visited sites in New York. Chelsea Piers, the crumbling remnants of the once vital Hell's Kitchen port, reopened as a massive playground, while on the east side the South Street Seaport became a sort of historical shopping mall. Another great wave of immigration brought even greater ethnic variety to the city, especially in Brooklyn (where much of the estimated half-million recent arrivals are Caribbean) and Queens; and in Manhattan (the Heights and Chinatown). The city's population rebounded by 10% between 1990 and 2000. And crime, the city's long-standing shadow empire, is to a substantial degree succumbing to the police department's continual investigations into corruption both external and internal. During the administration of Mayor Rudolph Guiliani, a former federal prosecutor, crime rates plummeted and are now at the lowest level in a half-century.

There can be no question, however, that the events of September 11, 2001, have forever changed this great city, sobering its financial, cultural, and architectural hubris. Yet it displayed the city at its best—heroic, united, determined. It has also demonstrated the inherent power of the American Dream: The Stature of Liberty lifts her lamp to illuminate the many monuments of both despair and hope. At press time, plans were underway to reopen the Statue to visitors; the new PATH terminal and Vesey Street pedestrian bridge had been opened to return traffic through lower Manhattan; and a network was taking shape of a dozen public parks and green spaces around the border of the island's southern tip. New York may wind up with an even greater sense of its "skyline" than it had before 9-11.

The Fictional City

There are few cities that have been the subject of more novels, plays, or stories than New York, and with the advent of television and movies, the landscape is even more familiar to nonresidents. But again, we want you to see the history beneath the surface of the city, the New York that its founders dreamed of, that its wealthy ordered and its working class constructed. So among some personal, evocative, and decidedly not modern favorites:

The Age of Innocence and *The House of Mirth,* by Edith Wharton, both titled with heavy irony, bring the heyday of Midtown society to life; so does Henry James's masterpiece *Washington Square.* (The lavish film versions of these books are worth a look for the look, at least.)

The Last of the Mohicans, by James Fenimore Cooper. Maybe its old-fashioned prose put you off as a child, but Cooper's history of the colonial state and the era of the French and Indian Wars is far more fascinating. (If you were enraptured by the equally fascinating movie, be warned: Hawkeye did not fall in love with Cora Monroe; he was old enough to be her father.)

Up in the Old Hotel, by Joseph Mitchell. In this astonishing collection of articles and stories, originally written for the *New Yorker,* Mitchell brings back to life the golden era of the oyster beds, the Fulton Fish Market, and the piers and warehouses and taverns of the West Side.

Winter's Tale, by Mark Halperin. A mystical vision of the city as an engine of pure energy, a sort of transmitter between this world and another—and no description of New York in winter can ever be more enrapturing.

Caleb Carr's two adventure novels *The Alienist* and *The Angel of Darkness,* take place around the turn of the century, when gangs roved the city, Teddy Roosevelt was a young reformer, and forensic evidence and psychology were new and mysterious sciences. In a similar vein is *Waterworks,* by E. L. Doctorow, with its fantastic vision of the old Croton Reservoir.

In *Time and Again,* Jack Finney manages to imprint the New York City of the late 19th century so thoroughly in his contemporary protagonist's mind that he is transported there and falls in love.

And of course, those least childish of children's books, E. B. White's *Stuart Little,* the picaresque novel of a mouse-sized Manhattanite, and the wonderful *Eloise* (by Kay Thompson), whose portrait hangs in the lobby of her beloved Plaza Hotel and in whose honor one of the authors was once allowed to ride on the back of a carriage horse in Central Park.

Part Two

Planning Your Visit to New York

When to Go

New York may sound "northern" to a lot of folks, and in winter it can certainly scrape some low temperatures and shine up the sidewalks; but in the heart of summer, especially August, it can be as thick and muggy as any Southern city, with the temperature nudging up toward the three-figure mark and sudden, sweeping rains that leave the asphalt steaming. Why do you think the Hamptons were invented? Of course, if you're inured to the humidity, or if business or school vacations require you to travel in July or August, you will still find a lot of free programs, indoors and out, all over town (and you can count on all the restaurants and museums cranking up the air-conditioning).

Actually, there's something to be said for almost any time of year. If you go for the sidewalk show, spring and fall are absolutely gorgeous in New York; average temperatures are in the 60s and 70s, making for perfect walking weather, and there are flower shows, the ballet and opera spring seasons, and circus rings.

Summer, as we've said, is freebie heaven: opera, classical music, and Shakespeare in Central Park; Tuesday night chamber concerts in Washington Square Park, weekend concerts at South Street seaport, and jazz in MoMA's sculpture garden; swing dance on Lincoln Center Plaza; at least one street fair every week; Fourth of July fireworks and sunbathing in Strawberry Fields.

Fall is one party after another, starting with Halloween and running through Thanksgiving; and Central Park is absolutely brilliant. For all its chill—the really brutal winds don't usually hit until after the New Year—New York is a city that really knows how to dress for the holidays, with musical programs, lighting displays, elaborate window settings, parades, and so on. (In fact, a parade is practically guaranteed for your visit: There are so many excuses for parading in this town, you'd have to look for a month to miss one.) Many parks, including the Bronx Zoo, light up and stay open late around the holidays; the atrium of the Citicorp Building holds a huge model train display, as does the New York Botanical Garden; the music of the Central Park and Rockefeller Center ice rinks fills the air. The South Street Seaport is a winter fantasy of lights, and the carolers—some of them puppets—are a family favorite. Department-store windows are almost worth the visit by themselves, particularly the tradition-minded Macy's and Saks and the extravagantly unpredictable Bergdorf-Goodman's (though lines to view the windows are enormous).

January may seem sort of an afterthought, but there are all those sales (including coats), Ice Capades at Madison Square Garden, perhaps an early Chinese New Year (of course there's a parade), and quiet time in the museums that are usually full of kids.

If you do wish to go during a major holiday or around a special event, such as Christmas, be sure to make your reservations well in advance and confirm at least once. Manhattan is a madhouse at prime time, although the excitement may be worth it. If you need your space, however, pick another time.

In any case, this really is the town that never sleeps. See the final section of the chapter for a calendar of special events.

What to Pack

Perhaps a little sadly, this once most elegant of societies has become extremely informal; you'll be unlikely to see a black tie or even a tuxedo outside of a wedding party unless you are fortunate enough to be invited to a serious social event. Even the old established restaurants rarely require a tie for lunch; most only "recommend" a jacket, although it's a good idea to have a tie on hand at night. (See the dress code advisories in our restaurant profiles.) However, the great majority of Manhattanites are dressed either for success or to impress, in classic style or not, so if you like to blend in with the shopping or art crowd, go for the reasonably neat look. All those gold- and silver-glittered sweatshirts just make you look as if you spent your adolescence in Atlantic City.

If you're simply sight-seeing, you can pretty much do as you please; streetwear is every-wear, especially during the day. Shorts, T-shirts, or polo shirts (athletic-logo sportswear for kids) are common well into autumn, and a casual dress or reasonably neat pair of khakis will make you look downright respectable. The one "touristy" craze we do not recommend is the fanny pack. Not only does it mark you as an outsider, it can be more easily cut off and stolen than wallets or even purses.

As to outerwear, try to get something with dual use. A rainproof top of some sort, a lightweight jacket you can layer, or a sweater is probably the most you'll need in the summer, just in case a breeze comes up at night.

However, remember that you will probably be going in and out of air conditioning. If you're planning to jump in and out of buses or stores or even theaters, a light jacket you can easily unbutton or remove and carry without difficulty will keep you from alternately sweating and freezing. (A medium-weight or heavy shawl, which can be both decorative and warming, is a great alternative and easy to pack.) Those small fold-up umbrellas are preferable to the traditional sort, not only because you can stash them in your bag but also because a crowd of people wielding pointed implements or hanging them on chair backs and such can be dangerous (they're available on the street if you lose or forget one).

Something along the lines of a trenchcoat with zip-in lining or a wool walking coat with a sweater will usually do in winter, though it's smart to have the anti-wind accessories—gloves, earmuffs, hats, or scarves—tucked in your bag. Coming down through those "tunnels" of skyscrapers, the gusts pick up some surprising force. And if you have pull-on, thin plastic galoshes or waterproof boots of some sort, it wouldn't hurt to bring them; snowstorms can move in pretty quickly. Fur coats are no longer much of an issue in the moral sense in New York, but unless you're planning to go to the nicer hotels and restaurants, you may find your fur more trouble to worry about than it's worth. Lugging a fuzzy through the Metropolitan Museum of Art gets to be extremely sweaty. Of course, if you're sticking to the Metropolitan Opera, fur away.

Just don't overload yourself. Frankly, years of travel (and packing) have convinced us that most people carry more clothes than they really need. (And these days, with stricter limits on carry-ons and baggage weights, it's even sillier to overindulge.) As obvious as those easy-packing tips you see in travel magazines may be (pick a basic color and a few bright accessories or a change of ties, things that don't wrinkle, lots of light layers, and so on), most visitors fill up their suitcases with whole new outfits for every day and evening event. Who are you trying to impress? Plan your packing the way you'd plan everyday life at home. Unless you have a really formal event to go to, high heels are tiring and take up a lot of room (though at least nowadays there are "comfortable" heels). Similarly, men can easily wear one nice jacket and carry assorted slacks, or a suit and different shirts, perhaps a vest. A dark suit is next to formality, anyway. Besides, it is difficult to resist buying something new and fashionable when you're visiting, and then you have even more clothes to carry.

Two really important things to consider when packing are comfortable shoes—this is a culture of the streets, and what isn't asphalt is concrete—and expandable or forgiving waistlines. Even if you don't think you're going to eat much, the scent of food is constantly in the air; every bar lays out those mixed nuts or something similar; and somehow even the most careful dieters seem to join the clean plate club when they visit one of the world's most famous restaurant centers. Seasoned travelers know that a change in schedule can often cause bloating as well as, paradoxically, dehydration. Make sure you have a change of shoes, too; this is not the place to save space, because wearing the same shoes through and after hours of walking or even standing around sight-seeing is a good way to have sore feet, if not worse. If you don't want to pack "fat day" clothes, you better be packing your running shoes, anyway. Or let them double as your walking shoes. A pair of shock-absorbent sole inserts can dramatically reduce foot and back pain as well.

The other traveling "musts" are over-the-counter medications and ointments. People tend to drink more coffee and more cocktails on vacation, or even when taking important clients out, so be sure to pack headache medicines, Alka-Seltzer, and the like. If you are on prescription medicine, carry a little more of it than you actually need: You might drop some while sight-seeing or find yourself staying a day or so longer than you expected for business or pleasure or even bad traveling weather. (It wouldn't hurt to photocopy the prescription or label, either, particularly if the medication contains any controlled substances.) If you are allergic to bites or stings, remember the antihistamines. For scratches and small annoyances, a small tube of Neosporin or other antiseptic ointment is helpful. You can get these things at a drugstore or the hotel shop, of course, but those little "travel sizes" are wildly overpriced; you'd be better off putting a small amount of each in your own containers. A good way to keep medications fresh, incidentally, is to use those small zip-plastic bags sold for jewelry (or even the sandwich-sized bags). Be absolutely sure to pack bandage strips and muscle-pain antidotes as well; blisters can ruin an otherwise wonderful trip. Similarly, you might want to bring an extra pair of eyeglasses or contact lenses.

Most better hotels have small sewing kits in the rooms for quick fixes, although bigger emergencies will be better served by valets or a cleaner's around the corner. But if you're staying in a basic hotel, a needle and thread may come in handy. So may a multitool pocket knife, though you must pack it with your checked baggage (any such implements in carry-on luggage, including corkscrews, will be confiscated). If you find that you forgot to take your grandfather's pocket knife out of your kit bag, find the nearest express office and send it home.

We have found three other tiny items extremely useful: a handkerchief, disposable stain-remover pad, and one of those tiny flashlights. We mean an old-fashioned man's handkerchief, not a pretty little showpiece. Between bad weather, allergies, air-conditioning, damp subway seats, and so on, a good 12-inch square is a lifesaver. If you plan to spend time on the subways or the sidewalks, you will be in near-contact with a lot of coffee cups, snacks, and so on; if you find yourself having an even closer encounter thanks to a jerking subway ride, one of those towelette-sized spot treatments can save you a lot of heartache. And as more and more museums have to lower or narrowly focus their lighting to protect fragile canvases and textiles, we increasingly find ourselves squinting at the plaques and captions. A penlight comes in handy (but be sure to train it only on the information, not the art).

And finally, not to be an alarmist, but this is a city that has a crime problem (as do most cities nowadays), so there is no good reason to walk around flashing a lot of expensive jewelry. Leave it at home and stick to the costume stuff, or leave it in the hotel safe except for the big party. That way, even if you lose an earring, you can replace it quickly and cheaply at the next vendor cart. You might be surprised what nice-looking silver you can find on the street.

For a more in-depth discussion on staying safe in the big city, see "How to Avoid Crime" in Part Four, Arriving and Getting Oriented.

Gathering Information

Brochures, historical background, and up-to-date schedules are available from the **New York Metropolitan Convention and Visitors Bureau** (NYMCVB), which updates its material quarterly. It's best to call in advance and get their information package mailed to you (call (800) NYC-VISIT) or go to the website (**www.nycvisit.com**), but they also have offices around Manhattan if you don't get to it beforehand (call (212) 397-8222). There you can pick up lots of maps, free tickets or discounts, shopping guides, and so on. One of the NYMCVB branches is in the Selwyn Theater in Times Square (229 West 42nd, between Seventh and Eighth), which also houses the Times Square Visitors Center and public transit information center. There are also visitors centers in Pennsylvania Station (34th Street side) and carts stationed inside the Empire State Building and outside (unless it's frigid) Madison Square Garden. Be sure to pick up the free subway map.

New York has a large gay and lesbian population and a great many services and attractions for the homosexual traveler. Among local publications reporting gay events are the *Village Voice* and *New York Press,* both free in the city; and the more specialized *Next* and *Blade,* a free weekly available at many bars and restaurants. The larger gay bookstores (see the relevant section in Part Nine, Shopping in New York) are also bulletin boards for community information.

When it comes to Internet and websites, no city outdoes New York. Among them are the online version of the weekly *City Guide* provided to hotels (**www.cityguideny.com**); Citysearch (**www.citysearch.com**); and the online site of the downtown monthly *Paper* (**www.papermag.com**). The *Village Voice* has its own site as well (**www.villagevoice.com**).

New York magazine puts cultural events and restaurant and entertainment listings up at **www.nymag.com.** Even the booming Times Square has a website with info on local attractions (**www.timessquarebid.org**).

Really serious museum-goers should try to get a subscription to *Museums New York* ($20), a sort of playbill for museums with features, phone numbers, and current exhibits for even the smallest streetside collections, plus discount coupons for many of them; call (212) 604-0877.

Once you are in New York, look for any free publications in your hotel room (most often the *New York Visitors Guide* and weekly editions of the *City Guide*); check current issues of *New York* and the *New Yorker* magazine and the daily *New York Times* for special events and performances. *Time Out* is a good source of entertainment and cultural opportunities, with a special gay-interest section. The Spanish language daily *El Diario* is available at most newsstands. There are also several entertainment and cultural hotlines to call for daily opportunities: see Part Eleven, Entertainment and Nightlife.

The main area code for Manhattan is still 212, though recent years have seen the addition of 646 and 917 (mostly for cell phones). Outer-borough area codes include 718, 347, and a few others. Despite the need to dial the area code when calling between boroughs, there are no additional charges for doing so.

For more suggestions on planning your vacations around special interests, see Part Seven, Sight-seeing, Tours, and Attractions.

Special Considerations

Traveling with Children

Of course, New York is most famous as a sort of adults' playground, but if you're considering a family vacation here, don't worry: For all the bars and "the-ah-tuh," New York is absolutely jam-packed with family-style attractions and hands-on, state-of-the-art children's museums both in and outside of Manhattan, not to mention the special events, such as the Macy's Thanksgiving Day Parade, holiday lights in the area zoos (four of them!) and botanical gardens, ice skating in Rockefeller Center, harbor tours, high views, antique carousels, and so on.

In fact, if you and your family are likely to become repeat visitors, you might consider joining the **Wildlife Conservancy Society:** a family membership ($75–$90 with varying benefits) gets you in free to the zoos in Central Park and Prospect Park, the famous Bronx Zoo, and the New York Aquarium in Coney Island, with its SeaWorld–style whale dances and sea lions. That way you can work your way around the boroughs and always have a safe kids' bet. Call (718) 228-5100 or surf (**www.wcs.org**) for information.

And sight-seeing with small children can be a bargain if you use public transportation: Kids under 44 inches ride free on the buses and subways (there are handy-dandy lines by the bus driver's seat and toll gates for comparison). Just remember that warnings about dehydration go double for small children, even in winter. For some specific recommendations, see the "Best Children's Fare" list in Part Seven, Sight-seeing, Tours, and Attractions.

If you do bring the kids but would like to have a little adults-only time, contact the **Baby Sitters Guild** (call (212) 682-0227), which has bonded members that will stay in or carry out, so to speak, to Central Park or some other play spot. Also check with your hotel; most have a list of reliable sitters.

Incidentally, if your "children" have four legs, contact the **Wagging Tail** in Tribeca (354½ Greenwich Street; (212) 285-4900; **www.thewaggingtail.com**), a canine and feline hotel and day spa with webcam contact for "parents."

In the case of illness or medical emergencies, first call the front desk of your hotel; many have arrangements with physicians for house calls. Otherwise contact **Dial-a-Doctor** (call (212) 971-9692). There are several 24-hour pharmacies in town, most run by the **Duane Reade** chain; the most centrally located are at Broadway and 57th Street (call (212) 541-9708) and Lexington and 47th (call (212) 682-5338).

Tips for International Travelers

All that visitors from the United Kingdom, western Europe, and Japan need to enter the United States is a valid passport, not a visa; Canadian citizens can get by with only proof of residence. Citizens of other countries must have a passport, good for at least six months beyond the projected end of the visit, and a tourist visa as well, available from any U.S. consulate. Some airlines and travel agents may also have forms available.

If you are taking prescription drugs that contain narcotics or require injection by syringe, be sure to get a doctor's signed prescription and instructions. Also check with the local consulate to see whether travelers from your country are currently required to have any inoculations; there are no set requirements to enter the United States, but if there has been any sort of epidemic in your homeland, there may be temporary restrictions.

If you arrive by air, be prepared to spend two hours or more entering the United States and getting through U.S. Customs. Every adult traveler may bring in, duty-free, up to one liter of wine or hard liquor; 200 cigarettes or 100 non-Cuban cigars or three pounds of loose tobacco; and $100 worth of gifts, as well as up to $10,000 in U.S. currency or its equivalent in foreign currency. No food or plants may be brought in.

The dollar is the basic unit of monetary exchange, and the entire system is decimal. The smaller sums are represented by coins. One hundred "cents" (or pennies, as the 1-cent coins are known) equal 1 dollar; 5 cents is a nickel (20 nickels to a dollar); the 10-cent coin is called a dime (10 dimes to a dollar); and the 25-cent coin is called a quarter (4 to a dollar). Beginning with 1 dollar, money is in currency bills (although there are some 1-dollar coins around as well). Bills come in $1, $2 (rare), $5, $10, $20, $50, $100, $500, and so on, although you are unlikely to want to carry $1,000 or more. Stick to twenties for taxicabs; drivers rarely make change for anything larger.

Banks in the United States are closed on federal holidays, including New Year's Day (January 1); Martin Luther King, Jr. Day (celebrated the third Monday in January); Presidents' Day (celebrated the third Monday in February); Memorial Day (last Monday in May); Independence Day (July 4); Labor Day (first Monday in September); Columbus Day (second Monday in October); Veterans Day (November 11); Thanksgiving (the fourth Thursday in November); and Christmas (December 25).

Credit cards are by far the most common form of payment in New York, especially American Express, Visa (also known as BarclayCard in Britain), and MasterCard (Access in Britain, Eurocard in Western Europe, or Chargex in Canada). Other popular cards include Diners Club, Discover/Novus, and Carte Blanche.

Traveler's checks will be accepted at most hotels and restaurants if they are in American dollars; other currencies should be taken to a bank or foreign exchange and turned into dollar figures. There are currency exchange booths in such major traffic areas as JFK and LaGuardia airports, Grand Central Station, Times Square, and even Macy's and Bloomingdale's.

If you need additional assistance, contact the **Traveler's Aid Society,** which has booths in JFK and Newark airports (call (718) 656-4870).

Public telephones require 35 cents; although area codes must be dialed for all calls inside or between boroughs, there is no additional charge. And throughout the United States, if you have a medical, police, or fire emergency, dial 911, even on a pay telephone, and an ambulance or police cruiser will be dispatched to help you.

Incidentally, New York has one of the most stringent antismoking programs in the country, something international visitors might need to consider in advance. Smoking is prohibited on buses, on subways, and in taxicabs; in public buildings or the lobbies of office buildings; in all but designated areas in theaters; in most shops and all museums; and in all restaurants and bars.

Tips for the Disabled

New York is far more receptive to the disabled tourist than its tough reputation might lead you to believe. City buses are equipped with wheelchair lifts and "kneeling" steps (though admittedly they don't always work), and disabled riders with a reduced-fare MetroCard pay half-fare ($1). Gray Line Tours has acquired a whole fleet of wheelchair-accessible double-decker touring buses. An increasing number of subway stops are wheelchair accessible as well; for a list, contact the **Transit Authority's Customer Service Department** (370 J Street, Suite 702, Brooklyn, NY 11201; (718) 330-3322). Visually impaired travelers can get a Braille subway map and other materials from the **Lighthouse** (call (800) 334-5497). The hearing-impaired can get similar help from the **New York Society for the Deaf** (817 Broadway, seventh floor; TDD (212) 777-3900).

A list of wheelchair-accessible museums, hotels, and restaurants is available from the **Society for Accessible Travel and Hospitality** (347 Fifth Avenue, New York, NY 10016; (212) 447-7284). A similar guidebook, "Audiences for All: A Guide for People with Disabilities to New York City Cultural Institutions," is available from **Hospital Audiences** for $5 (548 Broadway, 3rd Floor; (212) 284-4100 or (212) 575-7660). And many members of the volunteer **Big Apple Greeters,** warmly recommended in Part Seven, will partner handicapped visitors around town, but you should call at least several days in advance (phone (212) 669-2896; **www.bigapplegreeters.org**).

Visitors who use walking aids should be warned that only the larger museums and the newer shopping areas can be counted on to be wheelchair accessible. Many individual stores and smaller art collections are housed in what were once private homes with stairs, and even those at sidewalk level are unlikely to have wider aisles or specially equipped bathrooms. The restaurants that we profile later in the book all have a disabled access rating, as do most of the major attractions, but you need to call any other eatery or any store in advance. (In fact, you might check with some restaurants that were listed as not accessible at press time, as it's possible they've renovated their facilities since.) Similarly, you need to call any stores you're particularly interested in.

CALENDAR OF SPECIAL EVENTS

Here are the major celebrations and a sampling of the less well-known but unique events around New York and their approximate dates (specific ones where possible). Remember, if the event requires tickets, it's best to try to arrange them before leaving home; otherwise you may find yourself paying extra or being locked out entirely. Tickets for the U.S. Open Tennis Championships in August, for instance, go on sale in May, and the scalping fees are astonishingly high by the opening rounds.

Please note that many festivals, especially in the summer, move around from year to year, and that some close down or are replaced by others; so if you are interested, contact organizers as soon as possible. For many of the municipal functions, you may call the **Metropolitan Visitors and Convention Bureau** at (212) 397-8222. Parade routes and times will be listed in the *New York Times* on the appropriate days. The local newspapers (listed earlier) will also have numerous street fairs, arts shows, and concerts to tempt you, particularly in summer.

In addition to the contacts listed in the following section, **TicketMaster** may be able to supply tickets to particular events, although there will be an additional handling charge. Call (212) 307-1212.

January

Winter Antiques Show at the Armory   Third week in January. One of the largest and most prestigious (read: expensive) antiques gatherings in the city, this is held in the historic Seventh Regiment Armory on Park Avenue at 66th Street. Over the first weekend of the big collection, a sort of counter-show, featuring less established or edgier collectors, is held at the 26th Street Armory at Lexington Avenue, and shuttle buses run between the two. For information call (212) 452-3067.

Chinese New Year Parade   At the full moon in late January or early February. A fortnight of fireworks, street fairs, and food festivals leads toward the big dragon parade through Chinatown.

National Boat Show   Mid-January. Sailing vessels, yachts, cruisers, and powerboats fill the Jacob Javits Convention Center; call (212) 216-2000 or visit **www.javitscenter.com.**

February

Black History Month   Watch the newspapers and guides for cultural events, concerts, and lectures scheduled around the city.

Empire State Building Run   Early February. Hundreds of athletes race not horizontally but vertically: 1,575 steps from the lobby to the 86th-floor observation deck. The best make it in about 11 minutes. Contact the New York Road Runners at (212) 860-4455.

Gramercy Park Antiques Show   February and October. 17th-, 18th- and 19th-century porcelain, art glass, furniture, and fine art at the 69th Regiment Armory at Lexington and 26th Street; call (212) 255-0020.

Westminster Club Dog Show Mid-month. This most prestigious of canine parades brings thousands of familiar, unusual, and downright rare dogs, all blow-dried and ribboned for judging, to Madison Square Garden. Heck, this dog show's so big it's on cable TV. Call (800) 455-3647 or (212) 465-6741.

Valentine's Day February 14. A huge vow-one, vow-all mass wedding ceremony is performed at the wedding chapel in the Empire State Building; call (212) 736-3100.

Coliseum Antiques Show Not as elite as the Armory show, but huge and convenient: more than 100 dealers in the arena on Columbus Circle (late February or early March). For information, contact the NYMCVB at (800) NYC-VISIT.

March

International Cat Show The feline response to the Westminster show, also at Madison Square Garden and also the place for trendy types looking for the next trendy rare breed; call MSG at (212) 465-6741 or visit **www.thegarden.com.**

New York Flower Show One of the big stops on the flower circuit is the Horticultural Society of New York's annual competition/exhibition in the Coliseum on Columbus Circle; contact the NYMCVB at (800) NYC-VISIT.

Art Expo Early or mid-March. This huge affair at the Javits Convention Center specializes in what dealers call popular art, and that means anything from nice lithographs to the stuff you get on the sidewalk or see in chain motels. Good for a laugh and a possible find; call (212) 216-2000.

St. Patrick's Day Parade On March 17, everyone is Irish, so pack something green or get out of the way. The parade, at age 200 one of the oldest anywhere, includes an estimated 150,000 marchers; the route is along Fifth Avenue (of course) from 44th to 86th, with the thickest crowd around St. Patrick's Cathedral (of course).

Greek Independence Day Parade March 25. Zorba-style food and dance along Fifth Avenue from 49th to 59th.

New Directors/New Films Festival Mid-March. A cutting-edge cinematic collaboration between the Museum of Modern Art, which hosts the screenings, and the Lincoln Center Film Society. For more information call (212) 708-9480.

Triple Pier Expo Last two weekends in March. Vast antiques exhibit and sale on Piers 88, 90, and 92 (along the Hudson river). Call (212) 255-0020.

CALENDAR OF SPECIAL EVENTS *(continued)*

March (continued)

Ringling Bros. and Barnum & Bailey Circus Parade Late March. Another great traditional procession, this one is now (thanks to animal protests) a semisecret wee-hours train of elephants and lions and tigers making their way from Long Island City through the Queens-Midtown Tunnel to Madison Square Garden. For information call (212) 465-6741 or visit **www.ringling.com.**

Cirque du Soleil Late March. On alternate years watch for the appearance of the strange and fantastic Canadian one-tent circus; all acrobats and astonishing contortionists and eerie music, no animals; call (800) 678-5440.

Easter Parade Late March to mid-April. A parade so famous they made a Fred Astaire/Judy Garland movie about it. Don that bonnet—the bigger the better—and promenade along (what else?) Fifth Avenue from 44th to Central Park. Macy's flower show is scheduled for the week leading up to Easter Sunday; for information call (212) 494-4495.

Easter Egg Roll Saturday before Easter. In the East Meadow of Central Park; call (212) 360-3456 or (888) NYPARKS.

April

Baseball Season Opening Day Mid-April. If you're a pin-striper, or just an American Leaguer at heart, you can try for tickets by calling Ticket-Master or Yankee Stadium box office at (718) 293-6000. For fans of the senior league, those heartbreaking Mets are at Shea Stadium (call (718) 507-8499).

Rockefeller Center Flower Show Early–mid-April. One of the nicest free shows in town. Gardening companies and landscape designers fill the plaza between 48th and 51st Streets with fantasy getaways, Japanese rock gardens, arbors, and urban meadows. Call (800) NYC-VISIT.

Antiquarian Book Fair Mid-April. First editions, rare titles, and autographed copies fill the Seventh Regiment Armory on Park at 66th Street.

Seventh on Sixth The big spring collections of the haute couture world (i.e., Seventh Avenue) were staged for several years in Bryant Park (Sixth), but it has recently been trying out different homes, including Pier 92, so check the papers. All the shows are invitation only, but the celebrity-spotting is good. For information, contact the NYMCVB at (800) NYC-VISIT.

Cherry Blossom Festival Late April–early May. A celebration of the Japanese, or flowering Kwanzan, cherry trees of the Brooklyn Botanic Garden; call (718) 623-7200.

May

Bike New York   Early May. This ever-larger 41-mile for-fun bike race—it draws more than 35,000 wheelers and dealers—links all five boroughs, with the kickoff downtown and the finish line in Staten Island. Picnic at pedals' end. Call (212) 932-2453 or check **www.bikenetwork.com.**

Brooklyn Bridge Day   Second Sunday in May. Walk the bridge, admire its stunning structure, and enjoy a sort of street fair at the same time. For information, contact the NYMCVB at (800) NYC-VISIT.

International Fine Arts Fair   Mid-May. European and American artists are featured in this young but prestigious show at the Seventh Regimental Armory. For information, contact the NYMCVB or call (212) 472-0590 during the show itself.

Fleet Week   Mid-May. Ships ahoy! Naval and Coast Guard vessels of all sizes set up for tours and exhibitions. Call (212) 642-8572.

Martin Luther King, Jr. Day Parade   Third Sunday in May. A salute to the civil rights leader starts on Fifth Avenue at 44th and streams up to 86th.

Salute to Israel Parade   May. Along Fifth northward from 59th Street. Also, fashion sharks may find much to savor at the United Jewish Appeal's annual fundraiser; call (212) 836-1115.

Washington Square Art Exhibition   The last two weekends in May and the first two weekends of September. An old and revered Greenwich Village gathering, this huge outdoor art show is a giant block party, with easels (and food carts) in the streets all around the park. Call (212) 982-6255.

Ninth Avenue Food Festival   Third weekend in May. This was, and to a lesser extent still is, the international grocery strip of New York. A combination street fair and ethnic fare showcase, it stretches from 37th to 57th Streets. For information, call (800) NYC-VISIT.

Lower East Side Jewish Festival   Third or fourth Sunday in May. Combination historical tour and street party.

June

Shakespeare in the Park   From June to August, this now famous, free, and star-studded series (call (212) 539-8750) takes over the Delacorte Theater stage in Central Park. There are fewer than 2,000 seats, and the box office opens at 1 p.m. every day, but the line forms much earlier. (See "Ticket Tips" in Part Eleven, Entertainment and Nightlife.)

Concerts in the Park   June to August. Some of the concerts in Central Park, Prospect Park, and other city greens are put on by the New York Philharmonic (call (212) 875-5700 or visit **newyorkphilharmonic.org**) and the great Metropolitan Opera (call (212) 362-6000).

CALENDAR OF SPECIAL EVENTS *(continued)*

June (continued)

SummerStage   Similarly, there are free or nominally priced pop, rock, country, folk, reggae, and jazz concerts throughout the summer in Central Park: Remember Simon & Garfunkle? Garth Brooks? It's big, but it's fun. Call (212) 360-2777, or look up **www.summerstage.com.**

Puerto Rican Day Parade   First Sunday in June. A lively, musical march along Fifth Avenue from 44th to 86th Street. Call (800) NYC-VISIT.

Belmont Stakes   The second (occasionally the first) Saturday in June. The final leg of thoroughbred two-year-old racing's Triple Crown, and many warm-up races, go off at Belmont Park on Long Island; call (516) 488-6000 or visit **www.nyracing.com.**

Restaurant Week   Usually the third week. A sit-down Taste of the Town event, when some of the biggest-name restaurants offer special cut-price meals. As soon as you see the ads in the *New York Times* or elsewhere, listing the participating establishments, get on the phone or you'll be out of luck.

Feast of St. Anthony   Mid-June. Restaurant week or no, the saint of Padua must still be hungry: His street fair in Little Italy lasts two weeks.

Gay and Lesbian Pride Day Parade   Late June. A week-long series of public and private events culminates in the parade, commemorating the Stonewall Riot of June 27, 1969, that struts down (rather than up) Fifth Avenue from 53rd to the West Village. Call (212) 807-7433 or visit **www.nycpride.org.**

Mermaid Parade   Late June. A sort of pre-Halloween bash along the Coney Island–Brighton Beach Boardwalk. A few years ago, the Grand Merman, uh, Marshall, was former Talking Head David Byrne. Call (800) NYC-VISIT for information.

JVC Jazz Festival   Late June–early July. A series of top-name concerts in Bryant Park and venues around the city; watch the papers for schedules, or call (212) 219-3006 or (800) NYC-VISIT.

July

Fourth of July Festival   July 4. Independence Day celebrations include street fairs, the annual sailing of the Tall Ships in the harbor, and after dark, the famous Macy's fireworks over the East River. For information, call (212) 494-4495. All-day festivities in downtown around Battery Park climax with fireworks over the harbor.

Lincoln Center Festival   A dizzying array of dance, drama, ballet, children shows, and multimedia and performance art that involves both the repertory companies and special guests and that moves through the indoor venues and sometimes outdoors as well, through July and August. Call (212) 875-5928 or visit **lincolncenter.org.** There are also big-band dances (free lessons included) on weekends by the Lincoln Center fountain. And the Lincoln Center Plaza on Columbus is home territory to the two-week American Crafts Festival.

August

Lincoln Center Plaza concerts   Throughout the month. Some of the outdoor series taper off in August, but the music on the plaza (information at (212) 875-5400) or **lincolncenter.org**), along with another big crafts show late in the month keeps the joint jumpin'.

Dragon Boat Races   First two weekends in August. Some 50 teams of 22 rowers, plus drummer and helmsman, race Chinese-style 40-foot teak boats on the lake at Flushing Meadow–Corona Park in Queens; the winners travel to Hong Kong for the international trials. Call (718) 460-1312.

Harlem Heritage Week   Mid-August. Films, art exhibits, concerts, exhibition games, and street fairs celebrating the neighborhood's rich cultural history build up to the climax of Uptown Saturday Night, a combination block party and black arts expo along 125th Street between Lenox and Seventh Avenues.

Mostly Mozart   A famous phrase, and one of the most famous renditions (two weeks in mid- to late August) in the Lincoln Center's Avery Fisher Hall (call (212) 875-5030).

U.S. Open Tennis Tournament   Late August. In its expanded digs at Flushing Meadow, this Grand Slam event is one of the sport's hottest tickets—literally. Don't forget the water and the sunblock, if you can get in. For information call (888) 673-6849 or visit **www.usopen.org.**

New York International Fringe Festival   Last week of August to Labor Day. Round-the-clock multimedia, dance, theater, street and musical performances, many of them free, at venues around the Lower East Side and East Village. The "Fringe" has even spanned a farther fringe—the Pure Pop Theater Festival, which runs concurrently. Check local papers for listings.

September

Wigstock Parade   Labor Day weekend. Although this parade isn't as old as the Easter or Thanksgiving Day marathons, it's catching up fast in the fame department. The wildest and most royal drag event in the city, due to growth, it has moved a couple of times from its original East Village park space, most recently to the 11th Street Pier; contact the Lesbian and Gay Community Services Center for information at (212) 807-7433.

CALENDAR OF SPECIAL EVENTS *(continued)*

Broadway on Broadway   Early September. For one enchanted day and evening in Times Square—where else?—the casts of the big Broadway shows sing and step out in public; call (212) 563-2929.

West Indian Festival and Parade   Labor Day Weekend. It's big, it's loud, it's delicious, and it's relatively underpublicized (perhaps because it's in Brooklyn); but fans of world or Caribbean music, food, and dance won't mind the short trip to Crown Heights. For information call the Caribbean American Center of New York at (718) 625-1515.

Cloisters Medieval Festival   Early–mid September. Falconry, food, tomfoolery, jousting and feasting, all with a Middle Ages flavor. Call the Parks Department at (212) 360-2777.

New York Is Book Country   Third Sunday in September. A great indoor/outdoor book "mall" along Fifth Avenue from 48th to 59th Streets, with booths and racks of old, new, used, privately published, and rare volumes. Call (212) 207-7242.

One World Festival   Mid-September. International food, crafts, antiques, and street performance in a block party on East 35th between First and Second Avenues.

International Festival of Puppet Theater   Mid-September. On alternate years (including 2004), Muppet mavens Jim Henson Productions hosts this Manhattan family attraction. Call (212) 794-2400 or visit **www.henson.com.**

Feast of San Gennaro   Mid-September. This Little Italy street fest is pretty famous, probably because it lasts a long (two-weekend) week, although its rumored "family" connections have gotten a lot of publicity; along Mulberry Street. Call (212) 768-9320.

Broadway Cares/Equity Fights AIDS Annual Flea Market and Antique Sale   Last weekend of September. The theatrical garage sale, memento scuffle, and costume clearinghouse of the year. Shubert Alley and West 44th Street. Call (212) 840-0770 or see local listings for date.

Guinness/Red Stripe Cricket Tournament   Late September. "Limited over" tournament of the USA Cricket Association at Seaview Avenue and 88th Street in Canarsie Park. For information call (212) 273-2845.

New York Film Festival   Late September to early October. Not so avant-garde as the New Films series, this prestigious series in Lincoln Center's Alice Tully Hall lasts two weeks and usually has a big-name premiere or two on the schedule; call (212) 875-5610.

October

Big Apple Circus   October to January. You might have forgotten how this cheery little one-ring operation got its name; but watch the little big top go up in the park outside Lincoln Center and then try to resist; call (212) 268-2500.

Feast of St. Francis of Assisi   Early October. The Francis-like blessing of the animals at St. John the Divine used to be a fairly sedate affair, but nowadays it's a sort of well-bred circus, with snakes, rabbits, ferrets, exotic birds, and, yes, even elephants being offered for prayer. Call (212) 662-2133.

Gramercy Park Antiques Show   October and February. 17th-, 18th- and 19th-century porcelain, art glass, furniture, and fine art at the 69th Regiment Armory at Lexington and 26th Street; call (212) 255-0020.

NBA and NHL at MSG   Season openers. If you're a sports fan, you can read this. If not, it means that pro basketball (the Knicks) and ice hockey (the Rangers) are back in town at Madison Square Garden. Call (212) 465-6741 for information on both teams.

Pulaski Day Parade   Sunday nearest October 5. Polish-American festival, sometimes called Polish Day, marches Fifth from 26th to 52nd.

Columbus Day Parade   Second Monday in October. A combination Founder's Day, Italian pride, and star-spangled celebration down Fifth Avenue from 44th to 86th. Call (212) 249-9932 or (800) NYC-VISIT.

SoHo Arts Festival   Mid-October. This originally one-day event is up to nearly a fortnight now, with street theater, performance art, dance, and music indoors and out.

International Fine Arts and Antiques Dealers Show   Mid- to late October. The last (actually, the first, as dealers consider the season) of New York's major shows comes just in time for holiday shopping, if you can afford it. At least you can look. At the Seventh Regiment Armory; call (212) 642-8572.

Greenwich Village Halloween Parade   October 31. Yet another over-the-top and inimitable dress function, this annual party-on-legs (and some wheels) circles the Village; check local papers for the exact route. Walk-ups welcome; gather at Sixth Avenue just above Houston at dusk. Call (845) 758-5519 or visit **www.halloween-nyc.com.**

Next Wave Festival   October to December. The Brooklyn Academy of Music showcases avant-garde, experimental, and new music, dance, and performance; call (718) 636-4100 or visit **www.bam.org.**

CALENDAR OF SPECIAL EVENTS *(continued)*

October *(continued)*

New York City Marathon   Last Sunday in October or first Sunday in November. One of the big races—not counting the 2.5 million cheering onlookers and volunteers—and with one of the most scenic courses, which includes the Verrazano Narrows Bridge, stretches of Fifth Avenue, and a finish line at Tavern on the Green in Central Park. Call (212) 860-4455 for information.

November

Christmas Extravaganza at Radio City Music Hall   Mid-November to January. Traditional family favorite featuring the Rockettes in their Toy Soldier kick line, music, costumes, and so on. Call (212) 247-4777.

WTA Tour Championships   Mid-November. Madison Square Garden lays the courts for the old Virginia Slims women's tennis tourney; call (212) 465-6741.

Macy's Thanksgiving Day Parade   Late November. Well, how else would Santa Claus—not to mention Snoopy and Woodstock and Garfield and Bullwinkle and half of Broadway—make it to Herald Square on time? The parade begins at Central Park West and 77th and works down Broadway to the store at 34th Street. Santa takes up his station in Macy's beginning the next day. Call (212) 494-4495.

December

Lighting of the Christmas Tree at Rockefeller Center   The first Monday evening in December, the mayor pulls the switch, and people sing, ice skate, make wishes, you name it; the tree will be lit throughout the month. Call (212) 332-7654.

Lighting of the Hanukkah Menorah at Grand Army Plaza   Sometime in December, the first "candle" on this giant (32-foot) menorah at the corner of Fifth and 59th opens the Jewish holiday season; other candles are lit every night for the next week.

Antiques Show at the Seventh Regiment Armory Around the second weekend in December. Another blockbuster sale drawing 100 dealers in serious 17th-, 18th-, and 19th-century American, European, and Asian furniture and art. Call (212) 452-3067.

Nutcracker Ballet The Sugar Plum Fairy is absolutely everywhere, including the IMAX in Times Square. The American Ballet Theater version, for sentimentalists, is in the New York State Theater in Lincoln Center (call (212) 870-5570), but the local papers will list many others.

Messiah Sing-along at Lincoln Center Mid-December. Huge public performance of Handel's popular oratorio in Avery Fisher Hall, with rehearsals and coaching beforehand; call (212) 875-5030. Dozens of other sing-alongs, carolings, and family performances will be listed in the local papers.

Kwanzaa Celebrations Watch for listings of African-American ethnic festivities around town.

New Year's Eve December 31. Times Square must be one of the most famous addresses in New Year's folklore. It's a heck of a street party, complete with countdown and lighted ball. However, for those more intrigued by culture than alcohol, Manhattan's First Night celebration is one of the largest and finest progressive parties in the country, winding up with such old-fashioned touches as a dance in Grand Central Station and fireworks over the Tavern on the Green in Central Park; call (212) 873-3200. Or for those who have made their resolutions a day early, there's a midnight run through the park; call (212) 360-3456 or (888) NYPARKS or visit **www.tavernonthegreen.com.**

Part Three

New York Hotels

New Rooms in the Sky

Hotels keep going up here, with over 70,000 rooms in 2003. However, you can still find a room in New York and pocket a few bucks for the temptations of this hyper-metropolis. In fact, if you're savvy (and if you're reading this, you are indeed), you can find rooms well under NYC's $200 average, even with a private bath.

Following September 11th, several downtown area hotels were temporarily closed, representing 1,528 rooms. The **Marriott World Financial Center, Embassy Suites,** and the **Millennium Hilton** have since reopened, with improvements. Many weekends, it's hard to get a room; New York is back, big-time.

The newest New York lodging is often found in areas that have been neglected, room-wise and otherwise—including Harlem and the outer boroughs. Well-priced lodgings come on board continuously. Lower-priced hotel groups such as Apple Core, offer clean, budget accommodations, and bed-and-breakfasts are springing up throughout the five boroughs.

But never fear, big spenders: pricey establishments are increasing as well, even if top rates are a bit lower than recent years. These properties tend to be smaller and more niche-oriented. The trend of the last ten years continues: reconverting older commercial properties into boutique beauties, and upgrading faded hotels. The **Ritz-Carlton New York Central Park** on the site of the former St. Mortiz is a good example. And there still are dramatic hotels being built, often in conjunction with commercial and cultural components. One example is the **Ritz-Carlton Battery Park** atop a new skyscraper museum. The overall result is a bevy of smallish, "high-style" hotels—often with tiny, luxe rooms—which stress personal service and mid-to-high-priced luxury.

The most-talked about new hotel is the **Mandarin Oriental New York** at Columbus Circle. Besides offering lavish guest rooms, an elevator whisks guests to ultra-luxe shops and restaurants and Jazz at Lincoln Center, all within the same complex.

Other fine new hotels include the **Maritime,** with teak appointments and five-foot-diameter porthole windows, facing the Hudson. **Westin New York Times Square** is part of the brash and colorful E-Walk retail and restaurant complex, and **W Hotel Times Square Hotel** is not far away. Right next to the Nederlander Theater, **Hotel 41** has rooms starting at $99 per night. **City Club** is a small, stylish hotel where star-chef Daniel Boulud opened DB Bistro Moderne. **Le Marquis** is a boutique hotel, with rainshower showerheads and meticulous attention to detail.

A steady stream of refurbishments continues at the city's established hotels—from major penthouse-to-basement overhauls to cosmetic touchups. The **La Quinta Inn Manhattan** just had a $2.5-million makeover. The **San Carlos** had a 16-month, $22-million renovation, adding deluxe rooms and penthouse suites with fireplaces. The **Melrose Hotel** is the former Barbizon, with a $40-million luxury renovation.

To experience the city over the long term, extended-stay lodgings such as the Affinia properties (formerly Manhattan East, (866) AFFINIA; **www. affinia.com**), with kitchens and maid and shopping services, have been a long-time staple. But add on the newish luxury apartment-hotels and luxury hotels with kitchenette amenities, and you have excellent options in all price ranges. Indeed, the hotel scene continues to be tough but appealing—a melting pot worthy of New York, New York.

All Things Considered

New York hotels flaunt breathtaking views and grand lobbies, business services and concierges, superb restaurants and lavish bars. But even in luxury establishments, guest rooms are often miniscule, and recreational facilities will not match those in most major cities.

Why? Cost per square foot to build in Manhattan is outrageous, so to turn a profit, hotels opt for creating more guest rooms and appealing watering holes where payback is high. Thus, rather than health clubs, pools, and tennis courts, most otherwise great hotels offer only small fitness centers or passes to health clubs in the neighborhood.

The hotel scene here is different in other ways as well, since New York is as much a world city as an American one. Because about 20% of the Big Apple's visitors come here from around the globe, hotels must deal with a decidedly international aspect: Front-desk people speak many languages, translation services are easy to obtain, concierges abound even at small hotels, shops sell international goods familiar to overseas customers, and of course, many bathrooms have bidets.

Luxury—at least the illusion of it—is important, so uniformed door-men (these greeters are almost exclusively men), standard personnel at upscale city apartments, are also a tradition at good hotels, even if there is a revolving door. They exist as much for show and small services as for security: giving a friendly greeting, hailing cabs, holding umbrellas, and bringing luggage within the lobby.

Crime rates may be down, but danger remains a perception in these uncertain times, and as many guests are wealthy and/or famous, high-profile security is the norm. Elevator operators are a thing of the past—the **Pierre** is one holdout—but especially for women traveling alone, this would be a welcome bonus late at night. New York hotels usually provide key cards rather than keys and maintain regular floor checks by in-house guards. Loitering does not go unnoticed. Most upscale hotels have in-room safes, and all comply with strict city fire codes. The safest element of city hotels is that even in the wee hours of the morning, staff will be at the front desk, and usually you will find other guests in the lobby—New York does, after all, go on around the clock.

So which hotel should you stay in? Consider the following factors when choosing, and check their availability before booking. Our hotel chart at the end of the chapter will help in your selection, or you could call, peruse brochures, or access computer information. If you use a travel agent, explain carefully what matters most to you in selecting a hotel, and have the agent write those requests down.

Purpose of Stay   If you know why you're traveling, you'll know which hotel services and amenities are vital and what location is best.

- **On business?**   You might need special services, meeting space, banquet rooms, translation services, and extensive room facilities. Most big hotels are well equipped in these areas. But if you're a leisure traveler, why pay for them? Major chains such as **Marriott, Hilton, Hyatt,** and **Sheraton** will have the business facilities of course, but nowadays upscale independents such as **Thirty Thirty** often have state-of-the-art room facilities—such as cell phones—even if they lack meeting space. Hotels with excellent, upated meeting space include **Mandarin Oriental New York, Ritz-Carlton New York Central Park, Flatotel International, Grand Hyatt New York,** and **Jolly Hotel Madison Towers.**

- **Out to impress?**   Then concentrate on location, location, location. But different parts of Manhattan impress in different ways. The Upper East Side is the luxury address, but the Village and downtown are cutting-edge and creative. Public space and decor may be especially important if you're entertaining or on business, so you should scan brochures and Internet sites carefully. The **St. Regis, Four Seasons, Pierre, Carlyle, Mark, Waldorf-Astoria, Essex House, Lowell, Elysee, Soho Grand, Mercer,** and **W New York** are among the most impressive hotels for New York style of differing kinds.

- **Spending lots of time in your room?**   Then size, view, and amenities will matter more than if you're on the town 24/7. But everyone appreciates a VCR, CD player, big windows, and good lighting. Again, check out our chapter, chart, or hotel brochures, and have your travel agent ask about these features.

■ **Want to weave a romantic spell?**   Smaller, specialized hotels can add to the mood, and around-the-clock room service, king-sized beds, whirlpool tubs, and soft lighting will help. The **Elysee,** the **Inn at Irving Place,** and the **Hotel Casablanca** are oases of romance in this tough and hectic city.

Convenience   Time is perhaps your most precious commodity when traveling, especially in a city where crossing against the light to save a minute is a code of conduct. So think in terms of what you will be doing and where you will be doing it, then choose a hotel from our zone map, in close proximity to your needs. Also, check the information charts to see which hotels are closest to public transportation lines—safe, affordable, and efficient ways to get around. You can save big money if you don't have to spend it on long cab rides or parking fees.

For ultimate convenience, if you'll be spending a weekend seeing Broadway shows, stay at a nearby hotel such as the **Time, Westin Times Square, Marriott Marquis,** or the **Paramount.** Like to jog and enjoy the country? Stay as close to country as Manhattan gets—across from Central Park at the **Park Lane, Mayflower,** or **Essex House.** If you plan on lining up to get tickets for *The Late Show with David Letterman,* the **Ameritania** is around the corner. If you're visiting the Metropolitan Museum of Art, the **Stanhope** faces it, and the **Excelsior** is near the Museum of Natural History. Lincoln Center? The **Empire** is across the street. If you're strolling in Soho, check out the **Mercer.** The **Gorham** is directly across from City Center, with its many entertainment productions. When visiting your cousin in Westchester, you'll appreciate the **Grand Hyatt,** connected to Grand Central, and if your cousin is on Long Island, the **Metro Hotel** is near Penn Station. The time and money saved by being able to walk or take public transportation to your destination will make your stay more special.

View   What NYC lacks in horizontal space it makes up for in height, and a stunning by-product is the view. Whether a favorite landmark, river, or park, a hotel somewhere in this city is sure to overlook it. The zone map will help you locate which hotels are closest to whatever it is that you may want to overlook; these are the hotels that will offer your choicest views.

For example, if you like to watch the tugboats and water traffic and bridges of the East River, hotels along First Avenue, such as the **Beekman Tower** and **Regal U.N. Plaza,** overlook that watery scene (and the bonus of the United Nations complex). Hotels that rim the Park on Fifth Avenue, Central Park South, and Central Park West offer bucolic views in this hyper-urban environment. Midtown-east hotels in the 30s and 40s are most likely to include views of such landmarks as the Chrysler Building or Empire State Building. Hotels closest to the tip of Manhattan have rooms overlooking New York Harbor and the Statue of Liberty. Hotels near Broadway, such as **Novotel New York,** the **New York Marriott Marquis,** the **Renaissance New York Hotel,** and the **Crowne Plaza Manhattan** have blazingly colorful neon vistas. And the tallest (read: largest) hotels throughout the city provide panoramas that include huge sections of dramatic skyscrapers, rivers, and parks. When reservations are made, request a high floor and the best view possible, or, even more specifically, ask for a view of whatever it is that you want to see.

Noise   To a New Yorker the sounds of silence or a twittering bird can be off-putting, but the noise of a garbage truck grinding away, a wailing, piercing ambulance, or a car alarm at 3 a.m. is standard. You learn to live with it.

The city may never sleep, but you probably want to. Downtown (especially the financial district, at night) and Uptown are quieter than Midtown, which according to traffic experts has more vehicles per square mile than anywhere else in the country—some 700,000 motorists daily. Streets are generally less noisy than avenues—and avenues closer to the rivers than to Midtown are often quietest, although the West Side Drive along the Hudson and FDR Drive along the East River are heavily trafficked and often have emergency vehicles. If noise is a primary concern to you, stay away from hotels near hospitals, police stations, firehouses, or nightclubs. Major hospitals are at First Avenue and 16th Street, First Avenue and 32nd Street, York Avenue and 68th Street, East End Avenue and 88th Street, Park Avenue and 77th Street, Seventh Avenue and West 11th Street, and Tenth Avenue and West 59th Street. Ask for a room away from street noise (or elevator noise, if that matters). High up is better, but surprisingly, not all that much, as sound seems to echo against the skyscrapers. Older hotels, built before World War II, usually have the thickest walls, but most luxury hotels are exceptionally well insulated. Check our survey to make sure your hotel's windows are at least double-glazed; triple-glazing is even better and keeps most street noise out. Hotels on heavily trafficked routes, such as the **Kitano New York** on Park Avenue, are well soundproofed because of this. And some hotels, such as the **Hotel Casablanca,** have quadruple-glazed windows! Relatively quiet hotels include the **San Carlos, Sheraton Russell Hotel, Omni Berkshire Place,** and the **Drake Swissôtel.**

Amenities   New York City is the quintessential urban environment—culture, all-night action, superb restaurants, clubs, bars—and as a result many hotels offer only basic amenities. If you have special needs, mention them when booking. Physically challenged guests should clarify whether rooms designated for handicapped guests just have hand rails in bathrooms or have made-to-order furnishings and complete wheelchair access. If you have a car, a garage is a major convenience, and free parking a big bonus. If you are with your family or are planning a longer stay, a suite situation or a kitchenette can be a wonderful addition. Most New York hotels offer dataports, fax and copying services, and e-mail retrieval, and big hotels have conference rooms of all sizes, with state-of-the-art facilities. Some have kitchenettes.

The **Regal U.N. Plaza** offers both an indoor pool and tennis courts—a rarity in the city. But there are more unusual amenities as well. The **Four Seasons** provides toys for kids and food for pets. The **Doral Park Avenue Hotel** sets up backstage visits to some Broadway plays, and gourmet food to take with you to the airport. The **New York Palace** sets out personalized stationery and business cards in its Towers section. The **Benjamin Hotel** has ten types of pillows. The **Mark** offers cordless phones. The **Trump International Hotel & Towers** provides magnifying glasses and telescopes (presumably to look at Central Park vistas, not into other windows). The Premier at the **Millennium Broadway** offers champagne popsicles, and the **Algonquin Hotel** presents dinner and a cabaret show for guests. We have investigated to find other hotels with amenities that might appeal, so check out our hotel information chart at the end of the chapter.

Food and Drink   If you enjoy the convenience of dining en suite or a mere elevator ride from your room, check our charts at the end of the chapter for hotels that include restaurants. And when you book the hotel, ask for restaurant reservations at the same time; although hotel guests have priority, some of these restaurants are booked months in advance.

Most hotels in the city have at least a coffee shop or an adjacent restaurant, and you can otherwise count on minibars and coffeemakers to tide you over. If there's a restaurant, room service is also often available, especially at larger establishments. A pleasant trend, especially at smaller hotels, is a continental breakfast included in the price. Among hotels offering this are the **Avalon, Bentley, Franklin, Iroquois New York, Mansfield, Roger Smith, Roger Williams, Sheraton Russell Hotel, Shoreham,** and **Millennium Broadway.** Hotel dining establishments have become among the best in city, with star chefs, luxury decor, and multicourse tasting menus. Count on a three-course dinner at a top hotel restaurant costing at least $60 per person with a glass of wine, tax, and tip. Lunches are a better deal, and pretheater dinners or prix-fixe special meals are also good values.

As for watering holes where you can drink, nibble, and schmooze day and night, New York hotels have superb examples—and they may include light meals, sophisticated entertainment, or at least live piano music. The decor is often dramatic, as are the patrons—many of them power-brokers or stylish singles. You can people-watch in style.

Service   The level of service in hotels here varies from world-class polished and refined to straightforward, no-nonsense Noo Yawk–style, which can border on rude. The city is used to assertive people, and to hold your own in this competitive atmosphere, hang tough, as New

Yorkers do. Good manners are essential anywhere, but here you can ask a little louder or longer if there's something you'd like, or like changed. (Around here, that's called "chutzpah.") Although the service may vary from one front desk person to the next, good management ensures an atmosphere where "the guest is always right"—or at least starts out that way. The goals should be pleasing you and encouraging return visits.

Smaller hotels that cater to independent travelers are more likely to give better service, as they can't compete in terms of physical plant and amenities and focus instead on making guests feel special. So if you like to be pampered, luxury hotels and small independents will be best bets. Word-of-mouth based on the actual experience of travel agents, friends, or co-workers is a great indicator. Otherwise, note:

- Is there a service desk or service representative, such as a concierge? These show that a hotel is at least aware of the importance of service.

- How are you greeted? Is there a doorman? Are you taken to your room by a hotel representative? Are you provided with clear information and asked if you need anything?

- If you make a request, are your needs fulfilled promptly and courteously?

- What services are offered as standard—secretarial, translators, goods, baby sitters, concierges, luggage handlers, valet parking?

- Is your bed turned down at night, and towels replaced?

- Is there 24-hour room service?

Most luxury hotels pride themselves on service, which translates into luxury and in the final analysis is what often makes a hotel great. For example, the **Michelangelo** offers a kit with everything from dental floss to condoms, and the **St. Regis** provides 24-hour butler service. Other hotels with a rep for great service include the **Four Seasons,** the **Mark,** the **Lowell,** the **Carlyle,** the **Pierre,** and the **Peninsula.**

Size   Size-wise, most New York hotels, even the finest, have smaller rooms than in other major cities. But in a few cases, hotels such as **Flatotel International,** which have been converted from apartment houses (flat = apartment, get it?), offer huge units. Check our hotel information chart if bigger is better for you.

Families   Fictional Eloise and that *Home Alone* boy may be the most famous ones, but kids regularly stay and play in New York hotels (and in fact, the **Plaza,** where those two hung out, has some of the best kid programs in town). Suites, especially with kitchenettes, are a real cost-saver and a good idea. And many hotels offer free lodging staying in their parents' room. Some of New York's best hotels are surprisingly kid-friendly, with many family amenities, play rooms, increasingly lavish kids' programs, and in some cases, big discounts. Check when you reserve to make sure.

Some specifics: **Le Parker Meredien New York** has a family-friendly "Smart Aleck" service, which includes cartoons in the elevator to the rooftop pool. The **Westin New York Times Square** hosts a Kids Club; members receive a sports bottle, toys, coloring books, and a bedtime story. Toddlers get their own thing: an amenity box including step stool and potty seat. **DoubleTree Guest Suites Times Square** dedicates a playroom. The **Barclay New York** offers a backpack filled with goodies, including night lights, a baseball cap, and a guidebook of kid events.

Novotel New York provides a Kid's Corner, where the hotel's mascot, Dolfie, entertains. The **Gorham** has three-seater strollers, in case you have triplets; also, Operation Family offers family dens and pillow-fight menus. And the **Ritz-Carlton Battery Park** includes a toy menu from FAO Schwarz, a telescope for viewing the Statue of Liberty, and bikes to tour Battery Park. Ritz Kids also have their own butler to prepare a bubble bath, and leave a teddy bear on their pillow.

Other kid innovations? The **Waldorf-Astoria** hosts a children's tea, featuring etiquette tips. **Loews** hotels offers several packages specifically for grandparents and grandkids.

Pets   Can't bear to leave your four-legged family at home? Most hotels will only accept service animals, but a few choice properties allow pets under 20 pounds; be sure to mention your situation when booking. Hotels which may accept small animals include **Mayflower Hotel,** the **Michelangelo, New York Marriott Marquis,** the **Plaza,** and **Soho Grand. Loews** hotels provide a welcome kit, a pet menu, and a Puppy Pager, to get ahold of your pet in an emergency.

Tour and Convention Groups   Some New York hotels specialize in hosting convention or tour groups. For individual travelers, trying to compete with large groups can be time-consuming and frustrating. Even more maddening is to find yourself on the same floor with a tour group of 100 high-school seniors running up and down the corridor in the middle of the night, partying, and slamming doors. (We've been there.) The bottom line: in a large hotel, insist on a floor where no tour group is booked.

Be Hotel Wise

New Yorkers learn to use what's available and make do with what isn't. Here are some general tips to help:

- Check out rooms ahead of time if possible, by Internet or brochure. Try **www.hotres.com, www.hoteldiscounts.com,** or **www.quikbook.com.**

- Request a renovated room (even if you aren't sure there are any). New York hotels are constantly renovating, often floor by floor, and newest is usually best, often at the same price. Even if the hotel has not recently renovated, asking shows that you want the best available room for the price.

- If in doubt, visit the room before committing your luggage to it, and if you are not satisfied, ask for a better one. This is a common action in Europe, but New York hoteliers are not surprised by it. If you have a specific and legitimate gripe, such as size, poor housekeeping, lack of view, or noise, chances are you will get results and a better room.

- Maximize the concierge. The best NYC hotels have extensively trained profession-als who can book anything and advise about everything in the city. You can often acquire hard-to-get tickets this way, even at the last minute—if you're willing to pay the top fee for them; a good concierge has the savvy and connections needed. Even if a hotel just has a front-desk staff that goes out of its way, use their expertise. Book restaurants through concierges to get better tables, better service, and more response to complaints, as the restaurant doesn't want to offend the concierge and lose future business. If the meal was memorable and the reservation hard to get, factor part of your tip for the concierge.

- If you reserve in the hotel restaurant, be sure to mention if you are staying at the hotel. You'll probably get better attention.

- Be assertive. Don't accept the first "no" for major requests if you really want something.

- When you're on business, select a room with at least a portion of a sitting area. If you meet there, you'll save time, money, and hassle, and it will be more appropriate than sitting on a bed.

- Check in early and out late. Often you can extend your stay by several hours. If you arrive around noon for a 3 p.m. check-in, your room may already be made up. At worst, you can leave your bags in a locked room and return later. If you ask politely for a late check-out on your last day, you can often get it. But 2 p.m. check-out is usually the latest hotels are willing to give.

- If you're an independent traveler, small hotels will more often go out of their way for your business and to make you feel like a VIP. It's preferable to getting lost in the shuffle of larger groups.

- If you have a great view, open the curtains all the way! The greater your sense of place here in New York, the more you get for your money.

Hotel Neighborhoods

Unless business or friends and family take you to one of the outer bor-oughs, or you can't get a room otherwise, the place to stay is Manhattan. Within the narrow island are hundreds of choices—from the finest in the world to faded but acceptable structures.

But where in Manhattan?

Most New York hotels are clustered in the Midtown area, from 42nd Street to 59th. With the city on the upswing, fine new and refurbished hotels are turning up from the 90s, down to the Battery, from Soho and Chelsea to Chinatown, the Village, and the West Side. Generally, Down-town is trendy, Uptown is quiet, and Midtown is bustling, but anywhere in the city is exciting.

Downtown and Lower Manhattan

Here Peter Minuit bought Manhattan island from the Indians for the equivalent of $25, so the story goes. Today, in this pricey area, that hardly covers a room-service snack. Among the concrete canyons of the bulls and bears of Wall Street and the sight-seers at a rising Ground Zero are several modern hotels, geared to the business and leisure traveler. Because many visitors are on work assignments, most hotels in this area are large and offer complete business services. But visitors also flock to Battery Park, the Statue of Liberty and Ellis Island, the new Jewish Heritage Museum, South Street Seaport, Chinatown, and Little Italy. New restaurants and shops, recreational areas and bike paths—even water sports like parasailing in the Hudson River—make this an increasingly appealing part of the city. Many hotels will be converted from existing buildings in the next five years to add to the room inventory. Downtown is relatively quiet at night, with fewer nightspots than in the rest of the island. Also, although subways are convenient, bus service is erratic, and cab fares to Midtown are expensive. But the Staten Island ferry, with its great views, is free.

Greenwich Village and Soho

Restaurants, galleries, shops, and theaters abound, and NYU and the New School offer courses and cultural delights. Because of so many students, both the East and West Village remain undeniably hip. But surprisingly, until a few years ago you'd have to go elsewhere to sleep, and there still are only a few hotels here, including the **Washington Square Hotel** and the **Soho Grand.** In nearby Tribeca and the neighboring "meatpacking district," trendy new hotels reflect the renaissance of these now-stylish neighborhoods. This is a wonderful area to browse in, with artsy shops by day and action most of the night, and subway lines link you swiftly to other areas. But hotels remain scarce, and aside from bed-and-breakfasts and reconversions of small properties, the hotel scene has lagged behind the street scene. This is changing, however; in the next two years watch for ultra-luxe properties of architectural note.

14th to 30th Streets

The 30-acre Chelsea Piers sports complex on the Hudson River offers everything from bowling to volleyball to indoor golf. Artists are converting old buildings into studios and galleries. Many older buildings are ripe for renovation in this improving but still underrated neighborhood of businesses, universities, hospitals, and off-Broadway theaters, and a few hotels have already been opened. But for the most part, good hotels are few and far between. Visitors to the Chelsea Market and the Joyce, the city's modern dance theater, will like the **Chelsea Savoy** on the West Side. New and trendy hotels include the **Maritime** and the **Hotel Gansevoort.** The **Inn** at **Irving Place** is a tiny, choice place near leafy and quiet Gramercy Park on the East Side. Look for lots of small hotels developing from commercial buildings in the coming years as the area continues to upgrade.

31st to 41st Streets

This bustling area of offices, sports complexes, the Garment District, Macy's at Union Square (by the summer greenmarket), the Jacob Javits Convention Center, and transportation terminals is no-nonsense, and large. Midrange hotels reflect the group clientele and convention needs. Visitors to Madison Square Garden, by Penn Station, can stay at the small **Hotel Metro.** The proposed ribbon of greenery along the Hudson, with its bicycle paths and benches, should improve the West Side hotel scene. On the East Side, quiet Murray Hill, with its many historic town-houses, is home to the J. P. Morgan Library and nearby small hotels, such as the stylish **Morgans,** the **Avalon,** and the spiffy **Roger Williams.**

42nd to 59th Streets: The East Side

Midtown draws delegates and visitors to the United Nations, Carnegie Hall, Fifth Avenue shoppers, NBC and CBS sidewalk-studio gawkers, Rockefeller Center ice skaters, business travelers at corporate headquar-ters, and those who like being at the center of the city's energy. Some of the best hotels in the world offer great East River and landmark-building views. A beautifully refurbished Grand Central Station provides easy access to the northern suburbs and Connecticut. Among the dozens and dozens of fine skyscraper hotels clustered here are the classic Art Deco **Waldorf-Astoria** and the **Fitzpatrick Grand Central.**

42nd to 59th Streets: The West Side

In Times Square the neon is brighter than ever, and so is the spirit. Neighborhoods are cleaner and safer. Broadway, Carnegie Hall, theme restaurants, TV studios, and the office buildings along Columbus Circle and the Avenue of the Americas all draw visitors. Moderate chains, such as **Holiday Inn, Marriott, Howard Johnson,** and **Days Inn,** and older, slightly seedy hotels abound, catering to tour groups. But the **Michelan-gelo** and the great hotels rimming the southern end of Central Park, including the **Essex House,** are among the best in the city. And the **Peninsula,** just a hop west of Fifth Avenue, is grander than ever. Look for an increase in hotel rooms as buildings are converted and office-residential complexes developed—and watch for that comet-topped **Westin New York Times Square** at E-walk, just off Times Square.

60th Street and Above

Uptown—refined, fashionable, exclusive, cultural. Central Park is the oasis of this area, but there are also world-famous museums and top hospitals.

Two-storied Madison Avenue is one of the most fascinating shopping areas of the world, and Lincoln Center is a renowned cultural focal point. Great views of the park and the rivers abound. Not surprisingly, some of the fanciest hotels are here, including the **Carlyle,** the **Lowell,** and the **Mark.**

Can You Even Get In?

Even with increasing numbers of hotel rooms in New York City, with apologies to songwriters Kander and Ebb, if you can make a reservation (t)here, you can make one anywhere. It's up to you—and your resourcefulness—to get a room in NY, NY.

- Try **NYC & Company's** online reservation system (**www.nycvisit.com**) to check out almost 200 New York hotels. It's powered by 1800-usahotels.com and features day-to-day changes.

- Check out the **Peak Season Hotel Hotline.** It provides access to rooms at over 80 hotels in all price categories from September 1 to December 31. As a last resort, on nights when travel agents and consumers believe the city is "sold out," the hotline can find rooms. Call (800) 846-7666. And note the other reservations services listed later in the chapter.

- Book as far in advance as possible. Holidays are always busy, but even when occupancy is down in many parts of the country, rooms often are fully booked here, as huge conferences reserve blocks of hotel rooms years in advance, frequently at odd times. Check with the **NYCVB** at (800) 846-ROOM. Traditionally, the easiest time to get a room is during January and February. And Sunday is traditionally the slowest day of the week.

- Call just after 6 p.m. on the day you want to stay. That is when most properties cancel reservations not guaranteed with a credit card on the day of arrival. (In the industry, these nonguaranteed reservations are called "timers.")

- Try the Web. **Hotres.com** has blocks of reserved rooms at 30 midtown hotels, so lodging may be available even if a hotel says it's "sold out." Sites are always expanding and new ones popping up, so use a search engine like Yahoo! or Google to find a selection.

- Use travel and tour agencies that do lots of NYC convention business. They often have the clout to find a room, even when you're on your own. Usually the major agencies will do the most convention business; otherwise, inquire from friends or business associates who have traveled on business to New York, or ask around locally. As for tour operators, five who frequently handle New York City are **ATI** (American Tour International), **Allied Tours, T-Pro, CAUSA,** and **City Tours.** Your travel agent will help you reserve through tour operators.

- Be flexible. The more rigid your requests, the harder it may be to fill them. Ask what's available. Management may not have many standard rooms but can sometimes offer luxury suites or relatively unappealing rooms—poor view, low floor, not yet refurbished. If you're willing, you can often negotiate a deal for these white elephants.

- Think small. Hotels with few rooms are least likely to host huge groups, and surprisingly, you can often find a room at small places even at busy times.

- Think independent. When rooms are scarce, non-chain hotels often have availability, as they are less well known and have smaller advertising and marketing budgets than chains.

Because many working New Yorkers live outside the city, the metro and tri-state transportation network is the biggest in the country, and you can get to almost any borough or to the suburbs by public transport until the wee hours of the morning. So if you don't mind commuting, you can find a variety of accommodations outside Manhattan.

Queens, Brooklyn, Staten Island, and the Bronx have some chain hotels, and around Kennedy, LaGuardia, and Newark airports you will find many midlevel choices (see our hotel listings). But nearby Westchester County, southern Connecticut, and Long Island have a varied selection of luxury hotels, inns, resorts, and bed-and-breakfasts, with more recreational space at generally lower cost than comparable accommodations in the city. You may miss out on urban excitement, but you're more likely to get a room.

The following notable accommodations are in the suburbs within an hour or so of the city. All are near subway or train lines (taxis usually meet trains), are in safe neighborhoods, and they offer free parking, outstanding settings and decor, and excellent on-site or nearby restaurants.

Westchester County, NY

The Castle at Tarrytown Benedict Avenue, Tarrytown; (914) 631-1980; fax (914) 631-4612

Crabtree's Kittle House 11 Kittle Road, Chappaqua; (914) 666-8044; fax (914) 666-2684

Doral Arrowwood Anderson Hill Road, Rye Brook; (800) 633-6569; fax (914) 323-5500

Long Island

Garden City Hotel 45 Seventh Street, Garden City; (516) 747-3000; fax (516) 747-1414

The Inn at Great Neck 30 Cutter Mill Road, Great Neck; (516) 773-2000; fax (516) 773-2020

Southern Connecticut

The Homestead Inn 420 Fieldpoint Road, Greenwich; (203) 869-7500; fax (203) 869–7502

Hyatt Regency Greenwich 1800 East Putnam, Old Greenwich; (203) 637-1234; fax (203) 637-2940

The Inn at National Hall 2 Post Road W, Westport; (800) 628-4255, (203) 221-1351; fax (203) 221-0276

Slice the Price of Rooms in the Apple

The bad news: Average room rates are about $200 a night, and at top luxury hotels, standard rooms go for $400 or so—the highest rate in America. Tourists from around the world, it seems, will pay any price to visit New York.

The good news: Compared to many other great international cities, New York is a relative bargain. Remember that as you plunk down your plastic, signing off on what seems like the GNP of Honduras. Here are some helpful ideas for lowering costs:

- **Check out the Internet.** Last-minute bargains are now available online at sites such as **priceline.com, expedia.com,** and **travelocity.com.** You can judge comparative value for money by seeing a listing of hotels—what they offer, where they are located, and what they charge.

- **Choose a less-than-fashionable neighborhood.** New York is made up of many distinct enclaves, and this emphasis on address reflects itself in pricing. Unless you need to be there for convenience, it may not be worth it to you to stay on the Upper East Side when the same quality room on the Lower West Side may be half the cost. The East Side is priciest; Midtown and up to 96th Street is the fanciest area. The best deals are around Chelsea and on the Upper West Side. You will occasionally find a budget hotel in pricey areas, such as the Pickwick Arms, in the 50s on the East Side. Some other word-of-mouth recommendations for budget accommodations are **Habitat** and the **Lucerne.**

- **Leave your car at home.** Garaging a car overnight in New York can cost as much as a motel room off the highway (with donuts and coffee). And you really don't need a car here; most New Yorkers—even big spenders—don't bother with wheels, and many can't even drive. Taxis are abundant and public transportation is exceptional. Manhattan is a walkers' paradise, and most of the city is divided into simple grids. If you must drive, try for a rare hotel with free parking. See our survey.

- **For longer stays, try an apartment hotel.** These typically offer daily maid service, kitchen, and laundry facilities. Several upscale hotels offer an apartment option, including the **Waldorf-Astoria.** These hybrids combine hotel services with a kitchen and a residential feel and are wonderful for entertaining, or as an alternative to getting an apartment.

- **Seek a suite, which offers the potential of whole families in one room.** And if there's a kitchenette, even better. Several hotels, such as **Trump International Hotel & Towers,** offer kitchenettes even in standard rooms.

- **Stay at the worst room at a good hotel, rather than the best at a lesser one.** The cost differential can be considerable, although the rest of the hotel services, amenities, and public rooms remain the same. You're getting the biggest bang for your buck when you ask for the low-priced smallest room with the worst view on the lowest floor—at an otherwise good hotel.

- **Avoid room service and minibars.** Bring food up from delis, take-out groceries (which usually have salad bars), or sidewalk vendors, which purvey fresh fruits as well as hot dogs, falafel, and other ethnic delights. Most will provide utensils if needed, as New Yorkers are known for eating on the run. Or, if possible, make like a resident and have a restaurant deliver (frowned at by some hotels—check first). Neighborhood restaurants, especially the old-fashioned coffee shops and "ethnics," are good and surprisingly reasonable. If you eat like a local rather than a tourist, you can save big-time.

- **Accept shared baths.** Some hotels, such as the **Pickwick Arms,** are set up with some shared facilities, at around $100 a night. If price means more than privacy, you'll enjoy the savings.

- **Go really basic.** **YMCAs** and youth hostels are available in the city. Bare-bones, but cheap. There are Ys on the East Side (phone (212) 756-9600) and West Side (phone (212) 875-4100). **Hostelling International** offers a hostel on the Upper West Side (phone (800) 909-4776; **www.hinewyork.org**). Also try **NY Hostel** (phone (212) 932-2300). For dormitory accommodations, check with universities in the city, including New York University. Judith Glynn's **Manhattan Getaways** (phone (212) 956-2010; **manhattangetaways.com**) is a great source for home-style getaways, such as reconverted apartments and guesthouses.

- **Find a discounted rate.** Check out deals through ads, agents, special events, and openings. These include weekend and convention deals, frequent mileage clubs, automobile or other travel clubs, senior rates (some require ages as low as 50), military or government discounts, corporate or shareholder rates, packages, long-stay rates (usually at least five nights), and travel industry rates. Some hotels might even give lower rates if you are visiting because of bereavement or medical care.

Special Weekend Rates

Most hotels that cater to business, government, and convention travelers offer special weekend discount rates ranging 15–40% below normal weekday rates. Find out about weekend specials by calling individual hotels or by consulting your travel agent.

Corporate Rates

Many hotels offer discounted corporate rates (5–20% off rack rate). Usually you don't need to work for a large company or have a special relationship with the hotel—simply ask for this discount. Some will guarantee the discounted rate on the phone when you reserve.

Others may make the rate conditional on your providing some sort of bona fides—for instance, a fax on your company's letterhead requesting the rate, or a company credit card or business card on check-in. Generally, the screening is not rigorous.

Half-Price Programs

Larger discounts on rooms (35–60%), in New York or anywhere else, are available through half-price hotel programs, often called travel clubs. Program operators contract with an individual hotel to provide rooms at deep discounts, usually 50% off rack rate, on a "space available" basis. You can usually reserve a discounted room whenever the hotel expects less than 80% occupancy. A little calendar sleuthing to avoid citywide conventions and special events increases your chance of finding this kind of discount.

Most half-price programs charge an annual membership fee or directory subscription charge of $25 to $125. You get a membership card and a directory listing participating hotels. But note the restrictions and exceptions. Some hotels "black out" certain dates or times of year. Others may only offer the discount certain days of the week or require you to stay a certain number of nights. Still others may offer a much smaller discount than 50% off rack rate.

Programs specialize in domestic travel, international travel, or both. More established operators offer members thousands of hotels to choose from in the United States. All of the following programs have a heavy concentration of hotels in California and Florida, and most have a limited selection in New York City.

Encore	(800) 444-9800
Entertainment Publications	(800) 445-4137
ITC-50	(800) 987-6216
Quest	(800) 638-9819

One caveat: If something seems too good to be true, it usually is, and some hotels figure the discount on an exaggerated rack rate. A few may deduct the discount from a supposed "superior" or "upgraded" room rate, even though the room you get is standard.

But the majority of participating properties base discounts on the published rate in the *Hotel and Travel Index* (a quarterly reference work used by travel agents) and work within the spirit of their agreement with the program operator. As a rule, if you travel several times a year, your room rate savings will easily compensate for membership fees.

Deeply discounted rooms through half-price programs are not commissionable to travel agents, so you'll probably have to make your own calls and reservations. But if you travel frequently, your agent will probably do your legwork anyway.

Preferred Rates

This discount helps travel agents stimulate booking activity or attract a certain class of traveler. Most preferred rates are promoted through travel industry publications and are often accessible only through an agent. Sound out your travel agent about possible deals, but note that the rates shown on travel agents' computerized reservations systems are not always the lowest rates obtainable. Zero in on a couple of hotels that fill your needs in terms of location and quality of accommodations, then have your agent call the hotel for the latest rates and specials.

Hotel reps respond positively to travel agents because they represent a source of additional business. As we discussed earlier, there are certain specials that hotel reps will disclose only to travel agents. Also, a personal appeal from your agent to the hotel's director of sales and marketing will often get you a room.

Consolidators, Wholesalers, and Reservation Services

The discount available (if any) from a reservation service depends on whether the service functions as a consolidator or as a wholesaler. Consolidators are strictly sales agents who do not own or control the room inventory they are trying to sell. Discounts offered by consolidators are determined by the hotels with rooms to fill. Consolidator discounts vary enormously depending on how desperate the hotel is to unload the rooms. When you deal with a room reservation service that operates as a consolidator, you pay for your room as usual when you check out of the hotel.

Wholesalers have longstanding contracts with hotels to purchase rooms at an established deep discount. Some wholesalers hold purchase options on blocks of rooms, whereas others actually pay for rooms and own the inventory, so they can offer whatever discount is consistent with current demand. Most discounts fall in the 10–40% range, and you'll usually pay for your entire stay in advance with your credit card. The service then sends you a written confirmation and usually a voucher (indicating prepayment) to present at the hotel.

Reservation services are probably more useful when availability is scarce than to obtain deep discounts. Calling the hotels ourselves, we were often able to beat the reservation services' rates (when rooms were available). When the city was booked, however, the reservation services were able to find rooms at a fair price.

Ask for a rate quote for a particular hotel, or for their best available deal, in your preferred area. If you say you're on a budget, the service might even shave a bit off their profit.

Services that frequently offer substantial discounts include:

Accommodations Express	(800) 444-7666
Central Reservation Service	(800) 548-3311
Express Reservations	(800) 356-1123
Hotel Reservations Network	(800) 964-6835
Quikbook	(800) 789-9887
RMC Travel	(800) 245-5738
Room Finders USA	(800) 473-7829

How to Evaluate a Travel Package

Package vacations can be win/win. The buyer only has to make one phone call and deal with a single salesperson to set up the whole vacation: transportation, lodging, meals, guided tours, and Broadway shows. The seller eliminates separate sales, confirmations, and billing. Some packagers also buy hotel rooms and airfares in bulk on contract, like a broker playing the commodities market, which can mean a significant savings from posted fares.

Choose a package with features you are sure to use; you will be paying for them. If cost is more important than convenience, make a few calls to price individual components (airfare, lodging, shows, etc.). If the costs are about the same, the package is probably worth buying just for the convenience. If your package includes a choice of rental car or airport transfers (transportation to and from the airport), take the transfers. Driving in the city is difficult, and parking in a garage is expensive, often up to $50 for a 24-hour period. During the weekend, with most businesses closed and commuters and second-home types out of town, it's relatively easier to get around, and parking spaces may be available, if you want to chance it; but during the week, forget it. (If you do take the car, find a package that includes free parking at your hotel.)

Buyer beware. You're dealing with a lot of money and trust here, and alas, a packager could cash in on discounts without passing them on, or load packages with extras that cost next to nothing but inflate the retail price higher than the Empire State Building; a real New York–style con game. So if something seems "off," check with a supervisor or a major travel agency, and be sure you're with a reputable company.

Is Your Travel Agent NYC Savvy?

The city hotel scene is complex and constantly changing. Has your travel agent recently been to New York? And does the agency keep up-to-the-minute info?

Some travel agents unfamiliar with the Apple may try to plug you into a tour operator's or wholesaler's preset package, allowing the agent to set up your whole trip up with a single phone call—and still collect an 8–10% commission. And many agents will place almost all their New York business with only one or two wholesalers or tour operators, which doesn't provide much choice for you.

Agents will often use wholesalers who run packages in conjunction with airlines, like Delta Vacations or American's Fly Away Vacations, and because of the wholesaler's exclusive relationship with the carrier, these trips are easy to book. However, they can be more expensive than a package offered by a high-volume wholesaler who works with airlines in a primary New York City market.

To help your travel agent get you the best possible hotel deal, follow these five steps:

1. Determine which area is best for you, and if possible choose a specific hotel. Review the hotel information provided in this guide, and contact hotels that interest you, if necessary.
2. Check out the hotel deals and package vacations advertised on the Internet and in the Sunday travel sections of major newspapers such as the *New York Times, New York Daily News, Philadelphia Inquirer,* or *Boston Globe.* They often advertise deals that undercut anything offered in your local paper. See if you can find specials that fit your plans and include a hotel you like.

3. Call the hotels, wholesalers, or tour operators whose ads you have collected. Ask any questions you have concerning their packages, but do not book your trip with them directly.

4. Ask if your travel agent can get you something better. The deals in the paper will serve as a benchmark.

5. Choose from the options, then have your travel agent book the best one. Even if you go with one of the packages in the newspaper, it will probably be commissionable (at no additional cost to you) and will provide the agent some return on the time invested on your behalf. Also, as a travel professional, your agent should be able to verify the quality and integrity of the deal.

If You Make Your Own Reservation

Check out the Internet for immediate information; **priceline.com,** **travelocity.com,** and **expedia.com** are good options. Or call the specific hotel (as opposed to the hotel chain's national toll-free number where operators are usually unaware of local specials). Always ask about specials before inquiring about corporate rates—and don't be afraid to bargain. If you're buying a hotel's weekend package, for example, and want to extend your stay into the following week, you can often obtain at least the corporate rate for the extra days. However, do your bargaining before you check in, preferably when you make your reservations.

Are You Coming to NYC on Business?

Identify the zone(s) where your business will take you, then use the hotel chart to cross-reference the hotels located in that area. Once you have developed a short list of possible hotels that fit your budget and offer the standards you require, you (or your travel agent) can apply the cost-saving suggestions discussed earlier to obtain the lowest rate.

Convention Rates: How They Work and How to Do Better

If you're attending a major convention or trade show, your group has probably negotiated convention rates, and hotels have booked rooms at an agreed-on price, sometimes citywide.

Because the convention sponsor brings big business to New York and reserves many rooms, often annually, it usually can negotiate volume discounts substantially below rack rate. You may get a housing list that includes the special rates, and you can compare them with the rates using the strategies covered in the previous section.

If the negotiated convention rate doesn't sound like a good deal, try to reserve a room using an Internet bargain, a half-price club, a consolidator, or a tour operator. Remember, however, that deep discounts are usually available only when the hotel expects to be at less than 80% occupancy, a rarity when a big convention is in town.

Strategies for Beating Convention Rates—Easy as 1-2-3

1. Reserve early. Most big conventions and trade shows announce meeting sites one to three years in advance. If you book well ahead of the time the convention sponsor sends out the housing list, chances are good that the hotel will accept your reservation.

2. Compare your convention's housing list with the list of hotels presented in this guide. You may be able to find a suitable hotel not on the housing list.

3. Use a local reservations agency or consolidator. This is also a good strategy if you need to make reservations at the last minute. Local reservations agencies and consolidators almost always control some rooms, even during a huge convention or trade show.

Hotels Rated and Ranked

What's in a Room?

Unfortunately, in New York, some beautifully appointed rooms are cramped and poorly designed. *Unofficial Guide* researchers are aware of this and spend many weeks inspecting hotel rooms. Here are a few of the things we check.

Room Size   Spacious rooms are preferable, but New York's hotel rooms are generally smaller than those in other major cities, and the trend is high-style and cramped. Note the other luxuries, and if it will be a problem, ask about size when booking. (Smaller rooms can be cozy, but not if you bump your shins in the middle of the night trying to maneuver between the walls and the bed.) If a room is well designed, with big windows, mirrored walls, nooks and alcoves, it can compensate for lack of space. If size really matters, rooms at the Four Seasons, at 600 square feet, are just about the largest in the city—as large as many New York one-bedroom apartments—and are reputed to have cost about a million dollars each to design and furnish.

Temperature Control, Ventilation, and Odor   Hotel rooms should be odor-free and smoke-free and not feel stuffy or damp. The most quiet and responsive system is central heating and air-conditioning, controlled by the room's own thermostat. Next best is a room module heater and air conditioner, preferably controlled by an automatic thermostat, but usually by manually operated button controls. Central heating and air without any sort of room thermostat can leave you sweltering or shivering in the changeable New York climate, without much control.

Most hotel rooms have windows or balcony doors that have been permanently sealed. Though there are legitimate safety and liability issues involved, we prefer windows and balcony doors that can be opened. A room with a view is preferable, and a balcony or terrace is especially exciting (and rare) in New York City, not just because you can step outside but because of the full-length windows—and the "fresh" NYC air.

Room Security   We'll start with front desk staffers, who need to be discreet about calling out your room number. Better rooms have locks that require a plastic card instead of the traditional lock and key; card and slot systems allow the hotel to change the combination or entry code of the lock with each new guest. Though larger hotels and hotel chains with lock and key systems usually rotate their locks once each year, they remain vulnerable to hotel thieves much of the time, and many smaller or independent properties rarely rotate their locks.

In addition to the entry-lock system, the door should have a deadbolt, and perhaps a chain that can be locked from the inside, but a chain by itself is not sufficient. Peepholes allow you to check out visitors. Any windows and balcony doors should have secure locks. Room safes are becoming standard security devices, and the bigger the better, so that technical devices, cameras, and other large items can also be stored.

Safety   New York codes are tough. Fire or smoke alarm, clear fire instructions, and a sprinkler systems are musts for rooms. Bathtubs should have a nonskid surface, and shower stall doors are safest if they either open outward or slide side-to-side. Bathroom electrical outlets high on the wall and not too close to the sink are best. Balconies should have sturdy, high rails.

Noise   As we mentioned earlier, New York is a city filled with traffic and street noises round the clock. If this is a potential problem, check to make sure that windows are double- or triple-glazed. In better hotels, wall and ceiling construction effectively screen routine noise, carpets and drapes absorb and muffle sounds, and mattresses mounted on stable platforms or sturdy bed frames do not squeak much, even when challenged by the most acrobatic lovers. Televisions enclosed in cabinets, and with volume governors, rarely disturb guests in adjacent rooms.

Optimally, the air-conditioning and heating system operates without noise or vibration. Likewise, plumbing is quiet and positioned away from the sleeping area. Doors to the hall, and to adjoining rooms, are thick and well fitted to better block out noise. Remember, if you are easily disturbed by noise, ask for a room on a higher floor, off main thoroughfares, and away from elevators and ice and vending machines.

Darkness Control   Ever wake up at sunrise in a hotel room where the curtains would not quite meet in the middle? Thick, lined curtains that close completely in the center and extend beyond the edges of the window or door frame are ideal. In a well-planned room, the curtains, shades, or blinds should almost totally block light at any time of day.

Lighting   Poor lighting is a problem in American hotel rooms, and New York, sorry to say, is no exception. Lighting may be dramatic, and adequate for dressing, relaxing, or watching television, but not for reading or working. Light needs to be bright over tables and desks, and beside couches or easy chairs. Since many people read in bed, best is a separate light for each person, high enough to shed light on books, but illuminating a small area so that a sleeper will not be bothered by their roomate's light. A bedside console that controls most lights and electronics is especially desirable. The worst situation is a single bedside lamp, sometimes compounded by weak light bulbs.

Closet areas should be well lit, with a switch near the door that turns on room lights when you enter. Bathroom lighting should be adequate for grooming purposes—and a heat lamp is a nice bonus.

Furnishings Minimum sleep requirements are top-grade mattresses, pillows with nonallergic fillers, warm blankets, and bed linens changed daily. Better hotels usually provide extra blankets and pillows in the room or on request, and they sometimes use a second top sheet between blanket and spread. Duvets over down comforters, once a European luxury, are the New York standard of cleanliness and comfort. Better headboards are padded for comfortable reading in bed, and a nightstand or table on each side of the bed(s) is standard.

Dressers should be large enough to hold clothes for two people during a long stay, and a luggage rack and full-length mirror are useful. As for electronics, televisions today are expected to be large as well as cable-connected; ideally, with volume governors and remote controls, mounted on swivel bases, and, preferably, enclosed. A local TV program-guide helps. In-room movies and VCR capabilities are nice options. CD players and top-grade clock-radios are pluses.

Telephones should be touch-tone, capable of international direct dialing, conveniently situated, with easy-to-understand dialing instructions and a rate card. Local white and yellow pages should be provided. Better hotels install phones in the bathroom and furnish portable phones or equip room phones with long cords. Two lines, dataports for fax and laptop computers, and even cell and mobile phones are offered at luxury and business-oriented hotels.

A table with chairs, or a desk, and a sitting area—perhaps with screens or French doors to block off work and sleep areas—are important elements. Well-designed hotel rooms usually have armchairs and sometimes a sleeper sofa for lounging and reading. Nice extras in any hotel room include small refrigerators or minibars, irons and ironing boards, coffeemakers, and trouser presses.

Bathroom Marble, granite, and tile look best and are easy to keep clean. Two sinks are better than one, and you cannot have too much counter space. A sink outside the bath is a great convenience when one person bathes as another dresses, a separate toilet area is nice for privacy, and bidets are important options, especially for international travelers.

Better bathrooms have both a tub and shower with a nonslip bottom. Tub and shower controls should be easy to operate; adjustable shower heads are preferred, and whirlpool tubs and separate shower stalls are a plus. The bath needs to be well lit and should have an exhaust fan and a guest-controlled bathroom heater. Towels and washcloths should be large, thick, and generously supplied. An electrical outlet for each sink, conveniently and safely placed, is a big convenience when you're shaving or drying hair.

Magnifying mirrors, scales, bathrobes and slippers, phones, hair dryers, lines for TVs or extra speakers, and amenities such as fine soaps, shampoos, and lotions all add to the luxury of the bathroom.

Vending If there is no minibar, a complimentary ice machine and a drink machine should be conveniently located, or nibbles and drinks easily available from room service. Welcome additions at midrange properties include access to snacks and sundries (combs, toothpaste, etc.) in restaurants and shops. Luxury hotels will provide sundries in the room or on request.

Maintenance Your eyes, nose, and fingers will tell you how your room is maintained, and even if a room is large and luxurious, if it isn't clean it isn't habitable. On the other hand, a basic but clean room may be just fine. Check out whether the hotel offers daily maid service. Luxury hotels offer turndown service (and that nice chocolate—or more—on the pillow).

"You're the Greatest"
Our Favorite New York Hotels

With apologies to New York's own Ralph Kramden (of *The Honeymooners*), here's our totally subjective listing of superlative New York hotels. Some of these listings are not rated, but since they have special reputations for one particular aspect, we include them here.

Best Boutique Hotels

Bryant Park Hotel	Hudson Hotel	The Muse
City Club	Le Marquis	Library Hotel
Dylan Hotel	Mercer	

Large Rooms

Four Seasons Hotel	Flatotel International

Best Themes

Hotel Casablanca	Library Hotel	The Muse

NYC Icons

Algonquin Hotel	The Plaza	The Stanhope
The Carlyle	The St. Regis	The Waldorf-Astoria
The Pierre	The Sherry Netherland	

Bargains Under $150 (some with shared bath)

Cosmopolitan Hotel	On the Avenue	Tribeca Grand

Bargains Under $125 (shared/private bath)

Habitat Hotel   Pickwick Arms Hotel

Best Bed-and-Breakfasts/Under a Dozen Rooms

Akwaaba Mansion   Holmes Bed and   Inn on 23rd Street
Country Inn in the City   Breakfast   Le Refuge Inn (Bronx)
Harbor House (Staten   The Inn at Irving Place   Second Home on Second
   Island)   Inn New York City   Ave.

Classic Hotel Bars

The Bull & Bear at the   5757 at the Four Seasons   Mark's Bar at the Mark
   Waldorf-Astoria   King Cole Bar at the   Oak Bar at the Plaza
Fantino at Central Park   St. Regis Hotel
   Intercontinental

Trendy Hotel Bars and Lounges

The Grand Bar at the   Hudson Bar (with library   C3 Lounge at Washington
   Soho Grand   and purple pool table)   Square Hotel
The Grotto at the   at Hudson Hotel   Jack's Bar at Le Parker
   Michelangelo   Oasis at W New York   Meridien Hotel
                                                         Morgan's Bar at Morgans

Gay-comfortable Hotels

Chelsea Savoy   Washington Square Hotel

Best Complimentary Breakfast

Avalon   Iroquois New York   Sheraton Russell Hotel
Bentley   The Roger Smith   Washington Square Hotel

Best Brunch

Ambassador Grill at   Heartbeat at W New   Restaurant Charlotte at
   Regal U.N. Plaza   York   Millennium Broadway
Halcyon's Penthouse at   Norma's at Le Parker
   J.W. Marriott Hotel   Meridien Hotel

Best High Tea

The Pierre   The Ritz Carlton New   The St. Regis
The Plaza   York Battery Park   The Waldorf-Astoria

Best Hotel Restaurants

Adrienne at the Peninsula   Ilo at Bryant Park Hotel   Palladin at Time
Asiate at Mandarin   Jean Georges at Trump   Thom at 60 Thompson
   Oriental   International Hotel &   Town at Chambers—
C3 at Washington Square   Towers   a Hotel
   Hotel   Moda at Flatotel   Triomphe at the Iroquois
The Coach House at   Nadaman Hakubai at the   New York
   Avalon   Kitano New York   Virot at Dylan Hotel
District at the Muse   Le Cirque 2000 at the
Heartbeat at W New York   New York Palace

Drop-dead Elegant Hotels

The Four Seasons   The Peninsula   The Waldorf-Astoria
Mandarin Oriental   St. Regis Hotel

Best Public Rooms and Meeting Space

The Hilton New York	St. Regis Hotel rooftop	18th floor at the
Mandarin Oriental	The Sheraton New York	Waldorf-Astoria
The New York Marriott	Hotel and Towers	
Marquis		

Best Fitness Clubs and Spas

The Drake Swissôtel	The Peninsula	St. Regis Hotel
Mandarin Oriental	Regal U.N. Plaza	W New York
New York Palace	Ritz-Carlton New York	
Le Parker Meridien Hotel	Central Park	

Best for Romance

The Inn at Irving Place	The Peninsula	The Waldorf-Astoria
The Lowell	The Royalton	
The Mark	St. Regis Hotel	

Best People-watching

Peacock Alley at the	Lobby of the Royalton	Any downtown hotel less
Waldorf-Astoria	The Terrace at the	than a year old
King Cole Bar at the St.	Stanhope	Any hotel lobby where
Regis Hotel	Whiskey Blue at	the lowest rates are
The Regency at breakfast	W New York	more than $300 a night

Best Views

Beekman Tower Hotel	On the Avenue	Soho Grand (looking
DoubleTree Guest Suites	Regal U. N. Plaza	north)
Times Square	Ritz-Carlton New York	Hotels fronting Central
The Four Seasons	Battery Park	Park

Best for Long Stays

Trump International	The Waldorf-Astoria	Any east-side Manhattan
Hotel & Towers	towers	hotel

Kid-Friendly Hotels

The Barclay New York	Paramount	Ritz-Carlton New York
Essex House	The Plaza	Battery Park
The Gorham	Novotel New York	The Waldorf-Astoria
The Lucerne	Le Parker Meridien Hotel	

Pet-Friendly Hotels

The Muse (doggy room	Any Loews hotel, such as	On the Avenue
service and pooch	the Regency (puppy pagers	The Plaza
package)	provided)	

Computer- and Internet-friendly

Benjamin Hotel	The Muse	Time
The Drake Swissôtel	St. Regis	

Best Balconies and Terraces

Central Park	The Drake Swissôtel	On the Avenue
Intercontinental	The Lombardy	The Warwick Hotel

Best Quirky Hotels

The Box Tree	Inn on 23rd Street	Washington Square Hotel
Chambers—a Hotel	The Roger Smith	Westin New York Times
Hudson Hotel	The Sherry Netherland	Square
The Inn at Irving Place	Hotel	The Wyndham Hotel

Best Amenities

Benjamin Hotel (pillow menu)	The New York Palace (customized stationery and business cards)	The Ritz-Carlton New York Central Park (flat-screen TVs)
The Four Seasons (tubs that fill in 60 seconds)	Le Parker Meridien Hotel (homemade chocolate chip cookies)	Soho Grand (goldfish)
J.W. Marriott Hotel (heated toilet seats)	Regal U.N. Plaza (tennis court)	The Royalton ("intimacy kit")
The Mark (phones on either side of king bed, comp shuttle, Chinese tea classes)		Trump International Hotel & Towers (telescope, personal chef, laptop computer)

Hotel Ratings

Zone   The Zone column identifies the New York City zone where you will find a particular property.

Overall Quality   To distinguish properties according to relative quality, tastefulness, state of repair, cleanliness, and size of standard rooms, we have grouped the hotels and motels into classifications denoted by stars. Star ratings in this guide apply to New York–area properties only and do not necessarily correspond to stars awarded by Mobil, AAA, or other travel critics. Because stars carry little weight when awarded in the absence of common standards of comparison, we have linked our ratings to expected levels of quality established by specific American hotel corporations.

★★★★★	Superior	Tasteful and luxurious by any standard
★★★★	Extremely Nice	What you would expect at a Hyatt Regency; or Marriott
★★★	Nice	Holiday Inn or comparable quality
★★	Adequate	Clean, comfortable, and functional without frills (like a Motel 6)
★	Budget	Spartan, not aesthetically pleasing, but clean

Star ratings describe the property's standard accommodations. For most hotels, a "standard accommodation" is a room with either one king bed or two queen beds. In an all-suite property, the standard accommodation is either a one- or two-room suite. In addition to standard accommodations, many hotels offer luxury rooms and special suites not rated here. Star ratings are assigned without regard to whether a property has restaurant(s), recreational facilities, entertainment, or other extras.

Room Quality To In addition to stars (which delineate broad categories), we also employ a numerical rating system. Our rating scale is 0 to 100, with 100 as the best possible rating and zero (0) as the worst. Numerical ratings are presented to show the difference we perceive between one property and another. Rooms at the Sheraton New York, the Paramount, and the Avalon are all rated as four-star (★★★★). In the supplemental numerical ratings, the Sheraton is rated an 89, the Paramount an 88, and the Avalon an 84. This means that within the four-star category, the Sheraton and Paramount are comparable, and both have slightly nicer rooms than the Lucerne.

Cost Cost estimates are based on the hotel's published rack rates for standard rooms. Each "$" represents $80. Thus, a cost symbol of "$$$" means a room (or suite) at that hotel will cost about $240 a night.

How the Hotels Compare

Below is a hit parade of the nicest rooms in town. We've focused strictly on room quality and excluded any consideration of location, services, recreation, or amenities. In some instances, a one- or two-room suite can be had for the same price or less than that of a hotel room.

If you use subsequent editions of this guide, you will notice that many of the ratings and rankings have changed. In addition to the inclusion of new properties, these changes also consider guest room renovations or improved maintenance and housekeeping. A failure to properly maintain guest rooms or a lapse in housekeeping standards can negatively affect the ratings.

Finally, before you begin to shop for a hotel, take a hard look at this letter we received from a couple in Hot Springs, Arkansas:

We cancelled our room reservations to follow the advice in your book [and reserved a hotel room highly ranked by the Unofficial Guide]. We wanted inexpensive, but clean and cheerful. We got inexpensive, but [also] dirty, grim, and depressing. I really felt disappointed in your advice and the room. It was the pits. That was the one real piece of information I needed from your book! The room spoiled the holiday for me aside from our touring.

Needless to say, this letter was as unsettling to us as the bad room was to our reader. Our integrity as travel journalists, after all, is based on the quality of the information we provide our readers. Even with the best of intentions and the most conscientious research, however, we cannot inspect every room in every hotel. What we do, in statistical terms, is take a sample: We check out several rooms selected at random in each hotel and base our ratings and rankings on those rooms. The inspections are conducted anonymously and without the knowledge of management.

Although unusual, it is certainly possible that the rooms we randomly inspect are not representative of the majority of rooms at a particular hotel. Another possibility is that the rooms we inspect in a given hotel are representative but that by bad luck a reader is assigned a room that is inferior. When we rechecked the hotel our reader disliked, we discovered that our rating was correctly representative but that he and his wife had unfortunately been assigned to one of a small number of threadbare rooms scheduled for renovation.

The key to avoiding disappointment is to snoop around in advance. We recommend that you look on the web, ask for a photo of a hotel's standard guest room before you book, or at least get a copy of the hotel's promotional brochure. Alas, some hotel chains use the same guest room photo in their promotional literature for all their properties; a specific guest room may not resemble the brochure photo. Find out how old the property is and when your guest room was last renovated. If you arrive and are assigned an inferior room, demand to be moved.

HOW THE HOTELS COMPARE

Hotel	Zone	Overall Rating	Quality Rating	Cost ($=$80)
Ritz-Carlton Battery Park	1	★★★★★	98	$$$+
The Peninsula	9	★★★★★	98	$$$$$+
The St. Regis	9	★★★★★	98	$$$$$$$−
Mandarin Oriental Hotel	10	★★★★★	98	$$$$$$$+
Four Seasons Hotel	9	★★★★★	97	$$$$$$
Trump International Hotel & Towers	10	★★★★★	97	$$$$$$$−
Essex House Hotel Nikko New York	8	★★★★★	96	$$$
The New York Palace	9	★★★★★	96	$$$+
The Mark	13	★★★★★	96	$$$$
The Carlyle	13	★★★★★	96	$$$$$−
The Pierre	11	★★★★★	96	$$$$$$−
The Lowell	11	★★★★★	96	$$$$$$+
Benjamin Hotel	9	★★★★½	95	$$+
Central Park Intercontinental	10	★★★★½	95	$$$+
Le Parker Meridien New York	8	★★★★½	95	$$$+
Omni Berkshire Place	9	★★★★½	95	$$$+
The Waldorf-Astoria	9	★★★★½	95	$$$+
W Hotel Times Square	8	★★★★½	95	$$$$−
The Regency Hotel	11	★★★★½	95	$$$$$$−
Inn New York City	10	★★★★½	94	$$$$+
Mercer	2	★★★★½	94	$$$$+
The Kitano New York	9	★★★★½	94	$$$$$−

HOW THE HOTELS COMPARE *(continued)*

Hotel	Zone	Overall Rating	Quality Rating	Cost ($=$80)
Ritz-Carlton New York Central Park	9	★★★★½	94	$$$$$$–
The Lombardy	9	★★★★½	93	$$$–
Tribeca Grand	2	★★★★½	93	$$$–
Soho Grand	2	★★★★½	93	$$$+
The Inn at Irving Place	7	★★★★½	93	$$$$
J.W. Marriott Hotel	8	★★★★½	93	$$$
Flatotel International	8	★★★★½	93	$$$$–
The Michelangelo	8	★★★★½	93	$$$$–
Morgans	9	★★★★½	93	$$$$–
The Stanhope	13	★★★★½	93	$$$$–
City Club Hotel	9	★★★★½	93	$$$$$–
The Sherry Netherland	11	★★★★½	93	$$$$$–
The Drake Swissôtel	9	★★★★½	92	$$$–
Sheraton Manhattan Hotel	8	★★★★½	92	$$$–
W New York	9	★★★★½	92	$$$–
Millennium Broadway	8	★★★★½	92	$$$
The Plaza	9	★★★★½	92	$$$$
Renaissance New York Hotel	8	★★★★½	91	$$$–
Sheraton Russell Hotel	9	★★★★½	91	$$$–
Hotel Elysee	9	★★★★½	91	$$$$–
The Royalton	9	★★★★½	91	$$$$–
Embassy Suites NYC	1	★★★★½	90	$$–
Doral Park Avenue Hotel	9	★★★★½	90	$$$
Barclay New York	9	★★★★	90	$$$+
W New York Tuscany	9	★★★★½	90	$$$+
The Muse	8	★★★★½	90	$$$$–
Hotel Plaza Athenee	11	★★★★½	90	$$$$$–
Sheraton New York Hotel & Towers	8	★★★★	89	$$$–
The Gorham	8	★★★★	89	$$$
Regal U.N. Plaza	9	★★★★	89	$$$
The Shoreham	9	★★★★	89	$$$
Time	8	★★★★	89	$$$
The Warwick Hotel	9	★★★★	89	$$$
New York Hilton & Towers	8	★★★★	89	$$$+
Bryant Park Hotel	9	★★★★	89	$$$$–
Bed-and-Breakfast on the Park	16	★★★★	88	$$–
Bentley	11	★★★★	88	$$–
La Quinta Inn Manhattan	7	★★★★	88	$$–

HOW THE HOTELS COMPARE *(continued)*

Hotel	Zone	Overall Rating	Quality Rating	Cost ($=$80)
Fitzpatrick Manhattan Hotel	9	★★★★	88	$$$−
The Algonquin Hotel	9	★★★★	88	$$$+
Chambers—a Hotel	9	★★★★	88	$$$+
Hilton Times Square	8	★★★★	88	$$$+
Novotel New York	8	★★★★	88	$$$+
Paramount	8	★★★★	88	$$$+
Le Marquis	7	★★★★	88	$$$$−
Sofitel New York	9	★★★★	88	$$$$−
Hotel Gansevoort	4	★★★★	88	$$$$
60 Thompson	2	★★★★	88	$$$$+
Hotel Giraffe	7	★★★★	88	$$$$$$−
Westin New York Times Square	8	★★★★	88	$$$$$$−
New York Marriott Marquis	8	★★★★	87	$$$
Crowne Plaza United Nations	8	★★★★	87	$$$+
Maritime Hotel	6	★★★★	87	$$$+
W Hotel Union Square	7	★★★★	87	$$$$+
Roger Williams	7	★★★★	86	$$
The Wall Street Inn	1	★★★★	86	$$+
Beekman Tower Hotel	9	★★★★	86	$$$−
Hotel 41	8	★★★★	86	$$$−
Crowne Plaza Manhattan	8	★★★★	86	$$$
Hotel Casablanca	9	★★★★	86	$$$
Library Hotel	9	★★★★	86	$$$+
Iroquois New York	9	★★★★	86	$$$$−
Grand Hyatt New York	9	★★★★	86	$$$$+
Excelsior	12	★★★★	85	$$+
Fitzpatrick Grand Central	9	★★★★	85	$$$−
Dylan Hotel	9	★★★★	85	$$$
Hotel Bedford	9	★★★★	84	$$−
Hotel Wales	13	★★★★	84	$$
Avalon	7	★★★★	84	$$+
The Mansfield	9	★★★★	84	$$$
Thirty Thirty New York City	7	★★★½	83	$$−
Red Roof Inn Manhattan	7	★★★½	83	$$
Ameritania Hotel	8	★★★½	82	$$+
Courtyard by Marriott Manhattan Times Square South	8	★★★½	82	$$+
Clarion Fifth Avenue	9	★★★½	82	$$$−
Empire Hotel	10	★★★½	82	$$$
Hudson Hotel	8	★★★½	82	$$$

HOW THE HOTELS COMPARE *(continued)*

Hotel	Zone	Overall Rating	Quality Rating	Cost ($=$80)
The Melrose Hotel	11	★★★½	82	$$$$$−
Hotel Metro	9	★★★½	81	$$+
Le Refuge Inn	18	★★★½	80	$
Country Inn in the City	12	★★★½	80	$$−
The Franklin	13	★★★½	80	$$+
Roosevelt Hotel	7	★★★½	80	$$+
Jolly Hotel Madison Towers	9	★★★½	80	$$$−
On the Avenue	12	★★★½	80	$$$−
The Roger Smith	9	★★★½	80	$$$+
DoubleTree Guest Suites Times Square	8	★★★½	80	$$$
Lucerne	12	★★★½	79	$$+
The Metropolitan	9	★★★½	79	$$$−
Washington Square Hotel	4	★★★½	78	$$+
The Box Tree	9	★★★½	78	$$$
Second Home on Second Ave.	7	★★★½	77	$
Holmes Bed-and-Breakfast	12	★★★½	77	$+
Chelsea Savoy	6	★★★½	77	$$−
Inn on 23rd Street	6	★★★	76	$$+
Habitat	9	★★★	75	$+
Cosmopolitan Hotel	1	★★★	75	$$−
Akwaaba Mansion	16	★★★	70	$$
The Mayflower Hotel	10	★★★	69	$$$−
Harbor House	19	★★½	68	$−
Pickwick Arms	9	★★½	60	$+

NEW YORK HOTELS BY ZONE

Hotel	Overall Rating	Quality Rating	Cost ($=$80)
Zone 1: Lower Manhattan, Wall Street, and the Battery			
Ritz-Carlton Battery Park	★★★★★	98	$$$+
Embassy Suites NYC	★★★★½	90	$$−
The Wall Street Inn	★★★★	86	$$+
Cosmopolitan Hotel	★★★	75	$$−
Zone 2: Soho and Tribeca			
Mercer	★★★★½	94	$$$$+
Tribeca Grand	★★★★½	93	$$$−
Soho Grand	★★★★½	93	$$$+
60 Thompson	★★★★	88	$$$$+

NEW YORK HOTELS BY ZONE *(continued)*

Hotel	Overall Rating	Quality Rating	Cost ($=$80)
Zone 4: Greenwich Village			
Hotel Gansevoort	★★★★	88	$$$$
Washington Square Hotel	★★★½	78	$$+
Zone 6: Chelsea			
Maritime Hotel	★★★★	87	$$$+
Chelsea Savoy	★★★½	77	$$–
Inn on 23rd Street	★★★	76	$$+
Zone 7: Gramercy Park and Madison Square			
The Inn at Irving Place	★★★★½	93	$$$$
La Quinta Inn Manhattan	★★★★	88	$$–
Le Marquis	★★★★	88	$$$$–
Hotel Giraffe	★★★★	88	$$$$$$–
W Hotel Union Square	★★★★	87	$$$$+
Roger Williams	★★★★	86	$$
Avalon	★★★★	84	$$+
Thirty Thirty New York City	★★★½	83	$$–
Red Roof Inn Manhattan	★★★½	83	$$
Roosevelt Hotel	★★★½	80	$$+
Second Home on Second Ave.	★★★½	77	$
Zone 8: Midtown West and the Theater District			
Essex House Hotel Nikko New York	★★★★★	96	$$$
Le Parker Meridien New York	★★★★½	95	$$$+
W Hotel Times Square	★★★★½	95	$$$$–
J.W. Marriott Hotel	★★★★½	93	$$$
Flatotel International	★★★★½	93	$$$$–
The Michelangelo	★★★★½	93	$$$$–
Sheraton Manhattan Hotel	★★★★½	92	$$$–
Millennium Broadway	★★★★½	92	$$$
Renaissance New York Hotel	★★★★½	91	$$$–
The Muse	★★★★½	90	$$$$–
Sheraton New York Hotel & Towers	★★★★	89	$$$–
The Gorham	★★★★	89	$$$
Time	★★★★	89	$$$
New York Hilton & Towers	★★★★	89	$$$+
Hilton Times Square	★★★★	88	$$$+
Novotel New York	★★★★	88	$$$+
Paramount	★★★★	88	$$$+
Westin New York Times Square	★★★★	88	$$$$$$–

Hotel	Overall Rating	Quality Rating	Cost ($=$80)
NEW YORK HOTELS BY ZONE *(continued)*			
Zone 8: Midtown West and the Theater District (continued)			
New York Marriott Marquis	★★★★	87	$$$
Crowne Plaza United Nations	★★★★	87	$$$+
Hotel 41	★★★★	86	$$$−
Crowne Plaza Manhattan	★★★★	86	$$$
Ameritania Hotel	★★★½	82	$$+
Courtyard by Marriott Manhattan Times Square South	★★★½	82	$$+
Hudson Hotel	★★★½	82	$$$
DoubleTree Guest Suites Times Square	★★★½	80	$$$
Zone 9: Midtown East			
The Peninsula	★★★★★	98	$$$$$+
The St. Regis	★★★★★	98	$$$$$$$−
Four Seasons Hotel	★★★★★	97	$$$$$$
The New York Palace	★★★★★	96	$$$+
Benjamin Hotel	★★★★½	95	$$+
Omni Berkshire Place	★★★★½	95	$$$+
The Waldorf-Astoria	★★★★½	95	$$$+
The Kitano New York	★★★★½	94	$$$$$−
Ritz-Carlton New York Central Park	★★★★½	94	$$$$$$−
The Lombardy	★★★★½	93	$$$−
Morgans	★★★★½	93	$$$$−
City Club Hotel	★★★★½	93	$$$$$−
The Drake Swissôtel	★★★★½	92	$$$−
W New York	★★★★½	92	$$$−
The Plaza	★★★★½	92	$$$$
Sheraton Russell Hotel	★★★★½	91	$$$−
Hotel Elysee	★★★★½	91	$$$$−
The Royalton	★★★★½	91	$$$$−
Doral Park Avenue Hotel	★★★★½	90	$$$
W New York Tuscany	★★★★½	90	$$$+
Barclay New York	★★★★	90	$$$+
Regal U.N. Plaza	★★★★	89	$$$
The Shoreham	★★★★	89	$$$
The Warwick Hotel	★★★★	89	$$$
Bryant Park Hotel	★★★★	89	$$$$−
Fitzpatrick Manhattan Hotel	★★★★	88	$$$−
The Algonquin Hotel	★★★★	88	$$$+

NEW YORK HOTELS BY ZONE (continued)

Hotel	Overall Rating	Quality Rating	Cost ($=$80)
Zone 9: Midtown East (continued)			
Chambers—a Hotel	★★★★	88	$$$+
Sofitel New York	★★★★	88	$$$$−
Beekman Tower Hotel	★★★★	86	$$$−
Hotel Casablanca	★★★★	86	$$$
Library Hotel	★★★★	86	$$$+
Iroquois New York	★★★★	86	$$$$−
Grand Hyatt New York	★★★★	86	$$$$+
Fitzpatrick Grand Central	★★★★	85	$$$−
Dylan Hotel	★★★★	85	$$$
Hotel Bedford	★★★★	84	$$−
The Mansfield	★★★★	84	$$$
Clarion Fifth Avenue	★★★½	82	$$$−
Hotel Metro	★★★½	81	$$+
Jolly Hotel Madison Towers	★★★½	80	$$$−
The Roger Smith	★★★½	80	$$$+
The Metropolitan	★★★½	79	$$$−
The Box Tree	★★★½	78	$$$
Habitat	★★★	75	$+
Pickwick Arms	★★½	60	$+
Zone 10: West Side			
Mandarin Oriental Hotel	★★★★★	98	$$$$$$$+
Trump International Hotel & Towers	★★★★★	97	$$$$$$$−
Central Park Intercontinental	★★★★½	95	$$$+
Inn New York City	★★★★½	94	$$$$+
Empire Hotel	★★★½	82	$$$
The Mayflower Hotel	★★★	69	$$$−
Zone 11: East Side			
The Pierre	★★★★★	96	$$$$$$−
The Lowell	★★★★★	96	$$$$$$+
The Regency Hotel	★★★★½	95	$$$$$$−
The Sherry Netherland	★★★★½	93	$$$$$−
Hotel Plaza Athenee	★★★★½	90	$$$$$−
Bentley	★★★★	88	$$−
The Melrose Hotel	★★★½	82	$$$$$−
Zone 12: Upper West Side			
Excelsior	★★★★	85	$$+
Country Inn in the City	★★★½	80	$$−

Hotel	Overall Rating	Quality Rating	Cost ($=$80)
NEW YORK HOTELS BY ZONE *(continued)*			
Zone 12: Upper West Side (continued)			
On the Avenue	★★★½	80	$$$–
Lucerne	★★★½	79	$$+
Holmes Bed-and-Breakfast	★★★½	77	$+
Zone 13: Upper East Side			
The Mark	★★★★★	96	$$$$
The Carlyle	★★★★★	96	$$$$$–
The Stanhope	★★★★½	93	$$$$–
Hotel Wales	★★★★	84	$$
The Franklin	★★★½	80	$$+
Zone 16: Brooklyn			
Bed-and-Breakfast on the Park	★★★★	88	$$–
Akwaaba Mansion	★★★	70	$$
Zone 18: The Bronx			
Le Refuge Inn	★★★½	80	$
Zone 19: Staten Island			
Harbor House	★★½	68	$–

Top 30 Best Deals in New York

Having listed the nicest rooms in town, let's reorder the list to rank the best combinations of quality and value in a room. As before, the rankings are made without consideration of location or the availability of restaurant(s), recreational facilities, entertainment, and/or amenities. Remember that a ★★★ room at $120 may rank closely with a ★★★★ room at $240, but that does not mean the rooms will be of comparable quality. Regardless of whether it's a good deal or not, a ★★★ room is still a ★★★ room. These are the best room buys for the money, regardless of location or star classification, based on averaged rack rates.

TOP 30 BEST DEALS IN NEW YORK

Hotel	Overall Quality	Room Quality	Cost ($=$80)
1. Embassy Suites NYC	★★★★½	90	$$–
2. Bentley	★★★★	88	$$–
3. Thirty Thirty New York City	★★★½	83	$$–
4. Wall Street Inn	★★★★	86	$$+
5. Excelsior	★★★★	85	$$+
6. Washington Square Hotel	★★★½	78	$$+
7. The New York Palace	★★★★★	96	$$$+
8. Central Park Intercontinental	★★★★½	95	$$$+
9. Benjamin Hotel	★★★★½	95	$$+
10. Ameritania Hotel	★★★½	82	$$+
11. Time	★★★★	89	$$$
12. W New York	★★★★½	92	$$$–
13. Hilton Times Square	★★★★	88	$$$+
14. The Waldorf-Astoria	★★★★½	95	$$$+
15. Hotel Bedford	★★★★	84	$$–
16. Red Roof Inn Manhattan	★★★½	83	$$
17. Tribeca Grand	★★★★½	93	$$$–
18. Essex House Hotel Nikko New York	★★★★★	96	$$$
19. Soho Grand	★★★★½	93	$$$+
20. The Michelangelo	★★★★½	93	$$$$–
21. Morgans	★★★★½	93	$$$$–
22. Avalon	★★★★	84	$$+
23. Fitzpatrick Manhattan Hotel	★★★★	88	$$$–
24. Paramount	★★★★	88	$$$+
25. Sheraton Manhattan Hotel	★★★★½	92	$$$–
26. Sheraton Russell Hotel	★★★★½	91	$$$–
27. New York Hilton & Towers	★★★★	89	$$$+
28. Roger Williams	★★★★	86	$$
29. Hotel Wales	★★★★	84	$$
30. Habitat	★★★	75	$+

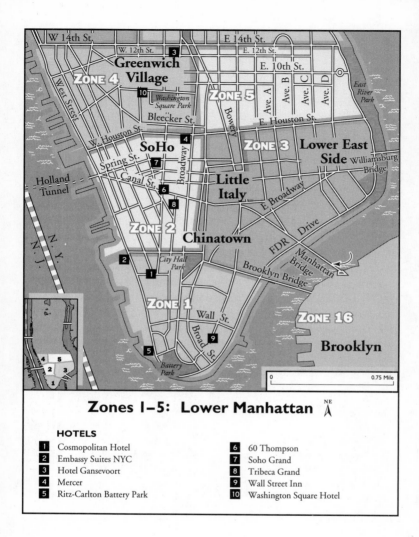

Zones 1–5: Lower Manhattan ⌃NE

HOTELS

1. Cosmopolitan Hotel
2. Embassy Suites NYC
3. Hotel Gansevoort
4. Mercer
5. Ritz-Carlton Battery Park
6. 60 Thompson
7. Soho Grand
8. Tribeca Grand
9. Wall Street Inn
10. Washington Square Hotel

Zones 10–13: East and West Side Manhattan

NE

HOTELS

1 Bentley	**13** Lucerne
2 The Carlyle	**14** Mandarin Oriental Hotel
3 Central Park Intercontinental	**15** The Mark
4 Country Inn in the City	**16** The Mayflower Hotel
5 Empire Hotel	**17** The Melrose Hotel
6 Excelsior	**18** On the Avenue
7 The Franklin	**19** The Pierre
8 Holmes Bed-and-Breakfast	**20** The Regency Hotel
9 Hotel Plaza Athenee	**21** The Sherry Netherland
10 Hotel Wales	**22** The Stanhope
11 Inn New York City	**23** Trump International Hotel & Towers
12 The Lowell	

Central Park S.

E. 59th St.

W. 57th St.

Queensbo

ZONE 9

W. 53rd St.

Museum of
Modern Art

W. 50th St.

E. 50th St.

Rockefeller
Center

ZONE 8

Midtown East

W. 45th St.

New York
Public Library

E. 45th St.

United
Nations

Midtown West

W. 42nd St.

E. 42nd St.

Port Authority
Bus Terminal

Times
Square

Madison
Square
Garden

Empire
State
Bldg.

Murray Hill

E. 34th St.

W. 34th St.

Broadway

Madison Ave.

Park Ave.

Lexington Ave.

3rd Ave.

2nd Ave.

1st Ave.

11th Ave.

10th Ave.

9th Ave.

8th Ave.

7th Ave.

Avenue of the Americas

5th Ave.

W. 23rd St.

E. 23rd St.

ZONE 6

Gramercy
Park

ZONE 7

Chelsea

Union
Square

W. 14th St.

E. 14th St.

W. 12th St.

**Zones 6–9:
Midtown
Manhattan**

ZONE 4

ZONE 5

NE

| 8 | 9 |
| 6 | 7 |

0   0.75 Mile

Washington
Square Park

Zones 6–9: Midtown Manhattan

HOTELS

1 The Algonquin Hotel
2 Ameritania Hotel
3 Avalon
4 Barclay New York
5 Beekman Tower Hotel
6 Benjamin Hotel
7 The Box Tree
8 Bryant Park Hotel
9 Chambers—a Hotel
10 Chelsea Savoy
11 City Club Hotel
12 Clarion Fifth Avenue
13 Courtyard by Marriott
   Manhattan Times Square South
14 Crown Plaza Manhattan
15 Crowne Plaza United Nations
16 Doral Park Avenue Hotel
17 DoubleTree Guest Suites Times Square
18 The Drake Swissôtel
19 Dylan Hotel
20 Essex House Hotel Nikko New York
21 Fitzpatrick Grand Central
22 Fitzpatrick Manhattan Hotel
23 Flatotel International
24 Four Seasons Hotel
25 The Gorham
26 Grand Hyatt New York
27 Habitat
28 Hilton Times Square
29 Hotel Bedford
30 Hotel Casablanca
31 Hotel Elysee
32 Hotel 41
33 Hotel Giraffe
34 Hotel Metro
35 Hudson Hotel
36 The Inn at Irving Place
37 Inn on 23rd Street
38 Iroquois New York
39 J.W. Marriott Hotel
40 Jolly Hotel Madison Towers
41 The Kitano New York
42 La Quinta Inn Manhattan
43 Le Marquis

44 Le Parker Meridien New York
45 Library Hotel
46 The Lombardy
47 The Mansfield
48 Maritime Hotel
49 The Metropolitan
50 The Michelangelo
51 Millennium Broadway
52 Morgans
53 The Muse
54 New York Hilton & Towers
55 New York Marriott Marquis
56 The New York Palace
57 Novotel New York
58 Omni Berkshire Place
59 Paramount
60 The Peninsula
61 Pickwick Arms
62 The Plaza
63 Red Roof Inn Manhattan
64 Regal U.N. Plaza
65 Renaissance New York Hotel
66 Ritz-Carlton New York Central Park
67 The Roger Smith
68 Roger Williams
69 Roosevelt Hotel
70 The Royalton
71 Second Home on Second Ave.
72 Sheraton Manhattan Hotel
73 Sheraton New York Hotel & Towers
74 Sheraton Russell Hotel
75 The Shoreham
76 Sofitel New York
77 The St. Regis
78 Thirty Thirty New York City
79 Time
80 W Hotel Times Square
81 W Hotel Union Square
82 W New York
83 W New York Tuscany
84 The Waldorf-Astoria
85 The Warwick Hotel
86 Westin New York Times Square

Hotel/website	Room Rating	Room Quality	Zone	Street Address
Akwaaba Mansion www.akwaaba.com	★★★	70	16	347 MacDonough Street New York, NY 11213
The Algonquin Hotel www.camberlyhotels.com	★★★★	88	9	59 West 44th Street New York, NY 10036
Ameritania Hotel www.nycityhotels.net	★★★½	82	8	230 West 54th Street New York, NY 10019
Avalon www.theavalonny.com	★★★★	84	7	16 East 32nd Street New York, NY 10016
Barclay New York www.interconti.com	★★★★	90	9	111 East 48th Street New York, NY 10017
Bed-and-Breakfast on the Park www.bbnyc.com	★★★★	88	16	113 Prospect Park West New York, NY 11215
Beekman Tower Hotel www.affinia.com	★★★★	86	9	3 Mitchell Place New York, NY 10017
Benjamin Hotel www.nycityhotels.net	★★★★½	95	9	125 East 50th Street New York, NY 10022
Bentley	★★★★	88	11	500 East 62nd Street New York, NY 10021
The Box Tree www.theboxtree.com	★★★½	78	9	250 East 49th Street New York, NY 10017
Bryant Park Hotel www.bryantparkhotel.com	★★★★	89	9	40 West 40th Street New York, NY 10018
The Carlyle www.rosewoodhotels.com	★★★★★	96	13	35 East 76th Street New York, NY 10021
Central Park Inter- continental new-york-central.intercontinental.com	★★★★½	95	10	112 Central Park South New York, NY 10019
Chambers–a Hotel www.chambersnyc.com	★★★★	88	9	15 West 56th Street New York, NY 10019
Chelsea Savoy www.chelseasavoy.qpg.com	★★★½	77	6	204 West 23rd Street New York, NY 10011
City Club Hotel www.cityclubhotel.com	★★★★½	93	9	55 West 44th Street New York, NY 10036
Clarion Fifth Avenue www.clarionfifthavenue.com	★★★½	82	9	3 East 40th Street New York, NY 10016
Cosmopolitan Hotel www.cosmohotel.com	★★	75	1	95 West Broadway New York, NY 10007
Country Inn in the City www.countryinnthecity.com	★★★½	80	12	270 West 77th Street New York, NY 10024
Courtyard by Marriott Manhattan Times Square South	★★★½	88	8	114 West 40th Street New York, NY 10018
Crowne Plaza Manhattan www.crowneplaza.com	★★★½	86	8	1605 Broadway New York, NY 10019

Local Phone	Guest Fax	Toll-Free Res. Line	Discounts Available	No. of Rooms	Room Sq. Ft.	Rack Rate
(718) 455-5958	(718) 774-1744			18	185	$$
(212) 840-6800	(212) 944-1419	(800) 555-8000		165	170	$$$+
(212) 247-5000	(212) 247-3313	(888) 96-HOTEL	Govt.	206	210	$$+
(212) 299-7000	(212) 299-7001	(888) HI AVALON	AAA, Govt.	100	200	$$+
(212) 755-5900	(212) 644-0079	(877) 660-8550		686	210	$$$+
(718) 499-6115				8	140	$$−
(212) 355-7300	(212) 753-9366	(800) 637-8483		172	250	$$$−
(212) 753-2700	(212) 715-2525	(800) 637-8483	AAA, Govt.	206	n/a	$$+
(212) 644-6000	(212) 207-4800	(888) 66 HOTEL		197	235	$$−
(212) 758-8320	(212) 308-3899			13	n/a	$$$
(212) 869-0100	(212) 869-4446	(877) 640-9300		129	300	$$$$−
(212) 744-1600	(212) 717-4682	(800) 227-5737		192	180	$$$$$−
(212) 757-1900	(212) 757-9620	(800) 327-0200		208	n/a	$$$+
(212) 974-5656	(212) 974-5657	(866) 204-5656		77	300	$$$+
(212) 929-9353	(212) 741-6309			90	n/a	$$−
(212) 921-5500	(212) 944-5544	(888) 256-4100		65	300	$$$$$−
(212) 228-5151	(212) 213-0972	(800) 668-4200	AAA, AARP	189	260	$$$−
(212) 566-1900	(212) 566-6909	(888) 895-9400		105	160	$$−
(212) 580-4183				4	550	$$−
(212) 391-0088	(212) 391-6023	(800) 321-2211	AAA, Govt.	244	n/a	$$+
(212) 977-4000	(212) 333-7393	(800) 243-6969	Govt.	770	n/a	$$$

Hotel	Meeting Facilities	Pool/ Sauna	Exercise Facilities	Window Glaze	Parking Per Day	Nearest Subway
Akwaaba Mansion				Sgl.	Free	20 min.
The Algonquin Hotel	✓		✓	Dbl.	Public lot 1 block $30	
Ameritania Hotel			✓ $20 access	Dbl.	$30	3 blocks
Avalon	✓		✓ access	Dbl.	$29– $39	1 block
Barclay New York	✓		✓	Sgl./ Dbl.	$38	0.5 block
Bed-and-Breakfast on the Park				Sgl.	Free	n/a
Beekman Tower Hotel	✓	Whirlpool, sauna	✓	Trpl./ Dbl.	$30	5 blocks
Benjamin Hotel	✓	Spa	✓	Trpl.	$35	1 block
Bentley			Discount access	Dbl.	$20	5 blocks
The Box Tree	✓			Sgl.	$23	5 blocks
Bryant Park	✓		✓	Dbl.	$45	0.5 block
The Carlyle	✓	Sauna, steam room	✓	Dbl.	$44	2 blocks
Central Park Intercontinental	✓	Sauna	✓	Dbl.	$37	1 block
Chambers—a Hotel	✓		Privileges	Dbl.	$35	1 block
Chelsea Savoy				Dbl.	$25	1 block
City Club Hotel				Dbl.	$20	0.5 block
Clarion Fifth Avenue		Sauna	Privileges $15	Dbl.	$25	2 blocks
Cosmopolitan Hotel	✓			Sgl.	$25	1 block
Country Inn in the City				Sgl.	n/a	2 blocks
Courtyard by Marriott Manhattan	✓		✓	Sgl.	$37	1 block
Crowne Plaza Manhattan	✓	Pool, sauna	✓	Sgl.	$39	2 blocks

Bar	On-site Dining	Extra Amenities	Business Amenities
	① African/Caribb./ Mediterranean	Free breakfast, terry cloth robes	
✓	③ Dinner show, pub fare, Continental		Dataport
✓	① Italian	Free cont'l	Dataport
✓	① American	Cont'l breakfast, concierge	Dataport, 2 phone lines
✓	① American		Courier, Internet, business center
	① American	Roof garden, free breakfast	
✓	② American	All-suite property	Dataport
✓	① American	Concierge	Dataport, 2 phone lines, fax, DSL
✓	① American	Cont'l brkfst, valet capppucino bar	Dataport, 2 phone lines
✓	① French Continental	Free breakfast	
✓	① Seasonal/European	Concierge	Dataport, 2 phone lines
✓	③ Dinner club, American/ French, Tea room	Cont'l cafe w/ live music	Dataport, 2 phone lines, fax
✓	① Continental	Concierge, 24-hr business center	Fax
✓	① American	Concierge, CD, DVD, library	Fax
✓	① Cafe		
✓	① Bistro		Internet, 2 phone lines, bath phone
	① Lunch & dinner	Free breakfast	Dataport, business center
			Dataport, fax, study desk
		Kitchenette, welcome basket	
✓	① Continetnal/European	Concierge, valet, dry cleaning	2 phone lines, Internet
✓	② American	Concierge	Business center, Internet

Hotel/website	Room Rating	Room Quality	Zone	Street Address
Crowne Plaza United Nations www.crowneplaza.com	★★★★	87	9	304 East 42nd Street New York, NY 10017
Doral Park Avenue Hotel www.doralparkavenue.com	★★★★½	90	9	70 Park Avenue New York, NY 10016
DoubleTree Guest Suites Times Square www.doubletree.com	★★★½	80	8	1568 Broadway New York, NY 10036
The Drake Swissôtel www.swissotel.com	★★★★½	92	9	440 Park Avenue New York, NY 10022
Dylan Hotel www.dylanhotel.com	★★★★	85	9	52 East 41st Street New York, NY 10017
Embassy Suites NYC www.embassysuites.com	★★★★½	90	1	102 North End Avenue New York, NY 10282
Empire Hotel www.empirehotel.com	★★★½	82	10	44 West 63rd Street New York, NY 10023
Essex House Hotel Nikko New York www.westin.com	★★★★★	96	8	160 Central Park South New York, NY 10019
Excelsior www.excelsiorhotelny.com	★★★★	85	12	45 West 81st Street New York, NY 10024
Fitzpatrick Grand Central www.fitzpatrickhotels.com	★★★★	85	9	141 East 44th Street New York, NY 10017
Fitzpatrick Manhattan Hotel www.fitzpatrickhotels.com	★★★★	88	9	687 Lexington Avenue New York, NY 10022
Flatotel International www.flatotel.com	★★★★½	93	8	135 West 52nd Street New York, NY 10019
Four Seasons Hotel www.fourseasons.com	★★★★★	97	9	57 East 57th Street New York, NY 10022
The Franklin www.boutiquehg.com	★★★½	80	13	164 East 87th Street New York, NY 10128
The Gorham www.gorhamhotel.com	★★★★	89	8	136 West 55th Street New York, NY 10019
Grand Hyatt New York www.grandnewyorkhyatt.com	★★★★	86	9	Park Avenue at Grand Central New York, NY 10017
Habitat www.habitatny.com	★★★	75	9	130 East 57th Street New York, NY 10022
Harbor House www.nyharborhouse.com	★★½	68	19	One Hylan Boulevard New York, NY 10305
Hilton Times Square www.hilton.com	★★★★	88	8	234 West 42nd Street New York, NY 10036
Holmes Bed-and-Breakfast	★★★½	77	12	157 West 91st Street New York, NY 10024
Hotel Bedford www.bedfordhotel.com	★★★★	84	9	118 East 40th Street New York, NY 10016

Local Phone	Guest Fax	Toll-Free Res. Line	Discounts Available	No. of Rooms	Room Sq. Ft.	Rack Rate
(212) 986-8800	(212) 986-1758	(800) 879-8836	AAA, AARP	300	248	$$$+
(212) 687-7050	(212) 808-9029	(877) 993-6725		188	270	$$$
(212) 719-1600	(212) 921-5212	(800) 222-TREE	AAA, AARP, Govt., Mil.	460	442	$$$
(212) 421-0900	(212) 371-4190		Govt.	495	300	$$$−
(212) 338-0500	(212) 338-0569	(800) 553-9526		107	210	$$$
(212) 945-0100	(212) 945-3012	(800) HILTONS	AAA	463	450	$$−
(212) 265-7400	(212) 315-0439	(888) 822-3555		376	160	$$$
(212) 247-0300	(212) 315-1839	(800) 645-5697	AAA, Govt.	597	170	$$$
(212) 362-9200	(212) 721-2994	(800) 368-4575		197	250	$$+
(212) 351-6800	(212) 818-1747	(800) 367-7701	AAA	155	500	$$$−
(212) 355-0100	(212) 317-0572	(800) 367-7701	AAA, AARP	92	450	$$$−
(212) 887-9400	(212) 887-9893	(800) FLATOTEL		168	n/a	$$$$−
(212) 758-5700	(212) 758-5711	(800) 819-5053		370	600	$$$$ $$
(212) 369-1000	(212) 369-8000	(877) 847-4444		47	150	$$+
(212) 245-1800	(212) 582-8332	(800) 735-0710	AAA, Govt.	116	360	$$$
(212) 883-1234	(212) 697-3772	(800) 633-7313	AAA, Senior	1,136	210	$$$$+
(212) 753-8841	(212) 829-9605	(800) 255-0482		300	100	$+
(718) 876-0056	(718) 420-9940		Multiroom	11	60	$−
(212) 840-8222	(212) 840-5516	(800) HILTONS	AAA, Govt.	444	300	$$$+
(212) 787-8796	(212) 595-6275			4	n/a	$+
(212) 697-4800	(212) 697-1093	(800) 221-6881		136	300	$$−

Hotel	Meeting Facilities	Pool/ Sauna	Exercise Facilities	Window Glaze	Parking Per Day	Nearest Subway
Crowne Plaza at the United Nations	✓	Whirlpool	✓	Sgl./ Trpl.	$40	2 blocks
Doral Park Avenue	✓	Whirlpool	Privileges	Dbl.	$40	3 blocks
DoubleTree Guest Suites Times Square	✓		✓	Sgl./ Dbl.	$35	0.5 block
The Drake Swissôtel	✓	Sauna	✓	Dbl.	$45	1 block
Dylan Hotel	✓		✓	Trpl.	$45	2 blocks
Embassy Suites NYC	✓		✓	Sgl.	$45	5 blocks
Empire Hotel	✓		Privileges	Dbl.	$37	0.5 block
Essex House Hotel Nikko New York	✓	Sauna, steam room	✓	Dbl.	$45	1 block
Excelsior	✓			Dbl.	$25– $35	0.5 block
Fitzpatrick Grand Central			Privileges	Dbl.	$38	Across street
Fitzpatrick Manhattan Hotel	✓	Pool, privileges	Privileges	Dbl.	$45	2 blocks
Flatotel International	Suites	Sauna, pool privileges	✓	Dbl.	$37	2 blocks
Four Seasons Hotel	✓	Whirlpool	✓	Tpl	$42	4 blocks
The Franklin			Privileges charges vary	Dbl.	$25– $35	1 block
The Gorham			✓	Dbl.	$33– $42	1 block
Grand Hyatt New York	✓			Sgl./ Dbl.	$45	0.5 block
Habitat					$28	2
Harbor House				Sgl.	Free	25 minutes
Hilton Times Square	✓	Sauna	✓	Sgl.	$34– $44	2.5 blocks
Holmes Bed-and-Breakfast				Sgl.	Free	4 blocks
Hotel Bedford				Sgl./ Dbl.	$22	1 block

Bar	On-site Dining	Extra Amenities	Business Amenities
✓	① Bistro		Dataport, 2 phone lines
✓	① New American		Dataport
✓	① American	Kitchenette, tour desk, robes	3 phone lines, Internet
✓	① American/Eclectic		Dataport, 2 phone lines, fax
✓	① Continental breakfast	Concierge, safe, valet	Dataport, voicemail, 2 phone lines
✓	② Steakhouse, American	Cocktails, breakfast	Fax, Internet, 2 phone lines
✓	② Steakhouse, American	CD library	Dataport, 2 phone lines
✓	③ French, Nouveau, American	Spa	Dataport, 2 phone lines, fax
	Charge for breakfast room	Library	Dataport, fax, 2 phone lines
✓	① Irish/American	Valet	Dataport, 2 phone lines
✓	① Cont'l	Irish theme	Dataport, fax
	① Breakfast only	Kitchenettes, free brkfst 24 hrs	Dataport, 2 ph. lines, business center
✓	① Contemporary American	Spa suite packages	2 phone lines
		Free breakfast	Some rooms: 2 lines, dataport, request ahead
✓	② Breakfast Room, Northern Italian	Whirlpools in suites	Dataport, 2 phone lines
✓	① American	Theater desk, fax	Business center
	Continental breakfast		Dataport, 2 phone lines
		Free cont'l brkfst.	
✓	① American	Valet, safe	Dataport, laptop, 2 phone lines, bus. ctr.
✓	① American/Italian	Kitchenettes, free breakfast	Dataport

Hotel/website	Room Rating	Room Quality	Zone	Street Address
Hotel Casablanca www.casablancahotel.com	★★★★	86	9	147 West 43rd Street New York, NY 10036
Hotel Elysee www.elyseehotel.com	★★★★½	91	9	60 East 54th Street New York, NY 10022
Hotel 41 www.hotel41.com	★★★★	86	8	206 West 41st Street New York, NY 10036
Hotel Gansevoort www.hotelgansevoort.com	★★★★	88	4	18 Ninth Avenue New York, NY 10014
Hotel Giraffe www.hotelgiraffe.com	★★★★	88	7	365 Park Avenue South New York, NY 10010
Hotel Metro www.hotelmetronyc.com	★★★½	81	9	45 West 35th Street New York, NY 10001
Hotel Plaza Athenee www.plaza-athenee.com	★★★★½	90	11	37 East 64th Street New York, NY 10021
Hotel Wales www.waleshotel.com	★★★★	84	13	1295 Madison Avenue New York, NY 10128
Hudson Hotel www.hudsonhotel.com	★★★½	82	8	353 West 57th Street New York, NY 10019
The Inn at Irving Place www.innatirving.com	★★★★½	93	7	56 Irving Place New York, NY 10003
Inn New York City	★★★★½	94	10	266 West 71st Street New York, NY 10023
Inn on 23rd Street www.innon23rd.com	★★★	76	6	131 West 23rd Street New York, NY 10011
Iroquois New York iroquoisny.com	★★★★	86	9	49 West 44th Street New York, NY 10036
J.W. Marriott www.marriott.com	★★★★½	93	8	151 West 54th Street New York, NY 10019
Jolly Hotel Madison Towers www.jollymadison.com	★★★½	80	9	22 East 38th Street New York, NY 10016
The Kitano New York www.kitano.com	★★★★½	94	9	66 Park Avenue New York, NY 10016
La Quinta Inn Manhattan www.lq.com	★★★★	88	7	17 West 32nd Street New York, NY 10001
Le Marquis www.lemarquisny.com	★★★★	88	7	12 East 31st Street New York, NY 10016
Le Parker Meridien New York www.parkermeridien.com	★★★★½	95	8	118 West 57th Street New York, NY 10019
Le Refuge Inn www.lerefugeinn.com	★★★½	80	18	620 City Island Avenue New York, NY 10464
Library Hotel www.libraryhotel.com	★★★★	86	9	299 Madison Avenue New York, NY 10017

Local Phone	Guest Fax	Toll-Free Res. Line	Discounts Available	No. of Rooms	Room Sq. Ft.	Rack Rate
(212) 869-1212	(212) 391-7585	(888) 922-7225		48	270	$$$
(212) 753-1066	(212) 980-9278	(800) 535-9733		99	300	$$$$−
(212) 703-8600	(212) 302-0895	(877) 847-4444		47	100	$$$−
(212) 206-6700	(212) 255-5850	(877) 726-7386		187	300	$$$$
(212) 685-7700	(212) 685-7771	(877) 296-0009		73	325	$$$$ $$−
(212) 947-2500	(212) 279-1310	(800) 356-3870		174	150	$$+
(212) 734-9100	(212) 772-0958	(800) 447-8800		152	300	$$$$ $−
(212) 876-6000	(212) 860-7000	(877) 847-4444		86	150	$$
(212) 554-6000	(212) 554-6139	(800) 444-4786		1,000	150	$$$
(212) 533-4600	(212) 533-4611	(800) 685-1447		12	360	$$$$
		(866) 823-9330		4	n/a	$$$$+
(212) 463-0330	(212) 463-0302	(877) 387-2323		14	215	$$+
(212) 840-3080	(212) 398-1754	(800) 332-7220		114	275	$$$$−
(212) 307-5000	(212) 533-4611	(800) 937-5454		12	360	$$$
(212) 802-0600	(212) 447-0747	(800) 221-2626	Packages	244	80	$$$−
(212) 885-7000	(212) 765-6530	(800) KITANO-NY	Govt.	500	460	$$$$ $−
(212) 790-2710	(212) 563-4007	(866) 725-1661	AAA, AARP, Govt.	182	160	$$−
(212) 889-6363	(212) 889-6699	(866) MARQUIS	AAA, AARP	112	200	$$$$−
(212) 245-5000	(212) 307-1776	(800) 543-4300	AAA	698	312	$$$+
(718) 885-2478				8	n/a	$
(212) 983-9653	(212) 499-9099	(877) 793-READ	Govt.	60	200	$$$+

Hotel	Meeting Facilities	Pool/ Sauna	Exercise Facilities	Window Glaze	Parking Per Day	Nearest Subway
Hotel Casablanca	Small conf. room	Privileges	Privileges free	Trpl.	$25	0.5 block
Hotel Elysee	✓ Small		Privileges	Dbl.	$26	1 block
Hotel 41			Privileges, $10	Dbl.	$30	0.5 block
Hotel Gansevoort	✓	✓	✓	Dbl./ Trpl.	n/a	1 block
Hotel Giraffe	✓			Trpl.	$28	1 block
Hotel Metro	✓		✓	Dbl.	$18	1 block
Hotel Plaza Athenee	✓		✓	Dbl.	$42	7 blocks
Hotel Wales		Privileges	Privileges + small on-site	Dbl.	$28	5 blocks
Hudson Hotel	✓		✓	Sgl.	$46	1 block
The Inn at Irving Place	✓		Privileges, $15–$20	n/a	$28	3 blocks
Inn New York City				Sgl.	Free	3 blocks
Inn on 23rd Street				Dbl.	n/a	2 blocks
Iroquois New York	✓	Sauna	✓	Sgl.	$29	2 blocks
J.W. Marriott	✓	Whirlpool, sauna	✓	Dbl.	$42	2 blocks
Jolly Hotel Madison Towers	✓	✓		Sgl.	$30	0.5 block
The Kitano New York	✓	Privileges	Privileges	Dbl.	$32	4 blocks
La Quinta Inn Manhattan	✓			Sgl.	$25	0.5 block
Le Marquis	✓	Sauna	✓	Dbl.	$35	0.5 block
Le Parker Meridien New York	✓	Pool	✓	Dbl.	$40	0.5 block
Le Refuge Inn				Dbl.	Free	n/a
Library Hotel	✓		Privileges, $15	Sgl.	$20	1 block

Bar	On-site Dining	Extra Amenities	Business Amenities
		Free cont'l brkfst., wine, hors d'oeuvres	Dataport, 2 phone lines
✓	① Continental	Wine, snacks, free cont'l brkfst.	Dataport, 2 phone lines
✓	① Bar food	Pet-friendly	Internet
✓	① Japanese	Roof garden, feather beds	Internet, 2 phone lines
✓		Wine/cheese, free breakfast, refrsmts.	Internet, 2 phone lines
✓	① Tuscan	Free cont'l brkfst. Family suite pkgs	Dataport
✓	① French		Dataport, 2 phone lines
	② American	Harp music in lobby, spa, videos, CD, free breakfast	
✓	① International comfort food	Valet, music	Internet, 2 phone lines
✓	③ Tea room, pub fare, Cafe	Library, cont'l breakfast	Dataport, 2 phone lines
		Kitchenette	
	① American Creative	Free breakfast	Dataport, 2 phone lines
✓	① American	Concierge, safe, CD	Dataport, 2 phone lines
✓	① New American	Live music in lounge	Dataport, 2 phone lines, fax
✓	② American, Italian		Dataport, 2 phone lines, Internet
✓	② American, Japanese	Safe	Dataport, 2 phone lines, fax
✓	② American, Chinese	Cont'l breakfast	Dataport
			Dataport, 2 phone lines, Internet
✓	② American/Continenetal, pub fare	Track, CD players, DVDs, health club	Dataport, 2 ph. lines, fax on request
	① Country French	Cont'l breakfast	
	① Northern Italian	Cont'l breakfast, wine, CD	Dataport, bus. ctr., 2 phone lines

Hotel/website	Room Rating	Room Quality	Zone	Street Address
The Lombardy www.lombardyhotel.com	★★★★½	93	11	111 East 56th Street New York, NY 10022
The Lowell www.lowellhotel.com	★★★★★	96	11	28 East 63rd Street New York, NY 10021-8088
Lucerne www.newyorkhotel.com	★★★½	79	12	201 West 79th Street New York, NY 10024
Mandarin Oriental Hotel www.mandarinoriental.com	★★★★★	98	10	80 Columbus Circle New York, NY 10023
The Mansfield www.mansfieldhotel.com	★★★★	84	9	12 West 44th Street New York, NY 10036
Maritime Hotel www.themaritimehotel.com	★★★★	87	6	363 West 16th Street New York, NY 10011
The Mark www.themarkhotel.com	★★★★★	96	13	Madison Avenue at 77th Street New York, NY 10021
The Mayflower Hotel www.mayflowerhotel.com	★★★	69	10	15 Central Park West New York, NY 10023
The Melrose Hotel www.melrosehotelnewyork.com	★★★½	82	11	140 East 63rd Street New York, NY 10021
Mercer www.mercerhotel.com	★★★★½	94	2	147 Mercer Street New York, NY 10012
The Metropolitan	★★★½	79	9	569 Lexington Avenue New York, NY 10022
The Michelangelo www.michelangelohotel.com	★★★★½	93	8	152 West 51st Street New York, NY 10019
Millennium Broadway www.millennium-hotels.com	★★★★½	92	8	145 West 44th Street New York, NY 10036
The Morgans	★★★★½	93	9	237 Madison Avenue New York, NY 10016
The Muse	★★★★½	90	8	130 West 46th Street New York, NY 10036
The New York Hilton and Towers www.hilton.com	★★★★	89	8	1335 Sixth Avenue New York, NY 10019
New York Marriott Marquis www.marriott.com	★★★★	87	8	1535 Broadway New York, NY 10036
The New York Palace www.nypalace.com	★★★★★	96	9	455 Madison Avenue New York, NY 10022
Novotel New York www.novotel.com	★★★★	88	8	226 West 52nd Street New York, NY 10019
Omni Berkshire Place www.omnihotels.com	★★★★½	95	9	21 East 52nd Street New York, NY 10022
On the Avenue www.ontheave-nyc.com	★★★½	80	12	2178 West 77th Street New York, NY 10023

Local Phone	Guest Fax	Toll-Free Res. Line	Discounts Available	No. of Rooms	Room Sq. Ft.	Rack Rate
(212) 753-8600	(212) 832-3170	(800) 223-5254		101	470	$$$–
(212) 838-1400	(212) 319-4230	(800) 221-4444	AAA	65	350	$$$$ $$+
(212) 875-1000	(212) 362-7251	(800) 492-8122	AAA, AARP, Govt. blacked out	250	204	$$+
(212) 805-8800	(212) 805-8888	(800) 526-6566		251	400	$$$$ $$$+
(212) 944-6050	(212) 764-4477	(877) 847-4444		123	150	$$$
(212) 242-4300	(212) 242-1188	(866) 601-9330		125	300	$$$+
(212) 744-4300	(212) 744-2749	(800) 843-6275		180	400	$$$$
(212) 265-0060	(212) 265-5098	(800) 223-4164	AAA, AARP blacked out	365	150	$$$–
(212) 838-5700	(212) 888-4271	(800) MELROSE		306	140	$$$$ $–
(212) 966-6060	(212) 965-3838	(888) 918-6060		75	320	$$$$+
(212) 752-7000	(212) 758-6311	(800) 695-8284		722	215	$$$–
(212) 765-1900	(212) 541-6604	(800) 237-0990		178	325	$$$$–
(212) 768-4400	(212) 768-0847	(800) 622-5569	AAA, Govt. blacked out	627	150	$$$
(212) 686-0300	(212) 779-8352	(800) 334-3408		113	240	$$$$–
(212) 485-2400	(212) 485-2900	(877) 692-6873	AAA	200	350	$$$$–
(212) 586-7000	(212) 315-1374	(800) HILTONS	AAA, AARP	2,041	320	$$$+
(212) 398-1900	(212) 704-8930	(800) 228-9290	Govt., Mil.	1,911	570	$$$
(212) 888-7000	(212) 303-6000	(800) NYPALACE	AAA, Govt. blacked out	900	320	$$$+
(212) 315-0100	(212) 765-5365	(800) 221-3185	AAA, Govt.	474	276	$$$+
(212) 753-5800	(212) 754-5018	(800) 843-6664	AAA, Govt.	396	300	$$$+
(212) 362-1100	(917) 441-0295	(800) 509-7598	AAA	196	375	$$$–

Hotel	Meeting Facilities	Pool/ Sauna	Exercise Facilities	Window Glaze	Parking Per Day	Nearest Subway
The Lombardy	✓ In rest.		✓	Dbl.	$21	3 blocks
The Lowell	✓ Small		✓	Dbl.	$45– $50	2 blocks
Lucerne	✓		Privileges	Dbl.	$25	1 block
Mandarin Oriental Hotel	✓	Pool, sauna	✓	Dbl.	$55–	0.5 block
The Mansfield	✓ Small		Privileges, $20	Dbl.	$25– $45	2 blocks
Maritime Hotel	✓		✓	Dbl.	$15– $36	1 block
The Mark	✓	Sauna, steam room	✓	Dbl.	$45	3 blocks
The Mayflower Hotel	✓		✓	Dbl.	$35	1 block
The Melrose Hotel	✓	✓	✓	Dbl.	$35	1 block
Mercer			Privileges	Sgl.	$40	1 block
The Metropolitan	✓		✓	Dbl.	$30	2 blocks
The Michelangelo	✓		✓	Dbl.	$38	2 blocks
Millennium Broadway	✓	Steam room	✓	Dbl.	$45	2 blocks
Morgans	✓		Privileges, free	Dbl.	$42	4 blocks
The Muse	✓		✓	Sgl.	$42	2 blocks
The New York Hilton and Towers	✓	Sauna	✓	Dbl.	$40	3 blocks
New York Marriott Marquis	✓	Sauna, whirlpool	✓	Dbl.	$45	3 blocks
The New York Palace	✓	Steam room	✓	Dbl.	$50	2 blocks
Novotel New York	✓		✓	Dbl.	$23	1 block
Omni Berkshire Place	✓		✓	Tpl	$25– $35	1 block
On the Avenue		Sauna privileges	Privileges $20	Dbl.	n/a	2 blocks

Bar	On-site Dining	Extra Amenities	Business Amenities
✓	① French	Kitchens, laundry	Dataport
✓	② Tea room, Steakhouse	Packages	Dataport, 2 phone lines, fax
✓	① Bar & grill	Cont'l breakfast	Dataport, 2 ph. lines fax in suites
✓	① French/Japanese	Bathrobes	Computer, Internet, cell phone rentals
			Dataport, access to copy and fax
✓	② Italian, Japanese	Banquet room	Dataport, 2 phone lines, Internet
✓	① French-American		Dataport, 2 phone lines, fax
✓	① Continental	Valet	Dataports
✓	① American	Audio library, Sign & Dine prog.	Dataport, 2 phone lines
	① American fusion	Valet, CD, safe	Dataport, 2 phone lines, fax, computer
✓	① American	Barber/beauty shop	Dataport
✓	① Italian	Free breakfast	Dataport, 2 ph. lines, fax, copy, print
✓	① Continental	Packages	Dataport, 2 phone lines
✓	① Japanese-Latino	Free breakfast	Dataport, 2 phone lines
✓	① American	Valet, safe, refreshments	Internet, 2 phone lines
✓	③ American, International, Italian	Spa pkgs.	Dataport, 2 phone lines
✓	④ Continental, Steak-house, American, deli	Hair salon, barber	
✓	② Mediterranean, French	Spa services	Dataport, 2 phone lines, fax
✓	① French	Live music in lounge wknts.	Dataport, 24-hour business center
✓	① Oriental-Mediterranean	Sundeck, electronic controls suite	Dataport, 2 phone lines, fax
		Hair dryers Irons	Dataport, 2 phone lines, fax

Hotel/website	Room Rating	Room Quality	Zone	Street Address
Paramount www.ianschragerhotels.com	★★★★	88	8	235 West 46th Street New York, NY 10036
The Peninsula www.peninsula.com	★★★★★	98	9	700 Fifth Avenue New York, NY 10009
Pickwick Arms www.pickwickarms.com	★★½	60	9	230 East 51st Street New York, NY 10022
The Pierre www.fourseasons.com	★★★★★	96	11	21 East 61st Street New York, NY 10021
The Plaza www.fairmont.com	★★★★½	92	9	Fifth Avenue/Cent. Pk. South New York, NY 10019
Red Roof Inn Manhattan www.redroof.com	★★★½	83	7	6 West 32nd Street New York, NY 10001
Regal U.N. Plaza www.millennium-hotels.com	★★★★	89	9	1 United Nations Plaza New York, NY 10017
The Regency Hotel www.loewshotels.com	★★★★½	95	11	540 Park Avenue New York, NY 10021
Renaissance New York Hotel www.marriott.com	★★★★½	91	8	714 Seventh Avenue New York, NY 10036
Ritz-Carlton Battery Park www.ritzcarlton.com	★★★★★	98	1	2 West Street New York, NY 10004
Ritz-Carlton New York Central Park www.ritzcarlton.com	★★★★½	94	9	50 Central Park South New York, NY 10017
The Roger Smith www.rogersmith.com	★★★½	80	9	501 Lexington Avenue New York, NY 10017
Roger Williams www.rogerwilliamshotel.com	★★★★	86	7	131 Madison Avenue New York, NY 10016
Roosevelt Hotel www.theroosevelthotel.com	★★★½	80	7	45 East 45th Street New York, NY 10017
The Royalton	★★★★½	91	9	44 West 44th Street New York, NY 10036
Second Home on Second Ave.	★★★½	77	7	7221 Second Avenue New York, NY 10003
Sheraton Manhattan Hotel www.sheraton.com	★★★★½	92	8	790 Seventh Avenue New York, NY 10019
Sheraton New York Hotel and Towers www.sheraton.com	★★★★	89	8	811 Seventh Avenue New York, NY 10019
Sheraton Russell Hotel www.sheraton.com	★★★★½	91	9	45 Park Avenue New York, NY 10016
The Sherry Netherland www.sherrynetherland.com	★★★★½	93	11	781 Fifth Avenue New York, NY 10022
The Shoreham www.boutiquehg.com	★★★★	89	9	33 West 55th Street New York, NY 10019

Local Phone	Guest Fax	Toll-Free Res. Line	Discounts Available	No. of Rooms	Room Sq. Ft.	Rack Rate
(212) 764-5500	(212) 554-6511	(800) 225-7474	AAA, Govt.	601	150	$$$+
(212) 956-2888	(212) 903-3949	(800) 262-9467		241	350	$$$$ $+
(212) 355-0300	(212) 755-5029	(800) 742-5945		350	100	$+
(212) 838-8000	(212) 940-8109	(800) 743-7734		202	455	$$$$ $$−
(212) 759-3000	(212) 759-3167	(800) 441-1414		805	380	$$$$
(212) 643-7100	(212) 643-7101	(800) REDROOF	AAA	171	n/a	$$
(212) 758-1234	(212) 702-5051	(866) 866-8086	AAA blacked out	427	240	$$$
(212) 759-4100	(212) 826-5674	(800) 233-2356		362	220	$$$$ $$−
(212) 765-7676	(212) 765-1962	(800) 236-2427	AAA, AARP blacked out	305	340	$$$−
(212) 344-0800	(212) 344-3804	(800) 241-3333	AAA	298	425	$$$+ −
(212) 308-9100	(212) 207-8831	(800) 241-3333	AAA, AARP	277	425	$$$$ $$−
(212) 755-1400	(212) 319-9130	(800) 445-0277	Govt.	136	204	$$$+
(212) 448-7000	(212) 448-7007	(888) 448-7788	AAA	200	300	$$
(212) 661-9600	(212) 885-6161	(888) TEDDY-NY	AAA, Govt.	1,033	200	$$+
(212) 869-4400	(212) 869-8965	(800) 635-9013		168	250	$$$$−
(212) 677-3161	(212) 677-3161			7	100	$
(212) 581-3300	(212) 541-9219	(800) 325-3535	AAA, AARP, Govt.	650	180	$$$−
(212) 581-1000	(212) 262-4410	(800) 325-3535	AAA, AARP, Govt.	1,750	180	$$$−
(212) 685-7676	(212) 889-3193	(800) 325-3535	AAA, Govt.	150	230	$$$−
(212) 355-2800	(212) 319-4306	(800) 247-4377		60	400	$$$$ $−
(212) 247-6700	(212) 765-9741	(877) 847-4444		178	250	$$$

Portland Square Hotel $700

Hotel	Meeting Facilities	Pool/ Sauna	Exercise Facilities	Window Glaze	Parking Per Day	Nearest Subway
Paramount	✓		✓	Dbl.	$45	2 blocks
The Peninsula	✓	✓	✓	Tpl	$45	3 blocks
Pickwick Arms				Dbl.	$35	2 blocks
The Pierre	✓		✓	Dbl.	$45	0.5 block
The Plaza	✓		✓	Dbl.	$45	Beneath hotel
Red Roof Inn Manhattan	✓		✓	Dbl.	$22	1 block
Regal U.N. Plaza	✓	Pool, sauna, whirlpool	✓	Dbl.	$24–$30	4 blocks
The Regency Hotel	✓	Sauna, whirlpool	✓	Dbl.	$47	2 blocks
Renaissance New York Hotel	✓		✓	Dbl.	$35–$48	Beneath hotel
Ritz-Carlton Battery Park	✓	Spa	✓	Sgl./ Dbl.	$50	0.5 block
Ritz-Carlton New York Central Park	✓	Spa		Dbl.	$50	0.5 block
The Roger Smith Hotel	✓	Sauna privileges	Privileges, $20	Dbl.	$35	2 blocks
Roger Williams				Sgl.	$27–$35	2 blocks
Roosevelt Hotel	✓			Sgl./ Dbl.	$40	1 block
The Royalton			✓	Dbl.	$40	4 blocks
Second Home on Second Ave.				Sgl.	n/a	2 blocks
Sheraton Manhattan Hotel	✓	Pool	✓	Dbl.	$27	2 blocks
Sheraton New York Hotel and Towers	✓	Privileges, $15	✓	Sgl.	$35	Beneath hotel
Sheraton Russell Hotel	✓ Small	Privileges, $20	Privileges Small	Dbl.	$41	5 blocks
The Sherry Netherland	✓ Small		✓	Sgl.	$45	0.5 block
The Shoreham		Privileges	Privileges free	Sgl.	$40	1 block

Bar	On-site Dining	Extra Amenities	Business Amenities
✓	① Continental	Pkgs.	Dataports, 2 ph. lines, new 24 hr. business ctr.
✓	① American, Continental	Marble baths, robes, mini bar, spa	Dataport, 2 phone lines, in-room fax
✓	② French, Continental		Business center at front desk, dataports
✓	② Continental, tea room	Piano music, hair salon	Dataport, 2 phone lines
✓	④ Continental, American, Steak, Seafood	Hair salon, spa	Dataports, 2 phone lines
✓		Concierge, free breakfast, paper	2 phone lines
✓	① New American	Harpist in lobby	Dataport, 2 phone lines, fax
✓	② Lounge, French-American	Hair salon, concierge, massage	Dataport, 2 phone lines, fax
✓	① American		Dataport, 2 phone lines
✓	② Steak house, Chinese	Telescope	Dataport, 2 phone lines
✓	① French/American	Telescope, robes, library	Internet, 2 phone lines
✓	① Continental/American	Free cont'l brkfst., gallery, videos	Dataport, computer available
		Free cont'l brkfst. free dessert buffet	Dataport, some have 2 phone lines
✓	② American	Concierge	2 phone lines fax, modem
✓	① American		Dataport, 2 phone lines
✓	① Bistro	Convention center, packages	Dataport, 2 phone lines, fax some rooms
✓	② Cafe, American	Convention center	Dataport, 2 phone lines, fax
✓	24-hour room service		Dataport, 2 phone lines, fax
✓	① Italian	Concierge, breakfast	Dataport, 2 phone lines, some have fax
✓	① French		Dataport, 2 phone lines

Hotel/website	Room Rating	Room Quality	Zone	Street Address
60 Thompson	★★★★	88	2	60 Thompson Street New York, NY 10012
Sofitel New York www.sofitel.com	★★★★	88	9	45 West 44th Street New York, NY 10036
Soho Grand www.sohogrand.com	★★★★½	93	2	310 West Broadway New York, NY 10013
The St. Regis www.strregis.com	★★★★★	98	9	2 East 55th Street New York, NY 10022
The Stanhope www.hyatt.com	★★★★½	93	13	995 Fifth Avenue New York, NY 10028
Thirty Thirty New York City www.thirtythirty-nyc.com	★★★½	83	7	30 East 30th Street New York, NY 10016
Time www.thetimeny.com	★★★★	89	8	224 West 49th Street New York, NY 10019
Tribeca Grand www.tribecagrand.com	★★★★½	93	2	25 Walker Street New York, NY 10013
Trump International Hotel & Towers www.trumpintl.com	★★★★★	97	10	1 Central Park West New York, NY 10023
W Hotel Times Square www.whotels.com	★★★★½	95	8	1467 Broadway New York, NY 10036
W Hotel Union Square www.whotels.com	★★★★	87	7	201 Park Avenue South New York, NY 10003
W New York www.whotels.com	★★★★½	92	9	541 Lexington Avenue New York, NY 10022
W New York Tuscany www.whotels.com	★★★★½	90	9	130 East 39th Street New York, NY 10016
The Waldorf-Astoria www.hilton.com	★★★★½	95	9	301 Park Avenue New York, NY 10022
Wall Street Inn	★★★★	86	1	9 S. William Street New York, NY 10004
The Warwick Hotel www.warwickhotels.com	★★★★	89	9	65 West 54th Street New York, NY 10019
Washington Square Hotel www.washingtonsquarehotel.com	★★★½	78	4	103 Waverly Place New York, NY 10011
Westin New York Times Square www.westinny.com	★★★★	88	8	270 West 43rd Street New York, NY 10036

Local Phone	Guest Fax	Toll-Free Res. Line	Discounts Available	No. of Rooms	Room Sq. Ft.	Rack Rate
(212) 431-0400	(212) 431-0200	(800) 325-3535	AAA, AARP, Govt.	650	180	$$$$+
(212) 354-884	(212) 782-3002	(800) SOFITEL		398	n/a	$$$$−
(212) 965-3000	(212) 965-3200	(800) 965-3000		367	275	$$$+
(212) 753-4500	(212) 787-3437	(800) 759-7550		313	425	$$$$ $$$−
(212) 288-5800	(212) 517-0088	(888) 649-6331		157	400	$$$$−
(212) 689-1900	(212) 689-0023	(800) 804-4480	AAA, Govt.	210	200	$$−
(212) 246-5252	(212) 245-2305	(877) 846-3692		194	235	$$$
(212) 519-6600	(212) 519-6700	(877) 519-6600	Govt.	203	n/a	$$$−
(212) 299-1000	(212) 299-1150	(888) 448-7867		167	n/a	$$$$ $$$−
(212) 930-7400	(212) 930-7500	(877) 946-8357	AAA, Govt., Mil.	509	210	$$$$−
(212) 253-9119	(212) 779-0148	(877) 946-8357	AAA, Govt.	286	390	$$$$+
(212) 755-1200	(212) 644-5951	(877) 946-8357	Govt., Mil.	700	200	$$$−
(212) 685-1100	(212) 779-0148	(877) 946-8357	Govt., Mil.	199	400	$$$+
(212) 355-3000	(212) 872-7272	(800) WALDORF		1,138	n/a	$$$+
(212) 747-1500	(212) 747-1900	(877) 747-1500		46	250	$$+
(212) 247-2700	(212) 957-8915	(800) 223-4099	AAA, Govt.	422	240	$$$
(212) 777-9515	(212) 979-8373	(800) 222-0418		180	120	$$+
(212) 201-2700	(212) 201-2701	(866) 837-4183	Travel agents	863	310	$$$$− $$−

Hotel	Meeting Facilities	Pool/ Sauna	Exercise Facilities	Window Glaze	Parking Per Day	Nearest Subway
60 Thompson	✓ Small		Privileges	Sgl.	$35	3 blocks
Sofitel New York	✓		✓	Trpl.	$40	2 blocks
Soho Grand	✓		✓	Trpl.	$34	1 block
The St. Regis	✓	Sauna, steam room	✓	Dbl.	$45	2 blocks
The Stanhope	✓		✓	Dbl.	$40	7 blocks
Thirty Thirty New York City				Sgl.	$25	2 blocks
Time	✓			Dbl.	$25	1 block
Tribeca Grand	✓	Pool	✓	Sgl.	$40	2 blocks
Trump International Hotel & Towers	✓	Pool	✓	Sgl.	$45	1 block
W Hotel Times Square	✓		✓	Sgl.	$45	0.5 block
W Hotel Union Square	✓		✓	Trpl.	$45	0.5 block
W New York	✓	Sauna, whirlpool	✓	Dbl.	$40	1 block
W New York Tuscany	✓			Dbl.	$40	2 blocks
The Waldorf-Astoria	✓	Whirlpool	✓	Dbl.	$45	1 block
Wall Street Inn	✓	Sauna, steam room	✓ Small	Dbl.	n/a	3 blocks
The Warwick Hotel	✓		✓	Dbl.	$25	2 blocks
Washington Square Hotel	✓ Small		✓	Sgl.	n/a	1 block
Westin New York Times Square	✓	Spa	✓	Dbl.	$38	0.5 block

Bar	On-site Dining	Extra Amenities	Business Amenities
✓	① American	Concierge, breakfast	Internet, fax
✓	① French	Concierge, radio	Dataport, DSL, computer
✓	① New England	Goldfish in room by request	Dataport, 2 phone lines
✓	② American, French	Live piano & harp in salon	Dataport, 2 phone lines
✓	① French Provincial	Concierge	Dataport, 2 phone lines
			2 phone lines
✓	① American		Dataport, 2 phone lines, fax, Webtv
✓	① American	Champagne, breakfast	2 phone lines, business center
✓	② American, French	Concierge, CD, safe	Dataport, 2 phone lines, fax
✓	① Seafood-Sushi	Spa, bathrobes, library	Internet, 2 phone lines, dataport
✓	① Italian	Concierge, CD, DVD, library	Dataport, 2 phone lines
✓			Dataport
✓	① Tuscan	Packages	Dataport, 2 phone lines
✓	③ French, American, Japanese	Cocktail terrace w/ pianist, salon, spa	Dataport, 2 phone lines, fax
		Free cont'l brkfst., hair dryers	Dataport, 2 phone lines
✓	① Italian Cafe	Packages	Dataport, 2 phone lines
✓	① American	Free continental breakfast	Dataport
✓	③ Steak house, American	Theater ticket desk	Dataport, 2 phone lines

Part Four

Arriving and
Getting Oriented

Getting into and out of Manhattan changed forever in the aftermath of the September 11th terrorist attacks. If you intend to drive a truck or van into the city, be forewarned that some bridges and tunnels may be closed to commercial vehicles. At all bridges and tunnels, all vehicles are subject to search at the discretion of the authorities. While a search itself is a minor inconvenience, the traffic backups attending such searches are not. Once arrived, be aware that there's still a lot of surface traffic congestion in lower Manhattan in the area surrounding Ground Zero. Our advice is to leave your vehicle outside the city and train in.

At the three area airports, you can expect the same security screenings as at other U.S. facilities, so be sure to arrive two or more hours prior to departure time. Train travel has been less affected by new security procedures than has air or automobile travel. If you had considered flying up from Washington or down from Boston on one of the air shuttles, you'll probably save time by switching from the plane to the train.

Arriving

Manhattan Island and the other boroughs that comprise New York City are situated near the mouth of the Hudson River off a narrow spit of land that dangles like an udder beneath the bulk of upstate New York. To the west, across the Hudson from Manhattan, is the rest of the United States, starting with New Jersey. Travel in any other direction and you will find yourself in one of New York City's boroughs. To the north of Manhattan across the Harlem River is the Bronx. Due east, on the opposite bank of the East River, is Queens. South of Queens and southeast of Manhattan is Brooklyn, and farther south and a little to the west sits Staten Island.

If you are an American, there's a good chance that your forebears entered the United States through New York, steaming west out of the Atlantic Ocean into Lower New York Bay, through the Narrows between

Staten Island and Brooklyn, north into Upper New York Bay, and finally past the Statue of Liberty to docks near the southern tip of Manhattan Island. Today, it's possible to arrive in New York by just about any means imaginable, making it one of the most accessible cities in the world.

By Car

If you are planning to arrive via automobile, you need this guidebook more than you ever imagined. Traffic in Manhattan comes in two basic modes: nutso and gridlock. With nutso you're moving, but everybody else is moving faster and usually at an angle that presupposes an imminent collision. Gridlock is gridlock. Bring a sandwich and a pocket edition of *War and Peace* and prepare yourself for some serious down time. Native New Yorkers will consider this a gross exaggeration, of course, but then most of them have cab-driver genes somewhere in their lineage.

If there were a driving school to prepare you for driving in Manhattan, it would emphasize the automobile as an offensive weapon and would teach you various foreign dialects so that you could converse with other drivers. The final exam would involve wedging your car on the fly into spaces too small for the average cephalopod.

And then there are parking and gas. Filling stations are rare and generally not conveniently located, while safe, off-street parking in Manhattan costs as much per night as a hotel room in most other cities.

Driving in the boroughs is somewhat less daunting but is still more challenging than motoring in most other large U.S. cities.

So, having been warned, in case you elect to bring your nice, clean, undented car into Manhattan, here's what you need to know.

- Manhattan is an island! This means that you must enter via a bridge or a tunnel.
- Rush-hour traffic clogs all the tunnels and bridges, so time your arrival for off-peak traffic times—10 a.m. to 2:30 p.m. and 7:30 p.m. to 6 a.m. on weekdays are best.
- Traffic in Manhattan is decidedly more civil on weekends, but avoid arriving during the late afternoon and early evening on Sunday.
- Fill up your gas tank before coming into Manhattan.
- If you will be lodging in Manhattan, use the hotel information chart in Part Three to find hotels with parking garages.
- Expect to pay at least $20 a day in parking in addition to the room charge.

Some Specific Directions

Coming from South or West of New York City   Coming from New Jersey, south of New York, you can take the Holland Tunnel into downtown Manhattan or the Lincoln Tunnel into Midtown. Both require tolls and both are accessed from Interstate 95. The Holland Tunnel is also accessible from I-78. Unless you are heading for lower (downtown) Manhattan, we recommend the more northerly Lincoln Tunnel. A third option is to take I-278 across Staten Island and into Brooklyn, and from there enter Manhattan via the Brooklyn–Battery Tunnel. This last is quite round-about and should only be considered when there is a traffic advisory for the Holland Tunnel.

Although it may sound less convenient, consider driving to the Metropark Station, leaving the car there ($2.50 a day instead of 20 times that) and buying a ticket on New Jersey Transit ($9–$12.20 round trip) into the city. (Amtrak also stops at Metropark, but is more expensive.) To reach Metropark, take the New Jersey Turnpike to the Garden State Park-way, then go about two miles to Exit 131 and into Metropark.

Coming from North of New York City   Coming from north of the city and west of the Hudson River, you can choose between the Lincoln Tun-nel or the George Washington Bridge, which crosses onto Manhattan at the northern end of the island.

East of the Hudson River, there's a dandy tangle of highways branch-ing south to New York City from upper New York State, Connecticut, Rhode Island, and points farther north. Coming south on I-87, pick up the Henry Hudson Parkway below Yonkers to enter Manhattan. From I-95 south you have several choices. Either stay on I-95 as it crosses the upper end of Manhattan Island, or branch off onto I-278 and enter New York City via the Triborough Bridge (toll).

Arriving and Departing by Airplane

The New York area is served by three major airports. LaGuardia Airport, located in Queens, is the closest airport, followed by John F. Kennedy International Airport (JFK), situated south of Queens on Jamaica Bay. To the west, in New Jersey, is Newark International Airport. LaGuardia services primarily domestic flights and carriers, while JFK and Newark handle both international and domestic air traffic.

In general, LaGuardia is closer and more convenient than JFK or Newark, though the difference is not all that great—about 20 or so addi-tional minutes and about $10 cab fare—to most Manhattan destina-tions. You may find bargain fares to Newark (and occasionally JFK) that more than make up for the longer commute.

However, there are free shuttles from JFK to the Howard Beach sub-way station, so you could make it into Manhattan for only $2. There is also bus service via **New York Airport Service Express Bus** (call (718) 875-8200) from JFK ($13) and LaGuardia ($10).

If you are visiting New York during the winter, we recommend flying into either Newark or JFK. These airports have longer runways and elec-tronic instrumentation that allows them to operate in weather that might shut LaGuardia down. In addition, because they are larger than LaGuardia, Newark and JFK can perform airplane de-icing operations adjacent to the active runways. At LaGuardia, planes in need of de-icing are usually detoured to a remote staging area.

Another way to hedge your bets during the winter is to fly into Baltimore/Washington International (BWI) and then take an Amtrak train directly to New York Penn Station. There are more than 20 trains a day, and there is an Amtrak station right at the airport. Conventional trains take about three hours and a quarter, whereas the Acela Express and express MetroLiners make the trip in two and a half hours.

Using BWI can also be a big dollar-saver. We flew Southwest Airlines, a discount carrier, to BWI for $112 round-trip from Birmingham, Alabama, and then transferred to Amtrak. Our total cost was $238— $112 round-trip air plus $126 round-trip rail from BWI—compared with airfares to LaGuardia, JFK, or Newark ranging from an economy $398 to a full coach fare of $788. Because the train deposits you right in the heart of Manhattan, you also avoid taxi or bus fares from the airport. Finally, if you can fly directly from your home airport to BWI, the plane/train combo can sometimes get you to New York faster than an air itinerary that requires a change of planes.

With the more stringent security enforced for carry-on luggage, you must be careful to pack the following items in your check-in luggage: scissors, nail files, nail clippers, pen-knives, razors or razor blades, or any other sharp object that could conceivably be used as a weapon.

TRANSPORTATION CHART

Name	Service	Phone
Amtrak	Train service	(800) 872-7245
Airporter	Airport-to-airport transfers	(609) 587-6600
Gray Line Air Shuttle	LaGuardia–NYC shuttle	(212) 315-3006
JFK International Airport	Airport	(718) 244-4444
LaGuardia Airport	Airport	(718) 533-3400
Long Island Railroad	Commuter railroad	(718) 217-LIRR
Metro-North Railroad	Commuter railroad	(212) 532-4900
New Jersey Transit	Buses & trains to NYC	(973) 762-5100
NYC Bridges & Tunnels	Bridge & tunnel info	(800) 221-9903
NYC D.O.T.	Parking, etc.	(212) CALL-DOT
NYC Taxi & Limo Commission	New York City taxis	(212) 302-TAXI
NYC Transit Authority	Subways & buses	(718) 330-1234
New York Airport Service	NYC–airport bus service	(718) 875-8200
New York Waterway	Commuter ferry service	(800) 533-3779
Newark International Airport	Airport	(973) 961-6000
Olympia Trails Express Buses	NYC–airport bus service	(718) 622-7700
PATH Train	New Jersey–NYC train	(800) 234-7284
Port Authority Bus Terminal	Bus & subway station	(212) 564-8484
Road Conditions	Road condition information	(800) 847-8929, (212) CALL-DOT

LaGuardia Airport

LaGuardia, the smallest of the New York airports, is located just off Grand Central Parkway in Queens. LaGuardia has four terminals. All airlines except Northwest, Delta, and US Airways use the Central Terminal. US Airways and Delta have their own terminals. Delta shares its main terminal with Northwest and also uses the Marine Air Terminal for its Delta Shuttle flights. Because the Delta Shuttle operates at the opposite end of the airport from Delta's other flights, make sure you know from which terminal your Delta flight departs.

If you plan to arrive by air (except during winter, as discussed earlier) from within the United States or Canada, flying into LaGuardia will usually get you to your Manhattan destination faster. How much faster depends on highway traffic conditions at the time of day you arrive. During nonrush periods it takes about 20–25 minutes by cab or limo and 35–45 minutes by bus from LaGuardia to Midtown. During rush hour, traffic flows both in and out of the city, and the convenience of flying into LaGuardia is sometimes offset by the snarled traffic of surrounding streets and highways. Although there is a water shuttle to the 34th Street Pier in Midtown, most arriving passengers commute to the city in cabs, limos, or buses. Getting into Manhattan from LaGuardia during rush hour, though a hassle (allow 35–60 minutes to Midtown), is doable. Going to the airport in afternoon rush traffic is problematic. If you are booked on a flight that departs between 4:30 and 8 p.m. on weekdays, leave Manhattan three hours in advance if traveling by cab, three and a half hours in advance if using an airport shuttle bus.

To get from LaGuardia to Manhattan, you have your choice of cab, limo, bus, or water taxi.

Public Transportation Routes from LAGUARDIA AIRPORT			
Service	**To**	**Departs**	**Travel time**
Gray Line Air Shuttle Fare: $14	Drop-off anywhere between Battery Park and 63rd Street; also stops at certain hotels between 63rd and 103rd Streets	6 a.m. to 11:30 p.m.	55–110 min. depending on destination
Cab Fare: $18–$26 plus tolls and tip	Any stop in Manhattan	At your convenience	20–35 min. depending on destination (nonrush)
Limo Cost depends on type of limo	Any stop in Manhattan	At your convenience	20–35 min. (nonrush)
New York Airport Service Fare: $10–$13	Grand Central Station & Port Authority Terminal	Every 30 minutes from 6:45 a.m. to midnight	35–45 min. (nonrush)

John F. Kennedy International Airport

JFK is a sprawling, confusing, nine-terminal facility that most savvy travelers go out of their way to avoid. Almost 100 airlines, including most foreign carriers, use JFK. International travelers make domestic connections at JFK, and U.S. carriers daily fly in thousands of passengers bound for international destinations. To get from JFK to Manhattan you have your choice of cab, limo, bus, or subway.

Public Transportation Routes from JFK AIRPORT			
Service	**To**	**Departs**	**Travel time**
Gray Line Air Shuttle Fare: $14	Drop-off anywhere between Battery Park and 63rd Street; also stops at certain hotels between 63rd and 103rd Streets	6 a.m. to 11:30 p.m.	55–110 min. depending on destination
New York Airport Service Fare: $13	Grand Central Station & Port Authority Terminal	Every 30 minutes from 6 a.m. to midnight	60 min. (nonrush)
Subway, "A" Line Fare: $2	Manhattan all stops from Fulton Street to 207th Street, Howard Beach Station to Midtown, plus stops in Queens and Brooklyn	Trains depart every 15–25 minutes	60–75 minutes
Cab Fare: $35 flat rate plus tolls and tip	Any stop in Manhattan	At your convenience	40–60 minutes
Limo Cost depends on type of limo	Any stop in Manhattan	At your convenience	40–60 minutes

Newark International Airport

Newark International Airport is located in New Jersey between Newark and Elizabeth. There are three terminals serving about 50 domestic and foreign airlines. All of the terminals and long-term parking lots are connected by monorail. Newark International is better organized and decidedly less intimidating than JFK and generally more efficient than LaGuardia. If your Manhattan destination is downtown or Midtown on the West Side, you should consider flying into Newark. Bus service, especially to downtown and to the Port Authority Terminal in Midtown, is excellent, with buses departing every 20 to 30 minutes 24 hours a day; and Amtrak offers train service from the airport to New York Penn Station.

To get from Newark International Airport to Manhattan, you can choose from among limos, cabs, buses, trains, or a combination of bus or cab, and train.

Public Transportation Routes from NEWARK INTERNATIONAL			
Service	**To**	**Departs**	**Travel time**
Olympia Trails Bus Fare: $11	Port Authority Terminal at 42nd and Eighth Ave,	Every 20–30 min. 24 hours a day	40–50 min.
Olympia Trails Bus Fare: $11	Grand Central Terminal or Penn Station	Every 20–30 min.	50–70 min.
Airlink Bus Amtrak & PATH to Newark Fare	Bus to rail connections at Newark Penn Station	Every 20–30 min.	15 min.
Cab Fare: $35–$55 rate plus tolls and tip	Any stop in Manhattan	At your convenience	40–60 minutes
Limo Cost depends on type of limo	Any stop in Manhattan	At your convenience	40–60 minutes
Train New Jersey Transit Fare: $12	New York Penn Station	Every 15–30 min.	30–45 minutes
Train Amtrak Acela Regional Fare: $24–$25	New York Penn Station	Every 25–60 min.	20 minutes

Getting into Manhattan from the Airports

When it comes to getting into the city from the airport, we opt for simplicity, even if it costs a dollar or two more. The fewer times you must heft your luggage around, the better, and likewise, the fewer stops or transfers necessary, the less complicated the trip.

From LaGuardia we always take a cab or limo (see above), unless we are arriving at the Marine Air Terminal at rush hour, in which case we sometimes use the Delta Water Shuttle. From JFK we take a cab or limo. The JFK A-train subway looks good on paper and is definitely the least expensive way to get into town, but it takes forever owing to countless intermediate stops. When it comes to Newark, we usually take the Olympia Trails express bus to the Port Authority Terminal on Manhattan's West Side in Midtown. Because of preferential treatment at the Lincoln Tunnel and a direct "buses only" throughway into the Port Authority Terminal, the bus can often make it to Manhattan faster than a cab (once the bus leaves the airport). From the Port Authority Terminal you can catch a cab or, if traveling light, a subway to your destination.

As an aside, the Port Authority Terminal is a huge, generally confusing maze of a building. After you disembark from the bus, your best bet is to make your way to ground level and exit the building on 42nd Street. You will find a cab stand just outside the door. If you plan to return to the airport via the terminal, locate the Airport Transportation Lobby on the first floor of the northern (42nd Street) side of the terminal. Though New York has made great progress in reducing crime in public places, the Port Authority Terminal is not a great spot to hang around. Unless, as we Southerners say, "you're fixin' to explode," wait until you reach your hotel to use the rest room. If you are considering a taxi, fares from Newark International to Midtown run about $45 plus tolls and tip—a bit pricey unless there are three or more in your party.

Amtrak opened a train station at Newark International in the fall of 2001. From the terminal, catch an AirTran monorail to the airport train station. The monorail is free if you have a prepurchased Amtrak ticket, or $5 if you don't. Trains from the airport station depart every 25–60 minutes, depending on time of day, and they stop at Newark Penn Station enroute. The commute via Amtrak takes only about 20 minutes, making it the fastest way into the city. It is also, however, the most expensive option short of a private cab, costing about $25 one way, not including any monorail charges. If you book your Amtrak itinerary on the Amtrak website, be aware that you must enter the airport code "EWR" rather than typing "Newark International Airport Station."

New Jersey Transit trains run almost the same route from Newark as their faster Amtrak counterparts, and they are much cheaper. At the entrance to the AirTrain monorail, there are vending machines that sell NJ Transit tickets. Follow the on-screen directions, and buy a ticket for New York Penn Station (about $12). Use this ticket to get through the AirTran turnstiles; the monorail will take you to the train station. Once your NJ Transit train arrives, board and find a seat. A conductor will come by to punch your ticket.

From LaGuardia and JFK, if there are two or more in your party, a cab is not much more expensive than the bus, plus it takes you right to your hotel. The Carey Bus from LaGuardia to Grand Central Terminal, for example, is $10 per head. A couple using the Carey bus would spend $20 to get to Grand Central and then would probably need a cab to reach their hotel. By the time you add it all up, the cost is very comparable to the price of a cab straight from the airport, including tolls and tip.

Each terminal at all three airports has a taxi queue, a designated place for arriving passengers to catch a cab. Because there are always lots of cabs at the airport awaiting fares, it usually takes only a couple of minutes in line to get a cab. Do not accept a ride from any person who approaches you in the terminal or on the sidewalk. Official, licensed cabs load only at designated taxi stands, supervised by a dispatcher.

Savvy travelers have discovered limo services. For sometimes even less than a cab, a limo and driver will meet your flight and transport you into Manhattan. Limos, which incidentally encompass a diverse assortment of vehicles in addition to stretch Cadillacs, can be reserved by the trip or by the hour. Rates range from $18 for a trip from LaGuardia to Manhattan in a modest sedan to over $150 for a ride to Newark International in something fancy. Although you can occasionally beat the price of a cab, the big advantage to reserving a limo is having somebody there waiting for you—i.e., no taxi queue. To reserve, call one of the operators listed below. Have your flight information handy, including airline, flight number, and arrival time. The service will also ask for your Manhattan destination. Although you can request that your driver meet you in the terminal, it's customary (and sometimes cheaper) to meet him or her curbside. Most limo services will accept prepayment by credit card, or alternatively, you can pay the driver. Tolls, parking fees, and gratuities are extra.

Garden State Limo (WEX)	(800) 532-3730 or (914) 592-9200
Super Saver by Carmel	(800) 924-9954 or (212) 666-6666
Classic Limousine	(800) 666-4949 or (631) 567-5100
Tel Aviv Car & Limo Service	(800) 222-9888 or (212) 777-7777
Dial Car	(800) DIAL 743 or (718) 743-8383

Getting to the Airports from Manhattan

Essentially, you have the same options available when it's time to go to the airport for your return flight. For LaGuardia and JFK, your best bet is a cab. For Newark, take a cab to the Port Authority Terminal and then board an Olympia Trails bus for the airport.

There is one additional option for commuting to the airports: ride-sharing services. These services offer reserved-space door-to-door transportation to the airports.

To LaGuardia or JFK	**Classic Airport Ride Share**	(631) 567-5100
To Newark International	**Gray Line Air Shuttle**	(212) 315-3006

With ride-share services, you call the service and advise them of your flight time. They integrate you into their pickup schedule and tell you what time to be ready to go. If you are the first person collected, you have a bit of driving to look forward to. On the other hand, if you are the last person in the van, it's straight to the airport you go. The service to Newark is a bargain at $14 and eliminates carting all your stuff through the Port Authority Terminal or paying big bucks for a cab. Ride-share service to JFK for one person will save you about $5–$10 over the cost of a cab. Going to LaGuardia, you're better off in terms of convenience and costs to take a taxi. For the record, the same companies also provide shared-ride service from the airports to Manhattan.

By Train

New York has excellent train connections south to Baltimore and Washington, D.C.; north to upstate New York, Boston, and New England; and west to New Jersey and eastern Pennsylvania. From these areas you can commute directly to Midtown Manhattan in a time span that rivals or betters that of traveling by air. From Baltimore, for example, we departed our hotel for the 10-minute ride to the Amtrak Station, waited less than 20 minutes for the train to arrive, and then buzzed up to New York's Penn Station in about two and a half hours—a total of just under three hours for the whole trip. (Using the new high-speed Acela Express trains, you can make it even faster.) By contrast, our colleagues commuted 20 minutes to the airport, then consumed two hours and 10 minutes checking in, walking to the departure gate, and boarding. The flight from gate to gate to LaGuardia took another hour. They had no checked luggage, but it took 15 minutes to unload and make it to the taxi queue, where the wait for a cab was a modest 5 minutes. Cabbing from LaGuardia to Midtown consumed a little over 20 minutes—for a total of 4 hours and 10 minutes.

Amtrak's Acela high-speed service from Washington, D.C. to New York, and from Boston to New York, is on a par with Europe's bullet trains. Reaching speeds of 150 miles an hour, Acela Express trains provide first- and business-class service, while Acela Regional trains (which make more stops) offer both business and coach accommodations. Plush seating, seatside electrical outlets for computers, conference tables, and a club car are standard on all Acela trains. Acela Express trains additionally offer a "quiet" car, as well as complimentary full meal and beverage service for first-class passengers. With departures throughout the day, and business and first-class fares comparable to air fares, it's hard to figure why anyone in the Boston/New York/DC corridor would opt to fly. For additional information, check out amtrak.com or call (800) USA-RAIL.

If you are traveling from points farther afield than the cities and areas listed above, the train probably requires more time than you are prepared to invest. Sometimes, however, the longer hauls offer some unexpected benefits. Bill, traveling from Atlanta to New York, caught the Amtrak Crescent at 7:30 p.m. With first-class accommodations, he enjoyed a sleeping compartment, and his meals were included as well. He arrived in New York at 2:10 the following afternoon. Because it was easy to work on the train, Bill had plenty of time to both relax and prepare for his afternoon meeting in New York. His partner, Jane, by contrast, spent a busy morning hustling to the airport, flying to LaGuardia, cabbing into the city, and then trying to catch a bite to eat on the run. Other eastern cities with fairly attractive Amtrak schedules and fares include Richmond, Norfolk, Raleigh/Durham, Charlotte, Charleston (SC), Birmingham, Savannah, Jacksonville, Orlando, Cleveland, Pittsburgh, Chicago, and Montreal. For information, call Amtrak at (800) 872-7245.

However, unless you're still in the backpacking years, it's still worth spending the extra money to get a ticket on a reserved-seating train; especially if you're traveling during a holiday or heavy convention time. (And in New York, there's never a light season.) Do it ahead of time, or it's possible you may even have to stand part of the way.

In addition to Amtrak, four commuter railroads serve the greater New York area. New Jersey Transit (call (973) 762-5100 or (800) 772-2222) operates two lines, using New York Penn Station along with Amtrak and the Long Island Railroad (call (718) 217-LIRR). The Metro-North Commuter Railroad, serving towns north along the Hudson River, arrives and departs from Grand Central Station.

By Ship

If you arrive in New York on a cruise ship you will probably tie up at the Passenger Ship Terminal on the far west side of the city between West 51st and West 52nd Streets. Cabs and limos provide transportation from the terminal to Manhattan and area destinations.

Getting Oriented

Laid out in a grid, New York is a very easy city to navigate. Avenues run north/south, and streets run east/west. Though some avenues have names (Park and Madison Avenues, for example) and some have names and numbers (Avenue of the Americas is also Sixth Avenue), most avenues just have numbers (First Avenue, Fifth Avenue, etc.). The numbering starts on the east side of Manhattan, with First Avenue, and ascends to Eleventh Avenue on the west side of the island.

Streets are a little trickier, but not much. Do you remember regular and irregular verbs from your English grammar studies? Well, in New York there are regular streets and irregular streets. Regular streets are numbered streets that run east/west, forming a nice grid with the avenues. Irregular streets are likely to run in just about any direction and generally have names instead of numbers. Most of the irregular streets are in the lowermost or uppermost parts of the island. In between the lower part and the upper part, in the 60% of Manhattan that comprises the middle, are the regular streets. Between 191st Street way Uptown (north) and 14th Street Downtown (south) there is a lovely, predictable grid. The only notable irregular street in this section of Manhattan is Broadway, which carves a lazy diagonal from northwest to southeast across the grid. Another exception, though it's not a street, is Central Park, a long north/south rectangle running from 110st Street south to 59th Street.

Going south from 14th Street toward the lower part of the island, the grid system prevails all the way down to First Street and Houston Street, but *only* on the east side. On the west side below 14th Street to Houston is Greenwich Village, which contains mostly irregular streets. From Houston Street on down to Battery Park at the tip of Manhattan is a crazy patchwork of irregular streets. Some of New York's more colorful neighborhoods and districts, including Chinatown, Little Italy, the Bowery, Soho, Tribeca, and the Financial District, are packed into this confined space. City Hall and the World Trade Center site now known as Ground Zero are also located here. If you are walking or driving in this area, the best way to stay oriented is to imagine a finger pointed down with the palm toward you. Wall Street is the crease at the first knuckle from the tip. The middle crease (second knuckle) is Canal Street, and the crease where the finger joins the palm is Houston Street. If you take a pen and draw a line down the middle of the finger from your palm to the tip, bisecting all three creases, that would be Broadway. If you can keep these streets and their relationship to one another straight, you will never be lost for long in Lower Manhattan. If you use this little memory aid in public, we strongly recommend that you use your index finger (the finger located closest to the thumb).

Things the Locals already Know

Tipping

As we've said, New York's unfriendly reputation is highly exaggerated, but the city requires a little "friendliness" on your part as well. This is a society accustomed to—one might almost say built on—the tipping system, and you should be prepared right from the start. Cabbies generally expect 15–20% of the fare as a tip, and you should certainly be generous if traffic is as bad as it generally is. If your hotel doorman gets you the cab, it's customary, though still optional, to slip him a dollar bill (besides, you don't want to have to wait next time, do you?). However, if you pick up the cab from one of the managed taxi stands at the train stations or airports, do not tip the traffic conductor.

Once at the hotel, expect to slip the bellman a dollar per suitcase ($2 if it's really heavy or clumsy); when you check out, leave behind at least $1 a day for the maids, $2 if the room has a second visit for turndown service or extra care. Tipping the concierge is a question of letting the reward fit the service: If she merely makes dinner reservations, a warm thank-you may suffice; but if she finagles them in the hottest restaurant in town, or gets opening-night tickets to a Broadway blockbuster, go for the 20% rule.

Bartenders typically get a dollar a drink; a bonus for a generous pour is always appreciated. Waiters generally get 15–20%, although you should look to see whether an automatic gratuity has been built into the total. If you check your coats, tip the attendant $1 per wrap when you pick them up, and perhaps another dollar for large umbrellas or briefcases. Legends to the contrary, it is rare that slipping the maitre d' a bribe will do you much good, and it makes you look like a rube unless some actual rearrangement has been necessary. If you have summoned the sommelier to consult on the wine choice, you should leave him something in the range of 10% of the cost of the bottle.

Any personal services you arrange, such as a massage, hair styling, manicure, or the like, also require a tip of about 20%. And if you get a shoeshine—an underestimated pleasure, incidentally—you should surely throw in a similar bonus.

Radio and Television Stations

New York has a thousand radio stations—well, maybe it just sounds that way, getting in and out of taxis and shopping malls —but among the most useful for out-of-towners are the National Public Radio WNYC (AM 820 and FM 93.9); sports WFAN (AM 660); and the all-news WBBR (AM 1130) and WINS (AM 1010). For the runners, etc., music choices include classical WQXP (FM 96.7); jazz WKCR (FM 89.9); rock Z100 (FM 100.3); Top 40 WPLJ (FM 95.5); classic rock WAXQ (FM 104.3); country WYNY (FM 107.1); and oldies WCBS (FM 101.1).

Most hotels have cable, and if you're lucky, the list of stations in your room will more or less correspond to what you actually get. The major networks are easy to find, however: CBS on Channel 2, NBC on Channel 4, Fox on 5, ABC on 7, and PBS on 13.

Public Accommodations

The *Unofficial Guides* are starting to get a reputation for worrying about rest rooms or, rather, about your being able to find them. This is a, uh, tribute to the relatively short staying power of our founder, Bob Sehlinger, and someday we'll stop teasing him about it. But he has a good point; being uncomfortable doesn't help you enjoy a walking tour or a museum. And especially in summer, when New York can be so hot, it's tempting to drink a lot. (When on a vacation is it not tempting to drink a lot?)

New York is experimenting with the automated kiosks familiar to European travelers, and you will spot them—they look something like circular phone booths—in City Hall Park and other public gathering spots. However, it is best to ask yourself the same question you ask the kids—Are you sure you don't have to go?—before you go, because the good rest rooms are not always easy to spot.

There are plenty of rest rooms in the transportation terminals, such as Grand Central and Penn Station, which are much cleaner and safer than they used to be; the large theaters (though most lobbies will be inaccessible during the day) and museums have them, too, but the lines can be rather long. In Central Park, look for the rest rooms near the Delacorte Theater at 79th Street; and there are public facilities behind the New York Public Library in Bryant Park on Sixth Avenue and 42nd Street. Castle Clinton in Battery Park is nice and not usually crowded. The nearby Robert Wagner Park facility is even better. Big tourist centers such as the Chelsea Piers development, department stores, and malls are good bets, though the quality varies with the age and general atmosphere (in the

Manhattan Mall, check the seventh floor). The large hotel lobbies have rest rooms, of course, although you should only take advantage of them in an emergency and when you are reasonably well dressed. If you are really in a pinch, go to a bar and at least order a soda before you hit the john.

How to Avoid Crime and Keep Safe in Public Places

Okay, let's face it. New York is not the sort of place where you can leave your door open. But you don't need a false bottom on your boot heel for your credit cards, either. All you need is a little common sense.

For many years, New York's "mean streets" were the national symbol of America's crime problem. Statistics were big; headlines were bigger. TV police shows and legal procedurals, series after series of precinct crime novels, and big-name movies played on that reputation. It wasn't organized crime that began to worry out-of-towners (although it did produce even more famous movie characters), or professional burglars, or con men; it was the independent and unpredictable punk, the street hood, the drug addict who might corner you on the subway or go "wilding" with his friends like the kids who gang-raped, beat, and left comatose a runner in Central Park.

But all of a sudden, in the last few years, the word *crime* is back on New Yorkers' lips—and they're smiling. Although analysts and politicians argue over who gets the credit, it is clear that crime has been sharply reduced in recent years. Homicide is at its lowest rate in three decades. Subway crime has been curtailed to an amazing degree: Robberies on the system, the threat of which formerly made late-night or solo travel worrisome, are down fully 80% since the beginning of the 1990s. (Intriguingly, transit police have demonstrated that one out of every six fare-evaders is either carrying a weapon or already has an outstanding warrant against him, so try to spot someone with a MetroCard and stick close.) And in one of those strange psychological victories, the renovation of many subway stations is improving users' attitudes toward the system; littering is down, on-board soliciting has nearly disappeared (except for the occasional itinerant musician or candy-seller), and the level of civility, as the president would say, has greatly increased.

One of the most obvious changes is around Times Square, once the byword for X-rated urban sleaze and now the site of a frenetic rebuilding and restoration movement. Crime is no longer much of an issue in the area, although the crowding and milling about does make some pick-pocketing possible.

Similarly, many of the neighborhoods that were once a little questionable after dark, especially in the southern part of Manhattan around Tribeca or Chelsea, are now busy with restaurants and young urban dwellers. Perhaps you still don't want to hang around the northern stretch of Central Park at night, and it never hurts to carry Mace or pepper spray and a strong whistle; but a reasonable amount of street smarts should keep you in good health.

Most of Manhattan is pretty safe during the day, but after dark you should stick to the more populated streets. Don't leave a lot of money or traveler's checks in your hotel room, even though the employees are probably dependable. And if you buy any valuables of the sort that can be easily pawned, such as silver, gems, or electronics, ask the hotel to lock them in the safe.

Ripoffs and Scams

A lively street scene is a veritable incubator for ripoffs and scams. Although pickpockets, scam artists, and tricksters work throughout Manhattan, they are particularly thick in the bus and train terminals, along Broadway and Seventh Avenue near Times Square, and along 42nd Street between Grand Central Station and the Port Authority Terminal. Although some of the scams are relatively harmless, others can be costly as well as dangerous.

Do not, repeat, *do not* carry your wallet and valuables in a fanny pack. Thieves can easily snip the belt and disappear into the crowd before you realize what's happened. Front pockets are safer than back pockets or suitcoat pockets, though with a little effort, pickpockets can get at front pockets, too. The safest place to carry valuables is under your arm in a shoulder-holster-style pouch.

Part Five

Getting around
New York

Taxis

When it comes to taxicabs, Manhattan is the land of plenty, a revelation for tourists from towns where you have to reserve one in advance. The main thoroughfares sometimes look like rivers of yellow, with four and five lanes of cabs whipping along. The New York City Taxi and Limousine Commission licenses and regulates the yellow "medallioned" taxis ("medallioned" refers to the illuminated light on top of the cab), and there are currently more than 12,000 Yellow Cabs alone. These taxis must be hailed on the street—in other words, you cannot call them on the phone to pick you up.

There is little trick to hailing one: First make sure you're not on a one-way street trying to wave somebody down on the wrong side. (This happens more often than you'd think.) Then stand at the edge of the curb—try not to walk out into traffic unless you're blocked by parked vehicles, and even then be very careful—and raise your arm high. You don't need to wave it about frantically unless you're in an emergency: Cabbies have a sort of radar. If you feel a little awkward at first pay a visit to the corner of Park Avenue and 49th Street; there you will find a J. Seward Johnson bronze of a very harried salaryman semaphoring for a cab in a sort of urban despair. It's rude to cut off someone who's already signaling by getting downstream (though it happens); however, you may approach a cab that's letting someone else out and wait by the open door.

To avoid unnecessary frustration, realize that in New York, unlike some other cities, passengers are guaranteed a private ride. That is, the cabbie cannot just veer over and see if you happen to be going in the same direction the first passenger is, and then pop you in the front seat. So don't swear at cabs with shadowy figures in the back. Of course, if there are several in your party who get in together, you can drop off some riders before others. Also note that the cab is not on duty unless the little light in the middle of the rooftop sign—the "medallion" that proves the cab is legit—is lit: If the yellow one in the middle that reads "off duty" is lit, he or she is headed home.

If you're staying at one of the nicer hotels, there is likely to be a doorman available to whistle a cab up for you. This also allows for a bit of cheating if you are a little timid or loaded down. You can walk into the hotel lobby from one entrance and pass through to the other side and, looking as though you just left your room, ask the doorman there to hail you one.

If you are not encumbered by luggage and the like, you can save yourself some time and money by walking to the closest one-way street heading in your direction and hailing a cab there. In a similar vein, if you find yourself gridlocked in a cab within a block or two of your destination, go ahead and pay your fare and proceed on foot.

Many New York cabbies speak only marginal English. You can expect them to be familiar with major hotels, train and bus terminals, and major attractions. For more obscure destinations or addresses, you will do yourself (and the cabbie) a favor by writing down the exact address where you want to go.

Once inside the cab, you should make sure the driver's license with photograph and name are clearly displayed on the passenger side visor. This is required for your protection in case of disagreement (for complaints, contact the Taxi and Limousine commission at (212) 221-8294). It doesn't hurt to notice the number, either, in case you leave something behind; perhaps then you can get the dispatcher to send the cab to your hotel.

In our experience, New York cabbies usually take the most direct route to any given destination. Sometimes there is a little fudging, as when a driver circles an entire block to deliver you to a corner address on a one-way street, but in the main you can count on cabbies to keep it short and simple. If you prefer, you can specify the route you want your driver to take, and sometimes on longer fares the cabbie will actually ask if you have a preference. Still, many New York first-timers are a bit paranoid about cabbies taking them for a ride. In particular, LaGuardia Airport to Midtown via the Triborough Bridge arouses suspicions, though it is a perfectly acceptable route.

In addition to the medallion on the roof, a legitimate cab will have an automatic receipt machine mounted on the dashboard so that you can get an immediate record. (Fares begin at $2, and the meter ticks over $0.30 for each fifth of a mile, or $0.20 per minute of standing time; there's a dark-hours surcharge of $0.50, and passengers are responsible for tolls.)

If you are making two stops—as when you are picking someone else up at one location and proceeding somewhere else—you need to tell the cabbie this. After you get in the cab, simply say, "Two stops," and provide your destinations in order. This lets the cabbie know not to turn off the meter when you reach the first destination.

Don't be surprised if your cabbie drives fast and aggressively. More often than not, you will feel like an extra in a movie chase scene as you careen through the concrete canyons, weaving in and out of traffic. The good news is that these guys are excellent drivers. The other good news is that cabs now have seat belts in the back.

Although cabs range throughout Manhattan and the boroughs, they are most plentiful in Midtown. If you find yourself below Canal Street after business hours or on a weekend, for example, finding an empty yellow medallioned taxi cruising down the street may be a challenge. Your alternative is to phone one of the many companies listed under "Taxicab Service" in the Yellow Pages. Although these companies are also licensed by the Taxi and Limousine Commission, their cars will probably not be yellow or have a medallion. Some companies dispatch cars on demand 24 hours a day, seven days a week, but others require advance arrangements. Fares, as you would expect, are generally higher than those of metered, yellow, medallioned cabs. Late at night, in bad weather, and/or in isolated areas, however, phoning for a taxi is a safer and less stressful option than trusting to luck on the street. For the lowest fares ask your concierge, hotel desk clerk, or restaurant maitre d' for a recommendation before hauling out the Yellow Pages. When you call, tell the dispatcher where you want the car to pick you up and where you are going, and ask to be quoted a fare. Almost all of the car-on-demand companies accept credit cards. As always, tips and tolls are extra.

Now, as to illicit taxis. New York has a lot of limousines and luxury cars because of all its executives and celebrities. Consequently, it also has a lot of chauffeurs with time on their hands. So frequently, when you are standing on the street trying to hail a cab—and this is particularly true if you are a woman or if it is clearly theater-rush or dinner time and you look a little harried—a nice-looking sedan or town car may pull over and the driver offer to take you to your destination. These are sometimes referred to as gypsy cabs; although few of them pose a threat in the sense that they are unlikely to kidnap you, they will almost certainly want to charge you a very hefty fee. If it's raining or snowing or you're really late, or you really want to make an entrance, you might want to take him up on it. Just be prepared to pay the fee—and realize that you won't have any legal complaint if you're ripped off.

The Subway

One of the first things that you notice about New York is the snarled traffic. But underground, far removed from the cursing, horn blowing, and bumper-to-bumper slog of the mean streets, is a fast, efficient subway system 250 miles in toto and carrying 3.5 million passengers 24 hours every day. Learn a little about how it operates and you will be able to get around New York quickly and affordably. The key to the city is just beneath the sidewalk, and it will set you free. For an online introduction visit **nycsubway.org** or **www.mta.nyc.ny.us.**

The Subway vs. Cabs

We recommend cabs whenever you are encumbered by luggage, multiple shopping bags, or anything large you must haul around. Cabs are also preferred for getting around in the evening after rush-hour traffic has abated and after 11 p.m. or so for safety reasons. If there are two or more in your party and you are heading to different destinations, sharing a cab makes more sense than taking the subway. Another good time to take a cab, provided you can find one, is when it's raining or snowing.

From 6:30 a.m. until about 7 p.m. on weekdays, New York streets and avenues are insanely congested. This is the time that the subway really shines. While cabs are stuck for three changes of the same traffic signal trying to crawl through a single intersection, the subways are zipping efficiently along. Plus, the subway is much less expensive.

Will the subway save you time? Maybe; it depends. With the subway, you must walk to the closest station, wait for the train, ride to your destination station, and then walk to wherever you're going. If you are traveling a relatively long distance, say 35 blocks or more, during business hours on a weekday, the subway will beat the cab about 60% of the time. If you are traveling a shorter distance, or if you must transfer on the subway to reach your destination, the cab will probably be faster. On weekends, when the streets are less congested and when trains run less frequently, the primary rationale for using the subway is to save money.

This latter, saving money, is no small potatoes. With fare and tip, the shortest cab ride will cost you about $5, compared to $2 on the subway. When we work in New York, we almost always use the subway, allowing enough time between meetings to walk to and from the stations and to wait for the train.

Finally, the subways do not run particularly close to the far east or the far west sides of the island. Thus, subway travel to such destinations as the Javits Center, the Passenger Ship Terminal, or the United Nations is not recommended.

Subway Basics

The New York subway system is one of the world's largest; almost 700 miles of track connect the four boroughs of Manhattan, the Bronx, Brooklyn, and Queens. There are close to 500 stations, so you are likely to find one near where you want to go.

The nexus of the system is the complex of stations and routes below Central Park extending to the southern tip of Manhattan Island. Though service to other areas of Manhattan and the outlying boroughs is more than adequate, this Midtown and Downtown ganglion of routes, connections, and stops provides the most frequent and flexible level of service that you are likely to find in any American city.

Safety

Once the butt of talk-show jokes, the New York subway system is now clean, scoured of (most) graffiti, and well policed. While not quite as secure as Disneyland, subway travel does not represent much of a risk. Muggings and violent crime are extremely rare these days, though riders on crowded trains and in crowded stations should continue to be alert for pickpockets.

In recent years, many stations have been renovated to include various kinds of artwork—murals, paintings, even mosaics—reflecting neighborhood attractions. The station at 81st Street near the Museum of Natural History has mosaics of reptiles, birds, butterflies, sharks, scorpions, and the like. In the Times Square station are murals by Jacob Lawrence and Jack Beal. Houston Street station shows a man sitting on a bench reading a newspaper while a whale kibbitzes over his shoulder. Alice—she of the "Adventures Underground"—and her Mad company are in evidence at 50th Street. Coffee cups and poetry come together beneath Bloomingdales, and 100 eyes, like Argus's, peer out at Chambers Street travelers.

From 6 a.m. until 11 p.m. or so, you can ride the subway with no more concern for your personal safety than you feel on the streets during business hours. After 11 p.m. it's wise to use the special "Off-Hours Waiting Areas" that are monitored by subway security. When the train arrives, we suggest that you ride in the same car as the train's conductor (usually one of the middle cars).

Any time of day, if you are carrying packages, a briefcase, or luggage, sit as far from the doors as possible. A favorite ploy of thieves is to grab the purse or package of a person sitting near a door and escape onto the platform just as the doors are closing.

Finding the Subway

An indispensable aid to locating stations and understanding the subway system is the New York City Transit Subway Map. The map shows all routes and stations and offers helpful information about fares and frequency of service, among other things. Once you know the address of your New York hotel, you can use the subway map to plan your travel around town. You can arrange to have a map mailed to you at home by calling Subway Travel Information at (718) 330-1234 (open 24 hours), or you can begin to familiarize yourself with the routes by logging onto **www.mta.nyc.ny.us.** If you forget to request a map before traveling to New York, you can usually pick one up at the airports, Penn Station, Grand Central Station, or the Port Authority Terminal. Some hotel front desks and concierges also stock a supply of maps. If all else fails, the

NYNEX Manhattan Yellow Pages book includes complete color maps of both the subway system and Manhattan bus routes; you'll find them at the beginning of the book.

If you are on the streets of Manhattan without a subway map, look for the lighted globes (about the size of bowling balls) that mark most subway entrances. A green globe means the subway entrance is open and staffed 24 hours a day. A red (or red and white) globe indicates that the entrance is open only during hours posted above the station. Some of the larger subway entrances are accessed through buildings. The majority of these have good street signage, although a few do not. Along similar lines, you may exit the subway at a station where the exits lead into a building, as opposed to directly back on the street. If this happens, simply exit the building and from there proceed to the nearest street corner to regain your orientation.

In Midtown and Downtown where various lines converge, there may be several stations located close together. The subway map will help you sort the stations out. If you don't have a map, descend into the closest station and check the system map displayed on the wall.

Reading the Subway Map

Each subway line is shown in a different color. Though some lines diverge into separate routes above Central Park in Manhattan and in the boroughs, they bear the color of the trunk (main) line. Each of the diverging routes is designated by a letter or number displayed in a circle or diamond of the same color. Terminals (ends of the line) are indicated by squares for normal service routes and diamonds for rush-hours-only routes.

The Lexington Avenue line, for example, is represented in green. Four routes—the 4-Circle, 5-Diamond, 5-Circle, and 6-Circle—originate in the Bronx and are likewise depicted in green. The routes converge in

Manhattan, where all four follow Lexington Avenue (from which the line takes its name). The end of the line for 6-Circle is City Hall, and the end for 5-Circle is Bowling Green, both in the Downtown tip of the island. 4-Circle and 5-Diamond cross out of Manhattan and head east into Brooklyn. 4-Circle terminates at Utica Avenue, and 5-Diamond ends at Flatbush Avenue. In this example we followed the routes south (downtown) from the Bronx. If we boarded the 5-Diamond subway at Flatbush Avenue and headed north (uptown), we would converge with the other green lines in lower Manhattan, follow Lexington Avenue north, and diverge at 138th Street to cross into the Bronx. If we stayed on to the end of the line, we would wind up at 241st Street in the Bronx.

Stations are represented on the map by:

Each station's name is shown in bold type. Station names are usually streets or avenues—for example, the Houston Street Station on the Red Line is shown on the map as **Houston St.** Some stations, however, have place names, such as **Penn Station** or **Times Square.**

Underneath the station name, the map shows which routes stop at that particular station. If the station is wheelchair accessible, the visual wheelchair graphic will be printed alongside the station name.

The 23rd Street Station on the Eighth Avenue (because the line follows Eighth Avenue) Blue Line looks like this on the map:

23 Street
C-E

This means that the C-Circle Train and the E-Circle Train both stop at this station. The A-Circle Train, which also runs on the Blue Line, does not stop here. If it did, the station would look like this:

23 Street
A-C-E

You might see a station where some of the routes are not depicted in bold, such as:

72 Street
1-2-3-9

This means that the 1-Circle, 2-Circle, and 3-Circle trains offer regular service but that the 9-Circle train only provides part-time service, in this case during rush hours Monday through Friday (you need the subway route chart for this last piece of information).

Where certain lines meet or come close to meeting, you will see little symbols that look like this:

This means that there is a pedestrian walkway or tunnel that connects two or more stations, thus allowing riders to transfer to other lines without exiting and reentering the subway system.

Fares

It costs $2 to ride the subway. (There is no charge for children under 44 inches in height.) Tokens are no longer accepted; you must buy a Metro-Card. A MetroCard looks like a credit card. Available at subway stations and at over 2,000 neighborhood stores, the MetroCard can be purchased in any amount from $2 (a single ride) to $80. (It's more economical to get at least $10 worth at a time; each five rides come with a free bonus sixth.) Each time you ride the subway you swipe your card—back to front, with the stripe facing you—through a little electronic reader on the right side of the turnstile. The electronic reader reads the amount of credit you have on the card and deducts $2 for every ride. When you use your card, your balance is displayed on the turnstile. All the accounting is maintained electronically, so there's no way to tell the fare credit remaining by looking at the card. If you want to check your balance, there are "reader" machines at most stations that will show the card's current balance without deducting anything. It is not necessary to get a new card when your balance gets low: All you have to do is take the card to a fare booth and pay to have your balance increased. When you buy a card or pay to increase your balance, always run your card through the reader (before you leave the fare window) to make sure your purchase was properly recorded. MetroCards expire after one year, but any amount remaining on the card can be transferred to a new card. For additional information on the MetroCard, call (212) METROCARD.

An even better bargain is the one-day, unlimited-ride MetroCard, which costs $7 (so after only four rides in a day you're already ahead); and which is good until 3 a.m. the morning after it's activated, so you can really see the town. Seven-day, unlimited-ride MetroCards cost $21, and if you're in town for the long haul, 30-day cards cost $70. In addition to being available anywhere regular MetroCards are sold, you can also buy these prepackaged cards at Hudson News and many drugstores.

Admittedly, we are not great fans of New York City buses, but you should know that with MetroCard you can transfer free from subway to bus, bus to subway, or bus to bus. You must use your MetroCard to start your trip and must make your transfer within two hours. Transfers from subway to subway are also free, with or without the MetroCard, as long as you do not exit the system. However, again, the unlimited-ride MetroCards are bargains, as they can be used for the buses all day as well as the subway.

Finally, be aware that the card was designed for New Yorkers, who, of course, are always in a hurry. In practical terms, this means you have to swipe your card fast! If you ease it through the turnstile device at a more leisurely tempo, it won't work. When in Rome . . .

Riding the Subway: A Primer

Looking at your subway map (or at one of the large poster-sized subway maps on display in the stations), try to locate the stations closest to your starting point and to your destination. If the station closest to your starting point does not offer service in the general direction you'll be going, check to see whether there are any other stations reasonably close by that do. Try to find a subway route that requires no transfers. It is generally faster to get within a few blocks of your destination on the subway and then cover the remaining distance on foot than it is to make a transfer. As a rule of thumb, it takes less than two minutes to walk the short blocks between streets. Walking crosstown, you can cover the long blocks between avenues in four to five minutes each.

Check to see which trains stop at stations you have identified. In general, the more trains, the better. Make sure that trains that stop at your departure station also stop at your destination station.

Almost all trains except the 7-Circle Flushing Local and the L-Circle 14th Street Canarsie Local (cross-town trains) travel generally north/south, or, in subway-speak, uptown (north) and downtown (south). Traveling on the subway is immensely simplified if you can determine whether you are traveling uptown or downtown.

If you want to go crosstown (east or west), you may need to know where the train terminates. Let's say you want to go from the west side to the east side on the E-Circle train. The signs for this train will not say "crosstown"; they will say "Jamaica/Queens," indicating the train's final destination. If you know (or learn by looking at the subway map) that this train travels cross-town en route to the borough of Queens, you will know to board in the direction of "Jamaica/Queens" to reach your crosstown destination. Incidentally, most trains that run cross-town also run part of their route north/south. Thus, signs for the E-Circle train may read "Uptown–Jamaica/Queens" or "Downtown–World Trade Center."

When you approach the station, there may be one or multiple entrances. If there is only one entrance, proceed inside and follow the signs directing you to the Uptown or Downtown train platforms, whichever applies. If you are standing at a street intersection and there is a subway entrance on all four corners, or on both sides of an avenue, the entrance(s) on the west side of the avenue will lead to Downtown platforms, and the entrance(s) on the east side of the street will lead to Uptown platforms. Normally there is good signage at the entrances identifying the line, trains (routes), and direction that the particular entrance serves. Usually, because you do not have to swipe your MetroCard until you are within spitting distance of the platform, you can verify that you have chosen the correct entrance by checking the signage on the platform. If you want to travel uptown and you descend to a platform that reads "Downtown," do not pass through the turnstiles. Instead, return to the street, cross the avenue, and descend to the Uptown platform.

Though most stations are served by only one line, there are a number of stations, particularly in Midtown and Downtown, that are served by several lines. What you have here, essentially, is a sort of double- or even triple-decker station. With these stations it's a little more complicated than uptown versus downtown. At these multiline stations you may have a choice of lines going uptown and downtown as well as, possibly, some cross-town lines. If you start your trip at one of these stations, locate the system map near the entrance and determine exactly which line you need and which direction you want to go. Armed with this knowledge, follow the signs to the correct platform.

Be aware that in the larger stations you may have to pay and go through the turnstiles before you get anywhere near the train platforms. Don't worry. The inside signage is good, and there are interior passages that will allow you to correct your mistake if you end up on the wrong platform.

Once on the platform, double-check the signs, and if necessary recheck the system map. The platform sign will show the trains that stop at that platform, indicate their direction (usually uptown or downtown), and specify the terminal (end of the line) for each route.

Sometimes a single waiting platform will serve two tracks. Trains arriving on one side of the platform will go in one direction, and trains on the other side will go in the opposite direction. If you descended a long way or had to navigate a spiraling stairwell, you may arrive on the platform somewhat disoriented. Check the signage to determine the correct direction for your travel. If the signs don't help, simply ask another waiting passenger.

If there are several trains that stop at both your departure and destination stations, you can take your choice. If you are going a relatively short distance (30 blocks or less), go ahead and hop on the first train that comes along. If it's a "local," it will make a lot of stops, but you will still probably arrive sooner than if you waited for an express. If you are going a long way, you may want to hold out for an express train.

When the train comes into the station, it will be well marked. The A-Circle train on the Eighth Avenue Blue Line, for example, will sport big blue circles with the letter A inside. The conductor usually rides in the middle of the train and will usually stick his head out of the window when the train stops. If you are really confused, ask him if the train goes to your destination station.

You've probably seen film footage of people crowding on and battling off subways. Although this does sometimes occur at the height of rush hour in the larger stations, usually things are much more civil. When the train stops, approach the door and wait for it to open. Allow passengers getting off to disembark, then step into the car. The conductor observes the loading process, so unless you're trying to leap on or off at the last second (not recommended), you shouldn't have to worry about getting caught in a closing door.

Once inside, take a seat if there is one available. If you are still a little confused, you will find a system map displayed on the wall of the car. Check the next scheduled stop for the direction you wish to travel. When the train pulls in, verify by the signs on the platform that you are traveling in the right direction. If you have mistakenly boarded the right train in the wrong direction, wait until the train stops at one of the larger stations where transfers are optional. These larger stations have internal passages that will allow you to cross over to the right platform without leaving the system and having to pay again to reenter.

Buses

In addition to being subject to all the problems that afflict Manhattan surface traffic, buses are slow, make innumerable stops, and have difficulty maneuvering. Even so, there are several good reasons to use public bus service. After 11 p.m. buses are safer than walking if you are not up to springing for a cab. Some buses, like the 1, 5, 6, 10, and 15, run very interesting routes and are a dirt-cheap option for sight-seeing (ride on weekends, when traffic is less problematic). Though subways excel in north/south, uptown/downtown service, there is less crosstown (east/west) subway service than one would hope (especially since no subways cross beneath Central Park). Buses fill this public transportation gap, running a goodly number of crosstown routes. You can get a vague idea of the bus's destination by noticing the initial that precedes the route number: "M" for Manhattan, "Q" for Queens, "B" for Brooklyn, and "Bx" for the Bronx. That's "up," remember? Finally, of course, buses are inexpensive to ride, especially with the MetroCard, which allows bus-to-bus, bus-to-subway, and subway-to-bus transfers. Maps of Manhattan bus routes can be found in the front of the NYNEX Manhattan Yellow Pages. MTA buses cost $2 and require either exact change or a MetroCard. For more information, check out **www.mta.nyc.ny.us.**

Walking

New York is a great town for walking. Like most cities, it has neighborhoods that are not ideally suited for an evening stroll, but these are easily avoided. If you observe a few precautions and exercise some common sense, you will find the sidewalks of New York not only interesting and exhilarating but also quite hospitable.

As you begin to explore, you will find that the blocks between the east/west streets are quite short. Thus, walking south (toward Downtown) on Seventh Avenue, most folks will be able to cover the blocks from 59th Street to 49th Street in about 12 minutes, even assuming a wait for traffic at several intersections. Crossing town from east to west (or vice versa), the blocks are much longer. A walk from First Avenue to Tenth Avenue along 42nd Street is a real hike, requiring more than 30 minutes for most people.

If you want to try a restaurant eight blocks away, and the address is north or south of where you are, you won't even need a cab. If the restaurant is eight blocks away across town (east/west), take a subway or hail a taxi.

If you become disoriented during a walk, proceed to the nearest street corner and see what the street is (as opposed to an avenue). Then walk one additional short block in either direction. If the next cross street is higher in number, you are heading north (uptown). East will be to your right, and west to your left. If the next cross street is lower in number, then you are walking south. East will be to your left, and west to your right.

Let's say, for example, that you just emerged from a subway station on the Avenue of the Americas (also called Sixth Avenue) and are not sure which way's which. Walking to the nearest corner, you discover that you are at the intersection of 24th Street and the Avenue of the Americas. You continue one more block on Avenue of the Americas and reach 23rd Street. You now know that you are going south and that First through Fifth Avenues are to your left (east) and that Seventh through Eleventh Avenues are to your right (west).

Or you can go by the traffic: Fifth, Park, and Lexington avenues are one-way streets going south; Park, Madison, and Third go north. Seventh and Broadway go south; Eighth goes north until it becomes Central Park West, when it is two-way (but of course, you can see the park from there anyway), and so on.

Because there is no better or more direct way to experience New York than to explore it on foot, we recommend that you do as much hoofing as your time and stamina permit. To help you organize your walking, we include several walking tours (guided and self-guided) in Part Seven, Sight-seeing, Tours, and Attractions.

Part Six

New York's Neighborhoods

The Sidewalks of New York

Now that you've decided which parts of the city you're most interested in seeing, it's time to hit the road. Actually, you can use the following neighborhood descriptions as armchair tours, and if you don't have time to see more than a little of the city this time, you might enjoy reading about the rest to see how all the pieces fit together.

The profiles in this chapter are designed to convey a little of the geographical layout, historical relevance, tourist attractions, chronological development, and general character of the neighborhoods—they're overviews to help you grasp the spirit of the area. We have included some phone numbers, but not all. Most of the buildings mentioned here are public structures, important for their exteriors; if they have particularly stunning lobbies, they will probably be open to the public during general office hours. Similarly, most churches welcome visitors, but a few smaller or older churches (or those with valuable antiques) may ask that you make an appointment to visit. In any case, apply common sense and courtesy; be quiet for the sake of those using the premises for its original purposes, and try not to interrupt religious services.

Some museums or collections may charge admission or ask for donations. Most will be closed on major holidays. (Remember, too, that Jewish museums and houses will probably be closed at least half a day Friday and all day Saturday.) A few of the most important historical buildings, museums, and landmarks in each zone are described in detail in Part Seven, Sight-seeing, Tours, and Attractions.

Zone I: Lower Manhattan, Wall Street, and the Battery

Always a major tourist area because of the **Statue of Liberty** and the view from the World Trade Center tower, lower Manhattan has become an even more emotionally powerful destination since the Trade Center was blasted off the skyline by the hijacked jetliners. And that is entirely appropriate, as New York's historical and spiritual footprint is at the tip of the island. The area below Chambers Street is the original New York—Nieuw Amsterdam, the port "bought" from the natives, and the village occupied by the British for virtually the entire Revolutionary War. The colonial administrators lived in the mansion on **Governors Island** out in the harbor; **Castle Clinton** (phone (212) 344-7220) on the west side of the Battery raised 28 cannon against the threat of invaders in 1811 (and a few years later became an entertainment venue). The Declaration of Independence was read aloud on the **Bowling Green** on July 9, 1776; the crowd then pulled down the statue of King George III that had stood there for almost half a century and melted it down into ammunition. George Washington prayed here, in the simplicity of **St. Paul's Chapel** on Broadway (phone (212) 602-0872); he bade farewell to his officers here, on the site of the **Fraunces Tavern Museum** at Pearl and Broad Streets (phone (212) 425-1778); he was sworn in as the first president here as well, on the site of what is now the Greek Revival **Federal Hall National Memorial** at 26 Wall Street (phone (212) 825-6888), probably just as the bronze statue on the steps there suggests.

The other thing to remember, though, is just how very small that original city was, not nearly so large even as this one zone. Nearly a third of it—including the entire **Battery Park** area and the eastern strip from Pearl Street to the East River, including the Franklin Roosevelt Drive and **South Street Seaport** areas—was actually constructed from landfill after the War of 1812. **Wall Street,** literally a wooden wall built in 1653, was the northern border of Nieuw Amsterdam; and even in colonial times the town was only 10 blocks square, counting the Bowling Green—which in those days really was one. It had an estimated population of only 20,000.

It wasn't until the early decades of the 19th century that the lawyers and stockbrokers had so taken hold of the Financial District that residences began to be built farther north. In fact, when **City Hall** was constructed in 1811, a little more than half a mile up Broadway, it was considered so far out of town that the north face was covered in brownstone instead of marble because city officials never expected anyone to view it from that side.

Nowadays, Lower Manhattan is one of the most fascinating areas of the city, still the financial capital of the nation—the **Federal Reserve Bank** (phone (212) 720-6130) on Liberty Street, the **New York Stock Exchange** (phone (212) 656-5165) at Broad and Wall Streets, the **American Stock Exchange** on Trinity Place (phone (212) 306-1000), and the **Mercantile Exchange** (1 North End Avenue; (212) 299-2000)—and, for so relatively young a city, very nearly the financial capital of the world. The various bank buildings along Wall Street and around the Exchange are New York's version of the Forum in Rome, veritable temples of finance.

From City Hall Park and the courthouse complex at the "north pole" of the neighborhood to Battery Park on the south, the **Fulton Fish Market** and **South Street Seaport** (phone (212) 748-8600) on the east and the glorious **Trinity Church** (phone (212) 602-0872) going eye-to-eye with Wall Street—God and Mammon in daily competition—it covers far and away the greatest range of New York history of any single region. From here the soaring **Brooklyn Bridge** joins Manhattan to one sibling borough; the **Staten Island Ferry** to a second; and Broadway, which runs all the way from Bowling Green to the Bronx, to a third.

This original Manhattan contains memorials ranging through New York's history, from its first sighting (the **Verrazano Monument** in the southwest corner of Battery Park) to its military heroes (the **New York Korean War Veterans Memorial** and **Coast Guard** tribute, both on the Battery, and the **Vietnam Veterans Plaza,** a simple glass-block fountain between Water and South Streets). The **New York City Police Museum,** with its collection of badges and weapons dating to 1658 and its third-floor tribute to 9/11 heroics, has moved into the old First Precinct station on Old Slip Street (phone (212) 480-3100). One site even exposes 400 years of city life—the **New York Unearthed** permanent archeological exhibit at State and Water Streets (phone (212) 748-8628). And just at water's edge is the new **Skyscraper Museum.**

This is also a good area to remember the melting pot of Manhattan history. The flagpole in **Peter Minuit Plaza,** a sort of corner of Battery Park near the ferry building, salutes the courage of New York's first Jewish immigrants, who had been caught up in the Portuguese-Dutch wars and were harried back and forth between Europe and Brazil, attacked by pirates, and finally carried to Nieuw Amsterdam, where they were allowed to settle in 1626. Another plaque salutes the 32 Belgian Hugenots who were turned away by the virulently anti-Catholic British in Virginia but allowed to land by the Dutch East India Company in 1724. The sculpture near Castle Clinton, with its eager arms and hopeful postures, is a tribute to the spirit of the millions of immigrants who landed here. The pair of circa-1800 townhouses at State and Water Streets were the family home of, and are now a shrine to, **"Mother" Elizabeth Ann Seton** (phone (212) 269-6865), the first American-born saint of the Catholic Church; it was also, appropriately, a home for immigrant Irish women, sheltering as many as 170,000 after the Civil War. And the recently discovered **African Burial Ground** near Broadway and Chambers Streets dates back at least to the 18th century and, archeologists say, quite likely to the 17th, a reminder that the labor of slaves, as well as so many others, built this city.

Perhaps the final addition to this minitour of New York history is the battered "world sphere" sculpture rescued from the ruins of the World Trade Center, that originally (ironically) represented global peace. The sculpture's temporary home here is also marked by an eternal flame.

Two museums remind us to remember the "forgotten peoples": the **National Museum of the American Indian** within the fine Beaux Arts **U.S. Custom House** (phone (212) 514-3700) at Broadway and Bowling Green; and the **Museum of Jewish Heritage—A Living Memorial to the Holocaust** in Battery Park City (phone (212) 968-1800). And it is from here, of course, that most visitors look to the **Statue of Liberty** (phone (212) 363-3200) and the **Ellis Island Museum of Immigration** (phone (212) 363-3200), perhaps the most lasting memorials to the American spirit anywhere.

Also out in the harbor is the 172-acre **Governors Island,** site of the 1988 Reagan-Gorbachev meetings, which has recently been returned to New York's possession after having been sold to the federal government for $1 in 1800. Summertime tours are available from Ferry Slip 7, visit **www.governorsislandnationalmonument.org** for information.

If you are interested in monumental views in architectural terms, be sure to walk up Broadway to **City Hall Park** and admire the elegant municipal buildings, including the French Renaissance **City Hall,** with its lobby murals, double hanging staircase, and exhibits of official gifts to the city; **Surrogate's Court** at Chambers and Centre, inspired by the Paris Opéra and arrayed with a pageant of sculpture and a neo-Egyptian mosaic ceiling in the lobby that, like Grand Central's, reproduces the zodiac; and the nearby court buildings of the **Civic Center,** especially the rotunda of 60 Centre Street, with its restored 1930s murals. Grab a snack from the park vendors while you're there. The statue of Benjamin Franklin at the south end of the park recalls a time when this stretch of Park Row was filled with newspaper presses, like London's Fleet Street.

Zone 2: Soho and Tribeca

Now that popular music and hip-industry logos have made odd capitalizations common, the names "Soho" and "Tribeca" don't stand out the way they used to. Both are purely physical descriptions, only in shorthand: Soho is SOuth of HOuston Street—it has nothing to do with the Soho of London—and Tribeca is an anagram for the TRIangle BElow CAnal, though it more closely resembles a slightly bottom-heavy diamond. (And note that Houston is pronounced "*house*-ton," not like the Texas city.)

Though it's now one of the two main art neighborhoods in the city, home to scores of galleries and the **New Museum of Contemporary Art** (Broadway between Houston and Prince; (212) 219-1222), Soho was largely rural until well after the turn of the 19th century. Remnants of the old Canarsie–Manate Indian tribe continued to live here throughout the Dutch and early British colonial eras. In the 18th century, it was largely farmland (like much of Manhattan) and country estates of the more prosperous residents. It was gradually consumed by townhouses after the turn of the 19th century; there is a four-block area at the north-central corner, bordered by Sixth Avenue, West Houston, and Varick and Vandam Streets, that is a historic district of its own; developed by John Jacob Astor in the late 1820s, it contains the city's largest concentration of Federal-style row houses.

But it came into its own in the mid-18th century, when the architectural movement sometimes called American Industrial—large, almost warehouse-sized spaces covered with pseudo-classical columns and cornices made of cast iron—swept in and transformed it into the light industrial and retail center of the city. It is still home to the largest concentration of cast-iron ornamentation in the city; and many of those oversized buildings have been transformed into art galleries, furniture display rooms, and even museums. The five cobblestone blocks of Greene Street from Canal to Houston are the centerpiece of the **Cast-Iron Historic District,** with more than 50 intact 19th-century buildings with façades in the neoclassical, Renaissance Revival, and Corinthian styles. The one at 72–76 Greene, a sort of duplex with a five-story Second Empire façade, is called the **"King of Greene Street."** The **"Queen of Greene,"** built by the same developer, Isaac Duckworth, is the mansard-roofed building at 28–30 Greene. (For more on this area, see "Great Neighborhoods for Shopping" in Part Nine.) The **New York City Fire Museum** at 278 Spring Street (phone (212) 691-1303) is the largest collection of antique firefighting equipment, engines, pumps, bells, and hydrants in the country.

Like Soho, Tribeca is a treasure trove of late–19th century commercial and industrial architecture: The cast iron and marble buildings along White, Franklin and Walker streets between Broadway and Church offer a quick tour, and the **Carey Building** at 105 Chambers Street is considered one of the finest examples of cast iron anywhere. Another can be found at **85 Leonard Street,** which was designed by cast-iron innovator James Bogardus.

And while you're in the neighborhood, check out the clock tower; you can actually climb the stairs and look out through the giant works.

Tribeca has become trendy more recently, and the shops are a little funkier still; but it has been getting a reputation (with good reason) as a restaurant and nightlife haven, possibly because of the many old and family-owned food/import businesses around. And thanks to the well-advertised presence of actor Robert De Niro, part-owner of such hotspots as the **Tribeca Grill** and **Nobu,** as well as restaurants from chefs David Bouley and David Waltuck (**Chanterelle**), Tribeca is developing a certain celebrity population.

Zone 3: Chinatown, Little Italy, and the Lower East Side

Time was when these three ethnic neighborhoods were not just distinct, they were rigorously segregated. More recently, however, the outlines of the three have blurred and overlapped, and Little Italy in particular is being subsumed as Chinese businesses spill north of Canal Street and up alongside the long strip of **Sara Delano Roosevelt Park.** Chinese immigrants have been one of the fastest-growing communities in the city for several decades, and an estimated 175,000 now live in Chinatown alone. In addition, Chinatown is now far more broadly Asian. The signs and sounds of Vietnamese, Thai, and Indonesian society are almost as common as Chinese.

At the same time, the eastward gradual expansion of Soho chic, and even some neo-1960s-style hippie culture from the East Village to the north, is turning parts of even **Orchard Street,** the heart of Lower East Side bargain territory, into the latest bohemian and art-warehouse hangout. Hence the latest "neighborhood" nicknames, Nolita—North of Little Italy—and Dumbo, for "Down Under the Manhattan Bridge Overpass."

The first Chinese residents arrived on Mott Street in the mid–19th century, and Chinatown's history is as convoluted (or as romantic, depending on your outlook) as any Manhattan neighborhood's, dominated by family networks, community associations, and more serious criminal gangs, but all operating in so closed a circle as to be nearly invisible to outsiders. It has little architectural style in comparison to, say, San Francisco's Grant Avenue area; but it is full of street vendors (most selling cheap knockoffs, but highly popular in themselves), produce and fish markets, restaurants, and import shops. More popular in recent years are the herbal apothecaries—herbal pharmacies with remedies dating back thousands of years.

The **Museum of Chinese in the Americas** at Mulberry and Bayard Streets (phone (212) 619-4785) is small, but its collection of old photographs, business leases, and oral histories is first-class; you might also be able to piggyback onto one of the walking tours the museum sometimes arranges. The **Eastern States Buddhist Temple** on Mott near Canal houses more than 100 golden statues of the Enlightened One (phone (212) 966-6229), and Confucius stands in monumental contemplation in **Confucius Plaza** on the Bowery near Pell Street. Ironically, the nearby block of **Doyers Street,** which takes a sharp turn between the Bowery and Pell, is what was known as Chinatown's "Bloody Angle," back when the opium dealers lured rivals into ambush. Pell Street was also a center of Italian crime, apparently: A waiter and hopeful entertainer named Irving Berlin, who worked in a bar at 12 Pell Street, complained to his manager about the clientele and was promptly fired.

Columbus Park, a small green oasis south of Bayard Street more or less at the juncture of Little Italy and Chinatown, was once the heart of the Five Points slum, one of the city's largest gang havens and red-light districts. The jagged Art Moderne **Criminal Courts Building** nearby used to be the jail, the last one built before Riker's Island.

As indicated earlier, Little Italy is a shadow of its former self, except perhaps during the Feast of San Gennaro in the fall and when the old-timers gather to play bocce in **Roosevelt Park.** Its most famous address is **Mulberry Street.** (Its most infamous address is probably the Bowery, thanks to that street's role in the *Bowery Boys* serials.) Although they are now intermixed with Asian and Hispanic businesses, there are still blocks of delis and family restaurants stoop to stoop. **Old St. Patrick's Cathedral** at Mott and Prince (phone (212) 226-8075), begun in 1809, is still the parish church, although the big St. Patrick's uptown is now the archdiocesan seat.

Especially if you loved those old *Untouchables* shows, you must stop at **Ratner's** at Delancey and Norfolk (phone (212) 677-5588). The restaurant's back room, now the neo-cocktail Prohibition-swank **Lansky Lounge,** is where gangster Meyer Lansky used to have breakfast, sometimes with childhood pal Lucky Luciano; Bugsy Siegel made his first hit on the corner outside the door, and there's an alley entrance to the bar that rumor has it was the old speakeasy slip-in. And the sidewalk in front of **Umberto's Clam House** at Broome and Mulberry (phone (212) 431-7545) was the scene of "Crazy" Joey Gallo's last meal—and last breath—in 1973.

To give equal time to the "coppers," walk by the luxury apartment building at Grand and Centre Streets, with its Baroque clock-tower dome, stone friezes, and guardian lions; it used to be the police headquarters, and gazing up the front steps at the guard's desk, you can just imagine how impressive it must have been to be hauled up in front of the sergeant in the heyday of New York's Irish finest. And at Lafayette and Hester Streets is the **Engine Co. No. 31,** an 1895 gem that looks more like a French country castle than a firehouse (it's now a community TV and film center).

The Lower East Side, generally on the south side of East Houston from the Bowery east, was not particularly desirable land in the early decades of New York development because it was largely wetlands. It had served as temporary quarters for a series of the poorest immigrants, first Irish victims of the potato famine and then German farmers whose own potato crops were gradually infected, followed by periodic influxes of Turkish and Greek families. However, the most famous and lasting immigration began in the late 19th century, when as many as 1.6 million Eastern European Jews arrived, creating the neighborhood famous from photographs of tenement houses, sidewalk carts, and orthodox scholars. It was both a slum and a cultural haven (not an unusual paradox for a people used to ghettos), filled with synagogues, debating clubs, and community banks as well as vendors and sweatshops. (For more on this area, see "Great Neighborhoods for Shopping" in Part Nine.)

In recent years, the Lower East Side has made a concerted effort to turn itself into a historical as well as retail tourist attraction. The irony is that many of the Jewish families have moved up-island to the wealthier areas on either side of the park and out to Brooklyn, and large numbers of Hispanic, black, and Asian families have replaced them. Nevertheless, the creation of the **Lower East Side Tenement Museum** (phone (212) 431-0233) on Orchard Street, in addition to the more organized promotion of the many family-owned clothing stores in that neighborhood (hearkening back to its merchant origins) has brought it a certain revived prosperity. The 1887 Moorish Revival **Eldridge Street Synagogue** between Allen and Canal Streets (phone (212) 219-0888), with its lavish stained glass, carved detailing, and chandeliers, is being restored to its full beauty; oral histories are welcome, and there is also a minimuseum of Jewish life in America in the building. **Schapiro's House of Kosher and Sacramental Wines** at 126 Rivington Street (phone (212) 674-4404) is the last winery still in operation in the city; you can tour it (by appointment) or purchase consecrated wine.

Incidentally, this is a good area for bridge enthusiasts. Only about a mile separates three of New York's major interborough spans: the Brooklyn, Manhattan, and Williamsburg Bridges. The **Brooklyn Bridge,** the oldest of the three, bears traffic away from near City Hall Park just south of Chinatown. The **Manhattan Bridge,** which has lost its allegorical sculptures to the Brooklyn Museum of Art but still has its triumphal arch, takes off from Canal Street, and the **Williamsburg Bridge** from Delancey Street.

Zone 4: Greenwich Village

This is probably the most famous neighborhood in New York, known even to outsiders as "the Village" and symbol of the city's artistic and literary history. It had originally been covered with largish "country houses" belonging to the businessmen from downtown and smaller homes along the riverfront built by marine craftsmen and merchants before it was sold off and subdivided. (Herman Melville lived here as a child, working around the docks before shipping off with whalers, being shipwrecked, and thinking twice about his choice of career.)

Because it was largely developed in the late 19th century before the grid system was put in place—the regular grid actually begins at 14th Street, the northern border of the Village—it has a number of diagonals, triangles, and bends that newcomers sometimes find confusing. The part of Greenwich Village east of Sixth Avenue more regularly ascribes to the numbered-street system, but on the west side, most streets have names rather than numbers, and even those few numbers don't behave very predictably: West 4th Street, for example, seems to move in the usual cross-island direction beneath Washington Square, but almost immediately begins making a series of elbow shifts north, and by the time it gets to the top of the Village, it's nearly gone perpendicular.

Think of the Village map as the left half of an opened fan: The area between Broadway and Sixth Avenue would be the fan's center, with the avenues as fairly upright spines. Seventh Avenue spreads out a little, and beyond that, the main avenues—Hudson Street, Washington Street, and West Street along the Hudson River—all bend a little farther out. (Greenwich Street squiggles a little, like a bent feather, between Washington and Hudson.) By the time the side streets are filled in, you have a series of trapezoids and triangles; it may be hard to negotiate at first, but it gives the area a true village atmosphere.

Washington Square, at the foot of Fifth Avenue, was one of Manhattan's first prestigious residential neighborhoods. The park was established in 1828, and it was surrounded by fine Greek Revival townhouses; several of the oldest are still standing, as is the Stanford White–designed archway. Even the mayor's official residence was here, at No. 8 (the façade is real, but the rest is not). Brothers Henry and William James grew up in the neighborhood; Henry James's *Washington Square* was set at No. 18, where his grandmother lived. James himself, Edith Wharton, and William Dean Howells all lived at various times at No. 1; John Dos Passos was living at No. 3 when he wrote *Manhattan Transfer.* All of those have been razed. (The so-called **Hanging Elm** in the northwest corner, a last reminder of the public executions of the early 19th century, is still hanging in there, though.) Nowadays, the park is alive with NYU students, aspiring musicians, chess players, dogs on play dates, kids on playground dates, and, on summer evenings, the legendary free Shakespeare performances of the Gorilla Repertory Company.

Patchin Place on West 10th Street just west of Sixth Avenue, a little cluster of rooming houses built in 1848, eventually housed such writers as e. e. cummings, Theodore Dreiser, and Djuna Barnes. The **Jefferson Market Public Library** on Sixth Avenue at West 10th Street, built in 1877, was modeled on one of Mad King Ludwig of Bavaria's castles, hiked up at one end with a clock tower and positively pockmarked with arched windows and pointed gables. It was actually a courthouse—and of all things, it was voted the country's fifth most beautiful building when it was completed.

As the money moved north, the Village became a more middle-class though still very desirable area, until the sprawling commercial development of the riverfront and the repeated waves of immigration threatened to pinch it between Hell's Kitchen and Little Italy. Townhouses were divided up into apartments, studio space became cheap, and the Village began to attract a second generation of writers and painters, either poorer or more naturally bohemian in outlook, among them Edna St. Vincent Millay, Walt Whitman, Mark Twain, Edgar Allan Poe, O. Henry, Louisa May Alcott, Albert Bierstadt, Gertrude Vanderbilt Whitney, Winslow Homer, and Edward Hopper.

The Village was also one of the first centers of theatrical experimentation (a tradition honored by the many street performers in Washington Square). The **Provincetown Playhouse** on MacDougal was Eugene O'Neill's first showcase, and the **Sullivan Street Playhouse** was home for more than 40 years and 16,000 performances of the quintessential off-Broadway hit *The Fantastics.* Dylan Thomas famously drank himself to death in the **White Horse Tavern** on Hudson at West 11th Street (phone (212) 243-9260), and the ghost of Aaron Burr is said to haunt the **One if by Land, Two if by Sea** Restaurant at 17 Barrow Street, not because he was poisoned by anyone's cooking (except perhaps his wife—see mention of the Morris-Jumel House in Zone 15) but because he lived in a house on that site.

Louisa May Alcott wrote *Little Women* while living at **130 MacDougal.** Ruth McKenney, and her sister Eileen, whose exploits eventually inspired the musical *On the Town,* lived at **14 Gay Street.** O. Henry supposedly modeled the scene of "The Last Leaf" on the gate at **10 Grove Street.** Hart Crane lived at **45 Grove,** and there was a tavern called Marie's Crises at **59 Grove** where Thomas Paine reportedly drafted "Common Sense." James Fenimore Cooper lived at **45 Bleeker Street,** and both Willa Cather and Richard Wright occupied **82 Washington Place.** There was a gentlemen's club at **83 West Third** where Poe worked on "The Raven."

The third and fourth generations, beats and bohemians, moved in after World War II, followed by the flower children and finally the retro-radicals. The **New York University** campus sprawls around Washington Square, and the **New School for Social Research** and **Parsons School of Design** are also here. The earlier artists left their mark by way of the dozens of off-Broadway theaters and jazz clubs, the later by way of the **New York Studio School of Drawing, Painting, and Sculpture** (the original home of the Whitney Museum) and **Parsons,** which combines art design and philosophy. Most appropriate of all might be the presence of the **Malcolm Forbes Gallery** on Fifth Avenue at West 12th (phone (212) 206-5548), the palace of playthings from the prince of capitalism.

This is a great spot for just walking, because of the mix of 18th- and 19th-century architecture (look for cobblestones on the west side), the ethnic assortment, and the mingling of social classes. It is also, of course, a famous refuge for gay and lesbian residents, though in recent years many gays have moved north into Chelsea and left the Village to the women. The gay scene centers around **Christopher Street;** the **Stonewall Tavern,** site of the infamous 1969 police/gay standoff, has moved about a little, but is now at 53 Christopher. (Gay Street, as it happens, was named after a family.)

Even if you only have a few minutes, the tiny area around Bedford Street from Christopher to Commerce is especially worth seeing. At 102 Bedford is the house called **Twin Peaks,** which looks a little like a Tudor cottage with a Hessian helmet on it; the original 1830 cottage was "done up" by architect Clifford Reed Daily to put a little more fun into the artists' community. The mansard-topped twins at **39** and **41 Commerce Street** around the corner were supposedly built in 1831 by a sea captain for his spinster daughters, who did not speak to each other; the central garden apparently did not bring them closer together, either. On Grove Street just off Bedford is a row of Federal townhouses, and in between **Nos. 10** and **12 Grove** is an alley of mid–19th century workingmen's cottages.

And the brick-covered clapboard house at No. 77 Bedford, the **Isaacs-Hendricks House,** is the oldest in the Village, built in 1800. And the house next door, the 1873 building at **75½ Bedford Street,** was Edna St. Vincent Millay's last New York home and was later home to John Barrymore and Cary Grant; only 9½ feet wide, it is the narrowest building in the city, built in what was once a passageway.

Zone 5: The East Village

The East Village—which, logically, extends east of Greenwich Village from Broadway to the East River—is topographically far more regular than its sibling: the avenues (here including Avenues A, B, C, and D, known as "Alphabet City," beyond First Avenue) run longitudinally, and the obediently numbered streets, from East First to East 14th, crisscross them more or less latitudinally.

Socially the population of the East Village is all over the map: a mix of Indian and Italian restaurateurs, Ukrainian boutiques, art students, street performers, and proto-punks. It's a hot club scene, studded with preserved churches and monuments to art movements of earlier days; it is also still a stronghold of the drug culture, though that is much less visible than in the 1970s. But it has many beautiful buildings and important cultural sites, and its history goes back to the days of Nieuw Amsterdam.

Peter Stuyvesant once owned the lion's share of what is now the East Village, and a fair amount of the island north of there as well (see Zone 7). The western border of the "bouwerie" was Fourth Avenue, which explains why that street becomes known as Bowery to the south. His country home was near 10th and Stuyvesant, and he had his own chapel, too, on the site of what is now **St. Mark's-in-the-Bowery** on East 10th at Second Avenue (phone (212) 674-6377), which itself goes back to 1799; he was buried in the ground beneath it. Poet W. H. Auden is memorialized there because he lived for many years at **77 St. Mark's Place.**

Astor Place, like Washington Square, was inhabited by the richest of the rich in the early 19th century. The Astor Place Opera House, actually the second famous theater in that park, was the site of what is known as the Astor Place Riots of 1849; it started as a quarrel between the paid adherents of two rival actors and ended in the death of several dozen people. In the same area are the **Public Theater,** originally the Astor Library building donated by John Jacob Astor and now best known as home of the year-round Shakespeare Festival founded by Joseph Papp; and **Cooper Union,** the famous free adult educational institution that was the first to accept women and students of all races and religions. Its columned Great Hall, where Lincoln delivered his "Right Makes Might" speech, is still the site of popular public debates. **Colonnade Row,** the homes from 428 to 434 Lafayette off Astor Place, was also known as "LaGrange Terrace" when the Astors themselves and the Vanderbilts and Delanos lived there, along with such temporary celebrity residents as Charles Dickens and William Makepeace Thackeray; but only four of the original nine buildings, and just the façades, survive.

The **Old Merchant's House** (phone (212) 777-1089), just south of the Public Theater at 29 East 4th Street, is an intact 1830s Greek Revival home with all its furnishings, paintings, and even books just the way they were when merchant Seabury Tredwell forbade his daughter Gertrude to marry a man he disapproved of. Gertrude then decided never to marry at all. Sex also used to be an issue at **McSorley's Old Ale House,** which from its founding in 1854 until the 1970s admitted only men; other than that, it's still the same old saloon (East 7th and Cooper Streets; phone (212) 473-9148).

On East 2nd Street between Second Avenue and the Bowery is the **New York City Marble Cemetery,** where many famous New York names are represented (and where one just-discovered unused vault is on the market for a six-figure sum). If you go into the alley on the other side of Second Avenue, you'll find another early–19th century cemetery, or, rather, the marble plaques above the underground vaults.

An odd little spire seems to poke up above Broadway, where it makes a funny little quirk around what was then an apple orchard; the spire leads down to the lovely Gothic Revival **Grace Church** at 802 Broadway (phone (212) 254-2000), designed by St. Patrick's architect James Renwick when he was 23 years old. It has particularly beautiful stained glass in the pre-Raphaelite style, and its moment in the celebrity sun occurred in 1863 when P. T. Barnum staged General Tom Thumb's wedding there.

If you've ever longed to lounge in one of those huge ornate public baths, here's your chance—the **Russian and Turkish baths** at 268 East Tenth (phone (212) 674-9250). Do call ahead: Some days are men-only, some women-only, and some coed.

If you hear the designation "Noho," it means "north of Houston," the area around Broadway and Lafayette whose commercial spirit has more in common with the West Village these days than the East.

Zone 6: Chelsea

When Captain Thomas Clarke acquired the land from Eighth Avenue to the Hudson River between West 14th and 25th Streets, he named it, in what must have seemed a rather ambitious flight of fancy, after a neighborhood in London famed for its high fashion and literary and artistic life. As it turned out, it was prophetic. Chelsea was the first Broadway, the original Hollywood, and over the years it has been home to dozens of artists and writers. It was an early fashion center and is still home to the **Fashion Institute of Technology** and the **"Fur District"** (between Sixth and Eighth Avenues and West 27th and 30th Streets), though the serious retail boutiques have long since moved farther uptown.

As noted in Part One, Understanding the City, most of Clarke's property was inherited by his grandson, Clement Clarke Moore of "'Twas the Night before Christmas" (disputed) fame. Among his gifts, the public-good component of his commercial development was the land for the **Theological Seminary** on Ninth Avenue between West 20th and 21st (phone (212) 243-5150). St. Mark's Library now has what is believed to be the largest collection of Latin Bibles in the world; the West Building is the oldest example of Gothic Revival architecture in the city.

But that is only one of several important religious-studies centers in the neighborhood: **The New Center for Jewish History** (15 West 16th Street; (212) 294-8301) incorporates the libraries of five major organizations, including **Yeshiva University** and the **American Jewish Historical Society,** as well as the publicly accessible **Genealogy Institute** and performance spaces for concerts and lectures. Across Ninth Avenue is **St. Peter's Episcopal Church** (346 West 20th Street); Moore insisted that it should be built in the style of a classical Greek temple, and the foundation was, but in midconstruction church officials shifted to the Gothic style then sweeping England.

The home at **Ninth and West 21st Street,** with the ornate peaked roof, is the oldest home in the neighborhood, built in the 1820s. When Moore subdivided the property in 1830, he required the residential developers to put gardens in front of the homes and trees along the street; the exteriors of the townhouses along **West 21st between Ninth and Tenth** are nearly intact, though many of the buildings are now apartments or shops. The Greek Revival row houses along **West 20th Street** in the same block were originally constructed as middle-class rental units in the late 1930s; notice the cast-iron detailing and the brownstone door frames that became a synonym for Manhattan homes.

The 19-story **Starrett-Lehigh Building,** which occupies the block between Eleventh and Twelfth avenues and 26th and 27th streets, was constructed in 1930 as a warehouse and freight terminal for the railroads; it is now a combination fashion mall and high-tech office campus (the old truck-sized elevator now carries occupants like Martha Stewart—and her car—directly to these nifty ninth-floor parking spaces.

The block bounded by West 23rd and 24th and Ninth and Tenth is taken up by the **London Terrace Apartments.** During the Depression, for some speculative reason, developers tried to play on the name by razing the mid–19th-century Greek Revival complex there and replacing it with this Mayfair-wannabe block with a garden in the middle and doormen dressed as London "bobbies." Across Tenth at 519 West 23rd Street is the **WPA Theatre,** one of the best-known off-off-Broadway venues; *Little Shop of Horrors* and *Steel Magnolias* began here, among others.

The **Chelsea Hotel,** which at various times was home or hotel to O. Henry, Mark Twain, Thomas Wolfe, Arthur Miller, Tennessee Williams, Brendan Behan, Vladimir Nabokov, Sarah Bernhardt, Dylan Thomas, Virgil Thomson, Jack Kerouac, and assorted touring rock stars, is on West 23rd between Seventh and Eighth avenues (phone (212) 243-3700).

The Gothic Revival **Marble Collegiate Church** at Broadway and West 29th Street (phone (212) 686-2770) is famous for its Tiffany windows and former pastor Norman Vincent Peale *(The Power of Positive Thinking)*. **St. John the Baptist** (phone (212) 564-9070) on West 31st Street just west of Seventh Avenue is like a geode—nearly obscured by the development around it, but glorious within.

Chelsea went through a long decline before urban renewal moved in, but nowadays, from its vantage point between the modern Theater District and Greenwich Village, it is at once a target for upwardly mobile young families, art and antiques dealers who have shifted north from the high-rent Soho, and (increasingly) a wealthy gay population. And with **Madison Square Garden** at one corner and the huge, renovated **Chelsea Piers** playground/tourist draw at the other, the famous Chelsea loft spaces are once again getting hard to find. (The original Pennsylvania Station was twin to the great Beaux Arts **Post Office** across Eighth Avenue, the one emblazoned with the famous "Neither snow nor rain . . ." slogan.)

If you're interested in fashion and design, you should stop by the free galleries at the **Fashion Institute of Technology** on Seventh Avenue at 27th Street (phone (212) 217-5779), which, like the better-known Costume Institute at the Metropolitan, assembles special exhibits that either trace a style through history or showcase designers or collectors and that sometimes detail a technique or material. One other Chelsea neighborhood worth noting is the **"Flower District"** along Sixth Avenue in the upper 60s. And part of Chelsea overlaps the infamous Tenderloin; see Zone 8.

Zone 7: Gramercy Park and Madison Square

This old and in many cases well-preserved section of Manhattan, which faces Chelsea across Sixth Avenue, is punctuated by squares and parks and white-collar firms. It is also the area that symbolized the commercial ambitions of the Gilded Age, home to the **Flatiron Building** in the triangle of Fifth Avenue, Broadway, and 23rd Street, which was the world's largest building when it was completed in 1903; the **Metropolitan Life Insurance Building** at Madison and 23rd, which topped it by adding a tower in 1909; the **Empire State Building,** which beat them both in 1931.

What was sometimes called "Ladies' Mile," a cluster of the first department stores—notably, the original Lord & Taylor and Tiffany stores—and custom shops catering to the carriage trade, ran along Broadway from Union Square to Madison Square—the heart of what is also sometimes known as the Flatiron District. ("Ladies" was a trifle sarcastic, as it had previously been a neighborhood of prominent brothels.) The Flatiron Building was actually named the Fuller Building, but its shape, something like the prow of a great ocean liner or an old press, inspired the nickname. Society figures and politicians made their homes here (Union Square was the home of Tammany Hall), and it was near enough to the theater district to attract the most important actors and writers as well. Edwin Booth, whose statue stands in the park, founded the famous **Players Club** on the south side. The **"Little Church around the Corner"** (also known as the Church of the Transfiguration) at East 29th and Fifth Avenue (phone (212) 684-6770), which became famous because it buried actors when some more "respectable" churches wouldn't, has a collection of theatrically inspired stained glass.

Before the Empire State Building was erected, the block of Fifth Avenue between West 33rd and West 34th Streets held two of the many Astor mansions, one belonging to William Waldorf Astor and the other to his aunt, Mrs. William Astor. An argument led to his moving out and putting up a hotel on the site called the Waldorf; almost immediately she moved out and built a connecting hotel, the Astoria. The two operated as a single company—though with the provision that she could block off the connection at any time—until 1929, when the Park Avenue hotel of that name was built and the Empire State Building begun.

Gramercy Park, the neighborhood centered on Gramercy Park at the foot of Lexington Avenue between West 20th and West 21st, was one of the first "gated communities," as we would call them now. In the 1830s, developer Samuel Ruggles bought a large chunk of the old Stuyvesant estate that included a creek shaped like a "crooked little knife," or "Crommessie." Ruggles wanted to entice a wealthy patronage, so he filled in the marshy creek area and laid out a London-style park in the heart of his territory, with one adjoining avenue named for the famous Revolutionary victory and one on the south side called Irving Place after writer Washington Irving. Astonishingly, it is still a private park, the only one in the city—area residents have keys to the lock—and the entire area is a historic district. Teddy Roosevelt was born on East 20th Street between Park and Broadway. The **Theodore Roosevelt Birthplace Museum** (phone (212) 260-1616) had to be reconstructed because the actual building was demolished during World War II, but the five rooms of period furniture, memorabilia, Teddy Bears, and campaign memorabilia are real enough.

Madison Square Park, between Fifth and Madison Avenues and between West 23rd and West 26th Streets, was part of the original grid plan of 1811, though only well into the mid–19th century did it become much more than a commons and parade ground (and "potter's field" or pauper's cemetery). This was the site of the second Madison Square Garden, the palatial exhibition hall/entertainment complex designed by Sanford White; its rooftop garden was also the place where White was shot to death in 1906 by millionaire socialite Harry Thaw, who believed White was having an affair with his showgirl wife, Evelyn Nesbit. The original New York Knickerbockers, the nation's first organized baseball team, played here; and before it was permanently hoisted into harbor-lighting position, the torch and upraised arm of the Statue of Liberty was exhibited here as well.

Overlooking Madison Square is the clock tower of the **Metropolitan Life Insurance Building,** nearly five feet taller than London's Big Ben. In the lobby are a series of historical murals painted by famed children's illustrator N. C. Wyeth. On the other corner, at Madison and East 25th, is the **New York State Supreme Court's Appellate Division,** believed to be the busiest appellate court in the world (among the former plaintiffs here: Babe Ruth, Charlie Chaplin, Edgar Allan Poe, and Harry Houdini). The many fine sculptures outside are matched by stained glass, murals, and carving inside, which you can see unless court is in session.

Among other old neighborhood names sometimes used by city residents or prestige-savvy developers are **Rose Hill,** a residential area north of Stuyvesant Square, and **Kips Bay,** for the area between Gramercy and Murray Hill (see Zone 9). Both names go back to old farming estates. The Kip family established their farm almost as soon as the Canarsie had sold Manhattan, and Rose Hill was sold off the Stuyvesant estate in the mid–18th century. The **"Block Beautiful"** is simply a well-preserved row of houses along East 19th Street between Irving Place and Third Avenue; theater great Mrs. Patrick Campbell and movie vamp Theda Bara both lived (at various times, of course) in **No. 132 19th Street.**

Union Square describes the area just north of the East Village between the actual Union Square Park and Stuyvesant Square. The rather stolid **St. George's Episcopal Church** overlooking Stuyvesant Square is where J. P. Morgan attended what one must imagine were safely conservative services. The night-lit clock tower that looks down from Irving Street at East 14th is part of the **Consolidated Edison** (ConEd) headquarters, but at various times this site held Tammany Hall and the Academy of Music. **Union Square** itself, at the intersection of Broadway and Park between West 14th and West 17th Streets, is the first of a series of squares marking the diagonal northward progress of Broadway. Though, like the East Village, it had become a famous drug market, the influx of boutique hotels and restaurants and the success of the open-air green market has revived it considerably.

Incidentally, this entire section of Manhattan was the "turf" of the original Gashouse Gang, so called because many of the factories that supplied the city's lights were located along the East River.

Zone 8: Midtown West and the Theater District

When people talk about Broadway, they rarely mean the street; they mean the **Theater District**—an area that ranges along both sides of Broadway from Times Square at West 42nd up to about 47th Street and between Ninth and Sixth Avenues. Nearby are many of the more important off-Broadway venues: the Shriner–Moorish Revival **City Center Theater of Music and Drama** on West 55th at 1212 Broadway (phone (212) 581-1212), **Carnegie Hall** on West 57th around the corner of Broadway (phone (212) 903-9600), and even the **Brill Building,** the one-time "Broadway" of pop music and the heart of Tin Pan Alley (between West 49th and West 50th Streets).

This is also the so-called **Garment District,** which began on the Lower East Side and gradually followed the department stores up Broadway. However, the most influential merchants decided that the showroom and the sweatshop shouldn't be so close together, and together they constructed large warehouses on Seventh Avenue at West 37th Street, which is why some of the Seventh Street signs have subtitles reading **Fashion Avenue.**

Among the most famous areas in this zone is **Times Square,** which until the paper's headquarters moved there in 1905 had been called Longacre Square, home to stables and blacksmiths and the occasional thief. This is where the famous ball drops to mark the New Year as it has every year since 1905; and although it had become notoriously seedy, studded with porno shops and cheap bars, the neighborhood underwent one of the most sweeping renovations in city history, perhaps second only to the development of Lincoln Center in place of the West Side slums. Times Square now draws an estimated 20 million visitors a year, making it one of the major tourist attractions in itself (not to mention a gridlock of pedestrian and vehicular traffic). In fact, things are opening so fast that you may want to pick up a copy of the neighborhood guide at the **Times Square Visitors Center** on Broadway between 46th and 47th streets; it offers full-scale tourist services, ATMs, tickets, Internet access, and handi-capped-accessible bathrooms. (Not all Times Square visuals are outdoors: Look for the newly expanded **International Center of Photography** on Sixth at 94th; (212) 857-4000.)

New theaters and renovated ones, trendy restaurants, comedy and music clubs, high-tech virtual playgrounds and megastores—plus those famous huge billboards and the *Times's* running-lights headline service—are bursting almost daily out from behind construction fences. The Disney Company restored the historic **New Amsterdam** on 42nd Street at

Seventh Avenue as a showcase for its extraordinary adaptation of *The Lion King.* (It's just behind the Disney superstore, but frankly, the theater lobby is the more fantastic of the two.) The **New Victory** across the street is a throwback to the golden age of children's theater. Two historic but aging theaters, the 1903 Lyric and the 1920 Apollo, have been replaced at a cost of $30 million by the single **Ford Center for the Performing Arts,** which will be the second-largest auditorium on Broadway.

The *New York Times* itself long ago had to move out of the old tower on the square to larger digs on West 43rd Street, but it is having an extraordinary 650-foot-tall glass tower constructed back in the "old neighborhood," and Reuters plans to follow suit. The Condé Nast magazine group, Viacom, Bertelsman (the German publisher that has acquired Random House and others), and MTV have moved into the "new" Times Square, along with the huge Ernst & Young advertising corporation. Other media-based entertainments include the huge **Warner Bros., Virgin,** and **Disney** megastores, the **World Wrestling Federation restaurant,** a **Rain Forest Café, B.B. King's Blues Room** and **Lucille's Café**, another **NBA/WNBA** store, the **Madame Tussaud's Wax Museum,** the sports-celebrity **All-Star Café,** the **ESPN Zone,** and the retro 1950s **Ellen's Stardust Diner.** A magic-theme restaurant from David Copperfield is in the works off and on (now you see it . . .). Another famous "running clock" is the **National Debt Clock** above Sixth Avenue between West 42nd and West 43rd; watch how fast it mounts up. The **Times Square Brewery** offers pizza bagels and house-brewed beer with a second-floor view of the action. And if you hang around the **MTV Studios,** whose mezzanine-level offices overlook the square from 44th to 46th; or watch the marquee outside **Cinema Ride,** one of those 3-D shows, you may see yourself among the models and billboards; there are hidden video cameras around the sidewalk.

Even odder is the sudden boom in old-fashioned moving "headline" signs known as "zippers." In addition to the *Times* news board, there are stock market quotation runners of the sort you might more reasonably expect down near Wall Street; one outside the **Dow Jones** offices at 1 Times Square, a **Morgan-Stanley** zipper on 1585 Broadway, and an even more astonishing **NASDAQ** board—$15 million worth and 125 feet high—on the Condé Nast building at 42nd and Broadway. **Reuters News Service** has a competing headline sign at 42nd and Seventh, just like the Fox News sign at 47th and Sixth and the NBC versions in Times Square and Rockefeller Plaza. And ABC—which, you may remember now belongs to the Disney company—has announced that it will construct a sidewalk-view studio for *Good Morning America* like the *Today Show* peek-in that packs Rockefeller Plaza every weekday at 7 Times Square. The same thing goes for Bryant Gumbel's *Early Show* at Fifth Avenue and 59th, across from the Plaza Hotel and Central Park.

Herald Square is named for the *New York Herald* newspaper building at West 34th, just as Times Square was named for the *New York Times*. And just as Times Square isn't really square, Herald Square is actually a triangle. (You could call it the Daily District: Greeley Square, another triangle one block south at West 33rd, was named for *New York Tribune* founder Horace Greeley.) Herald Square was the very center of the venomous **Tenderloin,** a thriving red-light and speakeasy district. It was partly the arrival of **Macy's Department Store** in 1901 that gave this area new respectability, and nowadays Herald Square is most famous for serving as the finale stage for Macy's annual Thanksgiving Day Parade and the arrival of Santa Claus.

The west side of this area also has a florid past, though not much of it is left to be seen. From Ninth Avenue west from the 30s to the 50s is what is most often known as **Hell's Kitchen,** the territory of the Irish gang of the same name, but also sometimes called Paddy's Market or Clinton, the name now coming back into style. There is even a Hell's Kitchen Flea Market on 39th between Ninth and Tenth avenues every weekend, when the block is closed to vehicular traffic. Nowadays the strip along Eleventh and Twelfth Avenues is mostly reduced to auto-body shops and a few X-rated theaters playing off (or off-off) the Broadway name. **Ninth Avenue,** however, particularly through the 40s, is a bazaar of small ethnic restaurants—Brazilian, Jamaican, Afghani, Peruvian, Greek, Turkish, Thai, Morroccan, Japanese, and even Burmese, as well as the relatively tame Italian and Mexican. Not only are these some of the better restaurants in the Theater District, they're much hipper (where do you think the actors eat?) and a lot less expensive. But for pretheater class, try **Restaurant Row,** the block on West 46th Street between Eighth and Ninth Avenues, home to the **Firebird, Orso,** celeb-spot **Joe Allen,** and **Becco,** among others.

Times Square is sometimes called "The Crossroads of the World," and it's also one of the major transportation crossroads of Manhattan: Several of the large subway transfer points, including 34th Street, Penn Station, Times Square, Rockefeller Center, 42nd Street, 49th Street, and Columbus Circle are in this area, and so is the Port Authority Bus Terminal. The Lincoln Tunnel runs west from West 38th. And the western edge of the zone is the unlovely but essential West Side Expressway.

North of the Javits Convention Center and Lincoln Tunnel, near Pier 86 at the foot of West 46th Street, is the popular **Intrepid Sea-Air-Space Museum** (phone (212) 245-2533). And at 237 West 51st Street is the baroquely extravagant **Times Square Church,** built as the Warner Hollywood movie palace in 1930 but quickly transformed into a playhouse (*Jesus Christ Superstar* was housed here, appropriately). The building opens at 5 p.m. Tuesdays and Fridays and 8 a.m. on Sundays; call (212) 541-6300 for more information.

Zone 9: Midtown East

This zone is for many tourists the heart of Manhattan: It includes **Rockefeller Center** (phone (212) 632-3975), **Radio City Music Hall** (phone (212) 247-4777), and the great shopping boulevard of Fifth Avenue; many of the city's most famous restaurants and such famous hotels as the **Waldorf-Astoria, New York Palace, St. Regis, Algonquin** (where you can still have a drink in the Rose Room and imagine the wits of the 1920s gathered around you), **Four Seasons,** and **Plaza.** The **Museum of Modern Art** is here (though closed for renovations) on West 53rd between Fifth and Sixth (phone (212) 708-9480), across from the **American Craft Museum** (phone (212) 956-3535) and the new, eight-level **American Folk Art Museum** (phone (212) 265-1040), and a block from the **Museum of Television and Radio** on West 52nd (phone (212) 621-6600). CBS Inc., the infamous **"Black Rock,"** is that monolith overshadowing the museum at Fifth and 52nd. The small but often uniquely satisfying **Dahesh Museum** has relocated to larger quarters at 580 Madison Avenue between 56th and 57th (phone (212) 759-0606). The **Sony Wonder Technology Lab** (phone (212) 833-8100) on Madison between 55th and 56th has become the city's hippest hands-on playground for both children (who talk with a robot, view the inner workings of the body, and surf the web) and electronic-trend fashion victims. There is even a miniature free branch of the **Whitney Museum of American Art** in the Philip Morris building on Park Avenue across from Grand Central with a sculpture garden and rotating exhibits from the main collection (phone (917) 663-2453).

This is also a living coffee-table book of monumental architecture. Among its landmarks are the lavishly restored Beaux Arts **Grand Central Terminal** at 42nd and Park Avenue (look up at the constellations winking in the ceiling, and be sure to peek into the Campbell Apartment above the West Balcony, a 13th-century Florentine-style hall); the gleaming, Buck Rogers–ish, Art Deco **Chrysler Building,** with its stainless steel "grill" crown and hood-ornament gargoyles saluting the spirit of the automotive age (Lexington at 42nd); the Mies van der Rohe–designed **Seagram Building** on Park Avenue between East 52nd and East 53rd Streets, elegant in its bronze and glass; the equally startling glass razor of the **Lever House** on Park at 54th; the literally gilded palace—now part of the **New York Palace** and Le Cirque 2000 restaurant—that was the **Villard House** on Madison between 50th and 51st Streets; the almost Disneyesque Gothic Revival **St. Patrick's Cathedral** on Fifth at 50th, the largest Catholic cathedral in this country; and the almost reticent but powerful **United Nations** complex, a perfect architectural metaphor, on the East River at 43rd Street (phone (212) 963-7713).

Rockefeller Center itself is a landmark, a total of 19 Art Deco buildings between Fifth and Seventh Avenues and 48th and 51st Streets, clustered around the famous plaza-cum–ice rink and including the eternally youthful Radio City Music Hall, with its Rockettes and classic revivals. Its façades are virtual museums of sculpture, bas-relief, gilding, mosaics, carvings, and molding; during the Great Depression, construction of the original 14 buildings kept a quarter of a million laborers and artists busy. The **Diamond District** is right next door, along West 47th Street between Sixth and Fifth, wall-to-wall and mall-to-mall shops hawking earrings, rings, and pins. It almost seems to bounce its lights upward toward the **Rainbow Room** (phone (212) 632-5000), which has a bird's-eye view of the skyline from the 65th floor of the tallest building of Rockefeller Center—and in fact, the Diamond District dates from almost the same era, when the Jewish merchants of Europe began fleeing the increasingly restrictive anti-Semitic laws.

The **Church of the Incarnation** (phone (212) 689-6350) on Madison Avenue at East 35th is modest on the outside, but its art collection—Tiffany stained glass window, Saint-Gaudens and Daniel French sculptures, and so on—is anything but modest. More obvious, perhaps, is the gold-leaf dome atop **St. Vartan Cathedral** on Second Avenue between East 34th and East 35th, but then it is the seat of the Armenian Orthodox Church in the United States. The Byzantine **St. Bartholomew's** on Park at East 50th is truly byzantine: part James Renwick, part Stanford White. St. Patrick's is the Gothic giant, but **St. Thomas'** just up the street at Fifth and 53rd is stubborn as a little David (phone (212) 757-7013). It's worth stopping in to admire its fantastic stone reredos, a wall of 60 figures behind the altar that represent Jesus and his apostles and family, saints, martyrs, prophets, and missionaries. And at the foot of the gallery stairs, to the right as you enter, is an "Adoration of the Magi" believed to be the work of Peter Paul Rubens.

The **New York Daily News Building** on 42nd and Second Avenue was used as the scene for the *Daily Planet* in the *Superman* movies, and there's an inside joke to that: The building has its own "planet," a huge revolving globe, in the lobby. Across the street is **Tudor City,** Henry VIII–style apartments, restaurants, shops, and services built in the 1920s as a sort of early urban renewal project.

The **Japan Society** on East 47th between First and Second Avenues (phone (212) 832-1155) offers changing exhibits of antique scroll paintings, textiles, ceramics, arms, and antiques as well as lectures and exhibitions; it also has a traditional Japanese garden. Be sure to step into the meditation garden of **Holy Family Church** a few doors west.

This wasn't really "good" territory until well into the 20th century. From Fourth Avenue (before it was called Park) east to the river lay stockyards and slums; there were railroad yards between Lexington and Madison, where Grand Central is now, and the gashouse, glue factories, prisons, workhouses, and asylums were all on what is now Roosevelt

Island in the East River. In fact, what seems to be a pretty series of gardens down the center of Park Avenue actually covers the remnants of the railroad tracks.

Consequently, there aren't a lot of old neighborhood names attached to this part of the island. **Beekman Place** is a two-block enclave that has been home to such theatrical greats as Lunt and Fontanne, Ethel Barrymore, Irving Berlin and "Auntie Mame"; climb the steps on 51st Street to the East River Promenade between 49th and 51st. **Sutton Place,** the southernmost section of York Avenue that runs between East 54th and 59th, was yet another, though later, London-style development aimed at the first families, and various of the Morgans and Vanderbilts in their turn lived here. The residence of the U.N. secretary-general is there now. In the park between 58th and 59th is a statue of a boar, which may seem strange unless you know that it's a copy of *Il Porcallino,* which stands in the market in Florence, Italy; pat its head for luck. And yes, Simon and Garfunkle fans, that is the 59th Street Bridge immortalized in "Feelin' Groovy," officially named the **Queensboro Bridge.**

You may also see references to **Murray Hill,** the prosperous residential area (and now the site of many luxury hotels and apartment buildings as well) from about East 34th to about 41st between Third and Madison Avenues. Legend has it that Mary Murray invited General Howe to tea in 1776, knowing he would be far too polite to refuse, and thus bought Washington time to escape up the island to Fort Tryon. On the east side of Third Avenue is **Sniffen Court,** a beautifully preserved mews of ten Romanesque Revival houses, built about 1850, at 150–160 East 36th Street.

On the other hand, Fifth Avenue along the 40s and 50s was the site of huge palaces during the Gilded Age, half a dozen belonging to the Vanderbilts alone and nearly as many to the Astors. One of the greatest of those old mansions is now a fine museum: the magnificent **J. Pierpont Morgan Library** at 36th and Madison (phone (212) 685-0008), which houses an unparalleled collection of illuminated medieval manuscripts, rare books, etchings, musical scores, and prints. Fifth Avenue may not be "Millionaire's Mile" anymore (unless you're paying the American Express bill after a shopping tour of the 50s), but you can stroll up the avenue feeling like a million.

Zone 10: The West Side

The West Side above the Theater District had never had much identity of its own until fairly recently. There was some port trade—the big cruise ships and liners still use piers in the lower 50s—and some hotel and theater spillover, but not of the better sort. In the early part of the 20th century it was a respectable if not particularly fashionable district, populated first by Jewish immigrants who prospered and moved out of the Lower East Side and later by middle-class blacks, who began to be pushed out again by

Puerto Rican immigrants and blue-collar white families from Hell's Kitchen. But with the creation of **Lincoln Center for the Performing Arts** (which involved the demolition of San Juan Hill, the Hispanic neighborhood in the West 60s, and the degenerating middle-class houses around it, exactly the area portrayed in *West Side Story*), businesses began to return.

The southwest corner of the zone is **Columbus Circle,** where Broadway, Eighth Avenue, and West 59th/Central Park South come together. The circle is dominated by the two glass spires of the new **Time Warner Center,** home of numerous upscale apartments, restaurants, bars, shops, and the **Mandarin Oriental Hotel.** The massively renovated **Trump International Hotel & Towers** (f.k.a. the Paramount Building, née Gulf & Western), with its minimall and chic eateries, is another tourist attraction in its own right.

Lincoln Center and its associated plazas and annexes pretty much take up the area from Columbus Avenue (the extension of Ninth Avenue, remember, not Eighth) and very nearly Broadway to Tenth Avenue between West 62nd and West 66th Streets. The law-school campus of **Fordham University** is just to its south, and the **School of American Ballet** and **Juilliard School of Music** are associated with the Lincoln Center complex, so the neighborhood is spotted with small cafes and shops that attract students and culture-lovers, as well as several health clubs and gymnasiums.

An offshoot gallery of the **American Folk Art Museum** (phone (212) 595-9533) is in what is called Lincoln Square on Columbus Avenue between West 65th and 66th. It specializes in textiles, furniture, and decorative arts from the 18th century, with particularly nice quilts and frequent lectures and demonstrations.

And if you ever wondered what "Tammany" really was, it, or rather he, was actually Tamanend, an Indian chief who supposedly befriended William Penn. The New York society, incorporated in 1789, was originally a Masonic-style fraternity with a Native American twist: 13 "tribes"—for the 13 colonies—and pseudo-Indian ceremonies and titles. If you look up at the weathervane in the museum atrium, you will see old Tamanend, looking sadly into the future, which would only associate his name with corruption.

No tourist-savvy city would be complete without an **IMAX theater** these days, and one of New York's is here, at Broadway and 68th. The screen is "seven elephants high" (phone (212) 336-5000).

There's plenty of streetside sight-seeing around these parts as well. The darkly Art Deco apartment building at 55 Central Park West (between 65th and 66th) served as the battleground between the demon Gozur and the Ghostbusters. The **Hotel des Artistes** on West 67th Street at Central Park West was actually constructed as artists' studios, with its two-story spaces designed to take advantage of the daylight (and exterior sculptures for inspiration), but now these are highly prized apartments. Noel Coward, Rudolph Valentino, Alexander Woollcott, Norman Rockwell, Isadora Duncan, and Howard Chandler Christy all lived there; Christy did the murals of romantic nudes in the popular **Café des Artists** (phone (212) 877-3500) in the lobby.

The towered apartment buildings along Central Park West mostly date to the 1920s, when building regulations allowed greater height in return for at least partial light (which is why so many New York skyscrapers have those angled or pointed tops). The pretty Art Nouveau building at West 64th and Central Park West is the home of the **New York Society for Ethical Culture** (phone (212) 874-5210). The **Spanish and Portuguese Synagogue** on the corner of West 70th Street at Central Park West, though built (with Tiffany windows) only in 1897, is home to the oldest Jewish congregation in the city, dating to the arrival in 1654 of fugitives from the Inquisition; it still adheres rigorously to Sephardic ritual (by appointment; (212) 873-0300).

Zone 11: The East Side

This is arguably the most beautiful area of Manhattan, fashionable and prosperous almost from the very beginning, and like the dowager of a good family, remarkably well preserved. It is an area of apartment houses open only to true millionaires (and not always open to them, either); of the most expensive of boutiques, art and antiques houses, elegant hotels, private clubs, and old-line restaurants, churches, and educational institutions.

The riverfront was the original draw; it was an in-town "beach" and resort area in the early 19th century before bridges made travel to the outer boroughs common. The wealthy (who still lived firmly downtown) built summer homes all the way up the East River to what is now Harlem, boating up- and downtown, taking carriages along the Boston Post Road (Third Avenue) and later the El. A huge complex called Jones's Wood filled the whole stretch east of the Post Road from near what is now the **Rockefeller University/Cornell University Medical Center** neighborhood in the 60s north to John Jay Park at East 76th; it offered genteel bathing facilities, theatrical entertainments, a beer garden, and parade grounds.

The apartment buildings on the East Side broke ground in several ways; they were so large that even families with whole staffs of servants might share them. (And nowadays, several families can fit within the various subdivisions of one formerly palatial apartment.) The new luxury townhouses had elaborate bathrooms, not just water closets. They were fully electrified, not just refitted. And of course they had the immense swath of Central Park for their front yard. Those that had to settle for views of Madison Avenue or Park Avenue offered elaborate lobbies and exterior detail instead: look at the outside of the building on the corner of **East 66th Street and Madison.**

Once Caroline Schermerhorn Astor—the same Mrs. William Astor whose feuding with her nephew produced the Waldorf-Astoria Hotel—actually moved all the way up Fifth Avenue as far as 65th Street, the last great millionaires' migration began. Several of their mansions are still visible, including the **Frick Collection,** home of steel boss Henry Clay Frick, on Fifth at East 70th Street; the extravagant Second Empire **Lotos Club** on East 66th just off Fifth Avenue, former home of pharmaceutical tycoon and civil rights activist William Schieffelin; and the onetime **George T. Bliss House** on East 68th just off Fifth Avenue, which has four giant columns for just one little overlook. No wonder Fifth Avenue became the semi-official parade route, with its blocks of balconies like reviewing stands along one side and the peoples' park on the other.

The Beaux Arts home of banker Henri Wertheim on East 67th just off Fifth is now the **Japanese Consul General's residence.** The side-by-side 1890s French Renaissance homes of Oliver Gould Jennings and Henry T. Sloane are now the **Lycée Français** on East 72nd Street between Fifth and Madison Avenues. What is now the **Explorer's Club** on East 70th between Madison and Park was built for Stephen Clark, owner of the Singer Sewing Machine Company and founder of the Baseball Hall of Fame in Cooperstown. The Venetian Revival home of Edwin Berwin, who had the coal monopoly for American warships, is now an apartment building at **Fifth and East 64th.** And the neo-Tudor **Lenox School** on East 70th between Lexington and Third Avenues was originally the home of Stephen Brown, head of the New York Stock Exchange. Astor's own home was torn down to make room for the partially Romanesque, partially Byzantine, and Astorially opulent **Temple Emanu-El.**

Hunter College has one of the most enviable locations in town, around Park Avenue between East 68th and 69th Streets. Hunter's community center is the **Sarah Delano Roosevelt Memorial House**—or, rather, houses—on East 65th between Park and Madison. FDR's mother famously commissioned these twin townhouses, one for herself and one for the newly married Franklin and Eleanor, with a single entrance and various connecting doors. It was in the fourth-floor front bedroom that FDR endured his long bout with polio, and Eleanor the almost equally paralyzing domination of her mother-in-law.

Among smaller museums of note in this area are the **Abigail Adams Smith Museum** on East 61st Street between York and First Avenues, named for—but never occupied by—the daughter of John Quincy Adams. She and her husband were the landowners, at least; they originally planned to build a country estate there called Mount Vernon in honor of George Washington, under whom William Smith had been a colonel. But they had to sell the land in 1799 without getting much farther than building the stone stable (later an inn) that is now the museum. It has been furnished in the Federal style, given a period garden, and stocked with antiques; and especially for children, the tour (by costumed members of the Colonial Dames of America, which maintains the house) is pretty interesting.

The **Asia Society** (phone (212) 288-640), housing the collection of John D. Rockefeller III, is on Park Avenue at East 70th Street; the space has been renovated, and a garden café installed. If you enjoy more commercial art, the **Society of Illustrators** at 128 East 63rd east of Park Avenue exhibits graphic arts, illustrations, and award-winning book jackets. The **New York Women's Exchange** on Third Avenue above East 64th is more than a century old, one of those cooperatives designed to help women make money from their handicrafts; it's still an interesting source of crafts and gifts.

The **Seventh Regiment Armory** on Park between East 66th and 67th, where many of the city's major art and antiques exhibits are held, looks like a oversized sand castle, but the inside, if you can see past the wares of the fairs, was furnished by Louis Comfort Tiffany.

Among other buildings with strange histories is the one at **131 East 71st Street** between Park and Lexington; it was built during the Civil War, but designer Elsie de Wolfe redid the façade in 1910 as a sort of silent advertisement of her own style. The **Knickerbocker Club** building on East 62nd at Fifth Avenue used to have a twin next door; it was famous as the home of Mrs. Marcellus Hartley Dodge, a Rockefeller cousin, who filled her five-story mansion with all the stray dogs she could rescue. Next to it is the **810 Fifth Avenue** building, onetime home to William Randolph Hearst, Richard Nixon, and Nelson Rockefeller—penthouse, bomb shelter, and all.

Madison Avenue is now more commercial than residential, but oh, what commercialism! (For more on Madison Avenue shopping, see "Great Neighborhoods for Shopping" in Part Nine.)

Although **Roosevelt Island** in the East River is now a residential community, it once held a rather exciting assortment of institutions—lunatic asylums, smallpox hospitals, workhouses, poorhouses, and prisons; it was almost the dark reflection of the wealth of the East Side. (It was once called Welfare Island, as a matter of fact, but of course that word isn't P.C. anymore.) There are a few historical buildings left, including a lighthouse; and the **Roosevelt Island Aerial Tramway,** a 250-foot-high sky ride, crosses over from Second Avenue and 60th Street about every 15 minutes (phone (212) 832-4543). The island is a particularly great place to watch the Fourth of July fireworks.

Zone 12: The Upper West Side

As suggested in the "Very Short History" section of Part One, development of the West Side was the stepchild of the Gilded Age. It required the daring of a few developers and the construction of the El up Ninth Avenue to persuade middle-class and professional Manhattanites that it was worth living above Midtown. On the other hand, because the land was a better bargain, many of the apartment buildings and brownstones were more gracious and seemed to have more elbow room. Broadway, in particular, has a European boulevardlike spaciousness in this area. Nowadays, it is a popular area for relatively affluent professionals, studded with restaurants, especially along Columbus Avenue.

In its heyday, Riverside Drive was the Fifth Avenue of the West Side, with mansions gazing out over their own Frederick Olmsted greenery, Riverside Park, instead of Central Park and with the Hudson River beyond that. Only a few of the old buildings remain; look for the turn-of-the-century **Yeshiva Chofetz Chaim,** the former Isaac Rice home, at West 89th for an example.

It was the construction of the **Dakota** on Central Park West at 72nd Street, the first luxury apartment building on the Upper West Side, in the 1880s that sparked a development boom. Designed by Plaza Hotel architect Henry Hardenberg for Singer Company heir Edward Clark, it is still probably the most famous apartment building in the city, used as the movie setting of *Rosemary's Baby* (Boris Karloff is said to haunt the building) and now, unfortunately, best known as the home and assassination spot of John Lennon.

Once the Dakota was in place, other developers hastened to get in on the act, and this resulted in such other extravagances as the Beaux Arts **Dorilton** at West 71st and Broadway; the **Alexandria** on West 70th, with its hieroglyphic detailing, monsters, and rooftop pharaohs; and the Belle Epoque **Ansonia Hotel** on Broadway at West 74th, which attracted such musical eminences as Toscanini, Caruso, and Stokowski. William Randolph Hearst was originally satisfied with the view from the top three floors of the 12-story **Clarendon** on Riverside Drive and West 86th, but after a few years he decided he needed the whole thing and bought it out.

The stretch of **Central Park West** between West 75th and West 77th is a historical district, dating from the turn of the 19th century. The double-towered **St. Remo** between 74th and 75th is a little younger, finished in 1930, but it has its pride; this is the co-op that turned down Madonna, though several other famous actors and musicians do live here. The same architect, Emery Roth, topped himself by giving the **Beresford** at West 81st Street three turrets a few years later.

One of the oddest corners is a little gated mews off West 94th Street near West End Avenue known as **Pomander Walk;** though built in 1921, it looks just like a movie set of old London—and in fact, it was modeled after the stage set of a popular play of the time called *Pomander Walk.* So it sentimentally attracted such tenants as Lillian and Dorothy Gish and Humphrey Bogart.

Although the Upper West Side can't rival the East Side's "Museum Mile," it does have some popular attractions. The **New-York Historical**

Society building on Central Park West between West 76th and West 77th houses an eclectic collection ranging from American-made fine silver and decorative arts to original prints for John J. Audubon's *Birds of America,* Hudson River School painters, furniture that marches through the building in chronological order, and Gilbert Stuart's portrait of Washington.

The **American Museum of Natural History,** newly refurbished and riding the crest of dinosaur fever, faces Central Park from West 77th Street to 81st and the stunning **Rose Center** and **Hayden Planetarium** annex. The **Children's Museum of Manhattan,** one of the city's first institutions to go heavily into interactive exhibits, is on West 83rd Street between Broadway and Amsterdam Avenue.

Symphony Space, which is a cult location both for its Bloomsday marathon readings of *Ulysses* every June 16 and its 12-hour free spring musical marathon, is on Broadway at West 94th Street.

And should you venture up to the little park at Broadway and 106th, you'll see a bronze called *Memory* looking into a wave-shaped pool and inscribed, "In their death they were not divided" (II Samuel). It was erected by Macy's employees after the death of store owner Isdaor Straus and his wife, Ida, on the *Titanic.*

Zone 13:The Upper East Side

This is the heart of "Museum Mile," that fantastic array of museums and collections ranging 20 blocks, from the **Metropolitan Museum of Art** at 82nd Street (phone (212) 535-7710) and the **Neue Gallerie** of German and Austrian decorative arts across the street (phone (212) 628-6200) past the **Guggenheim** (phone (212) 423-3500), the **Museum of the City of New York** (phone (212) 534-1672), the **National Academy Museum** (phone (212) 369-4880), and the **Cooper-Hewitt National Museum of Design** (phone (212) 849-8300), among others.

Like the rest of the East Side, it didn't really hit its stride until about a century ago, when the Fourth Avenue railroad became Park Avenue and the Met, as the Metropolitan Museum is almost universally known, had acquired a reputation rivaling the great collections of Europe (and when conditions in Midtown, increasingly crowded, middle-class, and noisy, made these "inner suburbs" more desirable). Like the area to the south, it is studded with the onetime homes of the wealthy; the French Renaissance **Jewish Museum** on Fifth Avenue at East 92nd (phone (212) 423-3200) was once the homestead of financier Felix Warburg, and the **Cooper-Hewitt** on East 91st at Fifth Avenue was originally Andrew Carnegie's home (he asked for something "modest and plain"). The **National Academy Museum** at 89th was Archer Huntingdon's home.

The shortest of strolls will be enough to show you what real wealth bought a hundred years ago. The current headquarters of the **Common-**

wealth Fund at East 75th and Fifth was built for an heir to a Standard Oil fortune; the Renaissance Revival mansion at **25 East 78th Street** and Madison Avenue was built for a railroad president. New York University's **Institute of Fine Arts,** down the block on 78th at Fifth, is housed in what was once the home of American Tobacco founder James Duke and was copied from a chateau in Bordeaux. And around the corner on Fifth Avenue between 78th and 79th Streets is the **French Embassy,** once the home of finance icon Payne Whitney, and more recently the site of an apparent Michelangelo sighting, although the Cupid in question has been removed from the lobby and consigned to experts' debates.

Consider the single block of East 91st Street between Fifth and Madison Avenues. Facing the Cooper-Hewitt at **No. 1 East 91st** is the last palace of **"Millionaire's Row,"** built for banker Otto Kahn and now a convent school; at No. 7 is the **Burden House,** the home of a Vanderbilt shipping heiress who married a Burden steel scion and a prominent society rental site (the spiral staircase, centered under a stained-glass dome, was known as "the stairway to heaven.") And next to that, at **No. 9,** is the house where jazz record producer John Hammond was "set up" by his wife's old-society family.

One of the ex–Mrs. Vanderbilts commissioned the French Revival mansion at **60 East 93rd Street** between Park and Madison. Flashy Broadway figure and party boy Billy Rose was a millionaire of a lesser sort, perhaps, but he lived well enough to build a great Scottish-romantic mansion of his own across the street at **No. 56** (now an alcoholism treatment facility). Even the **Synod of Bishops of the Russian Orthodox Church Outside Russia** across the street was once a private home, the mansion of banker George Baker; its collection of icons is a must-see for devotees of Byzantine and Eastern Orthodox art (by appointment only; 534-1601).

The block of East 80th Street between Lexington and Park also has three mansions lined up one after another, built for a Whitney (**No. 120**), a Dillon (**No. 124**), and another Astor (**No. 130**).

If these mansions start to overwhelm you, go east. **Gracie Mansion** (phone (212) 570-4751), the official residence of the mayor of New York and original home of the Museum of the City of New York, is in **Carl Schurz Park** overlooking the East River at East 88th Street. Its name salutes Scottish immigrant Archibald Gracie, who built a summer home here back in 1799, although an earlier house is known to have been destroyed during the American Revolution. It has only been the mayor's residence since the days of Fiorello La Guardia—like Lincoln Center, it was the brainchild of Parks Commissioner Robert Moses.

The newly repolished **Whitney Museum of American Art** (phone (212) 570-3600), too aggressively modern for Museum Mile, juts out in an inverse pyramid over Madison Avenue at East 75th Street. The **92nd Street Y** (phone (212) 996-1100), as the Young Men and Women's Hebrew

Association there is commonly known, is famous for its concerts, readings, and lectures by national and international as well as local artists and writers. The original **Playhouse 91,** home of the Jewish Repertory Theater, is on East 91st between First and Second (phone (212) 831-2000).

The **Russian Orthodox Cathedral of St. Nicholas** at East 97th and Fifth is like the whole Kremlin squashed together, with five onion domes and multicolored tile detailing—Moscow on, if not the Hudson, at least the East River (by appointment only; phone (212) 289-1915). It is also the repository of 34 icons that had been smuggled out and were about to be sold on the black market when customs officials rescued them; they are estimated to be worth more than $3 million and date to the mid-18th and 19th centuries. The **Islamic Center of New York** on Third at East 96th Street is the spiritual home to the city's Moslems of whom there may be as many as half a million; it was computer-measured to ensure that it faces directly toward Mecca.

A few old-time neighborhood nicknames persist. **Yorkville** is what used to be New York's Germantown but is now just as much black and Hispanic as European, running nearly the length of the Upper East Side from Lexington Avenue over to the river. Carl Schurz, for whom the park surrounding Gracie Mansion is named, was a German immigrant who became editor of the *New York Post* and *Harper's Weekly* and, after the Civil War, secretary of the interior. **Hell Gate** was not a gang hangout but the spot where the Harlem River and Long Island Sound converge into New York Harbor—perhaps a hellish spot for river pilots. **Carnegie Hill,** which ranges from the Cooper-Hewitt (formerly the Carnegie mansion) at 91st Street north atop off the boutique and café area of Madison Avenue, is a rapidly upscaling residential neighborhood.

Zone 14: Columbia University and Harlem

Though often overlooked by tourists, the Heights are filled with important educational institutions, historical sites, and beautiful churches, museums, and 19th-century houses. And Harlem, of course, is both New York's proudest and poorest black neighborhood: onetime center of a cultural renaissance and on the verge of becoming one again, but also the area with the highest death rate among young black men in the nation. East Harlem runs with an almost official harshness into the Upper East Side at 97th Street, despite the extension of Museum Mile up to **El Museo del Barrio** on 104th. Whole rooms from John D. Rockefeller's onetime mansion at Fifth and 51st Street have been moved to the **Museum of the City of New York** on Fifth at 103rd. But walk across 103rd to the east, and you'll find yourself in an area Rockefeller wouldn't have stabled horses in.

There are real "heights," or at least ranges of hills, that stand between the Upper West Side and such western neighborhoods as Morningside

Heights (between about West 110th and Martin Luther King Boule-vard); Hamilton Heights, also known as Harlem Heights, centered on City College of New York and running up to around Trinity Cemetery at West 155th Street; and Washington Heights above that (see Zone 15). The Heights run about four blocks west from the long green of Riverside Park; Harlem (and East Harlem, as the area beyond Fifth Avenue is called) runs to the East River and up alongside the Harlem River, an area of nearly six square miles.

Morningside Park, a sort of comma between Central Park and River-side Park, opened in the late 19th century and almost immediately became an enclave of scholars and theologians. **Columbia University,** whose campus ranges from about 116th Street to 124th from Morning-side to Riverside Drive, is the heart of this neighborhood, with **Barnard College,** the **Union Theological Seminary,** and massive **Riverside Church** on its western flank and the extraordinary and still-growing **Cathedral of St. John the Divine** on Amsterdam at 112th (phone (212) 316-7540).

Riverside Church, at 122nd Street, was another of John D. Rocke-feller Jr.'s gifts to the city, a 21-story Gothic beauty inspired by the cathe-dral at Chartres; its carillon of 74 bells is the largest in the world (one weighs 20 tons by itself), and the 22,000-pipe organ is one of the largest. It also offers a spectacular view of the river and the city from the observa-tion deck off the bell tower, nearly 400 feet high. Free tours are offered following Sunday services, about 12:30 p.m. (phone (212) 870-6700).

And if you want to know who's buried in **Grant's Tomb,** walk through Riverside Park to that mausoleum on the hill. (The answer, incidentally, is both Grant and his wife.)

On Morningside Drive at West 114th Street is a more intimate chapel, the **Eglise de Notre Dame.** It contains a replica of the grotto of Lourdes where young girls saw visions of the Virgin Mary; a woman who believed her son was healed there had the replica constructed in thanks.

If you drew a line extending Central Park West (Eighth Avenue) past Cathedral Parkway, which runs along the northern border of Central Park, and on up into the Heights where Eighth Avenue is called Frederick Doug-lass Boulevard, it would be a very rough estimate of the western edge of Harlem. In fact, **Hamilton Heights,** which has several beautiful blocks of row houses along Convent Avenue between about 141st and 145th Streets, was a highly desirable neighborhood for both turn-of-the-19th-century white and early-20th-century black residents, when it was nicknamed **Sugar Hill** and housed such jazz celebrities as Cab Calloway, Duke Ellington, and Count Basie. The current **Hamilton Heights His-toric District**—so named because the area was once the country estate of Alexander Hamilton—is centered on four blocks of finely preserved row houses, many of them now residences of City College (CCNY) faculty and administrators. (Hamilton's 1802 house, which has been moved to 287 Convent Avenue, is currently closed for historic renovation.) The watchtower just south of CCNY on Amsterdam at 135th Street and the gatehouses at 113th and 119th Streets are remnants of the old aqueduct system. More intriguingly, the three-level cast-iron tower in **Marcus Garvey Park** (East 120th to 124th and Madison) is a survivor if the Revolutionary Battle of Harlem Heights.

And speaking of remnants: **Our Lady of Lourdes Church** at 142nd Street and Amsterdam is a true miracle of salvage, having been put together in 1904 from bits of the old National Academy of Design at Park and East 23rd Street, the A. T. Stewart department store on the old Ladies' Mile, and the former Madison Avenue apse of St. Patrick's Cathedral, removed to make room for what is now the Lady Chapel.

At the top of Hamilton Heights are **Trinity Cemetery** and **Audubon Terrace,** which face each other across Broadway between West 153rd and 155th Streets. This whole area was once part of the estate of John James Audubon, and the naturalist himself, along with many of those whose names appear repeatedly in these pages—Astors, Schermerhorns, Van Burens, and Clement Clarke Moore—are buried at Trinity Cemetery. (Audubon's gravestone is, appropriately, carved with birds.)

Several institutions of more specialized interest are gathered at Audubon Terrace, including the **American Numismatic Society** (phone (212) 234-3130) and the **Hispanic Society of America** (phone (212) 926-2234), a little-known museum with a fantastic collection of Spanish art by Goya, El Greco, Velázquez, etc. The **American Academy of Arts and Letters,** which mounts periodic exhibitions featuring the works of members, is also here (phone (212) 368-5900). Audubon Terrace is a sort of family affair itself; Architect Charles Pratt Huntington designed the buildings, his philanthropist cousin Archer Huntington donated most of the money and the bulk of the Spanish art collection, and Charles's wife, Anna Hyatt Huntington, sculpted the Cid memorial. (This isn't even the only Huntington museum. Archer Huntington donated his private home on Fifth Avenue for the National Academy Museum and School of Fine Arts.)

Although Harlem is generally thought of as a black area, it is actually a mix of African American, Caribbean, and Hispanic (particularly Puerto Rican) families. East Harlem is often referred to as **El Barrio,** Spanish for "the neighborhood," or **Spanish Harlem.** However, in recent years, a growing Cuban/Caribbean community has flourished along Broadway north of Hamilton Heights as well.

In any case, Harlem certainly began as a black neighborhood; it was the first African slaves, in fact, imported by the Dutch, who blazed the original Broadway by moving up the island to Nieuw Haarlem in 1658. And though most of the area was taken up by the large farms and country estates, the East and Harlem riverfronts were an inevitable ramshackle assortment of immigrants and watermen. It was a popular upper-middle-class suburb for most of the 19th century, with its own commuter rail system, the New York and Harlem Railroad, to carry businessmen back downtown; but around the turn of the century, things began to go sour. Businesses went bankrupt, buildings emptied, and the continual north-ward press of development from the wealthier sections of Manhattan drove black and immigrant families into many of the poorer areas.

By the early 20th century, Harlem was the major community for blacks with all levels of income. The famous Harlem Renaissance of liter-ature, music, and philosophy had a powerful effect on both high art and popular culture, raising Harlem's profile and giving greater force to the growing civil rights debate.

Despite the predations of time, poverty, and unimaginative urban renewal, many old brownstones are still visible in such areas as the **Mount Morris Park Historical District,** a Victorian enclave that was dominated by German-Jewish families "moving up" from the Lower East Side. It covers about five blocks between Lenox Avenue and Marcus Gar-vey Park (formerly Mount Morris Park) between West 119th and 124th Streets, and there are several proposals for renovating buildings for bou-tique hotels or bed-and-breakfasts here. The fire tower in the park dates from 1856. **St. Martin's Episcopal Church** at Lenox and 122nd has a fine carillon of its own, about 40 bells strong.

A couple of blocks northwest of the park are the **Studio Museum of Harlem,** west of Lenox Avenue on 125th Street (phone (212) 864-4500), a small (but expanding) select collection of African, African American, and Caribbean fine arts that also offers lectures and educa-tional programs; and the famed **Apollo Theater** on West 125th between Adam Clayton Powell and Frederick Douglass Boulevards (phone (212) 749-5838), founded as a vaudeville house in 1914 and the major show-case of black talent well into the 1960s. It has been revived, and the Wednesday Amateur Night tradition is as strong and lively as ever.

From here it's only a block's walk to **Sylvia's,** a soul-food restaurant so famous that its gospel brunch is on many Harlem tours; it's located on Lenox between West 126th and 127th Streets (phone (212) 996-0660). Then head straight up Lenox to West 135th and the **Schomburg Center for Research in Black Culture,** the largest library of African and African-American cultural and sociological materials in this country (phone (212) 491-2200).

On West 138th Street between Lenox and Adam Clayton Powell Avenue is the **Abyssinian Baptist Church,** equally famous as the onetime pastoral seat of Powell himself and for its gospel choir; its Sunday services draw busloads of tourists from all around the world (phone (212) 862-7474). The blocks of West 138th and 139th from Adam Clayton Powell Avenue over to Frederick Douglass constitute the **St. Nicholas Historic**

District, another group of late–19th-century homes designed by several different prominent architects of the day. The neighborhood is also known as **Striver's Row** because it drew a pre-yuppie-era group of ambitious young professionals.

At the top of St. Nicholas Park at West 141st Street is the famous **Harlem School of the Arts,** which has come to rival the New York High School for the Performing Arts (the model for the school in *Fame*) with its music, dance, and theater classes (phone (212) 926-4100).

If you like walking, you can fairly easily follow the path we've laid out from Marcus Garvey Park back to Harlem Heights. Sadly, although conditions are improving, we still cannot recommend that you wander other parts of Harlem by yourself, especially after dark; it's best to stick to the most famous sites, take cabs, or hook up with a tour group.

If you are particularly interested in contemporary black theater, you may also wish to contact the **Frank Silvera Writers' Workshop** at West 125th and St. Nicholas (phone (212) 281-8832) and the small but prestigious **National Black Theater** at Fifth and East 125th Street (phone (212) 722-3800).

Zone 15: The Heights

The area north of Trinity Cemetery and Audubon Terrace, called Washington Heights, was the area to which Washington's troops retreated—the Morris-Jumel Mansion served as his headquarters—during the early battles of the American Revolution, and it centers on Fort Tryon Park. While the park's official highlights are the remaining defiant bulwark and its overlook, the 62-acre park offers a far finer overview of Manhattan's original beauty, the Hudson River and the fine woods and animal life; and it serves as a natural approach to the stunning Cloisters collection of the Met.

The **Morris-Jumel Mansion** at West 160th Street and Edgecrombe (phone (212) 923-8008), which dates from 1765, is one of the very few colonial buildings still standing in New York. It was a summer estate—its grounds stretched from Harlem to the Hudson—belonging to Roger Morris, a prominent Loyalist who had served as aide to General Braddock. Morris refused to act against his former colleague (and rumored rival for the hand of the wealthy Mrs. Morris) Washington, but even so, his estates were confiscated by the revolutionary state government, and the Morrises returned to England. Washington did in fact sleep here and briefly used it as a headquarters; so, ironically, did Sir Henry Clinton, the British commander. More amazingly, Washington, Jefferson, Hamilton, John Adams and his son John Quincy Adams met here for lunch in 1790. The "Jumel" part is equally intriguing: French-Caribbean Creole merchant Stephen Jumel bought it in 1810 and lavishly remodeled it with the help of his socially ambitious wife, Eliza; she allegedly slept her way through much of New York society, let her husband bleed to death so as to make her a very rich widow, and then married the ruined, aging Aaron Burr—only to divorce him on his deathbed. Her reputation for cold-bloodedness and the house's reputation for reproachful spirits led to its having been "cleansed" by a Haitian exorcist a few decades later. Among her furniture is a "dolphin" chair said to have been purchased from Napoleon.

Fort Tryon Park, which runs from Broadway to Riverside Drive between West 192nd and Dykeman Streets, is only part of the original Billings estate; the massive series of arches on Riverside Drive was the "driveway." It was landscaped, like most of New York's great parks, by Frederick Law Olmsted, and it has an incredible assortment of views and gardens. The effect is immediately visible and almost shocking as you get off the "A" train at 190th Street; although they have not yet been fully restored, the stone terraces down the hillside and the arched entrance to the park seem to bound a different world, a medieval one; it couldn't be a better setting for the **Cloisters.** Its various paths and roadways (watch out for buses) are popular with joggers and exercise walkers, but are rarely crowded. There is a marker, a bit of remaining battlement, on the hilltop of the park that recalls the defense of Fort Washington from the British. (A little gatehouse, down the slope from the marker, has been turned into a nice little cafe, good for a break.)

The Cloisters (phone (212) 923-3700) is actually the medieval collection arm of the Metropolitan Museum of Art (you can use the same admission badge to enter both on a single day), and it was constructed from wings of several medieval French and Spanish cloisters. This is one of New York's premier attractions, gloriously evocative and frequently nearly deserted. Astonishingly, the estate that is now Fort Tryon Park, the Cloisters buildings—painstakingly transported from Europe and reassembled here—as well as the Palisades across the Hudson River and the art and manuscripts of the collection itself were all gifts of philanthropist John D. Rockefeller, Jr.

Almost at the other end of the spectrum is the **Shrine of St. Frances X. Cabrini** on Fort Washington Avenue at 190th. Mother Cabrini, as she is usually called, is the patron saint of immigrants, and her remains (with the exception of her head, which is in Rome) are encased within the altar. The miraculous story here is that shortly after her death in 1917, a blind child was touched with a lock of her hair and received sight; naturally, he entered the priesthood. Mother Cabrini was the first American citizen to be canonized, but since she was Italian by birth, Mother Elizabeth Seton can honestly claim to be the first American-born saint (see Zone 1).

A few blocks from the Cloisters at Broadway and West 204th Street (phone (212) 304-9422) is the **Dyckman House,** the only surviving 18th-century Dutch farmhouse (circa 1783) on the island, authentically fitted out and surrounded by a smokehouse and garden.

Other sites of interest in Washington Heights include **Yeshiva University,** the oldest Jewish seminary in the country, founded in 1886 (at West 186th Street and Amsterdam Avenue); the old **Loews 175th Street Theatre** at Broadway, another of those fantastic movie palaces-turned-churches (it was called a "Wonder Palace," which seems appropriate); and the **High Bridge,** the oldest footbridge (and sometime aqueduct) between Manhattan and the mainland. Begun in 1839, it stretches across the Harlem River from Highbridge Park at West 174th Street to West 170th in the Bronx. And if your children have read *The Little Red Lighthouse and the Great Gray Bridge,* head to Fort Washington Park at about West 178th Street and you'll see the lighthouse just below the eastern tower of the George Washington Bridge.

Zone 16: Brooklyn

Brooklynites have good reason to resent all those jokes about accents and Coney Island culture. Even if it seceded from the rest of New York City, Brooklyn (from "Breukelen," Dutch for "Broken Land") would be the nation's fourth largest city, with enough famous landmarks, museums, and resorts to make it a long weekend's destination of its own.

Start by walking across the Brooklyn Bridge itself, which offers one of New York's best viewpoints in all directions. Fulton Ferry Landing is the site of Bargemusic, and beyond that is the **Brooklyn Heights Historic District.** Ranging from the riverfront Expressway to about Atlantic Avenue, this area is an amazing pre–Civil War enclave of more than 600 churches and homes (including those of Walt Whitman, Arthur Miller, W. H. Auden, Thomas Wolfe, and Truman Capote). **The Promenade,** along the East River, has a spectacular view of Manhattan, an almost idyllic grid of community gardens and playgrounds, and a marker for Four Chimneys, where George Washington billeted during the War of Long Island. **Smith Street** near Carroll Garden is the hot new restaurant and boutique enclave. The **Brooklyn Historical Society,** which spotlights local heroes ranging from the Brooklyn Dodgers to *The Honeymooners,* is in the historic district at Pierrepont and Clinton Streets (phone (718) 254-9830 or visit **www.brooklynhistory.org**). **St. Ann and the Holy Trinity Episcopal Church** at Montague and Clinton is in need of repair, but its extremely fine stained-glass windows by William Jay Bolton are the oldest set of figural windows made in the United States.

Brooklyn's population has always been a vital ethnic mix, but these days it has replaced Manhattan as the real melting pot. Its many distinct communities include Caribbean (especially Jamaican and Haitian), Spanish, Middle Eastern and Arabic, Scandinavian, Russian, Polish, Orthodox Jewish, and Italian. Many famous neighborhoods and destinations—not just Coney Island but also Brighton Beach and Rockaway Beach, Flatbush, Brooklyn Heights, Prospect Park, and Jamaica Bay—

are in this 75-square-mile borough. (Incidentally, be careful not to confuse the Broadway in Brooklyn with the Broadway in Manhattan; Brooklyn's runs southeast from the Williamsburg Bridge.)

It has also become a sort of second Harlem, in that it is developing a group of black cultural and social centers that could easily become another "Renaissance." The Fort Greene area in particular has a number of cafes that sponsor poetry readings, art galleries, and performance spaces. The most prestigious are the **Paul Robeson Theater** (40 Greene Avenue; (718) 783-9794) and **BAM Café** (30 Lafayette; (718) 636-4139), an outreach project at the Brooklyn Art Museum.

One of the most important neighborhoods for first-time visitors is the area around **Prospect Park,** at the junction of Eastern Parkway and Flatbush Avenue (phone (718) 965-8900). This, the Central Park of Brooklyn (designed by the same men, Frederick Olmsted and Calvert Vaux, and with similar facilities and features), includes a children's zoo, officially the **Prospect Park Wildlife Conservation Center** (phone (718) 399-7339), that is even larger than the more famous Bronx facility; an **antique carousel** as fine as Central Park's and rescued from Coney Island; a mid–19th-century Italianate villa; and a skating rink and croquet shed designed by Stanford White. It even has its own cemetery, a Friends (Quaker) burial ground where Montgomery Clift is interred.

The northern boundary of the park adjoins the **Brooklyn Botanic Garden** grounds, which then lead over to the **Brooklyn Museum of Art,** a collection nearly as comprehensive as the Metropolitan's but far more comprehensible. On weekends and holidays, a free trolley links these three major attractions. And serving as a grand foyer to it all is **Grand Army Plaza** at Plaza Street and Flatbush Avenue: Olmsted and Vaux's grand oval, with its triumphal Soldier's and Sailor's Arch and a monument bust of JFK.

In addition to these sites, Brooklyn has several other attractions of particular interest to families. At the closer end are the **Brooklyn Children's Museum** (phone (718) 735-4402), actually only another few blocks away from the parks we just discussed; and the newly renovated **New York Transit Museum** (phone (718) 243-8601), a little east of the Brooklyn Heights Historic District at Schermerhorn Street between Court Street and Boerum Place. A former subway station, it now houses a fine collection of vintage cars, signal equipment and signs, old photos, drawings, and subway mosaics that served as directions for the illiterate and non-English-speaking immigrants.

The other most intriguing area is the Brighton Beach–Coney Island area at the southern end of the borough. The famous **Coney Island** amusement park, somewhat less lustrous than in its heyday as "the world's largest playground" but still good for a stroll along the boardwalk, a ride on the teeth-rattling wooden Cyclone roller coaster (the skeletal remains of its predecessor, the Tornado, are almost scary), and an original Nathan's hot dog; the **New York Aquarium** (phone (718) 265-3474), with its shark tank, SeaWorld–style whale and dolphin "theater," and hands-on Discovery Cove is just alongside the park, and so is the new Brooklyn Cyclones (aka "Baby Mets") stadium; the Miami Beach–like Borscht Boardwalk of **Brighton Beach** is perhaps another mile down the way. Eat in the melting pot; have a hot dog at the game and a knish later. Or sushi—advertised in Cyrillic letters. Now you know why they call it "Little Odessa by the Sea." Even farther east is **Jamaica Bay Wildlife Refuge Center,** a ten-mile stretch of beach near Rockaway that is a migratory marker for more than 300 species of birds. Park rangers lead hikes on weekends (phone (718) 318-4340). The park even has its own subway stop at Broad Channel.

The **Brooklyn Academy of Music** (BAM) on Lafayette near Fulton Street (phone (718) 636-4100), as mentioned in Part Eleven, is not only a respected concert venue and home of the Brooklyn Philharmonic but also has its own opera house, the restored and aptly named Majestic Theater a block down Fulton Street, and several smaller performance spaces. As the BAM boosters like to point out, its history is every bit as lustrous as Broadway's: Bernhardt, Booth, Pavlova, Rachmaninoff, Sandburg, Churchill, and Caruso all performed here. Its October Next Wave Festival is extremely popular.

Zone 17: Queens

Queens, particularly the area called **Long Island City,** is suddenly being rediscovered, thanks primarily to the temporary (to early 2005 at least) relocation of the **Museum of Modern Art** while its 53rd Street building in Manhattan is being renovated and expanded. **MoMa QNS** (33rd Street at Queens Boulevard; (718) 708-9400), as it's being called, is easily accessed by subway. It's only a few minutes from the (also temporary) **Isamu Naguchi Museum** (phone (718) 204-7088) and the **Museum for African Art** (phone (718) 784-7700), both at 43rd Avenue and 36th Street. All this art has in turn sparked a flurry of neighborhood eateries. The Noguchi home, also being restored, is one of the few collections in the world devoted to one man's work, filling 12 galleries with his celebrated lamps and theatrical sets, and a gorgeous sculpture garden displays his larger pieces. The adjoining **Museum for African Art** is small but first-rate, exhibiting both traditional and contemporary arts. Queens offers another example of a fine day's sight-seeing, since most of what a visitor is likely to want to see is at **Flushing Meadows–Corona Park,** especially if you figure in the Mets' **Shea Stadium,** also used as a concert venue, and the **U.S. Tennis Association's** complex, where the U.S. Open is held. Here is Queens's main public park, with its own rowboat lake, ice rink, theater in the park, bike rentals, and so on, and frequent special events (phone (718) 520-5900); it was the site of two World's Fairs

(1939–40 and 1964–65) and is still home of the **New York Hall of Science,** the **Queens Wildlife Center** (phone (718) 271-1500), and the **Queens Museum of Art.** It's a world unto itself—that is, the 140-foot, 350-ton Unisphere globe, created for the 1964 World's Fair, still stands at the entrance. And this world, too, we owe to Robert Moses, who dredged out what had been a notorious swamp and rubbish pile to make a place worthy of an international exhibition.

Restored and renovated a couple of years ago, the park is now a sort of Disney Futurama of the past—what New Yorkers of 60 years ago expected of the 21st century. the "skyscape" is almost a space-scape, full of rocket ships and planets. And like Disney World's backwards glimpse at "progress," it reminds us that such marvels as robots, color film, synthetic fabrics, FM radio, and dishwashers were brand new in 1939. Space vehicles, elevated super-highways, and heliports were the hottest draws in 1964. Many of these exhibits have been preserved, along with time capsules, one from each fair, not to be opened for 5,000 years.

The **New York Hall of Science** (phone (718) 699-0005) was originally constructed as the Hall of Education for the 1964 World's Fair, but is scrupulously and often astonishingly up to date; it has interactive video stations that store outer-space transmissions, super-TV-sized microscope displays, and scores of hands-on demonstrations of light, music, color, and physical properties.

If Brooklyn's Museum of Art is like a miniature Metropolitan, the **Queens Museum of Art** (phone (718) 592-9700) is like a miniature New York: It was the original New York City Building of the fair. It houses a huge and detailed scale model (1 inch to 100 feet) of New York called the Panorama that was also constructed for the 1964 World's Fair and updated in the early 1990s. It includes all five boroughs, almost 900,000 individual buildings, a 15-inch Empire State Building, 35 bridges, and airplanes that actually "take off" from LaGuardia. The museum also has hundreds of bits of World's fair memorabilia, such as guidebooks, souvenir plates and pins, board games, and banners.

For history buffs, this building also has special significance: It served as the temporary headquarters of the United Nations from 1946 to 1951, and it was here that the nation of Israel was voted into existence.

There's a lot to see, but Friday through Sunday, trolleys circulate among the park attractions and the Willets Point/Shea Stadium subway; $1 buys you all-day access.

For foodies, the stretch of **Roosevelt Avenue** from about 60th Street to 90th Street is a famous world's fare, so to speak. Here you can sample Indian, Pakistani, Mexican, Korean, Cuban, Uruguayan, Filipino, Chinese, Thai, and even Texan cooking. Be sure to carry that Alka-Seltzer.

If you love over-the-top architecture, it might be worth ending the day with a side trip to Jamaica (to either the Parsons Boulevard or Jamaica

Center subway stops, accessible from the Forest Hills station at the east end of the park or the 74th Street station at the west side) to visit the **Tabernacle of Prayer for All People** at Jamaica and Merrick Boulevard. Constructed in the late 1920s as a movie palace, it is a rococo Spanish extravaganza of gold, enamel, cobalt, inlay, and even stars above. Open to visitors Friday evenings and Sundays; call (718) 657-4210 for information.

Astoria, the northwest part of Queens (the part that faces the Upper East Side across the East River), is home to the **American Museum of the Moving Image** at 35th Avenue and 36th Street (phone (718) 784-4520) and **PS 1** (Jackson Avenue at 46th Avenue; (718) 784-2084), one of the largest and most influential contemporary art centers. The "PS 1" name is short for Public School No. 1, which is what it originally was; now, it's an affiliate of the Museum of Modern Art.

In recent years, Queens has become a trendy destination for food-lovers as well. Flushing is flush with inexpensive Asian delights, and Corona is King of the Brazilian churrascaria. And Astoria's famous Greek ethnic community is second in size only to that in Athens itself; it is packed with restaurants, delicatessens, bakeries, and gift shops. Just stroll Broadway in the 30s and follow your nose.

Zone 18: The Bronx

There was a time when this was rich woodlands, then farmland (it was the 17th-century estate of retired sailor Jonas Bronck); it was genteel country estate territory in the 19th century; and even into the early 20th century it was a prestigious address. (Many neighborhoods, particularly Riverdale, still are.) Sadly, at this point in history those northward waves and ripples of alternating prosperity and decay have left the South Bronx in a slough. However, there is revived interest in the area, and some philanthropic and government funding is coming in for restoration.

Its most famous attractions, of course, are the **Bronx Zoo** (formally, the International Wildlife Conservation Park), the **New York Botanical Garden,** and **Yankee Stadium,** the House that Ruth Built—and when you come out of the subway at 161st Street, you'll see why the old Yankees-Dodgers contests were called "subway series": You can see right into the stands from the tracks. And it's here that you'll find the city's largest public green space, Pelham Bay Park, which is three times as large as Central Park.

The Grand Concourse, which is the great boulevard of the Bronx, runs from the Harlem River right up toward the botanical garden. The garden and the Bronx Zoo are neighbors, more or less, although there is a bit of a walk between the respective entrances. Both are near the campus of **Fordham University.**

The **Edgar Allan Poe Cottage** (phone (718) 881-8900) at Grand Concourse and East Kingsbridge Road is where Poe and the dying Virginia lived from 1846 to 1848, and it houses many of his manuscripts and memorabilia.

Toward the northern edge of the Bronx (and of the subway lines) are several historical estates, most notably the **Van Cortlandt House Museum** in Van Cortlandt Park (phone (718) 543-3344), a restored mid–18th-century mansion used by Washington as one of his headquarters (there was skirmish fire in the yard) and furnished with authentic period Dutch and American pieces as well as Delft ceramics. On the east side, Van Cortlandt Park adjoins **Woodlawn Cemetery** (phone (718) 920-0500), where the wealthy (Woolworths, Macys, Goulds, Belmonts, Armours, etc.) built eternal homes as elaborate as their temporal ones; get a map at the Webster Street entrance.

A few blocks west of Van Cortlandt Park is **Wave Hill,** the former estate of financier/conservationist George Perkins and at various points home to Theodore Roosevelt, Mark Twain, Arturo Toscanini, and so on. Take one glimpse of its view, over the Hudson River toward the Palisades, and you'll see why. The mansion is now used for concerts (in the vaulted Armor Hall), art exhibits ranging from sculpture to topiary, and demonstrations; the gardens and grounds are also open; call (718) 549-3200.

Although it requires a little more planning, those interested in sailing and whaling might want to visit **City Island** just off the northeast shore of the Bronx, a community of sailing vessels, boatyards (including the manufacturers of several America's Cup champs), marinas, and old-fashioned waterside eateries. Take the 6 subway to Pelham Bay and transfer to the Bx29 bus.

Zone 19: Staten Island

"I'll take Manhattan/The Bronx and Staten Island, too . . ." Staten Islanders could be forgiven for sometimes feeling as if they were an afterthought, famous primarily as the turnaround point for the Staten Island Ferry. In fact, Staten Island would still be part of New Jersey if the Duke of York hadn't put it up as a prize in a sailing contest in 1687. It wasn't even connected to any other borough until 1964, when the Verrazano Narrows Bridge between Staten Island and Brooklyn opened; it's the world's longest suspension bridge and still the only actual point of contact. And Staten Islanders have repeatedly voiced enthusiasm for breaking away from the rest of New York; a 1993 referendum on secession passed by a 2-to-1 vote.

Despite this apparent sense of independence, or perhaps because of it (too much progress can be a short-sighted thing), Staten Island is the site of several very old structures that might be worth an excursion, especially for families interested in American history. (For information on the ferry, see the section on Zone 1.) And though it's a little farther south than most tourists usually get, the **Greenbelt** (phone (718) 667-2165), or more formally High Rock Park, is nearly three times the size of Central Park—an outdoor paradise one could scarcely envision from the rusty environs of the ferry terminal.

The 28-building **Snug Harbor Cultural Center** at Richmond Terrace and Tysons Street (phone (718) 448-2500) was founded in 1801 as a home for aging sailors and served as one, at least in part, for nearly 150 years. Now converted to an arts center (the visitors center has listing of current exhibitions), it still has several fine Greek Revival structures dating to the 1830s. The oldest, Main Hall, with its seafaring-themed stained glass, is now the **Newhouse Center for Contemporary Art** (phone (718) 448-2500). Snug Harbor is also the site of the **Staten Island Children's Museum** (phone (718) 273-2060), which emphasizes performances as well as science, and the **Staten Island Botanical Garden,** with its lush orchid greenhouse and the brand-new traditional Chinese scholar's garden, built by local contractors with the assistance of 40 craftsmen from Suzhou (phone (718) 273-8200).

Overlooking the Narrows a little north of the Verrazano Bridge is the **Alice Austen House Museum** on Hylan Boulevard at the Bay (phone (718) 816-4506), a long, low, gracious cottage built in 1710. The prominent 19th-century photographer lived most of her life here and took more than 7,500 photographs of the evolution of New York life, but they went almost unnoticed, and at the age of 84, having lost everything in the stock market crash, she had to move into the poorhouse. But only a year later, she and her work were "discovered" by *Life* magazine, and she was able to spend her last years in a nursing home. Her photos are exhibited in the house on a rotating basis.

Historic Richmond Town (phone (718) 351-1611) on Clarke Avenue south of the Staten Island Expressway is even older, at least in part. It includes 29 buildings, about half of them open to the public, in a restored "village" something like a Williamsburg of the north. Among the open structures is the 1695 Voorlezer House, the oldest elementary school in the country; the 1839 Bennet House, now called the Museum of Childhood (see the toy room); and the 1840 General Store–cum–post office. Like Williamsburg, it is populated by costumed craftsmen and artisans who give demonstrations and sell reproductions as souvenirs in the Historical Museum gift store.

Thanks to a recent spate of movies and celebrity campaigns, there is increasing interest in Tibetan culture, and one of the few museums of Tibetan art is the **Jacques Marchais Center** (phone (718) 987-3500) at 338 Lighthouse Avenue, not far from Historic Richmond Town. "Marchais" was actually Asian art dealer Mrs. Harry Klauber, who built this replica of a Himalayan temple to house her private collection of Buddhas, religious artifacts, and other contemplative figurines. There are even life-sized stone Buddhas in the garden, and its visitors have included the Dalai Lama.

Central Park

As great cities go, New York is still young: brash, mercurial, simultaneously bursting out of its seams and shooting its cuffs. But that it early on considered itself the equal of any European capital is evident from its sweeping avenues and the long rise of Central Park, a project whose design and construction fascinated and eventually captured the imagination of people from every social class in the city. In fact, an early proposal to put it on the old Jones's Wood site (see the section on Zone 11) was furiously shouted down as being too niggardly and peripheral.

Ultimately, the construction of the park—the original construction, setting aside later additions—took 16 years. It covered almost 850 acres and required 5 million tons of fill dirt and rock (not counting the glacial rocks and schist that already stick up all over the park) and another 5 million trees, increasing the number of hardwood species from about 40 to more than 600, and more than 800 kinds of shrubs and bushes.

Nowadays, the park is an internationally recognized symbol of the city, attracting more than 20 million tourists every year, not to mention the thousands of residents who are drawn here every day. Its recreational facilities are particularly rich, including 22 separate playgrounds as well as the famous skating rink, and so on (for more information, see Part Ten, Exercise and Recreation). It has concessions stands and real restaurants, but there is an almost inexhaustible supply of other family attractions, plus long stretches of theme gardens, performance venues, and many miniparks, within the overall park.

When Central Park was begun, or rather, when the first attempts were made to clear out the squatters and renderers, Frederick Law Olmsted wasn't even a landscape designer; he was a journalist. But he was fascinated by the concept of a European-style commons, or "greensward," and backed by fellow writers Horace Greeley, William Cullen Bryant (who had been one of the first to inveigle against consuming development), and Washington Irving, he successfully applied to become superintendent of the park. A year later, in partnership with his friend Calvert Vaux, who was an architect and landscape professional, he secured the designer's position as well.

They did not always agree. Olmsted wanted no reservoirs or museums or structures of any sort beyond arches and bridges; Vaux himself designed most of the bridges, as well as the original Metropolitan Museum of Art building. Olmsted tried to block the construction of the Sheepfold, a haven for the flock that grazed what is still called the Sheep Meadow, but it was pushed through by Tammany Hall's Boss Tweed (it's now the Tavern on the Green restaurant). Nor did Olmsted and Vaux like the idea of mon-uments, though the park now has close to 100 busts, plaques, statues, and memorial gardens. What they would have said about the World War I–era proposal to put an airfield in, one can only imagine.

"New York's Backyard"

Central Park ranges nearly 50 blocks, from Central Park South (59th Street) to Central Park North (110th), and fills three avenues, from Fifth to Eighth. It is crossed from east to west in only five places, at roughly 65th, 72nd, 79th, 85th, and 99th Streets—"roughly" both because most of the transverse roads have pleasant curves rather than gridlike rigidity and because vehicular traffic is prohibited during the middle of the day and all weekend.

Several of the most famous children's attractions are in the southern-most segment of the park, including **Wollman skating rink** (restored by Donald Trump), the **Zoo** (officially the Central Park Wildlife Conserva-tion Center), and the **Carousel.** The Carousel (phone (212) 879-0244), a 1908 model with 58 hand-carved horses just south of the 65th Street transverse, was moved to Central Park from Coney Island in 1951, replacing a far less attractive merry-go-round. Back in the 19th century, real horses, on a treadmill beneath the carousel gazebo, pulled little car-riages around.

Looking north, the **Dairy** is to the right of the Carousel, closer to Fifth Avenue. The twin-peaked shed is now the main Visitors Center (phone (212) 794-6564), and Urban Park Rangers (phone (212) 360-2774) sometimes lead tours of the park from here. The **Chess and Checkers House,** a gift of financier Bernard Baruch, is on a rock just southwest of the Dairy. And beyond that, across Center Drive, are **Heckscher Play-ground** and the **softball fields,** which pretty much fill up the southeast part of this section to Columbus Circle.

The Pond, a reed-edged sanctuary filled with ducks and other wildlife, is curled up near Grand Army Plaza in the literal shadow of the St. Moritz and Helmsley Park Lane hotels.

The frontispiece of the zoo, near where East 64th Street runs into Fifth Avenue, is the **Arsenal** building (phone (212) 360-1311), which origi-nally earned its cannon, but in the years since it was built in 1851, it has been a weather station, a police station, a menagerie, the original Museum of Natural History, and finally, headquarters of the Parks and Recreation Department. The original Olmsted-Vaux plans for the park are exhibited here. The **Zoo** itself (phone (212) 861-6030) was renovated in the late 1980s; the parks department found new homes for the animals that were too large for such a crowded facility, and it constructed more contemporary, eco-sensitive settings for the animals that were kept. The monkey house is now a real jungle gym, the bats have an eternally nocturnal home, and the reptiles have a swamp that is almost a pre-Olmsted joke. Free tours daily at 2:30 p.m. and weekends at 10:30 a.m. as well.

(Don't just check your watch; check out the **Delacorte Clock** by the zoo entrance. Every 30 minutes, a bronze menagerie of musical animals appears to peal out nursery rhymes.)

Just above the 65th Street Transverse, almost to Central Park West, is the elaborate **Tavern on the Green** restaurant, with its famous conservatory style Crystal Room and the quainter upstairs dining rooms and lounge, still reminiscent of a sheepfold's loft. The **Sheep Meadow** is the 15-acre green alongside the Tavern (which has a new café, phone (212) 396-4100), and nearby is the **Bowling Green,** where top-ranked competitive collegiate and professional croquet teams still play.

Just to the right of the Sheep Meadow and Bowling Green, running just about down the middle of this second rung of the park's ladder, is a popular Rollerblading strip. And on the other side of that is **the Mall,** a formal promenade of elms that formed a sight line of ten blocks all the way up to Belvedere Castle atop Vista Rock. The bandshell there, the second on the site, is no longer used; summer concerts are now held on the adjoining playground, **Rumsey Field,** which, in case you need a good meeting point, is the one with the statue of Mother Goose.

Facing the old bandshell across Terrace Drive (the 72nd Street transverse) is **Bethesda Terrace,** a fountain setting at the edge of the lake that offers a grand view of the Ramble on the other side. The statue atop the fountain represents "The Angel of the Waters," from a story in the Gospel of John that says the touch of an angel gave healing powers to Bethesda pool in Jerusalem. **The Lake,** which is about one-third of the way up the park, is the second largest body of water in the park, pinched together in the middle and crossed by Vaux's 60-foot-high cast-iron **Bow Bridge.**

In the northeast corner of the Lake is **Loeb Boathouse** (phone (212) 517-2233), with its Venetian gondola and rowboat rentals—you can take a 30-minute ride from an Italian-trained gondolier for about $30. Just a short walk further is the **Boat House,** one of Manhattan's most popular scenic eateries for tourists. A little beyond Loeb toward Fifth Avenue is an unconnected, smaller lake called **Conservatory Water,** where the Kerbs Model Boathouse houses the miniature yachts that race every Saturday afternoon in summer. Nearby are the statues of the **Mad Tea Party** from *Alice's Adventures in Wonderland* and **Hans Christian Andersen;** Andersen's only permanent audience is a bronze bird, but his memorial is the gathering place for storytime on Saturdays at 11 a.m.

To the west of Bethesda Terrace is the **Cherry Hill** overlook, which offers a view of the Mall, the Lake, and the Ramble; beyond that, between the southernmost little finger of the Lake and the West 72nd Street entrance, is **Strawberry Fields,** Yoko Ono's memorial to John Lennon; it's across from the Dakota apartments, where he was assassinated. The mosaic, reading "Imagine," was a gift from the city of Naples, Italy; and the "peace garden" includes plants from 161 nations.

North of the Lake is **the Ramble,** 37 acres of woods and wildflower gardens and a haven for birds and bird-watchers alike; more than 250 species have been spotted here, many of which migrate along the Atlantic flyway. On the western shore of the lake at about 77th Street is the **Ladies Pavilion.**

Across from the Ramble, in the middle of the 79th Street transverse, is **Vista Rock** and its crowning glory, **Belvedere Castle,** a somewhat smaller but impressive replica of a Scottish stone castle—turrets, terraces, and all—that was just meant to be part of the decor back in Olmsted and Vaux's day. Today it houses the **Henry Luce Nature Observatory,** which arranges lots of family tours and programs (phone (212) 772-0210) and a branch of the National Weather Service that has information on wildlife and whose roof offers a splendid view of the park. West of the castle near Winter Drive are the **Swedish Cottage** (phone (212) 988-9093), a marionette theater originally built for the Philadelphia Exposition of 1876, and the **Shakespeare Garden,** a sort of Bard-lover's botanical Bartlett's; all the trees and flowers planted around the pools are mentioned in his works.

Visible across Belvedere Lake to the northwest is the **Delacorte Theater,** the 2,000-seat site of the popular summer Shakespeare in the Park shows, named for publisher George Delacorte, who also donated the animal fair clock at the zoo and the Mad Tea Party sculpture. In fact, he is said to have been the model, somewhat exaggerated, for the Mad Hatter himself.

Visible to the northeast is **Cleopatra's needle,** actually built by Thutmos III in 1600 B.C.E., despite its popular nickname. The obelisk and its twin were presented by the Khedive of Egypt to the city of New York and to Queen Victoria in 1881. Translations of the hieroglyphs, which have been nearly eradicated by modern air pollution, are engraved on plaques donated by that Cleopatra lover, moviemaker Cecil B. DeMille. Beyond Cleopatra's needle, along Fifth Avenue from East 81st to 84th, is the **Metropolitan Museum of Art.** And the great green oval in the center of the park from Belvedere Lake nearly to the 85th Street transverse is the 55-acre **Great Lawn,** with the brilliant Green Oval at its heart.

At least, now it's a lawn. It started out as a reservoir; it was the site of Central Park's Hooverville, as the Depression-era shantytowns were called, and later was used as an athletic field until the mid-1930s when Robert Moses, the great public works developer, created the great lawn. Most recently, resodded and regraded, it has been the venue for several famous concerts, including Simon and Garfunkle's 1981 concert, which drew a crowd of half a million; the even larger "No Nukes" show a year later; and Pavarotti's recital in 1993. It is also where the Metropolitan Opera and the New York Philharmonic stage their summer concerts.

The 85th Street transverse is geographically the waistline of the park. Above it is the 106-acre **Reservoir,** by far the largest of the park's half-dozen bodies of water, which takes up most of the area between the 85th and 97th Street transverses. It dates back to the original Croton reservoir system of 1862 and was in active use until only a couple of years ago. Now a popular jogging route, the trail around the reservoir has been named in honor of one of its most faithful visitors, Jacqueline Kennedy Onassis. The remaining corner of this section, northwest of the reservoir, is where the tennis courts are.

North of the 97th Street transverse are the large **North Meadow** and smaller **East Meadow,** which even for some city dwellers seems to be the end of the park. However, there are more gardens and even some historic sites above about 105th Street. The **Conservatory Garden,** actually three formal gardens (and no conservatory building) that were once part of the Cornelius Vanderbilt Mansion in Midtown, includes a "Secret Garden," with an appropriate statue of Dickon and Mary; the entrance gate, also from the Vanderbilt estate, is on Fifth Avenue between 104th and 105th.

Behind the Conservatory Garden is **the Mount,** which is now bare but once held a tavern (later a convent!) from which Washington's men held off the British. It looks down on **McGowan's Pass** at East 106th Street and beyond the pass to the former site of a pair of 1812 forts (now identified by markers only). Look for the blockhouse below East Drive (about West 109th Street) south or the Adam Clayton Powell Boulevard entrance.

At the opposite end of the park from Wollman Rink is **Lasker Rink,** another ice-skating rink—a wading pool in summer. Due to its location, this rink is cheaper and generally less crowded than Wollman.

Finally, at the top of the park beyond the **Harlem Meer** lake is **Charles A. Dana Discovery Center** (phone (212) 860-1370), once the boathouse and now an outpost of the Urban Park Rangers, dedicated to environmental issues.

Part Seven

Sight-seeing, Tours, and Attractions

Let Your Fingers Do the Walking . . . First

The nice thing about sight-seeing is that you can do it at your own pace, looking closely at what intrigues you, gazing appreciatively at what only pleases you, and pushing right on past what stirs not a flicker of interest. In New York, you can tour by land, sea, air, horse-drawn carriage, and even parasail. You can see historic spots or literary haunts, cathedrals or courts, authentic remnants or virtual realities. (And you can pay nothing or, well, something.)

You can see them all best if you get right down to street level. New York is particularly well suited to walking tours, and that's what we recommend. (Skylines are lovely, but you have to be at a distance to see them.) We want you to get up close and personal here. Keep your eyes open and your schedule a little loose: Several office buildings around town have minimuseums and free galleries on the street level; some technology firms such as Sony have informal try-out rooms.

But it's a little smarter to consider your preferences before you start off—before you leave home, if you have time, or maybe on the plane. New York offers so much that it can be confusing if not downright intimidating. So we've outlined some categories of special interest, suggested some specialized tours you might be interested in, and even sketched out a few starting points and highlights in Part Six, New York's Neighborhoods.

In Part Nine, Shopping in New York, we've combined souveniring with introductory walks around the most important neighborhoods (to visitors, at least), with a little background flavor and a few landmarks for orientation. Some of the most important museums, historic houses, and buildings are described in more detail in the attraction profiles at the end of this chapter.

On the other hand, we know that not everybody prefers do-it-yourself tours. Some people find it a bit distracting to try to read directions and anecdotes while walking, and others use packaged tours as a way of getting a mental map of the area. So we've also listed some of the most reputable guided tours available. (These are surely not all of them; tourism is a boom industry in New York, and you'll see flyers for new tours every month. If you do want to take a guided tour, check through the material at the information desks and visitors centers or even your hotel lobby; you may find a discount coupon lurking.)

We also realize that New York is not one-size-fits-all. Walking is wonderful if you're young and fit, but if your party includes children or seniors, make sure to pace yourself. Build in a timely stop in a park; split the touring day into "shifts" so that, if necessary, those with less stamina can head back to the hotel for a rest while the others continue; or lay out the schedule on the democratic scheme—that is, put the attractions everyone wants to see first, the could-be-missed intermediate ones later, and the only-for-fanatics excursions last. That way, whoever wants to drop out can.

If each member of the party has his or her own must-sees, then set a particular hour to split up and a clearly understood place to regroup. If you're worried about a teenager getting completely wound up in whatever museum or exhibit he's into and losing track of the time, schedule this separate tour session just before lunch; there are few things that can override a kid's stomach alarm, even a *T. rex* skeleton.

Finally, because the food and beverage lures are everywhere, especially around major tourist attractions, avoid stomach overload or whining children by carrying a supply of snacks in plastic bags. And don't forget water or soda: It's easy to become dehydrated when you're doing a lot of walking.

The former World Trade Center and environs, now known as **Ground Zero** after the terrorist attacks of 9/11, are the hub of a complicated and sometimes dangerous recovery effort. The roughly rectangular area (bounded by Barclay Street on the north, Church Street on the east, Albany Street on the south, and West Street on the west) is off-limits to everyone except recovery workers. For your own safety and that of workers (as well as out of respect for those who lost loved ones), sight-seeing in this area is discouraged.

However, recognizing the worldwide interest in Ground Zero, the City of New York has constructed a viewing platform to allow the public to see the area safely and without interfering with recovery work. The platform is at the south side of the site at Church and Maiden streets, and it's open daily, 9 a.m.–8 p.m. Tickets are no longer required, though security officers may limit access during heavy crowding. The pedestrian bridge at Liberty Street to the World Financial Center (and many neighboring buildings) also offer views of the area.

Categories and Recommendations

Best Children's Fare

Abigail Adams Smith Museum (Zone 11)

American Museum of Natural History (Zone 12)

Bronx Zoo (Zone 18)

Central Park

Forbes Magazine Galleries (Zone 4)

Hayden Planetarium (Zone 12)

IMAX Theater (Zone 10)

Intrepid Sea-Air-Space Museum (Zone 8)

Museum of the City of New York (Zone 13)

Museum of Television and Radio (Zone 9)

New York City Fire Museum (Zone 2)

New York City Police Museum (Zone 1)

New York Hall of Science (Zone 17)

New York Transit Museum (Zone 16)

Roosevelt Island Aerial Tramway (Zone 11)

Sony Wonder Technology Lab (Zone 9)

Best Views

Brooklyn Bridge (Zone 1/3)

Empire State Building (Zone 7)

Marriott-Marquis View Restaurant (Zone 8)

Riverside Church (Zone 14)

Rockefeller Center's Rainbow Room (Zone 9)

Statue of Liberty (Zone 1) (statue itself closed indefinitely)

Terrace on the Park (Zone 17)

Ethnic and "Roots" Exhibits

Ellis Island Immigration Museum (Zone 1)

Japan Society (Zone 9)

The Jewish Museum (Zone 13)

Lower East Side Tenement Museum (Zone 3)

El Museo del Barrio (Zone 13)

The Museum for African Art (Zone 2)

Museum of Chinese in the Americas (Zone 3)

The Museum of Jewish Heritage/Holocaust (Zone 1)

National Museum of the American Indian (Zone 1)

Schomberg Center for Research in Black Culture (Zone 14)

Smaller, Less-crowded Museums of Note

The Asia Society (Zone 11)

The Cloisters (Zone 15)

The Frick Collection (Zone 11)

Hispanic Society of America (Zone 14)

Isamu Noguchi Garden Museum (Zone 17)

jacques Marchais Center of Tibetan Art (Zone 19)

Museum of the City of New York (Zone 13)

New York City Police Museum (Zone 1)

New-York Historical Society (Zone 12)

Pierpont Morgan Library (Zone 9)

Free (or Pay What You Wish) Museum Hours

American Folk Art Museum, Friday 6–8 p.m.

The Asia Society, Friday 6–9 p.m.

Bronx Museum of the Arts, Wednesday 3–9 p.m.

Bronx Zoo, Wednesday 10 a.m.–4:30 p.m.

Cooper-Hewitt National Design Museum, Tuesday 5–9 p.m.

Solomon R. Guggenheim Museum, Friday 6–8 p.m. (pay what you wish)

International Center of Photography, Friday 5–8 p.m. (pay what you wish)

Jewish Museum, Tuesday 5–8 p.m.

Museum of Modern Art, Friday 4:30–8:30 p.m. (pay what you wish)

New Museum of Contemporary Art, Thursday 6–8 p.m.

New York Botanical Garden, Wednesday 10 a.m.–4 p.m.; Saturday 10 a.m.–noon

New York Hall of Science, Thursday and Friday (except July and August) 2–5 p.m.

Whitney Museum of American Art, Friday 6–9 p.m.

Touring Options

Packaged Tours

There are well over 1,000 licensed tour guides in New York, and many more unlicensed ones. And no wonder: The city draws 30 million visitors every year, and the numbers keep going up. That's good news and bad— good because you as a tourist have a huge number of tours and guides to choose from, and bad because it can be difficult to differentiate between the worthwhile and the time-consuming.

Frankly, we're not so enthusiastic about most packaged mass tours. We think it's more rewarding to select the attractions you're truly interested in and go on your own or with a more intimate group. After all, most of the "sights" on those sight-seeing tours are so famous you already know what the outside looks like, and a lot of the time that's all you see out the window, anyway. And you're a lot more likely to end the day feeling, just as you did in the morning, that Manhattan is a large, crowded, and loud place.

Besides, there are several drawbacks to taking these overview tours. For one thing, simply loading and off-loading passengers at every stop—not to mention dealing with traffic—takes up a substantial portion of the time you are supposedly sight-seeing. And a more recent twist is that more and more of the neighborhoods, from Soho to Harlem, are complaining about tour bus traffic and the noise and pollution created by idling vehicles. Commercial traffic is banned around some important historical areas, most notably Washington Square.

On the favorable side, you are apt to be swept around enough to get an idea of the island's layout, and if you plan to return frequently, that might be an advantage. Many of the longer tours have lunch or dinner and even a little entertainment scheduled right along with the ride, which may be a relief for those with sticker or map shock. Those with limited walking power might prefer to stay on the bus, in any case. Those shy of sidewalk adventures may find security in numbers. And you can hear a lot of history and humor in a single dose, if that's what you like. Note that prices frequently change; you might want to ask whether the tour company has discounts for members of AARP, AAA, and such.

Gray Line Tours, which has buses, a new fleet of eco-friendly (low-emission) and wheelchair-accessible double-decker buses, and trolleys, remains one of the most reliable packaged tour operators. You can spend from two hours to the whole day in the tour company's care; see the whole island or just a district or two; and get picked up from many major hotels as well as its headquarters at the side entrance to the Port Authority Bus Terminal on 42nd Street near Eighth Avenue (phone (800) 669 0051 or (212) 397-2600). A nice feature is that hop-on, hop-off tickets are good for two days, so you can spread it out if you don't want to make the whole circuit at once. Gray Line has tour guides who speak French, German, Italian, Spanish, and Portuguese as well as English. If you want to be picked up from the airport as well, call (212) 315-3006.

Harbor cruises lasting about 90 minutes and offering views of the Statue of Liberty and the downtown skyline are offered by **NY Waterways** (call (800) 533-3779); it leaves from Pier 78 (West 38th Street), but there's free bus pickup from various sites around town. *World Yacht* leaves from Pier 81 (41st Street) and goes down the west side of the island each night for dinner and weekends and Wednesdays for brunch (phone (212) 630-8100). **Seaport Music Cruises** swing around the Statue of Liberty and Ellis Island from the South Street Seaport in about an hour; they also offer two-hour jazz cruises on Thursday evenings and blues cruises on Wednesdays ($40–$55; (212) 630-8888). A somewhat more "exciting" version of the harbor tour, for the amusement-park thrill ride generation, is on the **"Beast,"** which uses 145-seat speed boats painted with Jaws-style grins and rock 'n' roll music to spice up a 30-minute, wet, and (fairly) wild tour available daily, April–October ($15; (212) 563-3200).

For a bird's eye view, take a helicopter tour: The **Gray Line** office sells no-reservation tickets for flights leaving continually from 9 a.m. to 6 p.m. weekdays (phone (212) 397-2620). Or try a 30-minute seaplane tour; call **SeaAir New York** (phone (212) 681-4779). **Liberty Helicopters** take off from 30th Street at Twelfth Avenue; call (212) 465-8905

More fun than a simple harbor cruise is the **Circle Line** tour, a surprisingly entertaining three-hour, 39-mile circumnavigation of Manhattan entirely by water. The ships, all former Coast Guard cutters or navy landing craft, head down the Hudson past the Statue of Liberty, back up the East River along the old Upper East Side, and through Spuyten-Duyvil Creek. In addition to the full three-hour tour ($26 adults, $22 seniors, $12 children), they also offer a two-hour Harbor Lights tour ($20 adults, $17 seniors, $10 children). The headquarters are at Pier 83 at West 42nd Street; three tours plus various shorter and evening tours leave daily April through mid-December (phone (212) 563-3200).

Guided Walking Tours

As we've said, we think walking tours, either independent or guided, are the way to really see New York. Just use a little common sense. Many walking tours are weather-dependent, so be sure to ask how to confirm whether the tour is on if the skies darken. The big tour companies are full-time, but many of the smaller tour groups (or personal guides) have more limited schedules. Most walking tours offered through museums or other groups are on weekends; so are most of the specialty tours, though you can often arrange for a weekday tour if you get in touch with the company in advance. Tips are appreciated by some but declined by others, particularly those arranged by nonprofit agencies; you can ask when you call.

Some of the best things really are free, even in New York. The **Urban Park Rangers** offer green-minded weekend walking tours through Central Park and other green areas in all five boroughs, and the guides are as family-friendly as the price. Call (212) 368-2345. The **Times Square Tours** have great guides, too—professional actors, in fact. The free tour starts at noon on Fridays, rain or shine, at the Times Square Visitors Center (phone (212) 768-1560) at 226 West 42nd Street or 1560 Broadway. And the Friday "Weekend" section of the *New York Times* often mentions special-interest tours arranged through nonprofit organizations or museums.

But if you want to set up a more personalized tour, or one with a specialized focus, contact **Big Apple Greeters,** who can put you in contact with an expert in your field if you give them a few days' notice (phone (212) 669-2896). The tour guides are volunteers, and the buddy-system tour, arranged though the Manhattan borough president's office, is free (though it would be nice if you offered to buy lunch or something). Similarly, you can start putting together a customized itinerary by calling **Signature Tours** (phone (212) 517-4306).

Of course, most tour guides are trying to make a paid living at this. Especially if you're interested in authentic flavor (as opposed to memorized brochure stuff), the neighborhood walking tours are the way to go.

Among the very best such tours are the **Big Onion Walking Tours** ("Long before it was dubbed the Big Apple, those who knew New York City called it the Big Onion," announces the brochure). Most of the Big Onion tours cover the historically polyglot region of Little Italy, Chinatown, Bowery, and the Lower East Side, but they have expanded their staff to cover Gramercy Park and Union Square, Historic Harlem, the East Village, Brooklyn Heights and the Brooklyn Bridge, gay and lesbian New York, "Revolutionary New York," Tribeca, and so forth.

Big Onion is the brainchild of two history scholars, Seth Kamil and Ed O'Donnell, and they and a staff of graduate students from NYU and Columbia University bring to life the eras of Tammany Hall, tenements, sweatshops and flophouses, and ethnic gang struggles. You can either take a sort of two-hour overview tour that covers the waterfront, so to speak, or sign up for the more in-depth walks titled "Before Stonewall: A Gay and Lesbian History Tour," "The Bowery," "Historic Harlem," "Immigrant New York," or "Jewish Lower East Side." And speaking of authentic flavors, you can even sign up for the "Multi-ethnic Eating Tours," in which you nosh a pickle, swipe a dumpling, and savor fresh mozzarella as you go. Tours range from $12 to $18 for adults (depending on whether food or museum admissions are involved) and from $10 to $16 for students and seniors; call (212) 439-1090 or visit **www. bigonion.com** for a schedule of tours or reservations.

Similarly evocative tours are the specialty of the **Adventure on a Shoe-string** folks, who put together itineraries such as "The World of Edith Wharton" and "Hell's Kitchen Hike" ($5; (212) 265-2663). **Michael Kaback** sponsors tours of such historic areas as the Garment District and "Bizarre and Eccentric" East Village (about $15; (212) 370-4214). For the exercise and history buff Kaback also leads six eight-mile hikes around Manhattan.

Georgette Blau's "Scene on TV" tours leads channel surfers past such building as the Jeffersons' high-rise, the West Village site of *Friends,* the Huxatables' Brooklyn brownstone—actually in Greenwich Village—and the Soup Nazi's kitchen, along with some very familiar-looking court-houses. The 90-minute bus tour leaves from the Times Square Visitors Center Saturdays and Sundays at 10 a.m., noon, 2 p.m., and 4 p.m. ($20 for adults, $10 children 6–12; (212) 410-9830).

If you're interested in historical sites in Harlem and African American culture, particularly jazz, gospel, and soul (as in food), contact **Harlem Spirituals** ($30–$95, depending on whether food is included, etc.; (212) 737-0425), which offers tours in a half-dozen languages—hey, gospel is hot! Or check out **Harlem Your Way** (phone (212) 690-1687; **www.harlemyourwaytours.com**) for the $25 "Sights and Sounds" tour, 10 a.m. Monday–Saturday, which meets at 129 West 130th; and the Gospel Tour, 10:30 a.m. Sunday, also $25; visit their website for details on champagne safari specials.

If architecture and design are of interest, try the **Municipal Art Soci-ety,** which offers a variety of tours around town that cost between $10 and $15 (phone (212) 935-3960 or (212) 439-1049; **www.mas.org**); or **NYC Cultural Walking Tours** (phone (212) 979-2388; **www.nycwalk.com**).

NYU/New School for Society Research professor **Joyce Gold** has been leading her walking tours of Manhattan neighborhoods for more than 20 years; the group tours are $12, but you can also arrange a private tour (phone (212) 242-5762). Queens College history professor **Harriet Davis-Kramm** offers a theme tour related to labor called "Manhattan Memories" (phone (212) 628-9517). Former high school teacher (aca-demics are big in the tour biz these days!) **Ruth Alscher-Green** can lead you "River to River" downtown ($35 for one person or $50 for two; group rates can be arranged; phone (212) 321-2823; river2nyc@ aol.com). Self-described "radical historian" **Bruce Kayton** arranges his "radical walking" tours off the beaten track on the beaten tracks. That is, his Greenwich Village tour points out sites of murder, riots, and general mayhem, and his Harlem tour is as much about the Black Panthers as it is the black arts scene ($12; (718) 492-0069).

Other highly regarded walking tours include the **New York City Cultural Tours,** either the Sunday public ones ($10) or customized private ones ($20–$30 an hour; phone (212) 979-2388); **A La Carte New York** (phone (212) 828-7360); **Landmark West!,** a non-profit group working to preserve the Upper West Side's architectural treasures (phone (212) 496-8110); and **Bravo New York** (call (718) 834-8655).

Some tours are, unfortunately, available only in warm weather (i.e., high tourist season). **The New-York Historical Society** sponsors summer walking tours through Central Park highlighting its history and evolution; tours are at 2 p.m. Fridays, Saturdays, and Sundays (phone (212) 873-3400; **www.nyhistory.org**). The occasional but fascinating tours offered by the **Museum of the City of New York** cover "Historic Harlem" and arts-oriented tours (but again, these are mostly good-weather options) every other Sunday from April to October ($12; (212) 534-1672 x206; **www.mcny.org**). You might also check the **Cooper-Hewitt National Design Museum** (phone (212) 849-8300) or the **92nd Street Y** (phone (212) 415-5500).

Self-guided Walking Tours

There are several books in print with in-depth walking tours of New York, but frankly, we're confident that what we've pointed out in Part Six, New York's Neighborhoods, will tell you most of what you want to know. However, in some neighborhoods, you can easily pick up additional guides as you go. Some of the very best are the **Heritage Trails/New York** maps of downtown prepared by a nonprofit state foundation and full of first-class historical information. If you are mostly interested in directions, there is a free map with highlights marked, but for $4 you can get a brochure with quite a lot of info; call (212) 825-6888.

Many other neighborhoods can supply do-it-yourself walking tour guides for a few dollars at most; **the Chinatown History Project** at 70 Mulberry Street has one for $1 (phone (212) 619-4785) and also offers occasional guided tours of the neighborhood.

Backstage and behind the Scenes

There are actually four separate tours of facilities at Lincoln Center, but the two finest—which are also two of the finest in town—are the backstage tours of the **Metropolitan Opera House,** led by members of the Opera Guild from October through June ($9 and reservations required; (212) 769-7020), and a general **Lincoln Center** tour that explores at least three theaters in the complex and comes with enthusiastic background info and the nicest kind of gossip ($10; tours usually from 10 a.m. to 4:30 p.m.). Venues toured depend on rehearsal, matinee, and set-construction schedules, so call ahead if you want to know which theaters are going to be included (phone (212) 875-5350).

Tours of **Carnegie Hall** are $6, offered at 11:30 a.m., 2 p.m., and 3 p.m. Mondays, Tuesdays, Thursdays, and Fridays; for more information call (212) 247-7800. Members of the Municipal Arts Society lead free tours of **Grand Central Terminal** every Wednesday at 12:30 p.m. (phone (212) 935-3960). Tours of the **New York Public Library,** like its neighbor Grand Central a gem of Beaux Arts design, are free at 11 a.m. and 2 p.m. (phone (212) 869-8089; **www.nypl.org**).

The **Radio City Music Hall** tour lasts about an hour, shows off the theater's wonderful Art Deco interior, and usually includes an up-close-and-personal appearance by at least one Rockette. Tours are Monday–Saturday from 10 a.m. to 5 p.m. and Sundays 11 a.m. to 5 p.m.; adult admission $18, children ages 12 and under $12. For information call (212) 307-7171. While you're in the neighborhood, ask about the **NBC Studio Tour** (phone (212) 664-7174; $19 for adults, $16 for children 6–16 or seniors 65 and older; no children under age 6). For $15 you can even get a behind-the-scenes tour of **Madison Square Garden** if you're a total sports nut (phone (212) 465-5800). **Rockefeller Center,** that land-mark of Deco idealism, offers a 75-minute tour that includes glimpses of **Rockefeller Plaza, Radio City Music Hall,** and the many vintage murals, mosaics, and statuary. Tours begin at the NBC Experience Store at Rockefeller Plaza and 49th Street ($10; (212) 664-7174.)

Several of the museums, especially the larger ones, offer highlights tours that give you an overview of the exhibits. The **American Museum of Natural History** (phone (212) 769-5100) offers highlights tours at 10:15 and 11:15 a.m., and 1:15, 2:15, and 3:15 p.m.; meet on the second floor in the Hall of African Mammals. The **Metropolitan Museum of Art** highlights tours are conducted in Italian, Spanish, French, Japanese, Korean, Portuguese, Russian, and German as well as English, at 10:15 and 11:15 a.m. and 1, 2, and 3:15 p.m.; tours leave from the great front hall (phone (212) 535-7710; **www.metmuseum.org**).

An Abundance of Riches

Okay, you've at least skimmed the neighborhood profiles in Part Six and the lists of sight-seeing recommendations earlier in this chapter, and hopefully you've settled on a few areas of special interest to you or your group. The following are more in-depth descriptions of a few of the most important attractions in each zone, to add to your enjoyment of each or perhaps help you winnow down the selection even further. After all, if you're faced with only a few hours, choosing among the museums in

Zone 13 alone might come down to whether you prefer Asian, European, or American art—or even ancient, medieval, or modern.

We try to estimate how long it will take to see, in any reasonable sense, the extent of the collection or building, although of course you must factor in both the extent of your own interest and your stamina when sketching out your schedule. We've also tried to convey the degree to which a particular museum or church might interest visitors of different ages and backgrounds so that you might be able to set up a tag-team plan allowing members of your group to divide up within a neighborhood and see things to their particular liking, then reunite. In that case, however, be sure to calculate not only the time involved in seeing an attraction but also the possible extra time required to stand in line. Again, if a particular teenager is boat- or book-crazy, she may score an otherwise two-star attraction a four.

Below, you'll find charts and maps that organize New York's attractions by type and zone. After that, we're provided some general commentary on the most popular areas for sight-seeing. Wrapping up are profiles of individual New York attractions, arranged alphabetically by attraction name.

NEW YORK CITY ATTRACTIONS BY TYPE		
Type and Name	**Zone**	**Author's Rating**
Churches		
Cathedral Church of St. John the Divine	14	★★★
St. Patrick's Cathedral	9	★★
St. Paul's Chapel	1	★★★★
Trinity Church	1	★★★
Famous Buildings		
Empire State Building	7	½
Lower East Side Tenement Museum	3	★★★
Library		
J. Pierpont Morgan Library	9	★★★★
Monuments		
Ellis Island National Monument	1	★★★★★
Statue of Liberty/Liberty Island	1	★★★
Museums		
American Museum of the Moving Image	17	★★★½
American Museum of Natural History	12	★★★★
Brooklyn Museum of Art	16	★★★★½
The Cloisters	15	★★★★★
Cooper-Hewitt National Design Museum	13	★★★

NEW YORK CITY ATTRACTIONS BY TYPE *(continued)*

Type and Name	Zone	Author's Rating
Museums (continued)		
Forbes Magazine Galleries	4	★★★½
The Frick Collection	11	★★★★★
Intrepid Sea-Air-Space Museum	8	★★★
Jewish Museum	13	★★★½
Metropolitan Museum of Art	13	★★★★★
El Museo del Barrio	13	★★★
Museum of the City of New York	13	★★★
Museum of Jewish Heritage	1	★★★★
Museum of Modern Art, Queens	17	★★★★★
Museum of Television and Radio	9	★★★
National Museum of the American Indian	1	★★★
Solomon R. Guggenheim Museum	13	★★★½
South Street Seaport and Museum	1	★★
Whitney Museum of American Art	13	★★★★
Parks and Gardens		
Bronx Zoo/International Wildlife Conservation Park	18	★★★½
Brooklyn Botanic Garden	16	★★★
New York Botanical Garden	18	★★★½

NEW YORK CITY ATTRACTIONS BY ZONE

Name	Description	Author's Rating
Zone 1: Lower Manhattan, Wall Street, and the Battery		
Ellis Island National Monument	Re-creation of immigrants' first with America	★★★★★
Museum of Jewish Heritage	Re-creation of Jewish culture of the last century	★★★★
National Museum of the American Indian	Part art collection, part anthropology lesson	★★★
St. Paul's Chapel	Small pre-Revolutionary church	★★★★
South Street Seaport and Museum	Historic district and maritime museum	★★
Statue of Liberty/Liberty Island	America's symbol of freedom	★★★
Trinity Church	Gothic Revival church from mid-19th century	★★★
Zone 3: Chinatown, Little Italy, and the Lower East Side		
Lower East Side Tenement Museum	Reconstructed early 20th-century slum	★★★

NEW YORK CITY ATTRACTIONS BY ZONE *(continued)*

Name	Description	Author's Rating
Zone 4: *Greenwich Village*		
Forbes Magazine Galleries	Fantastic collection of toys (for both kids and adults)	★★★½
Zone 7: *Gramercy Park and Madison Square*		
Empire State Building	Landmark tower with famous view	½
Zone 8: *Midtown West and the Theater District*		
Intrepid Sea-Air-Space Museum	Minifleet of retired military vessels	★★★
Zone 9: *Midtown East*		
J. Pierpont Morgan Library	Medieval and Renaissance books and drawings	★★★★
Museum of Television and Radio	Combination archives and rerun haven	★★★
St. Patrick's Cathedral	Largest Catholic cathedral in U.S.	★★
Zone 11: *East Side*		
The Frick Collection	18th- and 19th-century art in mansion	★★★★★
Zone 12: *Upper West Side*		
American Museum of Natural History	Popular and scientific collection	★★★★
Zone 13: *Upper East Side*		
Cooper-Hewitt National Design Museum	International design and design art	★★★
Jewish Museum	Ancient Judaica and Jewish art	★★★½
Metropolitan Museum of Art	One of greatest museums in the world	★★★★★
El Museo del Barrio	Pan-American Hispanic art and culture	★★★
Museum of the City of New York	Specific and often unusual collection of city history	★★★
Solomon R. Guggenheim Museum	20th-century European art	★★★½
Whitney Museum of American Art	20th-century American art	★★★★
Zone 14: *Columbia University and Harlem*		
Cathedral Church of St. John the Divine	Vast Episcopal cathedral	★★★
Zone 15: *The Heights*		
The Cloisters	Premier medieval art collection	★★★★★

NEW YORK CITY ATTRACTIONS BY ZONE *(continued)*

Name	Description	Author's Rating
Zone 16: Brooklyn		
Brooklyn Botanic Garden	Landscaped park with Japanese garden and greenhouse	★★★
Brooklyn Museum of Art	Cultural artifacts and fine art	★★★★½
Zone 17: Queens		
American Museum of the Moving Image	Entertainment history	★★★½
Museum of Modern Art, Queens	Premier collection of modern and contemporary art	★★★★★
Zone 18: The Bronx		
Bronx Zoo/International Wildlife Conservation Park	Famous old-fashioned zoo	★★★½
New York Botanical Garden	Gardens and greenhouse complex	★★★½

New York City Attractions

Notable Neighborhoods

Zone 1: Lower Manhattan, Wall Street, and the Battery

The good thing about riding the **Staten Island Ferry** (718) 815-BOAT) is that you can do it anytime, whenever your schedule is open for about a hour (or a little more, if you have to wait in line). You can choose to see Manhattan by dawn or sunset or even moonlight. It's a very cooling trip in summer and picturesque in the snow. And astonishingly, it's now free. On the other hand, once the thrill of the view of the Statue of Liberty and Lower Manhattan has paled, some children may be restless; there isn't anything else to do on board but wait for the other end. Ferries leave every 20 to 30 minutes during the day, more like every 45 minutes at night.

Incidentally, note that the Staten Island Ferry terminal is just a little east of Battery Park at the foot of Whitehall Street; the Circle Line/Statue of Liberty ferries leave from a little farther beside Castle Clinton.

If, under the constant press of stock-market news and inflation or recession stories, you'd like to see the **New York Stock Exchange** in action, get in line at 9 a.m. for a free but limited ticket, pick up a brochure at the main desk (20 Broad Street at Wall Street; (212) 656-5165), and then head directly to the glass-walled observation deck, where you can look down on the frantic hand-signals and such. The rest of the "exhibits" are a quick walk. If you're of a bearish temperament, the **Museum of American Financial History,** a one-room office formerly

Zones 1–5: Lower Manhattan Λ^{NE}

ATTRACTIONS

1 Ellis Island National Monument
2 Forbes Magazine Galleries
3 Lower East Side Tenement Museum
4 Museum of Jewish Heritage
5 National Museum of the American Indian

6 South Street Seaport and Museum
7 St. Paul's Chapel
8 Statue of Liberty/Liberty Island
9 Trinity Church

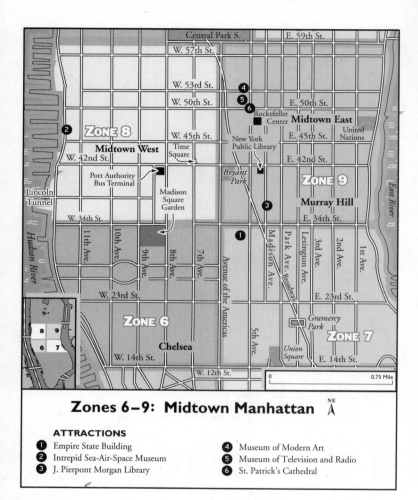

Zones 6–9: Midtown Manhattan

NE

ATTRACTIONS

1. Empire State Building
2. Intrepid Sea-Air-Space Museum
3. J. Pierpont Morgan Library
4. Museum of Modern Art
5. Museum of Television and Radio
6. St. Patrick's Cathedral

Zones 10–13: East and West Side Manhattan ᴺᴱ ⅄

ATTRACTIONS

1. American Museum of Natural History
2. Cooper-Hewitt National Design Museum
3. El Museo del Barrio
4. The Frick Collection
5. Jewish Museum
6. Metropolitan Museum of Art
7. Museum of the City of New York
8. Solomon R. Guggenheim Museum
9. Whitney Museum of American Art

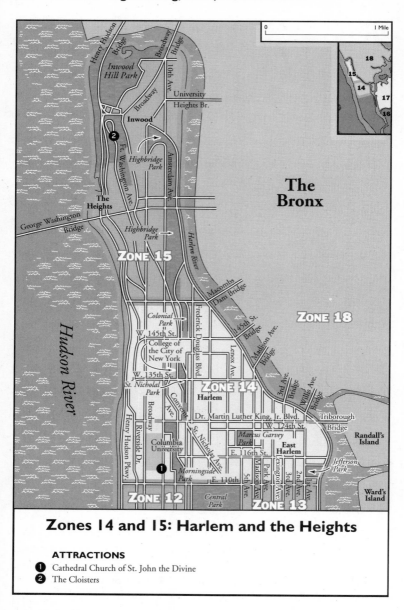

Zones 14 and 15: Harlem and the Heights

ATTRACTIONS

1 Cathedral Church of St. John the Divine
2 The Cloisters

occupied by Alexander Hamilton, later secretary of the Treasury (28 Broadway; (212) 908-4110 or (877) 98-FINANCE) exhibits various bits of Wall Street exotica including the only remaining bit of ticker tape from the infamous "Black Tuesday" crash of 1929. If, on the other hand, you prefer your assets in a more tangible form, you can tour the vaults of gold and museum exhibits at the **Federal Reserve Bank,** but you'll have reserve at least two weeks in advance (phone (212) 720-6130).

Zone 7: Gramercy Park and Madison Square

This neighborhood is also home to two small and particularly special-interest collections, the **Museum of Sex** (27th Street and Fifth Avenue; (212) 689-6337) and **Tibet House** (22 West 15th Street; (212) 807-0563). The former is a quintessentially American institution, with exhibits that range from the curious and even quaint (flyers for patent medicines, antique underwear, and nickolodeon-style film of pioneering ecdysiasts) to the X-tremely graphic (clips of hard-core films on repeating loops). Not surprisingly, no one under 18 is admitted. Tibet House, on the other hand, is a museum in exile, some 350 pieces of art that staffers hope to return to Tibet when that nation achieves independence.

Zone 8: Midtown West and the Theater District

As we've mentioned elsewhere, the Times Square corporations and the-aters have figured out that a booming tourist attraction requires a tour; if you'd like to find out how much there is here (some really historical, some purely commercial), head for the Times Square Visitors Center at 226 West 42nd Street, Fridays at noon.

Zone 9: Midtown East

As noted in Part Six, New York's Neighborhoods, this area is rich in attractions, many of them architectural. You don't need permission to stroll around **Grand Central Terminal** at East 42nd and Park Avenue, but if you'd like to know more about the classical sculptures and so on, contact the Municipal Arts Society (phone (212) 935-3960; **www.mas. org**), which leads free tours Wednesdays at 12:30 p.m. (For more on Grand Central, see Part Nine, Shopping in New York.)

The same is true of the **New York Public Library** on Fifth Avenue at 42nd, another civic treasure, with its signature lions (representing Patience and Fortitude) at the entrance, twin fountains (Beauty and Truth, which would please Keats), interior murals, paintings, documents (Jefferson's copy of the Declaration of Independence), and so on. The newly rededicated ceiling of the Guttesman Exhibition Hall sometimes outshines the exhibits.It's a 300-foot-long trompe d'oeil mural that seems to open the room to a classical sky inhabited by angels. And the glories of the great manuscripts and first-editions collection in Room 320 are pri-marily intellectual. But if you like, free tours leave from the front desk every day at 11 a.m. and 2 p.m.

Zone 17: Queens

Queens has recently opened an attraction that might seem more suited to Harlem, but that is completely at home here: **Louis Armstrong's** longtime home, extravagantly decorated in high 1940s style by his fourth wife, Walle Wilson. They lived here together until his death—in his beloved "wall to wall" bed (which is very nearly that wide)—in 1971; she lived there until her death in 1983. Highlights include the custom-built turquoise kitchen appliances, the gold-foil master bathroom, and the portrait of Armstrong by Tony Bennett. The house is located on 107th Street between 34th and 37th avenues, in Corona (phone (718) 997-3670).

Attraction Profiles

American Museum of the Moving Image   Zone 17

Type of Attraction Entertainment history as entertainment

Location 35th Avenue and 36th Street

Nearest Subway Station Steinway Street

Admission $10 adults; $6 seniors and college students with ID; $5 children; children ages 4 and under free

Hours Tuesday–Friday, noon–5 p.m.; Saturday and Sunday, 11 a.m.–6 p.m.; closed Monday

Phone (718) 784-0077; www.ammi.org

When to Go Weekends for film programs

Special Comments Admission includes screenings

Overall Appeal by Age Group

Pre-school ★½	Teens ★★★½	Over 30 ★★★½
Grade school ★★	Young Adults ★★★★	Seniors ★★★

Author's Rating Intriguing look at not only cinematic techniques but also the integration of "science" and "art," and the selling of both. ★★★½

How Much Time to Allow 1.5 to 4 hours

Description and Comments The museum is actually part of a larger movie-making complex—the restored historic Astoria Studios, where Valentino, the Marx Brothers, and Gloria Swanson worked in the 1920s and Woody Allen and Martin Scorsese have worked in the 1990s. In between it was used for army training films. Only the museum building is open to the public. It's a combination of memorabilia, costumes, props, posters, oddities (à la Planet Hollywood), reconstructed sets, and screening rooms. Smaller kids will get a kick out of exhibits that let them "enter" the set—speak through actors' mouths, put their heads on other bodies, and so on. The major exhibit, "Behind the Scenes," is an interactive explanation of the technology and history of the music biz, which allows visitors to make computer-animated shorts, step into the set of *The Glass Menagerie*, compare the tedious manual film-splicing process of yesteryear with modern digital editing, and the like. Screenings range from vintage rarities (silents are shown with music) to cutting-edge art films, and lectures are often lively and celebrity-studded; call for schedule.

American Museum of Natural History   Zone 12

Type of Attraction Popular and wide-ranging scientific and research collection

Location Central Park West at 79th Street

Nearest Subway Station 81st Street–Museum of Natural History or 79th Street

Admission "Suggested" $12 adults, $10 seniors and students, $7 children ages 12 and under; additional charge for some special exhibits; IMAX: $15 adults, $11 seniors and students, and $10 children (includes museum admission)

Hours Sunday–Thursday, 10 a.m.–5:45 p.m.; Friday and Saturday, 10 a.m.–8:45 p.m.; closed Thanksgiving and Christmas

Phone (212) 769-5100; IMAX, (212) 769-5200; www.amnh.org

When to Go Weekdays

Special Comments The standing exhibits at the Rose Center/Hayden Planetarium are included in museum admission, but Space Show (planetarium) admission is extra.

Overall Appeal by Age Group

Pre-school ★★	Teens ★★★½	Over 30 ★★★
Grade school ★★★½	Young Adults ★★★★	Seniors ★★½

Author's Rating Thanks to the museum's careful combination of adult and family-style exhibits, this will keep a whole group occupied really as long as you want. ★★★★

How Much Time to Allow 2–4 hours

Description and Comments This is a museum that inspires affection and frequently a kind of nostalgia; its dioramas of Africa and the evolutionary progress of humans and its gemstones (worth an estimated $50 million and including the famous Star of India sapphire) are perennial favorites, and they're the sort of exhibits we all seem to remember. The famous dinosaur skeletons are far more convincing since their cleaning and reconfiguration; the new exhibit halls are airy and the captioning first-rate. The museum's special exhibits have been headline-chasers, perhaps, focusing on the newly renovated dinosaur floor (and plugging into *Jurassic Park* fever) and the endless fascination of oversized diamonds, but they have certainly been blockbuster successes. There are several new hands-on and interactive exhibits, including the huge dinosaur of the Cultural African Republic Rainforest, and a children's Discovery Room opens on weekends from noon to 4 p.m. It has a couple of gift shops, but the one in the midst of the big cats is the most fun.

The stunning Rose Center of Earth and Space is a visible "universe"—a 95-foot glass cube enclosing a "floating" sphere that is the planetarium itself. The computer-assisted effects are as far beyond old star-light projections as *Star Wars* EFX were to *King Kong*. A Guggenheim-style ramp holds interactive displays, models, etc. Adjoining exhibits discuss the evolution of the universe and the likliehood of extra-terrestrial life.

The four statues atop the columns outside on Central Park West represent Lewis and Clark, Daniel Boone, and John J. Audubon. Walk around to the West 77th Street side or Columbus Avenue to try to see the museum as it looked at the turn of the century, with its Romanesque Revival structure already once expanded.

Touring Tips The museum offers highlights tours at 10:15 and 11:15 a.m. and 12:15, 1:15, 2:15, and 3:15 p.m.; meet on the second floor in the Hall of African Mammals. The museum has a cafeteria, cocktail bar, and restaurant. Even if you just walk by, be sure to see the Rose Center building; it's even more breathtaking at night.

Bronx Zoo/International Wildlife Conservation Park — Zone 18

Type of Attraction Famous old-fashioned zoo in transformation to modern times

Location Bronx River Parkway at Fordham Road

Nearest Subway Station Pelham Parkway

Admission $16 adults, $8 ages 2–12 and 65+

Hours Monday–Friday, 10 a.m.–5 p.m.; weekends and holidays until 5:30 p.m.; November to March, until 4:30 every day.

Phone (718) 367-1010; www.bronxzoo.com

When to Go Wednesday; weekdays

Special Comments Wednesday free; parking $7

Overall Appeal by Age Group

Pre-school ★★★	Teens ★★★½	Over 30 ★★★
Grade school ★★★★	Young Adults ★★★	Seniors ★★

Author's Rating Although several of the older facilities badly need upgrading (particularly the monkey house), the endangered snow leopards and Mexican wolves alone are worth the visit. ★★★½

How Much Time to Allow 1.5–4 hours

Description and Comments The main buildings date from the turn of the 19th century and for that reason are both wonderful (the monkey house has playful animals around the roof edge, the former big-cat house has lions and tigers around the frieze, etc.) and in some places looking a little sad. However, the zoo is moving quickly toward replacing all the old-fashioned cage-type enclosures with naturalistic ones, divided up by "continent," and some of these, including the wildlife marsh and savannah areas, are quite fine. The Wild Asia minizoo (with its glass-enclosed tropical rain forest, elephant plain, tiger hillside, and encircling monorail), the bat house, and the hands-on petting zoo are extremely popular. There are more than 4,300 creatures living here, representing 775 species.

The Congo Gorilla Forest is a park in itself—six-and-a-half acres that houses 300 primates and 75 species of smaller animals and birds such as okapi, red river hogs, and hornbills; 1,500 plants (400 varieties) that took a decade of greenhouse cultivation; 11 waterfalls; 55 artificial trees; mist machines; sound effects; and so on. It cost $43 million and is only open about eight months of the year. Its most popular resident is Pattycake, a New York native: She was born at the Central Park Zoo in 1972.

Like the nearby Botanical Gardens, the zoo goes all-out for kids from Thanksgiving past New Year's, staying open until 9 p.m. and filling the park with animal-shaped light "trees" and sculptures, with a special focus on reindeer and other seasonal topics. The hands-on Children's Zoo is great, but it may be a madhouse on weekends.

Touring Tips Frankly, the zoo is not a whole lot closer to the subway than the botanical gardens are (see "Touring Tips" in the Garden's description just below), and for out-of-towners, the route is a little confusing. It would be easier to use Metro North to the Botanic Garden stop and do a combination day (and perhaps even if you aren't stopping by the gardens, although you really should). The grounds adjoin, but the entrances don't; there's about a half-mile walk from the garden's main gate to the zoo, but at least it's a fairly straight shot. Or take a Liberty Line bus ($3 one way, $6 round trip; (718) 652-8400). There is a full-service café, plus seasonal concessions, stalls, and smaller cafés.

Brooklyn Botanic Garden   Zone 16

Type of Attraction Landscaped park with Japanese garden and greenhouse complex

Location Washington Avenue at Eastern Parkway

Nearest Subway Station Prospect Park or Eastern Parkway–Brooklyn Museum

Admission $4 adults, $2 seniors and students with ID; free for children ages 16 and under; free for seniors on Friday

Hours October–March: Tuesday–Friday, 8 a.m.–4:30 p.m.; weekends and holidays, 10 a.m.–4:30 p.m.; closed Monday. April–September: Tuesday–Friday, 8 a.m.–6 p.m.; weekends and holidays, 10 a.m.–6 p.m. Free admission on Tuesday and Saturday until noon.

Phone (718) 623-7200; www.bbg.org

When to Go Anytime

Overall Appeal by Age Group

Pre-school ½	Teens ★★	Over 30 ★★★
Grade school ★★	Young Adults ★★	Seniors ★★★

Author's Rating ★★★

How Much Time to Allow 1–1.5 hours

Description and Comments Even if you only walk through the grounds on your way from Prospect Park or the subway to the Brooklyn Museum of Art, it's worth a few minutes to look into the greenhouses, particularly the lily-pond room, the mini–rain forest (which includes several promising medicinal trees), and the bonsai garden; and it's absolutely essential to see the Japanese Tea Garden, with its many small pleasures and twists. If possible, see this in late April or May, when the thousands of Japanese cherry trees blossom (as they do more famously in Washington, D.C.), along with nearly 80 magnolias. Among other popular areas is the fragrance garden, which is heavily perfumed and has Braille labeling.

Touring Tips On weekends and holidays, a free trolley circles among the Botanic Garden, the Brooklyn Museum of Art, and the Prospect Park zoo; call (718) 965-8967.

Brooklyn Museum of Art   Zone 16

Type of Attraction World-class collection of cultural artifacts and fine art

Location Eastern Parkway at Washington Avenue

Nearest Subway Station Eastern Parkway

Admission $8 adults, $4 students and seniors (some special exhibits extra); free to children under 12

Hours Wednesday–Friday, 10 a.m.–5 p.m.; first Saturday of every month, 11 a.m.–11 p.m.; all other Saturdays, 11 a.m.–6 p.m.; Sunday, 11 a.m.–6 p.m.; closed Monday and Tuesday

Phone (718) 638-5000; www.brooklynart.org

When to Go Anytime

Special Comments Strollers are permitted in only a few areas on weekends.

Overall Appeal by Age Group

Pre-school ½	Teens ★★½	Over 30 ★★★★
Grade school ★★	Young Adults ★★★★	Seniors ★★★

Author's Rating In some ways, a more user-friendly mirror of the Met. ★★★★½

How Much Time to Allow 2–4 hours

Description and Comments Probably only in a city that already boasted the Metropolitan Museum of Art could the Brooklyn Museum be so often overlooked. (And if Brooklyn hadn't been absorbed into New York City, the original plans for the museum, might have been fulfilled, which would have made it the largest in the world.) Its collections may be a little smaller, but they're no less well exhibited; in fact, the Met can be so overwhelming that the Brooklyn Museum is almost nicer (and it's certainly less crowded). Its Egyptian and African holdings and the 19th-century American and European (particularly French) collections are world-renowned, and it has its own complex of 28 reconstructed rooms from the New York area going back to the 17th century and up to the Gilded Age (more Rockefeller Moorish-ness); but it has particular strengths in less familiar areas as well, including the art of Native American peoples, spectacular Persian paintings, and a smallish but exquisite gallery of Korean art. BMA's definition of "prints" should set a new dictionary standard: from Dürer woodblocks to Whistler lithographs, from Toulouse-Lautrec posters to Cassatt portraits, Winslow Homer engravings, and Picasso line drawings. In the past few years, the museum has also hosted several blockbuster exhibits, including "Monet in the Mediterranean" and "In the Light of Italy: Corot and Early Open-Air Painting."

Touring Tips   There is a nice little café on the ground floor. Also, check the schedule of the Brooklyn Academy of Music (call (718) 636-4100 or visit **bam.org**), which is only a pleasant walk or a couple of subway stops back toward Manhattan; you might be able to top off your day with a concert.

Cathedral Church of St. John the Divine   Zone 14

Type of Attraction   Vast (though unfinished) Episcopal cathedral
Location   Amsterdam Avenue at 112th Street
Nearest Subway Station   Cathedral Parkway (110th Street)
Admission   Suggested donation, $3
Hours   Monday–Saturday, 7 a.m.–6 p.m.; Sunday, 7 a.m.–8 p.m. unless there's a concert.
Phone   (212) 316-7540; www.stjohndivine.org
When to Go   Weekdays midmorning or afternoon to avoid disrupting services
Special Comments   Try to hook up with one of the tours; there's so much going on.
Overall Appeal by Age Group

Pre-school ★	Teens ★★	Over 30 ★★★
Grade school ★★	Young Adults ★★★	Seniors ★★★

Author's Rating   The continued ambitions (or is that aspirations?) of the builders are somehow moving, the adherence to traditional building methods even more so. ★★★
How Much Time to Allow   1.5–2 hours
Description and Comments   After more than a century, this almost symbolically style-embracing cathedral is still only two-thirds complete, and it may take most of a second century and half a billion dollars to finish it. But already it is a wonder, part Romanesque and part Gothic; a little Spanish, a little French, a little Italian. When finished, it will be the largest cathedral in the world—as large as Notre Dame and Chartres put together, with 300-foot towers and a 600-foot nave. There's a scale model in the gift shop that shows how at least the front half, from tower to tower, will look. Builders are trying to stick to real medieval methods. Up until recently, the stone blocks were being carved out just as they had been centuries ago (some Harlem students apprenticed under imported British master masons), and there are no steel supports. The portals were cast by the man who cast the Statue of Liberty; the so-called temporary dome has lasted nearly 90 years. Be sure to look closely at the stone carvings atop the columns and friezes. They're not all solemn; some feature famous New York landmarks and creatures.

  Inside, the "melting pot" philosophy has been extended to religion: The various chapels salute other major religions and ethnic groups, and the justly famous concerts and lectures are as often secular as sacred. One of the most popular events of the year is the annual Memorial Day concert by the New York Philharmonic; another is the famous blessing of the animals on the feast of St. Francis, the first Sunday in October, which each year attracts hundreds of not only dogs and cats but exotic birds, snakes, even a zoo animal or two.

Touring Tips   Tours are offered Tuesday through Saturday at 11 a.m. and 12:30 p.m.

The Cloisters   Zone 15

Type of Attraction Premier medieval art collection in evocative historical setting

Location Fort Tryon Park

Nearest Subway Station 190th Street

Admission "Suggested" $10 adults, $5 seniors and students; children ages 11 and under (with adult) free

Hours Tuesday–Sunday, 9:30 a.m.–5:15 p.m. (9:30 a.m.–4:45 p.m. November though February); closed Monday

Phone (212) 923-3700; www.metmuseum.org

When to Go Weekdays

Special Comments One ticket covers both the Metropolitan Museum of Art (includes main building) and the Cloisters on the same day.

Overall Appeal by Age Group

Pre-school ★	Teens ★★½	Over 30 ★★★
Grade school ★★	Young Adults ★★★	Seniors ★★½

Author's Rating It was a stroke of genius (and immeasurable philanthropy) to build a period home for part of the Metropolitan's medieval art collection. ★★★★★

How Much Time to Allow 1.5–2 hours

Description and Comments This fantastic assemblage of stone, with its serenely beautiful and stylistically otherworldly saints, stained glass, prayer-eroded blocks, and entombed crusaders, is like a dream. You're not even surprised to find, hanging on one wall, the frequently reproduced pictures of the hunting of the Unicorn. Or the almost-as-familiar illuminated *Belles Heures* of the Duc de Berry. The cloisters of the title—five of them, taken from the ruins of French monasteries dating from the 12th through the 15th centuries, plus a 12th-century Spanish apse and a Romanesque chapel—have been fitted together on two levels, so that you can actually stroll through them as the residents did. (They are actually organized chronologically, so you sort of circle from the Romanesque period, about 1000, to the Gothic era, ca. 1500.) The stone block benches of the chapter house are curved with the long erosion of centuries of use. One of the cloister gardens has been planted to match the courtyard garden seen in one of the huge tapestries, another with the herbs and medicinal plants of the Middle Ages. There is an air- and light-conditioned room of jewels, enamels, reliquaries, and manuscripts (this is one of those museums where a penlight might be helpful). There are also sculptures and altarpieces and a rare and extremely fine early 15th-century triptych of the *Annunciation* by Robert Campin of Tournai.

The Cloisters frequently offers lectures, some of them aimed at students, and wonderfully atmospheric concerts; call for schedules.

Touring Tips The museum itself is at least in part wheelchair-accessible (there is an elevator down by the security desk), but handicapped patrons would be well advised to spring for a cab, at least from the 175th Street subway station, which is accessible. Or take the M4 bus, which, though notoriously slow, stops right at the museum entrance.

Cooper-Hewitt National Design Museum   Zone 13

Type of Attraction Collection of international design and design art

Location East 91st Street and Fifth Avenue

Nearest Subway Station 96th Street or 86th Street

Admission $8 adults, $5 seniors and students; children ages 11 and under free

Hours Tuesday, 10 a.m.–9 p.m.; Wednesday–Saturday, 10 a.m.–5 p.m.; Sunday, noon–5 p.m.; closed Monday and federal holidays

Phone (212) 849-8400

When to Go Midafternoon

Special Comments This is a branch of the Smithsonian Institution; members get in free. Everyone gets in free Tuesday, 5–9 p.m.

Overall Appeal by Age Group

Pre-school ½	Teens ★★	Over 30 ★★★
Grade school ★★	Young Adults ★★★	Seniors ★★

Author's Rating The strength of the museum's appeal to younger visitors depends heavily on the special exhibits on view at the time, but adults will probably always find something to like. ★★★

How Much Time to Allow 1–1.5 hours

Description and Comments This was originally the "modest" home of Andrew Carnegie (the first private establishment in the city with an elevator, incidentally); the two families whose names are linked in the title collected textiles, jewelry, glassware, silver, furniture, and artisan paper from all over the world. Although the museum's collection as a whole is quite large, only a small fraction is on view at one time, but there may be several different exhibits coexisting; for example, most of one whole room may be given over to a line-up of six or eight intriguing chairs, while the library and the hallway may serve as a "rogue's gallery" of lettering styles. (Additional gallery space was created in the mid-1990s.)

Incidentally, this has one of the most intriguing museum shops in the city, with a lot of clever, attractive, and convenient writing implements, clocks and calculators, and other utensils.

Ellis Island National Monument   Zone 1

Type of Attraction Re-creation of immigrants' first contact with America

Location New York Harbor

Nearest Subway Station Bowling Green or South Ferry

Admission $8 adults, $6 seniors, children $3; ages 2 and under free (ticket covers ferry transport and admission to Liberty Island); $7 each for groups of 25+

Hours Daily, 9 a.m.–5:15 p.m.; extended hours during summer months and on some holidays; closed Christmas

Phone (212) 363-7620; ticket and ferry information, (212) 269-5755

When to Go Weekdays

Special Comments The museum is wheelchair-accessible and offers other disability assistance.

Overall Appeal by Age Group

Pre-school ½	Teens ★★★	Over 30 ★★★★★
Grade school ★★★	Young Adults ★★★★★	Seniors ★★★★

Author's Rating ★★★★★

How Much Time to Allow 1.5–2 hours

Description and Comments Few museums can have an association for as many Americans as this one; by some estimates, half of the nation's population has roots here. From 1892 to 1954, when the processing center was abandoned, as many as

10,000 immigrants per day, a total of more than 12 million, stumbled off often wretched boats into the waiting lines of Ellis Island, where they were examined, cross-examined (whether or not they could speak English), quarantined, frequently rechristened, and just as frequently turned away. And that total would be higher if the station hadn't been used to house German POWs during World War II. Many of the arrivals were children or orphans; the very first immigrant to set foot on the island, on New Year's Day, was 15-year-old Annie Moore.

Visitors follow the immigrants' route, entering through the main baggage room and up to the high-vaulted and intentionally intimidating Registry and then the bluntly named Staircase of Separation. Exhibits include the stark dormitories and baggage, dozens of rooms full of poignant photos and oral histories, video clips and dramatic presentations, and a thousand individual remembrances of home—crucifixes, jewelry, clothing, family heirlooms—donated by the families of those who passed through. The 1898 main building has been magnificently restored at a cost of more than $150 million, from the copper roofing to the rail-station-like glass and wrought-iron entrance-way; plans for the other buildings are uncertain. The Immigrant Wall of Fame lists half a million names, including the grandfathers of presidents from Washington to Kennedy, whose descendants contributed to the restoration. Except for the very youngest, who may get tired in the long lines, almost everyone will be taken with this experience—not only the older visitors, who remember the melting-pot era best, but also those school-age visitors for whom multiculturalism is a daily affair. First-and second-generation Americans will be especially affected.

Empire State Building   Zone 7

Type of Attraction Landmark tower with famous view

Location 350 Fifth Avenue (at 34th Street)

Nearest Subway Station 34th Street

Admission $11 adults, $9 military and seniors, $6 for children ages 5–11; free for children ages 5 and under

Hours Daily, 9:30 a.m.–midnight

Phone (212) 736-3100; www.esbnyc.com

When to Go After dark

Special Comments Some small children may find this rather scary.

Overall Appeal by Age Group

Pre-school ★	Teens ★★★	Over 30 ★★½
Grade school ★★½	Young Adults ★★★	Seniors ★★½

Author's Rating A nice view, but not the only choice. And since this is squarely on many bus tour routes, it can be very crowded. ½

How Much Time to Allow 30–45 minutes

Description and Comments There are two observation decks: one on the 86th floor, which is a glass-enclosed viewing area surrounded on all sides by open-air decks (from which, promoters say, you can see ships 40 miles out at sea); and an entirely enclosed one on the 102nd level, near the top of the spire, whose range, on the legendary clear day, is supposed to be 80 miles. The decks are open until midnight, when the view is even nicer and, oddly, less vertiginous. Its pride of reputation is shown in the lobby paintings, which picture the seven wonders of the ancient world and the "Eighth Wonder of the Modern World"—the Empire State Building. Currently the tallest building in the city, it's 1,454 feet tall (counting the transmitters and all; the 102nd-floor observatory is 1,250 feet up), and it took six months to build, required 10 million bricks, and weighs 360,000 tons. There are 1,860 steps, as veterans of the annual race up can attest, and 73 elevators. King Kong wasn't really here, of course; but the tower was struck by a fog-bound bomber back in 1945 just above the 78th floor, and it's still struck by lightning as many as 500 times a year. It has hosted more than 90 million visitors in its time, over 3.5 million every year. The exterior lights—always on, to avoid a second plane crash—are color-coded on holidays and special occasions: red, white, and blue on Independence Day; green for St. Patrick's; pink for Gay Liberation Day, and so on. Once it was lit blue to honor Frank "Ol' Blue Eyes" Sinatra.

The building now includes some more commercial tourist attractions as well. On the concourse, where the ticket booth is located, there's a Guinness World Records Exhibit Hall with dioramas and photos of some strange human endeavors. There are several other smaller simulated adventures, something like IMAX movies with motion, located in the building as well.

Touring Tips There's a snack bar at the 86th-floor level. Tickets are sold on the concourse level below the main lobby; you don't have to use the tickets on the same day you buy them. The ticket office closes at 11:30 p.m.

Forbes Magazine Galleries   Zone 4

Type of Attraction Fantastic collection of toys, both children's (tin soldiers, model boats) and adults (Fabergé) collected by Malcolm Forbes Sr.

Location 62 Fifth Avenue (at 12th Street)

Nearest Subway Station 14th Street–Union Square

Admission Free, but limited numbers admitted per day

Hours Tuesday, Wednesday, Friday, Saturday, 10 a.m.–4 p.m.; closed Sunday, Monday, and Thursday

Phone (212) 206-5548

When to Go Before lunch if there are children in the party, after if not

Special Comments Children ages 15 and under must be accompanied by an adult, and no more than four children per adult are allowed.

Overall Appeal by Age Group

Pre-school ★★★	Teens ★★★	Over 30 ★★★
Grade school ★★★★	Young Adults ★★★	Seniors ★★½

Author's Rating This says something about how some adults, particularly unrealistically wealthy ones (meaning both Forbes and the Romanovs), never have to outgrow childhood. Quite the escape even now. ★★★½

How Much Time to Allow 1–1.5 hours

Description and Comments If you think you've seen toy soldiers before, think again. The more than 12,000 flat and 3-D tin figures arranged in dioramas here—not just soldiers of every historical period and nation, but cowboys and Indians, Aztecs and Spaniards, knights and ladies, and so on—are only about one-tenth of Forbes's collection. The room built to match the famous "counterpane" illustration from Robert Louis Stevenson's *Child's Garden of Verse* has a glass bubble above the dummy figure allowing visitors to become the "child" in the picture. This labyrinth of galleries begins with a series of cases holding more than 500 vintage toy boats (not model boats, an interesting distinction) arranged in flotillas against a background of etched-glass Art Deco panels from the *Normandie;* it continues with a collection of period and special-edition Monopoly sets, trophies, sporting awards, and rotating exhibits of presidential memorabilia, including Nixon's letter of resignation and models of Washington's headquarters at Yorktown and Jefferson's bedroom at Monticello.

The grand finale is a collection of 300-plus Fabergé eggs, personal accessories, jewelry, and household items formerly belonging to the Romanovs of Russia, including the Imperial Diadem of diamonds, platinum, gold, and cobalt enamel. Forbes's collection of the famous eggs, 12 of the surviving 43, includes such spectacular examples as the Coronation Egg, presented by Nicholas II to Alexandria in 1899, which opens to reveal a tiny replica of the coronation coach. Finally, there is a gallery with changing selections of the paintings, prints, and autographs from the collection.

Touring Tips This can be so exhilarating for kids that they get a little loud, and the space is very small. Older adults may want to go at lunchtime to avoid the competition. The tight space and highly focused lighting can make this tiring for some older visitors. Also note that the galleries are occasionally closed on regular viewing days; it wouldn't hurt to call ahead.

The Frick Collection   Zone 11

Type of Attraction Collection of 18th- and 19th-century art in a gracious mansion

Location 1 East 70th Street (at Fifth Avenue)

Nearest Subway Station 68th Street–Hunter College

Admission $12 adults, $6 seniors and students; children under 16 must be accompanied by an adult; under 10 not admitted

Hours Tuesday–Saturday, 10 a.m.–6 p.m.; Sunday, 1–6 p.m.

Phone (212) 288-0700; www.frick.org

When to Go Weekdays

Special Comments Children under age 10 are not admitted.

Overall Appeal by Age Group

Pre-school —	Teens ★★	Over 30 ★★★★
Grade school ★½	Young Adults ★★★½	Seniors ★★★★

Author's Rating A personal favorite, glorious in both setting and collection. ★★★★★

How Much Time to Allow 1.5–3 hours

Description and Comments Maybe this betrays a Western romantic or even DWM-nostalgic mindset, but this is to our taste the perfect philanthropic collection, small by Met standards but studded with exquisite portraits (Whistler, Goya, El Greco, Titian, Vermeer, Sargeant, Holbein, Rembrandt), landscapes (Turner, Constable), allegories (Fragonard and an entire boudoir's worth of Boucher panels painted for Madame de Pompadour). Then there's the enamel Limoges miniatures, the garden court with its lily pond, the ghost of the pipe organ (the pipes are still there, in the hallway, though the works are gone), all those Oriental rugs (you are looking down, aren't you?), and just a smattering of fine furniture left from the days when steel magnate Henry Clay Frick and his family lived here.

Touring Tips This is only two blocks from the Asia Society collection at 70th and Park, which is a fine match in terms of temperament and pacing even if it is a world, or half a world, away in art.

Intrepid Sea-Air-Space Museum   Zone 8

Type of Attraction Minifleet of retired Navy and Coast Guard vessels, including the World War II aircraft carrier *Intrepid*

Location Pier 86, West 46th Street at 12th Avenue

Nearest Subway Station 42nd Street or 50th Street

Admission $14 adults, $10 veterans, seniors, and students, $7 children ages 6–11, $2 children ages 2–5; free for children under 2 and active military and travel professionals; half-price for disabled visitors.

Hours Summer: Monday–Friday, 10 a.m.–5 p.m.; Saturday–Sunday, 10 a.m.–7 p.m.; winter: Tuesday–Sunday 10 a.m.–5 p.m.; last admission 1 hour before closing

Phone (212) 245-0072; www.intrepidmuseum.org

When to Go Early or immediately after lunch

Special Comments Only limited areas of some of the six vessels, and the exhibit halls, are wheelchair-accessible, and other areas (particularly staircases) may be difficult for older visitors, small children, or the claustrophobic. In addition, these are not generally air-conditioned or heated facilities; dress accordingly. Note that the ticket office closes at 4 p.m.

Overall Appeal by Age Group

Pre-school ★½	Teens ★★½	Over 30 ★★★
Grade school ★★★	Young Adults ★★½	Seniors ★★★

Author's Rating This is really a sort of amusement park–cum–elephant graveyard, and for those with a real interest (or experience) in naval history, it's a four- or even five-star attraction. But don't underestimate this. If you add up the time recommended for touring the various vessels, it totals nearly five hours, and there are two exhibit halls as well. And there can be waiting lines for the guided tours. Better pick your spots. ★★★

How Much Time to Allow 2–5 hours

Description and Comments This complex includes half a dozen vessels and a mix of guided and self-guided tours. The centerpiece is, of course, the *Intrepid*, which has a 900-foot flight deck on which sit 40 real planes dating from the 1940s to the 1990s (including an A12 Blackbird spy plane). Visitors can wander through the bridge and most of the corridors and may well spend, as staffers estimate, three hours on the carrier alone. Only guided tours of specific areas are offered of the guided-missile submarine *Growler* (17 minutes), the Vietnam-era destroyer escort *Slater* (22 minutes), the Coast Guard lightship *Nantucket* (10 minutes), and the S.S. *Elizabeth* research ship; both (partial) guided and self-guided tours cross the fleet destroyer *Edson* (40 minutes). Pioneers Hall uses antique equipment, mock-ups, and some video to trace the history of flight; Technologies Hall showcases modern and futuristic methods of space and underwater exploration, including rockets, robots, and even some weapons.

Touring Tips As noted, this is almost a whole day's outing; it's best to pack snacks and water, particularly if there are children in your party.

J. Pierpont Morgan Library　　　　　　　　　　　*Zone 9*

Type of Attraction World-class collection of medieval and Renaissance illuminated manuscripts, rare books, and master drawings

Location 29 East 36th Street (at Madison Avenue)

Nearest Subway Station 33rd Street

Admission $9 adults, $7 students and seniors; children ages 12 and under free when accompanied by an adult

Hours Tuesday–Thursday, 10:30 a.m.–5 p.m.; Friday, 10:30 a.m–8 p.m.; Saturday, 10:30 a.m.–6 p.m.; Sunday, noon–6 p.m.; closed Mondays and holidays

Phone (212) 685-0008; www.morganlibrary.org

When to Go Weekdays; late afternoon

Special Comments There are child-friendly areas, but some special exhibits, say of children's books and illustrations, might have even higher appeal for young visitors.

Overall Appeal by Age Group

Pre-school ★	Teens ★★½	Over 30 ★★★★
Grade school ★★	Young Adults ★★★	Seniors ★★★

Author's Rating As admitted medieval history freaks and bibliophiles to boot, we think this is an incredible collection, and usually not very crowded. ★★★★

How Much Time to Allow 1.5–3.5 hours

Description and Comments Legendary financier J. P. Morgan may have been giving himself aristocratic airs when he built this Renaissance palace of a home, but he and his collection must have been a perfect fit for this warm, otherworldly complex. Gold and full-color manuscripts, the most delicate of red-chalk sketches, the almost illegibly tiny handwriting of the Brontë children, Mozart's own scores, Gutenberg's Bible, Voltaire's briefcase, Dickens's cigar case—the rotating pleasures of this museum are perhaps specialized, but they are certainly superior. The sheer number of books will fill you with envy, and the glorious murals, woodwork, plaster detailing will do the same.

Touring Tips There is a pretty little café on site that serves breakfast, lunch, and even, appropriately, tea, so true book-lovers can make quite a day of it.

Jewish Museum   Zone 13

Type of Attraction Surprisingly rich collection of ancient Judaica and Jewish art

Location Fifth Avenue at 92nd Street

Nearest Subway Station 96th Street

Admission $10 adults, $7 seniors and students; children ages 11 and under free

Hours Sunday, Monday, Wednesday, and Thursday, 11 a.m.–5:45 p.m.; Tuesday, 11 a.m.–8 p.m.; closed Monday, Friday, and Saturday

Phone (212) 423-3200; www.jewishmuseum.org

When to Go Anytime

Special Comments "Pay what you wish" on Tuesday, 5–8 p.m.

Overall Appeal by Age Group

Pre-school ½	Teens ★★★	Over 30 ★★★½
Grade school ★★	Young Adults ★★★½	Seniors ★★★★

Author's Rating One becomes so accustomed to seeing Christian relics and even Asian religious art that the age and variety of these ruins and sacred objects are startling. ★★★½

How Much Time to Allow 1–2 hours

Description and Comments This fine collection, now moving toward its centennial, centers around a permanent exhibition on the Jewish experience—religious and secular—that ranges back 4,000 years. Among its works are temple facades from Sumeria, wall paintings of biblical battles, Torah covers and crowns, fine art and sculpture, candelabras, flatware, manuscripts, ceremonial cups, and a gripping three-dimensional installation by Eleanor Antin and George Segal. The collection also includes many fine portraits of Jewish Americans and a computer/video library. Downstairs is a gallery used for special exhibitions.

Like many of the fine specialized museums in the city, this was originally a mansion, and the two-level wood-paneled library, which is filled with fine arks and altars and ceremonial items and holds an almost pulpitlike spiral staircase, is a beauty. There is also a family exhibit area designed for children and parents to visit together. Incidentally, the stonework in the rear extension was done by the same masons who are working on the Cathedral of St. John the Divine (see profile).

Touring Tips   This museum is extremely accessible for wheelchair users; but if you can use the stairs, be sure to come down stairwell No. 1, a glass-brick turret with a plaintively beautiful audio installation. There is a café in the basement.

Lower East Side Tenement Museum   Zone 3

Type of Attraction   Reconstructed early-20th-century slum
Location   90 Orchard Street (the actual tenement building is 97 Orchard)
Nearest Subway Station   Delancey or Grand Street
Admission $10 adults, $8 seniors and students
Hours   Gallery 90, the office/shop, is open Tuesday–Friday, 1–4 p.m.; Saturday and Sunday, 11 a.m.–5 p.m.; tours are offered during summer, Thursday evening only
Phone   (212) 431-0233; www.tenement.org
When to Go   Weekdays
Special Comments   Only guided tours are available; reserve in advance if possible.
Overall Appeal by Age Group

Pre-school ½	Teens ★★	Over 30 ★★★
Grade school ★½	Young Adults ★★★	Seniors ★★★

Author's Rating   The only way to understand 12 people living in one room is to see it. ★★★
How Much Time to Allow   1–1.5 hours
Description and Comments   In 1903, city officials reported that there were at least 2,200 people, most of them immigrants, packed into the single block bounded by Orchard, Delancey, Broome, and Allen Streets, in buildings like this 1863 tenement, restored in the main to turn-of-the-century conditions (it had no water, heat, or toilets until 1905). One apartment was left just as it was found in 1988, having been abandoned for about 50 years; another was restored to the (relatively) comfortable state it was in when the Gumpertz family lived there in 1878. The museum puts together changing exhibits portraying life of the neighborhood. Incidentally, this is not, as some people may think, a "Jewish museum"—it's very hybridized.

Touring Tips   The museum also offers hour-long neighborhood heritage tours weekends at 1 and 2:30 p.m., which leave from Gallery 90; you can buy either tickets for tours alone (also $10 and $8) or a combination ticket for a tenement tour and walking tour ($14 for adults and $12 for seniors and students).

   A block north at 89 Rivington Street is the Roumanian Shul, a continuously active 1881 Romanesque structure with handsome windows that, like the Eldridge Street Synagogue, is undergoing a thorough facelift.

Metropolitan Museum of Art   Zone 13

Type of Attraction   One of the greatest museum collections in the world
Location   Fifth Avenue between 80th and 84th Streets (entrance at 82nd)
Nearest Subway Station   86th Street
Admission   "Suggested" $12 adults, $7 seniors and students; children ages 11 and under free

Hours Sunday and Tuesday–Thursday, 9:30 a.m.–5:15 p.m.; Friday and Saturday, 9:30 a.m.–8:45 p.m.; closed Monday

Phone (212) 535-7710; www.metmuseum.org

When to Go Friday and Saturday evenings for dining and music; call (212) 570-3949 for special events schedule

Special Comments No strollers allowed on Sundays.

Overall Appeal by Age Group

Pre-school ★	Teens ★★½	Over 30 ★★★★
Grade school ★★	Young Adults ★★★★	Seniors ★★★★

Author's Rating We could visit this every time we were in New York and never feel as if we had seen it all. ★★★★★

How Much Time to Allow 1.5–5 hours

Description and Comments The figures are almost unbelievable: 3.5 million pieces of art, some dating back more than 5,000 years, and representing every culture in the world; 32 acres of exhibit space; 5 million visitors a year. It was founded in 1870 by New York's leading philanthropists and city boosters, who intended it to rival the great museums of Europe and prove New York the equal of any Old World center—and they were willing to pony up to make it happen. It worked, too.

You can't see it all, so pick a century, a style, or a special exhibit and start there. Or pick a centerpiece. For example, the American wing gently spirals down past Tiffany glass and Arts and Crafts pieces to the neoclassical sculpture in the garden court; the Temple of Dendur, which was erected by Augustus, has been reconstructed in a chamber of glass at the end of the Egyptian wing (a thank-you from the nation of Egypt for the United States' help in rescuing monuments threatened by the Aswan Dam); and the Astor Court, a replica of a Ming Dynasty–era scholar's garden created by artisans from Souzhou, China, using traditional techniques, is the jewel at the heart of the Asian art department on the second floor. Or you could luxuriate in medieval art, including ornately carved altarpieces and icons; all-American painting; or entirely reinstalled rooms—art, furniture, and all—from the Lehman townhouse on West 54th Street. And these are just the permanent exhibits. The Metropolitan continually hosts or initiates special collections of blockbuster art from other countries or by great masters.

Despite the museum's seeming austerity, there are several areas that even small children seem to like: the classical statues, the Egyptian mummies, and the reconstructed Temple of Dendur; the armor; the musical instruments; the furnished rooms, and so on. Depending on the exhibit, they may also get a kick out of the Costume Institute downstairs, which owns 45,000 pieces of clothing dating back to the 17th century. And there's a playground just outside, to the south, for emergencies.

Touring Tips There are several places to eat in the museum: the classical-looking but often loud full-service restaurant on the ground floor (phone (212) 570-3964); the sponsors' dining room on the second floor, open to the public on weekends; and the good-weather wine bar on the roof in the sculpture garden. The gift shop is famous. The Metropolitan also administers the Cloisters in the Heights (see profile); admission to one includes admission to the other on the same day. Across the street on Fifth between 83rd and 84th Streets is the small and specialized Goethe House German Cultural Center (phone (212) 439-8700), which often has exhibits of contemporary German art, films, and concerts.

El Museo del Barrio   Zone 13

Type of Attraction Smallish but distinguished collection of pan-American Hispanic art and culture

Location Fifth Avenue at 104th Street

Nearest Subway Station 103rd Street

Admission "Suggested" $5 adults; $3 seniors and students; children ages 11 and under free

Hours Wednesday–Sunday, 11 a.m.–5 p.m.; Closed Monday and Tuesday

Phone (212) 831-7272; www.elmuseo.org

When to Go Midafternoon

Overall Appeal by Age Group

Pre-school ★	Teens ★★★	Over 30 ★★★★
Grade school ★★	Young Adults ★★★½	Seniors ★★★½

Author's Rating Its cultural message is pointed without being at all preachy. ★★★

How Much Time to Allow 1–1.5 hours

Description and Comments This is not an especially large facility, and it shares its space with a training center, but its exhibits are well considered and well displayed, and the hands-on children's room, though small, is a good place to park the youngest members of the group. The collection includes religious carvings, textiles, prints, paintings, vintage photographs, pre-Columbian artifacts, and contemporary art; the exhibits often focus on thematic issues, such as dream symbols or regional developments.

Museum of the City of New York   Zone 13

Type of Attraction Historical collection that shines specific and often unusual lights on city history

Location Fifth Avenue at 103rd Street

Nearest Subway Station 103rd Street

Admission "Suggested" $7 adults, $4 seniors and children; $12 for families

Hours Wednesday–Saturday, 10 a.m.–5 p.m.; Sunday, noon–5 p.m.

Phone (212) 534-1672; www.mcny.org

When to Go Anytime

Overall Appeal by Age Group

Pre-school ★★½	Teens ★★	Over 30 ★★★
Grade school ★★★	Young Adults ★★★	Seniors ★★★

Author's Rating ★★★

How Much Time to Allow 1.5–2 hours

Description and Comments This might be the sort of museum in which families could split up to see different wings and then regroup—say, at the huge mezzanine-level model of what the museum will look like once its vast wing-addition is built in the 21st century. The rotating exhibits are often quirky and fascinating, focusing on such topics as the long tradition of circuses in New York (the theme music included a snatch from *Washington Week in Review,* perhaps a joke on media circuses!); the building of the Empire State Building and some of the art it has inspired; the Broadway tradition with posters and recordings. And there are some fine examples of native craftsmanship, furniture, household items, and the like. In the basement is a mini–fire museum and a selection of antique city maps. But the two best exhibits are the toys—including novelty banks, fire trucks and trains, tin soldiers and animals, and a series of dollhouses from the 18th, 19th, and even early 20th centuries—and the reconstructed Moorish-fantasy bedroom and dressing room from John D. Rockefeller's demolished mansion at Fifth and 51st. (You'll spot a matching room in the Brooklyn Museum of Art.) Just look at the stenciled canvas ceiling over the sleigh bed; or the woodwork in the dressing room, decorated with appropriate implements such as scissors and combs and mirrors worked in mother-of-pearl. There are other restored rooms and a display of custom Spode, Royal Doulton, Crown Derby, and Minton porcelain belonging to another prominent household. These rooms are up on the fifth floor and are quite frequently overlooked.

Museum of Jewish Heritage   Zone 1

Type of Attraction Re-creation of Jewish culture over the last century—that is, before, during, and after the Holocaust

Location 18 First Place, Battery Park City

Nearest Subway Station Bowling Green or South Ferry

Admission $8 adults, $6 seniors and students; children ages 5 and under free

Hours Sunday–Wednesday, 9 a.m.–5 p.m.; Thursday, 9 a.m.–8 p.m.; Friday, 9 a.m.–5 p.m.; closed Saturdays and Jewish holidays (museum closes at 4 p.m. the afternoon before Jewish holidays) and Thanksgiving

Phone (212) 509-6130 for information; for tickets call TicketMaster at (212) 945-0039

When to Go Anytime; tickets are timed and numbers restricted

Special Comments The museum is wheelchair-accessible. The third-floor reception room, with its panoramic view of the harbor, is available for rental.

Overall Appeal by Age Group

Pre-school ½	Teens ★★★	Over 30 ★★★★
Grade school ★★★	Young Adults ★★★★	Seniors ★★★★★

Author's Rating This seems to hit seniors (who remember the bad times) and teenagers (who may not previously have really understood the Holocaust) the hardest. ★★★★

How Much Time to Allow 2–3.5 hours

Description and Comments This carefully orchestrated collection, which begins in a subtle key, crashes into the Holocaust, and climaxes in a visual paean to the future and specifically to the United States, is subtitled "A Living Memorial to the Holocaust," with emphasis on the "Living," and it has a gentler, more affirmative, and in some ways more objective tone than the larger U.S. Holocaust Memorial Museum in Washington. Instead of placing visitors in the character of victims, as the Washington site does with its "passports," the New York museum tries to make all visitors, Jewish and not, feel included in the story by emphasizing the importance of tradition and faith. And although the Washington memorial is almost entirely focused on the Holocaust itself, this collection also speaks to the recovery of Judaism, the state of Israel—a happier present and future. The key to its mission is in the dual message carved in the wall of the foyer: "Remember ... NEVER FORGET." And right next to it, "There is hope for the future."

    The lower floor (one moves from the bottom up) spotlights the richness of Jewish family life in the late 19th and early 20th centuries, with clothing and artifacts from holidays and special occasions, such as a gorgeous silver and silk bride's headdress and belt, as well as simpler reminders of Sabbath and toys. (Wherever possible, the photograph of the item's owner—victim or survivor—is shown with it.) One of the most spectacular items is a handpainted Sukkah mural, almost Byzantine in its detail, showing life in Budapest in the 1920s and 1930s, along with biblical scenes and family portraits created by an untrained kosher butcher.

    The second story tells the story of the Holocaust itself, with thousands of photos of the executed (posted on the stall-like wooden slabs that symbolize the boxcars that carried Jews to the concentration camps); toys and mementos of both escapees and victims; and a salute to those who, like Raoul Wallenberg and the now famous Oskar Schindler, helped Jews escape the Nazis. (Notice how many of the smaller interior gallery spaces are six-sided, like the building itself.) The third floor, which spotlights the post-Holocaust era, is a bit of a letdown until one reaches the last gallery, a glass-walled expanse, almost blinding after all that granite darkness, that looks directly out upon the icons of Jewish freedom: the Statue of Liberty, Ellis Island, and the lesser-known but equally important railroad terminal on the Jersey shore, from which many immigrants began their new lives.

There are two dozen videos in the museum (many of the witnesses are part of Steven Spielberg's Shoah project). Intriguingly, the bulk of the museum's thousands of photographs and personal items are in storage so secret that most staff members don't know their location.

At press time, the museum's second wing, along with a living-tree installation on the roof, was nearing completion.

Touring Tips   There is no cafeteria in the museum, but just outside its parking lot is the new and understated Robert Wagner Park, a two-story brick structure that offers a fine view of the harbor and has clean public rest rooms as well as (from about April to mid-December) a nice little café.

Museum of Modern Art (closed until late 2004)   Zone 9

Type of Attraction   Premier collection of modern and contemporary art and design
Location   11 East 53rd Street
Nearest Subway Station   Fifth Avenue–53rd Street
Admission $12 adults, $8 seniors and students; children ages 16 and under free
Hours   Monday, Thursday, Saturday, and Sunday, 10 a.m.–5 p.m.; Friday, 10 a.m.–7:45 p.m.; closed Tuesday, Wednesday, Thanksgiving, and Christmas Day
Phone   (212) 708-9400; www.moma.org
When to Go   Weekdays; Friday afternoons
Special Comments   Friday 4:30–8:15 p.m. admission is "pay what you please." MOMA will re-open in late 2004 for its 75th anniversary celebration; see below for the museum's temporary location in Queens.

Overall Appeal by Age Group

Pre-school ½	Teens ★★	Over 30 ★★★★
Grade school ★★	Young Adults ★★★	Seniors ★★★

Author's Rating   Challenging and often difficult, but fascinating—clearly the world's leading modern art collection, just as advertised. As at many really first-rate museums, you can't really see it all in a few hours, but you can only take so much in at a time, any-way. ★★★★★

How Much Time to Allow   2–4 hours

Description and Comments   First-timers may be surprised at how many of these great paintings and prints they already "know," because so many of the most famous and frequently reproduced 20th-century works hang here, from those by the Impres-sionists to those by the Cubists to the Pop Artists and so on. (Stop by the main desk and ask for the self-guided tour; it points up many of these "greatest hits," including Van Gogh's *Starry Night,* Monet's *Water Lilies,* and Picasso's *Demoiselles d'Avignon.*) Not only two-dimensional but three-dimensional pieces are featured; late-19th- and early-20th-century painting and sculpture is on the second floor, postwar on the third. MoMA is also famous for its vetting of industrial and commercial design, from automobile bodies to typewriters, architectural models to appliances, even watches; one of Movado's most famous faces, the one with a single dot at the 12, is called "the Museum Watch" because MoMA approved of it so highly. The shop also has many disabled-friendly utensils.

Touring Tips Every Friday is Jazz Night in the Garden Café, and in good weather it's out in the Sculpture Garden. Also call and ask about film screenings, or check the local press; the museum's collection of films tops 10,000. The museum's Italian restaurant, Sette MoMA, serves until 10:30 p.m. Monday, Tuesday, and Thursday through Saturday.

Note that while the main museum has been closed for extensive renovations (and its collection temporarily housed in Queens, as described below), current plans call for its reopening as early as the end of 2004.

Museum of Modern Art, Queens (MoMa QNS)   Zone 17

Type of Attraction Temporary home-away-from-home for Museum of Modern Art

Location 33rd Street at Queens Boulevard

Nearest Subway Station 33rd Street

Admission $12 adults, $8.50 seniors and students with ID; ages 15 and under with adult free

Hours Saturday–Monday and Thursday, 10 a.m.–5 p.m.; Friday, 10 a.m.–7:45 p.m.; closed Tuesday and Wednesday

Phone (212) 708-9400; www.moma.org

When to Go Mondays and Thursdays

Special Comments Although all galleries and facilities are wheelchair-accessible, the 33rd Street subway station is not

Overall Appeal by Age Group

Pre-school ★★	Teens ★★	Over 30 ★★★
Grade school ★★	Young Adults ★★½	Seniors ★★★

Author's Rating A little frustrating, since although quality is high, limited space makes for limited quantity (and primitive hanging atmosphere); interest (and willingness to pay $12.50) depends heavily on special exhibit ★★½

How Much Time to Allow 1.5–3 hours

Description and Comments While its main building is being renovated, MoMA's directors made artistic irony out of necessity, turning a factory into warehouse-style hanging space a starving artist would appreciate, with long pale walls, translucent "window" blocks, and exposed ramps. There are several midsized rooms used for rotating exhibits such as the long-running Ansel Adams retrospective (a choice that seemed more populist than important); and three or four large rooms in which pieces from the permanent collection are arranged in greatest-hits style—one or two each from Cezanne, Picasso, Rousseau and Matisse; Oldenburg, Rauschenberg, and Jasper Johns; Ernst, Magritte, Dali, and Duchamps. Van Gogh's *Starry Night* is the Mona Lisa here, so much a draw that when it is not on view, a warning is posted out front.

Touring Tips Moma QNS is within a short walk of the Museum for African Art and its (also temporary) roommate the Noguchi Museum on 43rd Avenue at 36th Street; maps are available at information desk. There's a café and smallish store on premises.

Museum of Television and Radio   Zone 9

Type of Attraction A combination archives and rerun haven

Location 25 West 52nd Street

Nearest Subway Station 47th–50th Street/Rockefeller Center or Fifth Avenue–53rd Street

Admission $7 adults, $5 seniors and students, $4 for children ages 12 and under; members free

Hours Tuesday–Sunday, noon–6 p.m. ;theaters only, Thursday until 8 p.m., Friday until 9 p.m.; closed Monday, New Year's Day, Independence Day, Thanksgiving Day, and Christmas Day

Phone (212) 621-6600 for information; (212) 621-6800 for schedule; www.mtr.org

When to Go Early, at least to check schedule

Special Comments If you want to use the archives, add at least another hour, but the kids will be happy parked in one of the theaters. Note that the age group appeal may vary depending on the day's screenings.

Overall Appeal by Age Group

Pre-school ★½	Teens ★★★	Over 30 ★★★½
Grade school ★★★	Young Adults ★★★	Seniors ★★½

Author's Rating Although the computerized files are still being organized, meaning that it can be laborious to look some topics or subjects up, it's fascinating; and the rare films shown are a delight. ★★★

How Much Time to Allow 1–2.5 hours

Description and Comments A handsome if simple building, with five floors of exhibits, various-sized screening theaters, and radio listening room, all fully wheelchair-accessible and with listening-assist devices at the front counter and closed-captioning decoders in the library. The museum shop is good for gifts and souvenirs, too, mixing T-shirts and posters with industry coffee-table books.

Not so famous as most of New York's older museums, this is nevertheless a fine attraction, and one with strong interest for all ages. In fact, with its ongoing screenings on various floors, through which visitors are welcome to sit for as long or as short a time as they like, this is channel surfing to the max. In a single afternoon, for example, you might be able to see rare footage of Sinatra's "Rat Pack" in action, a segment of *The George Burns and Gracie Allen Show,* Jackie Kennedy taking CBS for a tour of the White House, a full-length *Wallace and Gromit* claymation adventure, bits of *Sesame Street* and *Fraggle Rock,* some *Beakman* science, a semiserious documentary on the evolution of sci-fi TV, and so on. The hallways are filled with changing photographic exhibits on such topics as journalists and special-effects makeup. The museum also produces salutes and series featuring the works of specific actors or directors, and many of these are shown in the evenings, making this an all-day bargain. Screenings begin at noon each day, and the full schedules are available at the counter, along with six months' advance schedules of the special exhibitions and series. There are special screenings of children's programming on weekends, but there is plenty of kid-vid all week long, too.

You can take a guided tour of the museum if you're curious about its history and collection (offered only a couple of times a day), but it's easily negotiated alone. The real treasure trove is the library, for which you need time-specific tickets (available at the front counter). You cruise the museum's library on computer, picking segments from 75,000 radio and TV programs and even TV and radio advertising, and then are sent to a private booth to screen (or hear) your selections. If you're not sure what you'd like to see, skim the category of 400 highlights, which are the segments most frequently requested by visitors—the final episode of *The Mary Tyler Moore Show,* for example.

Touring Tips There is no cafeteria on the premises.

National Museum of the American Indian   *Zone 1*

Type of Attraction Part art collection, part anthropology lesson

Location Old U.S. Custom House, 1 Bowling Green (near State and Whitehall streets)

Nearest Subway Station Bowling Green or South Ferry

Admission Free

Hours Daily, 10 a.m.–5 p.m.

Phone (212) 514-3700; www.nmai.si.edu

When to Go Anytime

Overall Appeal by Age Group

Pre-school ★½	Teens ★★★	Over 30 ★★★
Grade school ★★★	Young Adults ★★½	Seniors ★★½

Author's Rating There is beautiful work here, and surprising (to many Americans) diversity, but it may run into a generational guilt gap; it captures many children's attention faster than their parents'. ★★★

How Much Time to Allow 1–1.5 hours

Description and Comments This is a branch of the Smithsonian Institution, and not surprisingly, its captions and clarity of information are first-rate. It includes artifacts not only from the more familiar (from TV and movies) Plains Indians but also from the Aztec, Olmec, Mayan, northwestern, and even Siberian tribes. Voiceover narratives and mini–oral histories run into and over one another as you pass through various exhibits. There are often demonstrations of weaving or music in the center area, which children will enjoy.

Touring Tips Don't overlook the Beaux Arts Custom House itself, with its exterior sculptures of metaphoric goddesses by Daniel Chester French representing Asia (the meditative one), America (the optimistic one), Europe (with the vestiges of her empire), and Africa (unawakened). Well, it was pre-PC. Also, good and reasonable items are available in the gift shop.

New York Botanical Garden   Zone 18

Type of Attraction Half "natural," half formal array of gardens with dazzling greenhouse complex

Location 200th Street and Southern Boulevard

Nearest Subway Station Bedford Park Boulevard

Admission Grounds: $5 adults, $4 seniors and students, $2 children ages 2–17; greenhouse and tram tours additional

Hours October–April only: Tuesday–Sunday, 10 a.m.–6 p.m.; closed Monday, except holidays

Phone (718) 817-8700; www.nybg.org

When to Go Midweek

Special Comments Free admission on Wednesday

Overall Appeal by Age Group

Pre-school ★★★	Teens ★★½	Over 30 ★★★
Grade school ★★★★	Young Adults ★★★	Seniors ★★★★

Author's Rating Restful and restorative, and particularly family-friendly; four-star attraction for gardeners. ★★★½

How Much Time to Allow 1.5–4 hours

Description and Comments Within this 250-acre spread are a 40-acre forest with a variety of shortish but pretty trails through the sorts of hardwoods New York state had in abundance back in the last days of the Mohicans; and more than two dozen specialty gardens: a seasonal rose garden, a cherry valley, a picnic area, a giant water lily pond, a rock garden, orchid houses, a mini-maze, an herb garden, and so on. The real star is the Enid A. Haupt Conservatory, the glorious Crystal Exposition–style greenhouse complex, which recently completed a four-year, $25 million restoration and now encloses both upland and lowland rain forests (with mezzanine-level walkway), deserts from the Americas and Africa, and special collections. The garden's children's fare is first-rate, with special "treasure map" guides to the conservatory gardens, a hands-on adventure garden, family plant-your-own areas, and the like, plus a wide variety of special programs, children's walking tours, and demonstrations.

Incidentally, the gardens make a surprisingly buoyant addition to a holiday trip. The plants inside the conservatory are covered in lights, along with many outdoor trees; a huge model train exhibition winds through both imaginary and real miniature New York landscapes; special family concerts and performances are scheduled, and so on.

Touring Tips The garden is actually about eight blocks from the Bedford Park subway stop, and though it's downhill on your way there, it's a hard uphill return. However, Metro North commuter trains (phone (212) 532-4900) run from Grand Central right to a Botanic Garden stop a stone's throw from the side entrance in about 20 minutes. Also, during summer months, a shuttle operates among the American Museum of Natural History, the Metropolitan Museum of Art, and the botanical garden; call the garden's main number for information.

There is a full-service café between the conservatory and the train-side gate.

St. Patrick's Cathedral   Zone 9

Type of Attraction The largest Catholic cathedral in the country

Location Fifth Avenue between 50th and 51st Streets

Nearest Subway Station 47th–50th Street/Rockefeller Center or 51st Street

Admission Free

Hours Monday, 7 a.m.–9:30 p.m.; Saturday 7 a.m.–8 p.m.

Phone 753-2261

When to Go Late morning or midafternoon to avoid interrupting services

Overall Appeal by Age Group

Pre-school ½	Teens ★★	Over 30 ★★★
Grade school ★★	Young Adults ★★½	Seniors ★★★

Author's Rating Although this clearly has greater resonance for Catholic visitors, it is quite beautiful and well worth a visit, if only as a rest between other attractions. ★★

How Much Time to Allow 30–45 minutes

Description and Comments This looks almost as much like a fairy-tale castle as a cathedral, it's so busy with spires and arches and stained glass. Among the highlights are its huge and transporting organ (nearly 8,000 pipes) and the 26-foot Rose Window, both right over the main Fifth Avenue entrance; the Pietà in the rear near the Lady Chapel, which has its own set of gorgeous stained-glass windows; and the all-bronze baldachin that protects the high altar. (In the crypt below are the remains of Pierre Toussaint, a onetime Haitian slave who is likely to become the fourth American saint and the first black one.) Altogether there are 70 stained-glass windows, more than half from Chartres and Nantes.

Touring Tips This cathedral was designed by James Renwick at the request of John Hughes, the first archbishop of New York, shortly before the Civil War; it was not until 1889 that the 330-foot spires were raised in the religious art competition at the 1893 Chicago World's Fair. So much of the cathedral's power comes from the windows that sunlight (or reflected snow) really makes a difference; try to avoid going on a rainy day.

St. Paul's Chapel   Zone 1

Type of Attraction Small, remarkably peaceful pre-Revolutionary church

Location Broadway at Fulton Street

Nearest Subway Station Cortlandt or Fulton Street

Admission Free; donations requested for concerts

Hours Monday–Friday, 9 a.m.–3 p.m.; Sunday, 8 a.m.–3 p.m.; closed Saturday

Phone (212) 602-0872

When to Go Anytime

Special Comments George Washington's private pew and a few artifacts are preserved here.

Overall Appeal by Age Group

Pre-school ½	Teens ★★	Over 30 ★★★
Grade school ★★	Young Adults ★★★	Seniors ★★★

Author's Rating ★★★★

How Much Time to Allow 30 minutes

Description and Comments You might almost walk right by this little church without noticing it, it seems so beleaguered by development. But it's a blessing in its own right—warmly though simply painted, the wood lit by Waterford crystal chandeliers, and with President Washington's box unobtrusively roped off. It dates from the mid-1760s, and in one of those ironies of history, is purely Georgian—the style named for the kings New Yorkers would shortly renounce. More specifically, it is modeled on St.-Martin-in-the-Fields in London's Trafalgar Square and, like St. Martin's, is renowned for the quality of its concerts (noon, usually Monday and Thursday). It's one of the very few buildings to have survived the great fire of 1776, not to mention 9/11. In fact, it became a special sanctuary for rescue workers and support staff in the horrific days following the attacks.

Touring Tips Don't enter, as most people do, right off Broadway; that's actually the altar end. Walk around the yard (the cemetery once reached all the way to the river, providing a much grander setting) and come in at the "rear"; the effect is much more dramatic.

Also, from here go north a block to the Gothic Woolworth Building at 233 Broadway and walk into the elaborate and often hysterically funny interior; kids will go wild over the gargoyles, including caricatures of architect Cass Gilbert clutching a model of the building and F.W. Woolworth himself counting out coins—"fives and dimes," in fact.

Note that at press time, the Woolworth's lobby was closed for security reasons.

Solomon R. Guggenheim Museum   Zone 13

Type of Attraction Fine collection of 20th-century European art

Location Fifth Avenue at 88th Street

Nearest Subway Station 86th Street

Admission $12 adults, $8 seniors and students; children ages 11 and under free

Hours Sunday–Wednesday, 9 a.m.–6 p.m.; Friday and Saturday, 9 a.m.–8 p.m.; closed Thursday

Phone (212) 423-3500; www.guggenheim.org

When to Go Anytime

Special Comments Fridays, 6–8 p.m., pay what you wish. Though the spiral ramp seems good for wheelchairs and keeping kids interested, it can be hard on the legs.

Overall Appeal by Age Group

Pre-school ½	Teens ★★	Over 30 ★★★
Grade school ★★	Young Adults ★★★½	Seniors ★★★

Author's Rating ★★★½

How Much Time to Allow 1.5–3 hours

Description and Comments This is one of those museums more famous for its architecture than for its collection. Frank Lloyd Wright's upwardly expanding six-floor spiral, like a squared-off chambered nautilus (it's been called ruder things), frames the Great Rotunda and looks up to an often brilliantly lit glass dome; the exhibits fill the walls of the long ramp and lead off into the chambers. Among the permanent exhibits are major pieces by Klee, Picasso, Kandinsky, Chagall, and Modigliani; the museum also has a fine selection of French Impressionists, including Monet, Renoir, and Van Gogh.

Though in the shadow of the giant Museum of Modern Art collection, the Guggenheim, which has more European works, forms a strong duet with the Whitney Museum of American Art. (Also, it reaches back a little farther into the 19th century.) Guggenheim himself was aggressive in collecting avant-garde and new talent, and that was the reputation the museum was supposed to have, although it has been criticized for "maturing." Its new Soho branch (and the vast new branch in Bilbao, Spain) may give it new vitality.

South Street Seaport and Museum   Zone 1

Type of Attraction Combination historic district, shopping mall, and maritime museum

Location Water Street between John Street and Peck Slip

Nearest Subway Station Fulton Street

Admission Museum: $8 adults, $7 seniors, $5 students, $4 children

Hours October 1–March 31: 10 a.m.–5 p.m. (closed Tuesdays); April 1–September 30: 10 a.m.–6 p.m. (open until 8 p.m. Thursdays)

Phone General information, (212) 748-8600; www.southstseaport.org

When to Go Anytime

Special Comments The hours given above are retail area hours; restaurants may be open later.

Overall Appeal by Age Group

Pre-school —	Teens ★★	Over 30 ★★★
Grade school ★★	Young Adults ★★★★	Seniors ★★

Author's Rating ★★

How Much Time to Allow 1.5–4 hours

Description and Comments This is sort of a miniature theme park, covering 11 square blocks (some of them cobblestone) of real and reproduced seafaring New York. (It's a Rouse development, like Boston's Faneuil Hall and Baltimore's Harborplace.) In its heyday, the first half of the 19th century, it was so busy that South Street was nicknamed the "street of sails." But once steamships took over, the deeper-water piers on the Hudson River side gradually drew ship traffic away from this area. It wasn't until the early 1980s that its commercial potential was understood. From the Visitors Center in the former Pilothouse, where you pick up the free guide maps, you look right to the main food stand and shopping mall of Pier 17 and beyond that to the very real, 150-year-old Fulton Fish Market. One of the nicest stretches, in terms of architectural preservation, is Schermerhorn Row, Federal-style warehouses on the south side of Fulton Street between Front and South Streets dating from the very early 19th century (that's how far back the Schermerhorn money goes); they were later used as hotels and shops and are now boutiques and restaurants. A $21 million expansion has already uncovered such unique artifacts as Gaelic graffitti.

Quite frankly, most of the good stuff here is free: the view from Pier 17 (one of the most evocative and least publicized views of the harbor); craftsmen building and restoring small boats; and the view of the Brooklyn Bridge, which took 16 years to build and the lives of 20 of the 600 workers—many from the bends because they emerged too quickly from underwater assignments. (John Roebling, who designed it, had his foot crushed in a freak accident on the pier just before construction was to begin in 1869 and died three weeks later. His son took over, but repeated bouts of the bends left him partially paralyzed; finally Roebling's widow replaced him as supervisor.) The best reason to buy the museum ticket is to tour the tall ships anchored there: the 1991 *Peking*, the second largest sailing ship ever built, and the three-masted *Wavertree* of 1885. If you want to take a harbor tour from here, on the schooner *Pioneer* (March to November only), you can either make reservations up to two weeks in advance (phone (212) 748-8590) or take a chance on unreserved tickets at 10 a.m. Other commercial cruises also leave from here.

Touring Tips Walk past Fulton Fish Market to the corner of Peck Slip and Front Street and look at the mural on the ConEd substation; it's a trompe d'oeil painting of the Brooklyn Bridge (which in reality rises just beyond it), designed to make the station less obtrusive. Also look for the lighthouse at the intersection of Fulton and Water Streets. A memorial to the 1,500 passengers of the *Titanic* who perished in the 1912 catastrophe, it originally overlooked the harbor from the Seamen's Church near the current Vietnam Veterans Memorial but was moved here in 1976.

Statue of Liberty/Liberty Island   Zone 1

Type of Attraction America's premier symbol of freedom

Location New York Harbor

Nearest Subway Station Bowling Green or South Ferry

Admission $10 adults, $8 seniors, $4 children; children under age 3 free (combination ticket covers ferry transport and admission to Liberty Island)

Hours Daily, 9 a.m.–5:15 p.m.; extended hours during summer months and on some holidays; closed Christmas

Phone (212) 363-3200; ticket and ferry information, (212) 269-5755

When to Go Weekdays

Special Comments Wheelchair access extends only to the observation deck at pedestal height; only stairs ascend to the crown.

Overall Appeal by Age Group

Pre-school ½	Teens ★★½	Over 30 ★★★
Grade school ★★	Young Adults ★★★	Seniors ★★½

Author's Rating For all its very real emotional appeal, the actual impact of this attraction close-up may depend on the length of time you have to stand in line, making it problematic for small children. ★★★

How Much Time to Allow 1.5–4 hours

Description and Comments This most famous symbol of liberty is also a reminder of the revolutionary fervor often required to obtain it. It was a gift from the republic of France, a massive feat of both art (sculpted by visionary Frederic-Auguste Bartholdi, who used his mother as the model for that stern yet merciful face) and engineering (erected by Gustave Eiffel, whose own eventual monument would be the landmark tower in Paris). It was formally unveiled on October 28, 1896, and restored for its centennial at a cost of $70 million plus $2 million for the fireworks. However, the torch had corroded so badly that a replica, covered in 24-carat gold, was put in its place; the original is in the lobby.

There are four stations, so to speak: the outside of the base, engraved with Emma Lazarus's "New Prometheus" ("Give me your tired, your poor . . ."); the exhibit hall inside the base, with its record of Bartholdi's 17-year struggle and the many patriotic and commercial uses his figure has been put to; the observation decks at the top of the pedestal; and the view from the crown—the crowning touch, so to speak. Bartholdi's title for the massive sculpture was "Enlightening the World," and the crown's seven rays represent the seven continents and the seven seas.

While you're waiting, you can ponder the numbers: The statue itself is a little over 150 feet tall, twice that counting the pedestal and base; and it weighs 225 tons—100 tons of which represents the copper sheeting that covers the frame. There are 354 steps from the pedestal up into the crown, the equivalent of 22 stories. And don't feel bad about your own nose; hers is four and a half feet long.

Note that although the statue had been closed to visitors after 9/11, at press time, discussions on reopening it were underway.

Touring Tips If temperatures are predicted to go above 100°, only passengers from the first ferry of the day will be allowed to go all the way into the crown because of the even greater heat up there. All others will have to stop on the 10th floor pedestal level. That means you need to be among the first 600 people in line for the 8:30 a.m. ferry, so expect to be there at 7:30 a.m. And if the lines are very long, the staff may close them off early. Note also that the last ferries leave Lower Manhattan in midafternoon; call for exact times. (The only consolation for having to wait until late is that in winter you'll see the Manhattan skyline begin to light up.) Note again that tours are currently limited to the outside area following the events of 9/11; call for updates.

Trinity Church   Zone 1

Type of Attraction Fine Gothic Revival church from the mid-19th century
Location Broadway at Wall Street
Nearest Subway Station Wall Street (4, 5) or Rector Street (N, R)
Admission Free
Hours Monday–Friday, 9–1:45 a.m., 1–3:45 p.m; Saturday, 10 a.m.–3:45 p.m.; Sunday, 1–3:45 p.m.; free tours daily at 2 p.m. and Sunday after the 11:15 a.m. service. For group tours, call (212) 602-0872.
Phone (212) 602-0872; www.trinitywallstreet.org
When to Go Midafternoon
Special Comments Hearing-impaired services at 2 p.m.
Overall Appeal by Age Group

Pre-school ½	Teens ★★	Over 30 ★★★
Grade school ★	Young Adults ★★½	Seniors ★★★

Author's Rating ★★★
How Much Time to Allow 30 minutes
Description and Comments This church, as much as any other single edifice, is responsible for the Gothic Revival craze of the 19th century; its balance of interior extravagance (carved wood, stained glass, and ornate stone) and exterior restraint (itself a metaphor for religious faith) is striking. Actually, this is the third church on this

site: The first one was built in 1698 and burned in the conflagration of 1776; the second was razed in 1839. There's a small museum behind the altar with records of the congregation's homes. The brass doors are a tribute to Ghiberti's *Doors of Paradise* at the Duomo in Florence. Thanks to painstaking efforts by restorationists, who removed a supposedly protective layer of paraffin, the sandstone's original cherry tone is back. The 280-foot steeple pointed unrivaled to heaven until the late 19th century, and even surrounded by the towers of international finance, it has a certain obdurate confidence.

Romantics take note: This is where Founding Federalist and dueling victim Alexander Hamilton is buried, along with inventor Robert Fulton and other luminaries.

Touring Tips This is a wonderful place to hear music, either choral or concert. Come Sundays or check local listings for special events.

Whitney Museum of American Art   Zone 13

Type of Attraction World-class collection of 20th-century American art

Location Madison Avenue at 75th Street

Nearest Subway Station 77th Street

Admission $12 adults, $9.50 seniors and students; children ages 11 and under free

Hours Tuesday–Thursday, 11 a.m.–6 p.m.; Friday, 1–9 p.m.; Saturday and Sunday, 11 a.m.–6 p.m.; closed Monday

Phone (212) 570-3676; www.whitney.org

When to Go Anytime

Special Comments "Pay what you wish" Friday 6–9 p.m.

Overall Appeal by Age Group

Pre-school ½	Teens ★★★	Over 30 ★★★½
Grade school ★★½	Young Adults ★★★	Seniors ★★★½

Author's Rating ★★★★

How Much Time to Allow 1.5–3 hours

Description and Comments There is much to be said for an insider's eye, and since the Whitney was founded by sculptor Gertrude Vanderbilt Whitney, its collection of modern American art in many opinions rivals the international collection of the Museum of Modern Art. (She founded a new museum when the prestigious and no doubt somewhat pompous Metropolitan turned down her offer to donate the whole collection.)

Since its recent expansion and extensive exterior cleaning, this inverted concrete pyramid seems less forbidding and more quirky, though still mysterious; instead of seeming to lower, it seems to be playing at reticence, hiding its goods behind the drawbridge like a castle. It's a collection with a great deal of humor; and though it has many serious and dark pieces as well, it may surprise you how interested younger patrons may be in the cartoonlike Lichtensteins or robust Thomas Hart Bentons, the boxing art of George Bellows, Warhol's post-advertising art and other familiar elements of Pop Art, O'Keeffe's flowers, or the super-realistic Hopper paintings—or even many of the brilliantly colored abstracts. The famous Calder assemblage called "Circus" that used to be mounted just inside the main entrance has been moved upstairs; it is still the only piece on permanent display.

Touring Tips There is a café in the museum, a branch of the Upper East Side home-style restaurants called Sarabeth's (phone (212) 570-3670).

Dining and Restaurants

NYC EATs:
Everything, Anything, All the Time

No self-respecting New Yorker prepares meals at home more than four times a week. There are simply too many other options to entice the palate and relieve one from the kitchen. With food on offer from every part of the globe presented on paper plates to porcelain platters, New York boasts a plethora of culinary delights that would take months to fully digest. The longer you are here, the more adventurous and discerning your taste buds become. Trying the new, vying for reservations at the trendy, or simply sharing a meal at a neighborhood favorite is recreation, sport and entertainment for thousands of New Yorkers. When you get to the stage of knowing how to determine good dim sum and being able to assess a ceviche, the quest for insider information is insatiable and thus begins the NY obsession with food and the places that serve it.

You're hooked before you realize it. When new Latin American snacks, such as pupusas, make their appearance into your neighborhood or local newspaper, you'll be the first one lining up for them as soon as you find out how to order them with the correct pronunciation.

Rules of thumb include not judging an establishment by its tabletop. Some of the tastiest food can be served on formica whilst mediocrity can be hidden superficially on an expanse of starched linen. Price doesn't necessarily reflect quality, and we've found that many midrange restaurants tend to be the weakest link in the dining spectrum.

It used to be easier for restaurants to become hits because the owners were famous or the theme was fun (Britney Spears's **NYLA** a case in point); nowadays, with the culinary bar being raised ever higher, a restaurant has more chance of being successful for its food than for its founder—unless of course the founder is an established chef. So since the cachet of a restaurant is currently more about the chef, the location, atmosphere, and the décor, the chic aspect of the dining experience depends on the crowd. That said, the New York attitude towards food can be summed up nicely by Michael Romano, chef of 2003's (past years') most popular restaurant, **Union Square Café** (see profile): "For me, it's about a high level of quality for a lot of people versus the precious, rare commodity for a few. Food is too basic, too wonderful!" So lest there comes a time when too many expensive "glazed sea urchin testicles on a bed of wilted tropical palm leaves and caramelized baby scallions en jus" appear on menus, New Yorkers will revolt and eat elsewhere.

Manhattan alone has over 4,000 restaurants, and the range of food and flavors is exhilarating. The array of indigenous kitchens testify to the range of people who have chosen to settle on the New York shores. So whether you have a yen for Asian food or crave a zeppole, you'll find your dish and please your taste buds somewhere in the metropolis. Furthermore, if you're jet-lagged and hungry at 4 a.m., you'll be able to find a place other than a 7-11.

This chapter provides some insight and reviews a few highlights, but if you'd like more information check the *Village Voice, Time Out* reviews, or the Dining Out section in the Wednesday edition of the *New York Times*. You could also do several web searches (**www.citysearch.com**), and for specific advice on far-flung underground dining and opinions on a every type of food imaginable, visit sites like **www.chowhound.com** and **www.addyourown.com**.

Tireless foodies will go the extra mile to find the best dim sum (Flushing, Queens) an amazing falafel (Atlantic Avenue, Brooklyn) or real pierogies (Greenpoint, Brooklyn). For a quick culinary tour, we'll fill you in on just a few neighborhoods worth visiting for dining explorations: Sunset Park, Brooklyn—for Chinese, Vietnamese, and Mexican. If you're in town between May and September, visit the soccer fields in Red Hook, Brooklyn, on the weekend to savor some of the best homecooked Honduran, Mexican and other Latin American–inspired dishes. Bedford-Stuyvesant has soul food and renowned roti (**Ali's Roti Shop,** 1267 Fulton Street). Indian food can be found not just on East 6th Street, but also the "Curry Hill" area between 33rd and 26th streets between Third, Lexington, and Park avenues in Manhattan, and in Jackson Heights in Queens. Contrary to tourist belief, Little Italy is no longer the place to sample some of the best Italian fare on offer. You can find tasty Italian throughout the city, but Staten Island, not generally a mecca for discerning gourmets, is considered by natives to have a few exceptional Southern Italian establishments; the same can be said for areas in the Bronx, including Arthur Avenue.

Some might argue that there's a more interesting variety of food in the outer boroughs than in Manhattan, but we hope you have the opportunity to do the research firsthand. As you go forth on your eating exploits, we'd like to offer some words of advice. Be adventurous—make use of the NYC public transportation system, visit some of our suggestions, and talk to the locals. Above all: Enjoy your food, and come back to New York for seconds.

Hot Dogs to Haute Cuisine

A trip to the Big Apple isn't complete without tasting quintessential New York fare, such as a bagel, a slice of pizza, or a hot dog, as well as reserving a table at one of the upscale and established kitchens. The kitchens don't get much more established when you consider certain French restaurants (**La Caravelle,** 33 West 55th Street, (212) 586-4252; **La Grenouille,** 3 East 52nd Street; (212) 752-1495; **Le Perigord,** 405 East 52nd Street, (212) 755-6244; and **Lutece,** 249 East 50th Street, (212) 752-2225) that have been in New York for decades and have yet to serve a soggy baguette. They have basked in the glory of fine dining for years, but their prices are considerably steep (except at lunch), and their atmosphere is traditional. As for New York landmarks, restaurants that have stood the test of time include the **Four Seasons** (99 East 52nd Street; (212) 754-9494), **21 Club** (21 West 52nd Street; (212) 582-7200; **www.21club.com**) and **Café des Artistes** (1 West 67th Street; (212) 877-3500; **www.cafenyc.com**).

At the other end of the spectrum, but just as important, are the staples of New York snacks, light meals or brunches. If you can, try a New York bagel. **Murray's Bagels** (500 6th Avenue, (212) 462-2830; and 242 8th Avenue, (646) 638-1335) offers delicious, hand-rolled bagels from plain to "everything," with cream cheese and lox, otherwise known as smoked salmon. Hot dogs can be had at many a stand, but traditionalists like to go to **Nathan's Famous Hot Dogs** on the pier at Coney Island in Brooklyn. Many of these typical New York selections have heavy influences from Italy (pizza and calzones), and Eastern Europe. Besides bagels, some of the Eastern European selections include knishes, i.e potato pies (**Yonah Schimmel's,** 137 East Houston Street; (212) 477-2858), pickles (**Gus's Pickles,** 31 Essex Street) and whitefish salad (**Sable's Smoked Fish,** 1489 Second Avenue; (212) 249-6177; and **Russ & Daughters,** 179 East Houston Street; (212) 475-4880). For another New York dining experience, have lunch at a coffee shop and order anything in the realm of eggs, burgers, salads, sandwiches and grilled cheese, and wash it down with a milkshake or chocolate egg cream (seltzer, milk, and chocolate syrup). You'll feel the fast New York pace, and if you're lucky, you'll get a pleasantly churlish New Yorker as a waiter. If the bill is more than $24 for two people, then it's not a typical coffee shop.

Hot Spots

With the popularity of the Food Network and chefs writing their own cookbooks, it's no surprise that some chefs spend as much time behind the camera as they do behind the stove and therefore their reputation, be it through food or a show, precedes them. Many chefs are happy to leave traditional French cooking to the institutions mentioned earlier and experiment with new twists, fusion and fish. At press time, Marcus Samuelsson, of **Aquavit** (see profile) fame had just opened a Japanese-American restaurant called **Riingo** (in the Alex Hotel, 205 East 45th Street). Other eateries opening in 2004 are **Per Se,** Thomas Keller's (of French Laundry fame on the West Coast) restaurant to open in the Time Warner Center in Columbus Circle; and **Delouvrier,** Christian Delouvrier's (formerly from Lespinasse) new place to open in Midtown.

If you'd like to dine in hotels, we can recommend dinner at **Asia de Cuba** at the Morgan Hotel (237 Madison Avenue; (212) 726-7755) and **Le Cirque 2000** (see profile) at the New York Palace. Brunch is a fun affair at **Café Botanica** in the Essex House (160 Central Park South; (212) 484-5120) and is also festive at **Christmas** in the Palm Court at the Plaza Hotel (768 Fifth Avenue; (212) 546-5310).

Where's the Beef?

With the Atkins Diet bringing many people back to meaty protein, New York steakhouses have had a bit of a renaissance, although many of the waitstaff still prefer to be traditionally gruff. Most of the best steakhouses have been around for awhile ,and **Peter Luger** (see profile) has to go to the top of the list. **Palm** (837 Second Avenue; (212) 687-2953; **www. thepalm.com**) and its sister restaurant across the street at 840 Second Avenue (between 44th and 45th streets) has excellent sirloin steaks and cottage-fried potatoes. Another meat institution is **Smith and Wollensky** (201 East 49th Street; (212) 753-1530; **www.smithandwollemsky. com**) with hearty beef and a great wine list. After renovating, **Patroon** (160 East 46th Street; (212) 883-7373) altered the menu to add more than just steak, but it still has a good meaty base and a new rooftop terrace for cigar smokers. For meat with a South American flavor, try Brazilian rodizio at **Churrascaria Plataforma** (see profile).

The Dress Code: Silk or Sneakers

It's said that anything goes in New York, and in many cases this is true. However, there are some establishments that expect people to abide by a certain decorum that requires a jacket; we've noted where this is the case. Also, some places have jackets and occasionally ties on hand to loan, so as not to turn business away. Some pricey places will not require a jacket, merely a sense of chic, all black, or cockiness to get you through the door. If that's the case, chances are that the food isn't as important as the scene. Business casual to casual and/or funky are usually the norm for most of our profiled restaurants. However, should you be dining in one of these places on business, then your own sense of the importance of the meeting should dictate your clothing. Common sense and an air of confidence will go a long way.

Green Tip

We're not here to preach nor to make you eat your vegetables, but in the light of recent food debates discussing genetically modified food and "organic" counterparts, these issues have become more prominent for many New Yorkers. Restaurants, meat and vegetarian alike, that provide "GM free" ingredients and organic alternatives will probably gain more support in the next few years. Sustainably raised fish will also be a factor to consider, so before you tuck into a bowl of caviar or a medallion of monkfish, consider whether the produce has been obtained from a legal and ecologically sound source. You may be pleased to know that Arctic Char, the salmon-like fish, is currently in abundance and has graced many of the top restaurant menus—in part due to its good taste and ready availability.

Where to Find a Deal for a Meal

With the New York economy not yet back on its feet, finding a meal deal is easier now that restaurants want to lure the locals and tourists back to their dining rooms. Not all prix-fixe menus are cheap, but many lunch specials and prix-fixe menus exist in restaurants covering all price ranges. Two of the best lunch prix fixe in town are at **Lutece** (249 East 50th Street; (212) 752-2225) offering old-world fine French dining, at $29 per person; and a $5.95 lunch buffet at **Chennai Garden** (129 East 27th Street; (212) 689-1999) for wonderfully fresh and tasty kosher vegetarian Indian food. During June to Labor Day, many top restaurants sign up to be part of the Lunch and Dinner dining event, which means that they'll offer a prix-fixe menu at $20.04 for lunch and at $30.04 for dinner; the trend, so far, has been to add a penny for each new year. Some restaurants only have the offer for a week, so look out for the list in late May and June. The 2003 list included Tabla, Aquavit Café, Café Boulud, Montrachet, Artisanal, Tamarind, Patria, and many others.

The Restaurants

Our Favorite New York Restaurants

This survey of over 100 of New York's niftiest nosheries covers a wide spectrum of price categories, global origins, and New York neighborhoods, including tried and true oldies, popular trendies, off-beat ethnics, and local favorites. We give an overall impression of food and mood and what it will cost. Don't be surprised if some of our menu recommendations are not available on a particular day; many New York restaurants change their menus often to take advantage of ultra-fresh seasonal offerings. And though we've worked overtime to ensure the freshness of our opinions (places were checked at the very last minute before publication), do bear in mind that restaurants are works in progress. They're not static and are essentially a moving target. The only opinion that's 100% timely is your own, of your own meal as you eat it. Chefs change . . . or call in sick . . . or have bad days . . . or simply get bored and lose their edge. So . . . caveat eater!

We have developed detailed profiles for the best and most interesting restaurants in town. Each profile features an easily scanned heading that allows you to check out the restaurant's name, cuisine, star rating, cost, quality rating, and value rating.

Cuisine   The more entrenched imported cuisines are fragmenting—French into bistro fare and even Provençal, "new continental" into regional American and "eclectic"—while others have broadened and fused: Middle Eastern and Provençal into Mediterranean, Spanish and South American into nuevo Latino, and so on. In some cases, we have used the broader terms (i.e., "French") but added descriptions to give a clearer idea of the fare. Remember that experimentation and "fusion" are ever more common, so don't hold us or the chefs to too strict a style.

Overall Rating   The star rating encompasses the entire dining experience, including style, service, and ambience, in addition to the taste, presentation, and quality of the food. Five stars is the highest rating possible and connotes the best of everything. Four-star restaurants are exceptional and three-star restaurants are well above average. Two-star restaurants are good. One star is used to indicate an average restaurant that demonstrates an unusual capability in some area of specialization—for example, an otherwise unmemorable place that has great barbecue chicken.

Price   This is an expense description that provides a comparative sense of how much a complete meal will cost. A complete meal for our purposes consists of an entrée with vegetable or side dish and choice of soup or salad. Appetizers, desserts, drinks, and tips are excluded.

Inexpensive	$17 and less per person
Moderate	$18–$37 per person
Expensive	Over $37 per person

Quality Rating   The food quality is rated on a scale of one to five stars, five being the best rating attainable. The quality rating is based expressly on the taste, freshness of ingredients, preparation, presentation, and creativity of food served. There is no consideration of price. If you are a person who wants the best food available, and cost is not an issue, you need look no further than the quality ratings.

Value Rating   If, on the other hand, you are looking for both quality and value, then you should check the value rating. The value ratings are defined as follows:

★★★★★	Exceptional value; a real bargain
★★★★	Good value
★★★	Fair value; you get exactly what you pay for
★★	Somewhat overpriced
★	Significantly overpriced

Zone   The zone number will give you a general idea of where each pro-filed restaurant is located. We've divided New York into the following 19 geographic zones:

Zone 1   Lower Manhattan, Wall Street, and the Battery

Zone 2   Soho and Tribeca

Zone 3   Chinatown, Little Italy, and the Lower East Side

Zone 4   Greenwich Village

Zone 5   The East Village

Zone 6   Chelsea

Zone 7   Gramercy Park and Madison Square

Zone 8   Midtown West and the Theater District

Zone 9   Midtown East

Zone 10 West Side

Zone 11 East Side

Zone 12 Upper West Side

Zone 13 Upper East Side

Zone 14 Columbia University and Harlem

Zone 15 The Heights

Zone 16 Brooklyn

Zone 17 Queens

Zone 18 The Bronx

Zone 19 Staten Island

Payment   We've listed the type of payment accepted at each restaurant using the following code: AMEX equals American Express (Optima), CB equals Carte Blanche, D equals Discover, DC equals Diners Club, MC equals MasterCard, and VISA is self-explanatory.

Who's Included   Restaurants in New York open and close at an alarm-ing rate. So, for the most part, we have tried to confine our list to estab-lishments with a proven track record over a substantial period of time. The exceptions here are the newer offspring of the demigods of the culinary world—these places are destined to last, at least until our next update. Newer or changed establishments that demonstrate staying power and consistency will be profiled in subsequent editions. Also, the list is highly selective. Noninclusion of a particular place does not necessarily indicate that the restaurant is not good, only that it was not ranked by us to be among the best in its genre. Detailed profiles of individual restaurants follow in alphabetical order at the end of this chapter.

THE BEST NEW YORK RESTAURANTS

Type and Name	Overall Rating	Price	Quality Rating	Value Rating	Zone
American					
Grange Hall	★★★½	Mod	★★★★½	★★★★★	4
Gramercy Tavern	★★★½	Exp	★★★★	★★★	7
Blue Water Grill	★★★	Mod	★★★★	★★★★	7
Parsonage	★★★	Mod/Exp	★★★★	★★★★	19
Blue Ribbon	★★★	Mod	★★★½	★★★★	2, 16
The Pink Teacup	★★	Mod	★★★	★★★★	4
EJ's Luncheonette	★★	Inexp	★★★½	★★★½	12,13,4
Gray's Papaya	★½	Inexp	★★★½	★★★★★	12
American Southwest					
Mesa Grill	★★★	Exp	★★★½	★★★	7
Santa Fe	★★½	Mod	★★★½	★★★★	10
Argentinean					
Old San Juan	★★½	Inexp	★★★★	★★★★	8
Asian					
Cendrillon	★★★	Mod	★★★★	★★★★	2
Zen Palate	★★½	Inexp	★★★½	★★★★	12, 8, 7
Asian Fusion					
Union Pacific	★★★★½	Exp	★★★★½	★★★	7
Rain	★★★	Mod	★★★★	★★★	12, 13
Rice	★★★	Inexp	★★★½	★★★★★	3, 16
Barbecue					
Virgil's Barbecue	★★½	Mod	★★★	★★★	8
Belgian					
Petite Abeille	★★½	Inexp	★★★★	★★★★½	2, 4, 6
Bistro					
Artisinal	★★★½	Mod/Exp	★★★★	★★★	7
Florent	★★½	Mod	★★★½	★★★★	4
Pastis	★★½	Mod	★★★½	★★★½	4
Tartine	★★½	Inexp	★★★★	★★★★	4
Brazilian					
Churrascaria Plataforma	★★★	Mod	★★★★	★★★★	8
Cabana Carioca	★★½	Inexp	★★★★	★★★★★	8

THE BEST NEW YORK RESTAURANTS (continued)

Type and Name	Overall Rating	Price	Quality Rating	Value Rating	Zone
British					
Tea & Sympathy	★★★	Inexp/Mod	★★★½	★★★	4
Cantonese					
The Nice Restaurant	★★★½	Mod	★★★★½	★★★★	3
Chinese (see also Dim Sum)					
Ping's	★★★★	Mod	★★★★½	★★★★½	17
Shun Lee West, Shun Lee Café	★★★½	Mod/Exp	★★★★	★★★	10
66	★★★	Exp	★★★★	★★½	2
Joe's Shanghai	★★★	Mod	★★★★½	★★★★★	3, 17
Grand Sichuan International	★★★	Mod	★★★★	★★★★★	6
Kam Chueh	★★★	Mod	★★★★	★★★★½	3
Cuban					
Margon Restaurant	★★	Inexp	★★★½	★★★★★	8
Dim Sum (see also Chinese)					
Ping's	★★★★	Mod	★★★★½	★★★★½	17
The Nice Restaurant	★★★½	Mod	★★★★½	★★★★	3
Ethiopian					
Meskerem	★★★	Inexp/Mod	★★★½	★★★½	4, 8
French					
Le Bernardin	★★★★½	Very Exp	★★★★★	★★★	8
Chanterelle	★★★★	Very Exp	★★★★½	★★★★	2
Jean-Georges	★★★★	Exp	★★★★½	★★★	10
Le Cirque 2000	★★★★	Very Exp	★★★★½	★★★	9
Il Bucco	★★★★	Exp	★★★★½	★★★	5
Café Boulud	★★★½	Exp	★★★★½	★★★½	13
Montrachet	★★★½	Exp	★★★★	★★★½	2
Balthazar	★★★½	Mod/Exp	★★★★	★★★★	2
Les Halles	★★½	Exp	★★★½	★★★	7
La Boite en Bois	★★½	Mod	★★★½	★★★★	10
Greek					
Molyvos	★★★	Exp	★★★★	★★★★	8
Symposium	★★★	Inexp/Mod	★★★½	★★★★	14

THE BEST NEW YORK RESTAURANTS (continued)

Type and Name	Overall Rating	Price	Quality Rating	Value Rating	Zone
Indian					
Tabla	★★★★	Exp	★★★★½	★★★★	7
Tamarind	★★★½	Exp	★★★★	★★★	7
Shaan	★★★	Mod/Exp	★★★★	★★★★	9
Jackson Diner	★★	Inexp/Mod	★★★½	★★★★★	17
Namaaskar (buffet)	★½	Inexp	★★★½	★★★★★	2
Indonesian					
Borobudur Café	★★	Inexp	★★½	★★★	5
Irish					
Molly's	★★½	Mod	★★★★	★★★★	7
Italian					
Il Bucco	★★★★	Exp	★★★★½	★★★	5
Piccola Venezia	★★★★	Exp	★★★★½	★★★	17
Mulino	★★★½	Exp	★★★★½	★★★½	4
Babbo	★★★½	Exp	★★★★	★★★★	4
Pó	★★★½	Mod	★★★★	★★★★	4
Osteria Del Circo	★★★	Exp	★★★★	★★★	8
Piccolo Angolo	★★★	Mod	★★★★	★★★★	4
Iammo Bello	★★½	Inexp	★★★★	★★★★★	11
Becco	★★½	Mod	★★★½	★★★★★	8
Rosario's	★★	Inexp	★★★★	★★★★★	1
Italian (Northern)					
Paola's	★★★	Mod/Exp	★★★★	★★★★	13
Remi	★★★	Exp	★★★★	★★★	8
Orso	★★★	Mod	★★★½	★★★½	8
Italian (Tuscan)					
Coco Pazzo Teatro	★★½	Exp	★★★½	★★★	8
Japanese					
Nobu	★★★★	Exp	★★★★½	★★★	2
Tomoe	★★★½	Mod	★★★★½	★★★★	4
Sushisay	★★★½	Exp	★★★★	★★★★	9
Honmura An	★★★	Exp	★★★★	★★★	2
Menchanko-Tei	★★	Inexp	★★★½	★★★★	8, 9
Jewish Deli					
Mr. Broadway Kosher Deli	★★★	Mod	★★★★	★★★★★	8

THE BEST NEW YORK RESTAURANTS *(continued)*

Type and Name	Overall Rating	Price	Quality Rating	Value Rating	Zone
Jewish Deli (continued)					
Second Avenue Deli	★★½	Mod	★★★½	★★★	5
Korean					
Bo	★★★★	Inexp	★★★★½	★★★★★	17
Woo Chon	★★★	Mod	★★★★	★★★★	9
Latin American					
Patria	★★★½	Exp	★★★★	★★★	7
Calle Ocho	★★★	Mod	★★★★	★★★	12
Café con Leche	★★½	Inexp	★★★★	★★★★★	12
El Papasito	★★	Inexp	★★★½	★★★★★	8
Malaysian					
Penang	★★½	Mod	★★★½	★★★	12, 2
Jaya Malaysian	★★	Inexp	★★★½	★★★★½	3
Mediterranean					
Picholine	★★★★	Exp	★★★★½	★★★	10
Delphini	★★★	Mod	★★★½	★★★★	12
The Tree House	★★	Inexp/Mod	★★★½	★★★½	18
Mexican					
Gabriela's	★★★	Mod	★★★★	★★★★★	12
Rosa Mexicano	★★★	Mod	★★★★	★★★★	9
Middle Eastern					
Sahara East	★★½	Mod	★★★★	★★★★	5
Moroccan					
Café Mogador	★★½	Mod	★★★★	★★★★★	5
New American					
The River Café	★★★★★	Very Exp	★★★★★	★★★★½	16
Veritas	★★★★	Very Exp	★★★★½	★★★★	7
Union Square Café	★★★★	Exp	★★★★½	★★★★	7
Gotham Bar & Grill	★★★½	Exp	★★★★	★★★	4
Pasta					
Tre Pomodori	★★½	Mod	★★★★	★★★★★	7
Peruvian					
Rinconcito Peruano	★★★	Inexp	★★★★	★★★★★	8
Pizza					
Patsy's Pizza	★★★	Inexp	★★★★½	★★★★★	14
Otto	★★★	Mod	★★★½	★★	4

THE BEST NEW YORK RESTAURANTS (continued)

Type and Name	Overall Rating	Price	Quality Rating	Value Rating	Zone
Portuguese					
Cabana Carioca	★★½	Inexp	★★★★	★★★★★	8
Puerto Rican					
Old San Juan	★★★	Inexp	★★★★	★★★★	8
Russian					
Firebird	★★★	Exp	★★★★	★★★★	8
Petrossian	★★★	Exp	★★★★	★★★	8
Scandinavian					
Aquavit	★★★★½	Very Exp	★★★★★	★★★½	8
Seafood					
Union Pacific	★★★★½	Exp	★★★★½	★★★	7
Le Bernardin	★★★★	Very Exp	★★★★★	★★★★	8
Oceana	★★★½	Exp	★★★★½	★★★	9
Blue Water Grill	★★★	Mod	★★★★	★★★★	7
Soul Food					
Soul Fixin's	★★★	Inexp	★★★★	★★★★★	6
Jezebel	★★★	Exp	★★★★	★★★	8
Soup Take-out					
Soup Kitchen International	★★★½	Inexp	★★★★½	★★★★★	8
Spanish					
Il Bucco	★★★★	Exp	★★★★½	★★★	5
Xunta	★★★	Mod	★★★★	★★★★	5
Steak					
Peter Luger	★★★	Exp	★★★★	★★★★	16
Les Halles	★★½	Exp	★★★½	★★★	7
Tearoom					
Lady Mendl's Tea Salon	★★★	Mod	★★★★½	★★★	7
Thai					
Kway Tiow Thai	★★★★	Inexp	★★★★½	★★★★★	17
Jasmine	★★½	Mod	★★★★	★★★★	13
Vegetarian					
Candle Café	★★★½	Inexp/Mod	★★★★	★★★½	13
Kate's Joint	★★½	Mod	★★★★	★★★★	5

THE BEST NEW YORK RESTAURANTS (continued)

Type and Name	Overall Rating	Price	Quality Rating	Value Rating	Zone
Vegetarian (continued)					
Zen Palate	★★½	Inexp	★★★½	★★★★	12, 8, 7
Vietnamese					
New Pasteur	★★★½	Inexp	★★★★	★★★★★	3
Saigon Grill	★★★	Inexp	★★★★½	★★★★★	12, 13

THE BEST NEW YORK RESTAURANTS BY ZONE

Name	Type	Overall Rating	Price	Quality Rating	Value Rating
Zone 1: Lower Manhattan, Wall Street, and the Battery					
Rosario's	Italian	★★	Inexp	★★★★	★★★★★
Zone 2: Soho and Tribeca					
Chanterelle	French	★★★★	Very Exp	★★★★½	★★★★
Nobu	Japanese	★★★★	Exp	★★★★½	★★★
Balthazar	French	★★★½	Mod/Exp	★★★★	★★★★
Montrachet	French	★★★½	Exp	★★★★	★★★½
66	Chinese	★★★	Exp	★★★★	★★½
Blue Ribbon	American	★★★	Mod	★★★½	★★★★
Cendrillon	Asian	★★★	Mod	★★★★	★★★★
Honmura An	Japanese	★★★	Exp	★★★★	★★★
Petite Abeille	Belgian	★★½	Inexp	★★★★	★★★★½
Penang	Malaysian	★★½	Mod	★★★½	★★★
Namaaskar (buffet)	Indian	★½	Inexp	★★★½	★★★★★
Zone 3: Chinatown, Little Italy, and the Lower East Side					
New Pasteur	Vietnamese	★★★½	Inexp	★★★★	★★★★★
The Nice Restaurant	Cantonese/ Dim Sum	★★★½	Mod	★★★★½	★★★★
Joe's Shanghai	Chinese	★★★	Mod	★★★★½	★★★★★
Kam Chueh	Chinese	★★★	Mod	★★★★	★★★★½
Rice	Asian Fusion	★★★	Inexp		
Jaya Malaysian	Malaysian	★★	Inexp	★★★½	★★★★½
Zone 4: Greenwich					
Babbo	Italian	★★★½	Exp	★★★★	★★★★
Grange Hall	American	★★★½	Mod	★★★★½	★★★★★
Il Mulino	Italian	★★★½	Exp	★★★★½	★★★½
Pó	Italian	★★★½	Mod	★★★★	★★★★

THE BEST NEW YORK RESTAURANTS BY ZONE (continued)

Name	Type	Overall Rating	Price	Quality Rating	Value Rating
Zone 4: Greenwich (continued)					
Tomoe	Japanese	★★★½	Mod	★★★★½	★★★★
Gotham Bar & Grill	New American	★★★½	Exp	★★★★	★★★
Piccolo Angolo	Italian	★★★	Mod	★★★★	★★★★
Meskerem	Ethiopian	★★★	Inexp/Mod	★★★½	★★★½
Tea & Sympathy	British	★★★	Mod	★★★½	★★★
Otto	Pizza/ Enoteca	★★★	Mod	★★★½	★★
Petite Abeille	Belgian	★★½	Inexp	★★★★	★★★★½
Tartine	Bistro	★★½	Inexp	★★★★	★★★★
Florent	Bistro	★★½	Mod	★★★½	★★★★
Pastis	Bistro	★★½	Mod	★★★½	★★★½
EJ's Luncheonette	American	★★	Inexp	★★★½	★★★½
The Pink Teacup	American	★★	Mod	★★★	★★★★
Zone 5: The East Village					
Il Bucco	French/ Italian/Spanish	★★★★	Exp	★★★★½	★★★
Xunta	Spanish	★★★	Mod	★★★★	★★★★
Café Mogador	Moroccan	★★½	Mod	★★★★	★★★★★
Kate's Joint	Vegetarian	★★½	Mod	★★★★	★★★★
Sahara East	Middle Eastern	★★½	Mod	★★★★	★★★★
Second Avenue Deli	Jewish Deli	★★½	Mod	★★★½	★★★
Borobudur Café	Indonesian	★★	Inexp	★★½	★★★
Zone 6: Chelsea					
Grand Sichuan International	Chinese	★★★	Mod	★★★★	★★★★★
Soul Fixin's	Soul Food	★★★	Inexp	★★★★	★★★★★
Petite Abeille	Belgian	★★½	Inexp	★★★★	★★★★½
Zone 7: Gramercy Park and Madison Square					
Union Pacific	Seafood/ Asian Fusion	★★★★½	Exp	★★★★½	★★★
Tabla	Indian	★★★★	Exp	★★★★½	★★★★
Union Square Café	New American	★★★★	Exp	★★★★½	★★★★
Veritas	New American	★★★★	Exp	★★★★½	★★★★

THE BEST NEW YORK RESTAURANTS BY ZONE *(continued)*

Name	Type	Overall Rating	Price	Quality Rating	Value Rating
Zone 7: Gramercy Park and Madison Square *(continued)*					
Artisinal	Bistro/ Fromagerie	★★★½	Mod/Exp	★★★★	★★★
Tamarind	Indian	★★★½	Exp	★★★★	★★★
Gramercy Tavern	American	★★★½	Exp	★★★★	★★★
Patria	Latin American	★★★½	Exp	★★★★	★★★
Blue Water Grill	American/ Seafood	★★★	Mod	★★★★	★★★★
Lady Mendl's Tea Salon	Tearoom	★★★	Mod	★★★★½	★★★
Mesa Grill	American Southwest	★★★	Exp	★★★½	★★★
Les Halles	French/Steak	★★½	Exp	★★★½	★★★
Molly's	Irish	★★½	Mod	★★★★	★★★★
Tre Pomodori	Pasta	★★½	Mod	★★★★	★★★★★
Zen Palate	Vegetarian	★★½	Inexp	★★★½	★★★★
Zone 8: Midtown West and the Theater District					
Aquavit	Scandinavian	★★★★½	Very Exp	★★★★★	★★★½
Le Bernardin	French/ Seafood	★★★★½	Very Exp	★★★★★	★★★
Soup Kitchen International	Soup Take-Out	★★★½	Inexp	★★★★½	★★★★★
Mr. Broadway Kosher Deli	Jewish Deli	★★★	Mod	★★★★	★★★★★
Churrascaria Plataforma	Brazilian	★★★	Mod	★★★★	★★★★
Firebird	Russian	★★★	Exp	★★★★	★★★★
Jezebel	Soul Food	★★★	Exp	★★★★	★★★
Molyvos	Greek	★★★	Exp	★★★★	★★★★
Meskerem	Ethiopian	★★★	Inexp/Mod	★★★½	★★★½
Orso	Italian (Northern)	★★★	Mod	★★★½	★★★½
Osteria Del Circo	Italian	★★★	Exp	★★★★	★★★
Petrossian	Russian	★★★	Exp	★★★★	★★★
Remi	Italian (Northern)	★★★	Exp	★★★★	★★★
Rinconcito Peruano	Peruvian	★★★	Inexp	★★★★	★★★★★
Becco	Italian	★★½	Mod	★★★½	★★★★★
Cabana Carioca	Brazilian/ Portuguese	★★½	Inexp	★★★★	★★★★★

THE BEST NEW YORK RESTAURANTS BY ZONE *(continued)*

Name	Type	Overall Rating	Price	Quality Rating	Value Rating
Zone 8: Midtown West and the Theater District *(continued)*					
Coco Pazzo Teatro	Italian (Tuscan)	★★½	Exp	★★★½	★★★
Old San Juan	Argentinean/ Puerto Rican	★★½	Inexp	★★★★	★★★★
Virgil's Barbecue	Barbecue	★★½	Mod	★★★	★★★
Zen Palate	Asian/Veg.	★★½	Inexp	★★★½	★★★★
El Papasito	Latin American	★★	Inexp	★★★½	★★★★★
Margon Restaurant	Cuban	★★	Inexp	★★★½	★★★★★
Menchanko-Tei	Japanese	★★	Inexp	★★★½	★★★★
Zone 9: Midtown East					
Le Cirque 2000	French	★★★★	Very Exp	★★★★½	★★★
Oceana	Seafood	★★★½	Exp	★★★★½	★★★
Sushisay	Japanese	★★★½	Exp	★★★★	★★★★
Rosa Mexicano	Mexican	★★★	Mod	★★★★	★★★★
Woo Chon	Korean	★★★	Mod	★★★★	★★★★
Shaan	Indian	★★★	Mod/Exp	★★★★	★★★★
Menchanko-Tei	Japanese	★★	Inexp	★★★½	★★★★
Zone 10: West Side					
Jean-Georges	French	★★★★	Exp	★★★★½	★★★
Picholine	Mediter-ranean	★★★★	Exp	★★★★½	★★★
Shun Lee West, Shun Lee Café	Chinese	★★★½	Mod/Exp	★★★★	★★★
La Boite en Bois	French	★★½	Mod	★★★½	★★★★
Santa Fe	American Southwest	★★½	Mod	★★★½	★★★★
Zone 11: East Side					
Iammo Bello	Italian	★★½	Inexp	★★★★	★★★★★
Zone 12: Upper West Side					
Calle Ocho	Latin American	★★★	Mod	★★★★	★★★
Delphini	Mediter-ranean	★★★	Mod	★★★½	★★★★
Gabriela's	Mexican	★★★	Mod	★★★★	★★★★★
Rain	Asian Fusion	★★★	Mod	★★★★	★★★
Saigon Grill	Vietnamese	★★★	Inexp	★★★★½	★★★★★

THE BEST NEW YORK RESTAURANTS BY ZONE *(continued)*

Name	Type	Overall Rating	Price	Quality Rating	Value Rating
Zone 12: Upper West Side *(continued)*					
Café con Leche	Latin American	★★½	Inexp	★★★★	★★★★★
Penang	Malaysian	★★½	Mod	★★★½	★★★
Zen Palate	Asian/Veg.	★★½	Inexp	★★★½	★★★★
EJ's Luncheonette	American	★★	Inexp	★★★½	★★★½
Gray's Papaya	American	★½	Inexp	★★★½	★★★★★
Zone 13: Upper East Side					
Café Boulud	French	★★★½	Exp	★★★★½	★★★½
Candle Café	Vegetarian	★★★½	Inexp/Mod	★★★★	★★★½
Saigon Grill	Vietnamese	★★★	Inexp	★★★★½	★★★★★
Paola's	Italian (Northern)	★★★	Mod/Exp	★★★★	★★★★
Rain	Asian Fusion	★★★	Mod	★★★★	★★★
Jasmine	Thai	★★½	Mod	★★★★	★★★★
EJ's Luncheonette	American	★★	Inexp	★★★½	★★★½
Zone 14: Columbia University and Harlem					
Patsy's Pizza	Pizza	★★★	Inexp	★★★★½	★★★★★
Symposium	Greek	★★★	Inexp	★★★½	★★★★
Zone 16: Brooklyn					
The River Café	New American	★★★★★	Very Exp	★★★★★	★★★★½
Peter Luger	Steak	★★★½	Exp	★★★★	★★★★
Rice	Asian Fusion	★★★	Inexp	★★★½	★★★★★
Blue Ribbon	American	★★★	Mod	★★★½	★★★★
Zone 17: Queens					
Bo	Korean	★★★★	Inexp	★★★★½	★★★★★
Kway Tiow Thai	Thai	★★★★	Inexp	★★★★½	★★★★★
Piccola Venezia	Italian	★★★★	Exp	★★★★½	★★★
Ping's	Chinese/ Dim Sum	★★★★	Mod	★★★★½	★★★★½
Joe's Shanghai	Chinese	★★★	Mod	★★★★½	★★★★★
Jackson Diner	Indian	★★	Inexp/Mod	★★★½	★★★★★
Zone 18: The Bronx					
The Tree House	Mediter- American	★★	Inexp/Mod	★★★½	★★★½
Zone 19: Staten Island					
Parsonage	American	★★★	Mod/Exp	★★★★	★★★★

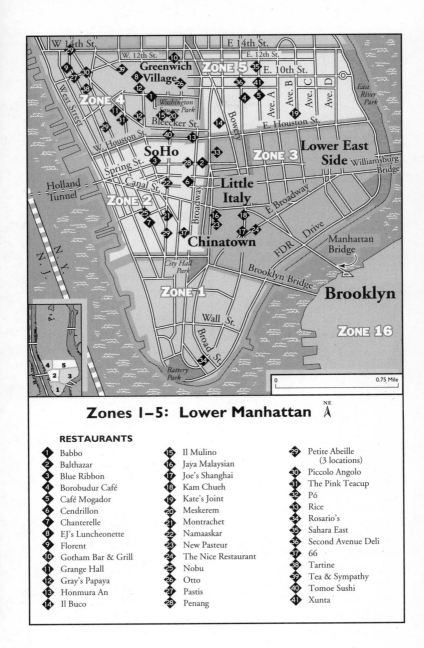

Zones 1–5: Lower Manhattan λ NE

RESTAURANTS

- ❶ Babbo
- ❷ Balthazar
- ❸ Blue Ribbon
- ❹ Borobudur Café
- ❺ Café Mogador
- ❻ Cendrillon
- ❼ Chanterelle
- ❽ EJ's Luncheonette
- ❾ Florent
- ❿ Gotham Bar & Grill
- ⓫ Grange Hall
- ⓬ Gray's Papaya
- ⓭ Honmura An
- ⓮ Il Buco

- ⓯ Il Mulino
- ⓰ Jaya Malaysian
- ⓱ Joe's Shanghai
- ⓲ Kam Chueh
- ⓳ Kate's Joint
- ⓴ Meskerem
- ㉑ Montrachet
- ㉒ Namaaskar
- ㉓ New Pasteur
- ㉔ The Nice Restaurant
- ㉕ Nobu
- ㉖ Otto
- ㉗ Pastis
- ㉘ Penang

- ㉙ Petite Abeille
  (3 locations)
- ㉚ Piccolo Angolo
- ㉛ The Pink Teacup
- ㉜ Pó
- ㉝ Rice
- ㉞ Rosario's
- ㉟ Sahara East
- ㊱ Second Avenue Deli
- ㊲ 66
- ㊳ Tartine
- ㊴ Tea & Sympathy
- ㊵ Tomoe Sushi
- ㊶ Xunta

251

Zones 6–9: Midtown Manhattan $\stackrel{NE}{\Lambda}$

RESTAURANTS

1. Aquavit
2. Artisinal
3. Becco
4. Blue Water Grill
5. Cabana Carioca
6. Churrascaria Plataforma
7. Coco Pazzo Teatro
8. El Papasito
9. Firebird
10. Gramercy Tavern
11. Grand Sichuan International
12. Jezebel
13. Lady Mendl's Tea Salon
14. Le Bernardin
15. Le Cirque 2000
16. Les Halles

17. Margon Restaurant
18. Menchanko-Tei (2 locations)
19. Mesa Grill
20. Meskerem
21. Molly's
22. Molyvos
23. Mr. Broadway Kosher Deli
24. Oceana
25. Old San Juan
26. Old San Juan Too
27. Orso
28. Osteria Del Circo
29. Patria
30. Petite Abeille
31. Petrossian
32. Rinconcito Peruano

33. Rosa Mexicano
34. Shaan
35. Soul Fixin's
36. Soup Kitchen International
37. Sushisay
38. Tabla
39. Tamarind
40. Tre Pomodori
41. Union Pacific
42. Union Square Cafe
43. Veritas
44. Virgil's Barbecue
45. Woo Chon
46. Zen Palate (2 locations)

Zones 10–13: East and West Side Manhattan

NE
ʌ

RESTAURANTS

1. Café Boulud
2. Café Con Leche
3. Calle Ocho
4. Candle Café
5. EJ's Luncheonette (2 locations)
6. Gabriela's
7. Gray's Papaya
8. Iammo Bello
9. Jasmine
10. Jean-Georges
11. La Boite En Bois
12. Paola's
13. Penang (2 locations)
14. Picholine
15. Rain (2 locations)
16. Saigon Grill
17. Santa Fe
18. Shun Lee, Shun Lee Café
19. Zen Palate

More Recommendations

The Best Brunch

Anglers and Writers   420 Hudson Street (212) 675-0810
Café des Artistes   1 West 67th Street (212) 877-3500
Café Botanica   Essex House, 160 Central Park South (212) 484-5120
Danal   90 East 10th Street (212) 982-6930
Good Enough to Eat   483 Amsterdam Avenue (212) 496-0163
Tartine   (see profile)
Zoe   90 Prince Street (212) 966-6722

The Best Burgers

Corner Bistro   331 West 4th Street (212) 242-9502
Cozy Soup & Burger   739 Broadway (212) 477-5566
Gotham Bar & Grill   (see profile)
Joe Allen   326 West 46th Street (212) 581-6464
Molly's   (see profile)
P. J. Clarke's   915 Third Avenue (212) 759-1650
Paul's Palace   131 Second Avenue (212) 529-3033
Steak Frites   9 East 16th Street (212) 463-7101
Wollensky's Grill   201 East 49th Street (3rd Avenue) (212) 753-0444
21 Club   21 West 52nd Street (212) 582-7200

The Best Cozy Tearooms

The Rotunda   At the Pierre 2 East 61st Street (212) 838-8000
Tea & Sympathy   108 Greenwich Avenue (212) 807-8329
Wild Lily Tea Room   511-A West 22nd Street (212) 691-2258

The Best Cappuccino

Fauchon   1000 Madison Avenue (212) 570-2211
Mudspot   307 East 9th Street (212) 288-9074
Via Quadronno   25 East 73rd Street (212) 650-9880

The Best Restaurants in Chinatown

Big Eat   97 Bowery (212) 219-9955
Grand Sichuan   125 Canal Street (212) 625-9212
Joe's Ginger   113 Mott Street (212) 966-6613
Joe's Shanghai   (see profile)
Kam Chueh   40 Bowery (212) 791-6868
Mandarin Court   61 Mott Street (212) 608-3838

The Best Restaurants in Chinatown (continued)

New Pasteur   (see profile)
Nha Trang   87 Baxter (212) 233-5948
The Nice Restaurant   (see profile)
Sweet and Tart Café   76 Mott Street (212) 334-8088

The Best Delis

Barney Greengrass   541 Amsterdam Avenue (212) 724-4707
Ben's Best   96–40 Queens Boulevard, Rego Park, Queens
  (718) 897-1700
Carnegie Deli   854 Seventh Avenue at 54th Street (212) 757-2245
Fine and Schapiro   138 West 72nd (212) 877-2874
Katz's Deli   205 East Houston (212) 254-2246
Mr. Broadway Kosher Deli   (see profile)
Second Avenue Deli   (see profile)

The Best Romantic Dining

Box Tree Inn   250 East 49th Street (212) 758-8320
Café des Artistes   1 West 67th Street (212) 877-3500
Café Nicholson   323 East 58th Street (212) 355-6769
King's Carriage House   251 East 82nd Street (212) 734-5490
March   405 East 58th Street (212) 754-6272
One if by Land, Two if by Sea   17 Barrow Street (212) 228-0822
The Screening Room   54 Varick (212) 334-2100
The River Café   (see profile)

The Best Family Dining

Churrascaria Plataforma (see profile)
City Crab   235 Park Avenue South (212) 529-3800
Popover Café   551 Amsterdam Avenue (212) 595-8555
Virgil's   (see profile)

The Best Fireplaces

The Black Sheep   39th and Third Avenue (212) 599-3476
Christer's   145 West 55th Street (212) 974-7224
I Trulli   122 East 27th Street (212) 481-7372
La Ripaille   605 Hudson Street (212) 255-4406
Molly's   (see profile)
Vivolo   140 East 74th Street (212) 737-3533

The Best Gardens

Barbetta   321 West 46th Street (212) 246-9171
Barolo   398 West Broadway (212) 226-1102
Boathouse Café   Central Park Lake, East Park Drive at 72nd Street
(212) 517-2233
Cloisters Café   238 East 9th Street (212) 777-9128
Gascogne 158 Eighth Avenue (between 17th and 18th streets)
(212) 675-6564
La Refuge   166 East 82nd Street (212) 861-4505
Le Jardin Bistro 25 Cleveland Place (between Kenmare and Spring)
(212) 343-9599
Rita's Antiques Café   167 8th Avenue (between 18th and 19th streets)
(212) 414-5775
Sahara East   (see profile)
Verbena   54 Irving Place (212) 260-5454

The Best Night-owl Prowls

Blue Ribbon   Closes 4 a.m. (see profile)
Café Noir 32 Grand Street (212) 431-7910; closes 4 a.m.
Cafeteria 119 Seventh Avenue (212) 414-1717; 24 hours
Corner Bistro   331 West 4th Street (212) 242-9502; closes 3:30 a.m.
Florent   24 hours (see profile)
Lucky Strike   59 Grand Street (212) 941-0479; closes 3 a.m.
Odean   145 West Broadway (212) 233-0507; closes 3 a.m.
Sahara East   Closes 2 a.m. (see profile)
Veselka   144 Second Avenue (corner of 9th Street) (212) 228-9682;
24 hours
Woo Chon   24 hours (see profile)

The Best Pizza

Arturo's Pizza   106 West Houston (212) 677-3820
Grimalda's   19 Old Fulton Street, Brooklyn (718) 858-4300
John's Pizza   278 Bleecker Street (212) 243-1680
La Pizza Fresca   31 East 20th Street (212) 598-0141
Lombardi's   32 Spring Street (212) 941-7994
Patsy's Pizza   Spanish Harlem (see profile)
Sal and Carmine's Pizza   2671 Broadway (212) 663-7651
Serafina   1022 Madison at 79th (212) 734-2676
Two Boots   42 Avenue A (212) 254-1919; 74 Bleecker (212) 777-
1033; 75 Greenwich Avenue (212) 633-9096
V & T Pizza   1024 Amsterdam Avenue (212) 663-1708

The Best Raw Bars

Aquagrill   210 Spring Street (212) 274-0505
Blue Ribbon   (see profile)
Blue Water Grill   31 Union Square West (212) 675-9500
Bongo   299 10th Avenue (212) 947-3654
Docks Oyster Bar & Grill   633 Third Avenue (212) 986-8080;
   Uptown, 2427 Broadway (212) 724-5588
Oyster Bar   Grand Central Station, Lower Level
   (212) 490-6650
Redeye Grill   890 Seventh Avenue (212) 541-9000

The Best Steakhouses

Churrascaria Plataforma   (see profile)
Frank's Restaurant   85 Tenth Avenue (212) 243-1349
Palm   837 Second Avenue (212) 687-2953
Palm Too   840 Second Avenue (212) 697-5198
Pampa   768 Amsterdam Avenue, near 98th Street (212) 865-2929
Peter Luger Steakhouse   (see profile)
Sparks steakhouse   210 East 46th Street (212) 687-4855

The Best Sushi

Japonica   100 University Place (212) 243-7752
Sushi of Gari   402 East 78th Street (212) 517-5340
Tomoe Sushi   172 Thompson Street (212) 777-9346

The Best Ultracheap Restaurants (under $8)

Bao Noodles   391 Second Avenue (between 22nd and 23rd streets)
   (212) 725-7770
Excellent Dumpling House   111 Lafayette Street (212) 219-0212
Gray's Papaya   (see profile)
Perbacco   234 East 4th Street (between avenues A and B)
   (212) 253-2038
Rosario Bistro   (see profile)
Soul Fixin's   (see profile)

So You Won't Drop while You Shop

Bodum Café and Homestore   413–415 West 14th Street (near Jeffrey,
   Stella McCartney, and other hot shops) (212) 367-9125
Café S.F.A.   Sak's Fifth Avenue, 611 Fifth Avenue, 8th floor
   (212) 940-4080

So You Won't Drop While You Shop *(continued)*

Fred's at Barney's   Lower level, Madison Avenue at 61st Street
(212) 833-2200

Le Train Blue   10 East 61st Street   (212) 705-2100

The Tea Box   Takashimaya, 693 Fifth Avenue   (212) 350-0180

The Best Legends and Landmarks

Algonquin Hotel   59 West 44th Street   (212) 840-6800 (stick to the lobby bar)

Chumley's   86 Bedford Street   (212) 675-4449 (former speakeasy)

Grand Ticino   228 Thompson Street   (212) 777-5922 (*Moonstruck* set)

Oyster Bar   Grand Central Station, Lower Level   (212) 490-6650

PJ Clarke's   915 Third Avenue   (212) 759-1650

Peter Luger Steakhouse   (see profile)

Pete's Tavern   129 East 18th Street   (212) 473-7676

Rao's   455 East 114th Street   (212) 722-6709

White Horse Tavern   567 Hudson Street   (212) 243-9260

The Best Vegetarian

Angelica Kitchen   300 East 12th Street   (212) 228-2909

Candle Café   1307 Third Avenue   (212) 472-0970

Caravan of Dreams   405 East 6th Street   (212) 254-1613

Hangawi   12 East 32nd Street (between Fifth and Madison avenues)
(212) 213-0077

Restaurant Profiles

Aquavit   ★★★★½

SCANDINAVIAN | VERY EXPENSIVE | QUALITY ★★★★★ | VALUE ★★★½ | ZONE 8

13 West 54th Street; (212) 307-7311   www.aquavit.org

Customers Business, curious foodies without a budget, New York elite **Wine Selection** Very Good **Reservations** Necessary **When to Go** Anytime **Bar** Full service, many housemade aquavits **Entrée Range** Prix fixe dinner, 3-course menu, $72 per person; 7-course chef's tasting menu, $90 per person; vegetarian 7-course tasting menu, $75 per person; "Aquavit Bite" multicourse tasting menu, $115 per person; prix fixe lunch, $32–$38 (2 or 3 courses); 5-course tasting menu, $48; à la carte lunch, $22–$26. Note that upstairs café is cheaper (see below). **Dress** Dressy casual to business and elegant **Payment** All major credit cards **Service Rating** ★★★★ **Friendliness Rating** ★★★★½ **Disabled Access** No

Lunch Monday–Friday, noon–2:30 p.m.

Dinner Daily, 5:30–10:30 p.m.; chef's tasting menus served until 10 p.m.; multicourse menu served until 9:30 p.m.

Brunch Sunday, noon–2:30 p.m.

Setting & Atmosphere Aquavit is housed in a stone building that requires one to descend a few outside steps and enter into the warm café and bar level of the space. To get to the main dining room, you need to proceed to another staircase that takes you downstairs past a few tables before you enter into the impressive atrium space. Subdued lighting and wall panels offset the soaring height of the enclosed atrium, which offers a window to the sky and taller surrounding buildings as well as office windows on lower floors. The piece de resistance is the 18-foot waterfall against the wall, appearing small in comparison to the six-story height of the atrium. Acoustics are very good, even when the room is full, due to soft-paneled wall coverings. Tables are situated in the middle of the room, as well as along the wall in semiprivate booths.

House Specialties Herring plate (various herring preparations served with Carlsberg beer and aquavit); lobster roll; gravlax and tandoori smoked salmon; seafood stew.

Other Recommendations Smoked Arctic char; brioche-wrapped salmon; sautéed halibut; Kobe beef ravioli.

Summary & Comments Swedish chef Marcus Samuelsson, who won the James Beard Foundation accolade of "Best Chef in New York City for 2003", has taken Aquavit to new levels of culinary prowess. If it weren't for the prices, we'd recommend a few return visits to try the tasting menu as well as some of the selections from the prix fixe. Housemade aquavits can accompany the fish appetizers perfectly; selections include pear, vanilla and black peppercorn, cloudberry, and citrus flavors. Presentation of all dishes is creative. The upstairs café is cheaper and worth a try. Keep in mind, though, that the café kitchen is separate from that of the main dining room; it is supervised by the executive chef and a little bit of overlap can be found. If you want Swedish meatballs, you can only get them in the café.

Artisanal ★★★½

BISTRO/FROMAGERIE | MOD/EXP | QUALITY ★★★★ | VALUE ★★★ | ZONE 7

2 Park Avenue (entrance on 32nd Street); (212) 725-8585

Customers Regulars, couples, professionals **Wine selection** Extensive **Reservations** recommended, but first come, first served at few tables by bar **When to Go** anytime **Bar** Full service **Entrée Range** $16–$27 Prix fixe lunch and dinners available **Dress** Business casual **Payment** All major credit cards **Service rating** ★★★ **Friendliness rating** ★★★ **Disabled Access** Yes

Brunch Saturday and Sunday, 11 a.m.–3 p.m.

Lunch Monday–Friday, noon–3 p.m.

Dinner Monday–Thursday, 5–11 p.m.; Friday and Saturday, 5 p.m.–midnight; Sunday, 5–10 p.m.

Setting & Atmosphere A large, bustling dining room with high ceilings, large windows, and happy diners. There's an upscale bistro/brasserie ambience and a buzz in the air, which can often be almost too loud. If you're looking for intimacy, go somewhere else. That said, there's something quite romantic about sharing fondue for an entrée and dessert . . .

House Specialties Cheese, fondue, and wine.

Other Recommendations Chocolate fondue; cassoulet; side of creamed spinach with parmesan; three-cheese onion soup; "chicken under brick"; tarte tatin.

Summary & Comments The great thing about Artisanal is that you don't need to have a full meal to enjoy and sample some of their specialties. Apart from lunch, dinner, brunch, and a late-night menu on offer after 9:30 p.m., you can come in and have a cheese and wine flight combination that offers three wines paired with three specific cheeses. Some of these preselected flight combinations include three choices from categories like International, Champagne, Italian, Alsatian, and Spanish; prices range from $29–$32. If you decide on the full meal option, go crazy with cheese, but make sure you have time for a walk afterwards. Fried fish and chips at $17.50 is hardly worth it, so opt for other dishes. Even if you are already cheese savvy, take advantage of the fromager to ask him/her questions about their selection of over 200 cheeses. A cheese plate takes on new meaning after you discuss your options and realize that a good way to go about selecting a five-cheese platter is to include "a goat, a cow, a sheep, a blue, and a cheddar." Fondue can be ordered in two sizes and a choice of varying cheese/herb/oil infusion combinations. There's always a fondue of the day. If you need something sweet besides a cheese plate, try the chocolate fondue or the tarte tatin with the cheddar cheese crust.

Babbo   ★★★½

ITALIAN | EXP | QUALITY ★★★★ | VALUE ★★★★ | ZONE 4

110 Waverly Place (between MacDougal and Sixth Avenue); (212) 777-0303
www.babbony.com

Customers Locals, professionals, celebrities **Reservations** A must **When to Go** Anytime you can get a reservation **Entrée Range** $15–$29; 7-course pasta tasting menu, $59; 7-course traditional tasting menu, $65 **Payment** All major credit cards **Service rating** ★★½ **Friendliness rating** ★★★ **Bar** Full service **Wine selection** Lots of Italian; ask for recommendations; fairly priced **Dress** Casual to dressy **Disabled Access** Main dining room and rest rooms

Dinner Sunday, 5–10:45 p.m.; Monday–Saturday, 5:30–11:15 p.m.

Setting & atmosphere Formerly home to James Beard's classic Coach House, this Greenwich Village bilevel space has been thoroughly updated to house Mario Batali's innovative Italian cooking. The main room is dressed comfortably in soft yellow, with banquettes running along the walls and a center table proudly displaying a beautiful bouquet of flowers. A majestic staircase splits the back of the room and leads up to a more serene second floor with white walls and a grand skylight. The main room brims with energy and resultant noise, and upstairs tends to be more relaxed and civilized.

House Specialties Marinated fresh anchovies; warm tripe parmigiana; mint love letters; pappardelle Bolognese; grilled lamb chops with broccoli rabe and shiitake mushrooms; saffron panna cotta with poached peaches.

Other Recommendations Mackerel tartare; beef-cheek ravioli with crushed squab livers; two-minute calamari, Sicilian lifeguard style; whole roasted fish with lemon-oregano jam; assortment of gelati and sorbetti; crespetta with blueberries and figs.

Summary & Comments Power team Molto Mario Batali (Po) and Joseph Bastianich (Felidia, Becco, Frico) have opened one of New York's most ambitious and most successful Italian restaurants. The room is raucous, and an open table comes up about as often as Halley's Comet, but it's worth the wait for Batali's fearless food. Batali pushes the limits of traditional Italian cooking, using ingredients most diners shun, like anchovies, calf's brains, and beef cheeks. More of it works than doesn't, but figuring it out is all the fun. For starters, Batali smartly tempers fresh silvery anchovies with dusky summer beans, softening the fish's sharper edges, and normally bland tripe gets a healthy dose of character from a spicy, hot tomato sauce. The surprisingly tender bites please almost instantly, and it's almost enough to make you a lifelong fan of this unusual delicacy. But certain pastas can be disappointing. Avoid overly rich preparations like duck liver ravioli, buried in an overly sweet, overbearing hoisin-like sauce, and beef-cheek ravioli, which may be too much for some. As for entrées, two-minute calamari is very good, but would work better as an appetizer. Stick with fish or the grilled lamb chops.

Balthazar ★★★½

FRENCH | MODERATELY EXPENSIVE | QUALITY ★★★★ | VALUE ★★★★ | ZONE 2

80 Spring Street; (212) 965-1785   www.balthazarny.com

Customers The "trendetti," celebrities, locals **Reservations** Recommended **When to Go** Anytime **Entrée Range** $16–$32 **Payment** All major credit cards **Service rating** ★★★ **Friendliness rating** ★★★ **Bar** Full service and usually full **Wine selection** Good and not overpriced; heavy on French options; house wine by the carafe is drinkable and inexpensive **Dress** Chic—upscale or down **Disabled Access** Yes

Breakfast Daily (continental), 7:30–11:30 a.m.

Brunch Saturday and Sunday, 11:30 a.m.–3:45 p.m.

Lunch Monday–Friday, noon–5 p.m.

Dinner Monday–Saturday, 5:45 p.m.–midnight; Sunday, 5:30–10:45 p.m.

Setting & Atmosphere Keith McNally, his advisors, and a fortune in francs (or dollars) turned what had been a leather store into a fabulous facsimile of a timeworn Paris brasserie that looks as though it has nestled on this East Soho street for years. Outside, red awnings mark the spot; inside, uneven old-gold-ocher walls, slightly scuffed and stained, peeling mirrors, a tiled floor, an old bar with a pewter top, and paper-covered wooden bistro tables set the trendy stage.

House Specialties Balthazar salad; steak au poivre; steak frites; beef short ribs; brandade de morue (puréed salt cod); warm goat cheese and caramelized onion tart; whole roast chicken.

Other Recommendations Duck and pistachio terrine; roasted halibut with crushed potatoes and warm tomato-almond vinaigrette; duck shepherd's pie; caramelized banana tart.

Summary & Comments Though not quite the place to see and be seen as when it first opened, Balthazar has more than held its own as a New York hot spot thanks to its laid-back, lively atmosphere and solid bistro fare. Bistro classics like steak frites and steak au poivre remain stellar, and garlicky brandade will have you coming back for more. Prices are surprisingly reasonable, but reservations are still hard to come by, so try to go for an upbeat and satisfying late lunch. If you can stand the wait, go for a super brunch. If you're on the go, the adjacent Balthazar Bakery offers an excellent selection of tasty breads, pastries, and sandwiches.

Becco ★★½

ITALIAN | MODERATE | QUALITY ★★★½ | VALUE ★★★★★ | ZONE 8

355 West 46th Street (between Eighth and Ninth Avenues); (212) 397-7597
www.becconyc.com

Customers Pre- and post-theater, tourists, locals **Reservations** Recommended; a must before theater **When to Go** Anytime **Entrée Range** $17.27–$29.95; prix fixe lunch, $16.95; prix fixe dinner, $21.95 **Payment** All major credit cards **Service rating** ★★★ **Friendliness rating** ★★★ **Bar** Full service **Wine selection** Good; there's a sizable list for only $18 **Dress** Casual, theater **Disabled Access** No

Lunch Daily, noon–3 p.m.

Dinner Monday–Saturday, 5 p.m.–midnight; Sunday, 5–10 p.m.

Setting & Atmosphere This thriving Restaurant Row-er is thronged with theater-goers. The narrow dining area in the front, with its beamed ceilings, has a few touches that suggest a country inn, but tables are so close together that the happy din can become daunting. The upstairs dining room, away from the noise and constant bustle, is a much better bet for a civilized dining experience, and the cute but smaller back room can be a pleasant diversion as well.

House Specialties Sinfonia di pasta, unlimited servings of three pastas that change daily; antipasto of grilled, marinated veggies and fish; homemade fruit sorbets; ricotta tart with orange caramel sauce.

Other Recommendations Osso buco with barley risotto; grilled swordfish with balsamic sauce; Italian stuffed peppers; rack of lamb.

Summary & Comments You get a lot for your lire at this popular Theater District trattoria run by the Bastianich family, who also run the famed **Felidia** (243 East 58th; 758-1479). For a mere $21.95, you get a choice of Caesar salad or assorted antipasto (go with the antipasti) and unlimited servings of three pastas of the day. Although you don't have a choice of what three pastas you get, there's usually a good assortment (including gnocchi and risotto on occasion), and the pastas are almost always home-made and usually surprisingly good; you'd be hard-pressed to find a better deal in the city. Entrées are good but for the most part unspectacular. Stick with the all-you-can-eat pastas and use the money you save on entrées to order a couple of extra bottles from their $18 wine list. This way you're guaranteed to leave both happy and satisfied.

Blue Ribbon ★★★

ECLECTIC AMERICAN | MODERATE | QUALITY ★★★½ | VALUE ★★★★ | ZONES 2, 16

97 Sullivan Street (near Spring Street); (212) 274-0404
280 Fifth Avenue (between 1st Street and Garfield Place); (718) 840-0404

Customers Local, trendies, night owls **Reservations** Only for parties of 5–8 **When to Go** Dinner only **Entrée Range** $9.50–$27 **Payment** All major credit cards **Service rating** ★★★ **Friendliness rating** ★★★ **Bar** Full service **Wine Selection** Interesting **Dress** Anything goes **Disabled Access** Yes, but very crowded

Dinner Tuesday–Sunday, 4 p.m.–4 a.m.; closed Monday

Setting & Atmosphere A smallish, square, very dark room that seems to be a magnet for young and not-so-young trendies. It's not the décor that does it. If you can see through the throng at the bar, you'll find a wall of painted dark red brick, dark red plush banquettes, and one large semicircular enclosure seating five or more, with a few interestingly odd paintings above and closely spaced tables. It's noisy.

House Specialties Fried chicken with collard greens and mashed potatoes; beef marrow with oxtail marmalade; anything from the raw bar; chocolate Bruno; banana split.

Other Recommendations Terrine of foie gras; sweet and spicy catfish; hanger steak with wild mushrooms and onion rings; french fries; crème brûlée. Skip "favorites" like the pu-pu platter and paella.

Summary & Comments This is the happening place in the happening Soho scene. Open until 4 a.m., it attracts a late-night crowd, local chefs included, but it's jammed from 8 p.m. on. Expect to wait at least one hour, and very possibly more, to sample chef Eric Bromberg's eclectic menu. Hanging out here is fun; the crowd is anything but dowdy. But if the waiting game is not for you, go north up Sullivan Street and see if you can get into **Blue Ribbon Sushi** (119 Sullivan Street; (212) 343-0404), Blue Ribbon's hip Japanese sibling restaurant. Or keep on going to **Jean Claude** (137 Sullivan Street; (212) 475-9232), another perfect Parisian transplant from St. Germain or Montparnasse—noisy, smoky, good bistro food, and not too expensive (cash only).

Blue Water Grill ★★★

AMERICAN/SEAFOOD | MODERATE | QUALITY ★★★★ | VALUE ★★★★ | ZONE 7

31 Union Square West (at 16th Street); (212) 675-9500
www.brguestrestaurants.com

Customers Professionals, locals, celebs, tourists **Reservations** Recommended **When to Go** Anytime **Entrée Range** $13.50–$21.95 **Payment** All major credit cards **Service rating** ★★★ **Friendliness rating** ★★★ **Bar** Full service **Wine Selection** Not particularly exciting, but not bad either **Dress** Casual **Disabled Access** In main dining room

Lunch Daily, 11 a.m.–4:30 p.m.

Dinner Monday–Thursday, 5:30 p.m.–12:30 a.m.; Friday and Saturday, 5:30 p.m.–1 a.m.; Sunday, 5:30 p.m.–midnight

Setting & Atmosphere Big, breezy, and beautiful, this converted bank built in 1904 features vaulted marble ceilings and marble walls, high columns and old-fashioned architectural details. Perfect-for-warm-weather seating is available outside just above street level, and during dinner you can listen to jazz while you eat downstairs. But the best seats in the house are the banquettes in the balcony of the main dining room. The epitome of laid-back and casual, the atmosphere at Blue Water Grill cannot be described as anything other than pleasant.

House Specialties Oysters on the half shell; Maryland crab cakes, roasted corn salsa, and classic tartar sauce; seared yellowfin tuna with artichokes and lemon pearl couscous; grilled fish from the wood-burning grill; brownie ice cream sundae.

Other Recommendations Chilled jumbo shrimp cocktail with three sauces; crispy skin salmon, wild mushroom risotto, and roasted garlic broth; blackened swordfish with sweet potato–crabmeat hash; blueberry and pineapple upside-down cake.

Summary & Comments People love Blue Water Grill. Whenever out-of-towners visit, New Yorkers invariably take them here. Not surprisingly, talk to anyone outside New York and they've all been here. And for one simple reason: Blue Water Grill knows how to make people happy. With its cool setting, casual atmosphere, friendly service, and something-for-everyone menu at prices that won't empty your wallet, Blue Water executes the game plan for success to perfection. And the food, although never great, is always good enough to ensure return trips. At the fresh raw bar, choose from the extensive and user-friendly list of oysters, each with a quick description and those for beginners marked conveniently with asterisks. Owner Steve Hanson has repeated his formula for success at uptown sibling **Ocean Grill** on the Upper West Side (384 Columbus Avenue; (212) 579-2300), and **Atlantic Grill** on the Upper East (1341 Third Avenue; (212) 988-9200) deserves an honorable mention for its fish and seafood menu.

Bo ★★★★

KOREAN | INEXPENSIVE | QUALITY ★★★★½ | VALUE ★★★★★ | ZONE 17

59-16 Kissena Boulevard (just north of Long Island Expressway); (718) 661-3775

Customers Queens College during day, local regulars at night **Reservations** Accepted **When to Go** Anytime **Entrée Range** $7.95–$16.95 **Payment** Cash only **Service Rating** ★★★★ **Friendliness Rating** ★★★★★ **Bar** None **Wine Selection** None **Dress** Casual **Disabled Access** Good; rest rooms not accessible

Lunch Monday–Saturday, 11:30 a.m.–3 p.m.

Dinner Monday–Saturday, 3–9 p.m.

Setting & Atmosphere Chef/owner Maria Cho has made the most of her small space; it's chic and sedate, and well-spaced tables lend a feeling of roominess. The elegantly minimalist décor is sleek in shades of white and beige. Exquisite Korean wall hangings are an impressive touch.

House Specialties Beef ribs, slow-potted for an eternity until meat is meltingly tender and the sauce richly concentrated; delicate potato or mung bean pancakes. Ginseng chicken (baby chicken, really, in a pot with sticky rice) is amazing. Specials are also good, as are the panchan (appetizer plates of pickles, vegetables, and such). It's hard to recommend when everything is so very delicious and cooked with such great feeling.

Summary & Comments Ms. Cho was once the pastry chef at splashy (now-defunct) Sign of the Dove, but returned to her Korean roots with this small, magical restaurant in a most unlikely neighborhood. This is one of the few places in New York for true Korean comfort food, the kind of home cooking otherwise unavailable in restaurants. It's a well-schooled hominess, however; everything is cooked with delicacy, subtlety, and great care. The kitchen is so honest, so genuine and loving, that homesick Koreans journey from far and wide to eat here . . . and equal numbers of occidentals (many from nearby Queens College) are also fiercely loyal.

Borobudur CafÉ ★★

INDONESIAN | INEXPENSIVE | QUALITY ★★½ | VALUE ★★★ | ZONE 5

128 East 4th Street (between 1st and 2nd Avenue); (212) 614-9079

Customers Ethnic, locals, regulars **Wine Selection** None–beer available **Reservations** Not necessary **When to Go** Anytime **Bar** None **Entrée Range** $6–$15 **Dress** Casual **Payment** V, MC **Service Rating** ★★★ **Friendliness Rating** ★★★ **Disabled Access** Yes

Open Daily, Sunday–Thursday, noon–10:30 p.m.; Friday and Saturday, noon–midnight

Setting & Atmosphere Small, simply designed, no-frills décor. Single-bulb lighting is softened with candlelight on each table in the evening. The exposed brick wall provides a sense of warmth.

House Specialties Special rice dinner for $30 per person, offering a selection of Indonesian specialties; gulai kambing (lamb cooked with curry, vegetables, and onions); martabak borobudur (fried fillo dough with ground beef, onion, and eggs with curry).

Other Recommendations Pempek (fried fish cake); balacan chilli sauce, sayur lodeh (a soup with vegetables in coconut milk); spiced iced tea with cinnamon and cloves. The gado-gado (light salad with peanut sauce) isn't what it could be.

Summary & Comments Apparently known in certain Indonesian circles, this unassuming restaurant serves consistently tasty Indonesian fare. The low prices may account for why the food lacks in presentation, but this has no effect on taste. The service is friendly, and they are eager to please and explain anything on the menu that may appear puzzling. If you're feeling adventurous, ask if they have any dorian (spiky fruit with sweet pulp inside that causes people to either writhe with pleasure or retch with disgust). If they have it and you want it, get a dorian milkshake.

Cabana Carioca ★★½

BRAZILIAN/PORTUGUESE | INEXP | QUALITY ★★★★ | VALUE ★★★★★ | ZONE 8

123 West 45th Street; (212) 581-8088

Customers Professionals at lunch; tourists, theater workers, ethnic at dinner **Reservations** None accepted for lunch; dinner only for 4 or more **When to Go** Lunch for buffet, dinner for bar specials **Entrée Range** $12.95–$19.95 **Payment** All major credit cards; cash only at the bar **Service Rating** ★★★ **Friendliness Rating** ★★★ **Bar** Full service **Wine Selection** Small **Dress** Casual **Disabled Access** Fair

Open Monday–Thursday, 11:30 a.m.–11 p.m.; Friday and Saturday, 11:30 a.m.–midnight; Sunday, 11:30 a.m.–10 p.m.

Setting & Atmosphere Service is offered on three levels, connected by steep steps (painted in garish Happy Colors). With tables close together and sound levels high, this is not the place for lingering or romance. Management tries for a fun, colorful, tropical look, but it's been a while since the last makeover, and things are starting to get just a tad seedy at the edges. Don't look too closely; just enjoy.

House Specialties These change daily. Examples include roast chicken, shrimp gumbo, pot roast, shell steak, caipirinhas.

Other Recommendations Caldo verdhe (potato soup with kale and chorizo sausage) is satisfying, almost a meal in itself for $1.90. Ask for some homemade hot sauce—vinegary and terrific (shake the bottle!)—and don't forget to spoon farofa (toasted yucca flour) over the beans.

Summary & Comments The buffet lunch is an astounding bargain: $9.95 ($6.45 on the third floor) buys you unlimited access to a large array of meat, salad, and vegetable dishes, as well as desserts (come early; the steam tables are less frequently replenished later on). But there's an even better deal: dinner specials, available only at the bars—and the tables near them—on all three levels, such as a crunchy, garlicky half roast chicken; homey pot roast; a huge mound of garlicky/spicy baby shrimp gumbo (not really gumbo, but tasty); or a pretty serviceable garlic-marinated steak. Each includes a heap of rice, excellent black beans, and lots of homemade thick-cut potato chips, plus unlimited access to the salad bar, all for well under $10. Amazing. But if you're here for a bargain, be wary of drinks; ordering beer or cocktails will almost double your tab (but they make good caipirinhas—Brazilian cocktails of distilled sugar cane and tons of limes). The spotty regular menu is not particularly recommended, nor is the feijoada (Brazilian black bean stew); stick with the bar and the buffet.

Numerological oddity: An address you'll never forget: 1-2-3 West 4-5 Street between 6th and 7th avenues.

Café Boulud ★★★½

FRENCH | EXPENSIVE | QUALITY ★★★★½ | VALUE ★★★½ | ZONE 13

20 East 76th Street; (212) 772-2600   www.danielnyc.com

Customers Business, locals **Reservations** Required **When to Go** Anytime **Entrée Range** $15–$39 **Payment** All major credit cards **Service Rating** ★★★★½ **Friendliness Rating** ★★★★ **Bar** Full service **Wine Selection** Extensive and reasonably priced **Dress** Nice casual–dressy **Disabled Access** Yes

Lunch   Tuesday–Saturday, noon–2:30 p.m.

Dinner   Every night, 5:45–11 p.m.

Setting & Atmosphere   On entering the restaurant you are met by a small sea of white linen–dressed tables, elegant ochre walls with muted pastel-toned oil paintings, and a few large mirrors. Black-and-white photographs line part of a wall leading to the well-appointed yet not over-the-top bathrooms. The atmosphere is more at ease than you might expect from such an Upper East Side establishment. There's an almost hushed sanctity within the restaurant which allows diners to talk in low to normal decibels and yet not be heard at the next table. It's possible to eat outside during warm weather.

House Specialties   The menu is divided into four sections: La Tradition, La Saison, Le Potager, and Le Voyage. La Tradition focuses on classic French dishes, La Saison concentrates on what's fresh in the market, Le Potager celebrates the vegetable (good choices for vegetarians), and Le Voyage highlights a chosen world cuisine and creates dishes within the genre. Le Voyage selections change monthly, and the others alter depending on the market and the chef. Some specialties have included lobster and seafood bisque; Peeky Toe crab salad; roasted beet and pear salad; roasted chicken with potatoes and bacon; and steamed wild striped bass.

Other Recommendations   Poached pear; warmed madeleines; raw and cooked tuna with beans, potatoes and quail egg; roasted monkfish.

Summary & Comments   Formerly housing Daniel Boulud's restaurant Daniel, Café Boulud took over when Boulud moved to a larger space and he decided to open another project. Café Boulud is designed to be more casual than its predecessor, yet created with the intent to maintain high-quality offerings. The food is clearly fresh and undoubtedly delicious, but not superb. The chefs seem to excel when working with fish, seafood, or vegetables. Meat dishes are a little disappointing. However, with each month bringing a new variation on a dish or a different flavor inspired by a new destination, the meat or chicken could be transformed into something very special. The choice of breads—such as sourdough, pumpkin seed, and olive— also varies depending on the chef's whim and the availability of ingredients. Service is well-paced and professional. Desserts are a little overly sweet except for the poached pear in wine sauce. The fresh, hot madeleines served at the table in a linen funnel at the end of the meal are a lovely treat. Take advantage of the prix fixe lunch menu before you commit to a hefty bill at dinner. If the season is right, though, you might find that dinner will be well worth the cost.

Café con Leche ★★½

DOMINICAN | INEXPENSIVE | QUALITY ★★★★ | VALUE ★★★★★ | ZONE 12

424 Amsterdam Avenue (between 80th and 81st streets); (212) 595-7000

Customers Locals **Reservations** Accepted Monday–Wednesday only **When to Go** Anytime; especially bargain weekday lunch specials **Entrée Range** $12.95–$25.95 **Payment** All major credit cards **Service Rating** ★★½ **Friendliness Rating** ★★★ **Bar** Full service **Wine Selection** Limited **Dress** Casual **Disabled Access** Small step up; rest rooms not accessible

Breakfast Daily, 8–11 a.m.

Lunch Daily, 11 a.m.–4 p.m.

Dinner Monday–Thursday, 4–11 p.m.; Friday–Sunday, 4 p.m.–midnight

Setting & Atmosphere This sunny café looks like any old joint from outside, but the interior is a pleasant surprise: a pizazzy, updated coffee shop with a colorful, tropical (carnival masks, silver trim on bright yellow walls) look.

House Specialties The pernil asado (roast pork) is intense, amazingly rich stuff; delicious, revisionist chicharrones de pollo (chunks of on-bone chicken) are herbacious and expertly deep fried with a batter that's more St. Louis than San Juan. Black bean soup is awesome, with good, crunchy onions, and sancocho (an ubiquitous, thick Dominican soup), often a special, is even better—an intense golden brown broth, clearly the product of long, careful cooking, with lovingly cooked root vegetables and a few chunks of pork. Beans and rice, served in appealing decorative bowls, are quite good (the rice is never dry here), and both tostones (starchy green plantains) and maduros (sweet ripe plantains) are skillfully fried.

Other Recommendations The condiments almost steal the show; there's a sensational hot sauce with incendiary flecks of black, green, and red and an innocent-looking thick white dressing that looks like sour cream but is actually potent garlic sauce . . . great on bread toasts. Not all the clever touches work: surprisingly light and greaseless mofungo (fried mash of plantains, pork, and garlic) comes with a fatally overwrought gravy, and the Cuban sandwiches taste too cleaned-up—not compressed, greasy, or garlicky enough for the flavors to come together.

Summary & Comments Café con Leche is the diametrical opposite of those trendy, pan-Latino fusion places. The latter tend to start with $4 million and a publicist and try to graft Latino flavors onto the kitchen's carefully designed Product. Café con Leche has solid Dominican coffeeshop credentials: the salsa recordings are what the staff wants to hear, not "Latin atmosphere"; the roast pork is rich and garlicky; and they shmoosh the bread slices when they toast them. Their innovative touches—e.g., that frothy purée of a garlic sauce replacing the standard emulsion of garlic chunks and oil—have grown organically from serious tradition. There's a second Café con Leche farther up Amsterdam Avenue (at #726), but it's nowhere near as good.

Café Mogador ★★½

MOROCCAN | MODERATE | QUALITY ★★★★ | VALUE ★★★★★ | ZONE 5

101 St. Marks Place; (212) 677-2226

Customers Local **Reservations** Accepted (necessary Wednesdays) **When to Go** Anytime (arrive by 8 p.m. for the Wednesday night belly dancing) **Entrée Range** $10–$14 **Payment** All major credit cards **Service Rating** ★★★ **Friendliness Rating** ★★ **Bar** Beer and wine only **Wine Selection** House **Dress** Casual **Disabled Access** Very poor

Brunch Saturday and Sunday, 11 a.m.–4 p.m.

Lunch & Dinner Daily, 9 a.m.–11:30 p.m.

Setting & Atmosphere Mogador looks less Moroccan than a standard-issue East Village bohemian café. It's a casual space below street level with tiny tables, faux oil lamps, and ceiling fans.

House Specialties Several flavors of tagine (a thick, complex stew made with chicken or lamb, served over rice or couscous), bastilla (an exotic dish of sweet and savory chopped chicken in flaky pastry) containing real saffron, homemade baklava (very sweet and cinnamony), and great fresh-squeezed pulpy lemonade, served with a mint leaf.

Entertainment & Amenities Wednesdays only: good live Arabic music at 8 p.m., belly dancing at 9 p.m. It's not just tourist shlock; the dancer's very good, and the musicians are some of the best in town. $3 music charge, $15 minimum meal; arrive by 8 p.m. for best seating.

Summary & Comments If you're a fan of Moroccan cooking—or are looking for an authentic experience—stay away. This leisurely East Village café doesn't purport to serve the Real Deal. But it's not fake tourist fodder, either—they do honest Moroccan American food, as if made from hand-me-down recipes from someone's great-grandmother. The little appetizer plates (you'll be shown a trayful of selections) are tempting simple things like spicy sliced carrots, peppery garlic potatoes, and long-stewed chicken livers. As with the rest of the menu, all are pleasing but none attention-grabbing; this is more everyday food than a special occasion eat. The café's relaxing (the busboys are too relaxed; you must beg and whimper for water), a rare Manhattan place where you can eat an exotic (but not too exotic) bite, look out the window, sigh, and daydream.

Calle Ocho ★★★

NUEVO LATINO | MODERATE | QUALITY ★★★★ | VALUE ★★★½ | ZONE 12

446 Columbus Avenue (between 81st and 82nd streets); (212) 873-5025

Customers Locals, trendies **Reservations** Recommended **When to Go** Anytime **Entrée Range** $16–$22 **Payment** All major credit cards **Service Rating** ★★★ **Friendliness Rating** ★★★ **Bar** Full service **Wine Selection** Heavy on Spanish, Argentinean, and Chilean **Dress** Casual, hip **Disabled Access** Dining room, yes; rest rooms, no

Brunch Sunday, 11 a.m.–3 p.m.

Dinner Monday–Thursday, 6–11 p.m.; Friday, 6 p.m.–midnight; Saturday, 5 p.m.–midnight; Sunday, 5–10 p.m.

Setting & Atmosphere Formerly home to Main Street, the front area has been transformed into a colorful bar/lounge, complete with its own singles scene and highlighted by a technicolor wall of brightly lit circles. The cavernous main dining room has the look and feel of a fancy airplane hangar, and may be just as loud. Bottom line: Downtown is uptown at this happening spot. Cool and fun are the operative words.

House Specialties Puerto Rican rum-glazed jumbo shrimp with crispy onions and avocado salsa; Caribbean lobster ceviche in a passion fruit mojo; Argentine hanger steak; coconut ice cream in a chocolate shell.

Other Recommendations Arepa with bacalao and vine-ripened tomatoes; shredded beef empanada; adobo-rubbed pork loin; crisp chicken cooked in lime; tobacco onion rings and yucca fries; banana fritters.

Summary & Comments Brought to you by the owners of Union Pacific and Rain, Calle Ocho brings sass and style to the Upper West Side restaurant scene. Chef Alex Garcia comes from Patria, and the pedigree shows in the lively presentation and brash blending of flavors. Appetizers are clearly the highlight here. Lobster ceviche comes heaped on top of fresh mangoes with passion fruit and a splash of hot sauce. Puerto Rican rum–glazed shrimp, the best of the lot, are big, bold, and fantastic. And fragrant arepa warms the soul with its deep, smoky bacalao. You may find yourself chewing longer than you normally would, as each sultry bite reveals a new layer of flavor. Entrées lack the same impact, though spicy adobo-rubbed pork loin is more than respectable, and carnivores will savor the Argentine hanger steak. Salt lovers will appreciate the chef's heavy-handedness. Fish entrées like the red snapper try too hard and come up short. The churros (elongated donut-type desserts) are made to order, making them a prime dessert choice. This is a super place for a date.

Candle Café ★★★½

VEGETARIAN/VEGAN | INEXP/MOD | QUALITY ★★★★ | VALUE ★★★½ | ZONE 13

*1307 Third Avenue (between 74th and 75th streets); (212) 472-0970
www.candlecafe.com*

Customers Regulars, locals, vegans, herbivores and even closeted carnivores **Wine Selection** A few choices of organic reds and whites **Reservations** Not necessary **When to Go** Anytime **Bar** Only juice bar **Entrée Range** $9–$16 **Dress** Casual and/or funky **Payment** All major credit cards **Service Rating** ★★★½ **Friendliness Rating** ★★★★ **Disabled Access** Yes

Open Monday–Saturday, 11:30 a.m.–10:30 p.m.; Sunday, 11:30 a.m.–9:30 p.m.

Setting & Atmosphere Except for off-peak times, Candle Café is often full of people and good vibes. The juice bar, with a good view of the vast selection of ripe fruits and veggies on offer and a bright chalkboard listing the drinks, dominates the entrance. Wooden tables line the walls along a medium-sized, rectangular space. Pro-veggie reading material is available at the bar.

House Specialties Anything from the juice bar; Aztec salad (barbequed seitan, pumpkin seeds, mixed greens, quinoa, black beans, corn and red onions); soba noodle salad; ginger-miso stir-fry; macrobiotic life platter.

Other Recommendations Carrot-ginger dressing; cornbread; chocolate cake; daily wraps; many of their daily specials; tofu club.

Summary & Comments Don't let the vegetarian label scare you away. The food here is well prepared and often so well executed that you might not even miss the taste of meat. Daily specials include combinations such as lemon parsley ravioli with artichoke filling served with spinach in a roasted tomato truffle sauce; and cumin seed–crusted tofu with eggplant and chickpea masala, coconut brown basmati rice, and lemondate chutney. Call beforehand or check the web for their daily specials. You can also stop here for a quick smoothie or fresh fruit or vegetable juice. Staff are knowledgeable and not militant about their food predilections, which makes for a calm dining experience, even when the place is packed. Candle Café has been so successful that they opened another, slightly more formal space, **Candle 79,** not far away at 154 East 79th Street (corner of Lexington Avenue).

Cendrillon ★★★

FILIPINO/ASIAN | MODERATE | QUALITY ★★★★ | VALUE ★★★★ | ZONE 2

45 Mercer Street (between Broome and Grand Streets); (212) 343-9012
www.cendrillon.com

Customers Ethnic, local **Reservations** Recommended **When to Go** Anytime **Entrée Range** $11.50–$23; appetizers $5.50–$11 **Payment** AMEX, MC, VISA **Service Rating** ★★★ **Friendliness Rating** ★★★ **Wine Selection** Good, and good range of prices **Dress** Casual **Disabled Access** Yes

Brunch Saturday and Sunday, 11:30 a.m.–4:30 p.m.

Lunch & Dinner Tuesday–Sunday, 11 a.m.–11 p.m.

Setting & Atmosphere A few twinkling lights on a relatively quiet street mark the entry to this unusually shaped but inviting Soho establishment. Comfortable booths with carved wooden tables front the open kitchen and lead to an airy, high-ceilinged back dining room. Exposed brick walls throughout, accented with touches of carved wood, hold changing exhibits of contemporary paintings.

House Specialties Amy's spring roll; grilled octopus salad with eggplant fritter; chicken adobo; Romy's spareribs; black rice paella with crab, shrimp, and Manila clams; banana crêpe with banana, rum, and cashew ice cream; blueberry and purple yam tart with young coconut sorbet.

Other Recommendations Grilled oxtail kare-kare; Balinese lamb shank with tomatillo and mango chutney; salt-roasted duck with cellophane noodles; warm chocolate cake with passion fruit sorbet.

Summary & Comments Chef/owner Romy Doroton offers fine Filipino fare and enhances his menu with a few "fusion" features that showcase his flare with Asian ingredients. Doroton and his staff are wonderfully helpful and friendly and make this an excellent place to try a new cuisine—still of the Asian persuasion, but different enough to make it fun and intriguing. Remember to leave room for one of the fine desserts and cleanse your palate with one of Cendrillon's rare exotic teas, brought directly from China. You can also buy Southeast Asian products and gifts.

Chanterelle ★★★★

FRENCH | VERY EXPENSIVE | QUALITY ★★★★½ | VALUE ★★★★ | ZONE 2

2 Harrison Street (at Hudson Street); (212) 966-6960 www.chanterellenyc.com

Customers Local **Reservations** A must **When to Go** Anytime **Entrée Range** Lunch, $38; prix fixe dinner, $84 and $95 **Payment** All major credit cards **Service Rating** ★★★★ **Friendliness Rating** ★★★ **Bar** Full service **Wine Selection** Excellent **Dress** Dressy **Disabled Access** Yes

Lunch Tuesday–Saturday, noon–2:30 p.m.

Dinner Monday–Saturday, 5:30–11 p.m.

Setting & Atmosphere Elegance prevails; peachy, sort of chanterelle-colored walls are punctuated with dark, carved wood panels. Polished brass chandeliers light the room warmly, and well-spaced tables make intimate dining more than a possibility.

House Specialties Grilled seafood sausage; lasagne of Louisiana crayfish; terrine of duck foie gras; softshell crabs with capers and cream; sautéed red snapper on a ragoût of vegetable and pig's feet; cheese cart.

Other Recommendations Steamed zucchini blossom with chicken and truffles; assortment of raw fish, Japanese style; roast beef fillet with honey and tomato; cod with Vidalia onion coulis; millefeuille of pineapple and kalamansi.

Summary & Comments Chanterelle is one of only a handful of restaurants to garner four stars from the *New York Times*, yet it isn't content to simply rest on its laurels. Chef David Waltuck changes the menu every six weeks, and every six weeks patrons will find creative, daring, and delicious food. One constant is the seafood sausage, always grilled to perfection and intensely satisfying. Though Chanterelle is well worth every penny and is a grand place to celebrate a special occasion, you might try it for lunch ($38 prix fixe) if your pennies are otherwise allocated.

Churrascaria Plataforma ★★★

BRAZILIAN | MODERATE | QUALITY ★★★★ | VALUE ★★★★ | ZONE 8

316 West 49th Street; (212) 245-0505   www.churrascariaplataforma.com

Customers Tourists, professionals (at lunch), pretheater **Reservations** Recommended **When to Go** Avoid weekend dinner crush; probably too heavy for lunch **Entrée Range** Prix fixe $38.95 ($27.95 for lunch); children under 5 years, free; ages 5–10 years, half-price **Payment** All major credit cards **Service Rating** ★ **Friendliness Rating** ★★★ **Bar** Full **Wine Selection** Decent selection **Dress** Casual **Disabled Access** Rest rooms not accessible

Lunch Daily, noon–4 p.m.

Dinner Daily, 4 p.m.–midnight

Setting & Atmosphere Enormous space, dominated by a monster salad bar at center. Desserts and cocktails are dispensed by beautiful young waitresses wheeling carts. The place is brightly lit, with refined, understated décor, but amid all the swirling meat and trips to the salad bar, who's paying attention? Sound level is high at peak times.

House Specialties All-you-can-eat meat, with all the trimmings (including gigunda Brazilian salad bar and good fried stuff).

Other Recommendations Caipirinhas are the traditional accompaniment; they're a cocktail of cachaça (a spirit similar to rum) and lots of fresh lime. Here, they also make them with passion fruit for an extra-tropical flavor.

Entertainment & Amenities Live Brazilian music Wednesday–Sunday nights.

Summary & Comments Rodizio is a Brazilian tradition where all-you-can-eat roast meats are brought to your table by skewer-bearing waiters. It's all very ritualized in Brazil, and this is the only one of a rash of local rodizios that observes all the rituals (it's also the only one that's Brazilian-owned and -run). You're served the traditional plates of fried yucca, french fries, batter-fried bananas, and particularly good fried polenta.

Management hopes you'll fill up on this cheap stuff, as well as the extensive salad bar (vegetarians will be more than sated: tons of salads, vegetables, and even a few entrées in their own rights, like the good shrimp moqueca, a peppery stew with coconut milk), but savvy diners hold out for the meat. Pace yourself carefully as more than a dozen cuts come around. The best thing of all doesn't come unless you ask for it, though: unbelievably delicious black beans, made from specially imported small and silky beans. Spoon farofa (garlicky toasted yucca flour) over them. If all the meat doesn't give you a coronary, the service will; confused and incompetent waiters take their cue from the managers, who pompously stroll through in suit and ties, scanning the room for trouble spots and summarily ignoring your desperate pleas for service, dessert, or the check. Bad service also extends to the reservations line; call three times and you'll get three different answers regarding table availability.

Coco Pazzo Teatro ★★½

ITALIAN-TUSCAN | EXPENSIVE | QUALITY ★★★½ | VALUE ★★★ | ZONE 8

224 West 49th Street; (212) 320-2929

Customers Theater, business **Reservations** Recommended **When to Go** Anytime **Entrée Range** Lunch, $12.50–$21; dinner $15–$32 **Payment** All major credit cards **Service Rating** ★★★ **Friendliness Rating** ★★★ **Bar** Full service **Wine Selection** Good, strong on Italian vintages **Dress** Casual, business, theater **Disabled Access** Yes

Lunch Monday–Saturday, noon–3 p.m.

Dinner Daily, 5–11 p.m.

Setting & Atmosphere Coolly attractive, this Theater District Coco sports blond wood; blue, green, and faux marble columns with clever box lights; and a still-life wall painting. The well-spaced tables are adorned with a pretty blue bottle topped by a potato holding an orchid sprig—pazzo, no?

House Specialties Grilled yellowfin tuna, spicy seafood stew; marinated veal; whole roasted fish; fettuccine al funghi.

Other Recommendations House-cured salmon with fennel and orange salad; "vegetali alla Morandi," seasonal vegetables in mushroom broth; grilled squab with wild mushrooms; veal chop.

Summary & Comments Fans of the now almost ubiquitous Pino Luongo–run Coco Italian restaurant chain know what to expect from this Theater District branch: good but not great food in a stylish atmosphere at decent prices. Prices here may be lower than those at the established, celebrity-strewn **Coco Pazzo** on the Upper East Side (23 East 74th Street; (212) 794-0205), but you get what you pay for, as the food doesn't quite match up either. Still, Teatro is a good choice before the curtain goes up or after it comes down.

EJ's Luncheonette ★★

AMERICAN | INEXPENSIVE | QUALITY ★★★ | VALUE ★★★½ | ZONES 4, 12, 13

432 Sixth Avenue (9th and 10th streets); (212) 473-5555; Zone 4
447 Amsterdam Avenue (81st & 82nd streets); (212) 873-3444; Zone 12
1271 Third Avenue (at 73rd Street); (212) 472-0600; Zone 13

Customers Locals and local children **Reservations** Not accepted **When to Go** Anytime **Entrée Range** $12–$20; appetizers, $5–$9 **Payment** Cash only **Service Rating** ★★★ **Friendliness Rating** ★★★ **Wine Selection** Limited; 3 house wines **Dress** Casual **Disabled Access** All on one level

Open Daily, 8 a.m.–11 p.m.

Setting & Atmosphere Think *Happy Days*. This luncheonette could just as well be on Main Street in Small Town, U.S.A. It's straight-up 1950s "Dinersville" all the way from the blue-and-white vinyl booths with Formica tables to the counter with blue-topped stools. The separate locations differ in detail only.

House Specialties Buttermilk or multigrain flapjacks with a dozen different toppings; ditto for the buttermilk or bran Belgian waffles; Caesar salad; EJ's club sandwich; salami and eggs, pancake-style; great home fries; Stewart's root beer float.

Other Recommendations Macaroni and cheese; grilled tuna club with wasabi; Thai chicken salad; EJ's chicken Reuben. Check the daily specials and the special kid's menu.

Summary & Comments This New York standby packs it in with people of all ages, solo diners, couples, and families small and large. They come for the large portions, kid-friendly atmosphere, and good, familiar food. There may be a wait, but service is so fast that once you sit down you'll be out before you can sing "Blueberry Hill." Great place for breakfast or brunch, but watch out for those weekend crowds.

El Papasito

DOMINICAN | INEXPENSIVE | QUALITY ★★★½ | VALUE ★★★★★ | ZONE 8

370 West 52nd (near 9th Avenue); (212) 265-2225 or (212) 265-2227

Customers Local Latinos **Reservations** Not required **When to Go** Anytime **Entrée Range** $7.75–$22 **Payment** All major credit cards **Service Rating** ★½ **Friendliness Rating** ★★ **Bar** Beer and wine only **Wine Selection** Minimal **Dress** Casual **Disabled Access** Small step up; rest room doors narrow

Lunch & Dinner Daily, 11:30 a.m.–11 p.m.

Setting & Atmosphere A colorful, inviting L-shaped space with mustard-yellow walls, neatly arranged tables with glass-covered green tablecloths, autographed photos of Dominican baseball players, and one bizarre black velvet flock painting with blinking electric lights. There's a bar tucked into a corner that's been built as a thatched Caribbean hut.

House Specialties New York is shockingly bean deprived, quality-wise, but El Papasito is legume heaven; several dishes (possibilities include white/pink/red/black beans, chick/pigeon peas, etc.) are made daily, each accorded the respect of its own recipe (silky, intense black beans have a hit of vinegar, pink beans are more starkly elemental). Mofungo—a fried mash of starchy plantains, garlic, and pork that's one of the heaviest dishes on earth (and easy to miss under the "side orders" heading)—here somehow manages to taste light and greaseless, served with a cup of delicious intense gravy that's instantly absorbed. Chicharrones are crunchy pieces of on-bone pork or chicken, not just fried skin (as the dish is often mistranslated); squirt lime over them. Asopado is a thick, intensely garlicky rice soup; one order is easily enough for three. Don't miss stewed goat when it's a special or the off-menu silky yucca (a yam-ish vegetable elsewhere cooked to death), served with great marinated onions that enhance the sweetness of the tuber. Chicken in any form (ubiquitous on the daily specials menu) is dependably good, and flan (caramel custard) is downright fantastic—just the right balance of ultra-eggy richness and lightness, with a non-cloying intense caramel sauce.

Other Recommendations Surprisingly, the café con leche is mediocre.

Summary & Comments This is the class act for Dominican cooking in lower Manhattan. El Papasito serves—in a jazzy, approachable ambience—great, fresh plates with all the soulful authenticity of a Spanish Harlem hole-in-the-wall. Servers are very friendly but utterly unprofessional; they speak decent English, but you'll ask twice for silverware, and the check is a major production (also, beware of the dreaded pre-dessert Windex tabletop spray-down). Perhaps the waiters figure that with food so good at such low prices, they don't need to do much more than carry plates . . . and they may be right.

Firebird   ★★★

RUSSIAN | EXPENSIVE | QUALITY ★★★★ | VALUE ★★★★ | ZONE 8

365 West 46th Street (between Eighth and Ninth avenues); (212) 586-0244
www.firebirdrestaurant.com

Customers Theatergoers, local, tourists **Reservations** Recommended **When to Go** Anytime **Entrée Range** $20–$38 (lower range includes hefty appetizer prices); $38 prix fixe **Payment** All major credit cards **Service Rating** ★★★ **Friendliness Rating** ★★★ **Bar** Full service, with a selection of 14 vodkas **Wine Selection** Good, with some surprisingly low-priced choices **Dress** Upscale casual, Theater District dressy **Disabled Access** Yes

Lunch Wednesday and Saturday, 11:45 a.m.–2 p.m.

Dinner Thursday, Friday, and Saturday, 5–11:15 p.m.; Sunday, Tuesday, and Wednesday, 5–8:30 p.m.

Setting & Atmosphere Two spruced-up brownstones stand behind gilt-edged gates manned by a Cossack costumed sentry. No, you're not really in imperial St. Petersburg, but you're close. The fabulously overdone, charmingly ornate interior, with eight rooms and two pretty bars, is decorated with chandeliers, lushly patterned carpets, Fabergé-ish objects, Russian wall hangings, ballet costumes, and ancient books. Despite the pomp, the greeting is gracious and the atmosphere not at all forbidding.

House Specialties Wild mushroom and three-grain soup; buckwheat blini with sour cream; lightly smoked salmon with cucumber salad and five-grain bread; crab and rice croquettes with mâche; grilled marinated sturgeon; Uzbek skewered quail; pelmeni Siberian.

Other Recommendations Kasha wild mushroom salad; roasted eggplant caviar; Karsky shashlik; roast chicken with bulgur-okra salad; Armenian yogurt-spiced lamb.

Summary & Comments Firebird prides itself on detail—the china was specially designed, the wait staff garbed by Oleg Cassini—and on serving the authentic cuisine of czarist Russia in the ambience of equal authenticity. Best of all, it's fun; you actually hear people say "Wow!" when they walk in. The seven-course "Taste of the Tsars" menu is $80 per person. It's a wonderfully theatrical addition to Theater District dining.

Florent   ★★½

DINER/BISTRO | MODERATE | QUALITY ★★★½ | VALUE ★★★★ | ZONE 4

69 Gansevoort Street (between Washington and Hudson streets); (212) 989-5779
www.restaurantflorent.com

Customers Anything goes **Reservations** Not accepted **When to Go** Anytime
Entrée Range $6.75–$19.50 **Payment** Cash only **Service Rating** ★★★ **Friendliness Rating** ★★★ **Bar** Full service **Wine Selection** Minimal **Dress** Anything goes
Disabled Access Yes

Hours Daily, 24 hours

Setting & Atmosphere Turn the corner of Hudson Street and you leave the bistrofied West Village for Manhattan's gentrified former meat market. Florent, an elongated
ur-diner, sits in the middle of the block and fits in perfectly. There's not a frill in sight,
unless you count the late-night/early-morning clientele and the occasional paper
streamers and strings of pearls festooning the interior. (Or as a charming waiter put it,
"We're always decorating with something tacky.") The atmosphere is set by the crowd
that ranges from debs and celebs to ordinary and extraordinary New Yorkers of every
hue and persuasion. Opened in 1985, Florent was hip way before the meatpacking district "packed up" and became the new place to be seen.

House Specialties Check daily specials; dry aged New York sirloin au poivre; meat
loaf with mashed potatoes; boudin noir with apples and onions; omelet with smoked
salmon and arugula (brunch); crème caramel; moules frites.

Other Recommendations Homemade rillettes with roasted garlic; moules frites;
steak (aged rib-eye) frites; chicken breast stuffed with wild mushrooms; many of the
soups du jour.

Summary & Comments This is a great after-hours spot—supper and breakfast are
served from midnight on—and it's just as good at other times. The food, a balance of
bistro and diner dishes, is hearty and plentiful, and the people-watching may not be
hearty, but it certainly is an eyeful. The wait staff, young and ebullient, seems to be having as good a time as the customers. The board over the bar always has some interesting, amusing, and/or cryptic messages.

Gabriela's   ★★★

MEXICAN | MODERATE | QUALITY ★★★★ | VALUE ★★★★★ | ZONE 12

685 Amsterdam Avenue (at 93rd Street); (212) 961-0574   www.gabrielas.com
315 Amsterdam Avenue (at 75th Street); (212) 875-8532

Customers Anything goes **Reservations** Not accepted **When to Go** Anytime
Entrée Range $5.75–$17.95 **Payment** Cash only **Service Rating** ★★★ **Friendliness Rating** ★★★ **Bar** Full service **Wine Selection** Minimal **Dress** Anything goes
Disabled Access Yes

Brunch Saturday and Sunday, 11:30 a.m.–3 p.m.

Lunch & Dinner Monday–Thursday, 11:30 a.m.–11 p.m.; Friday and Saturday, 11:30
a.m.–midnight; Sunday, 11:30 a.m.–10 p.m.

Setting & Atmosphere The room, like the food, is brighter and slicker than standard Mexican restaurants; décor is cheerful/colorful, with cactus murals on the walls
and mini-candelabras over each table. It's comfortable without pandering (à la Benny's
Burritos and other chains).

House Specialties Rotisserie chicken, posole (an ultra-satisfying huge bowl of pork
and hominy corn soup), crema de elote y poblano (spicy/creamy corn soup), tamales,
panucho yucateco (Yucatán-style stuffed tortillas), cochinita pibil (roast pork marinated in
orange juice and numerous spices), tinga poblana (crispy tortillas topped with shredded

pork), garnachas (tortillas filled with cheese, scallions, and hot peppers), licuados (fruit shakes), and aguas frescas (fresh fruit drinks).

Summary & Comments This is a relatively upscale, gringo-friendly establishment that cooks some unusual dishes with uncommon panache. It's the only place for rare Yucatán-style specialties like panuchos yucatecos (thick stuffed tortillas with black bean paste) and Yucatán roast chicken (there are also some touches from Oaxaca and Veracruz). Stick with more complex specialties, from the "platter" part of the menu, rather than simpler stuff like tortas, tacos, quesadillas, and enchiladas. Such antojitos (snacks) can be good here, but the kitchen's more consistent with ambitious items like cochinita pibil and crema de elote y poblano. Don't miss the five terrific varieties of tamales (one—made with mushrooms—is tucked under the "Vegetarian Platters" menu heading).

Gotham Bar & Grill   ★★★½

NEW AMERICAN | EXPENSIVE | QUALITY ★★★★ | VALUE ★★★ | ZONE 4

12 East 12th Street (between University Place and Fifth Avenue); (212) 620-4020

Customers Business, local **Reservations** Recommended **When to Go** Anytime **Entrée Range** $15–$37 **Payment** AMEX, MC, VISA **Service Rating** ★★ **Friendliness Rating** ★★ **Bar** Full service **Wine Selection** Very good **Dress** Business, dressy, casual chic **Disabled Access** No

Lunch Monday–Friday, noon–2 p.m.

Dinner Monday–Thursday, 5:30–10 p.m.; Friday, 5:30–11 p.m.; Saturday, 5–11 p.m.; Sunday, 5–10 p.m.

Setting & Atmosphere This lofty space has been tamed by sophisticated alterations: grand, fabric-draped overhead lighting fixtures, tables on varying levels, ocher columns, teal trim, bountiful bouquets of flowers on pedestals and on the imposing bar. All is dimly lit and austerely opulent.

House Specialties Soft-shell crab; seafood salad; seared yellowfin tuna; rack of lamb with garlic mashed potatoes; caramelized banana cake filled with bitter chocolate custard.

Other Recommendations Ricotta cheese ravioli; Chinese spiced duck breast with seared foie gras; red snapper in shellfish broth; lemon tart with warm blueberry compote.

Summary & Comments Chef Alfred Portale, a major influence on New American cuisine and mentor to many of its now successful practitioners, continues to turn out reliable, and memorable food. His soaring, structured presentations seem perfectly suited to the impressive room in which they are served. Gotham keeps its standing as a perennial favorite, both for the food and the welcoming predictability of it all.

Gramercy Tavern   ★★★½

AMERICAN | EXPENSIVE | QUALITY ★★★★ | VALUE ★★★ | ZONE 7

42 East 20th Street (between Broadway and Park Avenue South); (212) 477-0777

Customers Business, local, celebs **Reservations** Essential in the main dining room **When to Go** Anytime **Entrée Range** $33 prix fixe lunch, $65 prix fixe dinner **Payment** All major credit cards **Service Rating** ★★★ **Friendliness Rating** ★★ **Bar** Full service **Wine Selection** Excellent, many available by the glass or a 3-ounce tasting glass; $25 corkage fee **Dress** Anything goes **Disabled Access** Yes

Lunch Monday–Friday, noon–2 p.m.

Dinner Sunday–Thursday, 5:30–10 p.m.; Friday and Saturday, 5:30–11 p.m.

Setting & Atmosphere Lovely and inviting—flowers in profusion deck the entry, spill over a table near the open grill, ornament the dining spaces, even bloom in the rest rooms. Floor-to-ceiling windows front the tavern room, with its big, black-topped bar, and boldly colored paintings of fruits and vegetables brighten the upper walls. The lighting in the more formal, cathedral-ceilinged dining rooms goes from early American to trendy glass buckets; the decorations follow suit with a few American primitive portraits, a quilt, and large metal starfish. Somehow it all works well together.

House Specialties Fondue of Maine crabmeat with sweet pea sauce, smoked bacon, and pink peppercorns; tuna tartare with cucumber vinaigrette; roasted sirloin and braised beef cheeks with farro, morels, and red wine; individual nectarine tatin.

Other Recommendations Marinated hamachi; roasted cod; salt-baked salmon; chocolate pudding; selection of cheeses.

Summary & Comments Danny Meyer, the man who brought you Union Square Café (and Eleven Madison Park and Tabla), teamed up with chef Tom Colicchio to open this Gramercy-area winner in 1994. Gramercy has the same comfortable atmosphere and agreeable service that makes Union Square Café such a hit; the surprise lies in the food, which is more adventurous than that of its older sibling. The seafood fondues, a running theme at Gramercy, consistently please beyond expectation, and the meat entrées shine, especially the recently added roasted sirloin. Desserts are good but not memorable, so a selection of fine cheeses may be the way to go here. For a more informal and less expensive alternative, try the equally pleasing Tavern Room up front.

Grand Sichuan International   ★★★

CHINESE | MODERATE | QUALITY ★★★★ | VALUE ★★★★★ | ZONE 6

229 9th Avenue at 24th; (212) 620-5200

Customers Locals **Reservations** Accepted **When to Go** Anytime **Entrée Range** $10–$16.95 **Payment** All major credit cards **Service Rating** ★★ **Friendliness Rating** ★ **Bar** Beer and wine only **Wine Selection** Small **Dress** Casual **Disabled Access** Good, but tight path to rest rooms

Lunch & Dinner Daily, 11:30 a.m.–11 p.m.

Setting & Atmosphere To all appearances a generic, "nice" Midtown Chinese place, with track lighting, elegant shiny little black chairs, and nice tablecloths. Only the huge informational pamphlet-cum-textbook, unfurled across the length of the front window, tells you that is not just another mediocre joint for gringo moo-shoo. Foodie passersby stop and gape at the menu as if it were a Christmas window at Macy's.

House Specialties Terrific spicy Szechuan cuisine, with some other hard-to-find (and hard-to-find good) regional dishes from Hunan, Shanghai, and even a small selection of "Mao's Home Cooking," culled from the former leader's little black book of favorite recipes (he had good taste; they're mostly winners). You can't go wrong if you stick with hot/spicy stuff and the fancier exotic specialties (borrow the informational pamphlet and choose from the more extolled items); avoid duller-sounding and more clichéd offerings (chow fun or egg rolls, for example, are Wrong Orders, and your taste buds will be punished accordingly). Don't miss tea-smoked duck (so smoky, so addictive), the spicy double-cooked pork, or any of the Shanghai "red cooking" dishes (none of which, peculiarly, appear on Mao's list of faves). Dan dan noodles with chili sauce is a popular starter that will get the peppery fires going.

Other Recommendations Beware: Grand Sichuan looks like a neighborhood generic Chinese restaurant, and it really does serve that function for the area. Don't be tempted by the cheap lunch and dinner specials (pepper steak, chicken with broccoli, etc). Sit down and pay a few more bucks for what this place does well.

Summary & Comments Be warned: Sichuan (a.k.a. Szechuan) cuisine is spicy, hearty, and oily. Complaining about the greasiness of, say, Sichuan twice-cooked pork is like objecting to the wetness of soup; it's a raison d'être. So . . . don't come here if you're on a diet. The aforementioned pamphlet—a thick swath of information written in great enthusiastic detail—makes a super guide to the restaurant's offerings. Unfortunately you won't have much time to read it—despite Grand Sichuan's relatively upscale Midtown décor, the rushed service is strictly Chinatown style. Despite endless ownership infighting and debate on the rights to the name, GSI has four other nominal locations: 125 Canal Street, (212) 625-9212; 227 Lexington Avenue, (212) 679-9770; 745 Ninth Avenue, (212) 582-2288; and 1049 Second Avenue, (212) 355-5855. Different owners and styles, but good food all around.

Grange Hall ★★★½

AMERICAN | MODERATE | QUALITY ★★★★½ | VALUE ★★★★½ | ZONE 4

50 Commerce Street; (212) 924-5246

Customers Locals, couples **Reservations** Recommended **When to Go** Anytime **Entrée Range** Small dishes, $11–$18; main dishes, $30 per person **Payment** AMEX **Service Rating** ★★★★ **Friendliness Rating** ★★★★ **Bar** Full service **Wine Selection** Decent range of Americans **Dress** Nice casual or better **Disabled Access** Good (use Commerce Street entrance)

Brunch Saturday, 11 a.m.–3 p.m.; Sunday, 10:30 a.m.–4 p.m.

Lunch Monday–Friday, noon–3 p.m.; Saturday, 11 a.m.–3 p.m.; Sunday, 10:30 a.m.–3 p.m.

Dinner Monday, 5:30–11 p.m.; Tuesday–Saturday, 5:30–11:30 p.m.; Sunday, 5:30–11 p.m.

Setting & Atmosphere Situated on a twisty picture-postcard block in the most beautiful part of Greenwich Village, the exterior is inviting, and the interior even more so: smart and elegant, warmly lit and well-appointed, but not at all pretentious. The retro décor (1940s sophistication with a twist) doesn't intrude, and the jazz soundtrack wafts romantically; this is low-key urbane dining. There's a striking mural by artist David Joel.

House Specialties Acorn squash, freshly made sausage, potato pancakes, Yukon Gold scalloped potatoes, oven-roasted organic chicken, cranberry-glazed pork chops, farm vegetable platter, soups, salads.

Other Recommendations Those potato pancakes are an ideal bar snack if you just stop by for drinks.

Summary & Comments Grange Hall started out as the latest offering from a group known for their stable of theme eateries. This one was designed to be "Upscale Retro Blue Plate," but the restaurant has become loved on its own terms rather than as a contrived novelty. They've stocked the place with smart, funny young waiters and a great bar (good for solo dining and quite popular for martinis late into the night) and serve a seasonal menu of savvily cooked American dishes. The dishes use simple ingredients, but the chef's far too sophisticated to let his food devolve into clichéd comfort food; everything's cooked with flare, and simplicity never lapses into dullness. This is the perfect spot for carnivores to bring vegetarians; in addition to well-cooked meat dishes, there are numerous vegetable small plates that can accumulate into a meal. (Also, larger plates can be shared; it's all very mix-and-match.) If you've been dipping deep into New York's unparalleled ethnic food scene and want to relax with a more familiar—but still exciting—menu, this is the place.

Gray's Papaya ★½

AMERICAN | INEXPENSIVE | QUALITY ★★★½ | VALUE ★★★★★ | ZONES 4, 12

2090 Broadway (at 72nd Street); (212) 799-0243; Zone 12 Upper West Side
402 Sixth Avenue (at 8th Street); (212) 260-3532; Zone 4 Greenwich Village

Customers Anybody and everybody (except vegetarians) **Reservations** Not necessary **When to Go** Anytime **Entrée Range** $0.75 **Payment** Some loose change **Service Rating** ★ **Friendliness Rating** ★½ **Bar** None **Wine Selection** Only if grape juice counts **Dress** Pretty much anything, or nothing at all **Disabled Access** Drive-through accessibility

Open Daily, 24 hours

Setting & Atmosphere Cheery and cheap old-school orange counters, white tile, paper fruits hanging from the ceiling; décor is not exactly a priority here.

House Specialties Hot dog; hot dog with mustard; hot dog with sauerkraut; hot dog with sautéed onions; hot dog with mustard, sauerkraut, and sautéed onions. They toast their buns for a crispier hot-dog experience.

Other Recommendations Hot dog with ketchup; hot dog with ketchup and mustard; hot dog with ketchup, mustard, sauerkraut, and sautéed onions. You get the idea.

Summary & Comments New York wouldn't be New York without hot dogs, and Gray's is a New York institution. Although prices may have gone up by 50%, hot dogs are still only 75 cents a pop, and the recession special is by far the best deal in town at $2.45 for two dogs and a drink. The franks are grilled to perfection, leaving the skin crisp and locking in the flavor, and like all good wieners, come regular or well done. Everyone has a favorite, but all the fruity tropical drinks provide the perfect refreshment to wash down the best dogs in town.

Honmura An ★★★

JAPANESE (SOBA) | EXPENSIVE | QUALITY ★★★★ | VALUE ★★★ | ZONE 2

170 Mercer Street; (212) 334-5253

Customers Ethnic, local, Soho celebs **Reservations** Recommended for dinner **When to Go** Anytime **Entrée Range** $12–$21.75 **Payment** All major credit cards **Service Rating** ★★★ **Friendliness Rating** ★★★ **Bar** Wine, beer, and sake **Wine Selection** Fair **Dress** Casual **Disabled Access** No

Lunch Wednesday–Friday, noon–2:30 p.m.

Dinner Tuesday–Sunday, 6–10:30 p.m.

Setting & Atmosphere Plain wooden stairs with a few distinctly Japanese flower arrangements lead to a serene second-floor space that's the epitome of elegant understatement. Large pieces of plain white rice paper hang on the high brick walls, and polished wooden tables and dark green banquettes circle the room. A glass-enclosed corner is dedicated to the in-house production of the soba (buckwheat) noodles used in most of the main dishes.

House Specialties   Hot soba with sliced duck; anything soba; tempura, with rice in a lacquer box—and giant prawns specially shipped from a fish market in Tokyo; soba sushi, a sushi thick roll made of soba (what else!) with mashed prawns that must be ordered in advance.

Other Recommendations   Seiro soba (cold soba noodles with dipping sauce) and zaru soba (the same thing except the noodles are topped with nori, chopped dried seaweed).

Summary & Comments   The soba specialties, uncommon and superb, plus the tranquil setting and unobtrusive service make this an extremely popular Soho spot. Most of the appetizers tend to be disappointing, so stick with what this place does best, and that's soba. Though prices are a bit high for the portions, you won't find much better soba in the city. Zaru soba is a great snack in the summer, and you're likely to crave it throughout the year. This is a subtle cuisine that could fast become a healthy addiction. The $18–$24 prix fixe lunch makes a great intro, but the pricier $50 prix fixe soba dinner may not be worth it.

Iammo Bello   ★★½

ITALIAN CAFETERIA | INEXPENSIVE | QUALITY ★★★★ | VALUE ★★★★★ | ZONE 11

39 East 60th Street; (212) 935-9418

Customers Local, business **Reservations** Not accepted **When to Go** Early or late to miss the crowds, but queues move quickly even at peak hours **Entrée Range** $5.25–$8.50 **Payment** Major credit cards **Service Rating** ★★★½ **Friendliness Rating** ★★★ **Bar** None **Wine Selection** None **Dress** Casual **Disabled Access** No **Open** Monday–Saturday, 11 a.m.–5 p.m.; closed Sunday

Setting & Atmosphere A quick-moving queue snakes through this subterranean cafeteria, past myriad steam tables manned by hyperkinetic servers. All remaining space is crammed with long tables full of harried, ravenous eaters, forks and jaws working at a prodigious pace. It's all so fast-paced that you feel as if a request to pass the salt might elicit a hail of shakers flung at you from all directions.

House Specialties Wonderful heroes like chicken, veal, eggplant, or meatball parmigiana (with good, funky Parmesan cheese rather than the usual clots of bad mozzarella); zesty chicken francese (hot only on Thursdays, other days available cold at the antipasto bar); delicious homey lasagna; soups; well-fried calamari (Fridays only). Skip the deftly flavored pastas if you demand al dente (impossible to achieve in a steam table), but you'll be missing a pretty good alfredo sauce.

Other Recommendations There are various fancy pizzas (including one with nicely grilled vegetables) as well as regular slices (intriguingly different from the usual Gotham slice) available from a separate concession in the back. Up front, the abundantly stocked self-service antipasto bar costs $5.75/pound (don't miss the rice with vegetables).

Summary & Comments Iammo Bello means "come here, handsome," in Italian, but this no-frills bustling cafeteria depends more on its cooking than its looks to attract. Chicken francese is downright scrumptious, and even rough, unsubtle dishes like lasagna taste soulful. There's a certain satisfaction that comes from having eaten a really good $8 meal in a neighborhood filled with mediocre $30 lunches. As Italian cafeterias go, this isn't quite as good as Rosario's (see profile), but it's much more centrally located, and the food is certainly worlds above the heros, pastas, and salads served in local pizzerias.

Il Buco ★★★★

FRENCH/SPANISH/ITALIAN | EXPENSIVE | QUALITY ★★★★½ | VALUE ★★★ | ZONE 5

47 Bond Street; (212) 533-1932   www.ilbuco.com

Customers Local **Reservations** A must **When to Go** Anytime **Entrée Range** $16–$27 **Payment** AMEX **Service Rating** ★★★ **Friendliness Rating** ★★ **Bar** Full service **Wine Selection** Carefully selected collection of unusual (but savvy) choices **Dress** Expensive informal **Disabled Access** Good

Lunch Tuesday–Saturday, noon–4 p.m.

Dinner Monday–Thursday, 6 p.m.–1 a.m.; Friday and Saturday, 6 p.m.– 2 a.m.; Sunday, 5 p.m.–midnight

Setting & Atmosphere Antique store by day, restaurant by night, woody, atmospheric Il Buco has an old European farmhouse feeling quite unlike that of any other spot in the city. You eat at rough, candlelit tables surrounded by old furnishings and knickknacks, all for sale. It's tremendously romantic in its rustic way.

House Specialties Changing seasonal menu, but risottos, grilled octopus, homemade sausages, pastas, flourless chocolate cake, and plum cake are delicious fixtures.

Entertainment & Amenities The wine cellar allegedly was the inspiration for Edgar Allan Poe's story "A Cask of Amontillado," and it's got atmosphere galore; have a peek.

Summary & Comments Il Buco's cooking incorporates French, Italian, and Spanish influences, and the chef shows considerable command in all three culinary languages; the risotto is creamy, peasanty, and completely unpretentious; the octopus tastes like first-hand Mediterranean rather than a cooking school grad working from a recipe. This rogue kitchen has its own distinctive style; it follows no trends. Though not widely known, Il Buco is much loved by a discerning few, and the smallish place fills up most nights. This is an especially good locale for special occasions—long tables can be reserved either in the middle of the main room or in a rear alcove.

Il Mulino ★★★½

ITALIAN | EXPENSIVE | QUALITY ★★★★½ | VALUE ★★★★½ | ZONE 4

86 West Third Street (between Sullivan and Thompson); (212) 673-3783

Customers Business, local **Reservations** Highly recommended **When to Go** Anytime **Entrée Range** $22–$35 **Payment** All major credit cards **Service Rating** ★★★ **Friendliness Rating** ★★★ **Bar** Full service **Wine Selection** Good **Dress** Upscale, business suits **Disabled Access** Yes

Lunch Monday–Friday, noon–2:30 p.m.

Dinner Monday–Saturday, 5–11 p.m.

Setting & Atmosphere There's no mistaking this for a Village trattoria; low-key elegance and low-key lighting prevail from the small, pretty bar in the front to the single perfect rose and heavy white cloths on each table. Tall potted plants separate the dining room from the entrance; the ceiling is mercifully soundproofed, though this is hardly the place for a raucous crowd; and the walls that are not exposed brick are covered in soft, feathery wallpaper. The service is unobtrusively attentive.

House Specialties Check the daily specials; carpaccio; spaghettini carbonara; fillet of beef with caper sauce; rolled veal braised in wine, cream, and wild mushrooms; veal chop.

Other Recommendations Spaghettini with clams; spicy veal with anchovies, capers, and mushrooms; chicken and sausage in white wine; capellini Il Mulino; minnestrone.

Summary & Comments Most New Yorkers consider Il Mulino the best Italian in the the city, and with good reason. Complimentary appetizers, including delicious fried zucchini, superb salami, spicy bruschetta, and scrumptious chunks off the biggest slab of Parmigiano-Reggiano you've ever seen, will have your stomach running up the white flag before you've even ordered. The pastas prove addictive, like the rich capellini Il Mulino and perfect spaghettini carbonara, and the veal, in any of its multitude of preparations, is excellent. Portions are more than generous and one thing's certain—you won't leave here hungry. Finish your meal with a bang by taking in a glass of the potent homemade grappa.

Jackson Diner ★★½

INDIAN | INEXPENSIVE/MODERATE | QUALITY ★★★½ | VALUE ★★★★★ | ZONE 17

37–47 74th Street, Jackson Heights; (718) 672-1232

Customers Locals, ethnic, spice lovers **Reservations** Not necessary **When to Go** Anytime **Entrée Range** $8–$21 **Payment** Cash only **Service Rating** ★★½ **Friendliness Rating** ★★★ **Bar** Good Indian beer only **Wine Selection** None **Dress** Casual **Disabled Access** Two steps into restaurant; none for bathrooms

Lunch Daily, 11:30 a.m.–4:30 p.m.

Dinner Sunday–Thursday, 4:30–10 p.m.; Friday and Saturday, 4:30–10:30 p.m.

Setting & Atmosphere A large, high-ceilinged room filled with no-nonsense tables and chairs ready to house the crowds of regulars and soon-to-be converted. To be brief: There is no atmosphere! Banquet hall also available.

House Specialties Shrimp curry with coconut and spices; lentil cakes (iddly) and other variations of Southern Indian pancakes and crêpes; sag paneer (spicy spinach and homemade cheese cubes); murg lajwab (chicken cooked with tomatoes, ginger, and cilantro).

Other Recommendations lentil soup (mulligatawny); baignan bhurta (eggplant with onions, ginger, and tomatoes); dal diwan (yellow lentils with coriander and cumin); tandoori mix grill.

Summary & Comments So many of the dishes here hit the spot and tantalize the taste buds—assuming you appreciate Indian spice blends. This is not a place for the weak-hearted, although you're allowed to choose from mild, medium to hot; it seems that the chef feels a lot more comfortable farther up the spicy scale. Hardly a surprise when the food is so authentic. The main concern here is delivering good food at incredibly reasonable prices, so the atmosphere isn't given much attention. Jackson Diner has received its fair share of awards for its food, and no doubt it will continue to take home a few more accolades. From the chutney to the lassi and everything in between, you won't be disappointed.

Jasmine ★★½

THAI | MODERATE | QUALITY ★★★★ | VALUE ★★★★ | ZONE 13

1619 Second Avenue (at 84th Street); (212) 517-8854

Customers Locals **Reservations** Not accepted **When to Go** Anytime **Entrée Range** $9.50–$17.50 **Payment** All major credit cards **Service Rating** ★★½ **Friendliness Rating** ★★½ **Bar** Beer only **Wine Selection** Limited **Dress** Casual **Disabled Access** Yes

Lunch & Dinner Sunday–Thursday, noon–11 p.m.; Friday and Saturday, noon–midnight

Setting & Atmosphere Dark, candlelit with lots of dark red wood and wooden tables and chairs. Clean, new, and comfortable with some Southeast Asian touches like potted palms and bamboo wall hangings. Nicer than most neighborhood Thai places, but certainly no Vong when it comes to décor.

House Specialties Steamed shrimp dumplings with garlic-ginger sauce; pahd see yu (chow fun noodles with chicken or beef, Chinese broccoli, and eggs); spicy basil chicken with peppers, onions, and chili paste; gaeng penang (Thai red curry with beef or chicken, basil, coriander, pepper, and coconut milk).

Other Recommendations Po pia (spring rolls); tom kha gai (spicy Thai coconut milk soup); pahd thai noodles; khao pahd supparot (coconut fried rice with chicken topped with ground peanuts and fried onions); goong phao (grilled jumbo prawns with house special chili sauce); green curry chicken; Thai iced tea or iced coffee.

Summary & Comments The best Thai on the Upper East Side, this neighborhood favorite draws crowds for its well-prepared food and spicy change of pace. Though its menu is small, there's enough to choose from, and the things they do, they do very well. Start with one of the soups or excellent steamed shrimp dumplings. Of particular note are the spicy and fragrant Thai curries, tempered with coconut milk and a real treat. You can't miss with either gaeng penang with beef or green curry with chicken. Pahd thai and other noodle and rice dishes are above average, and to douse the flames in your mouth there's nothing better than soothing Thai iced tea or yummy Thai iced coffee.

Jaya Malaysian   ★★

MALAYSIAN | INEXPENSIVE | QUALITY ★★★½ | VALUE ★★★★½ | ZONE 3

90 Baxter Street; (212) 219-3331

Customers Ethnic, locals **Reservations** Not necessary **When to Go** Anytime **Entrée Range** $5–$18 **Payment** All major credit cards **Service Rating** ★★½ **Friendliness Rating** ★★½ **Bar** Beer only **Wine Selection** None **Dress** Casual **Disabled Access** No

Open Daily, 11 a.m.–10:45 p.m.

Setting & Atmosphere The storefront looks a little tacky, and it hardly convinces you that you've arrived at a place that serves authentic Malaysian food. Don't let the outside deter you; the restaurant is a fair size and can easily seat large groups. The décor consists of bamboo light fixtures, a wooden mesh ceiling, and one wall of painted plaster with seashells, rocks, dried sea creatures and vegetation, and other ocean motifs. The interior simply exists; it's neither offensive nor stimulating, and it certainly won't affect your enjoyment of the meal.

House Specialties Stingray in lotus leaf; shrimp with dried chili paste; various laksas (noodles in curried broth with either chicken, shrimp, seafood, or tofu); chendor (shaved ice with coconut, red beans, and green jelly); curry fish head pot.

Other Recommendations Thai-style fish cake; bean curd stuffed with cucumber and bean sprouts; lemongrass jumbo shrimp; carp with ginger-garlic sauce; Malaysian iced coffee; lychee iced tea.

Summary & Comments If possible, try to get here early because the place is full by 7:30 p.m., and the noise level can really rise. The menu is extensive, and there's everything from standard fried rice to more adventurous dishes such as crispy pork intestines. If this cuisine is new to you, try a shrimp, squid, or fish dish with curry, chili, and/or garlic. The stingray in lotus leaf is incredibly succulent, but it has a weird smell attributed to the leaf. It's also worth trying a selection of appetizers. Ask your waiter for some suggestions. If you need a shot of caffeine, don't forget to end the meal with an iced coffee—the condensed milk makes it heavenly. Jaya has another branch on the Upper West Side, but that location has a limited menu without the true spicy variety of this one in Chinatown.

Jean-Georges ★★★★

FRENCH | EXPENSIVE | QUALITY ★★★★½ | VALUE ★★★ | ZONE 10

1 Central Park West (at 60th Street); (212) 299-3900 www.jean-gorges.com

Customers Local **Reservations** Required **When to Go** Anytime **Entrée Range** $29–$35 entrées, $45 prix fixe lunch; $85 prix fixe dinner **Payment** Most major credit cards **Service Rating** ★★★★ **Friendliness Rating** ★★★ **Bar** Full service **Wine Selection** Excellent, good range of prices from $22 to $1,000 **Dress** Jacket required for men; dressy **Disabled Access** Yes

Lunch Monday–Friday, noon–2:30 p.m.

Dinner Monday–Saturday, 5:30–11 p.m.

Setting & Atmosphere Restaurant designer Adam Tihany has kept this large dining room simple and spare with subdued tones of beige and gray. The huge windows let in sun and sky and views of Central Park during the day; at night the lights of Columbus Circle and Central Park South twinkle in the distance, and the gargantuan globe that sits outside the Trump International Tower takes on extra prominence. The overall feeling is more cool than cozy, but definitely elegant.

House Specialties Foie gras and duck prosciutto roulade; asparagus with morel mushrooms; lobster tartine; baked arctic char; chocolate soufflé with warm raspberries and vanilla ice cream.

Other Recommendations Sea scallops in caper-raisin emulsion with caramelized cauliflower; broiled squab with corn pancake and foie gras; turbot uba Chateau Chalon sauce; rhubarb tart with rhubarb crème glacée.

Summary & Comments Jean-Georges, given four stars by the *New York Times*, is the eponymous jewel in Jean-Georges Vongerichten's culinary crown—he also owns JoJo, Vong, 66, and Mercer Kitchen. This is where Vongerichten concentrates on his signature French cuisine, the innovative, intensely flavored dishes that made his Restaurant Lafayette, now closed, a four-star hit. The food is superb, as is the service; each dish is finished at your table, and this kind of attention is rare indeed. Jean-Georges was a New York sensation from the moment it opened, and reservations are hard to come by, but try. The sleeker Nougatine Café, the front room and bar of the restaurant, serves breakfast as well as lunch and dinner. Entrées are less expensive there, and the atmosphere is somewhat less formal. The outdoor Mistral Terrace is open seasonally.

Jezebel ★★★

SOUL FOOD | EXPENSIVE | QUALITY ★★★★ | VALUE ★★★ | ZONE 8

630 Ninth Avenue (corner of 45th Street, entrance on 45th); (212) 582-1045
www.jezebelny.com

Customers Local, tourists **Reservations** Recommended **When to Go** Anytime
Entrée Range $20–$30 **Payment** All major credit cards **Service Rating** ★★★
Friendliness Rating ★★★ **Bar** Full service **Wine Selection** Not extensive **Dress**
Casual to dressy **Disabled Access** Yes

Dinner Tuesday–Thursday, 5:30–10 p.m.; Friday and Saturday, 5:30 p.m.–12:30 a.m.

Setting & Atmosphere It's easy to miss the low-key entrance, but open the door
and it's the Vieux Carré, sultry and seductive all the way. Fringed shawls hang from the
ceiling like Spanish moss; large potted palms, camellias, and vases of lilies bloom all
around the room; oriental carpets accent the polished floors; and the walls are covered
in posters—authentic French Art Nouveau, authentic American Andy Warhol, and a few
Josephine Baker biggies. Mirrored columns, white wooden swings, crystal chandeliers,
glass-topped tables with lace-bottomed clothes, wicker screens, and wrought-iron
chairs all add to the lushly romantic effect.

House Specialties She-crab soup; Gula curried goat; smothered pork chops; shrimp
Creole; barbecue spareribs.

Other Recommendations Smothered garlic shrimp; Jezebel's green pea soup;
coconut sweet potato pie; pecan pie.

Summary & Comments "Down-home" goes upscale here, and all is overseen by
Alberta Wright—the sophisticated yet soothingly savory soul food that comes out of
the kitchen and the fabulous festoonery of the dimly lit dining room. This is an unexpected wow of a Theater District restaurant, a performance in itself, and worth the trip
even if a show is not on the evening's schedule.

Joe's Shanghai ★★★

CHINESE | MODERATE | QUALITY ★★★★½ | VALUE ★★★★★ | ZONES 3, 17

9 Pell Street (between Mott and Bowery); (212) 233-8894; Zone 3 Chinatown
136–21 37th Avenue, Flushing (718) 539-4429; Zone 17 Queens

Customers Locals, foodies **Reservations** Only for parties of 10 or more **When to
Go** Off hours (between 2:30 and 5:30 p.m., or after 9:30 p.m.), to avoid wait **Entrée
Range** $9.95–$12.95 **Payment** Cash only **Service Rating** ★★★ **Friendliness Rat-
ing** ★★★ **Bar** Beer only, and a limited variety **Wine Selection** BYOB **Dress** Casual
Disabled Access Queens good, Manhattan fair (one step to dining room)

Open Manhattan, daily, 11 a.m.–11:15 p.m.; Queens, daily, 11 a.m.–10:30 p.m.

Setting & Atmosphere Several notches up from a Chinatown-style no-frills café,
always busy but comfortable. The big tables are shared, but that's part of the ritual.

House Specialties Crabmeat steamed buns, stewed pork balls, shredded pork with
pickled cabbage soup, anything with mushrooms, shrimp-fried rice cake, hot and sour
soup, pork shoulder (with honey glaze), Shanghai fried flat noodles, shredded turnip
shortcakes, soya (mock) duck.

Summary & Comments By all means, start with the crabmeat steamed buns, amazing soup-filled dumplings that New Yorkers have been going wild over. Wait for them to

cool a bit, then delicately (don't puncture—you'll lose the soup!) transfer a dumpling to a spoon into which you've pooled a bit of soy/ginger sauce and a dab of hot sauce. Nibble a hole in the skin, suck the soup, then down the dumpling. The shiitake mushrooms are great here, and the stewed pork balls are the lightest meatballs you've ever tasted, in a succulent sauce. Don't order typical Chinese restaurant fare, though—try to stick with the Shanghai specialties. Ask the harried but affable waiters for tips, or ask about good-looking dishes passing by. You can also check out **Joe's Ginger** (same owners) at 113 Mott Street, (212) 966-6613.

Kam Chueh ★★★

CHINESE | MODERATE | QUALITY ★★★★ | VALUE ★★★★½ | ZONE 3

40 Bowery (South of Canal Street); (212) 791-6868 or (212) 791-6866

Customers Good blend of Chinese and serious aficionados **Reservations** Large groups only **When to Go** Late **Entrée Range** $4–$22 **Payment** Cash only **Service Rating** ★★★½ **Friendliness Rating** ★★½ **Bar** Beer only **Wine Selection** None **Dress** Casual **Disabled Access** Small step up; rest rooms not accessible

Lunch & Dinner Daily, 11:30 a.m.–4 a.m.

Setting & Atmosphere Contented fish swim spunkily through crystal clear water in front window display tanks. Humans are accommodated in an only slightly less congenial habitat; the brightly lit dining room goes for an upscale look, with faux marble tiles and glittery cheap chandeliers.

House Specialties Razor clams (or jumbo shrimp) in superb black bean sauce; salt-and-pepper squid (basically top-notch fried calamari sans dipping sauce); chunks of excellent medium rare T-bone steak with flowering chives; sautéed mixed vegetables (order with off-menu foo yee sauce with briny fermented bean curd); super-delicate snowpea leaves; intense hot and sour soup; satisfying winter melon soup; flowering chives with clams; huge crabs with either ginger-scallion or black bean sauce.

Other Recommendations You can't go wrong ordering from the smaller specials menu listing exotic baby vegetables and fancier preparations many restaurants refuse to translate into English. Don't order egg rolls and such; the menu lists a few Chinese-American workhorses, but the chef is clearly not happy about it.

Entertainment & Amenities Each table is covered with a thick wad of white plastic sheeting; don't miss the meal-end spectacle when your waiter bundles up the remains inside the topmost sheet and hauls it back to the kitchen on his back, leaving behind a new layer of clean, virgin plastic.

Summary & Comments Kam Chueh descends from Cantonese royalty; it's the estranged brother of the late, lamented Shing Kee, Chinatown favorite of many cognoscenti. Their menu is nearly identical, and the cooking comes pretty close (their black bean sauce should be declared a cultural landmark by the city). This is an after-hours scene; it's quite the hangout at 2 or 3 a.m., as gigging musicians and snazzily dressed young Chinese clubbers converge here.

Kate's Joint ★★½

VEGETARIAN | MODERATE | QUALITY ★★★★ | VALUE ★★★★ | ZONE 5

58 Avenue B at 4th Street; (212) 777-7059

Customers Locals **Reservations** Only for parties of 8 or more **When to Go** Anytime **Entrée Range** $8–$12 **Payment** Most major credit cards **Service Rating** ★★ **Friendliness Rating** ★★ **Bar** Beer and wine **Wine Selection** Small **Dress** Casual **Disabled Access** Good

Lunch & Dinner Friday and Saturday, 9 a.m.–1 a.m.; Sunday–Thursday, 9 a.m.–midnight

Setting & Atmosphere Informal, mellow bohemian café with broodingly dark-colored walls and a good view of the East Village sidewalk parade.

House Specialties Mock-meat dishes; chile-con-tofu-carne, southern-fried tofu cutlets with mashed potatoes, un-turkey club.

Summary & Comments There are few vegetarian restaurants of merit in New York, but this is a notable exception. Chef/owner Kate Halpern cooks with a deft, knowing touch; her grilled vegetable hero is a knockout, her hummus assertively pungent and garlicky, and her mock meat dishes (made from carefully marinated tofu) both delicious and convincingly meatlike. Though the regular menu is reliable, daily specials are more hit-and-miss. Expect the usual spacy vegetarian restaurant service (it must be the meat deprivation). Kate's was a pioneer in the new restaurant row that's cropped up on formerly scary Avenue B; it's no longer a frightening area.

Kway Tiow Thai ★★★★

THAI | INEXPENSIVE | QUALITY ★★★★½ | VALUE ★★★★ | ZONE 17

83-47 Dongan Avenue, Elmhurst; (718) 476-6743

Customers Thai locals, questing aficionados **Reservations** Accepted **When to Go** Anytime **Entrée Range** $6.95–$22.95 **Payment** Cash only **Service Rating** ★★★★ **Friendliness Rating** ★★★★★ **Bar** None **Wine Selection** None **Dress** Casual **Disabled Access** Small step in; tight route to accessible rest room

Lunch Monday–Friday, 10:15 a.m.–3 p.m.

Dinner Monday–Thursday, 3–11 p.m.; Friday, 3–10:15 p.m.

Lunch & Dinner Saturday and Sunday, 10:15 a.m.–11:15 p.m.

Setting & Atmosphere A warm, well-lit, immaculate little dining room, with a few hard-to-find Thai products on display. Certainly not elegant, but invitingly bright and cheery in this neighborhood of inexpensive holes-in-the-walls. Comfortable seating.

House Specialties Start with larb (pronounced "lab"), ground pork with plenty of red onion, mint, lime, and pepper. All noodle dishes are beyond wonderful (pad thai is a revelation, with flavors fresh and focused, not all sweet and gunky like elsewhere). Chinese broccoli with crispy pork (really meaty cracklings) is amazing, and you can't go wrong with any other entrées (don't miss the curries, though). Specials of the day (often smoky, marinated pieces of roast chicken or Manila clams in a succulent brown sauce) are always good. Iced tea (served in a tall glass with milk) is bright orange, aromatic, and slightly smoky; Thai iced coffee is as rich and delicious as melted ice cream.

Other Recommendations Soups are good-not-great (but do feature nice, fresh galangal), and skip the stuffed chicken wings. For dessert, they offer "toast": thick-cut good white bread carefully, evenly toasted and carefully, evenly spread with butter and a light sprinkling of sugar (and, optionally, a light drenching of condensed milk), and it's a far cry from the stuff served with eggs in diners. There are also shaved ice desserts (choose from a large bar of toppings, including various beans, jellies, syrups, and squiggly things).

Do not by any means miss the fried bananas if they have them (they'll be on a platter by the cash register). They are a peak experience.

Summary & Comments There is no great—and precious little decent—Thai food in Manhattan. Long Tan and Thai Café in Brooklyn are good, but Kway Tiow alone is world-class. Not coincidentally, it's also one of the only Thai restaurants in town patronized by a largely Thai clientele. There is a battle among ethnic food devotees as to which is more important: authenticity or pure deliciousness. This place offers tons of both. Throw in friendly, sincere service by a family staff that clearly takes great pride in what they're doing, and you have an unbeatable combo. Kway Tiow Thai is very much worth a trip from anywhere in the city. The restaurant is a quick walk from the G/R subway (Elmhurst Avenue stop). Nearby and just as great (what a neighborhood!): **Ping's** (see profile) for Cantonese, and **Captain King** (82–39 Broadway; (718) 429-2828) for Shanghai/Taiwanese (and the best dumplings in town).

Lady Mendl's Tea Salon

TEAROOM | MODERATE | QUALITY ★★★★ | VALUE ★★★ | ZONE 7

56 Irving Place; (212) 533-4466

Customers Hotel guests, locals **Reservations** Accepted **When to Go** Anytime **Entrée Range** $30 prix fixe **Payment** All major credit cards **Service Rating** ★★ **Friendliness Rating** ★★★½ **Bar** Beer, wine, champagne, port, sherry **Wine Selection** Very small **Dress** Nice casual **Disabled Access** No

Open Wednesday–Friday, seatings at 3 and 4 p.m.; Saturday and Sunday, seatings at 2 and 4:30 p.m.

Setting & Atmosphere This tearoom, located in the pricey Inn at Irving Place, aims for an upscale English boardinghouse look. Unlike some of the Midtown hotel teas, this room—equipped with a working fireplace—is whisper-quiet.

House Specialties A five-course tea, with all the usual fixtures: crustless sandwiches of cucumber and smoked salmon; pâtés; warm scones; clotted cream; jams; tarts; and chocolate mousse cake, all served with a pot of tea per guest.

Entertainment & Amenities People-watching; The Inn at Irving Place is an exclusive hotel, so high-powered and celebrity guests are common.

Summary & Comments The food is nearly irreproachable; sandwiches are properly fussy, scones (perhaps the best item) taste homemade, and chocolate mousse cake is far better than the usual. There is a wide selection of teas and herbal infusions—all fancier than on-the-shelf brands—and each guest is served from one of the handsome antique pots collected by the owners. As you'd expect at a proper tea, everything's served on bone china. The one thing particularly out of character for a tea room is the increasing number of bridal and baby showers held in the space.

La Boite en Bois ★★½

FRENCH | MODERATE | QUALITY ★★★½ | VALUE ★★★★ | ZONE 10

75 West 68th Street (Central Park West and Columbus Avenue); (212) 874-2705

Customers Loyal locals, Lincoln Center attendees **Reservations** Recommended **When to Go** Anytime **Entrée Range** $32 per person **Payment** Cash and personal check **Service Rating** ★★★ **Friendliness Rating** ★★★ **Bar** Full service **Wine Selection** Good range, good prices **Dress** Casual **Disabled Access** No

Brunch Sunday, 11:30 a.m.–2:30 p.m. (except summer)

Lunch Daily, 11:30 a.m.–2:30 p.m. (except summer)

Dinner Monday–Saturday, 5:30–11:30 p.m.; Sunday (except summer), 4–10 p.m.

Setting & Atmosphere This cute, cozy, hole-in-the-wall bistro takes you from the sidewalks of Manhattan right into the French countryside. Only a few blocks from Lincoln Center, it's no wonder this is a preconcert favorite.

House Specialties Rack of lamb au jus; French string bean with wild mushroom salad; breast of duck with wild rice; tiny quail with lentils; seafood crêpe with tomato coulis; praline mousse.

Other Recommendations Pan-roasted chicken with herbs; pot-au-feu de poisson; côte de veau grillée au Calvados; crème brûlée.

Summary & Comments Popular with concertgoers in the know, this small space can get quite crowded, but by 7:45 p.m. it clears out and quiets down. The pretheater menu runs for $29, but an even better deal is three courses of your choice for $32 with no time constraints. The bread is wonderfully warm and tasty, the service personal and attentive, but the menu needs updating and the food, though decent, could use some fresh legs or at least a kick in the rear to get it going.

Le Bernardin ★★★★½

FISH/FRENCH | VERY EXPENSIVE | QUALITY ★★★★ | VALUE ★★★ | ZONE 8

155 West 51st Street (between Sixth and Seventh Avenues); (212) 489-1515
www.le-bernardin.com

Customers Business, local **Reservations** Required **When to Go** Anytime **Entrée Range** Dinner is prix fixe only, $75; $120 for the 7-course tasting menu; prix fixe lunch, $32–$43 **Payment** All major credit cards **Service Rating** ★★★★ **Friendliness Rating** ★★★★ **Bar** Full service **Wine Selection** Excellent **Dress** Dressy; jackets required for men **Disabled Access** Yes

Lunch Monday–Friday, noon–2:30 p.m.

Dinner Monday–Thursday, 5:30–11 p.m.; Friday and Saturday, 5:30–11:30 p.m.

Setting & Atmosphere Formal elegance, without arrogance, suffuses this grand space, and the clientele dress and act accordingly—this is, unmistakably, a luxurious setting for truly upscale dining. Blue-gray walls, adorned with fine classic maritime paintings in ornate frames, rise to a teak ceiling. Small roses top tables, handsomely set and graciously spaced.

House Specialties Yellowfin tuna carpaccio; lemon-splashed slivers of fluke with chives and lemon juice; warm lobster timbale in champagne-chive nage; seared, rare hamachi over sweet cherry tomato, onion, and portobello escabeche; steamed black bass with fresh coriander, ginger, and crab vermicelli in a tangy spiced citrus broth; spice-crusted cobia, duck sauce, sauté of cavaillon melon and preserved ginger; warm chocolate tarte with melting whipped cream and dark chocolate sauce.

Other Recommendations Spanish mackerel tartare topped with osetra caviar; shaved geoduck clam marinated with wasabi and soy-ginger dressing; pikytoe crab with green tomatoes and preserved lemon in a chilled gazpacho sauce; warm barbecue eel, sautéed black trumpet mushrooms, and chive blossoms; poached skate with caramelized baby fennel ragoût; lobster tail with shrimp sambal sauce and roasted mangoes; pan-roasted codfish on a bed of braised sweet peppers in their sweet and sour jus; sautéed Brazilian dorade, soft fresh corn purée, aged sherry, and portobello jus; passion fruit crêpe soufflé and Grand Marnier ice cream.

Summary & Comments Flawless fish, flawless service. Another New York candidate for number one—whether restaurant, fish restaurant, or French restaurant. Only the very finest fish and celestial shellfish are accorded the honor of appearing at table here, and these stars of the sea are prepared with panache and perfection by Eric Ripert, who has reached the same glorious gastronomic heights as Gilbert Le Coze, his renowned predecessor. Trying to choose from among the wide assortment of appetizers and entrées is like trying to choose a member of the Dream Team for your fantasy basketball team—you just can't go wrong. Steamed black bass is one of the best dishes in Manhattan; with soft citrus notes and fresh coriander that gives it an Indian edge, its subtle complexity will have you shaking your head in disbelief that food could ever be this good. Le Bernardin is on another level. Even the service is eerily psychic; simply stare at the back of your waiter's head as he walks 20 feet away and he'll turn around. To ease the stress of picking your own dishes, it might be best to go with one of the tasting menus. They may be ridiculously expensive, but if there was ever a place to justify such an expense, this is it. Eric Ripert also consulted on the menu for a restaurant called **Geisha** (33 East 61st Street; (212) 734-2676).

Le Cirque 2000   ★★★★

FRENCH | VERY EXPENSIVE | QUALITY ★★★★½ | VALUE ★★★ | ZONE 9

455 Madison Avenue (in the New York Palace Hotel); (212) 303-7788
www.lecirque.com

Customers Local, celebs, New York's social elite **Reservations** Recommended **When to Go** Anytime **Entrée Range** $26–$34 **Payment** All major credit cards **Service Rating** ★★★★ **Friendliness Rating** ★★★ **Bar** Full service **Wine Selection** Very good, and a wide range of prices **Dress** Dress-up time **Disabled Access** Yes

Lunch Monday–Saturday, 11:45 a.m.–2:30 p.m.

Dinner Daily, 5:30 p.m.–midnight

Setting & Atmosphere Any restraint Adam Tihany demonstrated in the low-key decoration of Jean-Georges, he's made up for in spades (Technicolor spades, that is) here. The grand, stately, turn-of-the-19th-century rooms of the Villard Houses that make up part of the Palace Hotel have been left in all their Gilded Age, chandeliered, marbled splendor. But Mr. Tihany has cleverly inserted a circus into the heart of these baronial walls: looping steel tubing with neon accents over the futuristic bar, high-backed purple chairs with multicolored clown buttons in the main dining room, red and white light columns in the grill room that complement the red and yellow banquettes and red high-backed, yellow-clown-buttoned chairs. The effect of these whimsical juxtapositions is giddy, over the top, but fabulous.

House Specialties Foie gras sauté; fish soup; cassolette of baby vegetables with black truffles; sweetbreads and veal kidney with shallot confit and caramelized endive; "paupiette" of black sea bass in crispy potatoes with braised leeks and Barolo sauce; duck magret; crème brûlée; Le Cirque stove.

Other Recommendations Lobster salad "Le Cirque"; potato gnocchi with scallops and lima beans; jumbo lump crabmeat with guacamole, peas, and tomatoes; risotto with lobster, coral, and rosemary; halibut fillet; chicken fricasée with ginger; Jacques' Napoleon; bomboloni.

Summary & Comments If there were any doubts that Sirio Maccioni could bring all the posh pizzazz and superlative food of his original Le Cirque to this new location, they have vanished. If a restaurant, like love, can be better the second time around, this is it. Maccioni, the magical master of this three-ring culinary circus, has truly done it again. Chef Sottha Khunn's creations are sensational, and Jacques Torres' desserts both dazzle and amuse (be sure to check out the chocolate stove). The service is superb, and the well-known faces that frequented the 65th Street establishment are back in force. It's usually quite difficult to get a reservation—keep trying.

Les Halles ★★½

FRENCH BISTRO/STEAK | EXPENSIVE | QUALITY ★★★½ | VALUE ★★★ | ZONE 7

411 Park Avenue South (between 28th and 29th Streets); (212) 679-4111
www.leshalles.net

Customers Locals, professionals **Reservations** Recommended **When to Go** Anytime **Entrée Range** $14.50–$28 **Payment** All major credit cards **Service Rating** ★★ **Friendliness Rating** ★★★ **Bar** Full service **Wine Selection** Well chosen; some good values **Dress** Casual **Disabled Access** Yes

Lunch & Dinner Daily, noon–midnight.

Setting & Atmosphere Don't expect a quiet, romantic evening for two at this boisterous, Gramercy-area French bistro/butcher shop. Patrons are packed elbow to elbow like, dare we say, cattle, and the noise quotient is high throughout most of the night. The glass-enclosed meat case at the front is a nice touch, and the room has a familiar, well-worn feel with dozens of posters and photos lining the walls. Throw in some cigarette smoke and you might as well be in Paris.

House Specialties Endive salad with apples, walnuts, and Roquefort cheese; steak frites; boudin aux pommes (blood sausage, caramelized apples); Onglet (hanger steak); warm chocolate and banana tart.

Other Recommendations Tarte Alsacienne (caramelized onion tart); homemade rillettes; steak tartare; moules marinières (mussels steamed in white wine); rib-eye steak; fresh apple tart with vanilla ice cream.

Summary & Comments Les Halles proves that predictability can be a good thing. If you're in the mood for a dependable bistro menu and train terminal atmosphere, Les Halles should be your call. Appetizers are win some, lose some. A good starter is the endive and arugula salad with walnuts and a bit of cheese. Chunks of fresh apples make this a refreshing beginning and serve to get rid of some of the impending guilt that arrives with the artery-clogging meat. Steaks here may not be up to par with Peter Luger's or any of the city's other big-name establishments, but they're good for what they are, and at $16.50, the steak frites is a great deal. Frites come with every steak and are meaty and delicious.

Margon Restaurant ★★

CUBAN CAFETERIA | INEXPENSIVE | QUALITY ★★★½ | VALUE ★★★★★ | ZONE 8

136 West 46th Street; (212) 354-5013

Customers Local, businessmen **Reservations** Not accepted **When to Go** Quick lunch **Entrée Range** $5.25–$7.25 (breakfast, $2–$5) **Payment** Cash only **Service Rating** ★★½ **Friendliness Rating** ★★★ **Bar** None **Wine Selection** None **Dress** Casual **Disabled Access** No

Breakfast Monday–Saturday, 7–10:30 a.m.

Lunch Monday–Friday, 10:30 a.m.–5 p.m.; Saturday, 10:30 a.m.–2:30 p.m.; closed Sunday

Setting & Atmosphere A harshly lit, bare-bones hustle-your-tray-through-the-line basement cafeteria.

House Specialties Roast chicken, octopus salad, rice and beans, fried plantains; all the standard-issue Latino luncheonette fare, but good!

Summary & Comments If you need to catch a quick lunch in Midtown, this place will get you in and out in a jiffy (don't sweat long lines; they move quickly), but patrons' fast-shoveling forks belie the high quality of the food. Everything's very fresh and made with care. There are precious few Latin lunch counters left in this part of town, and friendly, efficient Margon is a proud bastion.

Menchanko-Tei ★★

JAPANESE | INEXPENSIVE | QUALITY ★★★½ | VALUE ★★★★ | ZONES 8, 9

43–45 West 55th Street (between Fifth and Sixth avenues); (212) 247-1585
131 East 45th Street (between Lexington and Third avenues); (212) 986-6805
www.menchankotei.com

Customers Locals and local workers **Reservations** 45th Street: accepted; 55th Street: Only for parties of 5 or more **When to Go** If possible, avoid the 1 p.m. rush **Entrée Range** $7.75–$13 **Payment** All major credit cards **Service Rating** ★★★★ **Friendliness Rating** ★★ **Bar** Full service, with several sakes, Japanese beers, and spirits like shochu **Wine Selection** House **Dress** Nice casual **Disabled Access** Difficult (rest rooms not accessible) at both branches

Breakfast 55th Street: Tuesday–Sunday, 7–10 a.m

Lunch 55th Street: Daily, 11:30 a.m.–5 p.m.

Dinner 55th Street: Monday–Saturday, 5 p.m.–12:30 a.m.; Sunday, 11:30 a.m.– 11:30 p.m.

Lunch & Dinner 45th Street: Monday–Saturday, 11:30 a.m.–12:30 a.m.; Sunday, 11:30 a.m.–11:30 p.m.

Setting & Atmosphere Noodles are taken very seriously here, and the dignified décor immediately signals that this ain't no fooling around. The 55th Street Menchanko-Tei has stylish Midtown Japanese restaurant ambience: low ceilings, nice wood floors, halogen lights, some cursory Oriental tchotchkes, a low bar in front of an open (sparkling) kitchen, and a long line of tables for two and four (there's also a more peaceful dining room in back, painted a friendly mustard yellow). The 45th Street branch—airier and more Western—is also designed with a careful touch: higher ceilings, green carpet, potted plants, and a small dining spillover area upstairs near the rest rooms. Clientele in both is mixed, but predominantly Japanese.

House Specialties Several variations on souply themes: Menchanko itself is an egg noodle soup of profound delicacy; it can also be prepared with a miso base, and additions can include hot, pickled vegetables; fish balls; or a kitchen sink version called tokusei menchanko, dominated by chunks of fresh, flaky salmon that assertively flavor the delicate broth. There are two ramen soups, both topped with a succulent slice of yakibuta pork: hakata is a white broth (gingery and simple, but with great balance), and kikuzo is soy-based (the plainest of all, but no less worthy). Zousui soups are made with plump rice rather than noodles; Kimchi Zousui is particularly good, homey, and quite spicy from the hot, pickled cabbage. Nagasaki saraudon is frizzy, thin, fried noodles with a sweetish seafood sauce; Nagasaki chanpon is the same, but in soup.

Other Recommendations There are a handful of non-noodle options, few of them in a class with the soups: onigiri (rice balls wrapped in nori seaweed, containing stuff like umeboshi, salmon, or preserved cod fish roe) are perhaps too subtle for the unaccustomed palate. Oden are small appetizer plates; check out kinchaku—a deliciously exotic cake of fried tofu stuffed with sticky rice paste in a soothing broth/sauce. There are also side orders like yakibuta (pork), menma (tender bamboo shoots with a slightly caramelized flavor), or kimchi (hot, pickled cabbage). Ask for some yuzu-kosho—a red pepper paste flavored with yuzu fruit—to spoon into the soups.

A fuller menu is served nights at the 55th Street location; 45th Street offers Onigashima, a more full-service restaurant, upstairs.

Summary & Comments Fans of the film *Tampopo* will feel at home here in NYC's best Japanese noodle soup restaurant, where noodles are made with great care for a discerning clientele. These loyal customers come often; the 55th Street branch will sell regulars a full bottle of booze to keep on reserve (they have three months to drain it). Soups are served in heavy iron kettles, with a wooden ladle for transference to your bowl. Slurp loudly (silent noodle scarfing is an insult to the chef), but get out quick; despite the deliciousness, the well-appointed décor, the polite service, and the nonbargain prices (soups run as high as $13), this type of restaurant is considered fast food, so lingering is discouraged. The oden are better at 55th Street, but the soups may be slightly more complex at 45th Street (considered by many the superior location). Another great noodle place is **Sobaya** (229 East 9th Street; (212) 533-6966).

Mesa Grill ★★★

AMERICAN/SOUTHWEST | EXPENSIVE | QUALITY ★★★½ | VALUE ★★★ | ZONE 7

102 Fifth Avenue (15th and 16th streets); (212) 807-7400 www.mesagrill.com

Customers Local, business **Reservations** Recommended **When to Go** Anytime
Entrée Range $18–$34; appetizers, $7.50–$14.50 **Payment** All major credit cards
Service Rating ★★★ **Friendliness Rating** ★★ **Bar** Full service, with 20 different kinds of tequila **Wine Selection** Good **Dress** Casual; some business at lunch; no jacket required **Disabled Access** Yes, downstairs

Brunch Saturday and Sunday, 11:30 a.m.–3 p.m.

Lunch Monday–Friday, noon–2:30 p.m.

Dinner Monday–Sunday, 5:30–10:30 p.m.

Setting & Atmosphere Substantial columns, painted with bands of southwestern colors, hold up the two-story high ceiling. The lime green and yellow walls sprout tin lighting fixtures, and the banquettes are covered in a kitsch-cute "Hi-ho Silver" design. All this to let you know that you're in for spicy southwestern fare. The tables are close, and the noise level can rear up and buck like a bronco. Quieter late in the evening and at brunch.

House Specialties   Shrimp and roasted garlic corn tamale; spicy salmon tartare with plantain croutons and cilantro oil; blue corn tortilla–crusted red snapper; potato-corn taco and smoked red pepper–grilled onion relish.

Other Recommendations   Barbecue chicken quesadilla; grilled squid and Vidalia onion salad with smoked tomatoes and green chile vinaigrette; spicy maple-glazed veal chop with red onion marmalade and blue corn sweet potato taco; grilled striped bass with roasted corn–red pepper relish and buttermilk onion rings; miniature ice cream sandwiches.

Summary & Comments   Celebrity-chef Bobby Flay has pizzazz aplenty, and this smart venue is the perfect place for him to strut his southwestern stuff. Every dish has a spicy regional accent—even the romaine salad has red chile croutons, the red snapper is crusted with blue corn tortillas, and there's blue corn again in the biscotti. The appetizers are especially interesting and pretty on their Fiesta-ware plates, and the main courses are large enough to satisfy the hungry cowboys in the cookhouse, though some of the combos can be a little over the top. The clientele is trendy, the atmosphere animated.

Meskerem   ★★★

ETHIOPIAN | INEXP/MOD | QUALITY ★★★½ | VALUE ★★★½ | ZONES 4, 8

124 Macdougal Street (between Bleecker and West 3rd streets); (212) 777-8111
468 West 47th Street (between Ninth and Tenth avenues); (212) 664-0520
www.meskeremrestaurant.com

Customers   Local, ethnic, regulars   **Wine Selection**   Very small, but does offer Ethiopian honey wine   **Reservations**   Not required, unless large group; Village doesn't take reservations   **When to Go**   Anytime   **Bar**   Full service   **Entrée Range** $8–$13.50   **Dress**   Casual   **Payment**   MC, Visa   **Service Rating** ★★★½   **Friendliness Rating** ★★★★   **Disabled Access**   No for Village, yes for midtown

Open   Midtown: 11:30 a.m.–11:30 p.m.; Village: 11:30 a.m.–11 p.m.; lunch special both locations, Monday–Friday, 11:30 a.m.–3:30 p.m.

Setting & Atmosphere   Cheery, casual and almost always full of happy people sharing their food and looking almost guilty for not having to use utensils. Ethiopian prints, artifacts, and cloths can be found in both locations.

House Specialties   Shero wat (ground chickpeas with ground red pepper–berbere sauce); yebeg alecha (lamb with ginger, garlic and curry); kifto (chopped beef with butter and mitmita–ground chili pepper sauce, often served rare or raw); miser wat (lentils with garlic, onions and berbere sauce).

Other Recommendations   Timatim salad (tomatoes, onion, scallions, peppers); Meskerem combo dish with beef, lamb, and vegetables prepared in various ways.

Summary & Comments   This is an ideal place for at least four people with clean hands. This way you can try several dishes and have them all placed before you, collectively, on a huge circular platter, and then everyone gets to dig in on one plate using the injera (slightly sour, spongy, flat, soft bread made from an Ethiopian grian called tef) as the tool to collect, scoop, and place food into your mouth (or that of a friend's). Utensils are available for those unable or unwilling to suspend their usual cultural habits. A recommended way to order is one vegetarian combo entrée plus two to three meat entrées to get a full spectrum of tastes. Individual plates aren't provided unless you ask. You can wait by the bar (although it's quite small) for your table and order an Ethiopian honey wine as an aperitif.

Mr. Broadway Kosher Deli ★★★

JEWISH DELI | MODERATE | QUALITY ★★★★ | VALUE ★★★★★ | ZONE 8

1372 Broadway (between 37th and 38th streets); (212) 921-2152

Customers Locals, professionals **Reservations** Accepted **When to Go** Anytime **Entrée Range** $4.25–$21.75 **Payment** All major credit cards **Service Rating** ★★★ **Friendliness Rating** ★★★ **Bar** Beer and wine **Wine Selection** Small (kosher) **Dress** Casual **Disabled Access** Fair

Lunch & Dinner Sunday–Friday, 11 a.m.–10 p.m.; closed Saturday

Setting & Atmosphere From the front, this looks like just another of the area's many kosher fast-food spots, but the rear is classic Jewish deli, a bustling cavern with darting waiters, tables crammed with pickles and cole slaw, and regulars who look like they eat a lot of pastrami trying to squeeze their way through the tight floor plan.

House Specialties Outstanding garlicky baba ghanoush (eggplant salad); potato knishes; couscous; kasha varnichkes (oniony buckwheat with bow-tie noodles); potato pancakes (deep fried, but good); homemade french fries; chicken soup with matzo balls; falafel; derma (rich spicy stuffing in sausage casing); fried "Moroccan cigars" (pastry flutes stuffed with finely minced meat); homemade gefilte fish.

Other Recommendations There's a terrific self-service Middle Eastern salad bar up front, for take-out ($3.99/pound) or to accompany falafel and shwarma sandwiches.

Summary & Comments Mr. Broadway Kosher Deli & Restaurant is known by many names: it's also Me Tsu Yan Kosher Chinese Restaurant and Chez Lanu, serving North African dishes. The confluence of cuisines makes for some strange culinary juxtapositions, from customers smearing hummus on their hot dogs to the Moroccan couscous served with a homely piece of Eastern European roast chicken riding on top. For both Middle Eastern and deli specialties, Mr. Broadway is a winner. The kitchen somehow manages to turn out perfectly balanced baba ghanoush and flaky potato knishes without watering down the soulfulness of chicken soup or tender gefilte fish. Corned beef is, of course, of paramount importance in a Jewish deli; theirs is good and well cut but perhaps a bit too lean (everything's a tad lighter than usual here; perhaps it's the Sephardic influence). Chinese dishes—glatt kosher, like everything else—are handily available for those for whom real Chinese isn't an option. This place is only a few years old and unpedigreed in NYC deli history, but the more venerated delis seem grimily past their primes, while Mr. Broadway thrives.

Molly's ★★★

IRISH PUB FOOD | MODERATE | QUALITY ★★★★ | VALUE ★★★★ | ZONE 7

287 Third Avenue; (212) 889-3361

Customers Locals **Reservations** Limited **When to Go** Anytime **Entrée Range** $10.50–$21.50 **Payment** All major credit cards **Service Rating** ★★½ **Friendliness Rating** ★★ **Bar** Full **Wine Selection** Small selection **Dress** Casual **Disabled Access** Fair

Lunch & Dinner Monday–Saturday, 11 a.m.–4 a.m.; Sunday, noon– 4 a.m.

Setting & Atmosphere Classic Irish pub; woody and snug, complete with fireplace. Lots of booths and tables (the largest, a round table seating eight, is handy for after-work get-togethers).

House Specialties Cheeseburgers, shepherd's pie and chicken pot pie, respectable steak, mashed potatoes, and most fried items.

Other Recommendations Avoid specials; stick with the main menu. Ask for fried onions on your cheeseburger (they're sensational), and request the special walnut dressing on your salad.

Summary & Comments The area has plenty of anonymous Irish bar/restaurants to choose from, but this is the standout. Typical pub food is grand (best cheeseburgers and shepherd's pie in Manhattan), and they transcend type with touches like a surprisingly worthy bread basket and fresh (gasp!), not overcooked vegetable sides. Guinness stout, properly creamy and not overchilled, is among the best in town.

Molyvos

GREEK | EXPENSIVE | QUALITY ★★★★ | VALUE ★★★★ | ZONE 8

871 Seventh Avenue (between 55th and 56th streets); (212) 582-7500
www.molyvos.com

Customers Business, local **Reservations** Recommended **When to Go** Anytime **Entrée Range** $18–$34 **Payment** All major credit cards **Service Rating** ★★★ **Friendliness Rating** ★★★ **Bar** Full service; excellent ouzo selection **Wine Selection** Good; especially interesting Greek selections **Dress** Business, casual **Disabled Access** Fair; two steps to the dining room

Lunch & Dinner Sunday–Friday, noon–11:30 p.m.; Saturday, noon– 11:30 p.m.

Setting & Atmosphere An airy, comfortable Greek taverna with a bright front room and substantial bar that leads into a large, somewhat dimmer main dining room. Greek key panels top stenciled planks, the terra-cotta sponged walls are dotted with black-and-white photos of Molyvos, and all is accented with Hellenic objects, plates, amphorae, glass bottles, and the capital of a marble column.

House Specialties Marinated lamb shanks; moussaka; grilled baby octopus; meze; wood-grilled whole fish; loukoumades (dessert fritters with honey sauce).

Other Recommendations Rabbit stifado (rabbit stew with red wine and pearl onions); cabbage dolmades; grilled jumbo prawns; steamed mussels; ocean blackfish plaki; semolina and almond cake.

Summary & Comments With Molyvos, John Livanos (also owner of Oceana) pays homage to his hometown on the Greek island of Lesbos. The result is wonderful, authentic Greek cuisine and a great change of pace from more traditional New York upscale dining. The mouth-watering mezedes (little bites) such as tzatziki and grilled, marinated sardines alone can make a meal, but don't limit yourself or you could miss out on such great dishes as grilled baby octopus. Smoky and packed with flavor, the octopus needs little else to satisfy. With this dish and others, chef James Botsacos smartly chooses not to overpower the food with different flavors but instead to subtly complement it and entice the true flavors out. Simplicity never tasted so good. The super-fast service and great food make this an excellent stop either before or after a concert at Carnegie Hall.

Montrachet ★★★½

FRENCH BISTRO | EXPENSIVE | QUALITY ★★★★ | VALUE ★★★½ | ZONE 2

239 West Broadway (between Walker and White); (212) 219-2777
www.myriadrestaurantgroup.com

Customers Locals, professionals, oenophiles **Reservations** Necessary **When to Go** Anytime; Friday lunch **Entrée Range** $24–$36; tasting menu, $79 for 4 courses **Payment** All major credit cards **Service Rating** ★★★ **Friendliness Rating** ★★★★ **Bar** Full service **Wine Selection** One of the best in the city and top 100 in the country **Dress** Dressy casual to business **Disabled Access** Three steps up to enter

Lunch Friday, noon–2 p.m.

Dinner Monday–Saturday, 5:30–10 p.m.

Setting & Atmosphere This three-room Tribeca space is subtle and at ease. The front room boasts comfy plum-colored banquettes with narrow mirrors running just on top and modern art on the walls. The two back rooms remain simple with pale blue walls offset against dark wood tables and chairs. The mood reflects this easy relaxation and laid-back comfort.

House Specialties The menu changes regularly. Examples of some of the staples include warm oysters with champagne sauce and osetra caviar; salmon with fresh dill, cucumber, and mustard; roasted chicken with potato purée and fennel; crème brûlée; and chocolate brioche with pistachio ice cream.

Other Recommendations Coriander-encrusted red snapper with red peppers; foie gras; roasted lobster salad with sweetcorn, bacon, and chanterelles; chilled rhubarb soup and Long Island Duck.

Summary & Comments Often overlooked because of its hard-to-find Tribeca location, Montrachet quietly goes about its business, serving great food with an award-winning wine list in a low-key atmosphere. Chef Harold Moore has maintained the traditional French menu. The restaurant attracts a varied clientele, including the conservative business types, the glamorous, and the more casual. The food here is excellent in its own right, but the wine accompaniment and advice of the sommelier is part and parcel of the Montrachet experience. True, the wine itself can, at least, double the bill, but the assumption is that if you've decided to dine here, then you're well-prepared to give your wallet a decent airing. There's no need to be intimidated. The sommelier is patient, helpful and eager to help, advise, and explain the merits and drawbacks of any bottle. Descriptions such as "full-bodied," "oak-filled bouquet," and "fruity" have never had so many nuances. The chef is a little over-indulgent with salt, but the fresh ingredients and varied mix of herbs and spices help keep a balance. The chicken is absolutely melt-in-your-mouth succulent. Cappuccino is surprisingly disappointing, but the scrumptious petits-fours and desserts will keep you happy. Make sure to try some of the chef's complimentary preparations for tasting. Note that the lunch menu on Friday is similar to that of dinner's offerings, except the salmon is prepared differently.

Namaaskar ★½

INDIAN | INEXPENSIVE | QUALITY ★★★½ | VALUE ★★★★½ | ZONE 2

337 West Broadway (at Grand Street); (212) 625-1112

Customers Tribeca locals **Reservations** Accepted **When to Go** Lunch only! **Entrée Range** $9.95–$17.95; all-you-can-eat lunch buffet, $7.95 ($8.95 Sunday) **Payment** All major credit cards **Service Rating** ★★½ **Friendliness Rating** ★★½ **Bar** Full service **Wine Selection** Surprisingly good **Dress** Casual **Disabled Access** None

Lunch Buffet: Monday–Friday, noon–3 p.m.; Saturday, noon–4 p.m.

Dinner Sunday–Thursday, 5–11 p.m.; Friday and Saturday, 5 p.m.– midnight

Setting & Atmosphere Cramped at street level, but a casually elegant upstairs dining room has comfortable seating beside handsome antique windows framed with polished dark wood. Indian touches are scattered here and there, but they've tastefully avoided the over-the-top raj palace treatment.

House Specialties The buffet usually includes good creamy saag (spinach), and terrific tandoori chicken (if and only if you catch a fresh batch—see note below) has a properly crusty, spicy, smoky exterior and marinade thoroughly penetrating a meltingly tender interior. Raita (yogurt sauce) is extra creamy. Nan bread is mediocre, but paratha is better (though it's an ultracaloric oily kind). Speaking of oil, beware that dals (bean dishes, including delicious black lentils) are pretty rich with ghee (clarified butter). Lamb is served only at the Sunday buffet, which costs $1 more.

Other Recommendations Don't order from the menu (inconsistent in the extreme), and don't go for dinner (you'll be served buffet remainders in various guises).

Summary & Comments This is one of the best Indian buffet lunches in town; not for its lavishness, but for its comparatively high quality. Service is bumpy, alternately sycophantic and neglectful. Watch carefully for new batches of tandoori chicken and bread descending from the upstairs kitchen; freshness makes a huge difference.

New Pasteur ★★★½

VIETNAMESE | INEXPENSIVE | QUALITY ★★★★ | VALUE ★★★★★ | ZONE 3

85 Baxter Street; (212) 608-3656 or (212) 608-4838

Customers Ethnic, locals, foodies **Reservations** Suggested **When to Go** Avoid the peak hours of 8–10 p.m. **Entrée Range** $4.75–$11 **Payment** Cash only **Service Rating** ★★★ **Friendliness Rating** ★★½ **Bar** Beer and wine **Wine Selection** House **Dress** Casual **Disabled Access** Fair

Lunch & Dinner Daily, 11 a.m.–9:30 p.m.

Setting & Atmosphere Spare storefront with little decoration to detract from the memorable cooking. Be prepared to share tables.

House Specialties Any of the phos (elemental beef-based soups), barbecue beef (with vermicelli or on its own), shrimp rolls, fried spring rolls, barbecue shrimp roll on sugarcane, iced coffee.

Summary & Comments Year in and year out, homely New Pasteur (formerly Pho Pasteur) outclasses all new Vietnamese startups with no-nonsense first-class cooking. The barbecue beef is a marvel of gastronomic engineering, an entire beefy symphony compressed into each small nugget (wrap them in lettuce leaves, along with mint, cucumber slices, sprouts, and carroty fish sauce; the Vietnamese eat almost everything this way). If New Pasteur is full, as it often is, head up the block to larger and more upscale Nha Trang, whose food is nearly as good.

The Nice Restaurant ★★★½

CANTONESE/DIM SUM | MOD/EXP | QUALITY ★★★★½ | VALUE ★★★★ | ZONE 3

35 East Broadway; (212) 406-9510

Customers Business, families **Reservations** Suggested **When to Go** As early as possible for dim sum **Entrée Range** $10–$34 (up to $50 for specials); dim sum: $2–$6 **Payment** AMEX, VISA, MC **Service Rating** ★★★★ **Friendliness Rating** ★★½ **Bar** Beer only **Wine Selection** House **Dress** Nice casual **Disabled Access** Upstairs room not accessible; downstairs (closed Monday and Friday), one step up

Dim Sum Daily, 9 a.m.–noon

Lunch Daily, 11 a.m.–4 p.m.

Dinner Daily, 4–10:30 p.m.

Setting & Atmosphere Not as over-the-top as some of the more garish Hong Kong–style pavilions, the Nice is done up mostly in burgundy red (imagine a Chinese version of an upscale suburban catering hall). Noise levels run high, but it's an excited buzz, emanating from avid eaters.

House Specialties Minced conch and seafood with coconut curry sauce in conch shell; crispy seafood roll, minced squab with pine nuts in lettuce leaf; baby veal chops hot pot; tofu, minced chicken, and salted fish casserole; sautéed snow pea shoots with shredded dried scallops; stewed abalone in oyster sauce; crispy shrimp with walnuts.

Other Recommendations Dim sum: garlic har gow (garlic shrimp dumplings).

Summary & Comments The top end of Cantonese cuisine recalls that of France, what with the complexities of flavor, intricate presentation, attention to aroma and aftertaste, and strikingly unusual juxtapositions. The Nice Restaurant consistently attains these lofty heights; order well and you'll taste fancy Cantonese/Hong Kong banquet cooking at its best. Any of the above list of sensational—and largely off-menu—specialties will leave you forever convinced that Chinese food is much more than General Tso or shrimp in lobster sauce. The Nice puts on some of Chinatown's better dim sum, too, but arrive early, avoid fried things, and don't forget to special-order the amazing garlic shrimp dumplings from a manager.

Nobu ★★★★

JAPANESE | EXPENSIVE | QUALITY ★★★★½ | VALUE ★★★ | ZONE 2

105 Hudson Street (at Franklin Street); (212) 219-0500
www.myriadrestaurantgroup.com

Customers Local, business, celebs, ethnic **Reservations** Absolutely necessary **When to Go** Anytime **Entrée Range** $13–$31; multicourse "Omakase," chef's choice, $70 dinner, $45 lunch; sushi and sashimi à la carte, $3.50–$5 **Payment** All major credit cards **Service Rating** ★★★ **Friendliness Rating** ★★★ **Bar** Full service **Wine Selection** OK, but sipping sake might be better **Dress** Business, casual **Disabled Access** Fair; call in advance to arrange

Lunch Monday–Friday, 11:45 a.m.–2:15 p.m.

Dinner Daily, 5:45–10:15 p.m.

Setting & Atmosphere Birch tree columns, blond wood, high copper-leafed ceiling, plush banquettes, a wall of black river stones, and a large sushi counter are all part of the stunningly original million-dollar décor. Just as stunning are the number of well-known faces to be seen.

House Specialties The "Omakase" tasting dinner; toro tartar with caviar; black cod with miso; sea urchin in spinach; Matsushisa shrimp and caviar; yellowfin sashimi with jalapeño; squid "pasta" with garlic sauce.

Other Recommendations Broiled toro with spicy miso; shrimp and lobster with spicy lemon sauce; salmon tartar with caviar; sea urchin tempura; toro "to-ban" yaki.

Summary & Comments No doubt, Nobu is one of the most exciting eateries in New York—it's not the place to order simply sushi. Chef Nobuyuki Matsushisa's brilliant, innovative menu is as stunningly original as the décor and considered by some to be the city's best Japanese food, by others to be just the city's best food. The menu is huge, with over a hundred small and medium-size dishes—a grazer's paradise. Reservations are hard to come by, but you can get the same food without the formality at **Next Door Nobu.** This spot doesn't take reservations, though you may still have to wait up to an hour to get a table. Next Door is a bit more casual than the original but has many of the same menu items, including unforgettable toro tartar with caviar and everybody's favorite blackened cod with miso. You'll even find a few noodle dishes for good measure, something big brother lacks (though you can hardly call Nobu lacking).

Oceana ★★★½

FISH | EXPENSIVE | QUALITY ★★★★½ | VALUE ★★★ | ZONE 9

55 East 54th Street (between Madison and Park avenues); (212) 759-5941
www.oceanarestaurant.com

Customers Business, local **Reservations** Recommended **When to Go** Anytime **Entrée Range** Prix fixe only; lunch $45, dinner $65 **Payment** All major credit cards **Service Rating** ★★★ **Friendliness Rating** ★★★ **Parking** Garage, complimentary after 4 p.m. **Bar** Full service **Wine Selection** Excellent **Dress** Jacket and tie **Disabled Access** No

Lunch Monday–Friday, noon–2:30 p.m.

Dinner Monday–Saturday, 5:30–10:30 p.m.

Setting & Atmosphere This Midtown townhouse has been transformed into a luxury yacht, the kind captains of industry—and otherwise—and their wealthy pals ply the seas in. Downstairs, diners look out of faux windows on what might be Capri, maybe Antibes, or at a vintage ocean liner sailing by. The elegant, high-ceilinged upstairs bar serves oysters and the like and welcomes cigar smokers.

House Specialties Oysters; salmon tartare wrapped with smoked salmon and topped with osetra caviar, with pea shoots and toast points; lobster ravioli in a tomato-basil broth; seared Florida grouper fillet, fingerling potatoes, watercress, arugula, and pancetta with a whole-grain mustard vinaigrette; Oceana East Coast bouillabaisse; warm chocolate tart.

Other Recommendations Grilled marinated sardines; grilled fillet of rouget and orzo salad; soft-shell crabs (in season); jumbo lump crab cakes; Chilean sea bass steamed with ginger, soy, and fresh coriander; fresh fruit Napoleon.

Summary & Comments In case you couldn't tell from the name or the fact that you're basically seated inside a yacht, Oceana serves fish, and serves it well. Chef Rick Moonen turns out some of the best seafood in New York, drawing inspiration from around the globe, be it Asia, the Mediterranean, or down-home regional American. Regardless of the accents, Moonen's creations all speak the universal language of very good food. Unfortunately, the clientele mainly consists of what you would expect to find in such a yacht—men in suits—but service is impeccable and desserts are top-notch.

Old San Juan ★★½

PUERTO RICAN/ARGENTINEAN | INEXPENSIVE | QUALITY ★★★★ | VALUE ★★★★ |
ZONE 8

765 Ninth Avenue (51st and 52nd streets); (212) 262-7013

Customers Pretheater, ethnic, locals **Reservations** Not accepted **When to Go** Anytime **Entrée Range** $7.50–$22.95 **Payment** All major credit cards **Service Rating** ★★★ **Friendliness Rating** ★★★ **Bar** Full service **Wine Selection** Limited, heavy on the Argentinean **Dress** Pretheater, casual **Disabled Access** Everything on street level

Lunch & Dinner Sunday–Thursday, 11 a.m.–11 p.m.; Friday and Saturday, 11 a.m.– 2 a.m.

Setting & Atmosphere This addition to Ninth Avenue's restaurant roster is not big on décor. There's a luncheonette-like counter to handle the take-out crowd, plus a very small bar and a larger, low-ceilinged dining room with random Puerto Rican objects on the walls. But when you're welcomed by the owner, who says, with all sincerity, "I want you to be happy," who needs designer décor?

House Specialties Cazuela de mariscos, seafood in a casserole served over yellow rice; asopaos, soupy Puerto Rican rice stews, in various flavors; mofongo, a garlicky mound of mashed plantains and pork cracklings, with crab or roast pork; churrasco Argentino, a grilled skirt steak.

Other Recommendations Pasteles puertoriquenos, a comforting, tamalelike concoction steamed in a banana leaf; clams in garlic sauce; Argentinean empanadas; stewed goat; caramel-crusted bread pudding.

Summary & Comments Old San Juan successfully fills a rather surprising void in Manhattan's ethnic restaurant array. With its huge Puerto Rican population, the city should have more places accessible to non-natives that feature the island's hearty, savory dishes. It's crowded, but that doesn't diminish the service, which would be more than reputable in a far more expensive establishment. The daily lunch specials, at $6.50, are truly hard to beat. Similar fare can be had at the spin-off **Old San Juan Too** (Second Avenue and 26th Street; 799-9360).

Orso ★★★

NORTHERN ITALIAN | MODERATE | QUALITY ★★★½ | VALUE ★★★ | ZONE 8

322 West 46th Street; (212) 489-7212   www.orsorestaurant.com

Customers Theatergoers, theater people, locals **Reservations** Necessary at least a week in advance **When to Go** Anytime **Entrée Range** $18–$22 **Payment** Major credit cards **Service Rating** ★★★ **Friendliness Rating** ★★★ **Bar** Full service **Wine Selection** Italian only; house wine by the carafe is serviceable and well-priced. **Dress** Casual **Disabled Access** No

Brunch Sunday, noon–3 p.m.

Lunch & Dinner Daily, noon–11:30 p.m.

Setting & Atmosphere This star of Restaurant Row occupies a narrow space with a low-ceilinged bar area that leads to a vaulted back room where an active, open kitchen is fronted by a counter topped with large flower pots heaped with bread and lemons. Modesty prevails, the lights are low, adornment is limited to framed black-and-white photos, and, grazie Dio, there is soundproofing so that you can hear your dining companions and gather snatches of theatrical gossip from your neighbors.

House Specialties This menu changes daily, but there are always wonderful thin-crusted pizzas; pasta with porcini mushrooms; grilled vegetable plate; calf's liver with onions.

Other Recommendations Ultra-thin pizza bread with oil and rosemary; arugula salad with prosciutto; bruschetta; panzanella; gelato.

Summary & Comments Orso has been a winner for over 15 years, and it's still hard to get a reservation—so if this is your pretheater destination, book well in advance. The northern Italian dishes are expertly and authentically prepared, the waiters are cordial, the setting is relaxed, theater folk actually eat here, and prices are fair.

Osteria del Circo ★★★

ITALIAN | EXPENSIVE | QUALITY ★★★★ | VALUE ★★★ | ZONE 8

120 West 55th Street (between Sixth and Seventh avenues); (212) 265-3636
osteriadelcirco.com

Customers Business, local, tourist **Reservations** Recommended **When to Go** Anytime **Entrée Range** $16–$45; appetizers, $8.50–$26.50 **Payment** All major credit cards **Service Rating** ★★★ **Friendliness Rating** ★★★ **Bar** Full service; serves a top-notch "Negroni" **Wine Selection** Very good **Dress** Midtown melange of business and casual **Disabled Access** Yes

Lunch Monday–Saturday, 11:30 a.m.–2:30 p.m.

Dinner Monday–Saturday, 5:30–11 p.m.

Setting & Atmosphere From the tentlike red and yellow swaths of cloth that adorn the high ceiling to the trapeze ladder with hanging monkeys over the bar, designer Adam Tihany set out to create an atmosphere of fun—and he succeeded. The bright colors bring the room to life and the wide-open space and festive aura bring a smile to the face and create childlike anticipation for the main attraction: Mama Maccioni's food.

House Specialties Egi's ravioli; fresh Maine lobster with fennel in tomato confit, pink grapefruit, arugula, and red bliss potato salad; Zuppa alla frantoiana (Tuscan 30-vegetable soup); daily risottos; crème brûlée; bomboloncini (custard-, chocolate-, and raspberry-filled doughnuts).

Other Recommendations Cacciucco (Tuscan fish soup); any of the thin-crust pizzas; tripe stew with Parmesan; warm bread pudding.

Summary & Comments It's hard not to enjoy yourself at this Midtown Italian hot spot run by Sirio Maccioni's (Le Cirque) three sons. The room is spacious, the mood festive, and everyone seems happy to be there. The food, however, can be hit or miss. The lobster appetizer improves on the excellent lobster salad, which it replaced. The dish is a perfect marriage of contrasting flavors that come together on the palate. But the yellowfin tuna tartare is a flat and bland mush, held together barely by tender white beans on top. Egi's ravioli (a must-order), stuffed delicately with spinach, bitter greens, and sheep's milk ricotta, comes with a choice of sauces, but works best with the butter-sage. Unfortunately, agnolotti, half moon–shaped shrimp and corn ravioli in a curry sauce, fails miserably. Desserts, on the other hand, steal the show. The list is among the largest and best in the city, and the warm bread pudding topped with caramelized pecans is blissful and addictive. Although for now only a sideshow item that appears occasionally as a special on the menu, this scrumptious wonder deserves to be part of the big show.

Otto ★★★

PIZZERIA/ENOTECA | MODERATE | QUALITY ★★★★ | VALUE ★★ | ZONE 4

One Fifth Avenue (corner of 8th Street); (212) 995-9559   www.ottopizzeria.com

Customers Professionals, fashionistas, locals **Wine Selection** Extensive Italian **Reservations** Only for parties of 6 or more **When to Go** Off-peak so you won't have to wait too long **Bar** Full service **Entrée Range** $7–$14 **Dress** Casual and hip **Payment** All major credit cards **Service Rating** ★★★ **Friendliness Rating** ★★½ **Disabled Access** Yes

Open Daily, 11:30 a.m.–11:30 p.m.; pizza served all day

Setting & Atmosphere Although the space, including the bar and dining rooms, is large, the area doesn't seem cavernous, in part due to the partitions and shades of red, burgundy, and brown colors along with the wooden furniture and floor. The atmosphere is far from cozy, but it's warm with a sleek edge. Noise levels can be overwhelming when it's packed.

House Specialties Otto lardo pizza (yep—paper thin strips of pork fat and fresh rosemary over a pizza crust); gelato—all flavors; seasonal hot chocolate; fennel and bottarga pizza (fennel, fish roe, two cheeses, and tomato); Italian wine.

Other Recommendations Funghi misti (mixed mushrooms); ceci bottarga (fried chickpeas with fish roe); figs agrodolce.

Summary & Comments Mario Batali, of Babbo fame (along with a few other eateries), opened Otto in spring 2003 and it became, instantly, a controversial hit. The controversy is not about the pizzas (although the "otto lardo" pizza reached cult status in months), but more about the antipasti and whether Otto can justify charging $4–$21 for small to "grande" portions of various cuts of ham, preserved swordfish, cheese, olives, and various salads. We think the portion size is a bit lilliputian, but many of the dishes are well executed with subtle tastes worth trying in spite of the poor cost/size ratio. There are daily pizza and bruschetta specials, along with the regular "otto" and "classica" pizza varieties. Otto pizzas have untraditional toppings (see above for examples). The knowledgeable sommelier is on hand to discuss Italian wine accompaniments. As you wait for your table in the bar, we'd suggest indulging in a flight of wine for tasting. The gelato has already been graced with well-deserved awards; the olive oil, coffee, and hazelnut stracciatella flavors are superb.

Paola's ★★★

NORTHERN ITALIAN | MOD/EXP | QUALITY ★★★★ | VALUE ★★★★ | ZONE 13

245 East 84th Street; (212) 794-1890

Customers Locals **Reservations** Recommended **When to Go** Dinner only **Entrée Range** $17.95–$27 **Payment** All major credit cards **Service Rating** ★★★

Friendliness Rating ★★★ **Wine Selection** Good; a bit pricey **Dress** Casual **Disabled Access** Fair

Dinner Sunday and Monday, 6–11 p.m.; Tuesday–Saturday, 5–11 p.m.

Setting & Atmosphere Lovely and low-key; you could be sitting in a side-street establishment in Florence or Siena. The two rooms are small, the tables subtly lit with candles, the walls dark red with gilt-edged mirrors in a repeated pattern. When it fills up, the noise level can rise; in the warmer months, the noise spills out the windowed doors to the umbrella-topped tables of the sidewalk café.

House Specialties Pan-seared baby artichokes; homemade "malfatti," dumplings made of Swiss chard and ricotta; chicken and sweet sausage in wine sauce; ricotta cheesecake; cozze alla marinara (cultivated mussels sautéed in a light tomato sauce); macco (purée of fava beans over sautéed broccoli rabe with tomatoes and onions); casunsei ampezzani (beet-and-ricotta-stuffed pasta topped with poppy seeds).

Other Recommendations Mozzarella with tomatoes and basil; mixed baby greens with pears, walnuts, and shaved pecorino cheese; veal and chicken ravioli in a light tomato sauce; potato gnocchi; risotto del giorno; veal scaloppine.

Summary & Comments A cut or two above a neighborhood trattoria, this intimate Upper East Side Italian is worth the trip. The service is solicitous, and the food is authentic, homey, and very comforting. Chef/owner Paola Marracino has changed the menu very little over the years, and it's obvious she knows what she's doing with appetizers like pan-seared baby artichokes and mussels marinara that are the best versions of those dishes you'll find in Manhattan. Pastas are also first-rate, especially the stuffed variety, like ravioli and tortelloni. Great for a special occasion or a romantic night out.

The Parsonage

AMERICAN/ITALIAN | MOD/EXP | QUALITY ★★★★ | VALUE ★★★★½ | ZONE 19

74 Arthur Kill Road (corner of Clarke); (718) 351-7879

Customers Locals, Manhattanites in the know **Reservations** Recommended **When to Go** Anytime **Entrée Range** $14–$28 **Payment** All major credit cards **Service Rating** ★★★½ **Friendliness Rating** ★★★★ **Wine Selection** Modest, but varied and inexpensive **Dress** Nice casual/dressy **Disabled Access** Yes

Lunch Tuesday–Saturday, 11:30 a.m.–3 p.m.

Dinner Monday–Thursday, 5–10 p.m.; Friday and Saturday, 5–11 p.m.; Sunday, 1–9 p.m.

Setting & Atmosphere The Parsonage is an 140-year-old colonial house in the heart of historic Richmond on Staten Island. Wooden tables and chairs are arranged in a few rooms throughout the house. Features such as a beautiful old clock on a mantlepiece are included amongst the décor, whilst a few illustrations and paintings hang on the walls. The setting is uber-cozy—it's almost like being at your aunt's house for a special occasion.

House Specialties Creamy polenta with mushroom and sausage; oatmeal-crusted lamb with mint; veal ossobucco; monkfish; grilled portobella mushroom with asagi cheese.

Other Recommendations Homemade pizzas; chicken with sausage and peppers; Caesar salad; sesame-crusted salmon with shitake mushrooms; tartuffo.

Summary & Comments Proprietors Paul Montella and James McBratney really know how to make the guests feel at home. The service is unpretentious and very friendly. Their confidence and pride in both the restaurant and food are well-deserved.

The creamy polenta is delectably smooth and rich. Presentation isn't a high priority, but it seems like you can't go wrong whether you order a fish, chicken, meat, or pasta dish. Treat getting to the location as an adventure. If you take the ferry, simply get on the S74 bus which waits at the terminal, and ask the driver to tell you when you get to Arthur Kill Road; or simply ask for the Parsonage. Most people on the island know the place, and the bus stops directly outside the restaurant. Allow for a 25–30 minute bus ride.

Pastis ★★½

BISTRO/FRENCH | MODERATE | QUALITY ★★★½ | VALUE ★★★½ | ZONE 4

9 Ninth Avenue (corner of Little West 12th Street); (212) 929-4844
www.pastisny.com

Customers Locals, trendies, celebrities **Reservations** Recommended **When to Go** Anytime **Entrée Range** $9–$20 **Dress** Casual day; chic at night **Payment** All major credit cards **Service Rating** ★★★ **Friendliness Rating** ★★★½ **Bar** Full service, very popular **Wine Selection** Decent **Disabled Access** Accessible in front room and bathrooms

Breakfast Monday–Friday, 9:30–11:30 a.m.; pastries, Saturday and Sunday, 9:30–10 a.m.

Brunch Saturday and Sunday, 10 a.m.–5 p.m.

Lunch Monday–Friday, 12–5 p.m.

Dinner Daily, 6 p.m.–midnight.

Setting & Atmosphere Large restaurant with airy, crisp, bistro-French feel. Mirrors, brass, wood, and tile are the predominant materials used to decorate the expanse. Brunch and lunchtime brings a more relaxed feel to the restaurant, but come nighttime, the glitz shines in all its glory, and the front room with the bar becomes very crowded.

House Specialties Steak frites with Bearnaise sauce; onion soup, croque monsieur; croque madame; chicken sandwich with portobella and roasted peppers; crêpes suzette.

Other Recommendations Gratin dauphinois; skate; BLT with french fries; omelette.

Summary & Comments Pastis is not a place noteworthy for its food (though the coffee is excellent), but it has a high glamor factor, particularly at night. Its sibling Balthazar seems to have a better grip on food but has lost its hold on celebrities who seem to be flocking here instead. Come for brunch, get a feel for the place, and then decide if you'd like to tackle dinner here in another outfit. The bar scene is extremely lively and chic, so you could always forget dinner and stick to drinks. The food is standard, but brunch is fun if you order a drink and munch on the bread basket, a croque monsieur, or an omelette. One favorite beverage is the l'orchidee verte that consists of pastis, mint, and water; the crowning touch is its bold green color. The bathrooms are stylized for an old-fashoined, continental European feel; men and women wash their hands together in a trough-like sink, but use separate rooms for the toilets. In warm weather, sit outside where it feels a bit more relaxed (but it's harder to spot a celeb). Alternatively, you could enjoy the hyped atmosphere inside and join in on the eyeballing.

Patria ★★★½

LATIN AMERICAN | EXPENSIVE | QUALITY ★★★★ | VALUE ★★★ | ZONE 7

250 Park Avenue South (corner of 20th Street); (212) 777-6211

Customers Locals, business **Reservations** Recommended **When to Go** Anytime
Entrée Range $24–$34; tasting menu, $57; 5-course, $69; 7-course, $79 **Payment** All
major credit cards **Service Rating** ★★★ **Friendliness Rating** ★★★ **Bar** Full service **Wine Selection** Very good **Dress** Casual, business **Disabled Access** Fair; bathroom not accessible to wheelchairs

Lunch Monday–Friday, noon–3 p.m.

Dinner Monday–Thursday, 6–11 p.m.; Friday and Saturday, 5:30–midnight; Sunday,
5:30–10:30 p.m.

Setting & Atmosphere Bold and bright, animated with gold-ocher columns, colorful
mosaics on the floors and walls, big windows, big paintings, and a big bar in the center
of the action. It's cavernous and fun. There are comfortable booths and banquettes on
the lower dining tier and well-spaced tables on the two upper tiers.

House Specialties Ceviche of any kind! Ceviche Tiradito—Peruvian-style ceviche with
lime, onions and cilantro; coconut curry ceviche—lobster, shrimp, curried coconut, and aji
armarillo; Brazilian Vatapa—red snapper in coconut milk, with shrimp, cashews, and yuca.

Other Recommendations Black truffle tamal; plantain chips; churrasco—beef
steak with chimichurri, wine sauce, potatoes, and mushrooms; scallop ceviche.

Summary & Comments The "P" in Patria stands for "personality" and "presentation." From the bright, bold, and sassy two-level space to chef Andrew DiCataldo's
equally sassy and inventive Nuevo Latino cuisine, Patria is not so much a restaurant as
it is a revelation. Kickstart your meal with any of the fine ceviches. The ceviche arrives
potently in a martini glass and tastes like a refreshingly cold, spicy gazpacho. The red
snapper dish is one of the most imaginative and delicious ways to serve this fish. Each
dish is beautifully presented; the plantain chips look like a work of art as they come to
your table—each chip, resembling a small boomerang, is fanned in a circle towering
above a central area of salsa. The Latin music keeps your toes tapping as your tongue
wags for more! Amongst some of the desserts, pastry chef Alex Asteinza creates
chocolate bombones with café con leche ice cream, and Columbia and Cuba, which
consists of a white chocolate espresso cup filled with coffee cream and accompanied
with a chocolate-raspberry cigar. However, if you haven't had enough ceviche, you can
always finish off with the canteloupe-pear ceviche with a gazpacho sorbet.

Patsy's Pizza

PIZZERIA | INEXPENSIVE | QUALITY ★★★★½ | VALUE ★★★★★ | ZONE 14

2287 First Avenue; (212) 534-9783

Customers Locals, foodies **Reservations** Not necessary **When to Go** Anytime
Entrée Range Whole pizzas, $10–$19 (that's with three toppings) **Payment** Cash
only **Service Rating** ★★ **Friendliness Rating** ★★ **Bar** None **Wine Selection**
None **Dress** Casual **Disabled Access** Good

Lunch & Dinner Daily, 11 a.m.–midnight.

Setting & Atmosphere Though it's been in dire need of renovation for decades, the
new owner of Patsy's stubbornly refuses to fix the place up. The room with the oven
(where you order) is extremely dingy and harshly lit but permeated with the collective
spirit of a century of great pizza, so it might be a pity to lose that atmosphere (we hope
they never eliminate the pile of coal in front of the oven). Next door there's a room
with tables and friendly but amateurish waiter service.

House Specialties Fantastic unpretentious brick-oven pizza by the slice from an ancient coal-burning oven.

Entertainment & Amenities A semibroken black-and-white television blasting Spanish programs (ordering area only).

Summary & Comments Though this is the only top-notch brick oven pizzeria that will serve slices, you should really get a whole pie in order to experience the full grandeur (order slices—from pies that have been sitting—and you may face less crusty crust, though the taste is still tops). The neighborhood is Spanish Harlem, so taxi in after dark and remain on full alert. Across the street, open during warm weather only, Rex's is an eccentric spot serving some of the city's best Italian ices (avoid strawberry, though!). Important note: The other Patsy's Pizzas in Manhattan have merely licensed the name; they're not recommended.

Panang ★★½

MALAYSIAN | MODERATE | QUALITY ★★★½ | VALUE ★★★ | ZONES 2, 12, 13

240 Columbus Avenue (71st Street); (212) 769-3988
109 Spring Street (between Greene and Mercer streets); (212) 274-8883
1596 Second Avenue (83rd Street); (212) 585-3838

Customers Locals, ethnic **Reservations** Only for parties of 6 or more **When to Go** Anytime **Entrée Range** $11.95–$19.95 **Payment** All major credit cards **Service Rating** ★★★ **Friendliness Rating** ★★★ **Bar** Full service **Wine Selection** Limited, but the beers on tap seem to be the beverage of choice **Dress** Casual **Disabled Access** Upper West Side: fair, no access to bathrooms; Soho: none; Second Avenue: yes

Lunch West Side: noon–4:40 p.m.; Soho: 11:30 a.m.–closing; East Side: noon–4:30 p.m.; express lunch menu, noon–5 p.m. at all locations

Dinner West Side, Soho: Monday–Thursday, 4:30 p.m.–midnight; Friday and Saturday, 4:30 p.m.–1 a.m.; Sunday, noon–11 p.m.; East Side: Sunday–Thursday, 4:30 p.m.– midnight; Friday and Saturday, 4:30 p.m.–2 a.m.

Setting & Atmosphere Downtown, it's rain forest funk with a waterfall, no less. Uptown, it's wood paneling, wooden tables, windows, and bamboo with a few non–rain forest potted plants. The subterranean "lounge" is low on lights and high on decibels. There's more decoration outside—a large relief of plowing water buffalo—than in.

House Specialties Masak nenas, chicken or beef with fresh pineapple chunks and lemon grass, served in a pineapple shell; roti canai, Indian flat bread with curry dipping sauce; chicken with shredded mango and peppers served in a mango shell; spiced, deep-fried whole red snapper with a spicy sauce.

Other Recommendations Penang clay pot noodles with seafood; Malaysian nasi goreng; fried taro stuffed with seafood; beef rendang.

Summary & Comments Malaysia, the crossroads of the food world, incorporates into its cooking the best culinary qualities of nearby India, China, Thailand, and Vietnam, along with some European touches from the British colonizers. Though Penang has suffered from expansion and sometimes spotty food, it remains a viable venue for Malaysian cooking in Manhattan. Appetizers outpace entrées, so load up on those, especially the roti canai, warm, ultrathin ribbony bread that you tear up and dip into positively addictive chicken and potato curry sauce. **Nyonya** (194 Grand Street between Mott and Mulberry), by the same owners, has a wider selection of more obscure and authentic Malaysian dishes (try the Hainanese chicken rice and mee siam), but for the real thing, take the 7 train to Flushing and hit the original Penang (call (718) 321-2078); it's truly worth the trip.

Peter Luger ★★★½

STEAKHOUSE | EXPENSIVE | QUALITY ★★★★ | VALUE ★★★★ | ZONE 16

178 Broadway (Driggs Avenue), Brooklyn (Williamsburg); (718) 387-7400
www.peterluger.com

Customers Locals, business, tourists **Reservations** Required for dinner **When to Go** Anytime **Entrée Range** $30–$60 per person **Payment** Cash only **Service Rating** ★★★ **Friendliness Rating** ★★★ **Bar** Full service, proud of its "oversized drinks" **Wine Selection** Fair **Dress** Casual **Disabled Access** Yes

Lunch & Dinner Monday–Thursday, 11 a.m.–9:45 p.m.; Friday and Saturday, 11 a.m.–10:45 p.m.; Sunday, 1–9:45 p.m.

Setting & Atmosphere Just over the bridge in the Williamsburg section of Brooklyn, this 110-year-old landmark steakhouse is as plain as its menu. Scrubbed wooden tables, scrubbed wooden floors, a few beer steins, and crusty veteran waiters (who are actually very nice) are all right at home here. This is the way a steakhouse should be.

House Specialties USDA prime dry-aged (on the premises) porterhouse steak; creamed spinach; Luger's German fried potatoes; apple strudel with whipped cream.

Other Recommendations Double-thick loin lamb chops; steak sandwich; french fries; thick sliced bacon; cheesecake.

Summary & Comments What's a trip to New York City without a trip to the city's best steakhouse? Okay, so maybe Luger's isn't in the city, but it's close enough and more than worth the cab fare over the Williamsburg for the best steak in town. Why not start with a thick strip of bacon to loosen up the arteries a bit? Hey, if you're going to Luger's, you may as well go all the way. It's greasy, it's fatty, and it's good. But don't have too many strips, because you're going to need all the stomach room you can spare for that porterhouse, a huge cut of meat for two. Watch greedily as the waiter pours the excess meat juices and melted butter over the perfectly cooked slices for effect. Then take one bite of the tender, juicy meat and you'll soon know why many will never go to another steakhouse again. Just for fun, try ordering some chicken.

Petite Abeille ★★½

BELGIAN LUNCHEONETTE | INEXP | QUALITY ★★★★ | VALUE ★★★★½ |
ZONES 2, 4, 6

134 West Broadway (at Duane Street); (212) 791-1360
400 West 14th Street; (212) 727-1805
107 West 18th Street; (212) 604-9350

Customers Locals, business, expat Belgians **Reservations** Not accepted **When to Go** Anytime **Entrée Range** $10–$16.95 **Payment** Usually cash only; credit cards accepted with prior approval **Service Rating** ★★ **Friendliness Rating** ★★★ **Bar** None **Wine**

Selection None **Dress** Casual **Disabled Access** Good; staff helps with step

Brunch Saturday and Sunday, 9 a.m.–6 p.m.

Open Monday–Friday, 7 a.m.–7 p.m.; Saturday and Sunday, 9 a.m.–6 p.m.

Setting & Atmosphere Boxy but pleasant and fresh, with a distinctly European flair. There's a counter for take-out and drinks.

House Specialties Waffles (unadorned, as per Belgian tradition), carbonade (hearty sweet/savory beef stew), steump de carrot (ultra-homey carrot-flecked mashed potatoes), various sausage dishes, quiches, salads, and sandwiches.

Other Recommendations Brunch omelettes are tasty and fluffy, while coffee and cappuccino tend to be spot on.

Entertainment & Amenities They deliver.

Summary & Comments It's hard to decide whether you're eating in a really good restaurant masquerading as a cheap lunchroom or if this is simply a super-high-quality lunchroom. Don't expect gastronomic miracles, just skillfully cooked Belgian comfort food, unusual but accessible, easy to enjoy, and you can't beat the price. They offer a primitive variety of waiter service, but you'll do best by pitching in with trips to the counter to select things. The Hudson Street location has longer hours, a different menu, and particularly good pommes frites—though service can be peevish.

Petrossian   ★★★

RUSSIAN | EXPENSIVE | QUALITY ★★★½ | VALUE ★★★ | ZONE 8

182 West 58th Street (at Seventh Avenue); (212) 245-2217   www.petrossian.com

Customers Business, the ladies who lunch, caviar cravers **Reservations** Recommended **When to Go** Anytime **Entrée Range** $27–$40 **Payment** All major credit cards **Service Rating** ★★★ **Friendliness Rating** ★★★ **Bar** Full service **Wine Selection** Very good, especially the champagne by the glass **Dress** Upscale; jackets and ties **Disabled Access** No

Brunch Saturday and Sunday, 11:30 a.m.–3 p.m.

Lunch Monday–Friday, 11:30 a.m.–3 p.m.

Dinner Monday–Saturday, 5:30–11:30 p.m.; Sunday, 5:30–10:30 p.m.

Setting & Atmosphere Only one block from Carnegie Hall, this dimly lit caviar cave is nestled in a corner of the Alwyn Court. Art Nouveau lovelies grace the mirrors behind the polished granite bar. The dining area, mirrored, small, and darkly elegant, is appointed in rose, black, and well-buffed wood.

House Specialties Caviar! Beluga, sevruga, osetra, and so on, served with toast or blini and crème fraîche; "teasers," an assortment of a smoked fish appetizers with a touch of foie gras; sautéed loin of arctic venison; sea scallop soufflé with truffles.

Other Recommendations Borscht with piroshki; foie gras salad; steamed lobster; tropical fruit, vodka sorbets; Valrhona chocolate soufflé; lemon tart.

Summary & Comments You can blow a big budget on the caviar, but don't be intimidated—you can also dine surprisingly well on the $24 prix fixe lunch, which includes a glass of fine champagne or the $42 prix fixe dinner, graciously served throughout the evening. Brunch, too, is excellent. The Boutique offers caviar and foie gras to go, as well as table service for breakfast, lunch, or snacks.

Piccola Venezia ★★★★

ITALIAN | EXPENSIVE | QUALITY ★★★★½ | VALUE ★★★ | ZONE 17

42–01 28th Avenue (at 42nd Street), Astoria; (718) 721-8470
www.piccola-venezia.com

Customers Politicians, movie stars, and neighborhood folks who've been eating here for decades **Reservations** Necessary **When to Go** Avoid lunch (same menu, same stratospheric prices) **Entrée Range** $17.95–$33.95 **Payment** All major credit cards **Service Rating** ★★★★★ **Friendliness Rating** ★★★★ **Bar** Full service **Wine Selection** Extensive; mostly Italian **Dress** Elegant casual to dressy **Disabled Access** Good

Lunch & Dinner Monday–Friday, noon–10 p.m.; Saturday and Sunday, 2–10 p.m.

Setting & Atmosphere Spirited conviviality amid Old-World graciousness. This is a real class joint, from the quality table linens to the marble paneling and uniformed waiters, and it's filled to the rafters meal after meal with celebratory eaters (and celebrity eaters, too; there are more celeb sightings here than in nearly any Manhattan eatery). Venetian scenes decorate the walls; however, the management is actually Istrian (part of former Yugoslavia, though the region was once under Venetian rule).

House Specialties Excellent veal, especially the oversize veal porterhouse, veal chop giardiniera, or stunning veal franchaise. Don't miss fusi (a twisty Istrian pasta), with either grappa sauce or a traditional Istrian veal sauce. Fried calamari, roasted peppers, tricolor and house salad, tripe, chicken campagnola (basically chicken Marsala with mushrooms), and oniony sautéed Venetian liver are all dependably first-rate. With seafood, stick to specials (and ask your waiter for help—some days are better than others, and the waiters know). Terrific osso buco (get it with brown sauce if you can). Specials not to miss: venison, rabbit, seafood pasta with onions, veal valdestano, and Istrian sauerkraut soup). Avoid contadinas and other mixed grills, risotto. Pesto is best in summer (again, best when a special). Ask nicely and you may be granted some of these off-menu faves: roast loin of pork, scallops casino, stuffed artichokes, and shrimp or clams in vodka sauce.

Other Recommendations This was not always such an expensive ticket; it's a regular neighborhood restaurant that over the years has grown exorbitant. So while the plainer preparations are perfectly fine, they may not taste as sensational as their price tag. Avoid potential disappointments, such as the two lobster tail selections (whole lobster, when a special—e.g., wonderful lobster fra diavolo—is much more interesting), cold antipasto plate (just the usual cast of characters), minestrone soup, and filet mignon. Some whole-fish dishes can be a bit pedestrian as well. And definitely skip the ho-hum desserts.

Entertainment & Amenities Valet parking.

Summary & Comments Piccola Venezia, the most senior of several Astoria Istrian-Italians, has a fanatically devoted clientele. These folks know the waiters (old pros all) and count on them for guidance on matters of pesto freshness, seafood quality, etc. Newcomers are warmly served, but the staff may not go the extra mile for fresh faces. Unless you manage to establish a particular rapport with your waiter, stick with the above suggestions, the accumulated insights of several knowledgeable insiders.

Piccolo Angolo ★★★

ITALIAN | MODERATE | QUALITY ★★★★ | VALUE ★★★½ | ZONE 4

621 Hudson Street (Jane Street); (212) 229-9177

Customers Local **Reservations** Recommended **When to Go** Dinner only **Entrée Range** $12–17; pastas, $7.95–$12.95 **Payment** VISA, MC **Service Rating** ★★★ **Friendliness Rating** ★★★ **Wine Selection** Limited, mostly Italian; hold out for the inexpensive homemade "house" wine **Dress** Casual **Disabled Access** No

Dinner Tuesday–Thursday, 4–11 p.m.; Friday and Saturday, 4–11:30 p.m.; Sunday, 4–10 p.m.

Setting & Atmosphere This storefront West Village classic is small and crowded, but with good reason. The décor is limited to exposed brick with a few black-and-white prints. The tables are on top of each other and the noise level is high, but that doesn't stop regulars and a steady stream of newcomers from huddling in the doorway while they wait to be seated.

House Specialties Listen to the list of daily specials; fettucine with porcini mushrooms; linguine with white clam sauce; lobster ravioli; rack of lamb with Marsala.

Other Recommendations Hot seafood antipasto; shrimp Fra'Diavolo; grilled portobello mushrooms; eggplant rolitini; ricotta cheesecake.

Summary & Comments This place is family-run in the best sense. Renato Migliorini and his son, Peter, welcome customers and worry over the pint-sized kitchen, which somehow manages to turn out enough traditional, "home-cooked" Italian food to satisfy the full house expecting to be fed. When Papa lists the ample array of daily specials, it sounds more like a fast recitative from a Verdi opera. Listen closely; he's loathe to repeat, and these are the dishes to eat. Try to resist the irresistible garlic bread—you'll need room for the large, reasonably priced portions.

Picholine ★★★★

MEDITERRANEAN | EXPENSIVE | QUALITY ★★★★½ | VALUE ★★★ | ZONE 10

35 West 64th Street (between Columbus and Central Park West); (212) 724-8585

Customers Locals, business, Lincoln Center **Reservations** Recommended **When to Go** Anytime **Entrée Range** $26.50–$36; pretheater prix fixe, $52 and $62; tasting menus, $73 and $88; lunch, $17.50–$21; 3-course lunch for $28 **Payment** All major credit cards **Service Rating** ★★★ **Friendliness Rating** ★★★ **Bar** Full service **Wine Selection** Interesting selections in a good range of prices **Dress** Business, dressy, upscale casual; jacket required **Disabled Access** Yes

Lunch Tuesday–Saturday, noon–1:30 p.m.

Dinner Monday–Saturday, 5:30–11:45 p.m.; Sunday, 5–10 p.m.

Setting & Atmosphere East Side elegance on the West Side, with tapestries on the walls, lavishly framed paintings, ornate ceilings, shaded chandeliers, brocade banquettes, and some well-placed French country touches. The "picholine" (a small green olive) theme appears on the pretty plates and the warm olive green of the lower walls.

House Specialties Warm Maine lobster; foie gras, black mission figs, duck "prosciutto," and purslane; tournedos of salmon, horseradish crust, cucumbers, and salmon caviar; Jamison Farm organic loin of lamb; baked to order warm Valhrona chocolate tart; Picholine cheese cart.

Other Recommendations Tuna carpaccio; chilled white gazpacho; peekytoe crabmeat salad; wild mushroom and duck risotto; dayboat seafood selection; rabbit au Riesling; cheesecake mousse napoleon.

Summary & Comments By far the best restaurant on the Upper West Side of Manhattan, Picholine would more than hold its own against its East Side counterparts as well. Chef Terrance Brennan's Mediterranean-influenced French sparkles with originality and substance, like the white bean gazpacho filled with little surprises like white grapes, almond slivers, and tiny bits of chopped red pepper. Warm Maine lobster is absolutely sensual, and Brennan's perfectly balanced signature dish of salmon, cucumbers, and salmon caviar with a horseradish crust is an absolute must. There's no shortage of good food here, and the truly knowledgeable and pleasant staff will be happy to steer you in the right direction. Even desserts are excellent, but who has time for dessert when you have that incredible cheese cart running around the room? Maître de fromage Max McCalman chooses about 50 cheeses from Picholine's own cheese cave and sets about the room, offering suggestions for enthralled patrons and enthusiastically describing each cheese. For those with only a short-term memory, McCalman supplies a small index, noting the cheeses he has selected. Customers should feel welcome to stop in for cheese alone. A late-night stop for wine and cheese after a concert at Lincoln Center or even on a whim makes for a wonderful end to an evening (or maybe just a beginning).

Ping's ★★★★

CHINESE | MODERATE | QUALITY ★★★★½ | VALUE ★★★★½ | ZONE 17

83–02 Queens Boulevard, Elmhurst; (718) 396-1238

Customers Local Chinese and questing occidentals **Reservations** Accepted **When to Go** Before noon for dim sum; otherwise, anytime **Entrée Range** $18.95 and up **Payment** AMEX only **Service Rating** ★★★★ **Friendliness Rating** ★★★½ **Bar** Beer and wine only **Wine Selection** House **Dress** Nice casual **Disabled Access** Good (if the dim sum carts can get around, so can you!)

Breakfast (Dim Sum) Daily, 8 a.m.–3:30 p.m.

Lunch & Dinner Daily, 8 a.m.–4 a.m.

Setting & Atmosphere Despite its bleak Queens Boulevard location, Ping's is an elegant upscale Hong Kong banquet hall, with red velvet, gold tassle, and a wall of sparkling fish tanks. In spite of the grand décor (and suavely attired staff), many patrons come quite casually dressed.

House Specialties Very skillful and schooled renditions of classic Hong Kong dishes, plus the best Peking duck in town. Try the exquisitely fresh and delicate scallops in shell, whole sea bass (prepared in a variety of ways), snow peapod leaves (ultra-delicate greens) served with egg, any of the shellfish, pretty much anything on the specials menu, and the more ambitious-sounding offerings on the regular menu. Even less ambitious dishes like humble seafood pan-fried noodles are prepared with uncommon flair and served with great pizzaz (this one on an elegant white serving plate, garnished with a seamless bouquet of broccoli heads).

Other Recommendations Outstanding dim sum each morning, perhaps the city's best (it's crowded on weekends, but the selection is also wider). Don't miss the awesome roast pork triangles (xia siu so, pronounced "Cha Sill Sew"), with ultra-flaky pastry and rich, tender barbecue filling. For dessert, buns decorated with a yellow spiral, stuffed with potent coconut-spiked egg custard.

Entertainment & Amenities Free parking (you'll need it!) in a lot just across the side street. Don't forget to have your ticket stamped by the restaurant's cashier.

Summary & Comments The kitchen's elegance and flair bely the reasonable prices of many menu items. But while it's possible to make out quite well with noodles or chicken-n-cashew nuts here, don't waste your trip (or the kitchen's great skill) by bargain-hunting. This is a special-occasion place for exotic shellfish, rare baby vegetables, and fancy whole fish preparations. For especially special occasions, Ping's will put together a banquet meal (sky's the limit, price-wise; negotiate with a manager and be sure to carefully specify your party's squeamishness with unfamiliar ingredients). Service is excellent, with English-speaking managers in slick gray suits constantly walking the floor and offering help.

All the best action for Chinese food is happening in Queens these days, and although Flushing is a trek from Manhattan, Elmhurst—fast morphing into the city's fourth Chinatown—is much more accessible (a ten-minute ride once over the 59th Street Bridge, or take the E/F subway to Roosevelt Avenue, switch to the local G/R to the Grand Avenue stop). It's worth the trip, for dinner or dim sum; you'd have to go to Hong Kong to find much better food than this. For other superb eats in this area, see the profile for Kway Tiow Thai.

The Pink Teacup   ★½

SOUTHERN | INEXPENSIVE | QUALITY ★★★½ | VALUE ★★★½ | ZONE 4

42 Grove Street (between Bleecker and Bedford); (212) 807-6755
www.thepinkteacup.com

Customers Locals (mostly long-time regulars) **Reservations** Not accepted **When to Go** Great $7 lunch special (weekdays 11 a.m.–3 p.m.) **Entrée Range** $11–$15 **Payment** Cash only **Service Rating** ★★ **Friendliness Rating** ★★½ **Bar** None **Wine Selection** None **Dress** Nice casual **Disabled Access** Good; rest rooms not accessible **Open** Sunday–Thursday, 8 a.m.–midnight; Friday and Saturday, 8 a.m.–1 a.m.

Setting & Atmosphere Simple two- to four-person glass-topped tables filling a small space with one wall full of glossy black and whites of below-A-list actors, and another wall with a painted piece featuring Martin Luther King, Jr.

House Specialties The state of the art in fried pork chops; also, salmon croquettes (made with canned salmon, as per tradition), wonderful fried smoked bacon, ham and sausage, great collard greens and black-eyed peas (stir in Tabasco). Breakfast, available at all times, is the best meal; grits and home fries are especially good. For dessert, sweet potato pie is a better choice than the cakes.

Summary & Comments Lots of diners do wrong here by ordering the menu's less-distinguished offerings. Stick with breakfast; pork chops (try them with eggs and grits for breakfast), smoked meats, collard greens, and black-eyed peas are the way to go. Play some tunes on the Motown-and-funk–filled jukebox.

Pó ★★★½

ITALIAN | MODERATE | QUALITY ★★★★ | VALUE ★★★★ | ZONE 4

31 Cornelia Street (between Bleecker and West 4th streets); (212) 645-2189

Customers Local, aficionados from the boroughs and the burbs **Reservations** A must **When to Go** Dinner only **Entrée Range** $14–$18 **Payment** AMEX **Service Rating** ★★★ **Friendliness Rating** ★★★ **Wine Selection** Limited, but good and fairly priced **Dress** Casual **Disabled Access** Fair

Lunch Wednesday–Sunday, 11:30 a.m.–3 p.m.

Dinner Sunday, Tuesday–Thursday, 5:30–11 p.m.; Friday and Saturday, 5:30–11:30 p.m.

Setting & Atmosphere A thimbleful of space (with hardly more than a dozen tables), creamy buff walls, and the patterned tin ceiling so characteristic of old Village buildings. Mirrors above the simple banquettes and discreet lighting are the sole decoration, but the feeling is warm, informal, and inviting.

House Specialties Check daily specials; grappa-cured salmon; white bean ravioli with balsamic vinegar and brown butter; marinated quail with plums and pomegranate molasses; terrine of dark chocolate, amaretti, and vin santo with espresso caramel.

Other Recommendations Coach farm goat cheese truffle with balsamic onions, roasted peppers, and tapenade; linguine with clams, pancetta, and hot chiles; cool roasted veal breast with rucola grana and Ama oil; grilled lamb sirloin with merguez, white beans, and preserved lemons; campari-grapefruit sorbetto.

Summary & Comments The décor is not the draw here—it's the very well prepared, often inventive Italian food. The tradition began with former celeb chef Mario Batali and has since continued. Excellent white bean bruschetta, good bread, and olive oil come to the table to whet your appetite, but don't over-nibble; you'll need the room for what follows. If choosing is too taxing, try the six-course tasting menu for $40. The prices are as unpretentious as the setting; ditto for the service, helpful and friendly without fuss. Perhaps not as well kept a West Village secret as many of its repeat patrons would like: Reservations can be hard to come by, so plan ahead for this one.

Rain ★★★

ASIAN FUSION | MODERATE | QUALITY ★★★★ | VALUE ★★★ | ZONES 12, 13

100 West 82nd Street (Columbus Avenue); (212) 501-0776
1059 Third Avenue (between 62nd and 63rd streets) (212) 223-3669

Customers Locals **Reservations** Recommended **When to Go** Anytime **Entrée Range** $12–$24 **Payment** All major credit cards **Service Rating** ★★★ **Friendliness Rating** ★★★ **Bar** Full service **Wine Selection** Good **Dress** Informal, casual **Disabled Access** No

Brunch Saturday and Sunday, 11 a.m.–3 p.m.

Lunch Monday–Friday, noon–3 p.m.

Dinner Monday–Thursday, 6–11 p.m.; Friday, 6 p.m.–midnight; Saturday, 5 p.m.–midnight; Sunday, 5–10 p.m.

Setting & Atmosphere With a few simple strokes, the ground floor of this Upper West Side brownstone has taken on the sultry feel of Rangoon in the rainy season. Rattan settees with boldly flowered cushions cluster around low bamboo tables in the always crowded bar area, and the large dining area is simple and comfortable—tables covered with no-nonsense white paper; plain, polished wood floors; and slowly circling ceiling fans. Its new crosstown cousin has a more modern look, with a row of wooden booths bathed in soft lighting and separated by hanging swaths of linen along the wall.

House Specialties Crispy Vietnamese spring rolls stuffed with shrimp, vegetables, and glass noodles; Thai-style fajitas, a cross-cultural knockout that combines roast duck and Asian vegetables wrapped in moo-shu pancakes; a delicate salmon fillet roasted in a banana leaf and spiced with pepper and garlic.

Other Recommendations Daily specials; Malaysian chicken satay, with the traditional cucumber salad and peanut sauce; pad thai, rice noodles with chicken, shrimp, bean sprouts, and egg; crispy whole fish served with tangy "three-flavor" sauce. And if your sweet tooth needs satisfying, the fried coconut ice cream is a must. Asian eggs Benedict (with Malaysian sausage and a gingery hollandaise) on the brunch menu will spice up any lazy Sunday morning.

Summary & Comments Chef Taweewat Hurapan handles this combo of Southeast Asian cuisines—Thai, Vietnamese, and the lesser-known Malaysian—with ease and elegance. Traditional dishes alternate with innovative adaptations, and the presentations have a stylish pizzazz not often found in Asian restaurants. This is a very popular spot with the trendy and the non-, so book well in advance for weekend dinners. Only half the tables can be reserved; the rest are held for walk-ins, and that can leave you lifting libations in the bar for quite a while.

Rice ★★★

ASIAN FUSION | INEXPENSIVE | QUALITY ★★★½ | VALUE ★★★★★ | ZONES 3, 16

227 Mott Street (between Prince and Spring streets) (212) 226-5775
81 Washington Street; (718) 222-9880   www.riceny.com

Customers Locals, regulars, hipsters on a budget or a health kick **Wine Selection** Very small **Reservations** Not necessary **When to Go** Anytime **Bar** Beer, limited drinks **Entrée Range** $5–$13 **Dress** Casual or funky **Payment** Cash or checks only **Service Rating** ★★★ **Friendliness Rating** ★★★ **Disabled Access** Yes

Open Manhattan: Daily, noon–midnight; Brooklyn: daily, noon–10 p.m.; Brooklyn offers brunch on Sunday, noon–4 p.m.

Setting & Atmosphere Rice manages to perfect a combined atmosphere of calm, relaxation and stylish appeal. The background music is unobtrusive, but often tastefully selected. Simple wooden-topped tables and straight-backed chairs. The Brooklyn branch has a great outdoor patio for warm weather.

House Specialties Thai black rice with edamame peas; Asian coleslaw (no mayonnaise, and flavored with a delicious carrot ginger dressing); coconut curry shrimp; pear cider; banana leaf wrap dessert (sweet plantain rolled in sticky rice).

Other Recommendations Tea-smoked salmon salad; pad thai; eggplant maki; tamales.

Summary & Comments Rice caters to vegetarians and carnivores equally successfully, which is not always an easy task; tofu steak and chicken kabobs are given the same attention. Similarly, waifs and those with heartier appetites will be satisfied with the option of ordering either a small bowl of rice and topping instead of a larger size. The options are tasty and often healthy and the prices are low. Contrary to what might be considered a confused selection, the mixture of Thai, Indian, Mexican, and Japanese influences works for the menu as there aren't too many options for the mix to go over-board. Try to get to the Brooklyn branch as it's located in that borough's DUMBO (Down Under the Manhattan Bridge Overpass), which has a super view of Manhattan and has new galleries and a funky old factory appeal. If you're early enough (before 7 p.m. Monday–Saturday), visit the **Jacques Torres Chocolate Shop** (66 Water Street).

Rinconcito Peruano   ★★★

PERUVIAN | INEXPENSIVE | QUALITY ★★★★ | VALUE ★★★★★ | ZONE 8

803 9th Avenue (between 53rd and 54th streets); (212) 333-5685

Customers Peruvians from all over, locals **Reservations** For large parties only **When to Go** Anytime (weekends more choices) **Entrée Range** $6–$15 **Payment** VISA, MC **Service Rating** ★½ **Friendliness Rating** ★★½ **Bar** None **Wine Selection** None **Dress** Casual **Disabled Access** Good; rest rooms not accessible

Lunch & Dinner Monday–Friday, 11 a.m.–11 p.m; Saturday and Sunday, 10:30 a.m.–11 p.m.

Setting & Atmosphere A little touch of Jackson Heights, Queens, in Manhattan, with a modest, tidy little dining room. Although they seem to have learned restaurant management from a correspondence course, the Mom and Pop owners are lovely people (food this good doesn't come from cold-hearted cooks), and the good vibes that enliven the food permeate this humble parlor. Peruvians flock here, as do in-the-know Anglos.

House Specialties Tamales are the very epitome of corn; papas à la huancaina (the Peruvian classic of cold, boiled potatoes drenched in spicy cheese sauce) luxuriate in a rich, slightly chunky yellow sauce, not chalky or bland as elsewhere; papa rellena is an ungreasy fried ball of subtly spiced mashed potatoes stuffed with tender ground meat; aji de gallina is a casserole with chunks of tender chicken and good potato (along with ground walnuts, Parmesan cheese, and mirasol peppers) afloat in a sweetish sauce that's beautifully unified of flavor. Splendid fish ceviche (raw fish cooked through acidic limey marination) is quite spicy, the flesh so rich it's almost buttery; tacu tacu is smooth, irre-sistible soupy rice with white beans (also available with meat). For dessert, helado de lucuma is very smooth and deep-flavored ice cream made from a popular (but untrans-latable) South American fruit. Another dessert, choclo peruano, confronts you with a small ear of huge kerneled corn and a small brick of extremely mild cheese. At first you're not quite sure what to do, but nature quickly takes its course.

Other Recommendations The dynamite hot sauce contains some avocado; it's great for dunking bread in.

Summary & Comments Manhattan's been sadly lacking good South American food for years, but Rinconcito Peruano has upped the ante, serving Peruvian dishes worlds tastier than you'll find in even the best places in Queens and New Jersey (the food can't possibly be much better even in Peru!). It's so homey that nothing is ever made exactly the same way twice (much to the delight of the many regulars here, who seldom grow bored). The well-meaning staff is decidedly not ready for prime time, and the kitchen gets overwhelmed when crowds peak (so go at off hours). But gawd, is it ever worth it. To find most of the menu actually available, go for lunch on a Saturday or Sunday.

The River Café ★★★★★

NEW AMERICAN | VERY EXP | QUALITY ★★★★★ | VALUE ★★★★½ | ZONE 16

1 Water Street; (718) 522-5200   www.therivercafe.com

Customers Couples, loyal and deep-pocketed regulars, professionals, anyone celebrating extra-special occasions **Wine Selection** Extensive; over 500 selections **Reservations** Necessary, unless you wish to have drinks or order à la carte in the Terrace Room; call in advance to see if room is booked **When to Go** Anytime **Bar** Full service **Entrée Range** Prix fixe 3-course dinner, $70 per person; 6-course tasting menu, $90 per person; à la carte lunch menu, $23–$27 **Dress** Dressy for women, jacket required for men in main dining room; less formal in Terrace Room **Payment** All major credit cards **Service Rating** ★★★★½ **Friendliness Rating** ★★★★ **Disabled access** Yes

Brunch Sunday, 11 a.m.–3 p.m.

Lunch Monday–Saturday, noon–3 p.m.

Dinner Daily, 6–11 p.m.

Setting & Atmosphere It's hard to find restaurants with better views, and there's not even any elevation involved. The restaurant is directly on the waterfront on the Brooklyn side of the East River, just south and almost under the Brooklyn Bridge. Romantic and elegant in the evening, and inspiring (and a bit cheaper) during the day. At risk of belaboring the point, this may be one of the top ten places in New York for marriage proposals, wedding celebrations, and anniversary meals. Noise levels are controlled, and couples can be seated either next to the window, so they sit across form each other, or across from it against the wall along a comfortable banquette, so they can sit next to each other, hold hands, and look at the view together.

House Specialties Roasted pear salad; roasted "Bee Gee" shrimp; Maine lobster (seasonal preparations); rack of lamb; chocolate marquise Brooklyn Bridge dessert.

Other Recommendations Venison loin; most of their daily specials, especially the creative appetizers; the roquefort cheese soufflé is a decent vegetarian option, but can sometimes err on the heavy side.

Summary & Comments Tourist and locals are always in awe of the superb setting of the River Café. However, unlike other known spots, that may have great settings but mediocre food, the River Café excels in food and service—it's well worth a splurge on all levels. This is the place where several famed chefs once reigned, including Larry Forgione; Brad Steelman is currently at the helm. If the Terrace Room isn't booked, and you don't feel like paying for a full meal, enjoy some wine and an appetizer or two.

Rosa Mexicano ★★★

MEXICAN | MODERATE | QUALITY ★★★★ | VALUE ★★★★ | ZONE 9

1063 First Avenue (58th Street); (212) 753-7407   www.rosamexicano.com

Customers Local, ethnic, tourist **Reservations** Recommended **When to Go** Dinner only **Entrée Range** $17–$28 **Payment** AMEX, D, MC **Service Rating** ★★ **Friendliness Rating** ★★★ **Bar** Full service; emphasis on margaritas, especially the

pomegranate variation **Wine Selection** Limited **Dress** Casual **Disabled Access** Yes
Dinner Daily, 5–11:30 p.m.

Setting & Atmosphere It's always fiesta time here, with a boisterous bar scene in the front. Colorful cutout banners flutter from the dark rose ceilings over dusty rose adobe walls, star lighting fixtures twinkle, potted ferns add a little greenery, and traditional copper plates add a little elegance to the table settings. The smaller part of the L-shaped dining room is a tad quieter.

House Specialties Guacamole; crepas de cuitlacoche (Mexican corn fungus—a real delicacy); enchiladas de mole poblano; posole (a stew with pork, chicken, and hominy); alambres de camarones (grilled, skewered marinated shrimp).

Other Recommendations Ceviche of bay scallops; menudo (tripe stew); enchiladas de pato (duck with a green mole sauce); crepas camarones (crêpes filled with shrimp in a chile pasilla sauce).

Summary & Comments Above and beyond the usual Tex-Mex fare, this is as close to authentic, classic Mexican cuisine as you will find in New York. Be sure to order the made-to-order-at-your-table guacamole; it has become a renowned signature dish. The color and dash of the food and the setting are guaranteed to lift your spirits, even before you down a few divine margaritas. They also have another site at 61 Columbus Avenue (call (212) 977-7700). If you'd like to continue the price of paying a lot for Mexican fare, try **Dos Caminos** (373 Park Avenue South, between 26th and 27th streets; (212) 294-1000).

Rosario Bistro   ★★

ITALIAN | INEXPENSIVE | QUALITY ★★★★ | VALUE ★★★★★ | ZONE 1

38 Pearl Street; (212) 514-5454

Customers Professionals **Reservations** Not accepted **When to Go** Anytime
Entrée Range $5–$9 **Payment** All major credit cards **Service Rating** ★★★½
Friendliness Rating ★★½ **Bar** Beer and wine **Wine Selection** Three reds **Dress**
Casual **Disabled Access** Fair

Breakfast & Lunch Monday–Friday, 8 a.m.–3 p.m.; closed Saturday and Sunday

Setting & Atmosphere Bustling, no-nonsense cafeteria.

House Specialties Menu changes daily; familiar dishes like lasagna, veal or chicken or eggplant Parmigiana (dish or hero), escarole, penne à la vodka, minestrone, and so on.

Summary & Comments Rosario's makes their own mozzarella and their own pasta, and the food is extremely tasty, if inelegant. Prices are almost insanely low; they make their profit from volume, processing dozens of customers per minute with miraculous efficiency. Steam tables mean no al dente pasta; if that bothers you, stick with soups, heroes, and entrées. Why can't every neighborhood have a place like this?

Sahara East   ★★½

MIDDLE EASTERN | MODERATE | QUALITY ★★★★ | VALUE ★★★★ | ZONE 5

184 First Avenue; (212) 353-9000

Customers Locals, ethnic **Reservations** Accepted **When to Go** Warm weather
Entrée Range $10.95–$16.95 **Payment** Cash only **Service Rating** ★½ **Friendliness**

Rating ★★★★ **Bar** Beer and wine **Wine Selection** Small **Dress** Casual **Disabled Access** Poor (big step at front door)

Lunch Daily, 10 a.m.–5 p.m.

Dinner Daily, 5 p.m.–4 a.m.

Setting & Atmosphere A narrow little café, but pass through to the large garden in back decorated with lights and hanging knickknacks.

House Specialties Falafel, grape leaves, fattoush (salad with pita croutons), lamb or chicken shish kebab, lamb or chicken couscous.

Other Recommendations Shisha (aromatic tobacco, optionally flavored with apple), smoked from ornate water pipes fueled by glowing coals; bargain lunch specials.

Entertainment & Amenities Live music on Friday and Saturday, 9–11:30 p.m.

Summary & Comments Sahara can turn out some high-quality food, but the tiny kitchen gets overwhelmed when things are busy. The dilemma is that the place is most fun when crowded, so one must weigh food against ambience when choosing a time to eat here (busy nights are Thursday through Sunday). On nice clear evenings, the garden fills up, and the perfumed shisha smoke wafts as snakily as the music. Older Middle Eastern guys and East Village hipsters blend effortlessly into the scene, and it feels wonderful to be a part of it all. On these busy kitchen nights, stick with the dishes we've listed and you'll do fine. If, however, food is more important to you than setting, go on off nights and ask the friendly chef about the day's specials. In any case, service is very friendly but maddeningly slack. Put yourself on the same slow track, puff an apple shisha (try it—it's much mellower than cigarettes; this is the place that made shisha chic), and relax into the Egyptian groove.

Saigon Grill ★★★

VIETNAMESE | INEXPENSIVE | QUALITY ★★★★½ | VALUE ★★★★★ | ZONE 12, 13

620 Amsterdam Avenue (at 90th Street); (212) 875-9072   www.saigongrill.com
1700 Second Avenue (at 88th Street); (212) 996-4600

Customers Local **Reservations** Only for 5 or more (not accepted on weekends) **When to Go** Avoid peak hours, especially on weekends **Entrée Range** $8.50–$14.95 (much less at lunch) **Payment** All major credit cards **Service Rating** ★★½ **Friendliness Rating** ★★ **Bar** Beer only **Wine Selection** None **Dress** Casual **Disabled Access** No

Lunch & Dinner Daily, 11 a.m.–midnight

Setting & Atmosphere Clean, bright, no-frills bustling venue. Good for kids.

House Specialties Barbecue spare ribs, barbecue pork chop, barbecue chicken, crispy whole sea bass, grilled boneless chicken, summer rolls, coconut sticky rice, pickled vegetable salad.

Summary & Comments "Grill" is right: This place turns out some of the best grilled dishes around. Most Vietnamese restaurants in New York are run by Vietnamese of Chinese ethnicity, but here the two traditions run together. The wonderful barbecue spare ribs with peanut/plum sauce, for example, taste pretty Chinese. Hybrid or no, this is a real find, especially in an area where good Asian food is rare. Great as the grilled meats are, perhaps the best dish of all is the crispy whole sea bass (sweetly subtle sauce, ultra-flaky, and very fresh). Kids and adults will both like the wonderful coconut sticky rice (strewn with ground peanuts).

Santa Fe   ★★½

AMERICAN/SOUTHWEST | MODERATE | QUALITY ★★★½ | VALUE ★★★★ | ZONE 10

72 West 69th Street (Columbus Avenue and Central Park West); (212) 724-0822

Customers Locals, Lincoln Center **Reservations** Recommended **When to Go** Anytime **Entrée Range** $9.95–$22 **Payment** All major credit cards **Service Rating** ★★★ **Friendliness Rating** ★★★ **Bar** Full service **Wine Selection** Limited **Dress** Casual **Disabled Access** No

Lunch Daily, 11:30 a.m.–4 p.m.

Dinner Tuesday–Saturday, 4 p.m.–midnight; Sunday and Monday, 4–11 p.m.

Setting & Atmosphere The bottom floor of this Upper West Side townhouse has been washed in soft southwestern colors, coral walls, golden sand ceilings, white on the trim and on the candle-strewn, mirror-topped fireplaces. Acoma pots, decorated wooden bowls, handwoven Oaxacan rugs, and a few typical Santa Fe oil paintings foster the feeling that you're nestled below the Sangre de Cristo mountains.

House Specialties Southwestern shrimp jambalaya; Yucatán chicken; black bean and sweet potato burrito; chipotle chicken Santa Fe.

Other Recommendations Grilled cumin and chipotle pork chop; southwestern grilled vegetable pizza; scallop ceviche.

Summary & Comments One of the first around town to offer southwestern fare, this tranquil, pretty place has been going strong for 15 years. The upscale approach to both the traditional and the trendy cooking of the region, without any backsliding into Tex-Mex, margaritas that are mighty good and muy fuerte, and young, friendly waitpersons are reason enough to encourage a visit. And if Lincoln Center is your ultimate destination, this a fine choice, pre- or post-performance.

Second Avenue Deli   ★★½

JEWISH DELI | MODERATE | QUALITY ★★★★ | VALUE ★★★ | ZONE 5

156 Second Avenue; (212) 677-0606   www.2ndavedeli.com

Customers Locals, tourists **Reservations** Not accepted **When to Go** Anytime **Entrée Range** $10–$26 **Payment** All major credit cards **Service Rating** ★★★ **Friendliness Rating** ★★★ **Bar** Wine and beer **Wine Selection** Limited kosher **Dress** Casual **Disabled Access** Good

Breakfast, lunch, & dinner Sunday–Thursday, 7 a.m.–midnight; Friday and Saturday, 7 a.m.–3 a.m.

Setting & Atmosphere Classic deli, with wisecracking, kvetching meat slicers working up front and booths and pickle-filled tables.

House Specialties Freebie pungent health salad; great smooth chopped liver; authentic matzo ball soup; knishes; derma (rich stuffing—here with globs of paprika—in sausage casing); cholent (an ultra-slow-cooked meat and potato stew); sweet/orangy stuffed cabbage; homemade applesauce. There's much debate over the corned beef; theirs is very lightly "corned," but this allows more beefy flavors to emerge.

Other Recommendations Skip dessert; the deli may be open Friday nights and Saturdays, but they're kosher nonetheless, and desserts made with dairy substitutes aren't worth the calories.

Entertainment & Amenities They'll ship food anywhere via mail order.

Summary & Comments When people think of New York City restaurants, they think of delis. Ha. It's actually easier to find good corned beef in Montreal or Los Angeles than here. While Second Avenue Deli's offerings are spotty, it still makes a few dishes very well. Don't stray from our suggestions and you'll have the authentic New York deli experience, if not a fantastic taste experience. You'll find better consistency at Mr. Broadway Kosher Deli (see profile), but they have none of the history and little of the soul of this very traditional place.

Shaan ★★★

INDIAN | MOD/EXP | QUALITY ★★★★ | VALUE ★★★★ | ZONE 8

57 West 48th Street (between Fifth and Sixth avenues); (212) 977-8400

Customers Business, publishing types at lunch **Reservations** Recommended for dinner **When to Go** Anytime **Entrée Range** $10.95–$29.95 **Payment** All major credit cards **Service Rating** ★★★ **Friendliness Rating** ★★★ **Bar** Full service **Wine Selection** Small; Indian beer is a better choice here **Dress** Business, casual **Disabled Access** Fair; bathrooms downstairs

Lunch Monday–Friday, noon–3 p.m.

Dinner Daily, 5:30–11 p.m.

Setting & Atmosphere An island of subcontinental serenity in a spacious, well-appointed, marble-floored dining room with decorative weavings on the walls. The attractive bar area, done in soft green, has a lovely, noteworthy chandelier made from 37,000 gemstone beads. A buffet lunch is served downstairs in a slightly lower-ceilinged room that also serves for private parties. A cool but comfortable quietude prevails.

House Specialties Dali batata poori, stuffed flaky pastry topped with tangy tamarind sauce, is a fine opener; lobster krahi is a worthwhile splurge; shrimp Goa, a south Indian curry; pudina chaap, lamb chops tossed in a spicy mint sauce, a Parsi speciality.

Other Recommendations Chicken, lamb, and goat from the tandoor oven; gobhi alu matar, cauliflower, potatoes, and peas with onions, ginger, and spices; alu baigon dahiwala, potatoes and eggplant cooked in yogurt, for veggie-only folks. The poori bread is a puffy delight.

Summary & Comments This large, handsome room has gone through many incarnations over the years, starting as the Forum of the Twelve Caesars. It's still elegant, with tables far enough apart for private tête-à-têtes and confidential business discussions. The classy, interesting Indian cuisine is top-notch, as is the service. The $15.95 prix fixe lunch buffet (eight different main dishes) is a super buy, and there's an ample pretheater prix fixe dinner for $25 served until 7 p.m. A prix fixe tasting menu is also available for $23, served 7–11 p.m.

Shun Lee West, Shun Lee Café ★★★½

CHINESE | MODERATE/EXPENSIVE | QUALITY ★★★★ | VALUE ★★★★ | ZONE 10

43 West 65th Street; (212) 595-8895, (212) 769-3888 (Café)

Customers Locals, business, Lincoln Center **Reservations** Recommended **When to Go** Anytime **Entrée Range** $16–$32.50; in the café, most entrées are $16–$25 **Payment** All major credit cards **Service Rating** ★★ **Friendliness Rating** ★★ **Bar** Full bar **Wine Selection** Good **Dress** Dressy, business; casual in the café **Disabled Access** Yes

Lunch Daily, noon–4 p.m.

Dinner Daily, 4 p.m.–midnight

Setting & Atmosphere Dark and dramatic: Large silver-white dragons with little red eyes chase each other across black walls above luxurious black banquettes and black floors, and soft halogen lighting flatters the complexion. Silver-white monkeys swing over the small bar in the entrance, where you are greeted by tuxedoed maître d's. This is a snazzy take on the Chinese scene, and the clientele seems to revel in it.

House Specialties Szechuan wonton; steamed dumplings; beggar's chicken (order 24 hours in advance); Grand Marnier prawns; Cantonese sausage with Szechuan sausage; dim sum (café only).

Other Recommendations Sliced duckling with young ginger root; lobster in black bean sauce; rack of lamb, Szechuan-style.

Summary & Comments High-style chinoiserie, with high-style Chinese cooking to match, make this an upscale Lincoln Center favorite. Both food and mood are elegant, and both are reflected in the prices. Some of the same excellent food is available in the more casual café, which has its own entrance, for a lot less. The café, black-and-white checked from floor to ceiling, also offers very good dim sum from wandering carts and abrupt but rapid service.

66 ★★★

CHINESE	EXPENSIVE	QUALITY ★★★★	VALUE ★★½	ZONE 2

241 Church Street (between Leonard and Worth streets); (212) 925-0202

Customers Fashionistas, curious foodies, celebs, hipsters with thick wallets **Wine Selection** Good **Reservations** Necessary, but first come, first served at the long communal table by bar **When to Go** Dinner for the glitz and lunch for a cheaper, less crowded experience **Bar** Full service; interesting cocktails **Entrée Range** $18–$32; prix fixe lunch available **Dress** Business casual day, chic night **Payment** All major credit cards **Service Rating** ★★★ **Friendliness Rating** ★★★ **Disabled Access** Yes

Lunch Monday–Saturday, noon–3 p.m.; Sunday, 11:30 a.m.–3 p.m.

Dinner Monday–Thursday, 6 p.m.–midnight; Friday and Saturday, 6 p.m.–1 a.m.; Sunday, 6–10:30 p.m.

Setting & Atmosphere Sleek, geometric, and minimalist are the first adjectives that come to mind when describing 66. Once you pass the long and high-topped communal dining table, you enter the main dining space that has three partitions and high ceilings. Small aquariums with colorful tropical fish are in view from any table across one panel, as is the well lit and immaculate kitchen, viewed through glass above several tanks. The tables are made of a semitranslucent material that blends well with the white, silvery gray, and black décor. The similarities between 66 and a neighborhood Chinese restaurant begin and end with the lazy susans found on some of the large, round tables. Lunch is calmer and less crowded; dinner can be frenzied and a real scene.

House Specialties Peking duck; scallion pancakes; 66 sesame noodles; sweet and sour two-flavored shrimp (with condensed milk, mayonnaise, ginger); steamed cod with caramelized onions, ginger, and soy sauce; lobster.

Other Recommendations Marinated eggplant; Asian greens; lobster noodles; chili prawns; molten chocolate cake with spiced coconut ice cream; Vietnamese coffee flavored sorbet.

Summary & Comments 66 is a recent addition to the famed chef Jean-Georges Vongerichten's empire. The story is that he decided to open a Chinese restaurant that would celebrate flavors in the food without overwhelming a dish with too much indescribable sauce. Many of the dishes are well-executed with interesting combinations of flavors, but there is an ongoing debate as to whether 66 can justify the prices charged; some of the food has been likened to glorified cheap Chinese fare at top-dollar prices. We'd disagree with the "glorified cheap Chinese fare" bit, but the prices are steep. In contrast, critics have lauded 66 as a pioneering space that takes Chinese food to a new and exciting level. The dishes are carefully presented, and for those that require a bit of scene whilst munching on a steamed shrimp dumpling, then 66 is the place for you. The à la carte lunch menu is cheaper than the dinner menu, but the portions are smaller; if you wish to enjoy varied tastes and also fill your belly, several dishes must be ordered. The lunch prix fixe is an inexpensive though light feed. Sake is served with a hefty price tag and a frugal pour.

Soul Fixins'   ★★★

SOUTHERN/SOUL FOOD | INEXPENSIVE | QUALITY ★★★★ | VALUE ★★★★ | ZONE 6

371 West 34th Street; (212) 736-1345

Customers Locals **Reservations** Not accepted **When to Go** Anytime **Entrée Range** Lunch, $6–$7; dinner, $6.95–$9.95 **Payment** AMEX, MC, VISA **Service Rating** ★★ **Friendliness Rating** ★★½ **Bar** None **Wine Selection** None **Dress** Casual **Disabled Access** Good

Lunch Monday–Saturday, 11 a.m.–5 p.m.

Dinner Monday–Saturday, 5–10 p.m.; closed Sunday.

Setting & Atmosphere Minimal—this is mostly a take-out joint, but there are a bunch of self-service tables and chairs both inside and out on the sidewalk.

House Specialties Chicken in all forms—particularly barbecued; candied yams; collard greens; macaroni and cheese; cornbread; lemonade.

Summary & Comments It almost defies the imagination to realize that plates of truly soulful victuals can be had within a couple blocks of the Empire State Building (a neighborhood considered bereft of good eats) for five bucks. Soul Fixins' makes soul food as good or better than nearly any served Uptown for a loyal and largely African American clientele of Midtown workers. Everything's cooked with deft aplomb: chicken and pork chops are reliably tender and flavorful, collard greens have lots of smoke and are not at all mushy. Candied yams are individual halves of spuds neither overspiced nor oversweet, done to the perfect texture (no mean feat when you're cooking ahead for steam-table service). Homemade lemonade and iced tea are just right: smooth, not too sweet, and refreshing. Even the cornbread (often a throwaway in soul food take-outs) is very good. The kitchen takes a relatively healthy approach, using minimal pork and fat.

Soup Kitchen International ★★★½

SOUP TAKE-OUT | INEXPENSIVE | QUALITY ★★★★½ | VALUE ★★★★★ | ZONE 8

259A West 55th Street; (212) 757-7730

Customers Local regulars, tourists **Reservations** Not accepted **When to Go** Go late (after 3 p.m.) to avoid the worst crowds **Entrée Range** $6–$12 **Payment** Cash only **Service Rating** ★★★½ **Friendliness Rating** ★ **Bar** None **Wine Selection** None **Dress** Casual **Disabled Access** Good

Open Monday–Friday, noon–6 p.m. (sometimes later); closed Friday, Saturday, and all summer through November!

Setting & Atmosphere You wait in line, inching ever so slowly toward the venerated take-out window. Once at the head of the line, you peer in and glimpse a nervous high-pitched buzz like a Broadway backstage; assistants go about their souply tasks at full tilt, braced for the inevitable calamitous repercussions should they err in even the most trifling detail. A variety of signs—including an LED zipper—clearly state the Rules. At the center of this frenzy, a model of calm haughty efficiency, stands the Soup Man.

House Specialties There's always a chicken-based soup (either chicken vegetable or chicken broccoli), comparatively light and simple, with plenty of meat and carefully cut vegetables. The chef's personal favorites are the bisques—either seafood, lobster, or crab. These are the richest and most expensive choices, of an almost diabolical complexity. You'll find a not-very-spicy medium-thick chili (turkey, vegetable, chicken, or beef), and often Indian mulligatawny (extremely complex and sweetish). The remainders are seafood chowders, various peasanty soups, and delicious oddballs like mussels and spinach or bacon, lettuce, and tomato.

Other Recommendations In warm weather, there are cold soups like vichyssoise and gazpacho.

Entertainment & Amenities Watching newcomers fret and rehearse their order while in line.

Summary & Comments In spite of Jerry Seinfeld's famous sobriquet, owner/chef Al Yeganeh is not a Nazi. He's a very conscientious man who has a few irrefutably logical rules: Know what you want by the time you reach the window after your 45-minute wait (duh), have your money ready, and move to the left so the next person can step forward and order. Al—regulars refer to him as Al, though none would dare call him that to his face—feels sorry for those waiting (he keeps raising prices to discourage crowds, to no avail), so those who ignore his prominently posted rules—thus delaying service—receive no bread. Soup comes in small, large, or extra-large containers. If you order an extra-large, you'll be interrogated as to your intentions: Food shouldn't go unrefrigerated for long periods, so if you order a big one you'd best be prepared to convince Al that you and several friends intend to ingest forthwith. This isn't the most expensive soup; these ultra-nourishing concoctions (which come with bread, fruit, and a chocolate), are actually the cheapest four-star lunch in town. What's more, the price allows him to use the choicest ingredients: real saffron, the finest lobster, and so on. The hallmark of Al's soups is the incredible spectrum of textures: huge chunks down to microscopic in-suspension particles; dozens of ingredients collaborating in a soupy symphony, each arranged in perfect balance. Eat on benches one block north at the northeast corner of 56th Street and Eighth Avenue. You won't notice even the coldest winds while huddled with your take-out container of steaming soupy magnificence.

Sushisay   ★★★½

JAPANESE | EXPENSIVE | QUALITY ★★★★ | VALUE ★★★★ | ZONE 9

38 East 51st Street (between Madison and Park avenues); (212) 755-1780

Customers Ethnic, business, locals **Reservations** Recommended **When to Go** Anytime **Entrée Range** $16–$33; sushi available à la carte **Payment** All major credit cards **Service Rating** ★★ **Friendliness Rating** ★★★ **Wine Selection** Minimal **Dress** Casual, business **Disabled Access** No

Lunch Monday–Friday, noon–2 p.m.

Dinner Monday–Friday, 5:30–10:15 p.m.; Saturday, 5–9 p.m.

Setting & Atmosphere Startlingly simple, sharp-angled, and bright with off-white and light wood walls, and light wood tables. Understated Japanese floral arrangements add spots of vibrant color here and there, and a large, 20-seat sushi bar, manned by six sushi chefs and jammed with Japanese businessmen at lunch, forms the centerpiece.

House Specialties Special deluxe bento (appetizers, sushi, and sashimi served in an elegant lacquer box); special makimoto (three kinds of rolled sushi); sea urchin hand roll, spicy codfish sushi, Japanese mackerel sushi, and anything else that appeals on the à la carte sushi list.

Other Recommendations Cooked sushi assortment (good for sushi beginners); chirashi (assorted fish fillets on vinegar-seasoned rice); sushi deluxe (an assortment of fresh and cooked items).

Summary & Comments Celestial sushi and sashimi draws praise and crowds. An excellent Midtown choice for the freshest of fresh fish. Order the preselected assortments, or make individual selections from the extensive à la carte list of sushi and hand rolls. The ambience and service are friendly; the high prices reflect the location.

Symposium   ★★★

GREEK | INEXP/MOD | QUALITY ★★★½ | VALUE ★★★★ | ZONE 14

544 West 113th Street (between Broadway and Amsterdam avenues); (212) 865-1011

Customers Regulars, Columbia University staff and students, ethnic **Wine Selection** Small but includes Greek selections (besides ouzo) and sangria **Reservations** not necessary **When to Go** Anytime you have a yen for a stuffed grape leaf **Bar** Limited **Entrée Range** $8–$20 **Dress** Casual **Payment** MC, VISA **Service Rating** ★★★★ **Friendliness Rating** ★★★★½ **Disabled Access** No

Open Daily, noon–11 p.m.; lunch specials served noon–3 p.m.

Setting & Atmosphere The main dining room has a tavern feel with closely arranged dark wooden tables, a few booths, wood floor, paintings on the walls, and low ceiling. What it lacks in sleek modernity, it gains in sheer coziness and warmth. A feeling of dining community pervades: Everyone is there to have a good time and eat good Greek food. The enclosed garden practically doubles the amount of tables. It's cheerful and bright and hosts several hanging plants, white and green vinyl tablecloths, and wooden chairs, and two large trees have grown to a considerable height and girth there (the tree's canopies are way above the enclosure's roof).

House Specialties Mixed appetizer plate (especially the stuffed grape leaves, taramosalata, and eggplant dip); shish kebab (lamb and vegetables on a skewer); mousaka.

Other Recommendations Pastitsio (baked pasta and ground meat); vegetarian mousaka; spanakoppita (spinach and feta pie).

Summary & Comments It's clear that the owners (it's family-run) have a lot of confidence when the only route to the enclosed garden is through the kitchen. Symposium has been around for over 20 years and proclaims to serve genuine Greek cuisine, which we can't dispute. The best bet is to order the Symposium Salad for the table so you can sample a mixture of dips with a few olives and delectable stuffed grape leaves; warm pita bread accompanies the dish. The spinach pie is the right combination of spinach and feta, but sometimes the filo dough is not as crunchy as it could be. It's best to stick with the tried and true Greek specialties; rice and vegetables are served with the main dishes. The vegetarian mousaka is pretty decent as well. Service is very friendly.

Tabla ★★★★

INDIAN FUSION | EXPENSIVE | QUALITY ★★★★½ | VALUE ★★★★ | ZONE 7

11 Madison Avenue (at 25th Street); (212) 889-0667

Customers Locals, business, ethnic **Reservations** Recommended for main dining room **When to Go** Anytime **Entrée Range** 3-course prix fixe dinner, $57; 5- and 7-course tasting menus, $75 and $88 **Payment** All major credit cards **Service Rating** ★★★ **Friendliness Rating** ★★★ **Bar** Full service **Wine Selection** Well chosen for food; fairly priced **Dress** Casual or better **Disabled Access** Bread bar, yes; dining room, no

Lunch Monday–Friday, noon–2 p.m.

Dinner Monday–Friday, 5:30–10:30 p.m.

Setting & Atmosphere A dizzyingly beautiful crimson wood staircase separates two levels of space, each with its own distinct personality. The upstairs dining room is formal but hip, buzzing with excitement and alive with voluptuous colors—a perfect setting for the meal that follows. The room overlooks the street-level Bread Bar, which is more casual and doesn't require reservations.

House Specialties Goan spiced crab cake; tuna and seared baby squid, chickpea hummus, jicama, pickled ramps and peppers; rice-flaked crisped halibut; eggplant-stuffed braised Vidalia onion; vanilla bean kulfi.

Other Recommendations Nova Scotia lobster; foie gras torchon; lentil-crusted wild striped bass; rawa-coated soft-shell crabs; warm chocolate date cake.

Summary & Comments Danny Meyer, king of New York's New American establishments Gramercy Tavern, Union Square Café, and Eleven Madison Park, now brings you Indian fusion, and this may well be the best of the bunch. Perhaps realizing that New American just isn't that new anymore, Meyer hired Floyd Cardoz, a native of India, to literally add some spice to what is becoming an increasingly tired cuisine. Cardoz took him at his word, using ingredients like kokum, cumin, tamarind, and tapioca to breathe new life into dishes like crab cake, foie gras, and fettucine. Even the tandoori breads come in bizarre flavors like buckwheat honey and horseradish. Though fusion is more often than not a failed experiment, Tabla manages to pull it off with style, and then some. You've never tasted anything quite like the food here, and that's why you're sure to come back. But be warned, Tabla is not for everybody; some people love it, while others hate it, though everyone agrees the vanilla bean kulfi is one of the best desserts in Manhattan. Lunch upstairs can be a bit of a disappointment due to meager portions, so go for the awesome Bread Bar downstairs instead.

Tamarind ★★★½

INDIAN | EXPENSIVE | QUALITY ★★★★ | VALUE ★★★ | ZONE 7

41–3 East 22nd Street (between Park Avenue and Broadway); (212) 674-7400
www.tamarinde22.com

Customers Business, regulars, foodies on expense accounts **Wine Selection** Good with varied prices **Reservations** Recommended **When to Go** Anytime **Bar** Full service **Entrée Range** $14–$30 **Dress** Smart casual, chic, or business **Payment** All major credit cards **Service Rating** ★★★½ **Friendliness Rating** ★★★★½ **Disabled Access** yes

Lunch Daily, 11:30 a.m.–2:45 p.m.

Dinner Daily, 5:30–11:15 p.m.

Setting & Atmosphere This restaurant has a lot of style and warmth with a fresh, clean atmosphere. The style can be attributed to several elements, including the large glass windows at the front, skylight in the back, the fully stocked and well-appointed bar, the glass-enclosed kitchen, modern chairs, white-linen tablecloths, and freshly cut orchids on each table. The warmth is due to cream colors and soft lighting for the evening. You can eat at a table across from the bar in the narrow section of the restaurant, or you can sit at a table that opens out into a larger space towards the back. Private round tables are available around the periphery of the open room.

House Specialties Raji's tandoori scallops; lobster masala; raan e chengesi (lamb in garlic, ginger, and spices); murgh kola puri (spicy chicken with peppercorns); crab soup; tandoori items.

Other Recommendations Rosemary naan; lemon rice; luckhnow ki bhajia (incredibly crisp and light fritters with spinach, banana, and cheese); bhagarey baigan (eggplant with coconut, sesame, and peanut sauce); shrimp moiley (coconut-based sauce with mustard seeds, ginger, and curry leaves).

Summary & Comments Opened in 2001, Tamarind earned its culinary stripes almost immediately. The combination of spices is a treat to the senses. Luckily, there's a lot more than a linen tablecloth that sets this Indian restaurant apart from the other tasty and less expensive Indian counterparts. The difference lies in the delicate consideration of the ingredients used, the utmost freshest ingredients, and the daring to include lobster! The meats are as tender as the homemade cheese cubes that melt in the mouth. Presentation excels with the appetizers more than with the entrées; the succulent tandoori scallops are presented in a fried potato lattice cup that has become a signature dish. For a variety of chutneys and spices, try the vegetarian thali. Desserts range from chocolate soufflé to gulab jamun (pastry with dried milk and honey). The owner and manager are proud of their venture and are often seen shmoozing amongst the diners and ensuring customer happiness. The tearoom next door offers a wider selection of teas, desserts, and sandwiches in a more casual, cozy setting.

Tartine ★★★

FRENCH BISTRO | INEXPENSIVE | QUALITY ★★★★ | VALUE ★★★½ | ZONE 4

253 West 11th Street (corner of West 4th Street); (212) 229-2611

Customer Locals **Reservations** Not accepted **When to Go** Anytime **Entrée Range** $7.75–$16.95 **Payment** Cash only **Service Rating** ★★ **Friendliness Rating** ★★ **Wine Selection** Bring your own wine or beer **Dress** Casual **Disabled Access** For outside tables

Brunch Saturday and Sunday, 10:30 a.m.–4 p.m.; pastries, 9–11:30 a.m.

Lunch Tuesday–Friday, 11:30 a.m.–4 p.m.

Dinner Tuesday–Saturday, 5:30–10:30 p.m.; Sunday, 5:30–10 p.m.

Setting & Atmosphere This cute corner bistro on a pretty West Village street attracts lots of locals. There's usually a line waiting for the ten Formica-topped tables squeezed into the small exposed brick interior or for space in the outside café (weather permitting).

House Specialties Desserts—dacquoise, tarte tatin à la mode, custard-filled fruit tarts—are all made on the premises and are top-notch; salade basquaise; grilled salmon with citrus vinaigrette; croque monsieur made with brioche; beef mignonette aux poivres with frites.

Other Recommendations Onion tart, beet and endive salad; check daily specials.

Summary & Comments Basic bistro fare at very fair prices, the added savings of BYOB, and the cozy setting make Tartine a very popular place. Appetizers are hit or miss. Go with one of the salads or check out the daily specials, and skip the escargots. Of the entrées, beef mignonette aux poivres is very good, tender, and spicy, and accompanying frites are crisp and tasty, though a bit oversalted. Save room for desserts, though, especially the tarte tatin à la mode, served warm with caramelized apples. Service can be both charming and indifferent, depending on a variety of factors. Saturday and Sunday brunch at $10.95 is a great deal and very tasty; the prix fixe lunch is $12.95.

Tea & Sympathy ★★★

BRITISH | INEXP/MOD | QUALITY ★★★½ | VALUE ★★★ | ZONE 4

108–110 Greenwich Avenue (between Jane and Horatio streets); (212) 989-9735
www.teaandsympathynewyork.com

Customers Regulars, locals, homesick Brits, occasional celebs **Wine Selection** BYOB **Reservations** No **When to Go** Anytime **Bar** No, but lots of tea **Entrée Range** $6.50–$14.50 **Dress** Casual or avant garde **Payment** AMEX, MC, VISA **Service Rating** ★★★½ **Friendliness Rating** ★★★★ **Disabled Access** Yes, but not for bathroom

Open Daily, 11:30 a.m.–10:30 p.m; Sunday dinner, $18.95 or $25 with dessert and drink, served after 1:30 p.m. until they sell out

Setting & Atmosphere As you might imagine, with a name like Tea & Sympathy and a purpose to serve tea and comfort food, the décor is anything but minimalist. The restaurant is a cozy, square room with 10 small tables and a 22-seat capacity. A chalkboard lists the daily desserts, teas, and entrée specials. On the walls hang items of British kitsch, including caricatures of famous British icons, old-fashioned posters advertising British products, and shelves of mismatched china. The small kitchen is visible over the dessert case.

House Specialties Full afternoon tea (served anytime and includes watercress and egg salad, cream cheese and cucumber, chicken and tuna salad finger sandwiches, scones with clotted cream and jam, assorted cakes and cookies); shepherd's pie; bangers and mash (sausages and mashed potatoes); rhubarb crumble with custard; Sunday dinner (choice of roast beef, lamb or chicken, Yorkshire pudding, potatoes, and vegetables).

Other Recommendations Victoria sponge cake; baked beans on toast; Welsh rarebit (cheddar with mustard on toast); Stilton and walnut salad with beets; cheese and onion quiche; chicken and leek pie; tuna melt. The macaroni falls a little short.

Summary & Comments Due to the small size and addictive and delicious comfort food, it's not uncommon to have to wait outside for a table. The wait is well worth it, and since Tea and Sympathy is located in such a groovy part of town, you'll see interesting things to keep you occupied. This is not the place for a person on a strict diet; the tempting baked goods on display will entice you before you even look at the menu. Nicky, the owner, is often seen wandering between the restaurant and the shop next door, making sure customers are satisfied (and that they're behaving). She refuses to allow people to take a table unless everyone in the group is present; a few more of "Nicky's Rules" are displayed prominently on the front door window. The British selections excel, especially the shepherd's pie and vegetarian renditions. There aren't many places in NYC where you can find hot ribena and a Scotch egg on the menu. The afternoon tea is super and costs $19.95 for one person or $38 for two; if there are certain sweet things you don't like, let the server know beforehand so the selection can reflect your preferences. If you'd prefer fish and chips, the **A Salt and Battery** chip shop (also owned by Nicky) is next the adjacent tea shop.

Tomoe Sushi ★★★½

JAPANESE/SUSHI | MODERATE | QUALITY ★★★★ | VALUE ★★★★ | ZONE 4

172 Thompson Street (between Houston and Bleecker streets); (212) 777-9346

Customers Ethnic, locals **Reservations** Not accepted **When to Go** Anytime **Entrée Range** $15–$25 **Payment** AMEX **Service Rating** ★★ **Friendliness Rating** ★★★ **Bar** Beer and sake **Wine Selection** Stick to sake and beer **Dress** Very casual **Disabled Access** No

Lunch Wednesday–Saturday, 1–3 p.m.

Dinner Wednesday–Saturday and Monday, 5–11 p.m.; closed Sunday and Tuesday

Setting & Atmosphere The quintessential Village hole-in-the-wall with a few Japanese touches—lantern lights, prints on the wall, and a small sushi bar that seats a lucky five people at a time. Tomoe is about as big as the upper righthand section of a bento box, but that's part of its charm.

House Specialties Without a doubt, anything from the sushi bar; toro (fatty tuna), hamachi (yellowtail) belly; fresh salmon; amaebi (sweet shrimp); fresh king crab legs.

Other Recommendations Skip everything else. The shumai (boiled shrimp dumplings) are standard and the zaru soba (cold buckwheat noodles with dipping sauce) is subpar and much better elsewhere (try **Yodo** on 47th and Madison). Going to Tomoe for anything but raw fish is like going to a concert only for the opening act.

Summary & Comments Tomoe gives the phrase "fresh off the boat" new meaning. The sushi and sashimi here are wonderfully fresh, clean, and delicious. Pieces are big but not Yama-esque, just big enough to get the whole thing in your mouth comfortably. From there, just close your eyes and let the fish dissolve away. Buttery toro will melt in your mouth, and the huge king crab legs are so sweet and juicy you'll start to hear waves crashing around your eardrums. Tomoe boasts a great selection and reasonable prices, but get there early. Be prepared for small talk with those waiting in line; you might stand up to an hour, and it's worth every minute.

The Tree House Restaurant   ★★

MEDITERRANEAN | INEXP/MOD | QUALITY ★★★½ | VALUE ★★★½ | ZONE 18

273 City Island Avenue, City Island; (718) 885-0806

Customers Locals **Reservations** Not necessary **When to Go** Anytime **Entrée Range** $7–$23 **Payment** All major credit cards **Service Rating** ★★½ **Friendliness Rating** ★★★★½ **Bar** Full service **Wine Selection** Very small **Dress** Casual **Disabled Access** Yes, except bathrooms

Open Monday–Thursday, 11:30 a.m.–10 p.m.; Friday–Sunday, 11:30 a.m.–11 p.m.

Setting & Atmosphere An average-sized space opens up once you pass the bar on your right. The décor is pleasant, but nothing particularly worth mentioning apart from the lovely sea-view mural on one of the back walls. Tables are suitably spaced apart from each other, and the setting is clean. Little white lights in the front windows make the storefront look particularly homey.

House Specialties Chevapas (a favorite for expats of former Yugoslavia, also known as skinless char-grilled beef sausage); shunka wrapper (cheese rolled with bacon; warmed stuffed grape leaves); brick-oven pizza.

Other Recommendations Romanian steak marinated in Balsamic vinegar, olive oil and spices; Mediterranean chicken (chicken marinated in garlic and lemon and seasoned with peppercorns).

Summary & Comments What the Tree House lacks in presentation it gains in truly tasty dishes ranging from shunkas, grape leaves (absolutely fabulous—especially when served warm), chevapas, and Romanian steak. The Tree House also has the "best brick-oven pizza on City Island," featuring topping combos like the Ortolana (tomato sauce, mozzarella, smoked meat, eggplant, summer squash, onions, and fresh tomatoes). The chef hails from Montenegro, and he takes pride in preparing dishes from all over the Mediterranean region. Fish dishes are hit or miss, as is the pasta. Sticking with either the above dishes or a daily special is the best way to make the most of your meal. Don't bother with dessert. Part of the appeal of this place is simply going to City Island and checking out some of the little colonial houses, seeing the marina, and wandering along the main street, City Island Avenue. It's a welcome change of pace, which may also explain why the service is so friendly. If you stay late enough, you may even be offered a swig of something strong from the home country.

Tre Pomodori   ★★½

PASTA | MODERATE | QUALITY ★★★★ | VALUE ★★★★★ | ZONE 7

210 East 34th Street; (212) 545-7266

Customers Locals, professionals **Reservations** Recommended for large parties or at peak hours **When to Go** Anytime **Entrée Range** $8.95–$16.95; $5.95–$6.95 prix fixe lunch **Payment** Major credit cards **Service Rating** ★★½ **Friendliness Rating** ★★★½ **Bar** Beer and wine **Wine Selection** Small; South Americans best **Dress** Casual **Disabled Access** Fair

Lunch & Dinner Monday–Thursday, noon–11 p.m.; Friday and Saturday, noon–midnight

Dinner Sunday, 4–10 p.m.

Setting & Atmosphere A very narrow, cozy parlor with tiled floor, framed pictures dotting the walls, and candles flickering on tables.

House Specialties All pastas, especially linguine vongole (baby clams, oil, garlic), agnolotti al porcini (ultra-mushroomy pasta pockets), and linguine fra diavolo (black linguine with calamari and spicy tomato sauce); risotto; apple tart.

Summary & Comments This is not a great restaurant, but it is a useful one. If you're looking for a low-key place to get surprisingly tasty plates of pasta at bargain prices without getting gussied up (but you don't feel like a no-frills hole-in-the-wall either), this is a top choice, particularly when you're in East Midtown—where restaurants fitting that bill are hard to come by. The waiters will serve fast for those rushing back to work (or out to shows), but lingering is never discouraged. Avoid the spotty appetizers (specials are often better, and salads are always OK) and pricier entrées and cut straight to what they cook best: pasta. The linguine with baby clams is a splendid, classic version, very satisfying, and there's a broad range of other choices—18 in all. Risotto, sometimes a special, is also very good, as are the gratis crunchy toasts with tomato and basil. Desserts are only fair (best: apple tart). Service can be slightly confused but is always good-natured.

Union Pacific ★★★★½

SEAFOOD/ASIAN FUSION | EXP | QUALITY ★★★★½ | VALUE ★★★ | ZONES 7, 13

11 East 22nd Street (between Park Avenue South and Lexington); (212) 995-8500
www.unionpacificrestaurant.com
1742 Second Avenue (between 90th and 91st streets); (212) 831-8167

Customers Professionals, locals, celebrities **Reservations** Recommended **When to Go** Anytime **Entrée Range** Pretheater 3-course menu, $45, served until 6 p.m.; prix fixe 3-course dinner, $68; 5-course market menu, $85 **Payment** All major credit cards **Service Rating** ★★★ **Friendliness Rating** ★★★ **Bar** Full service **Wine Selection** Eclectic, a bit pricey **Dress** Upscale casual **Disabled Access** Main dining room

Lunch Monday–Friday, noon–2 p.m.

Dinner Monday–Friday, 5:30–10:30 p.m.; Saturday, 5:30–11 p.m.

Setting & Atmosphere Simple and understated, Union Pacific has one of the nicest rooms in the city. A small Japanese footbridge leads past a suspended curtain of falling water into a soaring space with arched metal beams overhead, a curved ceiling of frosted glass etched with constellations, comfortable banquettes, and Japanese cherrywood. As in the food, the Asian influence permeates; the room is immaculate and decidedly serene. Evening lighting is romantic; try lunch when the sunlight does the room justice.

House Specialties Bigeye tuna tartare with Asian pear and fresh wasabi; sautéed calamari with watermelon and avocado salad; kumamoto oysters with a Thai basil mignonette; sautéed skate with lime pickle Swiss chard and beurre noisette; caramelized veal chop; hazelnut success with gianduja cream.

Other Recommendations Ceviche of wild striped bass or rebolo with spring onions and lime; sautéed foie gras with green papaya and tamarind; lacquered squab with long beans and wild tarragon; poached halibut with young ginger and shallot cracklin'; baked peaches in brioche; warm chocolate cake with peanut butter ice cream.

Summary & Comments From the gorgeous room to the exhilarating food to the professional service, Union Pacific provides one of the best dining experiences in New York City. Chef Rocco DiSpirito's ingeniously creative food and bold clashing of flavors, temperatures, and textures will bring new life to even the most jaded of taste buds. With truly inventive dishes like sautéed calamari with watermelon and avocado, DiSpirito pulls no punches; he aggressively challenges the palate instead of giving in to it as so many other chefs do. His tuna tartare, the best in the city, burns with fresh wasabi, then cools with Asian pear. Sautéed skate, superior to many lesser imitations around the city, combines the perfectly cooked, butter-laden fish with lime pickle swiss chard and buerre noisette, an unlikely combination but one that seems destined from the beginning. In DiSpirito's dishes, everything counts, nothing is wasted, and all is carefully thought out. Although in isolation parts of a dish may seem discordant, juxtaposition brings harmony. DiSpirito is one of the best at combining different flavors that come together in the mouth and make you say, "Wow, now that's different—but it works." Here the whole is truly greater than the sum of its parts. And desserts are no different. One of the best desserts in Manhattan, hazelnut succes comes with candied wedges of pink grapefruit and whole hazelnuts, giving spark to what might otherwise be just a very good hazelnut mousse cake. Where others stop, Union Pacific pushes on, and that is the hallmark of a great restaurant.

Union Square Café ★★★★

NEW AMERICAN | EXPENSIVE | QUALITY ★★★★½ | VALUE ★★★★ | ZONE 7

21 East 16th Street (between Union Square and Fifth Avenue); (212) 243-4020

Customers Locals, business **Reservations** Recommended **When to Go** Anytime **Entrée Range** $16.50–$29 **Payment** All major credit cards **Service Rating** ★★★★ **Friendliness Rating** ★★★★ **Bar** Full service **Wine Selection** Excellent, both by the bottle and by the glass **Dress** Casual, business **Disabled Access** Fair

Lunch Monday–Saturday, noon–2 p.m.

Dinner Monday–Thursday, 6–10:15 p.m.; Friday and Saturday, 6–11:15 p.m.; Sunday, 5:30–9:45 p.m.

Setting & Atmosphere Airy dining spaces—a few steps down, a small flight up— with creamy beige walls, dark green chair rails, vibrant modern paintings, a mural of many merry maidens ("The Women of USC"), and bright bunches of fresh flowers. The cherrywood floors and a long, dark wood bar add to the warm, welcoming ambience. All is stylish without trying too hard.

House Specialties Be sure to check the daily specials; hot garlic potato chips; black bean soup; Union Square Café's calamari; crispy risotto cake; grilled, marinated filet mignon of tuna; crabmeat and artichoke tortelli; warm banana tart with honey-vanilla ice cream.

Other Recommendations Roasted lemon-pepper duck; peach pot pie. For lunch: yellowfin tuna burger with creamy cabbage slaw and the U.S.C. hamburger.

Summary & Comments For years, Union Square Café has been one of New York's most desired dining destinations. But one caveat, when Union Square Café is billed as New York's best restaurant, it's not for the food but the overall experience. Owner Danny Meyer and chef Michael Romano have set the standard for flawless, informed, amiable service in a laid-back setting, as well as dependable, usually delicious New American food. U.S.C. has all the elements of a classic, and it's one that's sure to keep running for years to come.

Veritas ★★★★

NEW AMERICAN | EXPENSIVE | QUALITY ★★★★½ | VALUE ★★★★ | ZONE 7

43 East 20th Street (between Park Avenue South and Broadway); (212) 353-3700
www.veritas-nyc.com

Customers Locals, business, oenophiles **Reservations** Necessary **When to Go** Anytime **Entrée Range** Prix fixe 3-course dinner, $68 **Payment** All major credit cards **Service Rating** ★★★★ **Friendliness Rating** ★★★★ **Bar** Full service **Wine Selection** Unbelievable and incredibly reasonable **Dress** Dressy casual, business **Disabled Access** Yes

Dinner Monday–Saturday, 5:30–10:15 p.m.; Sunday, 5–9:30 p.m.

Setting & Atmosphere This small one-room space has an elegant, modern look but a thoroughly comfortable feel. The room is decorated simply, with colorful hand-blown glass objets d'art set smartly into random spaces in the wall. The clean modesty of Veritas quickly translates itself into a relaxing and pleasant atmosphere; people seem genuinely happy to be here. Hint: Check out the bathrooms and the very cool sinks.

House Specialties Hamachi tartare with mint, green onions, soy, and osetra caviar; roasted sweetbreads; crisp skate, saffron-chive sauce, pistou, and orzo; braised veal; seared salmon with sautéed Asian greens and curry nage; caramelized peach tarte tatin; praline parfait.

Other Recommendations Seared foie gras, rhubarb compote, pistachio oil, and 20-year-old balsamic vinegar; sweet corn chowder with steamed clams; farm-roasted chicken; grilled black angus New York strip steak; chocolate souffle (cake); crème fraîche panna cotta; warm raspberry almond tart.

Summary & Comments Veritas has a small problem, though it's a problem most restaurants wished they had. When people think of Veritas, they think of wine, and with good reason. But because of that reputation, people might not go there to eat, and that would be a shame, because Veritas turns out some of the best food in the city. Chef Scott Bryan (also of Siena and West Village sleeper Indigo) is a master at using fresh, clean ingredients to mask the underlying complexity of his dishes. Sweet corn chowder sounds like it should be warm and comforting, but Bryan wakes it up with a sharp, lively hot broth and crunchy, juicy whole kernels of corn, then softens it with creamy clams—the perfect summer soup. Seared foie gras and hamachi tartare share a similar sensuality. And there's no dropoff with desserts either, as Cameron Irvin makes, among other things, a superb caramelized peach tarte tatin. The food at Veritas more than stands on its own, even if you don't order wine. But how can you do that? The size of a small bible, the wine list runs the gamut and has something for everyone, including a surprising number of quality bottles in the $18–$20 range. But perhaps the most pleasant surprise of Veritas is its lack of pretension. Despite the Ivy League–evoking name and the dedication to oenophilia, a subject traditionally associated with snobbery, Veritas goes out of its way to keep things down to earth. Eighteen-dollar bottles still bring out their top-of-the-line stemware; wine director Ben Breen and each of his four sommeliers are more than happy to pick out just the right bottle for you, and the entire staff is almost friendly to a fault. So go to Veritas, but don't just go for the wine. The wine list is great, but the food's even better.

Virgil's Barbecue   ★★½

BARBECUE | MODERATE | QUALITY ★★★½ | VALUE ★★★ | ZONE 8

152 West 44th Street; (212) 921-9494   www.virgilsbbq.com

Customers Professionals, tourists **Reservations** Recommended **When to Go** Anytime **Entrée Range** $8.95–$20 **Payment** All major credit cards **Service Rating** ★★★ **Friendliness Rating** ★★★½ **Bar** Full **Wine Selection** Small **Dress** Casual **Disabled Access** No

Lunch Daily, 11:30 a.m.–4:30 p.m.

Dinner Monday, 4:30–11 p.m.; Tuesday–Saturday, 4:30 p.m.–midnight; Sunday, 4:30–10 p.m.

Setting & Atmosphere Studied hillbilly, very Disney-esque—you expect the Country Bear Jamboree to strike up an Animatronic tune at any moment. Two levels: The top is for serious dining, and the ground level has tables, booths, and an inviting (and quite popular) long bar.

House Specialties Lamb barbecue sandwich, hamburgers, Brunswick stew, barbecue salad, hush puppies, onion rings, lemonade, Zapp's potato chips.

Other Recommendations The cornbread comes with really good maple butter; for a transcendent experience, ask for some as a dip for the hushpuppies.

Summary & Comments This restaurant is a great place for families, and you can't beat the convenient location, but foodwise, it's recommended only for a few certain things. The menu's unreliable, so rather than hunker down for an elaborate meal, head to the bar—or one of the informal tables downstairs—and grab a hamburger (redolent of hickory smoke) or lamb barbecue sandwich (very respectable, and much better than the ho-hum brisket or pulled pork), fabulous oniony hushpuppies (or merely good garlicky, funky onion rings), maybe a dish of Brunswick stew, and one of the impressive range of beers (lemonade's top-notch, too). If you don't stray too far from these tips and don't expect to make a Dining Experience of it all, you'll leave content—and without having emptied your wallet (this is one of those restaurants where prices look reasonable on the menu but the bill comes with smelling salts). Skip the chili and the barbecue plates (as opposed to sandwiches); forgo the ribs and desserts. Don't get fancy. Oh, and Virgil's bar (a happening nightspot, good for solo or group drinking) has friendly bartenders and is one of the only places in New York where you'll find wondrous Zapp's potato chips from New Orleans.

Woo Chon   ★★★

KOREAN | MODERATE | QUALITY ★★★★ | VALUE ★★★★ | ZONE 9

8 West 36th Street (near Fifth Avenue); (212) 695-0676

Customers Korean businessmen, aficionados **Reservations** Accepted **When to Go** Anytime **Entrée Range** $10–$20 **Payment** VISA, MC, AMEX **Service Rating** ★★★

Friendliness Rating ★½ **Bar** Beer and wine only **Wine Selection** Very limited **Dress** Nice casual or better **Disabled Access** Good

Open Daily, 24 hours

Setting & Atmosphere Two levels: a rather intense downstairs space (spotlit and dramatically appointed with lacquered calligraphy, dark wood, and Asian ink prints) and a slightly more laid-back upstairs room.

House Specialties Attention centers on the great bulgogi, sweetish garlic-marinated rib-eye prepared on the grill set into each table (wrap the beefy chunks in lettuce leaves with a little rice and dab on sweet soybean paste). Unfortunately, the tableside grills are outfitted for gas flame rather than glowing coals, but Woo Chon's awesome marinade—so delicious they bottle the stuff for sale—and top-quality meat easily compensate. Kalbi (beef short ribs) are equally recommended. Panchan, the traditional gratis assortment of little vegetable and fish starter plates, are unparalleled in their freshness, all flavors clearly focused and balanced (feel free to ask for extra helpings of your favorites). Yookgaejang (a restorative spicy beef soup) and dduk guk (a hearty dumpling soup) are both good choices, as are rice and noodle dishes that come with toppings for mixing in (look for "bibim" as a prefix), but be aware that the cold buckwheat noodle items serve more as palate-cleansers than main courses. Woo Chon elevates lowly pajun (crunchy/spongy pancakes with optional extras like seafood or kimchee) to an almost highbrow level, evoking subtle flavors from this snacky favorite. Also try gooksoo, a lot like shabu-shabu.

Other Recommendations Special $50 and $60 feasts may be ordered 48 hours in advance (bring a group and reserve a private room for the full effect).

Summary & Comments Though Woo Chon is a venerable name in New York Korean food, it's important to be aware of where its strengths lie. As in many Korean restaurants, the menu stretches well beyond those strengths in an effort to please a broad audience, so stick with the recommended dishes and avoid stews (jigae), intricate seafood or vegetable preparations, and homier items—this is no grandma kitchen; for down-home Korean, try Bo (see profile), Han Bat, or Cho Dang Gol. Management's haughty manner has unfortunately been adopted by many of the waiters. Woo Chon has a branch in Flushing at 41–19 Kissena Boulevard (phone (718) 463-0803).

Xunta   ★★★

SPANISH/TAPAS | MODERATE | QUALITY ★★★★ | VALUE ★★★★ | ZONE 5

174 First Avenue; (212) 614-0620   www.xuntatapas.com

Customers Young locals **Reservations** Only for 4 or more **When to Go** Before 7 p.m. to avoid crowds (Tuesdays are also light) **Entrée Range** $8–$23 **Payment** All major credit cards **Service Rating** ★★½ **Friendliness Rating** ★★½ **Bar** Full **Wine Selection** Good, Spanish **Dress** Nice casual **Disabled Access** Very poor (3 steps down)

Dinner Sunday–Thursday, 4 p.m.–midnight; Friday and Saturday, 4 p.m.–2 a.m.

Setting & Atmosphere Funky basement with Iberian touches and a young clientele. This seems more like a hangout than a restaurant; you'd certainly never expect to find good food here. This small space gets crowded on weekends.

House Specialties Pulpo a feira (octopus with paprika), tortilla española con cebolla (Spanish potato omelet with onion), lulas rechaeas (stuffed calamari), gazpacho, sardines, gambas ala plancha (grilled shrimp), cheeses, and hard-to-find Galician white wines (Albariños).

Entertainment & Amenities Live flamenco musicians and dancers Mondays and Thursdays at 8:30 p.m. (call to confirm day and time).

Summary & Comments The tapas craze hit New York in a big way, but this Galician bar is the only place that makes the Real Stuff. Holy grail tapas like octopus and potato omelet are closer to true Spanish style than at any other tapas bar in town. And the Albariños (young, tart white wines) are sipped the authentic way, out of white ceramic bowls. Items can be ordered either as small dishes (tapas) or larger raciones. Bear in mind that genuine tapas are unpretentious lusty accompaniments to drink, not haute cuisine, so the rollicking bar scene and crude seating are part and parcel of the experience.

Zen Palate ★★½

VEGETARIAN/ASIAN | INEXPENSIVE | QUALITY ★★★½ | VALUE ★★★★ |
ZONES 7, 8, 12

34 Union Square East (16th Street) (212) 614-9345
663 Ninth Avenue (Corner of 46th Street) (212) 582-1669
2170 Broadway (between 76th and 77th streets); (212) 501-7867

Customers Ethnic, locals **Reservations** Not accepted **When to Go** Anytime **Entrée Range** $8–$10; $2.50–$9 for pastas and soups **Payment** All major credit cards **Service Rating** ★★★ **Friendliness Rating** ★★ **Wine Selection** No liquor license; BYOB **Dress** Casual **Disabled Access** Upper West Side, yes; Midtown, yes; Downtown, no

Lunch & Dinner Upper West Side: Sunday–Thursday, noon–10:30 p.m.; Friday and Saturday, noon–11:30 p.m.; Midtown: daily, 11:30 a.m.–11 p.m.; Downtown: lunch daily, 11:30 a.m.–3 p.m.; dinner, Monday–Saturday, 5:30–11 p.m.; Sunday, 5–10:30 p.m.

Setting & Atmosphere This laid-back trio offers pockets of peace, with soft ocher walls, clouds on the ceiling in Midtown, patterned latticework Uptown, and dramatic architecture in the Union Square branch.

House Specialties Vegetable dumplings; spinach linguine salad with sesame peanut dressing; Zen lasagna; eggplant in garlic sauce; tofu honey pie.

Other Recommendations Basil moo-shu rolls; stir-fried fettuccine; Zen ravioli with special sauce; fresh-squeezed vegetable juice.

Summary & Comments An inexpensive oasis for noncarnivores, but you don't have to be a vegetarian to get the good karma and good vibes that come with the more than soul-satisfying cuisine here. The veggie variations are flavorfully inventive, and some are surprising in their intensity.

Part Nine

Shopping in New York

Keeping Your Eyes on the Prize (and the Price)

It may seem almost redundant to talk about a shopping guide to Manhattan. In fact, it's almost impossible *not* to shop in a city whose souvenirs—miniature Statues of Liberty, Empire State Buildings, (little) Big Apples—are so instantly familiar. There are Fifth Avenues in a million cities, but no dedicated follower of fashion will mistake that address for any other. Nearly every toney hotel lobby now comes complete with a fancy gift shop, if not a couple of name-brand boutiques. And then there are the street vendors, the shopping marts, the jewelry malls, the flea markets . . .

In fact, if you're not careful—even if it's exactly what you have in mind—you could find yourself spending your whole visit, and more than your budget, haphazardly acquiring things. That seems like a waste in more ways than one. When every city you visit seems to have the same designer shopping malls filled with the same stores and labels, New York is a treasure trove of specialty items, one-of-a-kind gifts, and real connoisseur's delights. We can't list them all (have you hefted a Manhattan Yellow Pages lately?), but we have picked out some we particularly like.

And as usual, we have tried to pick out ways that you can combine your shopping expeditions with explorations of neighborhoods, which have much nicer views than all those prepackaged malls and dispense with some of the hype in favor of the rich variety of New York. Sure, this is prime window-shopping territory, and you can see, and buy, a little of almost everything just by wandering around; but intriguingly, communities of merchants seem to have evolved that coincide with great walking opportunities, so if you know what sort of purchases you want to make, you can look them over for hours and see history at the same time.

For example, are you longing to personalize your suburban townhome with unusual furniture and home accessories? Head to Soho. Love gazing at art galleries? You could spend a whole visit in Soho and its sibling rival, Chelsea. Designer couture? Fifth Avenue, of course, but also upper Madison Avenue. You can get discounts on clothes at a factory-shop mall, but why not wander the Lower East Side, the neighborhood that made discount shopping famous? New York is famous for gourmet foods, and supermarkets such as Dean & Deluca and Zabar's are classics, but what about noshing on real pickles or fresh-from-the-oven matzo? And if you're looking for a real ethnic experience, skip the markets in Little Italy in favor of Arthur Avenue in the Bronx and see the neighborhood groceries out there.

For those collectors who are more single-minded, we have included a selection of stores and purveyors of specific goods. Rare books, black ties, vintage rock and roll—you want it, we got it.

All Together Now: Department Stores, "Malls," and Flea Markets

The Big Names

We're not by any means suggesting that you settle for department-store shopping in New York, but sometimes traveling is a matter of so many gifts, so little time. In that case, you need a lot of options at one address. Besides which, there are some stores in New York so famous in and of themselves that they almost qualify as tourist attractions. (And there are a couple, perhaps not so well-known, that might change your vision of department stores.) Or you may like the spontaneity and treasure-hunt aspect of flea markets. Or, especially if you want to get that souvenir stuff out of the way in a hurry, you might just want to hustle through the company-logo superstores that are the gift shop equivalents of amusement parks.

Probably the best-known names in department-store shopping in Manhattan are Barney's, Bergdorf Goodman, Bloomingdale's, Macy's, and Saks.

Barney's original Chelsea store is on 18th Street between Seventh and Eighth avenues (phone (212) 716-8817), but nowadays the main Barney's is the $100-million Midtown megastore on Madison Avenue at East 61st (phone (212) 826-8900).

The B&G logo of **Bergdorf Goodman** (phone (212) 753-7300) has been at the cornerstones of Fifth and 57th, both literally and metaphorically, for generations; and maybe that's exactly the reason it recently embarked on a very modern retooling. The seventh-floor housewares department, already a magnet for forward-thinking brides and newly promoted partners, is now 3,000 square feet larger and arranges its own exhibitions. Famed chef Daniel Boulud helped set up the new tea salon, and while so many stores are cutting back on either prices or service, Bergdorf is booming: It now has a whole men's store, called simply Bergdorf Goodman Men, on the opposite side of the street. Bergdorf is so dependable that should you suddenly discover that the dinner you're invited to is black-tie, you can call the gender-appropriate store to dispatch a personal shopper to your hotel with an armful of outfits for you to try on.

Bloomingdale's is the designer version of a department store, and it looks it. Everything is name-brand—you could hang your clothes out in the living room and never worry about feeling label-challenged—from Polo to Petrossian (yup, a caviar stand). It even has an American Express office (on Third Avenue at East 59th Street; (212) 355-5900).

Macy's may be a giant—it covers more than a million square feet—but it's the most moderate-priced of the bunch. Perhaps its merchandise isn't as cutting-edge as some; but it covers nearly all the bases, from kitchen goods (and carry-out) in the basement to antiques on the ninth floor, and from haircuts to pedicures. And its rather stubborn nostalgia is fairly represented by that famous Thanksgiving Day Parade (Broadway between West 34th and 35th; (212) 695-4400).

Saks Fifth Avenue (phone (212) 753-4000) is just where you'd expect it to be, on Fifth between 49th and 50th streets next to St. Patrick's Cathedral. This is an old-money outlet with an old-money outlook on fashion, jewelry, fine foods, and even lunch; the Café SFA on the eighth floor has views of the cathedral and Rockefeller Center across the street.

Henri Bendel remains a temple for the haute and the ultra-hip (712 Fifth Avenue, between 55th and 56th streets; (212) 247-1100).

Our personal favorite is much less famous, far more limited in stock, and on the expensive side, but it is so beautifully appointed—even the store hardware is gorgeous—that it's worth a look. **Takashimaya** (Fifth Avenue between East 54th and 55th; (212) 350-0115), in a fine six-story townhouse, begins with a tea shop in the basement and rises through a flower shop, spa, and art galleries to men's, women's, and home furnishings. One visit, and you'll have a whole new respect for interior design.

Malls and All

Even less do we suggest you look for a shopping mall in Manhattan (especially as the streets are already full of Gaps, etc.). If you must run off a quick list, however, there are a couple of shopping towers ("malls" in the city are more likely to be vertical than horizontal) that won't be far off your path.

The **Manhattan Mall** at Sixth Avenue and 33rd Street has about 120 shops on nine levels of shops, a typical food court, and a useful brochure-heavy visitors center on the seventh floor (phone (212) 465-0500). Even handier, it's right next to Macy's. The fourth and fifth floors of **Trump Tower** on Fifth Avenue between 56th and 57th streets are full of shops: The really big names—Bruno Magli, Ferragamo, Chanel, etc.—are right at street level; and the pink marble atrium with its astonishing waterfall/waterwall is something of a tourist attraction in itself. **Rockefeller Center** also has a minimall that you can tour while admiring the Plaza display of the moment, the skating rink, the Deco buildings, and so on (just off Fifth between 49th and 50th). And the renovated **South Street Seaport,** part of the built-up Lower Manhattan area near the Fulton Fishmarket at Water Street, is now an attractive, if somewhat predictable, mall of shops, restaurants, and marine-history souvenir stores.

The most attractive one-stop shopping destination for now is the renovated **Grand Central Station,** which has more than 120 boutiques, service stores, coffee shops, and carryouts. And of course, it also has several serious restaurants to choose from, including Michael Jordan's Steakhouse, with its view of the Grand Concourse; a mezzanine bar; the famed Grand Central Oyster Bar; the third-floor cocktail lounge in the long-neglected Campbell Apartment, built in the 1920s as a private office and modeled on a 13th-century Florentine palazzo; and a trendy faster-food and trattoria concourse on the lower level complete with fish and meat markets. At press time, stores in the chic new **Time Warner Center** (at Columbus Circle, 59th Street and Central Park West) were just beginning to open; check it out for some primo boutiques and chains.

Flea Markets

We do recommend this very characteristic diversion. What would shopping in Manhattan be without a visit to the flea markets? Of course, we mean semi-pro shopping—not the sort of amateur souveniring you can do anywhere, but spot, dash, and bargain stuff. Frequently there are serious antiques dealers as well (see more on antiques centers later in this section), but with flea markets, you need to be a little more careful about derivations and aging.

Some flea markets are regularly scheduled, some are more impromptu (especially in good weather), and a few are more like block parties with vendors involved, especially downtown. A few general rules apply to all, however. Don't expect dealers to accept credit cards, although a few whose merchandise is particularly expensive (antique furniture and so on) might. In most cases, expect to pay cash and carry your prize off with you. If you want to skim off the cream of the crop, go early; if you're hoping to score a real bargain, wait until the afternoon, when some dealers may be willing to shave the price so they don't have to pack everything up. Some markets may charge a nominal entrance fee of a dollar or two.

These are the most dependable spots to shop, but the Weekend section of the *New York Times* may mention some special fairs; also check the classified ads.

The most famous, the original, is the **Annex Antiques Fair and Flea Market**—popularly known as the "26th Street flea market"—which brings more than 500 vendors together every weekend in a trio of parking lots that stretch along Sixth Avenue from West 24th toward West 27th. The antiques area, around 26th, is open both Saturdays and Sundays from 9 a.m. to 5 p.m., but the general market at the southern end is open only on Sundays—and that's the one to see if you're hoping to celebrity-hunt while you're trying to distinguish the Tiffany from the trash. (This is also a good place to learn more about such merchandise, as many of the dealers are extremely professional.) From there it's a short walk to the **Chelsea Antiques Annex,** a.k.a. "the Garage," along West 25th Street between Sixth and Seventh, which is run by the same people and opens and closes in tandem with the outdoor market.

But unless you are a flea-market veteran, you may find it easier to grasp the opportunities at the somewhat smaller **Soho Antiques Fair and Flea Market,** which sets up Saturdays and Sundays from 9 a.m. to 5 p.m. at the corner of Broadway and Grand Street. Another good smaller flea market is the **Greenwich Village Flea Market** at P.S. 41 on Greenwich Avenue near Seventh; it is open Saturdays only from noon to 7 p.m.

If you have the stamina, you can do the East Side/West Side two-step over the weekend by swinging through the upscale flea markets at **P.S. 183** on East 66th Street between First and York Avenues (Saturday only, 6 a.m.–6 p.m.) and the "Greenflea" indoor/outdoor market at **Intermediate School 44** on Columbus Avenue at West 77th (Sunday only, 10 a.m.–5:30 p.m.).

One-stop Shopping: Museum Shops and Theme Stores

Art-ifacts: The Museum Shops

If you're sick of the cookie-cutter gift list, treat yourself to a mall of the mind, so to speak. Along two straight lines, one in Midtown and the other on the East Side, are clusters of the smartest—meaning chic and brainy—shops, all a little different and all, so to speak, of museum quality.

The first line, of course, is along Museum Mile, that stretch of Fifth Avenue between 82nd and 104th Streets along which nine major collections are assembled. All have some sort of gift shop, but it's fair to say that the **Metropolitan Museum of Art** at 82nd Street (phone (212) 897-5500) has one of the most stunning collections anywhere, filled with not only merchandise relating to current and hit exhibits—replica jewelry, Egyptiana, art-design scarves, notepaper, and the like—but also classic reproduction posters, decorative glass, books, T-shirts, desk accessories, card cases, calendars, vases, reproduction statuary, Impressionist umbrellas, Munch and Dalí wristwatches, and even rugs. It has its own bridal registry, too. Check out some of the art being sold on consignment upstairs. And if you don't make it up to Museum Mile, the **Metropolitan Museum** has a two-story branch in Rockefeller Center at 15 West 49th Street (phone (212) 332-1360), where you can find a full selection of its merchandise, rugs and all; there's also an outpost in Soho at 113 Prince Street (phone (212) 614-3000).

The **Jewish Museum** on Fifth at 92nd (phone (212) 423-3200) has a small but striking collection of jewelry, menorahs, and scarves, many with designs adapted from religious or historical works.

The **Cooper-Hewitt National Museum of Design** at 91st (phone (212) 849-8300) is design central for those whose taste in silver, platters, and small personal and office items such as pens, bath luxuries, salt-and-peppers, and coasters tends to an earlier, more sensual age than the sleek modernity of MoMA's collection (this is, after all, the former Carnegie mansion). But if you do like that smart postmodern look, step into the shop at the **Guggenheim** at 89th Street (phone (212) 423-3615) and peruse their fine selections.

A short stroll away, though not literally in "the Mile," are the **Frick Collection** (Fifth and 70th), which has lovely notepaper, calendars, postcards, and notebooks; the **Whitney Museum's** (Madison and 75th) store with its sometimes elegantly spare (Shaker-influenced), sometimes witty assortment of ties, toys, and other home and closet whimsy; and the **Asia Society** bookstore has been newly renovated and expanded (Park Avenue between 70th and 71st; phone (212) 517-2742; **asiasociety.org**), and stocks not only adult and children's books on Asian culture, cooking, language, and design but also toys, jewelry, teapots, chopsticks, Indonesian carvings, and unusual paper goods.

Along a somewhat more imaginary aisle in Midtown Manhattan, on a line that cuts from West 53rd to West 49th streets between Fifth and Sixth avenues (though closer to Fifth), you'll find half a dozen more museum shops within easy reach.

The **American Craft Museum** and the **Museum of American Folk Art** on West 53rd are both exhibit spaces and among the finest art-gift shops in town (40 West 53rd; (212) 956-3535). Though the selection is not large, the jewelry is particularly attractive, sometimes spectacular, and there are often some glassworks as well as paperweights and other decorative items.

The **MoMA Design Store** (44 West 53rd Street; (212) 767-1050) has for good reason inspired one of the great mail catalogs of our box-stuffing era. Every one of these products—glassware, writing pens, kids' flatware, vases, photo frames, even watches and ties—have passed such muster with the museum's design mavens that they have become part of the per-manent collection. And smart as they are, they are frequently great bar-gains: Among our personal favorite acquisitions have been spiral-twist stretch bracelets, something like Slinkies for the wrist, for $8–$12. And **MoMA's bookstore** (across the street in the lobby at 11 West 53rd; (212) 708-9700), which stocks more than 6,000 coffee-table books, cata-logs, and quality paperbacks, is also packed with educational videos, software, art posters, calendars, and so on. For downtowners, there is another MoMA shop in Soho at 81 Spring Street (phone (646) 613-1367) and also one at the MoMa QNS at 33rd Street and Queens Boulevard.

Just around the corner (straight through the block, if you could do it) on 52nd Street is the **Museum of Television and Radio** (phone (212) 621-6800), which has a small store ideally suited to those whose kids (or spouses) still have crushes on Mary Tyler Moore or Captain Kirk. It stocks videos, T-shirts, posters, vintage radio shows, and stocking stuffers with character, so to speak.

The **International Center for Photography** at Sixth Avenue and 43rd Street (phone (212) 860-1777) is the only museum anywhere that collects and exhibits only photographs; its calendars, prints, and coffee-table books are first-rate. The **Museum of the City of New York** has such urban memorabilia as stickball sets and vintage posters (Fifth Avenue at 103rd Street; (212) 534-1672).

Among other attractive stops are the trio of stores at the **Metropolitan Opera House** in Lincoln Center: the Met shop on the main floor (phone (212) 580-4090); the broader Performing Arts shop on the lower level (phone (917) 441-1195); and the Poster Gallery (phone (212) 580-4673), which stocks not only great records and biographies but also diva (and danseur) T-shirts, mugs, and the sort of unabashed art lover's acces-sories that fill PBS catalogs. The shop at the **National Museum of the American Indian** (phone (212) 514-3700) in the old Customs House at 1 Bowling Green downtown near Battery Park has Native American music and meditation tapes, beadwork kits, and turquoise jewelry of the sort that is once again popular with young people, plus T-shirts, arrow-heads, and reproductions of famous paintings of the West. And if you're headed down that way, you might want to check out the maps, model ships, and other old-salt stuff at the **South Street Seaport Museum Shops** (phone (212) 732-8257).

Brand Loyalty: Theme Stores

The 1990s gave birth to a whole new boom in merchandising: stores spe-cializing in movie and television tie-ins, corporate brand names, celebrity properties, and so on. They are virtually theme parks disguised as stores, and if your kids are determined to have these sorts of souvenirs, there are several along almost any major tour route.

Along Fifth Avenue near the foot of Central Park are the **Coca-Cola Store,** the **Warner Bros. Studio Store,** and the **Disney Studio Store.** (Both Disney and Warner Bros. have stores in Times Square as well.) The multistory **Niketown** is on 57th just around the corner toward Madison Avenue, as is the **Original Levi's Store.** There are **NBA/WNBA** stores in Times Square and on Fifth at 52nd. The **WWF New York** at Broadway and 43rd has floor-to-ceiling TV screens for video replays and a stage for live "performances," frequent in-house and celeb drop-bys as well as paraphernalia and food (phone (212) 398-2563).

The **NBC Studio Store,** in Rockefeller Center, is stocked with T-shirts, coffee mugs, and caps from *Seinfeld, Frasier, Friends, The Tonight Show, Saturday Night Live,* and so on.

And since more and more restaurants have their own in-house merchandise stores, check out the **Harley-Davidson Cafe** (Sixth Avenue and West 56th; (212) 245-6000), the **Jekyll & Hyde Club** (Sixth and 57th; (212) 541-9505), **Planet Hollywood** (phone (212) 333-7827), at Broadway and 45th, and the **Hard Rock Cafe** (West 57th between Seventh and Broadway; (212) 459-9320). These are all close enough to serve as an instant playground pub tour.

Of course, if your particular brand loyalty lies with a famous designer, you're headed uptown, so see the following sections on Fifth Avenue and Madison Avenue.

Great Neighborhoods for Shopping

Windows on the World: Fifth Avenue

There are a few streets whose stores and window displays are so famous that they don't even need city names attached. Rodeo Drive. Champs-Elysées. Via Veneto. And Fifth Avenue.

Fifth Avenue was nicknamed "Millionaire's Row" at the turn of the century, when the Vanderbilts, Astors, and Goulds all built palaces for themselves along the road, and it's never quite given up that expensive spirit. A few of the 19th-century mansions are still standing, and the churches of the area give you an idea of the luxury such tycoons expected even in their houses of worship. (Remember that Fifth Avenue is the east/west dividing line, and don't let addresses on the numbered streets confuse you. Cartier at East 52nd Street faces B. Dalton at West 52nd.)

To get a serious sense of both the retail and historical beauties of Midtown, start at the corner of 49th Street and head north toward Central Park. On your left: **Rockefeller Center,** which fills the blocks between

Fifth and Sixth Avenues and West 48th and 51st Streets and incorporates Radio City Music Hall and the NBC Studios (look around the corner onto West 49th and you'll see that famous window into the *Today* show). There are also many shops in the lower levels of the complex, and the famous ice rink/outdoor café (a Jekyll and Hyde trick that follows the seasons) and gardens, as well as many seasonal displays on the plaza. There is actually a minimuseum of the complex on the concourse level at 30 Rockefeller Plaza, with photos and video, and a walking tour guide is available free at the information desk in the lobby. Notice the gilded gods of industry on the front, the bas relief, and the Art Deco detailing.

Across the street are **Saks Fifth Avenue,** one of the city's finest department stores; and St. Patrick's Cathedral, which was built by James Renwick, Jr., in the 1880s. Just above that is the elaborate facade of the famous jeweler **Cartier** at the corner of East 52nd, which is one of the few turn-of-the-19th-century mansions still intact. Legend has it that the original owner traded the house to Pierre Cartier for a string of pearls.

The French Gothic St. Thomas Church at the corner of Fifth and 53rd was built in 1914; the University Club at 54th was built in 1899 by Charles McKim (a partner of Stanford White) in imitation of the Italian palazzos. McKim also designed what is now the Banco di Napoli across the street. The Fifth Avenue Presbyterian Church, built in 1875, was where the Roosevelts, Auchinclosses, and Walcotts worshiped, helping give it the reputation of being the city's most influential congregation.

Now the credit-card boutiques begin to thicken: **Christian Dior** at Fifth Avenue and East 55th; **Takashimaya** (discussed earlier) and **Elizabeth Arden** between East 54th and 55th; **Façonnable** and **Gucci** at East 54th; and **Henri Bendel** between West 55th and 56th.

Harry Winston, diamond designer to the rich and famous, is on Fifth at West 56th, and the other three famous "Four Carat" neighbors, **Tiffany, Van Cleef & Arpels,** and **Bulgari,** are all at the intersection of 57th. (The building that houses Bulgari at 730 Fifth was the first home of the Museum of Modern Art.) Between 56th and 57th look for **Ferragamo** and O.J. favorite **Bruno Magli; Steuben,** the art-glass company; **Burberry's; Chanel;** and **Fendi. Norma Kamali** is just around the corner on 56th.

Bergdorf Goodman and **Bergdorf Goodman Men** (discussed earlier) fill the blocks from West 57th to 58th. And as you get to the bottom of the park, where Fifth meets 58th Street, you'll see **FAO Schwarz,** one of the most famous (though now insolvent) toy stores in the world.

Clothing on the High Side: The East Side

If you love that Italian-label look but don't have time to fly to Rome, relax. These days, the signs along Madison Avenue in the 60s and 70s read like satellite transmissions from the Via Veneto, with just enough American and international designer boutiques to keep you grounded.

Some of the big-name stores have set up along the numbered streets between Madison and Fifth Avenues, so that the old couture row, the new Madison, and the museum district are beginning to merge. As an example, start east along 57th Street from Fifth Avenue and you will see the signs for **Christian Dior, Chanel, Charivari, Yves Saint Laurent, Hugo Boss, Jil Sander, Montblanc, Bur-berry's, Coach, Prada, Louis Vuitton,** and **Gurkha;** turn the corner onto Madison for **Tourneau,** the watch temple. **Emporio Armani** is on Madison at 58th; **DKNY** and the **Calvin Klein** flagship are on the corner at East 60th. **Hermès** is on Madison at 62nd; **Shanghai Tang** at 63rd; **David Yurman** at 64th; and **Emilio Pucci** is just around the corner on 64th Street between Madison and Fifth.

But the real name-label parade begins at the northwest corner of West 65th and Madison with the **Giorgio Armani** boutique, a stunning white four-story showplace that resembles the National Gallery's East Building (not to mention Armani couture itself). It gazes serenely across at the **Krizia** and **Valentino** boutiques and shelters the **BCBG/May Azria** shop on its left.

Across 66th are the new **Bulgari** showroom, **Cerutti** children's clothing, **David Berk Cashmere, Jean-Paul Gaultier,** and **Nicole Miller,** who is to ties as the *New Yorker* is to cartoons. **Emmanuel Ungaro** holds down the corner of Madison and 67th. Cross 67th to **Kenzo, Moschino, Davide Cenci,** and **Frette** Italian linens, and peek around the corner to 21 East 67th for the classic English country tweeds, cufflinks, and other gentry goods at the boutique of the 150-year-old **House of Dormeuil.**

Above 67th you'll find **Joseph Tricot** London sweater chic. Above 68th Street are the complete ready-to-wear collections of **Gianni Versace** (in a negative-image Roman temple with black capitals and silver-gilded capitals); **MaxMara; Malo,** the European cashmere king; **Jaeger** sportswear; **Donna Karan; Bogner** ski couture; and **TSE Cashmere.** The **Dolce & Gabbana** store at the corner of Madison and 69th is 7,000 square feet of retro-rococo chic; **Prada** preens nearby at Fifth (phone (212) 664-0010) and Madison (phone (212) 327-4200).

Cross 69th to **Missoni, Chloë, Maraolo** Italian shoes, **Romeo Gigli, Miu Miu, Fila,** and **Andrea Carrano.** If you're crazy for natural fibers or custom-woven linens, it's dueling designer labels: the Italian **Pratesi** versus the French **D. Porthault.**

Yves Saint Laurent's couture store and his **Rive Gauche** boutique are side by side on Madison between 70th and 71st Streets, along with **Gianfranco Ferre, Sonia Rykiel, Frederic Fekkai,** the hairdresser-cum-designer, and **Santoni's** handmade Italian footwear.

Ralph Lauren has four floors of Polo clothing, accessories, and home luxuries on the west side of Madison between 71st and 72nd Streets and a whole second building full of Polo Sport casualwear and his trademark weathered look on the east side. **Givenchy's** haute couture store is on Madison at East 75th near **Carolina Herrerra,** and **Issey Miyake's** is at 76th along with **Michael Kors.**

Clothing on the Hip Side: Soho

Fashion- and/or bargain-conscious visitors have a great reason to wander the Soho area—aside from the fun of the street theater, that is. (Besides, the shops and names play musical addresses so often you may have to wander around to find again that great find you found before.) Remember that weekends are prime wandering time, too, so that quite a few Soho shopkeepers close on Monday.

Retro, nouveau, haute, and so-so, Soho and surroundings are big boutique territory, so unless you want to have an Armani T-shirt just like everybody else's, you can get more in-circle designerwear at places such as **Scoop** (532 Broadway; (212) 925-2886); **Morgane Le Fay,** Liliana Ordas's splendidly mysterious cave of dresses and capes (67 Wooster Street; (212) 219-7672); and Laura Whittcomb's **Label** (265 Lafayette Street; (212) 966-7736).

Other specialty shops include **Kate Spade** (59 Thompson Street; (212) 274-1991) and her husband **Jack Spade's** men's shop around the corner (56 Greene; (212) 625-1820); **Alexander McQueen** (417 West 14th Street; (212) 645-1797); **Anna Sui** (13 Greene; (212) 941-8406); the lower-case upper-class **agnes b.** (13 East 16th; (212) 741-2585) and **agnes b. homme** (79 Green; (212) 431-4339); the London legend **Vivienne Westwood** (71 Greene; (212) 334-5200); Rei Kawakubo at **Commes des Garçons** (520 West 22nd; (212) 604-9200); the pricey but irresistibly distinctive **Yohji Yamamoto** (103 Grand; (212) 966-9066); rock-star child **Stella McCartney** (429 West 14th Street; (212) 255-1556); neo-Mod **Cynthia Rowley** (112 Wooster; (212) 334-1144); **Balenciaga** (54 West 23rd Street: (212) 206-0872); **Vivienne Tam** (99 Greene; (212) 966-2398); **Diane von Furstenberg** (389 West 12th; (212) 486-4800); and Miuccia Prada at **Miu Miu** (100 Prince Street; (212) 334-5156). An amalgam of Miu Miu, Jil Sander, Prada, Fendi, etc. is all in one at **Jeffrey New York** (449 West 14th Street; (212) 206-1272). One of **Betsey Johnson's** several New York locations is 138 Wooster (phone (212) 995-5048); **Nicole Miller Soho** is at 134 Prince (phone (212) 343-1362). Also check out **Product** (71 Mercer Street; (212) 274-1494); **Kirna Zabête** (96 Greene Street; (212) 941-9656); **Palma** (521 Broome Street; (212) 966-1722); **Alpana Bawa** (41 Grand Street; (212) 965-0559); and Beastie Boy Mike D's **X-Large** (Lafayette Street; (212) 334-4480).

Perhaps a symbol of the next consumer boom is the huge **Prada** flagship at Broadway and Prince (phone (212) 334-8888), a $40-million,

23,000-square-foot art loft with computers in the racks, stadium seating in the shoe department, and handbags in the elevators.

The first name in vintage chic, of course, is **Harriet Love,** author of the best-selling guide to the stuff and maven of the store that outfitted onetime-employee-turned-pop-singer Cyndi Lauper (126 Prince Street; (212) 966-2280). **What Comes Around Goes Around** stocks more than 60,000 vintage pieces, designer to denim (351 West Broadway; (212) 343-9303). Also check out **Alice Underground** (481 Broadway; (212) 431-9067), **Screaming Mimi** (382 Lafayette; (212) 677-6464), **Stellas Dallas** (218 Thompson; (212) 674-0447), and **Arkle & Sparkle** (216 Lafayette; (212) 925-9699). For the traditional Japanese look, as opposed to Tokyo modern couture, try **Kimono House** (131 Thompson Street; (212) 505-0232).

There are also hot spots for last year's, or even last season's, designer consignments and sell-offs: check **INA** (21 Prince; (212) 334-9048) and **INA Men** (262 Mott; (212) 334-2210), for high style—Prada, Helmut Lang, Joseph—at cut-rate prices. Also look into **NANA** (New and Almost New) at 65 Mercer (phone (212) 226-6677), **Cherry** (185 Orchard; (212) 358-7131), and **Yu** (151 Ludlow; (212) 979-9370) to score Yohji Yamamoto and Commedes Garçons on the rebound.

As with home furnishings, art, and hipness in general, the neighborhood is filling out through Little Italy, making Mott and Elizabeth Streets a trendy transition to the bargain-minded Lower East Side. Imelda Marcos wannabes must make a beeline for **Sigerson Morrison** (242 Mott; (212) 219-3893), unless you already have kid leather pumps the color of a swashbuckler's wine and velvet loafers for your dinner jacket. Milliner **Kelly Christy** (235 Elizabeth Street; (212) 965-0686) makes hats to order from a set of designs with names Ben & Jerry would love (though not at ice cream prices), such as the Jackie Kennedy–style pillbox called O and the fruit-topped Cherry Swirl. Softer chapeaux of fleece and fake fur and felt come in both adult and baby sizes at **Lisa Shaub**'s hat store (232 Mulberry; (212) 965-9176). **Geraldine** does avant-garde (246 Mott; (212) 219-1620) while **Milena** does the Imelda Marco thing (252 Mott; (212) 226-4711). So do **Shoe** (197 Mulberry; (212) 941-0205) and **Goffredo Fantini** (248 Elizabeth; (212) 219-1501). **Mayle** delivers the casual chic assembled by former model Jane Mayle (252 Elizabeth Street; (212) 625-0406), while traditional ethnic prints and sari scarves are put together in untraditional ways at **Calypso** (280 Mott; (212) 965-0990). **Zero** showcases Modernist designer Maria Cornejo (225 Mott Street; (212) 925-3849), and **P.A.K.** hangs out Corey Pak (229 Mott; (212) 226-5167). And **Living Doll** is for those who love vintage at even lower prices (49 Prince; (212) 625-9410).

Incidentally, if you have a certain craving for name-brand architecture as well as couture, skip down to 119 Hudson Street in Tribeca and see the Frank Gehry-designed **Issey Miyake** boutique, with its titanium "ribbons" that run from cellar to ceiling.

Clothing on the Bargain Side: The Lower East Side

The Lower East Side has been famous for years as the place bargains were best; serious shoppers flew in to gawk along Orchard Street, where last season's department store and even designerwear could be had for, well, if not a song, then a chorus or two. These days, with sales so much more common and outlet malls thriving, the trek is a little lower on some visitors' itineraries, but the merchants of the neighborhood, now being more aggressively promoted as the Historic Orchard Street Bargain District, have banded together to raise their profile again. So if you do have that bargain bug—and, after all, how many of your office mates can tell last year's classics from this year's?—head east from Soho into this evocative old section.

More than 300 businesses in this neighborhood are still family-owned, and with just a little imagination (and maybe a stop in the Lower East Side Tenement Museum or other historic landmark), you'll be able to see it as it was when the pushcart and peddler era was melding into the wholesale world—especially if you go on a Sunday, when a lot of the area streets are blocked off for pedestrian traffic and turned into open-air vendor markets. And you'll definitely still hear the rhythms of the Yiddish millions of East European Jews stamped on the bargaining patter of the vendors, even though the community's ethnicity now ranges from South American to Southeast Asian. You may find 19th-century echoes in some stores' cash-only, or at least no credit card, policies and the haggling over prices you may get into every once in a while. But there are a few entirely modern things you should remember as well. The first is that many of those sidewalk vendors are hawking bootleg or counterfeit goods. And maybe you shouldn't flash your cash too carelessly. But if you like the hurly-burly of contact-sport shopping, this is the place, and you might get a real bargain if you work at it.

To keep from getting disoriented in all this retail abundance, stop by the offices of the **Historic Orchard Street Shopping District** at 261 Broome Street (phone (212) 226-9010) and pick up a brochure/map of the neighborhood; or if you drop by **Katz's Deli** at the corner of Ludlow Street and East Houston (phone (212) 254-2246) any Sunday at 11 a.m. from April through December, you can hook up to a free hour-long shopping tour. (If Katz's looks particularly familiar to you, it's probably because the most famous scene in *When Harry Met Sally*—the, uh, loud one—was shot here.) Meanwhile, a few spots to get you started.

Feet first: Check into the likes of **Giselle Sportswear** (143 Orchard; (212) 673-1900); cashmere at **Fishkin Knitwear** (around the corner at 314 Grand; (212) 226-6538); and the really big-name double-breasteds at **Jodamo International** menswear (321 Grand Street; (212) 219-1039). Lingerie lovers linger at **A. W. Kaufman** (73 Orchard; (212) 226-1629) and **Louis Chock** across the street (74 Orchard; (212) 473-1929). Try on the leather coats at **Carl & Sons** (172 Orchard; (212) 674-8470). Actually, you can't escape leather shops on Orchard Street, any more than you will run out of any other kind of clothing; walk around a little before you buy, or at least try to bargain a little.

Do a hat trick at **Stetson's** (101 Delancey; (212) 473-1343). For designer handbags, look to **Fine & Klein** (119 Orchard; (212) 674-6720), **Ber-Sel Handbags** (75 Orchard; (212) 966-5517), and **Sole of Italy** (125 Orchard; (212) 674-2662). If you really just want another Samsonite or American Tourister rollalong, there's plenty of that stuff to be found as well. On the other hand, there's just one place for umbrellas, **Salwen's** (45 Orchard; (212) 226-1693), because if you don't hear Irving Salwen play Yiddish folks songs on the guitar, you haven't really gotten the Lower East Side experience.

Marcesa hangs up imported evening gowns from French and Italian designers (108 Orchard Street; (212) 674-6344), and that Soho chic-boutique thang is headed east, so keep your eyes peeled for iconoclastic designers setting up shop. The fabric stores are clustered along Hester and Orchard Streets, and the tailoring shops are clustered north of Delancey toward East Houston along Rivington Street, Allen Street, and Stanton; get something custom-made. If you sew yourself, or even if you don't, take a gander at the incredible variety of zippers at **A. Feibusch,** from doll-sized to double-length (27 Allen Street; (212) 226-3964).

Thanks to chic creep, so to speak, the strip of Orchard Street between Houston and Delancey is on the verge of becoming another youth-oriented bar-and-boutique area—O-Ho, perhaps. Many of these are retro-hip spots, with overtones of funk and psychedelia as well as hip-hop and sometimes a little ethnic or one-world flavor. If the shopping expedition covers two generations, this could be the answer.

Art Galleries: Chelsea and Soho

It's almost a battle between these old villages for the city's art scene crown. In the last two or three years, both have seen the number of galleries and exhibit spaces increase several times.

Soho is estimated to house 250 art galleries; its art scene has grown so rapidly that its annual September arts festival boomed from 60 events in 1965 to 200 in 1996 and spread out to 11 days of visual arts exhibits, performances, and dance in 1997. Festival director Simon Watson puts out a monthly newsletter called "Simon Says" (available at neighborhood galleries) listing 40 recommendations for art-gazing, and he also organizes Saturday afternoon museum/gallery walks led by area dealers.

Almost any Soho block has an art, photography, or print shop mixed in with the boutiques, if you just want to trust to chance. The two buildings at 415 and 420 West Broadway by themselves house well over a dozen galleries, including the famed **Leo Castelli Gallery** (420 West Broadway), and one of the branches of the **Dia Center for the Contemporary Arts** is a few doors down at 393 West Broadway. **Louis K. Meisel** is at 141 Prince, **Martin Lawrence** at 457 West Broadway, **Pace Gallery** at 142 Greene, and **Phyllis King** at 136 Greene.

But a stroll down Broadway between Prince and Houston offers more than a full day's worth of art-gazing and architectural interest. The six-story loft at 575 Broadway, formerly used as the Guggenheim Museum Soho, was originally designed for owner John Jacob Astor II as a garment manufacturing and retailing complex. The **New Museum of Contemporary Art** at 583 Broadway is not so establishment (in the prestige sense), but serves as almost a preview space for cutting-edge artists. (The museum is planning to move to a larger building on the Bowery at the terminus of Prince Street.) The **Alternative Museum** is only one of several galleries inside 594 Broadway, but it sometimes mixes poetry readings and music with the visuals.

Although the cast-iron facade of the **Museum for African Art** at 593 Broadway, which moved from its smaller Upper East Side space in 1993, is original, the interior spaces were designed by Maya Lin, architect of the Vietnam Veterans Memorial (the "black wall") in Washington. It is the only museum other than the Smithsonian's Museum of African Art that focuses on sub-Saharan cultural artifacts: life-sized carvings, masks, weavings, jewelry, and so on.

The easiest way to take in some of Chelsea's major galleries is to stroll back and forth along the streets from West 20th to West 26th Streets between Tenth and Eleventh avenues. The four-story **Dia Center for the Arts,** which arguably sparked the neighborhood movement when it expanded here from Soho, is at 548 West 22nd.

In the 500 stretch of West 21st Street, for example, **Bonakdar Jancou Gallery** has joined **Paolo Baldacci** at 521 West 21st Street near **Paula Cooper** (534 West 21st Street). Former Cooper Gallery directors **Christopher D'Amelio** and **Lucien Terras** now have their own eponymous gallery around the corner at 525 West 22nd Street, which is also the address of Lisa Spellman's **303 Gallery** and **Jason McCoy. Matthew Marks Gallery** is at 522 West 22nd, and **Max Protetch** has relocated to 511 West 22nd (leasing part of the space to the Wild Lily Tearoom); **Thomas Healey** and **Pat Hearn** are both at 530 West 22nd. **Fredericks** is at 504 West 22nd.

The stunning Art Deco building across 11th Avenue stretching from 26th to 27th is the Starrett-Lehigh Building, originally constructed over the Lehigh Valley Railroad yards and with elevators that hauled whole freight cars, fully loaded, into the warehouse. It is now a multigallery complex that includes not only visual arts spaces, such as **Pamela Auchincloss,** but also **Jan van der Donk** rare books and the even more fantastic **Bound and Unbound** conceptual art bookstore.

Note that most Soho galleries are open on Saturday and closed on Sunday and Monday; Chelsea galleries used to be open on Sunday, but many are now shifting to Saturday hours instead. Be sure to check ahead if you have weekend wandering in mind.

If you prefer to stick to Midtown, you can spend a lot of time amid the old, fine, and famous cluster of galleries in the area bounded by 56th and 57th streets and Park and Sixth avenues, particularly the **Fuller Building** at the corner of Madison; though most of these are also closed on Sundays, a fair number are open on Mondays. Among the most prominent galleries are **Pace Wildenstein** at 12 East 57th; **Edwynn Hook,** which specializes in big-name photography, at 745 Fifth Avenue; modern art specialists **Joseph Helman** at 20 West 57th; **David Findlay, Jr.,** where you may spot a John Singer Sargent, at 41 East 57th; and a branch of the international **Marlborough** galleries at 40 West 57th.

Home Furnishings and Interiors: Soho

The lower end of Soho around Greene and Broome Streets sweeps the market in cool furniture and home design, a number of them partial boutiques from the artisans who own them, including **Moss** (146 Greene Street; (212) 226-2190), **Totem** (83 Grand; (212) 219-2446), **Aero Studios** (132 Spring Street; (212) 966-1500), **Design by Mary Jaeger** (51 Spring Street; (212) 941-5877), **Armani Casa** (97 Greene; (212) 334-1271), and **Todd Hase** (261 Wooster Street; (212) 334-3568; **toddhase. com**). A little more commercial but still intriguing are the multi-culti **Coconut Co.** (131 Greene; (212) 539-1940); **Anthropologie** (375 West Broadway; (212) 343-7070), which mixes clothing for the urban frontierfolk with artistically weathered furniture; **Zoo** (83 Grand; (212) 505-0500) and **Language** (238 Mulberry; (212) 431-5566), which are part department store, part art gallery; **Portico Home** (72 Spring; (212) 941-7800); and **Dialogica** (484 Broome; (212) 966-1934). Also look into **Grass Roots Garden** (131 Spring; (212) 226-2662) and **Terra Verde** (120 Wooster; (212) 925-4533) for that Garden Design–approved casual chic. **Apartment** is the reality show of design stores, with its own kitchen and chef (101 Crosby Street; (212) 219-3066).

Astonishing varieties and textures of tile, including platters and planters, are on display at the 3,500-square-foot branch of Milan's prestigious **Bisazza** (43 Greene Street; (212) 463-0624), **Artistic Tile** (79 5th; (212) 727-9331), and around the corner at **Country Floors** (15 East 16th; (212) 627-8300). **Jeffrey Ruesch**'s Art Deco and Nouveau furniture is upstairs from **Fred Silberman's** Art Deco furniture and lighting (39 Bond Street; (212) 226-4777); the **Wooster Gallery** also caters to Deco-dent redecorators (86 Wooster; (212) 219-2190).

Urban-country outfitters (particularly in the southwestern and neo-Italian styles) include **Distant Origin** (153 Mercer; (212) 941-0025), **Uproar** (121 Greene; (212) 614-8580), and **Modern Stone Age** (54 Greene; (212) 219-0383). Italy is the spiritual home, and often the actual one as well, of the ceramic designs and linens at **Ceramica** (59 Thompson Street; (212) 941-1307); while the decor deluxe at **Jamson Whyte** (47 Wooster; (212) 965-9405) hails from Singapore and Southeast Asia. Those with super-sensitive skins, or simply with ecological concerns, would be grateful for gifts from **Ad Hoc Softwares,** which has nothing to do with computers, but rather has everything to do with unbleached and chemical-free bed linens, natural body products, and the exquisitely designed Global Japanese knives (136 Wooster; (212) 925-2652). Deco-devoted celebrities head to **Depression Modern** (150 Sullivan Street; (212) 982-5699).

But the home furnishings neighborhood is expanding—don't they always?—and in the single block of Lafayette Street between East Houston and Prince (which was once considered Little Italy, but is rather rapidly shifting toward the city's hip pocket), you can find astonishing antique etched-glass doors, Deco lighting fixtures, huge marble tubs, wrought-iron gates, ritzy toilet paper holders, and even the occasional elevator box at **Urban Archaeology** (143 Franklin; (212) 431-4646; **www.urbanarcheology.com**); custom retro at **Salon Modern** (281 Lafayette; (212) 219-3439); Tuscan-rustic tidbits for the meditation garden at **Rooms & Gardens** (7 Mercer Street; (212) 431-1297); late–19th- and 20th-century antiques at **Secondhand Rose** (138 Dwayne; (212) 393-9002); funkier fringe is-it-old-or-is-it-just-camp Americana at **Coming to America** (276 Lafayette; (212) 343-2968); and one-of-a-kind Howdy-Doody-meets-the-Mad-Hatter-in-Manhattan accessories and furniture at **Lost City Arts** (18 Cooper Square; (212) 941-8025 or (212) 375-0500). **BAC** has some of the most important names in mid-20th-century French design on its books (16 Crosby Street; (212) 431-6151); and **Saigoniste** deals in, as the name suggests, Vietnamese trays, bowls, pillows, and chopsticks (239 Mulberry; (212) 925-4610).

For smaller accessories, check out the desktop toy-techs at **Dom USA** (382 West Broadway; (212) 334-5580). If you wander beyond Lafayette toward the Lower East Side, look for the mod-minimalist housewares at **Shi** (233 Elizabeth Street; (212) 334-4330). **Just Shades** (21 Spring

Street; (212) 966-2757) stocks exactly what it says, but here you can dress your windows with rice paper, silk, burlap, parchment, and a host of custom designs. And at the **Apartment,** the medium truly is the message . . . it's hard to tell whether it's a shop or someone's co-op (101 Crosby Street; (212) 219-3666).

If there is any possibility that you have not found what you want in the Soho neighborhood—or at **ABC Carpet and Home** on Broadway at East 19th (phone (212) 443-3000)—there is also a large number of home furnishing shops in the East Village, especially along East 9th Street and on Duane and Franklin streets in Tribeca. Among the Franklin Street high spots are another branch of **Totem** (71 Franklin; (212) 925-5506); **Antik** (104 Franklin; (212) 343-0471); **R 20th Century** (82 Franklin; (212) 343-7979); **Dune** (88 Franklin; (212) 925-6171); and **Intérieurs** (149 Franklin; (212) 343-0800).

Specialty Shopping

If you're already a collector or are shopping for someone who is, you can almost certainly find whatever it is in New York. In fact, you can probably find too many or get waylaid by all the other goodies in town. There are whole volumes devoted to shopping in Manhattan, and we ain't just talking the phone book; but unless shopping is your life, or you plan to move to town permanently, this list should help you get started.

Antiques It would be impossible to pick the finest antiques dealers in a city like this, so we've only mentioned a few and their specialties. (Also look through this section for specific items.) Don't overlook the auction houses, especially **Christie's,** which has a 24-hour hotline for auction information (20 Rockefeller Plaza; (212) 636-2000); its somewhat lower-scale—relatively speaking—branch, **Christie's East** at 219 East 67th (phone (212) 606-0400); **Sotheby Parke Bernet** (York Avenue at East 72nd Street; (212) 606-7000) and its junior gallery, **Sotheby's Arcade** (phone (212) 606-7409); and **Swann Galleries** (104 East 25th Street; phone (212) 254-4710). All of these and several other reputable firms advertise previews and auctions in the *New York Times.* Also be sure to refer to the "Flea Markets" section, since one woman's flea is often another woman's find.

If you like just to walk in and out of shops to see what catches your eye, the area around East 60th Street between Second and Third avenues is treasure alley. If you like to ground yourself in a single building and see as many dealers as possible, head for the **Chelsea Antiques Building** at 110 West 25th Street (phone (212) 929-0909), which has 150 dealers spread over 12 floors; or the **Manhattan Art and Antiques Center,** with 100 galleries of Asian, African, American, and European works (1050

Second Avenue between 55th and 56th; (212) 355-4400). **Antiques at the Showplace** houses 100 dealers on two huge floors (40 West 25th Street; (212) 633-6063), but like its neighboring flea markets, it's open only on weekends.

Among the Upper East Side galleries are the John Rosselli group: **JR Antiques** (255 East 72nd Street; (212) 737-2252), **John Rosselli International** (423 East 73rd; (212) 772-2137), and his lighting and accessory store, **John Rosselli & Associates** (979 Third Avenue, Suite 700; (212) 993-2060).

Down in Soho, one of the big names in designer circles is **Niall Smith,** who specializes in late–18th- and early–19th-century European neoclassical furniture (96 Grand Street; (212) 941-7354). **Eileen Lane** refurbishes Deco for redecoration (150 Thompson; (212) 475-2988). For something your neighbors will never be able to get from Pier 1, look into **Rabun & Claiborne Gallery,** which specializes in late–19th-century American pieces and iron furniture by Omer Claiborne, whose daughter Leslie Cozart co-owns the gallery (115 Crosby Street; (212) 226-5053).

Architectural Remnants   In addition to Soho's **Urban Archaeology,** mentioned earlier, Brooklyn's **Architectural Salvage Warehouse** in the Williamsburg area (phone (212) 487-6800) was established by the New York Landmarks Preservation Commission to supply historically minded New Yorkers (you don't have to show ID) with doors, mantels, wrought iron, chandeliers, and so on. The trick here is that you'll have to arrange your own shipping. Also check out **Irreplaceable Artifacts** (914 Second Avenue; (212) 777-2900).

Asian Art and Antiques   For Japanese woodblocks, contact **Ronin Gallery** (605 Madison Avenue, fourth floor; (212) 688-0188); **Things Japanese** (127 East 60th Street, upstairs; (212) 371-4661); or the very fine **Joan B. Mirviss, Ltd.** (by appointment; (212) 799-4021). New Orleans's prominent Asian art and textiles specialist **Diane Genre** shows in New York several times a year; call (504) 595-8945 for an appointment. **Art of the Past** (1242 Madison Avenue; (212) 860-7070) specializes in Asian art and antiques.

For chinoiserie, try **Ralph M. Chait Galleries** (12 East 56th Street; (212) 758-0937) or **Chinese Art and Antiques** (825 Broadway; (212) 505-0549).

Autographs   Forget those mall stores with their preframed sports photos and replicated signatures. Head to the East Side to **James Lowe** (by appointment, 30 East 60th; (212) 759-0775), **Kenneth Rendell** (989 Madison Avenue; (212) 717-1776), or **Tollett & Harman** (by appointment, 175 West 76th; (212) 877-1566; **tollettandharmonautographs. com**) for authentic signed letters, manuscripts, photographs, and other documents. Inquire about their searching for specific persons' autographs or professional evaluations if you have such items to insure or sell.

Baby and Children's Clothing   If you coo over pictures of babies in medieval lace, head for **La Layette et Plus** (170 East 61st Street; (212) 688-7072) or **Au Chat Botté** (1192 Madison Avenue; (212) 722-6474). Modern-day French designs are the only sweets at **La Petite Etoille** (746 Madison; (212) 744-0975) and **Jacardi** (787 Madison; (212) 535-3200). In the Gap Kids era, **Tartine et Chocolat** hearkens back to the more romantic ideal of smocked dresses and prep school shorts (1047 Madison Avenue; (212) 717-2112).

Beads   Agate, cinnabar, ivory, porcelain, faux and real amber, jade, amethyst, seed, brass, silver—all sizes, types and prices of beads are at **Leekan Designs** in Soho (Mercer and Spring; (212) 226-7226) along with sake and tea sets and wonderful bargain trinkets from Asia.

Bones   Since the auctioning of Sue the *T. rex* at Sotheby's, bones have become big business. Actually, they already were starting to be, but for most tourists, the skeletons, teeth, fossils, and anatomical charts at **Maxilla & Mandible** will be a revelation (451–55 Columbus Avenue; (212) 724-6173). It's just around the corner from the American Museum of Natural History, where dinosaurs are truly king, Rex or no; so this is a natural for kid's day. M&M owner Harry Galiano used to work at the American Museum of Natural History, in fact, and his museum-quality merchandise is impeccably treated.

If you're down in Soho, look into **Evolution,** which also has a fascinating assortment of bugs, skulls, horns, feathers, shells, and fossils—plus T-shirts to match (120 Spring Street; (212) 343-1114).

Books   If you have the title, they have the book, or at least they can get it for you (and maybe wholesale). Manhattan is crammed with general-interest bookstores, of course, including the original **Barnes & Noble, B. Dalton,** and **Doubleday** stores; and most neighborhoods have at least one hangout that caters to night owls. **Rizzoli** (31 West 57th; (212) 759-2424) must be one of the prettiest stores in town, especially now that the big megastores have pretty much dispensed with decor.

But not surprisingly, the capital of American publishing is also a haven for fine antique, rare, used, and specialty books, several of them on the Upper East Side. Contact **Baum on Rare Books** (535 Madison Avenue, (212) 751-0011; and 301 Park Avenue, Waldorf-Astoria Hotel, (212) 759-8300); **Imperial Fine Books** (790 Madison Avenue, 2nd floor; (212) 861-6620), **Ursus Books** (981 Madison, (212) 772-8787; and 132 West 21st, (212) 627-5370), **Archivia** (1063 Madison, 2nd floor; (212) 439-9194); **Martayan Lan** (48 East 57th Street; (212) 308-0018), or **James Cummins** (699 Madison Avenue, 7th floor; (212) 688-6441). The most famous secondhand bookstore in New York is the **Strand** (828

Broadway; (212) 473-1452), which has an estimated 16 miles of shelves at rock-bottom prices, plus some first editions, autographed copies, and serious rare books (on the third floor) for those on lavish budgets. The **Gotham Book Market,** though not as huge, is a prestigious shop of the old literary-salon sort (41 West 47th Street; (212) 719-4448). **Argosy Books** (59th Street between Park and Lexington; (212) 753-4455) is six floors of maps, posters, antiquarian books, political cartoons, and autographs: It was here that one collector purchased the boundary papers for Washington, D.C., signed by then–Secretary of State Thomas Jefferson, but most items are more affordable than that.

Manhattan's three gay bookstores are all downtown: the **Oscare Wilde Bookshop** in Greenwich Village (15 Christopher Street; (212) 255-8097), **Creative Visions** in the West Village, and **Bluestockings Women's Bookstore** on the Lower East Side.

Hacker Art Books has a huge inventory of books on fine and decorative arts, architecture, techniques, and you-name-it (45 West 57th Street, fifth floor; (212) 688-7600). **Biography Bookshop** in Greenwich Village is just what it sounds like, incorporating not only straight biographies but also diaries, children's versions, and biographical fiction (400 Bleecker Street; (212) 807-8655). **Drama Book Shop** (250 West 40th Street; (212) 944-0595; **www.dramabookshop**) is the place to go for titles on the performing arts.

Books of Wonder in Chelsea is the sort of children's bookstore you never grow out of, one where authors and illustrators pop in for pleasure as well as for autographings (16 West 18th Street; (212) 989-3270). **Printed Matter Bookstore** (535 West 22nd Street; (212) 925-0325) is a nonprofit outlet for books designed and produced by artists, often by hand; but most of the thousands of volumes are quite inexpensive.

With homestyle fare back on the trend menus (and container gardening a Martha Stewart–style craze), you may be furrowing your brow for just that particular zucchini casserole recipe. **Joanne Hendricks Cookbooks** is heaven for culinary wannabes, including those who remember their moms working out of treasures that have long been out of print (488 Greenwich Street; (212) 226-5731). An even larger selection, more than 7,000 titles both in and out of print, is available at **Kitchen Arts and Letters,** the love child of former Harper & Row editor Nachum Waxman (1435 Lexington Avenue; (212) 876-5550).

Kinokuniya is a shop in Rockefeller Plaza that sells books on Japanese food, culture, art, martial arts, and fine literature in both English and Japanese; it's a branch of the Japanese Barnes & Noble, so to speak (10 West 49th Street; (212) 765-7766). And in the Rockefeller Center Promenade is the **Librarie de France/Libreria Hispanica,** a.k.a. the Dictionary Store, which has thousands of French- and Spanish-language records, books, magazines, and newspapers, and more (610 5th Avenue;

(212) 581-8810). **Liberation Books** specializes in African American history and literature (421 Lenox Avenue; (212) 281-4615).

Murder Ink (2486 Broadway, between 92nd and 93rd; (212) 362-8905) is so full of mystery choices it's a crime to miss it—unless you're a Sherlockian, in which case you should head to the **Mysterious Bookshop** of Baker Street Irregular Otto Penzler (129 West 56th Street; (212) 765-0900); or find your Watson at **Partners & Crime** (44 Greenwich Avenue; (212) 243-0440). Science fiction fans head to the **Forbidden Planet** (840 Broadway; (212) 473-1576). For comic books (admittedly a paperback of a different color) head down to **Village Comics** (214 Sullivan Street; (212) 777-2770) or **St. Mark's Comics,** which carries underground, limited-edition, and other hard-to-find copies (11 St. Mark's Place; (212) 598-9439).

Bridal Gowns   Here the first (and second) name in wedding designs is **Vera Wang** (by appointment only, 991 Madison Avenue; (212) 628-3400). For more downtown tastes, try **Jane Wilson-Marquis** in Soho (by appointment only, 155 Prince Street; (212) 477-4408), **Mika Inatome** (11 Worth Street; (212) 966-7777), or **Mary Adams** (159 Ludlow; (212) 473-0237). For the bridesmaids, try the **Bridal Garden** (122 East 29th; (212) 252-0661) or **Bridal Party** (243 East 82nd; (212) 861-2318). And if you don't mind playing Secondhand Rose go see **Michael's** (see Consignment Clothing below).

Caviar   **Petrossian** is the most famous name in mail-order caviar, and for good reason, but their headquarters are proof that good taste goes both ways. Whether you're buying beluga by the tin or just dropping by for a snack, this beautiful marble room, something like an ice cream parlor for sophisticates, is a great stop-off. There's a classic dinner menu as well, and it's a fine one (West 58th Street at Seventh Avenue; (212) 245-2214). Over on the East Side, try **Caviarteria** right beneath the Christie's auction house (Park Avenue at 59th; (212) 759-7410).

Cheese   For those who consider cheddar the vanilla of cheeses, New York is *fromage* heaven. Check out the tasting menus at **Artisinal** (East 32nd Street and Park Avenue; (212) 725-8585), **Ideal Cheese** (942 First Avenue; (212) 688-7579), or **Murray's Cheese** (757 Bleecker Street; (888) 692-4339). Don't worry about smelling up your suitcase; they ship.

Chocolate and Confections   Designer desserts? But of course! One look at the petits-fours at **Ceci-Cela** (55 Spring Street, (212) 274-9179; and 166 Chambers, (212) 566-8933), or the 200 chocolates in 25 flavors Kee Ling Tong sets out at her **Chocolate Garden** (80 Thompson Street; (212) 334-3284), and you'll never waste your money on grocery-store candy again.

Classic Records   For the widest selection in vintage vinyl, particularly rock and roll, try **Strider Records** (22 Jones Street; (212) 675-3040) in

Greenwich Village; or head to **St. Marks Sounds** (16 St. Marks Place; (212) 677-3444). For Broadway cast recordings or early jazz, try **Footlight Records** in the East Village (113 East 12th; (212) 533-1572) or **Jazz Record Center** (236 West 26th; (212) 675-4480).

Consignment Clothing   This is one town where resale is still high-fashion, so you can really come back from a New York trip wearing designer clothing at department-store prices. A lot of them, not surprisingly, are uptown. Big-name evening dresses are the hottest items at **Designer Resale** (324 East 81st Street between First and Second; phone (212) 734-3639) and **Encore** (1132 Madison Avenue between 84th and 85th; (212) 879-2850). In the same general neighborhood are **Michael's** (1041 Madison, 2nd floor, between 79th and 80th; (212) 737-7273), **Tatiana** (860 Lexington; (212) 717-7684), and the just-as-chic men's designer boutique called **Gentlemen's Resale** (322 East 81st, between First and Second; (212) 734-2739). Farther downtown you can slide into **Riflessi's** for Armani, Ermenegildo Zegna and Cerutti, and in sizes up to 60XL (260 Madison; (212) 679-4875). (Look also at the section on shopping in Soho, above.) For kids' consignments try **Second Act Childrenswear** (1046 Madison Avenue; (212) 988-2440). Intriguingly, this is just across the street from the French children's boutique Tartine et Chocolat, listed above.

Cookware and Kitchen Goods   The hottest styles in stoves, namely the porcelain-coated, restaurant-quality Garland stoves that the chefs, chef's critics, and celebrities with private chefs now buy for home use, are sold with a smile at **Mazer Store Equipment** in the Lower East Side (207 Bowery; (212) 674-3450). **Broadway Panhandler** (477 Broome; (212) 966-3434) gives "baker's dozen" a whole new meaning: It stocks not just dozens but hundreds of kinds of cake pans. For serious cookware in the French style, try **Bridge** (214 East 52nd; (212) 688-4220). **Fish's Eddy** has overstocked, de-accessioned, and leftover lots of plates, glassware, and platters from restaurants and hotels, and sometimes even ships; they have fun designs and logos and in many cases are institutionally sturdy (Broadway and 19th, (212) 420-9020; and Broadway at 77th, (212) 873-8819; **fishseddy.com**).

Cosmetics and Skin Care   Nobody cares more about facial products and cosmetics than Big Apple women (and men); none are more into earth-friendly brands than those in and around Soho. Try **Aveda** (233 Spring Street; (212) 807-1492) or **M.A.C. Soho** (113 Spring Street; (212) 334-4641) for new looks and counseling (ask for a discount if you're in the modeling or theatrical biz) or **Face Stockholm,** with its palette of 140 eye shadows (110 Prince Street; (212) 966-9110). For all-natural herbal cosmetics and body products, try **Erbe** (Prince and Spring Streets; (212) 966-1445) or the Estée Lauder—owned but still honorable

Origins (402 West Broadway; (212) 219-9764). Even the venerable **Helena Rubenstein** has moved downtown in a big way—8,000 square feet, that is—at 135 Spring Street (phone (212) 343-9966).

Farther uptown, **Bergdorf Goodman** carries several cult lines of cosmetics from other countries, such as Japan's Kanebo and Paris's Yon-Ka, as well as the Spa to Go goods from top resorts (Fifth Avenue at 57th; (212) 753-7300). It's also home to the **Susan Ciminelli Day Spa** on the ninth floor (phone (212) 872-2630). For youthful labels (poppy, Bloom, Versace, Club Monaco) try **Sephora** (Fifth at 51st; (212) 245-1633).

For deeper treatments—facials, peels, aromatherapies, and the like— book some time in **Bliss** (568 West Broadway, 2nd floor; (212) 219-8970) or **Bliss57** (9 East 57th Street; (212) 219-8970), the **Urban Oasis Day Spa** (108 East 16th; (212) 254-7722), **Anuslaka Spa and Cellulite Clinic** (241 East 60th Street; (212) 355-6406), **Greenhouse Spa** (127 East 57th Street; (212) 644-4449), **Qiora** (535 Madison Avenue; (212) 527-9933), the Korean-style **Juvemex** (25 West 32nd Street, 5th floor; (212) 733-1330), **Ula Day Spa** in Tribeca (8 Harrison Street; (212) 343-2376), or the **Aveda Esthetique** (456 West Broadway; (212) 473-0280).

And if you're tired of trying to find that perfect lipstick, check out **Three Custom Color** (at Henri Bendel, 712 Fifth Avenue, or one-on-one by appointment; (212) 247-1100). They can custom-blend lipsticks or glosses to your specification (two for $55), matching something you always loved but can't find anymore, or a make-up artist will spend about one hour working with you for our own color ($25); or you can choose from their ready-to-wears ($15 apiece). If you left that old favorite at home, just go to Bendel and ask for one of the mail-back packages.

Kiehl's Since '85 (109 Third Avenue; (212) 677-3171) has, as the name implies, been a Manhattan watchword for nearly a century and a half, still owned and operated by the same family and still making its body treatments, shampoos, and skin care items by hand from all-natural ingredients.

Decorative Arts   With all the revived interest in imperial Russia, Fabergé, and so on, it's fascinating to step into **A La Vielle Russie** (781 Fifth Avenue; (212) 752-1727), which has been selling Russian enamels, jewelry, and, yes, Fabergé, since the Romanovs were in power.

If it's early-20th-century style you seek, you can indulge your craving for Art Deco at **DeLorenzo** (958 Madison Avenue, 55 East 65th; (212) 772-1080) or **Barry Friedman** (32 East 67th; (212) 794-8950). Tiffany classics are the house specialty at **Macklowe Gallery & Modernism** (667 Madison Avenue; (212) 644-6400).

Furs   The center of the retail fur trade in Manhattan is on Seventh Avenue between 28th and 29th streets in Chelsea, a neighborhood often called (a little grandly) the Fur District. Among the most reliable names here are **G. Michael Hennessy** (phone (212) 695-7991) and **Gus Goodman** (phone (212) 244-7422), both in the 345 Seventh Avenue building, though on different floors—Hennessy on the 5th and Goodman on the 16th. But the greatest bargain, especially for the nonrich and unknown, is the **Ritz Thrift Shop** at 107 West 57th Street (phone (212) 265-4559), which buys, refits, and reconditions estate-sale furs, turns antique coats into linings or novelty coats, and sometimes just offers nice but not premium new coats at half-price or even lower. They'll buy their own coats back, too, although at a very much lower price and so long as they're still in very good condition; so you can keep trading up.

Gourmet Foods In search of the perfect pickle or real old-fashioned sauerkraut? Where else but the Lower East Side, where **Guss Pickle Products,** the city's oldest (and one of the major "characters" of the film *Crossing Delancey*), is still dishing 'em out (35 Essex Street; (212) 254-4477). With that get the matzo to go at **Streit's Matzo Company** (150 Rivington Street; (212) 475-7000). From dried fruit to nuts, go nuts at **A. L. Bazzini's** in Tribeca, which smells like honey-roasted heaven and sells a real PB&J sandwich that would have given Proust fits (339 Greenwich Street; (212) 334-1280).

Greenwich Village is dangerous territory for foodies. Olives, all colors, sizes, and brines of them, are the hot items at the **Gourmet Garage in Soho** (453 Broome Street; (212) 941-5850). Imported coffees are easy enough to come by these days, but **McNulty's Tea and Coffee Co.** in Greenwich Village also stocks a few hundred types of tea leaves (109 Christopher Street; (212) 242-5351); **Aphrodisia** has a few hundred leaves to choose from, too—in this case herbs, spices, and herbal remedies (264 Bleecker Street; (212) 989-6440).

Of course, if you like all your temptations under one roof, there are New York's three most famous names in food: **Zabar's, Balducci's,** and **Dean & DeLuca.** Zabar's, on the West Side, just goes to show you what a serious Jewish deli can be (2245 Broadway; (212) 787-2000). Balducci's may not be the Village veggie stand any more, but it's still run by the same folks (424 Sixth Avenue; (212) 673-2600). D&D, the Bloomingdale's of food, is located at 560 Broadway (phone (212) 226-6800).

Jewelry If you want diamonds, you have to cruise the **Diamond District,** a continuous wall of glittering store windows and minimalls along 47th Street between Fifth and Sixth Avenues, traditionally operated by Orthodox Jewish and (increasingly) Middle Eastern dealers, where somehow if you cannot find just the setting you want, it can be made in about 24 hours. The most eye-bulging pieces already set with precious and semiprecious stones are in an even more glittery row along Fifth Avenue between 56th and 57th, including **Tiffany & Co.** (phone (212) 755-8000), **Harry Winston** (phone (212) 245-2000), **Bulgari** (phone (212)

315-9000), and **Van Cleef & Arpels** (in the Bergdorf-Goodman building; (212) 644-9500). **Cartier** is a few blocks away at 52nd (phone (212) 753-0111) and on Madison Avenue at 69th (phone (212) 472-6400).

But if you want the one-of-a-kind look without the Indian-curse pedigree or the shah of Iran price tag, visit **Reinstein/Ross,** Susan Reinstein's boutiques in Soho (122 Prince Street; (212) 226-4513) or the upper East Side (by appointment; 29 East 73rd; (212) 772-1901); **Doyle & Doyle Estate and Fine Jewelry** on the Lower East Side (189 Orchard Street; (212) 677-9991), **Me and Ro,** the Robin Renz/Michele Quan shop in NoLiTa (29 Elizabeth; (212) 237-9215), or **Pedro Boregaard** in Midtown (18 East 53rd Street, 15th floor; (212) 826-3660). For custom-made pieces, go to **Belenky Brothers,** still in family hands after more than a century and now showcasing contemporary art as well as fine jewelry in its Soho building (151 Wooster Street; (212) 674-424); or, check out **Stuart Moore,** near Reinstein's (128 Prince; (212) 941-1023).

Mikimoto's pearls are the most famous, of course (730 Fifth Avenue; (212) 664-1800), but **Sanko Cultured Pearls** (45 West 47th Street; (212) 819-0585) also has a fine reputation, though you have to make an appointment.

Jukeboxes   Refurbished Wurlitzers, slot machines, and soft drink dispensers are among the nostalgia for sale at **Back Pages Antiques** in Soho (125 Greene Street, (212) 460-5998; and 1891 Coney Island, Brooklyn).

Musical Instruments   The **Steinway & Sons** store on West 57th is as much museum as shop, and it's not alone: Even the rankest amateur would recognize the names on the violins and cellos at **Morel & Gradoux-Matt** (250 West 54th; (212) 582-8896). And anyone whose taste runs to blues and rock 'n' roll will know the more modern names (Muddy Waters, Peter Frampton) on the guitars at **Sam Ash** (155 West 48th; (212) 719-2625). For less common international string and and percussion instruments, try **Music Inn World Instruments** (169 West 46th; (212) 243-5715.

Neon   If you've discovered the artsy side of neon (and argon, and all the other colors of the electrified rainbow), head for **Let There Be Neon** in Tribeca (38 White Street; (212) 226-4883), home of artist Rudi Stern.

Perfumes   Depending on your allegiance, try **Floris of London** (703 Madison Avenue; (212) 935-9100), the all-American **Caswell-Massey** (518 Lexington Avenue; (212) 755-2254), London-based **Jo Malone** in the Flatiron Building on 23rd (phone (212) 673-2220), or the **Anglo-French Creed** (9 Bond Street; (212) 228-1732)—perfumeries to Hollywood and European royalty.

Photography   Cindy Sherman is just one of the big names whose work can be found at **Metro Pictures** in Soho (519 West 24th; (212) 206-

7100), and hours of browsing won't begin to exhaust the fine options at **Laurence Miller Gallery** (20 West 57th; (212) 397-3930). Although it's really a little farther south in Tribeca, the **Soho Photo Gallery** is the oldest, most comprehensive co-op in the country (15 White Street; (212) 226-8571). Uptown, your best bets include **Pace Wilderstein MacGill** (32 East 57th Street; (212) 421-3292), **Goodman** (24 West 57th; (212) 977-7160), and **ICP** (Fifth Avenue at 94th; (212) 860-1777).

Sports Souvenirs   Athletic logo clothing is in every shopping mall these days, but "official" T-shirts, warm-up jackets, and even home-game tickets can be scooped up at the **Yankees Clubhouse** stores (110 East 59th Street, (212) 768-9555) or the **Mets Clubhouse** (143 East 54th; (212) 888-7508). Or, of course, you could go to a real game . . .

Spy Stuff   Cold War or no, the **Counter Spy Shop** (or Shoppe: it's a Bonded branch of a Mayfair, London, operation) has all the mini-mini-cams, bulletproof vests, night-vision binoculars, scramblers, and lie detectors you could ever need. For heaven's sake, try not to look too shady (444 Madison Avenue; (212) 750-6645).

Tea   Fauchon, the famous Parisien tratteur, has two locations in Manhattan with more than 100 kinds of tea, as well as caviar, candies, and pastries (1000 Madison Avenue at 78th Street; and 442 Park Avenue at 56th, Drake Swissôtel).

Toys   Everyone knew the dearly departed FAO Schwarz, of course; but more people should know **The Enchanted Forest** in Soho (85 Mercer Street; (212) 925-6677), which describes itself as "a gallery of beasts, books, and handmade toys celebrating the spirit of the animals, the old stories and the child within." And it is. The equally imaginative **Dinosaur Hill** in the East Village (306 East 9th Street; (212) 473-5850) is intentionally hard to find, like a fairy tale treasure; look for the name set in marbles in the sidewalk. But the buzz these days is all about the four-story **Toys R Us** store in Times Square, with its 60-foot-high Ferris wheel, toy-themed cars, and Lego versions of the Empire State and Chrysler buildings.

Vintage Posters and Cartoons   The best collection of Toulouse-Lautrec and the like—in fact, the only complete collection of his "advertising" posters—belongs to *Wine Spectator/Cigar Aficionado* tycoon Marvin Shenken. Unfortunately, unless you're invited to his offices, you probably won't be able to see them, but you can pick up a few items almost as rare at **La Belle Epoque** on the Upper West Side (282 Columbus Avenue; (212) 362-1770) and Soho (827 Broadway; (212) 254-6436). **Poster America** specializes in modern posters, but it's equally famous for its home in the old stables that once served—literally—the carriage trade of the 1880s (138 West 18th Street; (212) 206-0499). Movie buffs can try **Triton Gallery** (323 West 45th Street; (212) 765-2472); or for foreign titles, try **Cinema Paradiso** (162 Bleecker Street; (212) 677-8215) or **Chisholm Larsson Gallery** (145 Eighth Avenue; (212) 741-1703).

Fans of the *New Yorker* can make an appointment to view some of the famous cartoon collection for sale at the Times Square offices (phone (212) 286-5795). If it's animation cels you want, head for **Animazing Gallery** in Soho (474 Broome; (212) 226-7374), the only authorized Disney and Warner Bros. art gallery in the city.

Watches   Counterfeit Rolexes, Piagets, and Movados are all over town, and for $25 or $30 bucks they can be a fun souvenir, although whether they'll run for 24 hours or 24 months is a matter of pure chance. So is whether the hands work, incidentally. Try **Mostly Watches** (200 West 57th Street; (212) 265-7100). For guaranteed models of those luxury names—the ones that shout platinum! titanium! white gold! and so on— visit **Tourneau,** whose double-page ads in the *New York Times* and luxury magazines are whole catalogs in themselves. In fact, it's practically an avenue in itself, with stores along Madison Avenue at 52nd, 57th, and 59th, as well as West 34th and Seventh Avenue; you can reach any of them through the main switchboard (phone (212) 758-3671). For more unusual vintage timepieces and clocks, try **Fanelli Antique Timepieces** (790 Madison Avenue; (212) 517-2300), **Central Watch Band Stand** (Grand Central's Roosevelt Passage; (212) 685-1689), **Time Will Tell** (962 Madison Avenue; (212) 861-2663), or **Aaron Faber** (666 Fifth Avenue; (212) 586-8411).

Wines   **Sherry Lehmann's** inventory is famous, and not by accident; it's probably the largest in the world. The catalogs, which come out every couple of months, make great souvenirs and gifts as well (Madison Avenue at East 61st Street; (212) 838-7500). But for atmosphere, and for a wine bar right next door, try **Morell & Co.** at 1 Rockefeller Plaza (phone (212) 688-9370), one of Manhattan's best-respected shops.

Vintage New York in Soho stocks only wines produced in the state, as many as 150 labels (482 Broome Street, (212) 226-9463; and 2492 Broadway between 92nd and 93rd, (212) 721-9999).

Manhattan is also home to a new kind of wine store, **Best Cellars,** where the less label-conscious can find help and hope. Here, wines are arranged not simply by varietals (since having drunk a lot of California Chardonnay will not necessarily give you a fair concept of French or Aus- tralian Chardonnay) but by "taste"—that is, "fresh" (light-bodied), "lus- cious" (round, richly flavored), and so on. So you just go after the sort of wine you like. And most of them are bargain-priced, to boot (Lexington at 87th; (212) 426-4200).

Wrought Iron   Not the old, but the old-style new-custom stuff: beds, lamps, étagères, and fencing from brother Carfaro, whose grandfather smithed in Turin, at **Desiron** (139 West 22nd Street; (212) 414-4070).

Part Ten

Exercise and Recreation

Double Your Pleasure, Double Your Fun

A few years ago, it would have seemed silly to put a chapter on exercise in a vacation guide—particularly a guide to a city as famous for self-indulgence as New York. But most of us at the *Unofficial Guides* are into some form of aerobic exercise, if only as a matter of self-preservation. It reduces stress, helps offset those expense account and diet-holiday meals (no, it's not true that food eaten on vacation has no calories), and even ameliorates some of the effects of jet lag. Even more remarkably, we have discovered that jogging, biking, and just plain walking are among the nicest ways to experience a city on its own turf, so to speak; and we're happy to see that more and more travelers feel as we do.

Even more intriguingly, New York is a paradise for workout buffs, since the gyms and exercise clubs in this town are often on the front lines of alternative routines. If you've read about Pilates or capoeira or some other new style but you haven't seen a lesson offered in your hometown yet, this is the place.

One good thing about indoor workout gear is that is takes up relatively little room and, at least until that step class, may double as walking-about wear. Also, if you are staying in one of the ritzier hotels, such as the New York Palace, the fitness center may have T-shirts and even shoes you can borrow for your workout, thus lightening your load even more. And if you're caught short, there are certainly T-shirts and shorts to be had on the street, if not at the gym.

If you are an outdoor type, however, consider the seasonal weather that time of year when you're packing. In the summer months, when it can be not only hot but extremely humid, it's really a good idea to schedule exercise early in the day or in the first cool of the evening; those late-afternoon showers can make a nice difference. (On the other hand, insects prefer the cooler hours, too, so pack some bug spray—better yet, double up and get some of that sunscreen with repellent built in.) Holiday decorations can make for wonderful jogging in cold weather, if the sidewalks aren't slick; but again, it may be damp, so be sure to pack a weather-resistant layer. And remember that first-aid kit: We go nowhere without sports-style adhesive strips (get the flexible ones), ibuprofen or some other analgesic, petroleum jelly, and a small tube of antiseptic. And consider doubling your socks.

Chelsea Piers and Central Park

The redevelopment of the old Hudson River pier area between 17th and 23rd Streets into the **Chelsea Piers Sports and Entertainment Complex** may have cost millions, but it's sure bringing it back in now. Among its attractions are one of those Japanese multilevel golf driving ranges with 52 stalls and a 200-foot fairway—which, considering how crowded the courses are in the neighboring boroughs, is likely to be your best shot (phone (212) 336-6400); two outdoor roller rinks (phone (212) 336-6200) and two indoor ice rinks (phone (212) 336-6100); a huge field house with basketball, yoga, spinning, volleyball, batting cages, gymnastics bars, and the like (phone (212) 336-6500); and a mega–workout club, the **Sports Center at Chelsea Piers** (phone (212) 336-6000), with running track, boxing ring, bowling alley, pool, 10,000-square-foot rock-climbing wall, and weight-training areas—even indoor horseback riding and blading fitness classes. Sports club passes are $50 a day; skating costs $7–$14 for adults, $6–$10 for kids, and $15–$25 for skate rental. Spend the whole day: There's an Origins spa next door for post-workout massages, manicures, and so on (phone (212) 336-6780), a sundeck and a brewpub for rewards (phone (212) 336-6440).

Central Park is where all outdoor sports meet—and meet up with Ultimate Frisbee, softball, pick-up flag football, and the like. Within Central Park, just for starters, there are rowboats at Loeb Boathouse (phone (212) 517-2233), which is also where rental bikes are found; rock-climbing classes around 97th Street; a half-dozen baseball diamonds and four soccer fields; tennis courts; regulation croquet (the competitive game, not the backyard version) near West 67th and lawn bowling near West 69th; the Wollman ice-skating/roller-skating rink; and a front nine of miniature golf, thanks to Donald Trump, near the Wollman Rink in summertime.

If you're fond of folk-dancing, you'll find plenty of partners of a Sunday evening near the East 81st Street entrance toward Turtle Pond. There is even a bird-watching hotline that keeps up with unusual sightings and nestings (phone (212) 979-3070), and with more than 100 species hanging around, that can be a lot. We once thought we had caught a young man yelling obscure obscenities at a playground full of kids in the park; eventually we realized he was practicing bird calls. For information on other areas to play, call the Manhattan Department of Parks and Recreation (phone (212) 360-8133). Also read the description of Central Park in Part Six, New York's Neighborhoods.

Working Out

Workout Clubs and Gyms

As we've said, New York has such a body-conscious culture that you can try out almost anything—and since that world overlaps with the competitive business world, there are even 24-hour clubs where the most obsessive of networkers can go in the wee hours.

Among the hottest workout clubs—the ones always written up in fitness magazines—are **The Sports Center at Chelsea Piers** (see above); the 24-hour **Crunch Fitness** clubs (404 Lafayette, (212) 614-0120; 1109 59th Street, (212) 758-3434; 162 West 83rd Street, (212) 875-1902; and 54 East 13th Street, (212) 475-2018), **Equinox Fitness** clubs (344 Amsterdam Avenue, (212) 721-4200; and 897 Broadway, (212) 780-9300), the **IP PowerStrike Studios** (115 West 74th Street; (212) 496-1254), founded by aerobics pro Patricia Merno and black belt Ilaria Montagnani, and the **Reebok Sports Club** (160 Columbus Avenue; (212) 362-6800). If you go with a member, you can get a one-day pass for either Equinox Fitness or Reebok Sports Clubs.

Yoga is incredibly hot in New York (and we don't just mean the steamy bikram classes, either); check out the studio list at **www.yogaalliance. com** for the closest studio.

Buffing is a particularly strong draw for gay New Yorkers, and the most gay-friendly gyms are toward the Village and Chelsea, among them the **YMCA** branch at 224 East 47th Street (phone (212) 756-9600; 1-day pass for $25), **19th Street Gym** (22 West 19th Street; (212) 929-6789; 1-day pass for $25), and the **Chelsea Gym** (267 West 17th Street; (212) 255-1150).

For more traditional swimming, racquetball, track, etc., the big **West Side YMCA** is the largest of the 19 branches, with two pools, basketball and volleyball, racquetball and squash, massage rooms, free weights, and more offers a $20 daily pass (5 West 63rd Street; (212) 875-4100). Other popular branches are the **Midtown YWCA** (610 Lexington; (212) 755-4500; $20 daily pass) and the **Vanderbilt YMCA** (224 East 47th; (212) 756-9600; $25 daily pass). Also check out the **92nd Street YMHA** (1395 Lexington; (212) 996-1100; $25 daily pass).

So far less famous, and so not crowded, is the gym and track facility at **Staten Island's Pier 6.**

Walking

Considering how strongly we've urged you to do your touring on foot, you may have already guessed that we find not agony but ecstasy in de feet. It's almost impossible not to enjoy the sidewalks of New York, and it's unfortunate that many of its most beautiful sections, particularly downtown, have been so reduced to the tour-stop circuit that most tourists never experience it. If you go out a little early, say 7:30 or 8 p.m., before the sidewalks get so crowded, you can walk Fifth Avenue or Madison Avenue at a fairly brisk pace, too; but you'll have to deal with the traffic signals.

The most obvious walking area, of course, is **Central Park,** where you can either stick to the 7-mile Outer Loop, the 4-mile Middle Loop (from 72nd Street south), or the 1½-mile reservoir track; but it's even more fun to just take whatever asphalt trails attract you. You can't really get lost—some part of the outer world's skyline is almost always visible, and you'll come back across the main road several times—but there is always something new to discover that way: statues (have you found the Mad Tea Party yet?), lakes, ornate old bridges, gingerbread-trimmed buildings, the carousel, flower beds, dancing dogs, tiny transmitter-driven sailboats reminiscent of *Stuart Little,* chess players, stages, and so forth.

Another popular park for walkers is **Riverside Park** on the Upper West Side between West 72nd and 145th Streets, so if you're really interested in seeing the natural sights, you can turn out of Central Park along the main crossroads at West 86th, 97th, or even at the top of park, 110th Street/Cathedral Parkway, and go four blocks to the Hudson and Riverside Park, which is another four miles long.

Running and Jogging

If you hadn't already guessed that Central Park was also runners' central, a quick glance will convince you. Central Park Drive, which has a dedicated biking/running lane, is about seven miles long, or you can come in halfway at 72nd Street and do the southern part of the loop for about four miles; the famous track around the Reservoir (now with a beautifully restored fence) is just over a mile and a half. The road is closed to traffic from 10 a.m. to 3 p.m. every weekday (except, please note, during the holidays, when the traffic crush is too heavy), and all weekend, starting at 7 p.m. Friday. There are runners there at most any (daylight) hour, especially on weekends; feel free to join the pack. For group therapy, call the **New York Road Runners Club** (phone (212) 860-4455; **www. nyrrc.org**), or hook up with their regular runs: about 6:30 and 7:15 p.m. weekdays and 10 a.m. Saturdays and Sundays. Meet at the club at East 89th Street or catch up at the starting point, just inside the park at Fifth and 90th. Handicapped joggers can hook up with the **Achilles Track**

Club at 42 West 38th Street for safe runs through Central Park (phone (212) 354-0300).

Another popular stretch for runners, as for walkers, is Riverside Park by the Hudson River, discussed in the preceding section. There is another two-mile stretch along the **Hudson Promenade** in the Village near the piers at the foot of Christopher Street; there's a track along the East River between the **Queensboro Bridge** and Gracie Mansion; Brooklyn's **Prospect Park** has a 3½-mile trail that begins near the boathouse entrance. If you'd like a short but sharp and visually stunning interval run, take the mile-long **Brooklyn Bridge** over and back, and consider the view of the Manhattan skyline a reward for chugging that high curve.

Biking and Blading

New York has some of the most elaborate bike stores in the country, including **Metro Bicycles,** which will rent some of its models out for the day (360 West 47th and other locations; (212) 581-4500), and **Pedal Pusher Bicycle Shop** (1306 Second Avenue, between 68th and 69th; (212) 288-5592). If you're sticking with Central Park (a good idea, especially for newcomers), you can rent bikes right at the **Loeb Boathouse,** which is near East 74th Street (phone (212) 517-2233). A few of the bike-tour organizers—such as **Bite of the Apple Central Park Bike Tours** (phone (212) 541-8759), which lead two-hour rides through the lower part of Central Park—include bike rental in the fee ($30 adult, $20 child). Really experienced riders who prefer longer tours or races should contact the **New York Cycle Club** (phone (212) 828-5711).

Central Park is the place for recreational biking not only for its beauty but also because it has a designated biking/jogging lane that stretches for about seven miles. (See the preceding section, "Running and Jogging," for auto-free hours.) You must stick to the road, however; no impromptu mountain or trail riding allowed. If you'd like to see the park by moonlight, and you're in town on the last Friday of the month, wheel over to Columbus Circle at 10 p.m. Or you can combine the **Riverside Park** path from West 110th Street to West 72nd down the bike lane through **Hudson River Park** all the way to **Battery Park City.** Both the **Five Borough Bicycle Club** (phone (212) 932-2300 x115) and the **New York Cycle Club** (phone (212) 828-5711) organize weekend group rides).

If you're more into blades, either ice or in-line, **Blades** has a half-dozen locations that teach, rent, and sell ice skates and rollers (they also equip you with protective gear). Among the most convenient locations are those at Columbus and Broadway at 72nd (phone (212) 787-3911); in the Village at Bleecker and Third (phone (212) 477-7350); at the Chelsea Piers development (phone (212) 336-6299); and at the Sky Rink itself at the Piers (phone (212) 336-6100). Blades also sponsors free clinics at the 72nd Street entrances, both East and West, weekend afternoons from April to October. The **Achilles Track Club,** mentioned above, also escorts in-line skaters through the park.

Central Park's **Wollman Rink** is open for in-lining in summer and, more famously, ice skating in winter (phone (212) 439-6900); you can hear the music almost any time. You can rent skates for the rink or for the rest of the park. Even more famous, of course, is the **Rockefeller Plaza** ice rink, also seasonal (phone (212) 332-7654). For group skates and lessons, contact **Sky Rink** at Chelsea Piers, which offers lessons (phone (212) 336-6100) and a little pickup hockey as well.

If you are a serious blader, into the semiguerilla sorts of expeditions, contact the **Night Skates,** who meet at various sites around town, including Columbus Circle, Union Square, or skate shops (ask for information), and pick a route for the night. Also look over the biking and running routes mentioned in the preceding sections.

Other Recreational Sports

Despite the success of Neil Simon's "Brighton Beach" trilogy, many tourists are surprised to discover that New York has beaches. They are easily accessible by subway: the **Rockaways** by the A train; **Coney Island** by the B, D, F, or N; and nearby **Brighton Beach** itself by the D or Q.

Only a few hotels have swimming pools; so if lapping is your thing, check into Chelsea Piers or Asphalt Green, another of those we-do-it-bigger sports facilities. They have an Olympic-sized lap pool at York Avenue at 91st Street (phone (212) 369-8890; $20), but the pool is members-only between 3 and 8 p.m.

There are 30 Har-Tru **tennis courts** in Central Park that you can get for $5 an hour, though you need a permit (phone (212) 280-0201) and you have to sign up on a first come, first served basis. Sheets go up on the half-hour for the next hour's slot. Riverside Park's clay courts are maintained by volunteers (do your part) and first come, first served. If you don't mind paying for your time, call **Crosstown Tennis** (14 West 31st Street; (212) 947-5780) or **Sutton East Tennis Club,** favored by clay-courters (York Avenue at 60th Street; (212) 751-3452), where rates go as high as $125 an hour. The Midtown Tennis Club has four courts inside and four outside (on the roof, which is a lot of fun); $50–$80 an hour (341 Eighth Avenue; (212) 989-8572; **midtowntennis.com**).

Horseback riding through the park is legendary, and so is the Claremont Riding Academy on West 89th, a couple of blocks from the park (phone (212) 724-5100). Rental for experienced riders is $45 an hour; $50 buys you a 30-minute private lesson or one-hour group lesson.

You'll see **rock climbing** in Central Park—they call it Rat Rock, and it's near Fifth Avenue around 62nd Street—but if you want something tougher, drop $15 at the **Manhattan Plaza Health Club** (482 West 43rd Street; (212) 974-2250), **ExtraVertical Climbing Center** (61 West 62nd Street; (212) 586-5718), or check the gyms mentioned above.

Romantics can go *en garde* at **Metropolitan Fencing** (45 West 21st Street, Chelsea; (212) 463-8044).

Pick-up softball, basketball, and **volleyball** are visible all over town, but the competition is really tough, especially when it comes to B-ball: Just watch a few minutes outside the cages at West Fourth and Sixth Avenue near Washington Square, famous as the original stomping grounds of Dr. J. There are more than a dozen golf courses in the city, but if you wish to waste most of a day in New York leaning over a little white ball, you're on your own. For information on the new USGA Museum, see Part Seven.

Kayakers should check out **Chelsea Pier 60** (phone (212) 924-1788) or the **Downtown Boathouse** at Pier 26 (phone (212) 385-2790).

There is even a **bowling alley** in the Port Authority Bus Terminal (625 Eighth Avenue; (212) 268-6909). For more opportunities to join in, pick up the weekly sports handout in gyms and sports stores around town.

Spectator Sports

New York's pro sports teams are legendary and seemingly legion; it's no wonder that Madison Square Garden is a cable network as well as a venue. However, this is one time when "New York" means all five boroughs, and a little more. Both NFL teams, the **New York Giants** and the **New York Jets,** play "at home" at Giants Stadium in the Meadowlands of New Jersey—and frankly, tickets are almost impossible to get, unless you're visiting friends with connections (or you're willing to pay a high price to a scalper). Besides, unless your friends are also driving, you'll have to catch a bus from the Port Authority to the stadium. However, if you feel like making a stab at it, you can call the Meadowlands box office at (201) 935-3900. You can also see if there are any odd seats left with TicketMaster at (212) 307-7171 or check the newspaper classified ads for tickets or ticket resale packagers.

The more frankly named **New York/New Jersey MetroStars** also play their soccer matches at the Meadowlands, but tickets may be easier to come by. Ditto another NBA team, the **New Jersey Nets,** and one of three area NHL teams, the **New Jersey Devils;** call the box office or TicketMaster. Another NHL team, the **New York Islanders,** is actually in New York—Long Island's Nassau Coliseum—but farther out in Uniondale, and it takes both the Long Island Railroad (to Uniondale) and then a bus (N70, 71, or 72) to get there, so only fanatics need apply. The women's soccer team, the **New York Power,** also plays in Uniondale, but at press time all WUSA league play had been suspended.

But you don't have to leave town to score. If you aren't lucky enough to live in an area where you can see baseball live, you have never seen baseball. (And you'll never see baseball fans the way you'll see them in New York, for good or evil.) **Yankee Stadium**—the House that Ruth Built—is in the Bronx, though at the end of so easy a subway ride that going to a game there is on our list of recommended things to do. If you're staying on the West Side, catch the B or D line; if you're on the East Side, get the No. 4 train. All deliver you right to the 161st Street/Yankee Stadium station. (*Hint:* Transfer to the D line at Columbus Circle or 125th Street, as it's an express during peak times.) Do not take a taxi; it's not only about 20 times more expensive, it might also take you 5 times longer to get there. Besides, you'd miss an essential part of the experience: joining the fan crowd. Call the box office at (718) 293-6000 or TicketMaster at (212) 307-7171. Get there early enough to wander around and check out the plaques beyond the outfield saluting Mickey Mantle, Babe Ruth, Lou Gehrig, Joe DiMaggio, and others. They used to be actually in play, flat in the turf, but cooler heads prevailed.

The **New York Mets'** Shea Stadium is in Queens—in Flushing Meadow, alongside the U.S. Tennis Association complex, where the U.S. Open is held—and is also easily reached by subway. To get to Shea, take the 7 line from the big 42nd Street station (Times Square) right to the Willett Street/Shea Stadium stop. You can quite possibly walk up and get tickets, but it might be better to call the stadium box office at (718) 507-8499.

But minor-league baseball, which many aficionados swear is better, is all around the town. There are three stadiums, each holding around 6,500 seats, opening in the boroughs. The Mets have a brand-new $30 million stadium for their Class A minor league baseball team, the **Cyclones,** on the Boardwalk at Brooklyn's Coney Island, which repaid the investment by winning the New York–Penn League pennant its first year out (phone (718) 449-8497). The Yankees are spending $71 million to put a Class A team (also called the Yankees) on Staten Island, accessible via the tourist-friendly ferry (call (718) 720-9265). And the **Newark Bears,** a team of baseball veterans (both Canseco brothers) owned by former Yankees catcher Rick Cerone, play in the Atlantic League (call (973) 848-1000).

Both the NHL **New York Rangers** and the NBA **New York Knicks** call Madison Square Garden home. Unfortunately, they have a pretty regular following, so tickets are problematic. Call (212) 465-6741 for Rangers info, (212) 465-JUMP for the Knicks, or TicketMaster at (212) 307-7171.

Even hotter these days is women's pro basketball, and the **WNBA New York Liberty** also tend the Garden. So do the **Golden Gloves** boxing cards in January and February; the **National Invitational Tournament** college basketball championships in March; and the **Women's Tennis Association Tour championships** (what used to be known as the Virginia Slims Championship) every November. For any of these events, call the Garden box office (465-6741) and TicketMaster (307-7171).

The **U.S. Open** is held in the weeks leading up to Labor Day weekend at the U.S. Tennis Center in Flushing Meadow, and even with its new Arthur Ashe grandstand court, it's frequently a sell-out. Unless you're already in the loop for finals tickets, they'll cost you a very close haircut, but earlier tickets may be around. Call the office at (718) 760-6200 for more information or check in with our friends at TicketMaster. If you're curious about cricket, take the orange line subway (1 or 9) to **Van Cortlandt Park** at 242nd Street on a Saturday or Sunday afternoon.

Horse racing has a long and aristocratic tradition in New York, and though the crowds may be more democratic these days, the thoroughbred bloodlines are as blue as ever. You can take the subway (Far Rockaway A) to **Aqueduct Stadium** in Queens from mid-October to May (for information call (718) 641-4700) or the Long Island Rail Road's Belmont Special from Penn Station to **Belmont Park** (call (718) 641-4700) from May to July and again from Labor Day to mid-October. (In between, the very old-style racing circuit moves upstate to hallowed Saratoga Springs.) The Belmont Stakes, the third jewel of the Triple Crown, is the first or second Saturday in June.

If you prefer harness racing, the standardbreds wheel around **Yonkers Raceway** Mondays, Tuesdays, Thursdays, Fridays, and Saturdays year-round; for race information call (718) 562-9500. For that, you'll have to catch the Liberty Line's BXM4C bus from Madison Avenue at 39th Street (for schedule information call (914) 682-2020). The Meadowlands has both Thoroughbred racing in the fall and harness racing from mid-December through August (call (201) 935-8500).

Part Eleven

Entertainment
and Nightlife

Lights, Tickets, Action . . .

It's hard to beat the scope and breadth of entertainment options in NYC, and if you haven't already figured it out, there are countless events, free or otherwise, occurring every single day and night. Modern, classical, jazz, international and experimental forms of dance, music, opera, and theater (including comedy) are presented in all areas and many venues. Some performances are even found in the subway, on the sidewalk, and especially in the parks, particularly with good weather.

To try and combat the overwhelming feeling of not knowing where to start, you can break down the options before delving into the choices. Consider the following: area of town you'd like to be in, budget, genre of entertainment, how late you're prepared to stay out, and ticket availability. Once you've assessed these parameters, you can peruse the columns of listings with confidence; alternatively you could mark a random point on a page and act on a whim. For the latest information, check either the websites or the papers including *Time Out, Village Voice, 'L' Magazine,* the *New Yorker,* and *New York* magazine. The *New York Times* has an informative Arts & Leisure section, which expands over the weekend for some of the latest previews and reviews. Keep in mind that the latter part of this chapter profiles several club and bar options which can be enjoyed before or after your chosen diversion.

Embrace the spirit of the city's offerings, and be open to a bit of spontaneity. If you can't get tickets to one thing, there are other options, and you may end up going to something even better. Talk to people during intermission and see if you can pick up any more suggestions. NYC is at your fingertips, so use make use of those hands and enjoy!

Ticket Tips

There's a certain cachet to having opening-night seats for a big performance. Often with big-time events, such seats are taken up by the press, luminaries, and those with connections and/or deep pockets. However, the performance takes precedence over the night you see it. Below you'll find some useful numbers and websites, and possible ways of how you can avoid going bankrupt in the process.

NYC/On Stage (phone (212) 768-1818) gives recorded listings and schedules for a variety of performing arts and will transfer you to the phone-charge company that handles the selected tickets. **Theater Direct** (phone (212) 541-8457 or (800) BROADWAY; **www.theatredirect.com**) offers group ticket sales at reduced prices, as long as you have a group of at least ten people (sometimes more depending on show).

The main ticket handling agencies for New York are **Telecharge** (phone (212) 239-5258 or (800) 545-2559; **www.telecharge.com**), **TicketMaster** (phone (212) 307-4100 or (212) 307-7171; **www.ticketmaster.com**) and **CityTix** (phone (212) 581-1212; **www.citytix.com**). Be warned that all of these agencies charge a handling fee, and sometimes there are additional "convenience fees" up to $9 per ticket.

Other ways of trying to snag otherwise sold-out seats is to go directly to the venue's box office about an hour and a half before show time (you can call the box office to confirm) and stand in (or start) the "returns and cancellation" line. Such tickets, if available, are released soon before the curtain rises and are a real coup to acquire. Depending on the reason for the return, the tickets are either resold or given free (usually as a result of an extra press pass, or a kind soul approaches you on the line to offer an extra ticket). It's a common occurrence for venues, arts and sports included, to also release house seats. Broadway shows, Lincoln Center, and Carnegie Hall have nightly cancellation lines too, but remember: There's no guarantee of getting a seat by depending on the kindness of strangers.

You're also more likely to score a ticket if you are willing to sit alone, or if you can go at an off-peak time, such as Monday, Tuesday, or after (but not during) holidays.

There are plenty of ticket resellers who are sort of corporate scalpers; they manage to find tickets to sold-out shows (look under "Tickets" in the Yellow Pages, or do a Web search). And there are other "convenient" ticket centers at places like the Plaza Hotel, which bank on the idea that you don't have the patience or leisure to call the big, automated phone-charge networks yourself; however, one round with the surcharges may dissuade you from this convenience. Still, if money's no object or time is at a premium, they are easy and reliable sources. Among some reputable firms are **Prestige Entertainment** (phone (800) 243-8849) and **Manhattan Entertainment** (phone (212)382-0633).

If you have an American Express gold card, call (800) 448-8457 to see if there are any special promotional seats available (this usually applies only to hot, trendy shows). A final caveat: You are apt to find scalpers outside theaters and big sports events offering tickets, but this can be tricky; an increasing number of these tickets are counterfeit.

Economizing

It "ain't cheap puttin' on a show," and ticket prices, often, reflect the costs. Whether the venue is off-off Broadway or at the Metropolitan Opera House, salaries and/or rent needs to be paid; costumes, lights, and props need to be rented, borrowed, made, and/or insured; and publicity needs to be generated. Chances are that an off-off Broadway production won't cost more than $20 and will more likely be $5–$12. However, the bigger the event, the more expensive, and tickets for some events can be, easily, upwards of $100 before a handling or scalping fee is even added. An average Broadway or Lincoln Center ticket costs about $60, though the full range is about $26 to $90. But deals do exist.

A good place to start is **TKTS** (phone (212) 221-0013). This is a place where same-day tickets to various theater and other cultural events are available for 25–50% off, plus a $2.50 surcharge; the only trick is that you have to go in person and take your chances on getting into a show you want to see. The best idea is to have three alternatives, in order of preference, already in your head; that way, if your first choice is sold out and there are only obstructed or nosebleed seats for your second choice, you'll still have something else to go for.

The main TKTS outlet is located at the north end of the Times Square area at 47th and Broadway, a multiline striped tent on its own little island in the traffic, officially called Duffy Square. (The statue there, incidentally, is of George Cohan, who wrote "Give My Regards to Broadway," among other songs.) The day's options are listed on a board overhead; you can study it while in line. Windows open at 3 p.m. and stay open until 8 p.m. (which just gives you time to sprint for the theater door) Monday through Saturday; they open for matinee tickets (Wednesday and Saturday) from 9 a.m. to 2 p.m., also curtain time; and Sundays from 11 a.m. to 7:30 p.m. The other TKTS outlet is located by the South Street Seaport, at the corner of John and Front Streets; hours are Monday–Saturday, 11 a.m.–6 p.m.; and Sunday, 11 a.m.–3:30 p.m. Wednesday matinee tickets are sold on Tuesday evening, but only at this location. Note that TKTS does not take credit cards, but traveler's checks are as good as cash. Also beware that TKTS is not a secret to residents or tourists; the formidable queues at Times Square form some time before the actual opening.

Other ways to trim costs: Go directly to the box office of the show you want to see with cash or a credit card and avoid the handling charge; this also frequently allows you to look at a seating chart and pick the best ticket available. If you are interested in one of the longer-running shows rather than a new hit, or don't care so much which show you see, look for discount coupons (some coupons are known as "twofers," i.e. two for one) at the various Convention and Visitors' Bureau branches and stalls.

You might consider tickets to previews (full dress run-throughs of shows that have not officially opened yet and are still being polished), which are frequently less expensive; or matinees, although since older New Yorkers favor these earlier hours, they can be crowded. Or you might just go for a rehearsal, like those of the New York Philharmonic (see below).

Some of the cultural institutions have discounts for students or senior citizens, but be sure to carry ID when you go to seek tickets. And if you are a sturdy sort, inquire about standing-room tickets at the bigger venues; they aren't always free, but it's a show (and some people will probably leave at intermission . . .).

Cameras and Close-Ups

If it's one of the television talk shows you're interested in, you most likely need to try to get tickets ahead of time—say, six or eight weeks. In the case of *Saturday Night Live,* it's a matter of seasons rather than weeks. Tickets for the whole taping season are awarded by a lottery drawing every August, meaning that postcard requests gathered in the 11 months previous are also in the pot, and even then winners only get two seats. Address postcards to *Saturday Night Live,* NBC Tickets, 30 Rockefeller Plaza, New York, NY 10012.

Most shows are a little easier, but almost all requests should be sent in at least two or three months in advance, and probably longer. Of course, if you regularly watch the shows, you probably already know this. What happens if your favorite personality gets canceled in the meantime? Hey, that's showbiz.

On the other hand, nobody likes empty chairs, even a couple, to show in the audience. So if you're still longing for that wild and crazy *SNL* moment, and you feel lucky, go over to Rockefeller Plaza early on Saturday morning, stand around on the sidewalk on 49th Street between Fifth and Sixth, get your face on television in the background of the *Today Show,* and keep an eye on the 49th Street entrance to 30 Rockefeller Plaza. At about 9:15 a.m., not every week and with no guarantees, a few standby tickets to *Saturday Night Live* may be passed out. If you do get in, prepare to be seated at 8:30 p.m. for the dress rehearsal and 11:30 p.m. for the taping. You could also duck inside the main NBC lobby at 30 Rockefeller Plaza and hope for *Late Night with Conan O'Brien* passes. These tickets may be handed out at 9 a.m., but the line is already long by 7:30 a.m.

The Late Show with David Letterman tapes Mondays to Thursdays at 5:30 pm (twice on Thursday, 5:30 p.m. and 8 p.m. to cover the Friday show). For advance tickets, send a postcard to Late Show Tickets, Ed Sullivan Theater, 1697 Broadway, New York, NY 10019. You can also try your luck by calling (212) 247-6497 at 11 a.m. on the day of a show for standby tickets; the phones are answered until the tickets are gone. You can also show up for standby tickets for *The View* by going to ABC Studios at 320 West 66th Street before 9:30 a.m.; first come, first served.

Or just horn in on the al fresco audiences for the morning shows; see the section on Times Square in Part Six, New York's Neighborhoods.

For more information on how to get future tickets to *Montel Williams,* call (212) 830-0364; for *Ricki Lake,* call (212) 352-8600; for *Regis and Kelly,* call (212) 456-3537; for *Total Request Live* on MTV, call (212) 598-8549.

Performing Arts

The Big Tickets: Lincoln Center and Carnegie Hall

Live from Lincoln Center is almost an understatement. This venue draws an estimated 5 million patrons a year, and even if you only worked your way through all its programs and never set foot farther down Broadway, you could still fill up most of a week. Since the mid-1960s, the **Lincoln Center for the Performing Arts (www.lincolncenter.org)** has been home to New York's most prestigious companies: the New York Philharmonic, the Metropolitan Opera and the New York City Opera, the New York City Ballet and American Ballet Theater, the Repertory Company of Lincoln Center, Wynton Marsalis's Lincoln Center Jazz Orchestra (now housed down the block at Time Warner Center), the Chamber Music Society, the Lincoln Center Film Society, and, for several years, though no longer, the New York Shakespeare Festival, plus the Juilliard School and the School of American Ballet.

The six-building complex, a cluster that looks out toward Broadway and Columbus Avenue between West 62nd and 65th, includes five theaters; the opera house, Bruno Walter Auditorium concert hall, and Alice Tully Recital Hall; two theaters and a recital hall within Juilliard; an outdoor bandshell; and branches of the New York Public Library and the Library and Museum for the Performing Arts. Huge renovations are due to take place over the next few years to give some buildings a facelift and improve acoustics.

Despite a near split, **Philharmonic,** under the direction of Lorin Maazel, is still in residence at Avery Fisher Hall from September to May, with its popular and relaxed "Mostly Mozart" series during the summer. Open rehearsals during the season are held Thursdays at 9:45 a.m. For more information call (212) 875-5030.

The **Metropolitan Opera House,** with its crystal chandeliers and Chagall murals, is worth a tour of its own (see Part Seven, Sight-seeing, Tours, and Attractions). The Met Company, directed by James Levine, holds the stage from mid-September to April; the American Ballet Theater has been using it the rest of the year, and sometimes performs at City Center (see below). For more information, call (212) 362-6000.

The **Vivian Beaumont Theater,** next to the opera house behind the reflecting pool with the Henry Moore sculpture, is shining after a $5 million renovation (phone (212) 239-6277). Under the Beaumont is the smaller (only 325 seats) and more cutting-edge **Mitzi Newhouse Theater** (phone (212) 239-6277).

The **New York State Theater** (phone (212) 870-5570), on the south side of the opera house, was designed by Philip Johnson and looks it, with its sequential entrances like layers of architectural curtains drawing back, its gilded ceiling, and its four banks of balconies. The New York City Ballet is in residence from around Thanksgiving through February (the *Nutcracker* pretty much fills up the schedule until January) and again from April through June. The New York City Opera, under the direction of Paul Kellog, performs July through November.

Alice Tully Hall is the home of the Lincoln Center Chamber Music Society and also often hosts concerts by Juilliard students; it turns cinematic in fall for the International Film Festival (phone (212) 875-5050), and the **Walter Reade Theater** upstairs hosts the New York Film Festival (phone (212) 875-5600). Special recitals are sometimes held in the three venues at Juilliard (phone (212) 799-5000). Check out the library exhibits, costumes, stage sets, prints, and scores.

The plaza outside is called **Damrosch Park** and is the site of various fine arts and crafts shows during the year and the Big Apple Circus in winter. It is also where the Guggenheim Bandshell is located and where free concerts, dance programs, and family shows organized by Lincoln Center Out-of-Doors pop up all through the summer; watch the papers.

Few concert halls have attracted as many legends as **Carnegie Hall** (**www.carnegiehall.org**) and no wonder: The premier concert was conducted by Tchaikovsky; the New York Philharmonic played here in the heyday of Mahler, Toscanini, Stokowski, and Bernstein; and a concert date here has for the past century been recognized as a mark of supreme artistry. Nowadays it hosts pop concerts as often as classical, but its astonishing acoustics—it was overhauled in the late 1980s—and its displays of memorabilia make it a genuine experience. Its new 700-seat underground venue, **Zankel Hall,** is a more intimate space that already has bookings for Yo-Yo Ma, Emmylou Harris, Emmanuel Ax, the Julliard String Quartet, the New World Symphony, and Mitsuko Uchida. Carnegie Hall is at 154 West 57th, near Seventh Avenue (phone (212) 247-7800).

Nearby is the **City Center of Music and Drama** at 131 West 55th (581-7907), which is once again drawing touring shows, dance performances, and concerts. (The Moorish-Spanish facade is a hint that it was originally a Shriners' Temple.)

Two other frequently star-studded venues, a little less accessible to first-timers but often astonishing in their offerings (and not hard to get to): The **Brooklyn Academy of Music** (phone (718) 636-4100; **www.bam.org**) affectionately known as BAM, hosts film, theater, dance, opera, and music from local and international companies, as well as the Brooklyn Philharmonic. The **New Jersey Performing Arts Center** in Newark (phone (973) 642-8989; **www.njpac.org**), stages many major international ballet, opera, and dance touring companies, not to mention world class jazz and classical concerts.

Broadway

So when the lights "go out" on Broadway, which happened most recently in March 2003, for a musicians' strike and later that same year in August, during the the blackout, people around the world know. Besides having a large number of theaters opening up in the Times Square area, the arrival of the New York Times Building in 1904, changed the name of the former Long Acre Square to Times Square. More theaters, including the opening of the Empire Theater at 1430 Broadway at West 40th Street, increased traffic and human interest to the area. With the increased illumination of Broadway and Times Square, along with the new *New York Times* Building, the area was dubbed "The Great White Way" in deference to all of the lights. Recently, the Broadway and Times Square area are often in the news because of the increasingly advanced technology of the billboards, news screens, and visible television studios.

The "official" Broadway theater district spans a 12 block stretch with a southern boundary at West 41st Street where the Nederlander stands, to the northern boundary of Broadway and West 53rd. Ironically, there are only 4 theaters situated on Broadway itself: The **Marquis** at 46th, the **Palace** at 47th, the **Winter Garden** at 50th and the **Broadway** at 53rd Street. All other theaters are located to the east or west of this stretch. For current shows, schedules and phone numbers of all theaters, check the local newspapers or the listings at the beginning of this chapter.

For the record, Broadway is the only "true" north/south thoroughfare in Manhattan that crosses the city diagonally, thus forming Times Square, Union Square, Columbus Circle, Dante Park by Lincoln Center, and the oddly shaped area around West 72nd Street.

Off- and Off-off-Broadway

The spiritual line between some on-Broadway and off-Broadway venues is getting fuzzier. Many of the more "uptown" off-Broadway houses have pretty much been assimilated, whereas the downtown off-Broadway troupes, many of whom may once have been rather anti-establishment, are threatening to mellow into the high-culture circuit. And yet such theaters as the **Playwright's Horizons** (416 West 42nd; (212) 564-1235) and **Roundabout** (231 West 39th; (212) 719-9393), despite their central White Way addresses, have off-Broadway attitudes.

Among the best-known venues are the **Provincetown Playhouse,** famous as Eugene O'Neill's first dramatic home; the ambitious **Minetta Lane Theater** (18 Minetta Lane; (212) 420-8000); **Cherry Lane,** founded by Edna St. Vincent Millay (38 Commerce Street; (212) 989-2020); the **WPA Theater** (159 West 25th Street; (212) 206-0523); **Classic Stage Company** (136 East 13th Street; (212) 677-4210); **Jean Cocteau Repertory** (Bowery and Bond; (212) 677-0060); **Joyce Theater** (Eighth at West 19th; (212) 242-0800), featuring many dance genres; Joseph Papp's six-hall **Public Theater** in the onetime free library near Astor Place (425 Lafayette Street; (212) 398-8383), and the lower-profile **Astor Place Theatre** across the street (434 Lafayette; (212) 254-4370); **Players Theatre** near Washington Square (115 MacDougal Street; (212) 254-5076); **Union Square Theater** (17th Street and Park Avenue; (212) 505-0700); **Actors Playhouse** (100 Seventh Avenue South; (212) 239-6200) and the **Sheridan Square Playhouse** across the street (99 Seventh Avenue South).

Again, off-off-Broadway refers less to an address (generally downtown, though it may be Village, East Village, Soho, etc.) than to a mindset. It used to imply experimental or avant-garde productions, satires, debut productions, and sometimes just deeply serious art, and to a great extent it still does; but sometimes productions that are destined (or at least intended) to make their way to Broadway get their final editings here. Among the most interesting venues are the **Performing Garage,** home of the Wooster Group (33 Wooster Street; (212) 966-3651); **Manhattan Theater Club** (261 West 47th Street, the Biltmore, and Stage I and II at City Center; (212) 399-3000; **www.mtc.nyc.org**); the multimedia-minded **Kitchen** (512 West 19th Street; (212) 255-5793); and **Ohio Theater** in Soho (66 Wooster Street; (212) 966-4844); the four-stage **Theater for the New City** (155 First Avenue; (212) 254-1109); and nearby **P.S. 122**—not Public School, here, but Performance Space—in the East Village (150 First Avenue at East Ninth; (212) 477-5288); and **Theater Workshop** (79 East Fourth Street; (212) 460-5475).

Something for Free?

It may be hard to believe, but New York does have free theater, and it is commonly known as **Shakespeare in the Park.** Central Park's Delacorte Theater is the summer home to the company that otherwise holds forth at the Papp Public Theater. It's a matter of principle, or at least of sentiment, for some of the biggest stars of stage and screen to do their stint in the open air: Patrick Stewart, Andre Braugher, Kevin Klein, and Michelle Pfeiffer have all bellowed the Bard here.

Tickets are given out on a first-come, first-served basis at the Delacorte Theater beginning at 1 p.m. the day of show, but you'd better be there long before that. You might double your chances of getting in by sending a confederate down to the Public Theater box office (phone (212) 398-83838) between 1 and 3 p.m.; you can only get two tickets, but that's better than none. Furthermore, on selected dates, tickets will be distributed in each of the five boroughs; call (212) 539-8750 or visit **www.publictheater.org** for details. Even in winter, the Public Theater is a great, steeply intimate place to see innovative productions of Shakespeare with equally big-name stars.

The **New York International Fringe Festival** (**www.fringenyc.org**), although not free, offers premieres, improvisations, lectures, readings, storytellings, Shakespearean declamations, character studies, one-person shows, comic interpretations, and dance performances for relatively decent prices. You may even be surprised by the quality of the free subway entertainment. Although some performances aren't officially sanctioned by the MTA, the MUNY (Music Under New York) program allows musicians to perform "legally" and grants them a special banner to prove that they have succeeded in getting through the application process that includes a competitive audition. Over 100 acts, individuals or ensembles, are sanctioned and perform over 150 times, somewhere in the subway system, during the week; locations change, although Times Square and Union Square are usually fixed spots. Impromptu, free entertainment can also be found during the summer months in many of the NYC parks.

Other Major Venues

As mentioned earlier, the New York City Ballet calls Lincoln Center home; but that is far from the only premier dance troupe that plays Manhattan. The American Ballet Theater and Alvin Ailey American Dance Theater (phone (212) 767-0590; **www.alvinailey.org**) use **City Center** at 131 West 55th (phone (212) 581-1212); other companies book into the **Joyce Theater** (175 Eighth Avenue; (212) 242-0800), which is home to the Eliot Feld Ballet, or the **Sylvia and Danny Kaye Theater** at Hunter College (68th between Park and Lexington Avenues; (212) 772-4448). The **Florence Gould Hall** at the French Institute (55 East 59th Street; (212) 355-6160), hosts some theatrical and literary performances; **Makor** (35 West 67th Street; (212) 601-1000; **www.makor.org**) shows films and hosts lectures, music, and discussions. The **Aaron Davis Theater** at City College (West 139th Street and Convent Avenue; (212) 650-6900) hosts ethnic dance troupes. Also watch for listings for such locally based companies as **Merce Cunningham** (phone (212) 691-9751), **Dance Theater of Harlem** (phone (212) 690-2800), and **Dance Theater Workshop** (phone (212) 924-0077).

Various chamber, orchestral, and recital performances take place at **Juilliard** in Lincoln Center (phone (212) 799-5000) and the nearby **Merkin Concert Hall** (129 West 67th; (212) 501-3330); in the **Tisch**

Center at the 92nd Street Y (at Lexington Avenue; (212) 996-1100); in Miller Theater at **Columbia School of the Arts** (Broadway at 116th Street; (212) 854-7799); and at the **Harlem School of the Arts** (St. Nicholas at West 141st; (212) 926-4100). The **Amato Opera Theater,** a weekend-only venue, is very popular with serious music lovers (Bowery at Second Street; (212) 228-8200). By far the most unusual venue is **BargeMusic**—just what it sounds like, a boat transformed into a concert hall—but the acoustics, and the names on the schedule, will make a believer out of you (across the East River at Fulton Ferry Landing just south of the Brooklyn Bridge; (718) 624-2083).

Major rock/pop/reggae/soul/country concerts are apt to be held, like most everything else, in **Madison Square Garden** (phone (212) 465-6741); but other common concert venues include MSG's smaller annex, the **Paramount;** the **Orpheum** (126 Second Avenue; (212) 307-4100); the revived **Apollo** (West 125th and Frederick Douglass Boulevard; (212) 749-5838); the **Beacon Theater** (2124 Broadway; (212) 496-7070); the **Hammerstein Ballroom** at Manhattan Center (311 West 34th Street; (212) 564-4882); **Symphony Space** (Broadway and 95th; (212) 864-5400); **Roseland** (239 West 52nd Street; (212) 247-0200); and the **Westbeth Center** in Chelsea (111 West 17th Street; (212) 691-2272). Occasionally more mainstream names show up in **Town Hall** (123 West 43rd Street; (212) 840-2824), Avery Fisher Hall.

If lectures, poetry, and readings are your bag, call the **92nd Street Y** (1395 Lexington Avenue; (212) 415-5440); or the home of the "poetry slam," the **Nuyorican Poet's Café** in the East Village (236 East Third Street; (212) 505-8183); or the **New School/Academy of American Poets** series (66 West 12th; (212) 229-5600). Or call the **Academy of American Poets** headquarters at (212) 274-0343 to inquire about its poetry readings around town.

New York Nightlife

For some of your own bootie shakin', you'll have to hit the dance clubs or exercise your elbow for some liquid indulgence. There's a place and space for all types of people any night of the week. To wet your whistle, we suggest places that offer good beer, sake, sumptuous cocktails, jazz, rock, cabaret, country, alternative sounds, comedy, cigars, hookah pipes, and literary discussions. It's a taste of the options, but a good place to start.

Keep in mind that New York nightlife is alive and well, but it took a bit of a blow with the March 2003 smoking ban. A very few bars have smoking licenses (see profiles for **Kush** and **Club Macanudo**), but others either had to ban smoking or blatantly ignore the rules and risk huge fines. Whilst the air in many bars has greatly improved since the ban, many smokers are now regularly congregating outside of a venue (causing other noise or smoke problems for neighbors on higher floors) for a quick butt; the whole pick-up art of either asking for a light or being on the ready to offer one has been extinguished, unless of course you happen to be walking down the street. Some people try to get around the problem by either going to unofficially organized loft parties or finding outdoor garden space (not too effective in cold months). Although private clubs are officially subject to smoking rules too, acquiring pricey and exclusive membership for such places has become popular with a select group. Clubs like the **Soho House** (29–35 Ninth Avenue) attract both Europeans and New Yorkers, and although we can't advise how to get in, knowing about such places may be good for nightlife conversation. We hope that with all the bar and club choices New York has to offer, you'll be motivated to do some regular night-owl exploration.

Jazz

Jazz may have originated in New Orleans, but for decades New York has been the center of the jazz universe. If you have even the slightest interest in this style, you'll want to check out one or two of the following clubs; be prepared to stay up late, especially if you'd like to catch a jam session.

See profiles for **Village Vanguard, Smoke, Blue Note, Kavehaz, Knitting Factory, Tonic,** and **Zinc Bar.**

Cleopatra's Needle (2485 Broadway at 92nd Street; (212) 769-6969) has live music nightly and jam sessions Wednesday–Saturday, 12:30 a.m.–3 a.m.; $10 minimum per set.

C-Note (157 Avenue C; (212) 677-8142) is a little divey, but staff are friendly and there's lots of music. Jazz jam session on Saturday—quite early, 4–7 p.m.! They also have an original cocktail-table version of the classic video game Galaxian.

55 Bar (55 Christopher Street; (212) 929-9883) is a no-nonsense Greenwich Village joint with music that is often surprisingly good. Two-drink minimum.

Iridium (48 West 63rd Street; (212) 582-2121), with its over-the-top ultramodern decor, is a trippy exception to the rule that jazz is often played in drab spaces.

Sweet Rhythm (88 Seventh Avenue South; (212) 255-3626) was formerly the jazz-only Sweet Basil, but it now hosts world music with a bit of jazz thrown in.

Rock and Alternative

Rock clubs in Manhattan mostly fit into three categories. There are the bar/venues that host big-name acts for big cover charges—places like **Irving Plaza** (17 Irving Place; (212) 777-6800), **Bowery Ballroom** (6

Delancey Street; (212) 533-2111; **www.boweryballroom.com**), and **Roseland** (239 West 52nd Street; (212) 247-0200). Then there are the showcase places where newly signed bands preen for industry insiders— **Southpaw** (125 Fifth Avenue, Brooklyn; (718) 230-0236; **www. spsounds.com**) and **Mercury Lounge** (see profile). At the bottom of the ladder are the vanity clubs where amateurish weekend warriors and ambitious startups play short sets (**Acme Underground,** the **Baggot Inn, Pyramid,** and **Elbow Room**). The multiband nights are hit or miss; one good band in a line-up of four is a welcome surprise.

The problem is that if you just want to have a beer and listen to professional-quality local guys who play live for a living—a real *bar* band—you're in the wrong place. The country's best bar bands have long played their hearts out in nearby New Jersey and Long Island (remember the origins of Southside Johnny, Bruce Springsteen, the Rascals, etc.), but Manhattan, right between those two areas, has few groups (or venues to present them) dedicated to entertaining a bar. The showcasing kids angle more for A&R attention than for a grooving good time for the house crowd, and an evening in one of the name venues means buying expensive tickets and standing amid rapturous crowds; you're basically at a concert, not hanging out in a bar.

If you don't mind your rock filtered through other influences, **Rodeo Bar** (see profile) presents good, professional hang-out bands (most are rockabilly/country/funky). **Hank's Saloon** (46 Third Avenue at Atlantic Avenue, Brooklyn; (718) 625-8003) offers country music and a divey saloon vibe. Other venues include:

Arlene Grocery (95 Stanton Street; (212) 473-9831) has a $3 cover Friday and Saturday, $5 Sunday (draft beer is $5). Considered a prestigious showcase for indie bands; medium to heavy rock.

Bitter End (147 Bleecker Street; (212) 673-7030; **www.bitterend.com**) has been around for years, hosting some great and not-so-good music. Worth a visit just for the tradition it represents.

CB's 313 Gallery (313 Bowery; (212) 677-0455; **www.cbgb.com**) sports a $5 cover. Mostly acoustic bookings in this "nice" twin (hung with paintings) to the legendary punk mecca CBGB's (phone (212) 982-4052) next door (which is still going, though its time is clearly past). There's a huge sprawling cozy basement with sofas and pizza.

Living Room (84 Stanton Street; (212) 533-7235) charges no cover; one-drink minimum. Medium rock to folk.

Luna Lounge (171 Ludlow Street; (212) 260-2323; **www.lunalounge. com**) charges no cover. Particularly cutting edge; medium to heavy rock.

Sidewalk Café (94 Avenue A; (212) 473-7373) no cover, two-drink minimum. Medium rock to folk. Avoid Monday's open-mic night.

South of Houston Street, the music is often edgier and more experimental. **Tonic** (see profile) is a bastion of quality performances. The **Walker Stage** (56 Walker Street; (212) 905-2845), run by S. G. Music Media, hosts interesting music shows and has great acoustics.

Regardless of your age, always bring ID with you . . . some of these places wouldn't let in Rip Van Winkle without photo ID.

Dancing

Apart from weird cabaret laws prohibiting dancing in bars unless they're licensed, dancing is alive and well in NYC. Clubs, both underground and mainstream, abound and satisfy all music and style tastes. Herein lies the rub—some of the best beats are spun by DJs that travel and host club parties at various venues; some stationary clubs have nonstop style, but not always the best music, as hip takes precedence over harmonics. We won't list the DJ parties, as they often change, but *Time Out* has a good weekly clubs section listing. As for the trendy clubs, we'll give you an intro, but blink and they may already be passe.

Avalon (47 West 20th Street; (212) 807-7780), moving in where Limelight once reigned, is trying to hark back to the 1980s heyday of glitter and disco. **Glass** (287 10th Avenue; (212) 904-1580) has an exclusive club feel, with house-lounge music (sometimes Latin). **Cielo** (18 Little West 12th Street; (212) 941-1540) is a relative newcomer in the hot Meatpacking District, although dancing is definitely taken seriously once you get past the door. Glass has a neat unisex bathrooms so passersby on the street can see you preening in the two-way mirror. Other new clubs include **Crobar** (530 West 28th Street; (212) 629-9000) and **Quo,** also to open on West 28th Street, almost across from Crobar. For no scene and lots of fun, try **B3** (33 Avenue B; (212) 619-9755) for dancing in the basement.

For salsa dancing in a setting more down-home than glossy, choices include nightspots such as **S.O.B.'s** (see profile); or warm, artsy **Nuyorican Poets Café** (236 East 3rd Street; (212) 505-8183). For a stylized and authentic evening of salsa dancing and live bands, leave your jeans and sneakers at home and visit **Wild Palm** (1601 Bronxdale Avenue; (718) 518-1247; **www.wildpalmnightclub.com**) in the Bronx; call ahead for schedule. You can also enjoy the billiards room. Yet another option is **Swing 46** (see profile).

Cabaret

Some of New York's notable cabaret bars include **Firebird Café** (see profile), **Joe's Pub** (see profile), and, notably, **Feinstein's at the Regency Hotel** (540 Park Avenue; (212) 339-4095) featuring namesake/owner Michael Feinstein and other legends. Old standbys (and we mean *old;*

some of the following have been in operation for decades) include **Duplex** (61 Christopher at 7th Avenue; (212) 255-5438), **Judy's Chelsea** (169 Eighth Avenue; (212) 929-5410), **Danny's Skylight Room** (346 West 46th Street; (212) 265-8133; skip the Thai food), **the Oak Room** (see "Hotel Bars" below), **Don't Tell Mama's** (343 West 46th Street; (212) 757-0788), and **Café Carlyle** (see profile).

For more info on NYC cabaret, check out **www.svhamstra.com** and **www.cabaret.org.**

Irish

Irish pubs are a safe bet to find good beer, pub grub, and fine "craic." You may even get some live music, complete with fiddle or two. The following are of particular interest:

An Beal Bocht (445 West 238th; Riverdale, Bronx; (718) 884-7127) offers great music Wednesday–Saturday; it's a trek to get to, but they serve the best Guinness of all (warm fire too).

Mona's (224 Avenue B; (212) 353-3780), a real ultra-dive, serves cheap beer and hosts Monday-night jam sessions starting at 10:30 p.m.

Paddy Reilly's (515 Second Avenue; (212) 686-1210) has music nightly.

Swift's Hibernian Lounge (34 East 4th; (212) 260-3600) has music on Tuesdays, and great beer to boot.

Thady Con's (915 Second Avenue; (212) 688-9700) serves up authenticity and good Bass Ale.

Fine Drinks

One of the best things about New York is the substantial number of people who seek out the best food and drink with with obsessive zeal and passion. Mind you, the city has a plethora of corner bars where Bud Lite is drunk unrepentantly. But for those on a mission to enjoy only the finest drinks, there are zillions of aficionado places whose selection will astound. And for those who aren't professional bon vivants, the true believers populating these bars will gladly help clueless novices. New Yorkers may be rude and blasé, but once they start enthusing, it's hard to keep 'em down.

If you're online, the *NYC Beer Guide* provides exhaustive annotated listings of pubs, tastings, and local microbrews at **www.nycbeer.org.** The best bars and restaurants for good beer:

Blind Tiger Ale House (518 Hudson Street; (212) 675-3848) has 24 quality taps, plus hand-pumps.

Brewsky's (41 East Seventh Street; (212) 420-0671) serves a multitude of bottled brews.

The Brooklyn Brewery (79 North 11th Street; (718) 486-7422; **www. brooklynbrewery.com**) in Williamsburg offers free brewery tours on Saturday at 1, 2, 3, and 4 p.m.; they're also open on Friday, 6–10 p.m. Worth a visit.

Café de Bruxelles (118 Greenwich Avenue; (212) 206-1830) fries great pommes frites and offers a small but smart selection of Belgian bottles.

Chumley's (86 Bedford Street; (212) 675-4449) is located in a hidden former speakeasy.

DBA   See profile.

Ear Inn (326 Spring Street; (212) 226-9060) is a bohemian little café with especially good Guinness.

The Ginger Man   See profile.

John Street Bar and Grill (17 John Street; (212) 349-3278) is an informal beery basement in the Financial District with a fine selection.

McSorley's Old Ale House (15 East Seventh Street; (212) 473-9148) is a tourist fave, with old New York ambience and mediocre beer swilled alongside rambunctious frat boys.

Old Town Bar (45 East 18th Street; (212) 529-6732) has a halfway decent beer selection, plus great, traditional ambience.

Peculier Pub (145 Bleecker Street; (212) 353-1327) is expensive and incredibly mobbed on weekends, but the selection's amazing.

Ruby's Taphouse (1495 Second Avenue; (212) 987-8179) offers 26 taps on the Upper East Side; bar scene is very college-oriented.

Silver Swan (41 East 20th Street; (212) 254-3611) cooks terrific German food and stocks plenty of good German bottles.

Waterfront Ale House (540 Second Avenue; (212) 696-4104) has an excellent tap selection, with some ultra-rare specials and good pub food.

Heartland Brewery (35 Union Square West; (212) 645-3400) and **Chelsea Brewing Company** (Pier 59, Chelsea Piers; (212) 336-6440) are decent microbreweries, both with outdoor seating in the summer.

Japanese and Sake

There are two loci of Japanese culture in Manhattan: the East Village, where hip bohemian Japanese kids live and hang out, and Midtown, where a more suit-and-tie crowd have their bars and restaurants, many private. Each scene has its own custom-tailored sake bar. **Decibel** (240 East 9th Street; (212) 979-2733) is a knickknack-filled haven, a very cool little basement space to talk and drink any of tons of sakes from your choice of unique cups. You can also try plum wine or a lychee martini. For other Japanese-flavored nightlife, see profiles for **Angel's Share, Chibitini,** and **Hole in One.**

Hotel Bars

Some of the most elegant bars in town are located in hotels. These are places where beer takes a back seat to the Cosmo and martini hybrids.

The Algonquin (59 West 48th Street; (212) 840-6800) is full of good drinking options: There's the famous Oak Room, as well as their elegant and relaxing lobby bar and the woody/clubby Blue Bar.

The Carlyle Hotel (35 East 76th Street; (212) 744-1600) contains not only the famous Café Carlyle (see profile) but also Bemelmans Bar, which features tinkling piano and a clubby atmosphere, with watercolors on the walls.

5757 at the Four Seasons Hotel (57 East 57th Street; (212) 758-5700) is huge and Gothic, designed by I. M. Pei.

Grand Bar at the Soho Grand Hotel (310 West Broadway; (212) 965-3000) has a very atmospheric lounge area, all inside hotel lobby; very hip.

Holiday Inn (440 West 57th Street; (212) 581-8100) has a pool and bar on their roof. Pay them a fee and you can swim and sip to your heart's content.

The Hudson Bar   See profile.

Monkey Bar at the Elysee Hotel (60 East 54th Street; (212) 838-2600) is anything but restrained and stuffy; it attracts an exuberant crowd, and laughter—sometimes even singing, if you get there late enough—drowns out clinking glasses.

Morgans Bar at the Morgan Hotel (237 Madison Avenue; (212) 726-7600) serves up attitude, romantic atmosphere, and pricey but good mixed drinks.

The Royalton   See profile.

The Top of the Tower at Beekman Tower Hotel (3 Mitchell Place—East 49th Street and First Avenue; (212) 355-7300) is a blessedly mellow spot for a late-night drink with a handsome East Side view, especially enjoyable at one of the outdoor tables.

Town Bar   See profile.

The View at the Marriott Marquis (1535 Broadway; (212) 704-8900) is the only revolving bar in New York. Don't eat the food.

Sex

Single life in New York seemed very appealing on *Sex and the City*. It almost tempted those in committed relationships to jump ship and test the waters. Television aside, being single and young at heart in the Big Apple offers many opportunities to either sow your wild oats or have a great time in places that don't flaunt the pick-up vibe. For those who prefer to "meat" and greet the old-fashioned way (rather than through online personals) there are ample choices. Try **Rolf's** (a German restaurant with a popular late bar, 281 Third Avenue; (212) 473-8718); **Asia de Cuba** (237 Madison Avenue; (212) 726-7755); **Grange Hall** (see profile); **Tao** (42 East 58th Street; (212) 888-2288); **Drip** (489 Amsterdam Avenue; (212) 875-1032), which offers a novel computer-assisted way of finding a match; **Au Bar** (41 East 58th Street; (212) 308-9455), **The Bubble Room** (see profile); **Nell's** (see profile); and the chic and grown-up **King Cole Bar** at the Regis Hotel (2 East 55th Street; (212) 339-6721) for power pick-ups.

For those looking for a something a little racier, fancy strip clubs like **Scores** (333 East 60th Street; (212) 421-3600) and **VIP Club** (20 West 20th Street; (212) 633-1199) offer super examples of plastic surgery gone wild (and very steep bar tabs). More low-key is the very laid-back— almost rural—**Baby Doll Lounge** (24 White Street; (212) 226-4870).

Beware of clip joints like **Nude Legz Diamond** (231 West 54th Street; (212) 977-6826), many of which pass out promotional flyers on Midtown streets; these are full-nudity places that bypass restrictions by serving no alcohol. Your cranberry juice will cost you dearly, and talkative women hired by the bar will attempt to pressure you into buying them even more outrageously priced drinks (and, eventually, fake champagne).

Gay Nightlife

The latest scenes change at a dizzying pace; widely available publications like *Time Out* and *New York Blade* are good sources for information, as is the **Lesbian, Gay, Bisexual, and Transgender Community Center** (208 West 13th Street; (212) 620-7310; **www.gaycenter.org**). The following are some spots with longevity.

The grandaddy of all piano bars is **Don't Tell Mama's** (343 West 46th; (212) 757-0788). **Stonewall Bar** still stands at 53 Christopher Street (it's since gone through several incarnations; phone (212) 463-0950). A walk down Christopher Street and environs will reveal a plethora of clubs and bars. **The Monster** (80 Grove Street; (212) 924-3557) has an upstairs piano bar for an older crowd, plus a downstairs mirrored disco that's more of a pickup joint. The crowd's diverse, and while things can get silly, it's always fairly tasteful and safe.

Don Hill's (511 Greenwich Street; (212) 334-1390) is a much more fringey scene. **The Cock** (188 Avenue A; (212) 777-6254) may be dark and divey, but it's *very* serious about partying.

The Works (428 Columbus Avenue; (212) 799-7365) is a "nice" uptown place (well . . . *clean,* anyway) for yuppies and out-of-towners. **Barrage** (401 West 47th Street; (212) 586-9390) and **SBNY** (50 West 17th Street; (212) 691-0073) have good pick-up potential.

On the Upper East Side: **The Townhouse** (236 East 58th Street; (212) 754-4649) is a place where Young Men Who Want to Meet Guys Who Wear Coats and Ties meet guys who wear coats and ties who want to meet Young Men Who Want to Meet Guys Who Wear Coats and Ties.

The Roxy (515 West 18th Street; (212) 645-5156) hosts gay roller disco on Wednesday nights, and a gay disco party on Saturday. **Henrietta Hudson** (458 Hudson Street; (212) 924-3347) has live bands and DJs. **Starlight** (167 Avenue A; (212) 475-2172) is hip and suits all crowds.

Meow Mix (269 East Houston Street; (212) 254-0688) is a landmark lesbian bar that hosts particularly debauched parties, often with live bands. **Cubby Hole** (281 West 12th Street; (212) 243-9041) is more mellow and intimate.

Out of Manhattan, check out **Excelsior** (see profile) and **Ginger's** (see profile) both in Park Slope, Brooklyn.

Comedy

Comedy clubs are often looked down upon by Manhattanites as strictly for tourists (or, worse, for Bridge-and-Tunnelers—the derisive name for suburbanites drawn to the island for weekend entertainment). Indeed, the average New Yorker is at least as funny as some kid working the mike at Larry's Laughter Lounge. But if you must indulge in such shamefully uncosmopolitan pleasures, there are a few nationally known clubs, plus some intriguing cutting-edge comedy venues where you can both yuck it up and feel hip.

The best mainstream clubs are **Caroline's** (see profile), **Gotham Comedy Club** (34 West 22nd Street; (212) 367-9000), and **the Comic Strip** (1568 Second Avenue; (212) 861-9386). Gotham feels serious and intimate—upscale but no baloney or showbiz touches; just a room with mic and audience. The Comic Strip, best on weekends, is even less slick. Celebs are fairly common at the Monday night showcase at the Comic Strip, but otherwise the show's very hit-or-miss. Those three get the best-known acts and have the most upscale ambience. Beware "new talent nights" at the big clubs: Audiences paying a hefty cover and two-drink minimum often see not the brightest young talent but those newcomers who've promised club owners they'll pack the club (and thus its coffers) with friends and family. **The Comedy Cellar** (117 MacDougal Street; (212) 254-3480) and **Stand-up NY** (236 West 78th Street; (212) 595-0850) are also worth visiting.

Ye Olde Tripple Inn (263 West 54th Street; (212) 245-9849) is a rowdy place with a long-standing reputation for comedy (Freddie Prinze used to emcee). The audience for the Tuesday and Saturday night free shows (10:30 p.m.–12:30 a.m.) consists of a strange blend of insiders, dart throwers, and off-the-bar walk-ins; there's a screen for showing short films, plus improv and sketch groups.

Another place offering comedic sketches and improv stylings is the the **Upright Citizens Brigade Theater** (307 West 26th Street; (212) 366-9176; **www.ucbtheater.org**); chances are you won't be disappointed, and performances are fairly inexpensive.

For information on all flavors of comedy, *Time Out* magazine features very complete listings.

NEW YORK NIGHTCLUBS BY ZONE	
Name	**Description**
Zone 2: Soho and Tribeca	
The Bubble Lounge	Champagne bar
The Knitting Factory	(Very) alternative music club
No Moore	Relaxed drinking space, occasional live music
S.O.B.'s	Latin and world music/dance nightclub
Zinc Bar	Bar and jazz club
Zone 3: Chinatown, Little Italy, and the Lower East Side	
Chibitini	Hip sake bar
Kush	Funky Moroccan-themed bar
Tonic	Grungy but chic new music club
Zone 4: Greenwich Village	
The Blue Note	Jazz club
Bowlmor Lanes	Hip bowling with attitude
Village Vanguard	Jazz club
Zone 5: The East Village	
Angel's Share	Secret hideaway cocktail oasis
DBA	Mecca for ultra-high-quality drinks
Fez	Hip Moroccan-style bar with subterranean nightclub
International Bar	Local dive bar
Joe's Pub	Lush nightclub
Mercury Lounge	Rock showcase
Webster Hall	Disco theme park
Zone 6: Chelsea	
Bongo	Trendy hangout/oyster bar
Coral Room	Dance club with mermaids
Kavehaz	Gallery/jazz café
Nell's	Warm living room-ish dance club with hot disco basement
Zone 7: Gramercy Park and Madison Square	
Flatiron Lounge	Chic cocktail lounge
The Ginger Man	Giant-sized beer bar
Rodeo Bar	Cowboy bar with high-quality eclectic live music

NEW YORK NIGHTCLUBS BY ZONE (continued)

Name	Description
Zone 8: Midtown West and the Theater District	
Caroline's	Comedy club
Firebird Café	Cabaret
Le Bar Bat	Gothic nightclub/restaurant/disco
O'Flaherty's Ale House	Irish pub after-show hideaway
Swing 46	Swing dance club
Town	Chic cocktail bar
Zone 9: Midtown East	
Hole in One	Whisky and Japanese food bar
Pen-Top Bar at the Peninsula Hotel	Rooftop hotel bar
PJ Clarke's	Old-time New York bar
Saka Gura	Hidden suave sake bar
Zone 10: West Side	
Hudson Bar	Chic hotel bar
Zone 11: East Side	
Club Macanudo	Upscale cigar and whisky bar
Zone 12: Upper West Side	
Smoke	Jazz club
Zone 13: Upper East Side	
Café Carlyle	Sophisticated New York nightspot
Zone 16: Brooklyn	
Excelsior Bar	Swish, neighborhood gay bar
Galapagos	Bar and performance space
Ginger's	Friendly gay bar with pool table
Halcyon	Funky wine bar with DJs

AT-A-GLANCE CLUB GUIDE

Sake Bars/Japanese

Angel's Share	Hole in One
Chibitini	Saka Gura

AT-A-GLANCE CLUB GUIDE *(continued)*

Sake Bars/Japanese

Whiskey/Cocktails/Champagne

Angel's Share	DBA
The Bubble Lounge	Hole in One
Club Macanudo	Town
Flatiron Lounge	

Jazz Clubs

The Blue Note	Village Vanguard
Smoke	Zinc Bar

Music Venues—Various Genres

Galapagos	Mercury Lounge
Joe's Pub	S.O.B.'s
The Knitting Factory	Tonic
No Moore	

Chic/Trendy

Bongo	Hudson Bar
Fez	Excelsior
Flatiron Lounge	

Anti-chic

International Bar

Arty

Galapagos	The Knitting Factory
Halcyon	Mercury Lounge
Kavehaz	Tonic
Kush	

Dance/Disco

Le Bar Bat	Rodeo Bar
Coral Room	S.O.B.'s
Joe's Pub	Swing 46
Nell's	Webster Hall

Hotel

The Bar at 44—Royalton Hotel	Pen-Top Bar at The Peninsula
Café Carlyle—Carlyle Hotel	Town—Chambers Hotel
Hudson Bar—Hudson Hotel	

AT-A-GLANCE CLUB GUIDE *(continued)*

Gay

Excelsior   Ginger's

Cozy

Angel's Share   O'Flaherty's Ale House
The Bubble Lounge   Pen-Top Bar at The Peninsula
Chibitini

Bowling

Bowlmor Lanes

Comedy/Cabaret

Café Carlyle   Firebird Café
Caroline's

Beer/New York Landmarks

The Ginger Man   PJ Clarke's
O'Flaherty's Ale House

Zones 1–5: Lower Manhattan

NE
Λ

NIGHTCLUBS

1 Angel's Share	**7** Fez	**13** Small's
2 The Blue Note	**8** Go!	**14** SOB's
3 Bowlmor Lanes	**9** Joe's Pub	**15** Tonic
4 The Bubble Lounge	**10** Kavehaz	**16** Village Vanguard
5 Chibitini	**11** The Knitting Factory	**17** Webster Hall
6 DBA	**12** Mercury Lounge	**18** Zinc Bar

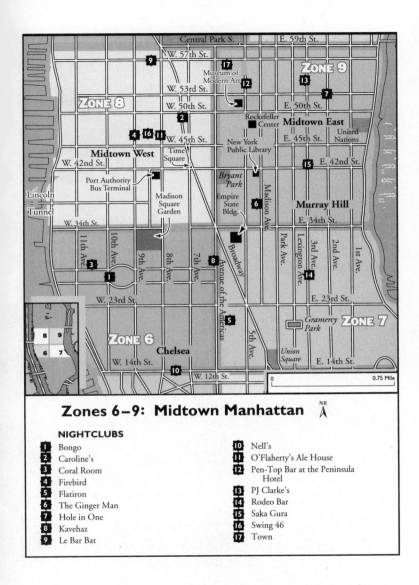

Zones 6–9: Midtown Manhattan ^{NE}

NIGHTCLUBS

1 Bongo
2 Caroline's
3 Coral Room
4 Firebird
5 Flatiron
6 The Ginger Man
7 Hole in One
8 Kavehaz
9 Le Bar Bat

10 Nell's
11 O'Flaherty's Ale House
12 Pen-Top Bar at the Peninsula Hotel
13 PJ Clarke's
14 Rodeo Bar
15 Saka Gura
16 Swing 46
17 Town

Zones 10–13: East and West Side Manhattan

NE

NIGHTCLUBS

1 Cafe Carlyle   3 Hudson Bar
2 Club Macanudo   4 Smoke

Nightclub Profiles

Angel's Share

SECRET HIDEAWAY COCKTAIL OASIS

Who Goes There 25–45; the beautiful, the hipsters, and the bohemian East Village Japanese

8 Stuyvesant Street (2nd floor); (212) 777-5415   Zone 5

Cover None **Minimum** None **Mixed Drinks** $6–$8 **Wine** Bottles $25–$60 **Beer** $5–$18 **Dress** Elegant casual or anything black. Dress-up's fine, but not flashy. **Food Available** Small menu of excellent Korean/Japanese snacks; great fried oysters.

Hours Daily, 6 p.m.–2:30 a.m.

What Goes On You go up steps with pink neon banisters, turn left through the sushi restaurant, and open an unmarked door to enter a mega-atmospheric little den of hip urbanity. Inside, there are suave young Asian bartenders crafting cocktails with single-minded intensity (they sample your drinks and tweak, often several times, before serving), soothing jazz played over a fine sound system, a few romantic tables with great views, and a bar filled with an interesting, intelligent, attractive clientele. Martinis are awesome, as are gimlets and fresh fruit daiquiris (not too sweet), plus you'll find wonderful selections of spirits like whisky and bourbon—there's not a single dumb bottle in the room. Service is classy but utterly unpretentious. The bristling intensity of the bartenders electrifies the place; it's the ideal choice for an intelligent date. The "no standing" rule can make it frustratingly difficult to get in (especially on crowded weekends), but provides uncommon tranquility when you do.

Setting & Atmosphere A narrow sliver with a bar on one side and a dramatic view up Third Avenue through tall, draperied windows on the other. A huge mural of an Asian angel baby sets the tone of elegance with a sardonic twist. Tables are mostly for two—this isn't a destination for groups.

If You Go Fridays and Saturdays you may find Japanese jazz duos strumming in a cramped corner, but the stereo is far more pleasing (yet another reason to avoid weekend prime time).

The Bar at 44 (Royalton Hotel)

SWANKY BUT STRANGELY COZY HOTEL LOBBY BAR

Who Goes There 30–60; tourists, businessmen, predinner drinkers

44 West 44th Street; (212) 944-8844   Zone 8

Cover None **Minimum** None **Mixed Drinks** $10–$15 **Wine** $14–$17 by the glass; $35–$390 for bottles **Beer** $10 **Dress** Mostly suits in evenings; looser later **Food Available** Light fare and desserts (from the kitchen of adjacent Restaurant 44)

Hours Daily, noon–1:30 a.m.

What Goes On This is an ideal break-the-ice meeting place for a predinner drink, be your companions business associates, in-laws, or a hot date. It's just swanky enough to set an elegant tone, but comfy enough (lots of well-cushioned couches and chairs positioned for maximum intimacy) not to intimidate. Urbane conversation flows easily; as you look around the room, you notice that everyone seems very very engaged, very very glib. It's not just the clientele; it's the room. Good lighting combined with the atmospheric coziness also make this a choice spot for a late-night tête-à-tête.

Setting & Atmosphere The cocktail area occupies a dramatic, long, sunken strip to your left as you walk through the narrow lobby. Toward the back, the lounge morphs into an airily open restaurant of similar design. Decor is what used to be called "futuristic": beige Jetsons couches, love seats, and chairs of odd shape in off-white fabrics. Jaded types might describe the look as Early Airport Club.

If You Go Peer into the tiny vodka/champagne/grappa bar hidden to the right as you come in the front door. This claustrophobic sci-fi transporter room sports circular padded walls and flickery candles. Check out the bathrooms.

The Blue Note

JAZZ CLUB

Who Goes There 22–90; tourists

131 West Third Street; (212) 475-8592   www.bluenotejazz.com   Zone 4

Cover $10–$55 at tables, $5–$45 at bar; brunch: $12–$20/person **Minimum** $5 at tables, one drink at the bar **Mixed Drinks** $6–$12 **Wine** Bottles, $30–$200 **Beer** $5 **Dress** Fancy shmancy **Specials** Monday nights are bargains; Fridays and Saturdays after the last set, late-night show until 4 a.m. for $5 cover. No minimum till 4 a.m. **Food Available** Full menu, for the gastronomically reckless

Hours Shows at 9 and 11:30 every night. Saturday and Sunday; jazz brunch, noon–6 p.m., with shows at 1 and 3:30 p.m.

What Goes On It's amazing how many tourists think that the Blue Note is a historic jazz institution, even though the place didn't open until the late date of 1981. But hordes of them continue to pay stratospheric prices to sit in uncomfortable chairs packed *way* too close together in a small, dark, boxy room. It's worth it, however, when they bring in acts who normally don't play clubs (Ray Charles, Herbie Hancock, etc.), many of whom shine in the more intimate setting. But the entertainment here can be more "jazzish" than jazz; people like Roberta Flack, Tito Puente, and Steve Allen have played here. The Village Vanguard (see profile) and Iridium (see introduction to this chapter) are far more pure-minded in their bookings.

Setting & Atmosphere Claustrophobic and tacky, done in dark tones and mirrors. A cheesey neon Manhattan skyline is the only "classy" touch.

If You Go As at all jazz clubs in New York, avoid crowds by arriving for the last set or during bad weather (budget option: the revamped bar area now has good sight lines). Late jam sessions are cheap and sometimes quite good.

Bongo

TRENDY HANGOUT/OYSTER BAR

Who Goes There Stylish small groups, couples, singles

299 10th Avenue; (212) 947-3654   Zone 6

Cover None **Minimum** None **Mixed Drinks** $6 and up (but they're huge) **Wine** $6–$8 **Beer** $4–$5 **Dress** Cool; suits may feel out of place after 8 p.m. **Specials** None **Food Available** Superb oysters on the half shell, perhaps the best in town

Hours Monday–Wednesday, 5 p.m.–2 a.m.; Thursday–Saturday, 5 p.m.–3 a.m.

What Goes On While there are times when one wants to be in the center of things (and there's no better place than Manhattan for feeling "plugged in"), there are times when one prefers to retreat to the sidelines. Bongo, is a tiny storefront hardly worth a second look from the outside. Yet despite the gritty area, you'll certainly not be roughing it inside, where cool ambience, great shellfish, and oversized cocktails are in the offing. It's no bargain, but there is a compelling coolness factor of knowing to take your date or business associate to this hip little place on the West Side. For those who like to nurse their drinks (pace is slooow here) and turn the intensity down a notch—and chat up companions away from bustling crowds and prying ears—this alluring scene is a five-minute cab ride from Midtown.

Setting & Atmosphere A tiny but chic storefront with ironically retro couches and chairs, soft lighting, and sultry music. The comfortable bar faces a backlit stage of trendy vodka bottles and other intriguing drinks. Staff is aloof and cooler-than-thou (chalk it up to mystique).

If You Go Don't miss the extraordinarily good (and well-priced) oysters, especially rich, sweet kumamotos. Mixed drinks are good (they spray your glass with atomized Vermouth for a *really* dry martini). The place can get crowded later, though there's usually space at the bar. Skip the expensive lobster rolls (lots of fresh lobster, but overwhelmed by olive oil and basil).

Bowlmor Lanes

HIP BOWLING WITH ATTITUDE

Who Goes There Stylishly pierced and ironic 20–30 somethings

110 University Place; (212) 255-8188; www.bowlmor.com   Zone 4

Cover Weekdays, $5.95 per person per game before 5 p.m., $7 after 5 p.m.; Friday night and weekends, $7 ($5 for shoes) **Minimum** None **Mixed Drinks** $6.50–$8.50 **Wine** $5.50 and up **Beer** $4.75–$7 **Dress** Jeans and T-shirts (though some do dress up) **Specials** Monday night, unlimited bowling for $20 per person, ages 13 and up; kids' birthday parties available weekend afternoons **Food Available** Surprisingly good (eat at the bar or take delivery directly to your lane!), including some of Manhattan's better burgers; beware the $25 credit card minimum

Hours Monday and Friday, 11 a.m.–4 a.m.; Tuesday and Wednesday, 11 a.m.–1 a.m.; Thursday, 11 a.m.–2 a.m.; Saturday, noon–4 a.m.; Sunday, noon–1 a.m.

What Goes On Very very hip, very very ironic bowling, with a crowd of chic 20–30-somethings sprinkled with some oblivious oldsters. As the place is fond of saying, "this is not your father's bowling alley."

Setting & Atmosphere A real old-time bowling alley (built in 1938) partially morphed into a way-cool hangout. Just because the ball-return lanes are painted baby blue and balls and pins are fluorescent pink and yellow doesn't mean Uncle Ernie and Aunt Ethel (who've come here for 30 years) don't feel at home bowling a few frames among the packs of 22-year-olds. There's a handsome old semicircular bar and old-fashioned tile floors. The place hasn't been totally revised—this is not so much a complete MTV makeover of a 1950s bowling alley as a slightly trippy touch-up. Enough of the old remains that the effect is more eerie than contrived.

If You Go Call ahead to check lane availability ... this is not Paramus, New Jersey, so there's only space for a limited number of lanes. Try glow-in-the-dark bowling night (call for schedule).

The Bubble Lounge

CHAMPAGNE BAR

Who Goes There 21–60; slinky well-heeled lounge chicsters and locals

228 West Broadway; (212) 431-3433   www.bubblelounge.com   Zone 2

Cover None **Minimum** $25 at tables **Mixed Drinks** $7–$10 **Wine** Champagnes $7–$35/glass, less for half-glasses **Beer** $6 and up **Dress** Way chic, dark colors **Specials** Live jazz Tuesdays at 7:30 p.m. **Food Available** Typical champagne accompaniments like oysters, caviar, salmon, foie gras, sorbets; all quite pricey

Hours Monday and Tuesday, 5 p.m.–2 a.m.; Wednesday and Thursday, 5 p.m.–2 a.m.; Friday, 5 p.m.–4 a.m.; Saturday, 6 p.m.–4 a.m.; closed Sunday.

What Goes On A champagne and cigar bar (excellent ventilation tames the smoke) where chic poseurs peacefully coexist with more down-to-earth locals, all feeling very very grown-up. The bubbly itself is quaffed more as a style thing than as serious wine pursuit (sniff and swirl your glass like an oenophile here and you'll get some strange looks), but there's no denying that sipping Dom Perignon without shelling out big bucks for a whole bottle is a good thing. Twenty-three champagnes are available by the glass, 280 champagnes and sparkling wines by the bottle.

Setting & Atmosphere An L-shaped space lush with red velvet draperies, exposed brick, couches, flickering candles, highly lacquered wood, and highly preened waitresses. Dracula would feel at home.

If You Go Check out the downstairs Krug room, a champagne/wine cellar with waitress service.

Café Carlyle

SOPHISTICATED NEW YORK NIGHTSPOT

Who Goes There 25–90; grown-ups

35 East 76th Street; (212) 744-1600   www.thecarlyle.com   Zone 13

Cover $50–$90/table, $10/bar **Minimum** None **Mixed Drinks** $10 and up **Wine** $10–$13.50 by the glass **Beer** $10–$12 **Dress** Jackets required, of course, but you'd do well to pull out all the stops and wear your very best duds. **Specials** Save $20 on the cover charge by watching from the café (reservations aren't accepted, though, and you'll pay full price even if there's only standing room). **Food Available** Old-fashioned New York food served by old-fashioned professional New York waiters—expensive and available 6 p.m.–midnight

Hours Daily, 6 p.m.–1 a.m., shows at 8:45 p.m. and 10:45 p.m. (no second show Monday and Tuesday)

What Goes On Singer/pianist Bobby Short is the main man, and though some nights he can seem just a tad tired of it all, he's always drolly debonair. Short-less nights don't always draw as well, though replacements are reliably top-drawer.

Setting & Atmosphere One of the most famous cabarets in the world, Café Carlyle sets a nearly unreachable standard of elegant and intimate supper-club ambience. A splendid assortment of Vertes murals adds greatly to the magic.

If You Go Have a low-key drink before or after the show (or instead of the show entirely if you're on a budget) in the hotel's Bemelmans Bar, an urbane time capsule of an older New York with fine—if less famous—piano entertainment.

Caroline's

COMEDY CLUB

Who Goes There 21–60; suburbanites on weekends, tourists and fans during the week

1626 Broadway; (212) 956-0101   www.carolines.com   Zone 8

Cover $15–35, depending on the act **Minimum** 2 drinks **Mixed Drinks** $5–$8 **Wine** $6–$8 **Beer** $4–$8 **Dress** Casual **Food Available** TGIFridays-type menu (with cutesy comedy-theme dish names) in the monstrously commercial upstairs Comedy Nation restaurant. Snack menu in the club.

Hours Daily, 5 p.m.–until, shows at about 8 and 10:30 p.m. weekdays, 12:30 a.m. weekends (call for info)

What Goes On With a location smack-dab in the middle of Times Square, Caroline's 10:30 p.m. late set is a magnet for theatergoers insatiable for more entertainment. Like Broadway these days, the club relies on a steady diet of Big Names to pull in crowds, and this well-run operation—the most "upscale" of the big New York comedy clubs—gives them their money's worth.

Setting & Atmosphere Though the Comedy Nation restaurant at street level is an utterly soulless space (comedy insiders call it "Planet Ha-Ha-Hollywood"), the actual club area, downstairs, is a nice loungey hang, a decent place for drinks even if you're not attending the show. The room doesn't have the mic-and-a-room pure minimalism of Gotham, but on entering it one feels that something exciting is about to occur—and with the top-flight talent booked here, it often does.

Chibitini

HIP SAKE BAR

Who Goes There 20's–50's; locals, hipsters, sake lovers (this brings the age up)

63 Clinton Street (between Rivington and Stanton)   (212) 674-7300   Zone 3

Cover None **Minimum** None **Mixed Drinks** $10–$12 **Wine** Not much selection but LOTS of sake, $7–$11; $20 bottles **Beer** Bottled only—6 to choose from, including Belgian, $7–$10 **Dress** Casual or cool **Specials** None **Food Available** Light snacks, including sweet and savory dumplings, $8–$13

Hours Sunday and Tuesday–Thursday, 5 p.m.–midnight; Friday and Saturday, 5 p.m.– 1 a.m.

What Goes On Socializing and sake.

Setting & Atmosphere Small and intimate place: six bar stools and padded benches along two walls with tables and chairs. Candles on each table, red-orange wall,s and a prominent photo of Chibi, the the owner's French bulldog and the bar's namesake. Jazz or trippy electronica is usually playing in the background.

If You Go This is the place to wise up on the sake scene by ordering a flight (a selection of three different sakes), either regular or deluxe at $15 or $20 respectively. It's a good way to try unfiltered sake, sake with an apple taste, and even a lightly sparkling sake. All sakes available here are served cold.

Club Macanudo

UPSCALE CIGAR AND WHISKY BAR

Who Goes There 30–65; middle-aged suits, often stag but some towing either bored wives or trophy babes; some younger shmoozers

26 East 63rd Street; *(212) 752-8200* *www.clubmacanudo.com* *Zone 11*

Cover None **Minimum** None **Scotch** $9–$300 **Wine** Vintage/tawny ports $12–$40 **Beer** $9 **Dress** Jackets for men, no sneakers or jeans **Food Available** Overpriced; stick with appetizers/tapas (Monday, Tuesday 5 p.m.–11 p.m.; Wednesday–Saturday 5 p.m.–12 a.m.)

Hours Monday and Tuesday, 5 p.m.–1 a.m.; Wednesday–Friday, 5 p.m.–2 a.m.; Saturday, 6 p.m.–2 a.m.; Sunday, closed.

What Goes On Some might expect that cigars and whisky are fun things to be enjoyed lightheartedly. These people will not dig Club Macanudo. This place takes itself seriously. If it all wasn't very very serious, people might not be inclined to fork over $800/year to rent tiny personal humidors here (complete with shiny brass nameplate), they might wince at the over-the-top chummy/clubby/woody interior, or they might even break a smile. But the scotch selection *is* pretty serious stuff—it's America's only bar serving rare bottlings from the Scotch Whisky Society—and the friendly bartenders (as devoted to scotch 'n' smoke as many regulars) are knowledgeable guides for neophytes. Go late enough that plenty of scotch has already been ingested, and you may strike up a stogie-based friendship with an exec who'd otherwise never take your calls.

Setting & Atmosphere It's like being in an enormous cigar box (complete with wooden Indians)—and nearly as claustrophobic, especially on weekends and Thursdays (the "hot" night).

If You Go Don't worry too much about ordering the wrong thing; there are few dumb choices, drink- and cigar-wise. But do bone up on proper stogie cutting and lighting; do it wrong and you'll elicit gasps of horror.

Coral Room

NIGHTCLUB WITH DANCING AND HIGH NOVELTY APPEAL

Who Goes There 20's–30's; locals, hipsters, and mixed crowd depending on event and DJ

512 West 29th Street (between Tenth and Eleventh avenues); (212) 244-1965 *www.coralroomnyc.com* *Zone 6*

Cover Wednesday and Thursday—no cover unless special event; Sunday no cover; Friday $10, Saturday $15 **Minimum** None **Mixed Drinks** $6–$12 **Wine** $6–$10 **Beer**

$5–$8 **Dress** Casual, funky or event appropriate **Specials** Events are announced on website; no happy hour **Food Available** None

Hours Wednesday–Sunday, 10 p.m.–4 a.m.

What Goes On Drinking, dancing, fish and mermaid/merman ogleing. Friday features DJ Abby and once-a-month live music; Saturday hosts DJ Reach, from Last Call with Carson Daly, spinning hip hop, funk, and R&B; Sunday is Stingray party with Merman Matt, DJs, and host Lyle Derek.

Setting & Atmosphere The main appeal of this place is the 35-foot-long, 9,000-gallon aquarium situated, conveniently, behind the bar. It holds almost 200 fish of 15 species, not including the *Homo sapiens* who swim and/or cavort in the tank for a few minutes every hour. Mermaids change depending on the night, and some change costumes with each appearance. The VIP room (separated by velvet rope in the club) and dance area are are supposedly designed to appear as if on a ship (complete with portholes), but the effect is minimally successful at best. The bathrooms are divided from the main space by a wall dotted with smaller mini fish tanks visible from both sides, so you can eyeball your crush through the tank for a water-distorted vision of his/her wait for the rest rooms. There are comfortable couches, low stools, and a small 1950s-style living room complete with driftwood lamps, paintings, and a wood-paneled TV playing black-and-white aquatic themed films. Music quality varies with night, as does the crowd, but when the music/crowd ratio feels right, this is a great place for a fun evening of fish and frolics.

If You Go Expect considerable attitude at the door, unless you arrive very early or very late. Make sure you stay for at least one mermaid appearance.

DBA

MECCA FOR ULTRA-HIGH-QUALITY DRINKS

Who Goes There 21–50; drink freaks, ranging from nerdy homebrewers to assured sybarites

41 First Avenue; (212) 475-5097 Zone 5

Cover None **Minimum** None **Mixed Drinks** $5.50 and up **Wine** $7 by the glass **Beer** $4–$25 **Dress** Casual but hip **Specials** Happy hour every day, 1–7:30 p.m. ($1 off everything) **Food Available** None

Hours Daily, 1 p.m.–4 a.m.

What Goes On No Schlitz here; rather, you'll find hand-pumped British (and British-style) ales, a whole bunch of taps (dated, so you can gauge freshness), and zillions of bottles. This is the only place in New York that serves properly poured ales and lagers at the proper temperature (never frigid, hand pumps at cellar temperature) in the proper glasses, and there's a fine bourbon, scotch, and tequila collection, as well. Servers have attitude, as do some of the customers.

Setting & Atmosphere Low-lit, contemporary, and spare, this invariably crowded spot doesn't have much decor to distract the reverent drinking, but it's certainly far more refined than your average skanky beer hall. Nice garden out back, open only in warm weather.

If You Go Not sure what to order? Ask advice from any of the beer geeks at the bar and you'll be guided by some of the city's most knowledgeable drinkers.

Excelsior Bar

SWISH, NEIGHBORHOOD GAY BAR

Who Goes There 20–50; locals, gay, straight and hip.

390 Fifth Avenue (between 6th & 7th Streets); (718) 832-1599   Zone 16

Cover None **Minimum** None **Mixed Drinks** $6–8 **Wine** $6–$7 **Beer** On tap and bottled **Dress** Casual or cool **Specials** Happy hour, Monday–Friday, 6–8 p.m.; Saturday and Sunday, 2–7 p.m. **Food Available** None, but you may call for deliveries

Hours Monday–Friday, 6 p.m.–4 a.m; Saturday and Sunday, 2 p.m.–4 a.m.

What Goes On There's usually a good rapport at the bar—whether you're here for just a drink or to do some subtle cruising. From pretty boys to straight men and everything in between, all will enjoy themselves.

Setting & Atmosphere Friendly, relaxed, and sophisticated cool atmosphere. Sleek decor which mixes pseudo-Mondrian-esque designs with 1970s tackiness. There's a lot of red and angular lines; overall the setting is crisp and clean. Old fans on the ceiling loom over clean wooden floors.

If You Go Check out the jukebox, and after your selection has played, spend some time outside on the deck, or go downstairs into the garden and admire the two plastic pink flamingoes. You could also bar-hop to **Ginger's** across the street or get an order of tasty french fries at the **Chip Shop** (383 Fifth Avenue; (718) 832-7701).

Fez

HIP MOROCCAN-STYLE BAR WITH SUBTERRANEAN NIGHTCLUB

Who Goes There 21–45; brisk pre- and post-concert biz, otherwise pretentious comely hangsters mixed with relaxing locals

380 Lafayette (at Fourth Street); (212) 533-2680   www.feznyc.com   Zone 5

Cover $10–18 in nightclub, none in bar **Minimum** 2 drinks in nightclub, none in bar **Mixed Drinks** $5.50–$9 **Wine** $5.50–$7 **Beer** $5–$6 **Dress** Designer casual **Food Available** Stripped-down version of Time Café menu

Hours Monday–Thursday, 6 p.m.–2 a.m.; Friday–Sunday, 6 p.m.–4 a.m. (bar); nightclub varies, so call for info.

What Goes On Downstairs is one of the city's best alternative (largely acoustic) music spaces, hosting sultry/loungey acts from jazz to world beat. The sound is fine, and the vibe is hip and exciting (booths and long tables comfortably accommodate groups). The bar above feels like a secret opium den, and the café up front is a popular spot for late-night retrosnacks.

Setting & Atmosphere Enter through the Time Café, a brightly lit retro-luncheonette, then pass through a bead-curtained arch into a sexy Moroccan lounge outfitted with mosaic-tiled octagonal tables, flickering mock oil lamps, Alhambra-esque arches, and paintings of Arabic singers. Luxuriate on well-padded couches and cushiony bar stools and enjoy jazz on the excellent sound system. Fez achieves that elusive combination of chic atmosphere and low-key coziness. Downstairs in the nightclub (both lounge and nightclub are called Fez): low ceiling, red velvet, intimate clubby ambience with gleaming bar.

If You Go The most popular act downstairs is the Thursday-night nutsy jazzy way-hip Mingus Big Band, but they sell out, so reserve ahead. Few real clinkers play here, so go ahead and take potluck. There's also another branch at 2330 Broadway (and 85th Street), phone (212) 579-5100.

Firebird Café

CABARET

Who Goes There Older crowd, many couples

363 West 46th Street; (212) 586-0244   Zone 8

Cover $20–$30 **Minimum** $15 **Mixed Drinks** $6–$10 **Wine** $7–$10 **Beer** $5–$7 **Dress** Dressy **Specials** Occasionally no cover for late night **Food Available** Appetizers and desserts from Firebird (Russian restaurant next door)

Hours Sunday through Tuesday, closed except for special shows; Wednesday through Saturday, shows at 7 p.m., 9 p.m., or 11 p.m.

What Goes On Firebird presents the brightest up-and-comers on the cabaret scene, with occasional bigger names, in one of the most comfortable settings in town. Lots of choices for the vodka enthusiast.

Setting & Atmosphere Supremely intimate; no seat is more than a few feet from the stage. The cabaret room is nowhere near as lavish as the Russian restaurant next door (so over the top it would embarrass a czar), but it's an elegant, dramatic space. You're served by the same waiters in faux red or green Russian military officer uniforms as in the restaurant.

If You Go If the room is *too* intimate for you (one sneeze will make you part of the act), stroll out to the bar for a few tunes. You can still see and hear okay, and the bartender is a riot. Also, Firebird restaurant next door is one of the few worthy eats on this "Restaurant Row."

Flatiron Lounge

CHIC, SPECIALIST COCKTAILS

Who Goes There 20's–40's; cocktail connoisseurs, chic lounge-types mixed with business suits and professionals

37 West 19th Street; (212) 727-7741   www.flatironlouonge.com   Zone 7

Cover None **Minimum** None **Mixed Drinks** $8–$12 **Wine** $8–$12 **Beer** $8 but you don't come here for beer **Dress** Chic or suited **Specials** Downstairs room may be on offer for parties and special events **Food Available** Only free bar nibbles

Hours Monday–Thursday 5 p.m.–2 a.m.; Friday and Saturday 5 p.m.–4 a.m.

What Goes On Cocktail consumption, socializing, looking fantastic.

Setting & Atmosphere Great setting that comes at a price for the drinks. The space is Art Deco inspired and designed, with an arched ceiling at the entrance, dark wood and plush, private group banquettes along the wall, beside open tables and a 30-foot bar. The bar was renovated to its "original splendor" from its origin in the 1920s. There's a romantic quality to the place.

If You Go Indulge in one or two of their special cocktails using some of their own infused spirits; alternatively, you could order a flight of cocktails ($18) that provides a selection and avoids excessive alcohol consumption. The mixologist prepares drinks such as a "Metropolis" that includes pearl vodka infused with green apples and finished with a touch of French apple brandy cider. A spiced pear drink is made with vodka infused with pear and cloves. Some drinks are prepared for certain seasons only.

Galapagos

BAR AND PERFORMANCE SPACE

Who Goes There 20–50; locals, art set, hipsters

70 North 6th Street; (718) 782-5188   www.galapagosartspace.com   Zone 16

Cover Free, except back room performances, including music, theater, dance, and films (usually $5–$10) **Minimum** None **Mixed Drinks** $6–$9 **Wine** $6–$8 **Beer** $5–$8 **Dress** Grunge, casual, or simply cool **Specials** Frequent special events; happy hour Monday–Saturday, 6–8 p.m. **Food Available** None, but you may call for deliveries

Hours Sunday–Thursday, 6 p.m.–2 a.m.; Friday and Saturday, 6 p.m.–4 a.m.

What Goes On Galapagos is a solid reason to get out of Manhattan for an evening. It has won several awards of distinction for its performance space, its bar, and for being a top nightclub destination. These accolades are well-deserved. There's almost always something going on—whether it be a DJ, art installation, film, music, theatre, or dance performance. You can go simply for a drink or to soak up a bit of culture, no pressure—it's all very laid-back and comfortable.

Setting & Atmosphere Housed in an old mayonnaise factory, Galapagos suitably fills the lofty space. You'll either be taken aback or mesmerized by the expanse of water that meets you as you enter. An art piece usually hovers over the water. The water has been described as a "reflecting pool," but it's easy to get caught in the optical illusion tricking you to think that the water is bottomless. Lighting is dimmed and full of candles and colored lights. For those not wanting beer, the bartender makes a good vodka lemondrop. High tables and stools are close to a stage in the main space, and a few lower tables are arranged by the reflecting pool. The back room has several theatre-style seats in the back and round tables near the stage. Although the music may be loud in back, the front room usually is usually quiet enough for conversation.

If You Go Have a drink in the main space and then take a peek in the back room to see if the scheduled event strikes your fancy. The lovely and simple women's rest rooms are candlelit, fragranced with fresh flowers, and have stalls hidden only by white muslin curtains. North 6th Street has several bars, and Bedford Avenue is a nightlife hotbed; combine your visit to Galapagos with an exploration of Williamsburg.

The Ginger Man

GIANT-SIZED BEER BAR

Who Goes There 21–60; throngs of businessmen and yuppies after work, varied at other times

11 East 36th Street; (212) 532-3740   Zone 7

Cover None **Minimum** None **Mixed Drinks** $5 and up **Wine** $5–$6 **Beer** $4–$10 **Dress** Casual **Food Available** A few simple bar snacks; Guinness Stout stew

Hours Monday–Wednesday, 11:30 a.m.–2 a.m.; Thursday–Friday, 11:30 a.m.–4 a.m.; Saturday, 12:30 p.m.–4 a.m.; Sunday, 3 p.m.–midnight

What Goes On On paper, this is New York's best beer hall. It boasts a mind-boggling 60 taps, nearly all well-chosen; decent Guinness stew to eat; friendly bartenders; and a comfy living room in the back. Prices are fair, and this is a late hang in an early-closing nabe. But there are problems: The beer's too cold (fine for light lagers, but some of the fancier British and Belgian ales turn flavorless at ballpark temperature), and peak hours—5:30–10 p.m. and all night on weekends—can be a crowded hell of noise, so time your visit carefully. Off-peak times can be almost depressingly dead, however.

Setting & Atmosphere The huge, high-ceilinged space is classic New York, dominated by a mile-long bar and copper-plated Wall o' Taps. There are tables up front by the floor-to-ceiling windows and a relaxing parlor in back with sofas and armchairs.

If You Go Midafternoons and late weeknights you'll have the place largely to yourself; bring 20 or 30 friends, no problem!

Ginger's

FRIENDLY GAY BAR

Who Goes There 20–70; locals, gay, straight; truly diverse crowd

363 Fifth Avenue (between 5th and 6th streets); (718) 788-0924 Zone 16

Cover None **Minimum** None **Mixed Drinks** $6–$9 **Wine** $6 **Beer** $4–$7 **Dress** Anything goes **Specials** Monthly drink specials **Food Available** None

Hours Monday–Friday, 6 p.m.–4 a.m.; Friday and Saturday, 2 p.m.–4 a.m.

What Goes On This is a great neighborhood bar, embracing all kinds. Lesbians are especially welcome. Amenities include pool table, outdoor garden, and the jukebox. Many have hailed the jukebox as being quite varied, but it sometimes plays a little too much Melissa Etheridge. Camaraderie is rampant, and you needn't sip your drink alone for long.

Setting & Atmosphere The front part of the space is narrow with the bar spanning one side. This is a very lively area and tends to get noisy and crowded quickly. The regulars know each other and it's a good place to people-watch. The back room is more spacious and conducive to a quieter conversation—unless there's a dispute at the pool table. Ginger's is packed with knickknacks on the walls and loads of black and white photos. It's an incredibly cozy and homey space. The bar staff are very friendly and pour a good pint.

If You Go Consider playing pool in the back room—but beware that some of the ladies take their game very seriously. When it's warm, you can enjoy the outdoor garden.

Halcyon

FUNKY WINE BAR, DJ VENUE, MUSIC AND FURNISHINGS SHOP

Who Goes There Locals, mellow hipsters, DJ groupies, vegetarians, appreciators of literary pursuits and kitsch

227 Smith Street (between Butler and Douglass streets) (718) 260-9299 www.halcyonline.com Zone 16

Cover None **Minimum** None **Mixed Drinks** Wine, beer, and sake only **Wine** Decent selection, $5.50–$7.50 **Beer** Bottled only $4–$11 **Dress** Casual, funky, hip **Specials** None **Food Available** Vegetarian snacks, entrées, desserts

Hours Sunday–Thursday, 11 a.m.–1 a.m.; Friday and Saturday, 11 a.m.–2 a.m.

What Goes On A little bit of everything takes place. If you time it right, you could come here for a tasty brunch, stay for a literary discussion, wait longer for the guest DJ, and then go home with a newly bought lamp and CD. Live music is also performed as are screenings. Music of some sort is featured every night.

Setting & Atmosphere Some think the atmosphere is wired with too many studied cool vibes, while others embrace the scene, pick a couch or deep bucket chair, relax, indulge in a drink (good espresso and teas too), and absorb the music. During the day, a true sense of calm pervades, and reading and chilling out is highly encouraged; evenings can get more frenetic depending on the DJ on deck and types of video and/or slide installations. Music ranges from psychedelic to electronic grooves, trance, techno, hip hop, and funk. The setting features sofas, mosaic coffee tables, lamps, bookshelves, and kitsch artifacts inspired by the 1950s—all for sale. The back hawks a wide selection of vinyl and CD remixes and imports for the budding spinner. All material can be sampled via headphones.

If You Go Keep in mind that you don't need to be a DJ junkie or know trance to appreciate the scene. There's a wide variety on offer, and usually, it's not too loud. If you're not interested in the installations, you can play one of the board games found on the bookshelves.

Hole in One

WHISKY AND JAPANESE FOOD BAR

Who Goes There 28–70; well-heeled Japanese businessmen

1003A 2nd Avenue at 53rd Street (2nd floor); (212) 319-6070   Zone 9

Cover $25 +20% service charge **Minimum** None **Mixed Drinks** $14.50–$980 **Wine** $14.50 per glass **Beer** $7.50–$8.50 **Dress** Jackets and dresses **Food Available** Exquisite Japanese bar food is not to be missed: little plates (for about $10) of things like mackerel sushi, free-range strips of chicken shioyaki (the skin broiled to crispy perfection), consummately fried baby eels, delicious sautéed burdock. No English menu, but staff will attempt to translate.

Hours Monday–Friday, 7 p.m.–2:30 a.m.

What Goes On This is one of the world's best single-malt whisky bars—if you can find it. The entrance is marked only by a discreet brass sign . . . in Japanese. But although Hole in One is hidden and costly, and the clientele's almost entirely Japanese, it's not private. You're buzzed through an interior door, you pass up a flight of steps, and then you enter whisky heaven. Owner Koichi Iraiwa has amassed a treasure trove of whiskeys, 250 bottles in all (more if you count blends), many original bottlings from distilleries long ago closed (such as a bottle of St. Magdalene [Linjithgow] 12-year that may be one of the last remaining in the world). The rarest cost upward of $1,000 a glass; but many less exorbitant bottles are still more than worthy (e.g., Clynelish for $33, Edradour 10 for $19.50, and Port Ellen 15 for $19.50). There is a particularly broad range of Springanks, from 10 years ($14.50). Avo and Griffin cigars are also for sale, as are good cognacs, gins, vodkas, and bourbons.

Setting & Atmosphere A cozy but sleek, windowless room with a few dozen seats at intimate tables and a long bar facing the sea of bottles. Unintentionally silly Scottish knickknacks—plenty of golf clubs, for example—are scattered everywhere.

If You Go Bring a big wad of money (or a platinum card); if you love Japanese food or scotch whisky, this is a worthy splurge. But this male bastion may make unaccompanied women feel out of place. Friday, the slow night, might be best for those who want to mount a serious tasting undistracted by crowds.

Hudson Bar

CHIC HOTEL BAR

Who Goes There 22–50; the beautiful, the trendy, and those interested in modern architecture.

356 West 58th Street; (212) 554-6343   www.hudsonhotel.com   Zone 8

Cover None **Minimum** None **Mixed Drinks** $10–$15 **Wine** Bottles $50 and up; $7–$15 by the glass; cognac $9–$35 by the glass **Beer** $6–$7 **Dress** Casual dressy to ultra chic or interestingly different; black always works **Specials** None **Food Available** None, but hotel has restaurant and other food options

Hours Daily, from 4 p.m.–3 a.m.

What Goes On This is a great place to go on an expense account, expensive date, or our for some extravagant fun. The Hudson Bar oozes cool and style, and it still manages to offer a genuinely friendly staff. The DJ nights aren't particularly stunning—many prefer the CDs pumped through the speakers on other evenings.

Setting & Atmosphere Expectations are high when you enter an Ian Schrager hotel, and you won't be disappointed with the Hudson. Subtlety is key from the sidewalk until you enter through the glass doors and proceed up the chartreuse-hued, illuminated escalators. Once off the escalators, turn around and walk up a few stairs to the Hudson Bar. Before the stairs there are a few tables in hidden corners and low light—up the stairs you're met with a long bar and a vast floor comprised of large, illuminated lit square tiles. There's plenty of space—one wall has pillowed banquettes with clear tables and a mixture of faux-period and ultra-modern, clear-plastic high-backed chairs. The ceiling isn't too high, but you won't mind as you sip a strawbellini (strawberry puree and champagne) and gaze at the dozens of candles throughout the room; your eyes may even happen upon a famous face.

If You Go Don't go if you're having a bad hair day. Also visit the Hudson Private Park bar—a beautifully decorated outdoor bar which can be viewed through the lobby. This bar is open Monday–Friday, 7:30 a.m.–1 a.m.; and Saturday and Sunday, 8:30 a.m.–1 a.m.; the bar is closed during colder months. It has incredibly comfy chairs and love seats; you could easily become addicted to the atmosphere. Coffee and food available. During the winter you could also try the Hudson Library Bar, which is wood-paneled and cozy but not particularly chic.

International Bar

LOCAL, ANTI-CHIC DIVE BAR WITH CLASS

Who Goes There 20's–60's; locals, regulars, those in search of conversation and NO scene

120½ First Avenue (between 7th Street and St. Mark's Place)   (212) 777-9244 Zone 5

Cover None **Minimum** None **Mixed Drinks** $4–$6 **Wine** $4–$5 **Beer** $2–$4 **Dress** Anything goes **Specials** Prices this low are special anyway, but you might get every 3rd drink free if you come between 2 and 7 p.m. **Food Available** None

Hours   Daily, 2 p.m.–4 a.m.

What Goes On   This is one place where fresh college grads, East Villagers, tattooed and pierced punk rockers, old regulars, and the odd tourist might find themselves peacefully rubbing elbows and downing a few. Conversation is definitely an option even when the jukebox is on.

Setting & Atmosphere   Don't be put off by the spray-canned graffiti on the door, or the year-round white Christmas lights in the windows—International is quite a welcome retreat if you need to find a place for a cheap drink without the posing. As an antithesis to chic, the place revels in its dive quality. Bar staff are very friendly and, once you pass the bar, the place widens out a bit in the back to allow for a few tables. A thoroughly nondescript, small outdoor space is open for good weather.

If You Go   Make sure you play a round of Ms. Pac-Man on the upright game machine— still only a quarter. Unless you're really hard-up, forego the $2 canned beer, and spring for the $3–$4 choices. Make use of the eclectic jukebox; the selection is wonderfully varied and has a little bit of everything, except anything remotely top ten.

Joe's Pub

LUSH NIGHTCLUB

Who Goes There   A smart, chic set (younger later)

425 Lafayette Street; (212) 539-8770 (x778 for reservations, x454 for show schedule) www.joespub.com   Zone 5

Cover $10–$35 (call to check) **Minimum** Usually 2 drinks (call to check) **Mixed Drinks** $9–$11 **Wine** $8 **Beer** $4–$6 **Dress** Elegant on cabaret nights, elegantly sexy on dance nights **Specials** Pretheater prix fixe dinner, 6–7:30 p.m. **Food Available** Full menu until 1 a.m.

Hours   Daily, 6 p.m.–4 a.m.; shows usually start around 8 and/or 11:30 p.m.

What Goes On   Lots of cabaret (the more theatrical style, à la Ute Lemper—this is no piano bar). Also some rock-ish (Ricki Lee Jones has played here), jazz-ish, and well-chosen alternative bands (with music kept at a reasonable volume). Late Wednesday nights are a high point, with dancing to hot live salsa bands; likewise Tuesdays for reggae. Cabaret attracts a mixed audience, late and dance nights an especially attractive crowd. The name is a joke—"Joe" is Joseph Papp, the highly respected director of the Public Theater, and this certainly is no mere pub . . . though it makes a good pun.

Setting & Atmosphere   Carpeted with high ceilings, French windows, and softly glowing lamps. Highly atmospheric (where are the fog machines?) and very dramatic (not surprising, given their locale inside the Public Theater), Joe's Pub feels like a 1930s musical set—Marlene Dietrich would fit in well here. Yet it's not at all kitsch or contrived; it's just a great dark, sexy transportive place to dance, drink, or listen to music.

If You Go   Reserve tickets ahead of time. And don't forget to mix your low culture with some high culture by enjoying a film or theater performance in the Public Theater.

Kavehaz

GALLERY AND JAZZ CAFÉ

Who Goes There   22–90; locals, artsy folk, jazz and blues-minded people

37 West 26th Street; (212) 343-0612   www.kavehaz.com   Zone 6

Cover None **Minimum** 2-drink minimum except at the bar **Mixed Drinks** $6–$10 **Wine** Bottles $20 and up, big selection; $6–$8 by the glass **Beer** 5 beers on tap as well as bottled; $5–$8 **Dress** Casual to chic **Specials** Each night hosts at least one band. **Food Available** Full menu, including salads, pastas, sandwiches, and tasty desserts; served until half-hour before closing

Hours Sunday–Thursday, noon–midnight; Friday, noon–2 a.m.; Saturday, noon–2:30 a.m.

What Goes On Each visit to the Kavehaz is a little different, since the artwork on the walls changes every month, and the featured bands change nightly. Daytime finds the Kavehaz mellow and somewhat sophisticated, and by night it becomes more sultry as a jazz café. Wednesday nights are especially busy due to performances by the Ray Vega Latin Jazz band; Vega used to play with Tito Puente. Monday nights feature a singer's showcase.

Setting & Atmosphere Formerly located in Soho, the new Kavehaz has pretty much the same vibe, but the space is a little smaller. The artwork often dictates mood. Photographs tend to make the scene seem sophisticated, while the paintings give the space a very avant-garde feel. The ambience in the evening is subdued with candlelight. Above all, the service is friendly, and the atmosphere is more focused on a café-style relaxed vibe—it's never pretentious and is usually enjoyable (unless of course the band is bad).

If You Go Try one of the featured wines by the glass. If you decide to teetotal and simply absorb the atmosphere, have a cappuccino, served in a bowl.

The Knitting Factory

(VERY) ALTERNATIVE MUSIC CLUB

Who Goes There 21–45; varies with the music, black-clad hipsters to shaved heads and multiple piercings; a broad age range for the less rock-ish groups.

74 Leonard Street; (212) 219-3055   www.knittingfactory.com   Zone 2

Cover Varies by show **Minimum** None **Mixed Drinks** $5 and up **Wine** $5 and up **Beer** $4 and up **Dress** Black T-shirts and black jeans always work **Specials** Happy hour, 5–7 p.m., free live music in downstairs bar every night from 11 p.m. until late **Food Available** None

Hours Vary, call for info

What Goes On A world-famous venue for alternative music and klezmer to thrash. Some of the jazzier and more intellectual performers have switched their allegiance to upstart **Tonic** (see profile) across town, but this is still a mecca for those open-minded enough to listen to "free" jazz, traditional Hanukkah melodies deconstructed by punk groups, or tuba quartets covering Jimi Hendrix. The staff has tons of attitude.

Setting & Atmosphere A nice mellow bar at street level, large two-level performance space within (very European), and a tiny Alterknit Room presenting groups of still narrower appeal. The old office's downstairs bar is dark, atmospheric, and quite the destination on late nights when hipper-than-hip bands set up there.

If You Go Check your email or surf the Web for free at the club's Internet connection in the main corridor. Try and see what's happening on every level of the space.

Kush

FUNKY, MOROCCAN-THEMED BAR WITH VARIED ENTERTAINMENT

Who Goes There 20's–40's; locals, hipsters, smokers, and those interested in world music and belly-dancing

183 Orchard Street (between Houston and Stanton)   (212) 677-7328   Zone 3

Cover None, except Sundays $5 for Afro-Cuban music and DJ **Minimum** None **Mixed Drinks** $6–$12 **Wine** Not big selection, but has Lebanese wine, $7 **Beer** Bottles $5–$10 **Dress** Casual or cool. **Specials** Happy hour, 6–8 p.m. Monday–Saturday; 7–9 p.m. Sunday **Food Available** Middle Eastern snacks, including fresh mint tea

Hours Monday–Saturday 6 p.m.–4 a.m.; Sunday 7 p.m.–4 a.m.

What Goes On Live, DJ, or "organic electronic" music played each night. Kush offers interesting entertainment, including belly-dancing, percussion, and Bulgarian harmonics. This is one of the few places where tobacco smoking (not just hookahs) is permitted, so by default, Kush would be crowded even if it didn't have a good vibe.

Setting & Atmosphere Kush is divided into two parts: the long, narrow space along a bar, and the other side of the room that has tables, a tiny stage, and a smaller bar (connected to the main bar on the other side) with stools. Morrocan decor, low lighting, and a serene scene prevail, in spite of weekend crowds.

If You Go Make sure you catch some of the entertainment, and if you are inclined to smoke, rent a hookah with specially flavored tobacco for $15 (inhaling not required).

Le Bar Bat

GOTHIC NIGHTCLUB/RESTAURANT/DISCO

Who Goes There 25–50; suburbanites on weekends, locals and professionals weeknights, musicians on Monday night

311 West 57th Street; (212) 307-7228   www.lebarbat.com   Zone 8

Cover Sunday–Wednesday, $10; Thursday, $15; Friday and Saturday, $20 **Minimum** None **Mixed Drinks** $6–$10 **Wine** Bottles, $25 and up, $6–$7.50 by the glass **Beer** $5–$10 **Dress** Anything from white tie to nice casual (dress code Thursday–Saturday: no jeans, sneakers, T-shirts) **Specials** Ladies' night Friday **Food Available** Full continental/Southwestern sit-down menu; late bar menu till 2 a.m. Wednesday–Saturday, till 1 a.m. Sunday.

Hours Bar open 5 p.m.–4 a.m. daily; kitchen open Sunday–Thursday, 5–11 p.m.; Friday and Saturday, 5 p.m.–midnight.

What Goes On This wacky, labyrinthine party joint long preceded all its plasticky theme-bar neighbors. First and foremost, it's a supper club, presenting R&B, blues, funk, dance, and pop/rock bands (jazz vocals on more informal Sunday nights) in a lush cabaret setting. Rather than dine, you can buzz around the bat bar at the back of the room; view and sound are fine. If you're bored with the music—or simply want to change channels—go upstairs to the balcony (perfect for loners and voyeurs), recede into the comfortable Borneo Room, or take the all-out sensory stimulation route in Pandora's Box (opens at 9 p.m. nightly).

Setting & Atmosphere Trippy Gothic cathedral look, complete with fluorescent blue semimolten bats hanging from the ceiling. The main room centers on the stage. The upstairs balcony has more seating and a bird's-eye view of the action; a passageway leads back to the Borneo Room, an inner sanctum with low lighting, comfy loveseats, handsome copper bar, and jukebox. In the basement, Pandora's Box is a disco complete with cool light system, big bar, and crowds of partiers.

If You Go The musical range is quite wide, so find out who's playing—not that it matters much; with myriad rooms to choose from, it's easy to escape the nightclub area if the music fails to please. Though formality is by no means de rigueur, this is a good spot for drinks after a black-tie event. There are frequent singles events and other special parties (or throw your own; they'll accommodate groups from 10 to 1,500); call for details. Monday nights feature jam sessions, mainly blues.

Mercury Lounge

ROCK SHOWCASE

Who Goes There 21–40; serious music fans, bohemian Lower East Side clubbers, some grunge

217 East Houston Street; (212) 260-4700 www.mercurylounge.com Zone 5
Cover $5–$12 **Minimum** None **Mixed Drinks** $3.50–$5.50 **Wine** $3.75–$5 **Beer** $3.50–$4.50 **Dress** Black and hip **Food Available** None

Hours Daily, 6 p.m.–4 a.m.; shows every night at 8 p.m.

What Goes On A showcase for newly signed (and hot about-to-be-signed) rock bands with an excellent sound system. The performance space is perfect for listening to an eclectic mix of groups, from surprisingly big names (playing here to maintain their hip credentials) to up-and-comers and cult favorites. If you've never heard of a band playing here, you probably will soon.

Setting & Atmosphere You enter through a mysterious-looking black bar with black curtains, and the music's through a door in the back. It's basically a box of a room, but exposed brick and great sound (blessedly, never head-bangingly loud) and lighting create an ambience that feels right.

If You Go Walk down nearby Ludlow Street after the show to explore some cafés, music clubs, and late-night shops.

Nell's

WARM LIVING ROOM–ISH DANCE CLUB WITH HOT DISCO BASEMENT

Who Goes There 25–40; sexy clubbers and chic music scenesters

246 West 14th Street; (212) 675-1567 www.nells.com Zone 6
Cover Sunday–Wednesday, $10; Thursday–Saturday, $15; **Minimum** None **Mixed Drinks** $6–$8.50 **Wine** $5 **Beer** $5 **Dress** To kill (no sneakers, no jeans) **Specials** Ladies' night (free admission); call for info **Food Available** Light pub food

Hours Daily, 10 p.m.–4 a.m.

What Goes On This is the Dorian Gray of dance clubs; Nell's never goes out of fashion and never tarnishes with age. The main room (if you make it there past the snide and intimidating doormen without killing or being killed) is a cozy, funky living room that plays host to excellent bluesy/jazzy/funky/Latin-ish live bands. Each night has its musical theme (e.g., tango Mondays, jazz Saturdays, international Fridays, and Tuesday open mics where some talented vocalists sit in with the house soul/R&B group). It's a great scene for hair-down dancing; this room is sort of an anti-disco for those who hate loud, flashy, pounding dance floors. Downstairs is the loud, flashy, pounding dance floor. Just as live music styles rotate nightly upstairs, each night a different DJ spins his or her own groovy mix in the basement, like house/reggae on Tuesdays, soul/R&B on Saturdays, and the eclectic Sunday night stylings of Jonny Sender. Schedules shift, so call the club for info.

Setting & Atmosphere Victorian British men's club ambience upstairs, all dark wood and red velvet with couches and armchairs, with an incongruous dance floor facing the central stage; downstairs, a packed disco dance floor plus adjacent couchy lounge with Persian rugs and coffee tables.

No Moore

RELAXED DRINKING SPACE WITH OPTION FOR LIVE MUSIC

Who Goes There 20's–50's; locals, regulars,

234 West Broadway (corner of North Moore Street) (212) 925-2595 *Zone 2*

Cover Sometimes there's a cover for music in downstairs space; but no cover for ground-floor space **Minimum** None **Mixed Drinks** $6–$10 **Wine** $6–$9 **Beer** $5–$8 **Dress** Casual **Specials** Happy hour, Monday–Saturday 4–7 p.m. **Food Available** No, but you're welcome to call for deliveries and menus are provided at the bar.

Hours Monday–Thursday 4 p.m.–3 a.m.; Friday and Saturday, 4 p.m.–4 a.m.

What Goes On Relaxation, drinking, and (sometimes) music.

Setting & Atmosphere No Moore is slightly post-hip, which gives it a more relaxed appeal—it's not trying to be anything other than a decent space for a drink. Live music is on offer when the downstairs section is open. The ground floor has an open feel, large windows, and a serviceable jukebox.

If You Go Enjoy your drink in a cool space and check out the music downstairs. After your drink, walk west to the Hudson River Park promenade.

O'Flaherty's Ale House

IRISH PUB AFTER-SHOW HIDEAWAY

Who Goes There 25–55; locals and tourists until the 11 p.m. influx of the after-theater crowd (many actors and musicians)

334 West 46th Street; (212) 581-9366 Zone 8

Cover None **Minimum** 1 drink **Mixed Drinks** $4.50–$5 **Wine** $4.50 **Beer** $4–$4.50 **Dress** Anything from suit and tie to jeans and T-shirt **Food Available** Surprisingly extensive Irish menu (shepherd's pie in several incarnations, stews, fried stuff)

Hours Daily, noon–4 a.m.

What Goes On The beer's not super, but one of the selections is an interesting house-brewed honey lager. This is a great spot because among the windy passageways and copious alcoves there's an ambience to please almost anyone. The energy level picks up as theater people stop by for an after-work drink, and much of the crowd stays late. Part of the draw is the old-fashioned Irish bartenders, probably hired as much for their brogues as for their gregariousness.

Setting & Atmosphere Choose your surroundings: a book-filled study in the back with comfortable chairs and a pool table; a front corner of couches (great for groups); a handsome wraparound bar with adjoining dart board; an outdoor garden with antique-style park benches. There's a nook or cranny for any occasion. It's all alcoves; there's no "main section" to speak of.

If You Go If you're looking for a livelier time on this same block, see the profile for **Swing 46**, a jive-talking swing-dancing nightspot.

Pen-top Bar at the Peninsula Hotel

ROOFTOP HOTEL BAR

Who Goes There 30–65; after-workers, trystin' smoochers, one-last-drinkers

700 Fifth Avenue; (212) 247-2200   www.peninsula.com   Zone 9

Cover None **Minimum** None **Mixed Drinks** $10–$15 **Wine** $15 and up, by the glass **Beer** $10 and up **Dress** Sophisticated and expensive **Food Available** Small selection of upscale snacks like smoked salmon, cheese platter, and shrimp; good free-bie bar snacks come with drinks

Hours Monday–Thursday, 5 p.m.–midnight; Friday and Saturday, 5 p.m.–1 a.m.; closed Sunday

What Goes On There are higher bars with more breathtaking views, but the great thing about this 23rd-floor perch is that you see Manhattan not from the bottom or top but from the middle. You're surrounded by the top thirds of buildings (like the beautiful St. Regis Hotel across the street), an odd and striking geometric landscape cluttering the nighttime sky. It's a dramatic setting for an outdoor drink in good weather, and the indoor bar is hyper-romantic when it snows. Friendly, professional service.

Setting & Atmosphere A romantic little bar surrounded by three outdoor spaces, each with its own great view: a large spillover area (full after work) with plastic tables and chairs; a standing-only balcony with a view up Fifth Avenue (good for cooing couples); and an elegant green carpeted rectangle with comfortable chairs and flickering lamps.

If You Go Go on the late side; from 5 to 7 p.m. the office crowd takes over. The bar's essentially hidden: take the elevator to the top floor, then ascend the dramatic glassed-in circular staircase.

PJ Clarke's

OLD-TIME NEW YORK BAR

Who Goes There Businessmen after work, extremely varied later

915 Third Avenue; (212) 317-1616   www.pjclarkes.com   Zone 9

Cover None **Minimum** None **Mixed Drinks** $7 and up **Wine** $6–$8 **Beer** $4–$8 **Dress** Anything **Specials** None **Food Available** Raw bar plus full menu, including burgers, fries, salads, chicken, steak, desserts

Hours Daily, 11:30 a.m.–4 a.m. (dining room closes at 3 a.m.)

What Goes On A real New York legend, and one of the only old-time bars that hasn't turned cloyingly self-conscious. PJ's is a magnet for advertising people after work, but later the crowd turns amazingly diverse, from tourists to hard-boiled old guys to corporate moguls to Ratso Rizzo, with lots of interaction. A great jukebox plays well-chosen show tunes, swing, and rock.

Setting & Atmosphere "Renovation" was a dirty word for the regulars, but after a year's closure, the place looks surprisingly similar, except with stronger floorboards and an upstairs bar/dining room. Luckily, this single skinny little brick building has stubbornly remained. The atmosphere inside is so authentically old New York it's practically gas-lit. There's an oversized wooden bar; big foggy mirrors plastered with photos of presidents, Irishmen, and deceased bartenders; and smoke-filled dining rooms where meals are served on tables with red-checkered tablecloths.

If You Go Check out the antique men's urinals—tourist attractions in their own right. On the subject, other notable rest rooms are the unisex see-through (until you close the latch) stalls at **Bar 89** (89 Mercer Street; (212) 279-0989).

Rodeo Bar

COWBOY BAR WITH HIGH-QUALITY ECLECTIC LIVE MUSIC

Who Goes There Aging hippies, urban cowboys, music fans

375 Third Avenue; (212) 683-6500 www.rodeobar.com *Zone 7*

Cover No **Minimum** None **Mixed Drinks** $5–$11 **Wine** $4 **Beer** $4–$5 **Dress** Jeans and whatever **Specials** Happy hour, 4–7 p.m. weekdays **Food Available** Tex-Mex (full meals or bar munchies)

Hours Daily, 10 p.m.–until; music Monday–Saturday, 11:30 p.m.–4 a.m.

What Goes On Rodeo Bar isn't taken terribly seriously by New York music scene cognoscenti, but it offers something extremely rare: good bar bands in regular rotation. Styles range from electric to rockabilly to country rock, but the musical sensibility is always more New York hip than the saddles 'n' barrels decor would suggest; even the most country acts are *funky* country. The same bands play regularly, building audience and repertoire and honing skills. As a result, performances here are more polished than at nearly any other club in town, and there are loyal fans who come here first when they want to drink a beer and hear some dependably solid tunes without dropping dozens of dollars.

Setting & Atmosphere So Wild West that you half expect Calamity Jane to come whooping past the bar; this place is tricked out with barrels, stirrups, rope-handle door knobs, peanut shells, the works. Someone was decorating for a square dance, but thank goodness the music's much hipper than Cowboy Bob. A huge bull stares inquisitively at the performers from the side of the stage. Yee-haw.

If You Go If the cow-punching vibe is too much for you, cross over to the adjoining restaurant next door for a quick city fix.

Saka Gura

HIDDEN SUAVE SAKE BAR

Who Goes There 30–55; Japanese businessmen, sake aficionados

211 East 43rd Street; (212) 953-SAKE www.sakagura.com *Zone 9*

Cover None **Minimum** $10 **Mixed Drinks** $7–$15 **Wine** $4–$25 for sake **Beer** $5–$8 (Japanese only) **Dress** Most people in jackets, but nice casual will do **Food Available** Excellent simple Japanese dishes like udon (noodle soup) and kinpira (marinated burdock root)

Hours Monday–Thursday, noon–11 p.m.; Friday, noon–2 a.m.; Saturday 6 p.m.–2 a.m.; Sunday, 6 p.m.–midnight

What Goes On A treasure trove of sakes, plain, pricey, and odd. The drier sakes are usually the most interesting, and those who find sake an overly subtle drink should try nama zake, which has a much wider flavor of considerable complexity. If you can afford them, the aged koshu sakes (a particularly good one is kamo izumi koshu, for $15 a glass) have the length and complexity of great wine. Don't make the faux pas of ordering your rice wine hot; the good stuff is drunk cold or at room temperature (very dry ones can be warmed a little). A couple of options: You can choose to sip from a masu (wooden box) rather than a cup, or a hire (nontoxic blowfish fin) can be added to impart a mellow, smoky flavor.

Setting & Atmosphere Enter through a glarey office building lobby, walk back toward the elevators, and descend a dank staircase to get to this supremely inviting inner sanctum that's all sleek lines and open space. There are some secluded tables, but there's lots more action at the big handsome bar. It's sexy and peaceful, rarely crowded. Rest rooms are hidden inside huge round wooden fermenting barrels.

If You Go Try to talk your way into the odd private karaoke club; the door is just to your left as you enter the building's lobby.

Smoke

JAZZ CLUB AND LOUNGE

Who Goes There All ages; jazz lovers, musicians and any other affiliates

2751 Broadway (between 105th and 106th streets); (212) 864-6662
www.smokejazz.com Zone 12

Cover Varies, usually $10, but no cover Tuesday–Thursday, 5–8 p.m. **Minimum** Varies; sometimes a $10 "cover" is good for two drinks, sometimes it's separate **Mixed Drinks** $6–$7 **Wine** $6–$8 **Beer** Bottled and draft, $5–$6 **Dress** Casual; lounge and/or accessorize with instrument, sheet music, or drum sticks **Specials** "Retro Happy Hour," Monday–Saturday 5–8 p.m.; $2 pints of cider and $4 apple martinis **Food Available** None, but you're welcome to order in

Hours Monday–Saturday, 5 p.m.–4 a.m.; Sunday 5 p.m.–2:30 a.m.

What Goes On There's music every night of the week, most of it incredibly good. Smoke takes over from where the former Augie's Jazz Bar left off, so a great music tradition continues in this renovated space. You'll never know who'll be in the crowd listening or who'll come to the stage for a jam set, so no visit is ever the same.

Setting & Atmosphere An intimate, warm, relaxed setting for some great music; space can get tight since there's only seating for 70, but the overflow crowds at the bar, and everyone gets a decent view. There's a real jazz-club ambience, with bar and lounge area complete with small octagonal tables, plush sofa and chairs, dark wood, red velvet curtains, candle sconces, and a few low-hanging, unobtrusive chandeliers; the only missing accoutrement is the club's namesake (eliminated by the smoking ban). Musicians and listeners alike praise the sound system; performances, including jam sessions, are given due respect and attention.

If You Go Be prepared to listen, relax, and perhaps even be inspired.

S.O.B.'s

LATIN AND WORLD MUSIC/DANCE NIGHTCLUB

Who Goes There 21–40; music fans, salsa dancers, ethnic music trollers like David Byrne

204 Varick Street; (212) 243-4940 www.sobs.com *Zone 2*

Cover Varies ($10–$25, more or less) **Minimum** $10 at tables **Mixed Drinks** $6–$9 **Wine** $6–$8 **Beer** $5–$7 **Dress** Colorful and flashy **Specials** Free entrance Fridays before 7 p.m., Tuesday before 9 p.m.; free salsa dance lessons Monday, 7–8:30 p.m. (stay free for show) **Food Available** Pretty good overpriced pan-Latino and Brazilian dishes

Hours Monday–Saturday, 6:30 p.m.–4 a.m. (closed Sunday in fall and winter); music usually starts after 9 p.m.

What Goes On This is a fun enough club just for hanging out and listening, but for those who like to dance, it's one of the best parties in town. Monday nights smoke with famous salsa groups (the dance class will get your hips up to speed); other nights feature music from Brazilian to reggae—anything funky and tropical. The bands are tops in their genres; this is a great place for world music neophytes to familiarize themselves with different styles. It's more nightclub than disco; bands are listened to as much as danced to, and even unaccompanied women feel "safe" on the dance floor.

Setting & Atmosphere Large stage with sunken dance floor; the bar faces the stage, but visibility is bad in crowds. There are tables to the side of the stage. Bright and colorful, with lots of tropical touches.

If You Go Bear in mind that things can get crowded; meet the $15 minimum by ordering a bottle from the surprisingly good wine list. FYI, S.O.B.'s stands for "Sounds of Brazil."

Swing 46

SWING DANCE CLUB

Who Goes There 25–90; swing dance aficionados old and young, cool barflies

349 West 46th Street ; (212) 262-9554 www.swing46.com *Zone 8*

Cover $5–$15 **Minimum** 2 drinks at tables **Mixed Drinks** $6–$10 **Wine** $6–$8 **Beer** $5–$7 **Dress** Anything goes; dancers dress up **Specials** Free dance lessons every night after first set **Food Available** Expensive dinners plus reasonably priced snacks (burgers, etc.)

Hours Daily, 5 p.m.–2 a.m.

What Goes On Live music seven nights a week; big bands and combos playing swing. Lindy hoppers and jitterbugs are as hot as the music, and the place bristles with energy even on weeknights. The bar is as cool as the dance floor is hot, populated by older swing fans who prefer to sit and take it all in without getting personally involved. If you can overlook all the silly hepcat daddy-o spiel, it's all a pretty wild good time (neophyte dancers will not feel uncomfortable). Tap jam on Sunday.

Setting & Atmosphere The bar's up front, cut off from the frenzied action further inside, but the bands can be clearly heard. The dance/nightclub room, framed with beige paneling, has a low ceiling and is close but not overly so. Tables have flickering candle lamps, and the dance floor is right up next to the band. An outdoor sunken terrace in front of the club is filled with tables in summer.

If You Go Restaurant Row is actually a better block for bars than for restaurants. On this same street, check out **O'Flaherty's Ale House** (see profile).

Tonic

QUALITY ALTERNATIVE MUSIC CLUB

Who Goes There Intellectual music fans and scenesters

107 Norfolk Street; (212) 358-7501   www.tonic107.com   Zone 3

Cover $12 and up **Minimum** None **Mixed Drinks** $5–$8 **Wine** $5 **Beer** $4 **Dress** In black **Specials** None **Food Available** Limited; sandwiches, desserts, soup at bar **Hours** Show times vary; call. Box office opens at 7:30 p.m.

What Goes On The **Knitting Factory** (see profile) is still the best-known name in the city's avant garde music scene, but it has lost a good deal of its creative edge. Tonic now plays host to many of the Knit's former performers and draws many of the new music scene's most cutting-edge bands. Programming runs the gamut, from semi-acoustic jazz to klezmer to "free" jazz to that hard-to-categorize point where many diverse styles meet.

Setting & Atmosphere An arty narrow space with high ceilings, rough semipainted concrete, red velvet curtains, and red scrimlights. A small bookstore near the entrance sells 'zines and books on subjects you never knew existed. Sound is good; staff is friendly.

If You Go Have a drink afterward at **DBA** (see profile), take a walk down nearby Ludlow Street (lots of bars, cafés, shops, and music), or catch some less-challenging East Village music (see the "Alternative Rock" section in this chapter's introduction). Visit the downstairs space, Subtonic, to dee DJs spin in a trippy dimension—oftentimes way off the map.

Town Bar

COOL, CHIC COCKTAIL BAR

Who Goes There 20's–60's; professionals, deep-pocketed chicsters, hip hotel guests, cocktail aficionados

15 West 56th Street (between 5th and 6th avenues), in Chambers Hotel
(212) 582-4445   www.townnyc.com   Zone 8

Cover None **Minimum** None **Mixed Drinks** $10–$22 **Wine** Good selection, $8–$20 **Beer** Bottled only, and what's the point when the drink and wine selection is so extensive? **Dress** Smart casual, cool, elegant, or chic **Specials** None **Food Available** Delicious light meals, prepared in the Town restaurant kitchen, $12–$24

Hours Sunday–Friday, noon–midnight; Saturday, 5 p.m.–1 a.m.

What Goes On Town is bustling with a well-heeled, after-work crowd between 6 and 8 p.m.; afterwards, the scene is less frenetic and decidedly sophisticated. This is not the place to indulge recession blues, with quality champagne flowing in many a cocktail and gold leaf floating in drinks that sell for $22 a pop. Cocktails are taken seriously, and the mixers, from fruit purée to infusions, are all fresh.

Setting & Atmosphere Ultra-chic environment, with a choice of four areas to drink: the lobby, main bar, mezzanine, or balcony. The main bar is small and narrow; warm, subtle lighting helps everyone look their absolute best. The staff are friendly and knowledgeable.

If You Go Understand and accept that even though you may part with more cash than is normally sane for a round of drinks, you will enjoy the experience (unless you order beer). Ask the bartender (a.k.a. bar chef) about any recently concocted potions and request an explanation of the myriad infusions, spices, and ingredients displayed on the bar. A look at the vanilla-infused rum used for the mojitos is enough to make a sworn vodka tippler try a change of pace.

Village Vanguard

JAZZ CLUB

Who Goes There 25–90; jazz pilgrims and Japanese tourists

178 Seventh Avenue South; (212) 255-4037   www.villagevanguard.com   Zone 4

Cover $25–$30 (includes $10 drink minimum) **Minimum** $25 for tables, $10 plus two drinks at bar **Mixed Drinks** $5–$8 **Wine** $5–$7 **Beer** $4.50–$5 **Dress Dressy** or nice casual **Food Available** None

Hours Open 8 p.m. every night, closing time varies. Sets start at 9 and 11 p.m.; call to see if a third set is scheduled.

What Goes On This is it—the most famous jazz club in the world. Over the last 60 years almost every major jazz musician has gigged in this room (many recorded landmark live albums here as well), and the ghosts are palpable. The service is crabby and the seating's cramped, but you become a tiny part of jazz history simply by walking in the door. The music is *finally* straying from strictly straight-ahead jazz and bebop: fusion, Latin, and even fresh blood are being heard here.

Setting & Atmosphere Dank basement with a small bar in back ... but the acoustics are wonderful, and it feels like jazz. Table service.

If You Go Check out the Monday Night Vanguard Jazz Orchestra (Thad Jones/Mel Lewis's band, sans leaders). On any night, reservations are a good idea; this small club fills up fast.

Webster Hall

DISCO THEME PARK

Who Goes There 21–35; equal parts NYU freshmen, beautiful party people, and paunchy 30-somethings clutching beers and looking wistful

125 East 11th Street; (212) 353-1600   www.webster-hall.com   Zone 5

Cover None–$30 **Minimum** None **Mixed Drinks** $6.50–$8 **Wine** $6.50 **Beer** $6–$7 **Dress** No sneakers, baseball hats, ripped jeans, dress to impress **Specials** $15 admission discounts are available through their website **Food Available** Probably somewhere; look around

Hours Thursday–Sunday, 10 p.m.–5 a.m.; Monday–Wednesday, closed.

What Goes On An enormous disco theme park with dance floors, lounges, a (temporary) tattoo parlor, and a coffee bar. There are spending opportunities everywhere you look; even the bathroom attendants reign over little concession stands, selling candy, mouthwash, and hair products. Fridays and Saturdays are monstrously crowded mainstream disco free-for-alls, and Thursdays have a psychedelic 1960s theme. The staff seems to be instructed to act as peevish as possible. Lots of DJs; ladies get in free all Thursday night, while men get in for $10 before 11:30 p.m.

Setting & Atmosphere Ground level is mostly a classic disco, complete with go-go girl behind the bar. Upstairs you enter a cavernous ballroom, like a junior high school auditorium taken over by aliens with superior technology: amazing lighting tricks and a SenSurround-style bass response that makes your chest feel like it's going to explode. More go-go girls, and androgynous characters on stilts. Still further upstairs is a balcony with tarot readings, temporary tattoos, body painting, and a tranquil lounge (wicker chairs, ferns) that hosts live bands Thursday and Friday nights (also check the bar here for drink specials). In the basement, yet another dance floor, this one with burning incense.

If You Go Conceal no weapons (or beer bottles)—no happening disco would be complete without a security pat-down at the front door, and this is no exception.

Zinc Bar

BAR AND JAZZ CLUB

Who Goes There 22–55; locals, night-owls and jazz aficionados.

90 West Houston Street; (212) 477-8337   www.zincbar.com   Zone 2 Soho

Cover $5 **Minimum** 1 drink **Mixed Drinks** $7–$12 **Wine** Bottles $25 and up; $6–$8 by the glass **Beer** $7–$8 **Dress** Casual to chic **Specials** None **Food Available** None

Hours Sunday–Thursday, 6 p.m.–3:30 a.m.; Friday and Saturday, 6 p.m.–4 a.m.

What Goes On This is a great place to watch some purely amazing musicians in an intimate setting. Occasional impromptu audience participation occurs during performances. It's also cozy for a tête-à-tete with drinks. You can sit in the back room if you don't want to watch the set—but you will hear it. Poetry readings take place on Sundays at 6:30 p.m.

Setting & Atmosphere Once you go down a few steps, pass the curtain and move into a low-light, narrow bar, you will already be in a mood to hear music. The Zinc Bar has two rooms—the first room hosts the main bar with stools on one side, and small round tables with a padded bench, along the wall, on the other side. This is where the musicians perform. The dominant color is red. The second room is a little more sizable and exposes red brick and wooden floors. One side has banquettes—perfect for groups—and the other side, once again, has a padded bench along the wall with a few cocktail tables.

If You Go Make sure you manage to catch at least one set; the last one can start as late as 2 a.m.

Restaurant Index

Page numbers in **bold** type indicate restaurant profiles.

Nightclub Index

Page numbers in **bold** type indicate nightclub profiles.

Subject Index